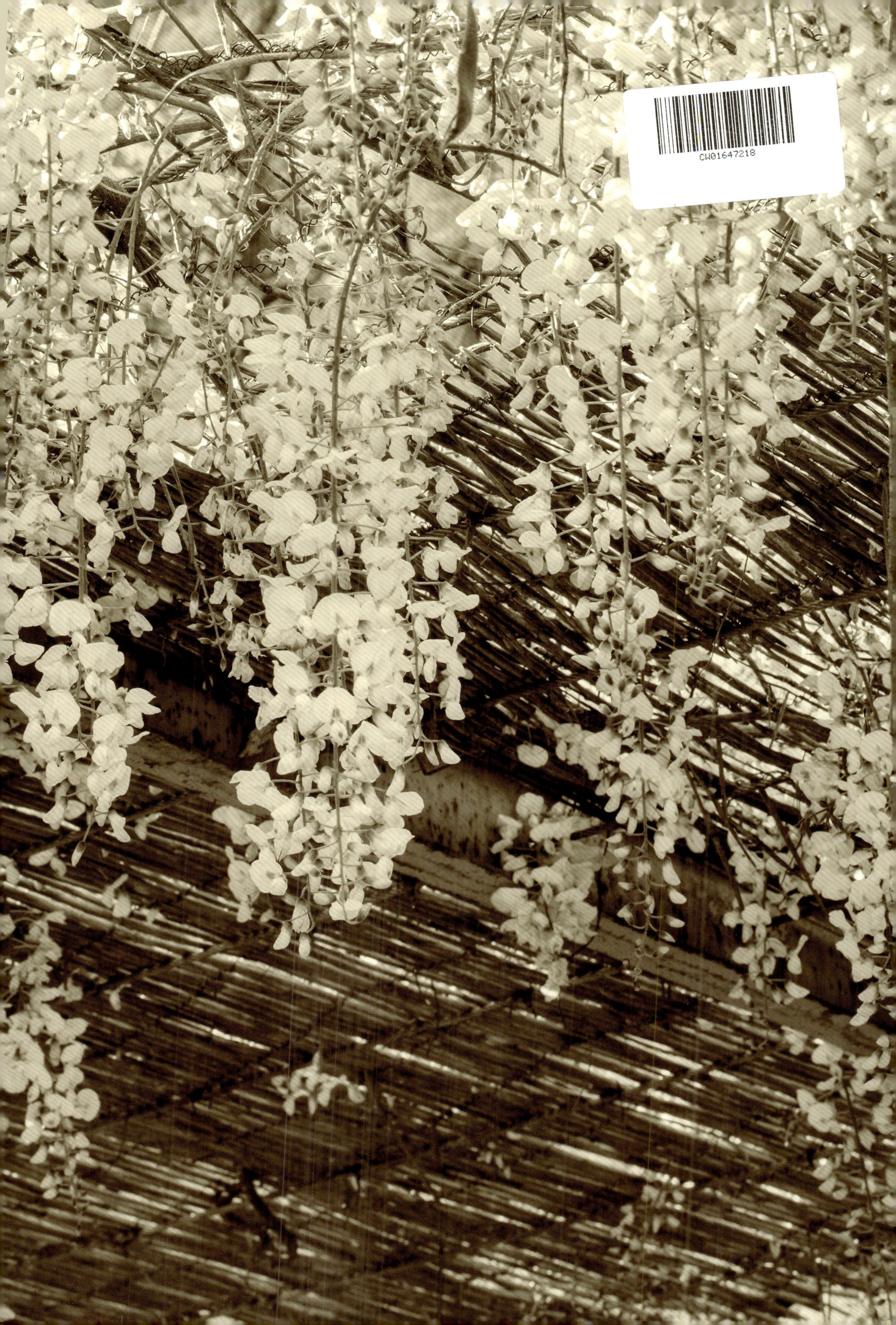

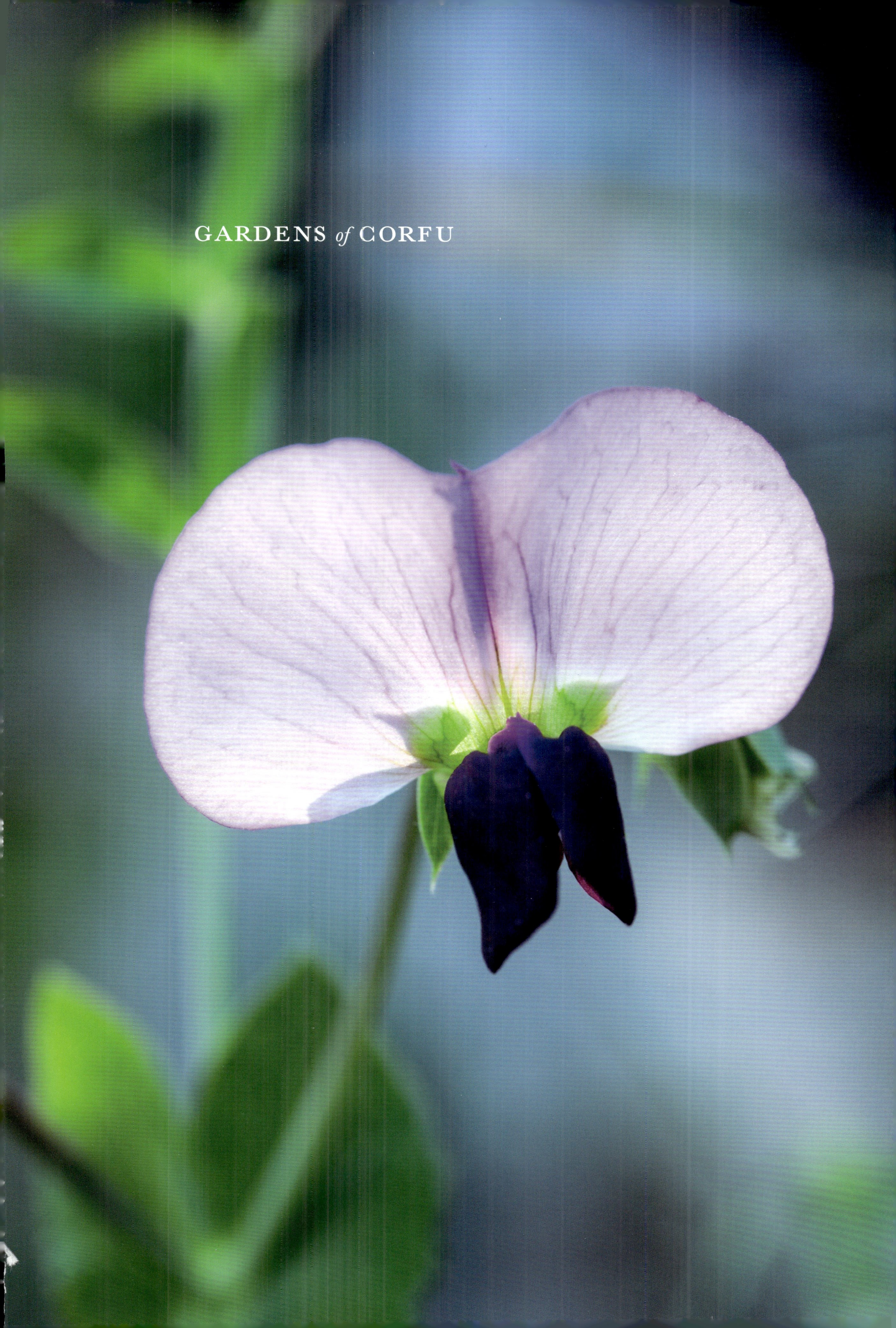
GARDENS *of* CORFU

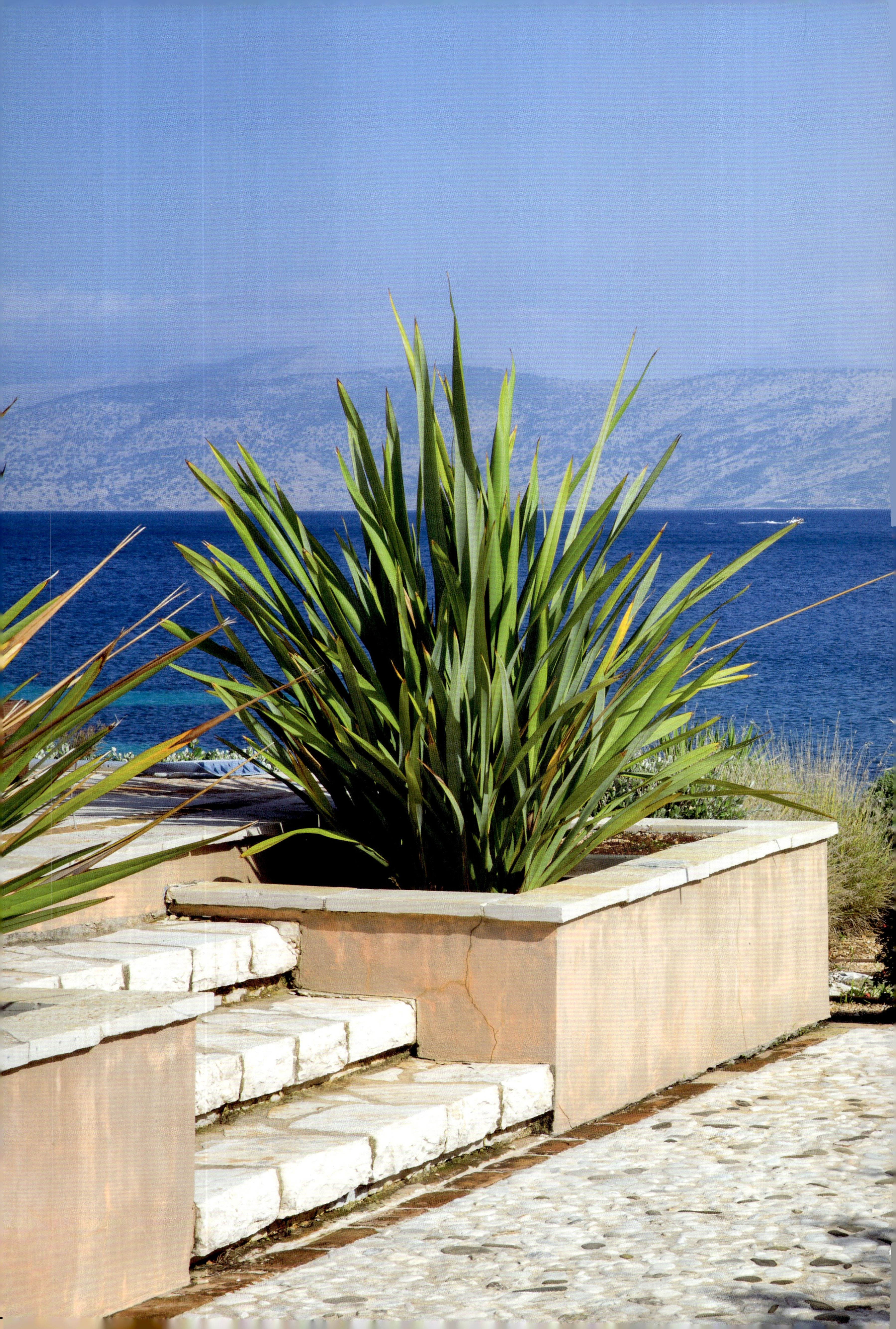

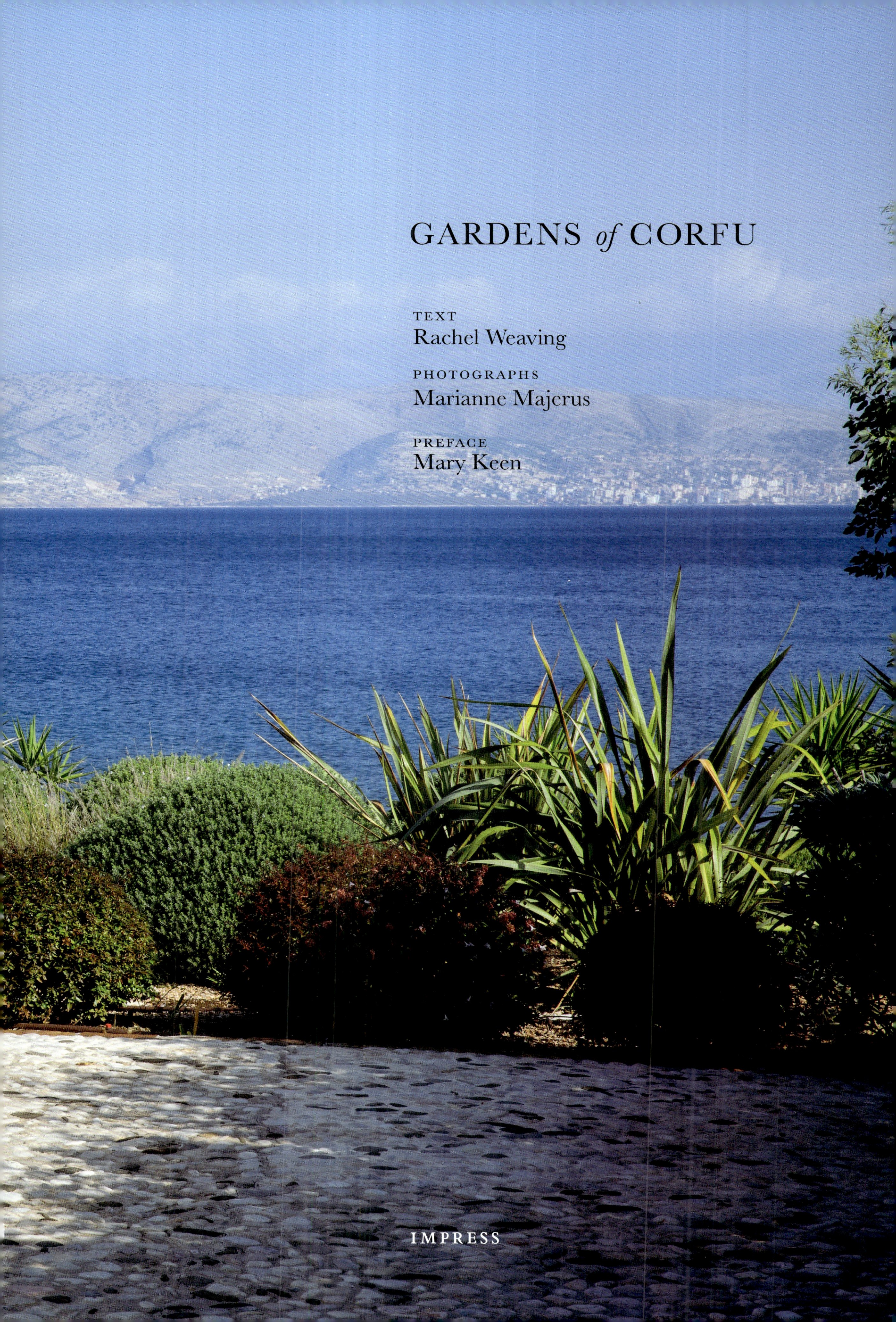

GARDENS *of* CORFU

TEXT
Rachel Weaving

PHOTOGRAPHS
Marianne Majerus

PREFACE
Mary Keen

IMPRESS

HALF TITLE
Delicate wild pea (*Pisum sativum*) grows in moist grassland and shady places.

TITLE
The garden at Villa Levánta opens on to the sea.

AUTHOR'S NOTE

This book is a partial portrait rather than a comprehensive survey of Corfu's gardens; many more, equally beautiful, exist across the island.

Plant names quoted are, for cultivated plants, those used in the Royal Horticultural Society's horticultural database (see http://apps.rhs.org.uk/horticulturaldatabase/), and, for wild plants, those used in Marjorie Blamey and Christopher Grey-Wilson, *Wild Flowers of the Mediterranean* (London: A. and C. Black, 1988, second edn. 2008).

As has become common practice, throughout this book 'Mediterranean' with a capital M refers to the Mediterranean Sea, the countries around it, and their plants; 'mediterranean' with a lower-case m refers to the climate, other parts of the world that share this climate (e.g. South Africa or California), and their plants. By 'pan-mediterranean' we mean 'spanning the various areas that have a mediterranean climate'.

Published in the UK in 2018 by *Impress*
Editorial Department [156]
95 Wilton Road
London, SW1V 1BZ
impress-publishing.com

ISBN 978-1-9997825-1-1

Design by Prof. Phil Cleaver and Matthew Jackson, *et al design consultants*

Printed and bound in the UK by *DLM Creative*

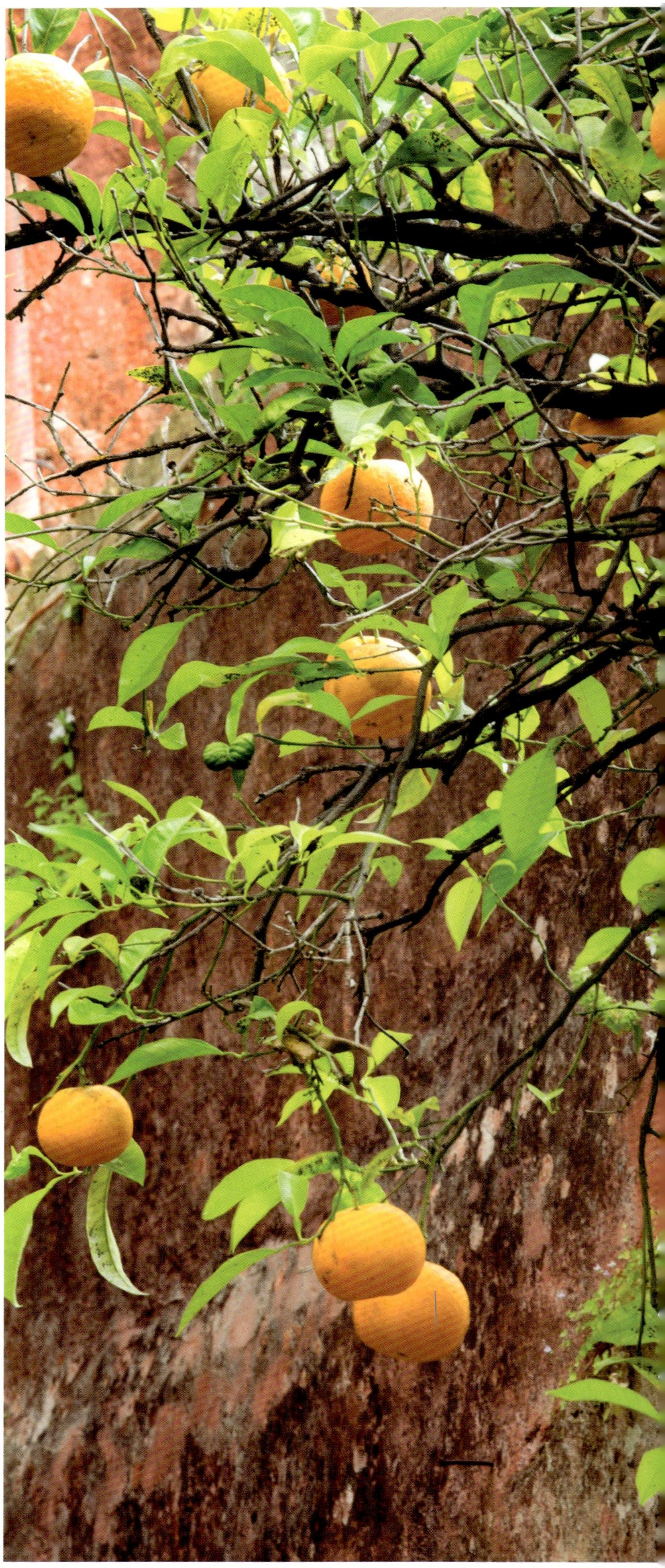

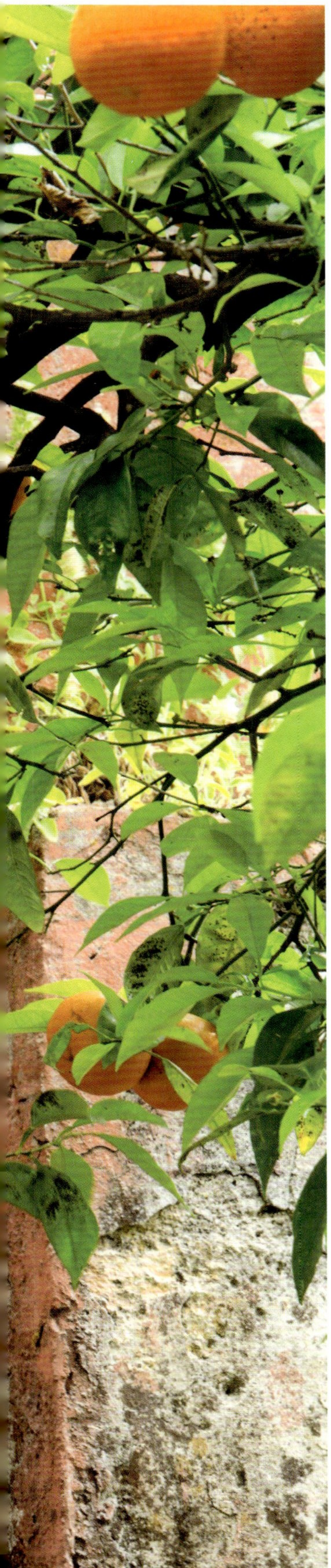

Oranges against a wall at San Stefano.

PREFACE

Mary Keen

The title Lawrence Durrell chose for what is still the best guide to Corfu was *Prospero's Cell*. While scholars may dispute the claim that it was the setting for Shakespeare's *The Tempest*, there is no doubt that Corfu is the most magical of all the Greek islands. Corfu has also been called 'The Garden Isle'. Blessed with more rainfall than anywhere in the Aegean and with a legacy of ancient olive trees from the Venetian rule, the place and its flowers have always enchanted visitors. Especially the British, who occupied Corfu for almost fifty years after the Napoleonic wars. Indeed, among the pages of this book, those on the British Cemetery made me wonder why I had never visited this garden of wild orchids and summer roses. The mixed heritage and the unusual climate may account for the fact that Corfu has its own special atmosphere.

On my first visit to the island, almost half a century ago, there were few roads—only chalky dirt tracks that curled down to the glittering sea. Today inland there are still traces of unchanged Corfu, but tourism has eroded the edges and beaches. The magic has been shattered a little, but those who love Corfu have spun their own spell around the various properties portrayed in this book.

When I started to work on the garden at Kanónas I found that the atmosphere, the genius of the place, was so strong that it was hard to change a thing. Sea, stone, and olive trees are what matter here. Cyclamen and iris sprinkle the olive groves and Primavera flowers—pink dandelions, field gladiolus, marigolds, and wild geraniums—paint the grass every spring. It is good to read that so many garden makers in this book have respected the spirit and beauty of the island and that gaudy *Bougainvillea* tends to be less frequently planted than native plants.

Much of the earth in Corfu is a thin layer of calcareous soil over rocks and although more rain falls annually than it does in London, summers are increasingly hot. So it makes sense to adopt what Rachel Weaving refers to as a 'pan-mediterranean style'. Even gardeners in cooler climates will find they can learn from the descriptions of ways of husbanding water and respecting local distinctiveness.

Lovers of Corfu and of gardens will find plenty of magic in the pages that follow.

Contents

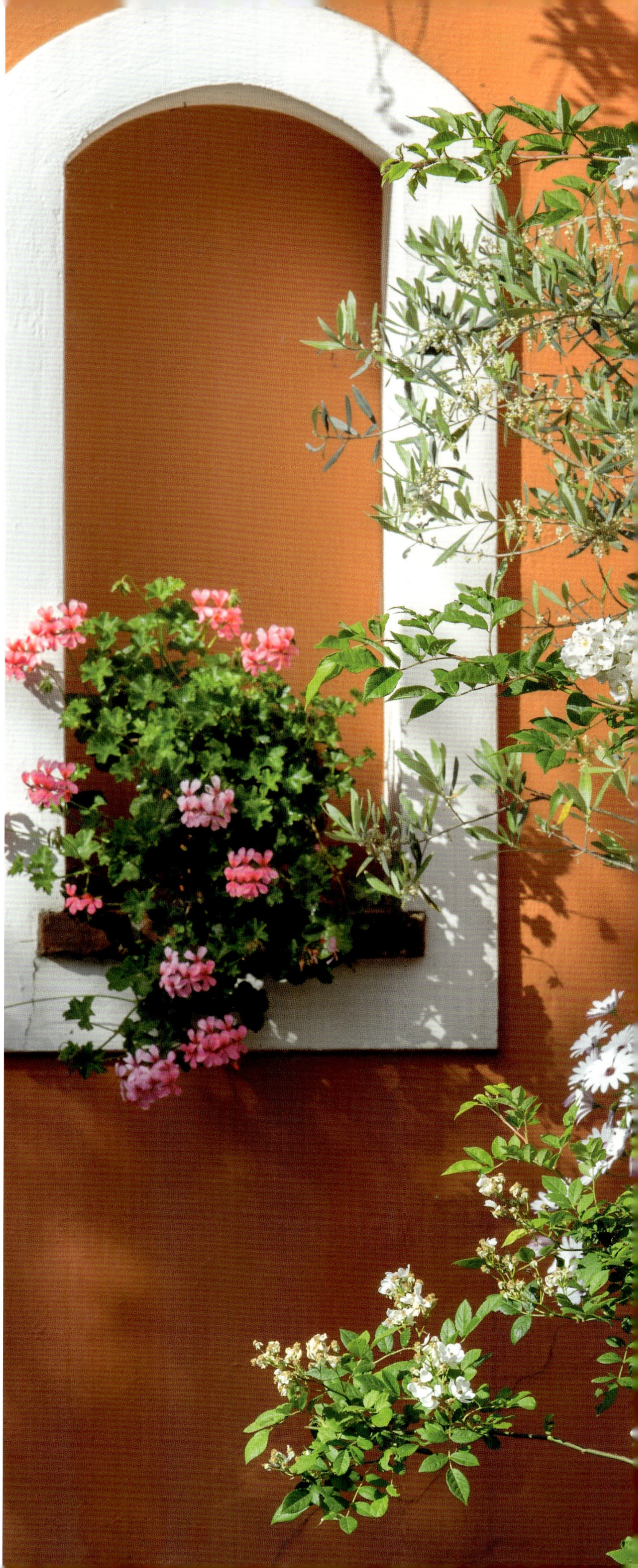

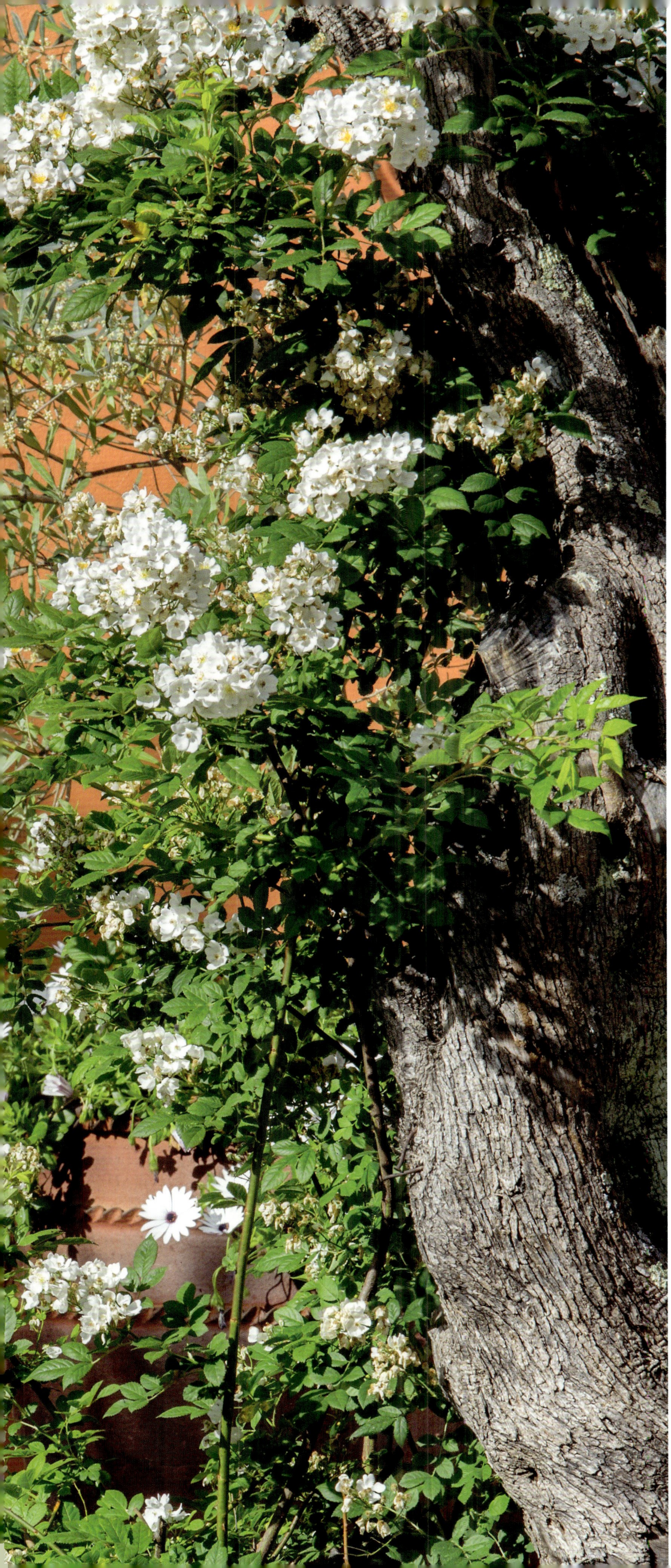

At Soukiá, climbing roses, olive, and pelargonium with a wall painted in typical Corfiot style.

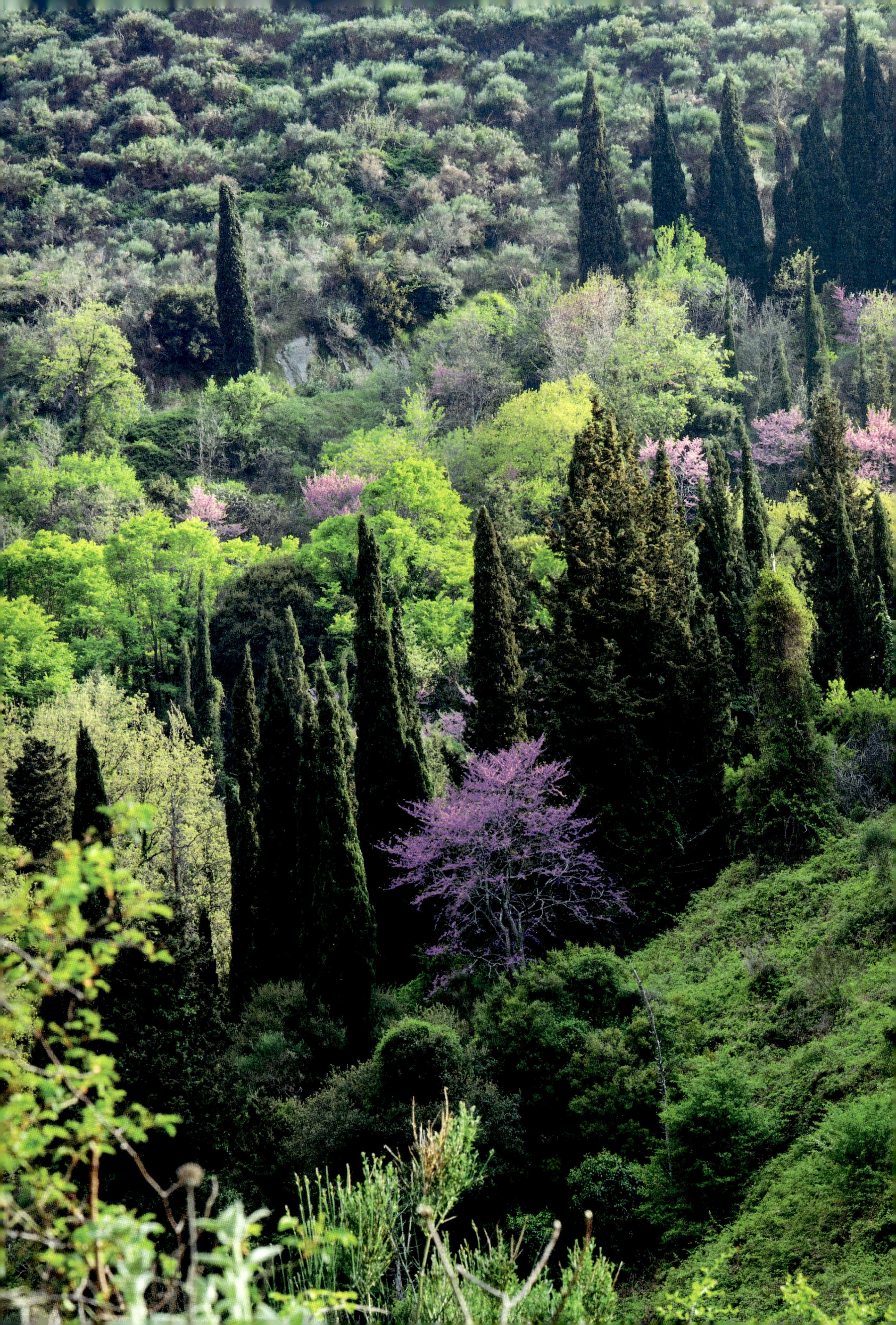

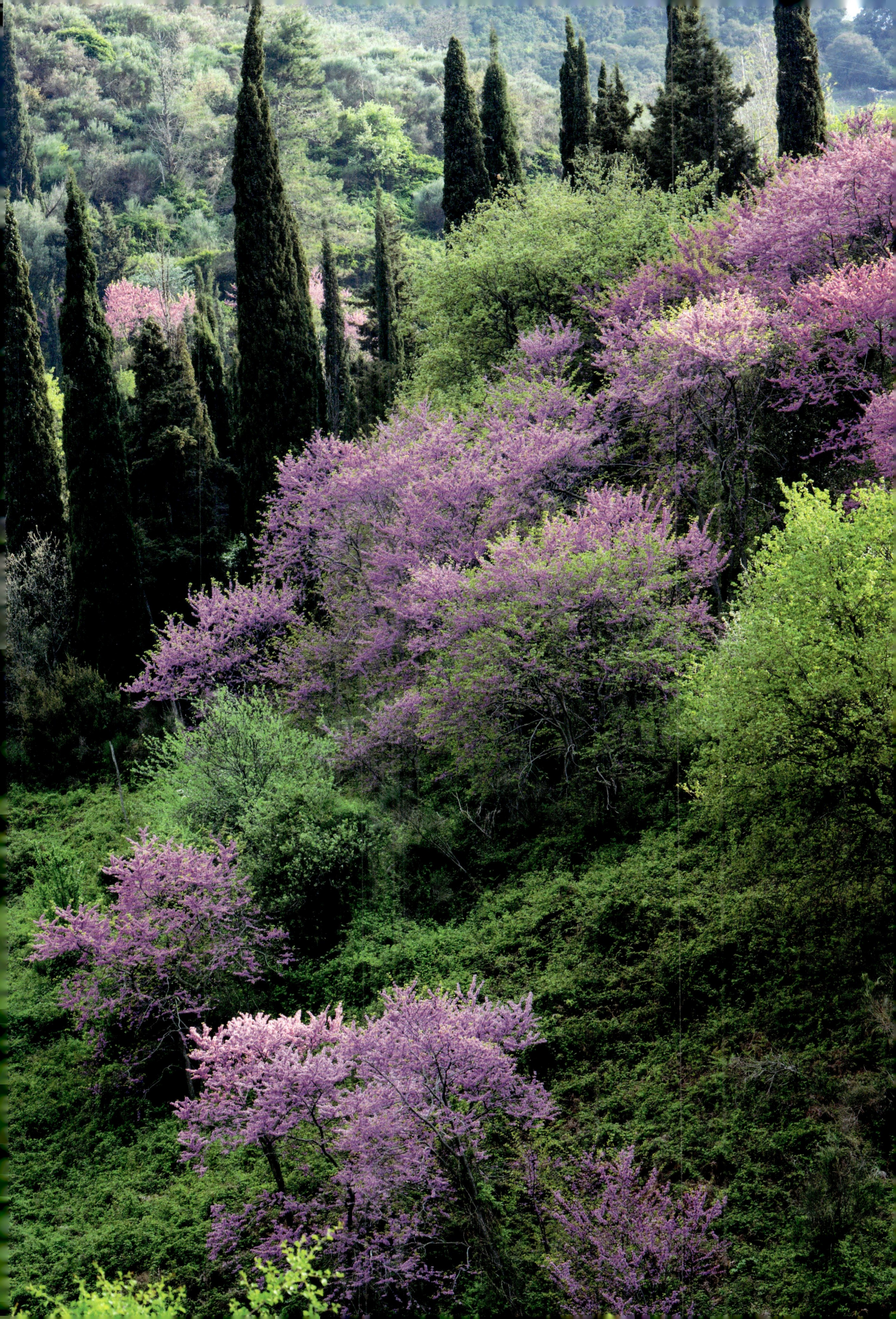

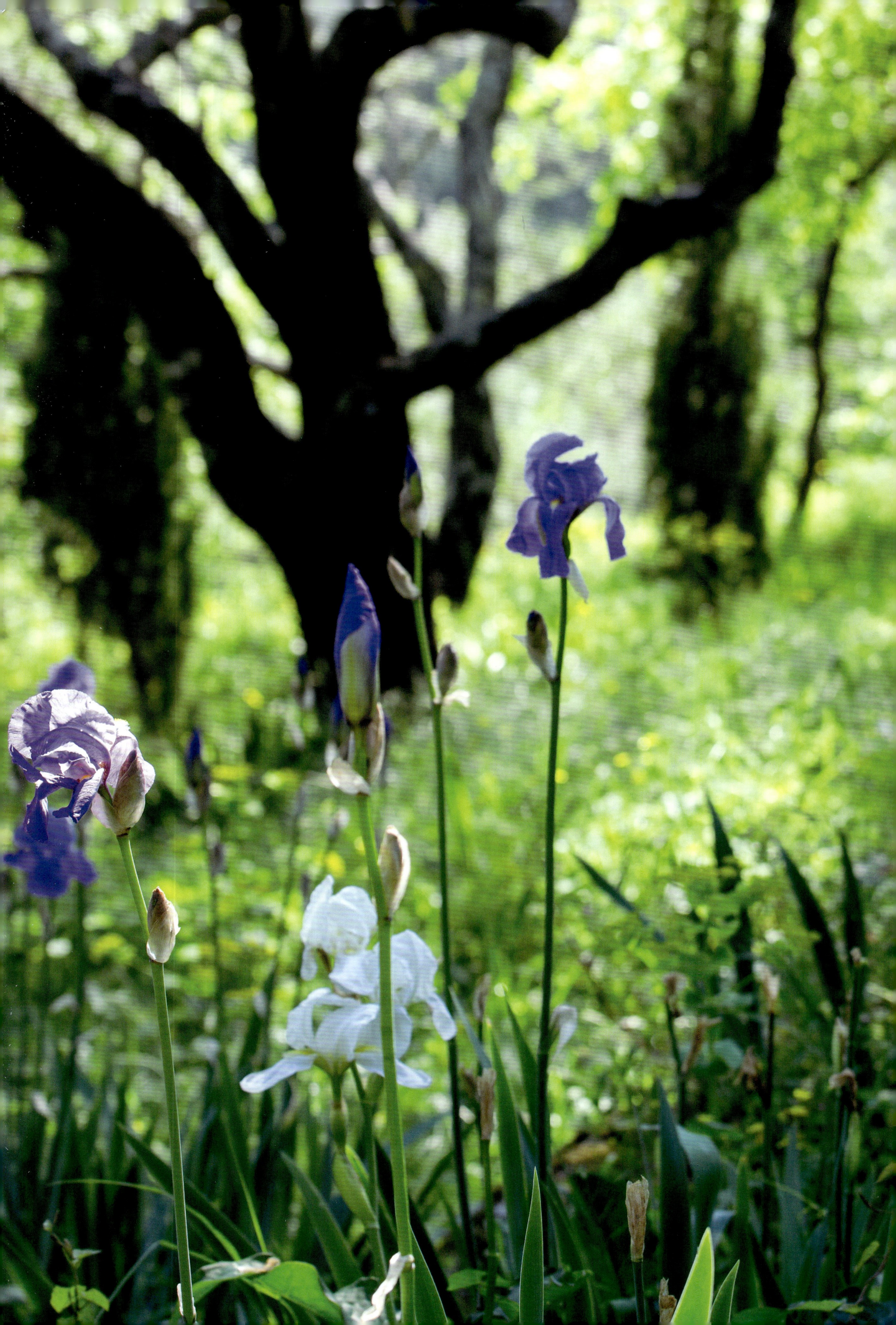

CHAPTER ONE

Corfu Gardens: Ancient Myth and Modern Magic

OPPOSITE
Bearded irises flower under ancient olive trees at Katsafaláta, home of Derek and Daphne Johns.

Greenest of the Greek islands, Corfu exerts a powerful magic. For those who seek them out, its natural landscapes and private gardens evoke a sense of wonder: expansive and intimate, restorative and energising, they offer joy and solace in a stressful world.

It was in pre-Classical times that Corfu emerged as the subject of a potent myth—a concept that the island is itself a garden. Scholars tell us that Corfu was Homer's model for the island of the Phaeacians, where shipwrecked Odysseus found the garden of King Alcinous 'full of beautiful trees—pears, pomegranates, and the most delicious apples. There are luscious figs also, and olives in full growth. The fruits never rot nor fail all the year round, neither winter nor summer, for the air is so soft that a new crop ripens before the old has dropped... In the furthest part of the ground there are beautifully arranged beds of flowers that are in bloom all the year round.'[1]

PREVIOUS
Corfu is often called 'the garden isle'. Here, wild Judas trees *(Cercis siliquastrum)* flower in April on Mount Pantocrátor.

Writing in the fourth century BC, Xenophon recorded the island as a fertile cultivated paradise.[2] Much later, perhaps inspired by descriptions from contemporary travellers such as Fynes Moryson[3] or George Sandys,[4] Shakespeare took Corfu as the basis for Prospero's enchanted island in *The Tempest.*

Nineteenth-century visitors also fell under Corfu's spell. In spring then, as now, they would have found Corfu carpeted with flowers: 'This is the characteristic scene for miles: ferns, asphodels, myrtles, hyacinths, cyclamen, irises, anemones, crocuses, and violets and an endless variety of other wildflowers grow under the trees in great profusion'.[5] British artist and writer Edward Lear, who spent almost four years on the island, wrote of 'gardens dark with orange and lemon groves, their fruit sparkling golden and yellow against the purple sea and the amethyst hills'.[6]

The building of two nineteenth-century palaces helped popularise

1. Homer, *The Odyssey*, Book VII, translated by Samuel Butler. 2. Xenophon, *A History of My Times*, Book VI (London: Penguin Classics edition, 1966). 3. See Fynes Moryson, *An Itinerary Concerning His Travel to the Twelve Dominions* (Glasgow: James MacLehose and Sons, 1617, Vol. II). 4. See George Sandys, *Sandys Travels: A Relation of a Journey begun in An. Dom. 1610* (London, 1621). 5. Letter by military officer J. D. Shakespear, 1850s, exhibited at Mon Repos. 6. As quoted in Peter Nahum, 'Edward Lear', in Frank Giles, ed., *Corfu: The Garden Isle* (UK: John Murray and USA: Abbeville Press 1994), p. 177.

Corfu's image as a garden paradise. Mon Repos, built by British High Commissioner Frederick Adam, was surrounded with English-style rose gardens, and by 1830 its grounds contained a botanical garden with four thousand plants, including trees from parts as distant as Australia. Not far south of Corfu Town, Empress Elisabeth of Austria built the Achílleion Palace to reflect her dreams of Greek antiquity: 'a palace with pillared colonnades and hanging gardens, safe from prying eyes—a palace worthy of Achilles'.[7] Her gardens were planted with exotic trees and shrubs, many of them quite new to Europe at the time; several of these survive today.

Closer to our time, artists and writers both Greek and foreign have helped the island weave its magic. Corfiot Angelos Giállinas, Greece's most famous watercolourist, painted olive and citrus groves and gardens with cypresses and irises, sometimes against the background of a luminescent blue sea. American painter John Singer Sargent summered at the Villa Sotiriótissa in Kontókali in 1909 and 1910. In the luxuriant garden there, he captured the indolence of summer days—but also the stark, startling, and peculiarly Greek quality of Corfu's summer light. British novelist Lawrence Durrell later described this same light: the 'dancing magnesium-flare quality of the sunlight blazing on a white wall; in the depths of the light there is blackness which throbs with violet—a magnetic unwearying ultra-violet throb.'[8] Both Lawrence and his naturalist brother, Gerald Durrell, wrote of the piercing beauty of the island that Gerald called the 'Garden of the Gods'.[9]

In Corfu's gardens of today, the myth lives on. Their richness and diversity might seem surprising in an island so small. Partly it stems from generous winter rainfall, mild winters, and a large variety of microclimates and soils, which allow the cultivation of a wide range of plants. But also it stems from Corfu's unusual social and cultural history. Under successive regimes—Venetian, French, British, and Greek—Corfu's prominent residents have kept in touch with artistic developments and garden fashions in European cultural centres and seen that these could be replicated and adapted locally. To be sure, at some of the island's old estates, only the vestiges remain of formerly grand gardens, their ruined walkways and staircases shrouded in wisteria and mystery. But other old estate gardens are still lovingly cared for and several have been sensitively brought up to date. And

7. Empress Elisabeth of Austria, instructions to Austrian Consul Baron Warsburg, as quoted in Frank Giles, ed. *Corfu: The Garden Isle*, p. 106. 8. Lawrence Durrell, 'Corfu', in *The Greek Islands* (London and Boston, MA: Faber, 1978). 9. Gerald Durrell, *Corfu: Garden of the Gods* (London: Harper Collins, 1978).

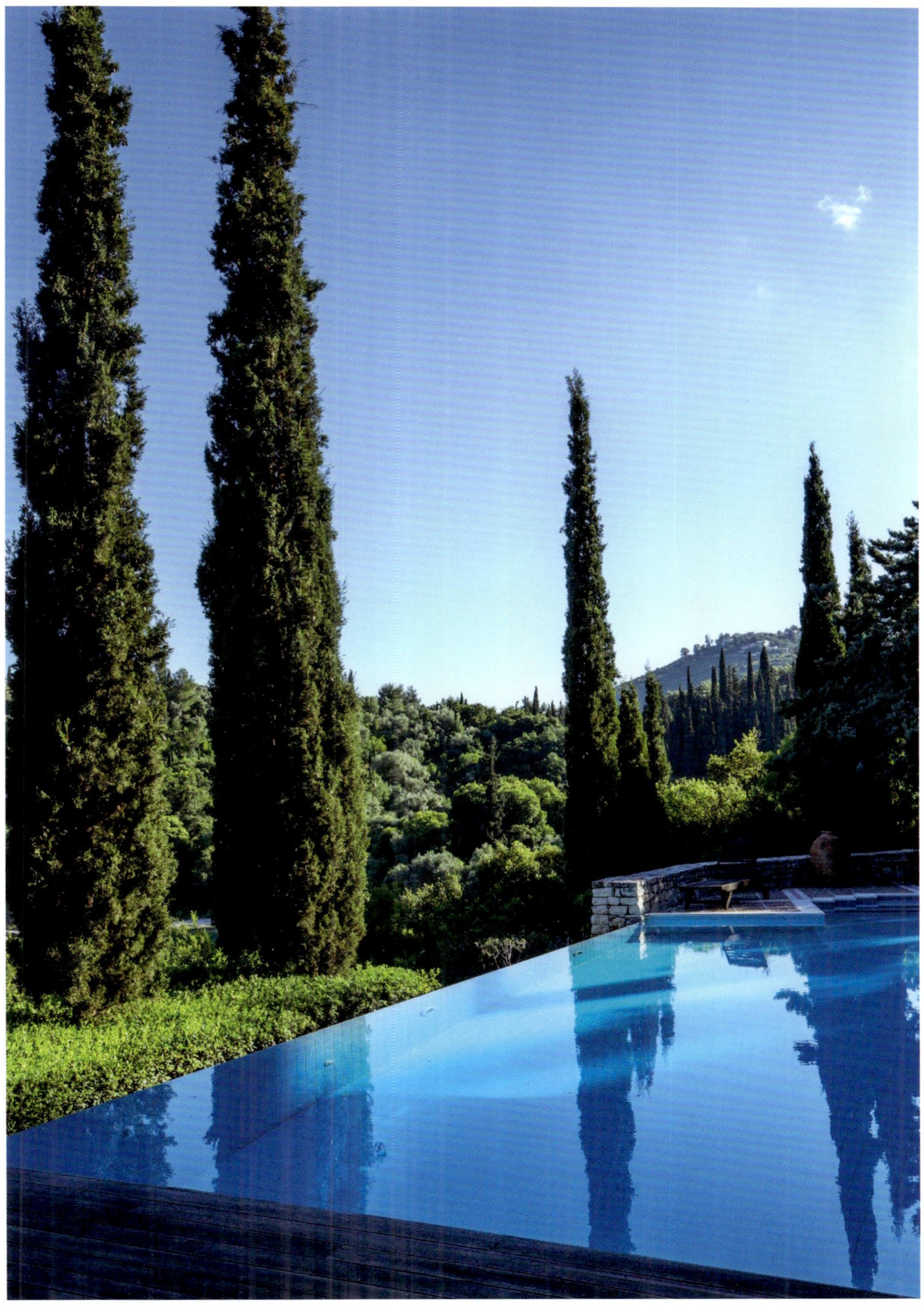

The intense blue of a summer sky is reflected in the pool at Petróti, home of Robert and Sara Lucas.

though parts of Corfu are now marred by the ugly trappings of mass tourism, a crop of remarkable new gardens has been created in the past twenty years. On rocky coastal promontories and on the outskirts of hillside villages, dream homes of well-to-do Corfiots and Athenians perch next to those of artists, writers, celebrities, and businesspeople from across Europe and beyond. Their gardens reflect the talent of contemporary international designers and increasingly take inspiration from their natural surroundings, seeking to complement and enhance the natural beauty of the island landscape.

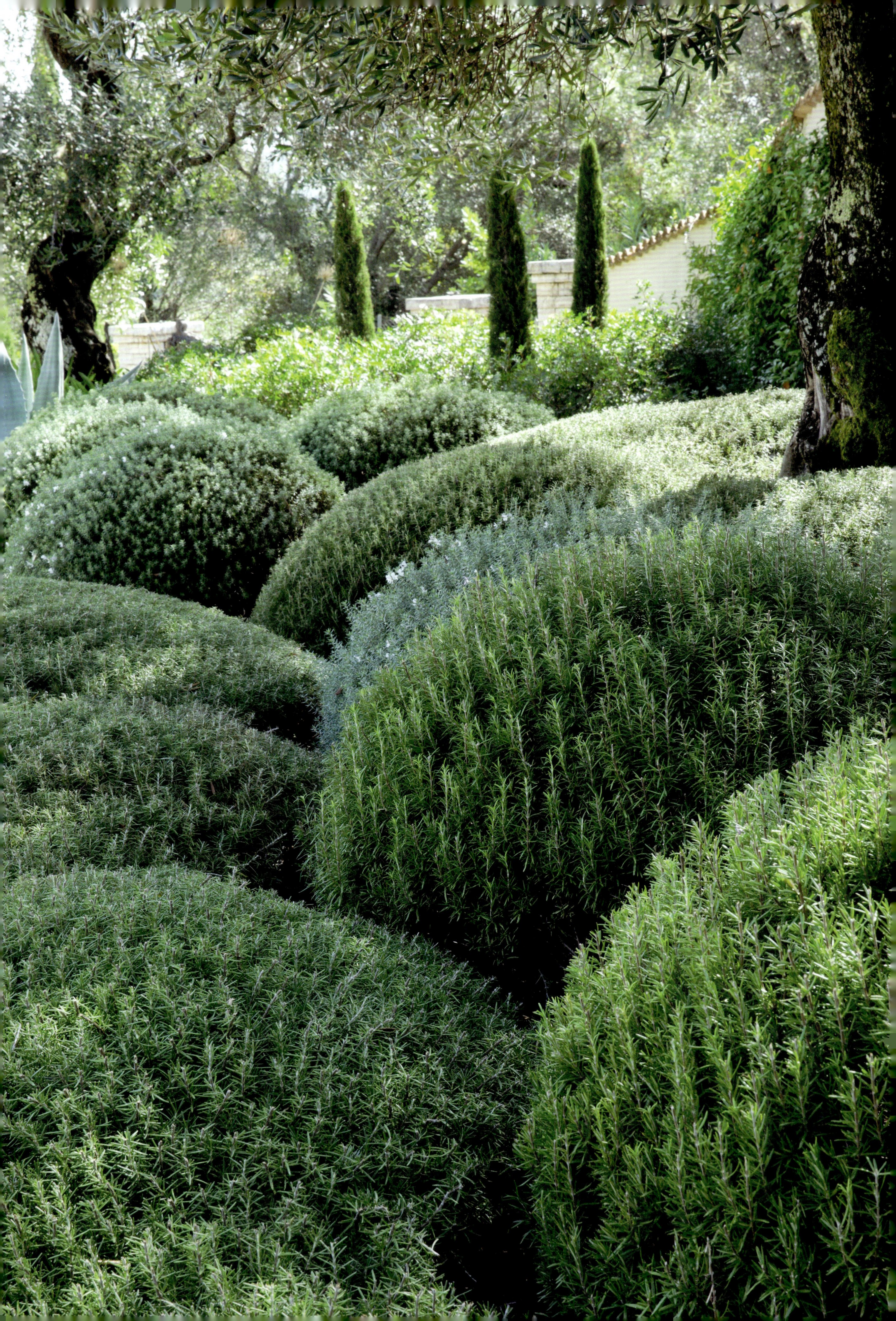

CHAPTER TWO

Garden Making in Corfu: Elements of Style

Any successful garden respects the features of its site—the surrounding landscape, physical features such as soil and water supply, altitude and aspect, weather patterns, and light and shade—and is sensitive to the basic materials in common local use.

How have designers and gardeners in Corfu responded to the local conditions? Is there a distinctively Corfiot style?

OPPOSITE
The olive trees predated the garden at Villa Zografiá. Under them, a simple planting of evergreen shrubs (*Westringia fruticosa* and *Rosmarinus officinalis*) creates mystery. Design by Alithea Johns, pruning by Ben Carter.

DIALOGUE WITH THE LANDSCAPE

Most of the island's distinguished gardens, old or new, accept and celebrate natural—or inherited agricultural—features of their sites, and deliberately evoke elements of the landscape beyond their walls. The vernacular gardens in villages and towns have probably changed little over the centuries, but for more ambitious gardens intended as art the design ideals have changed greatly. The Italian and English models that inspired Corfu's nineteenth and twentieth-century garden makers have given way to an international pan-mediterranean style, whose proponents take their inspiration from a garden's surrounding landscape and, often, from the natural features of the site itself. Strong emphasis is given to respecting and enhancing the 'spirit of place'. For example, Jennifer Gay has said of her work at Kassiopia Estate that 'The design philosophy capitalised on the natural habitats existent on site, and these became the framework for the garden'.[10] Calí Doxiádis, whose influence is seen in many Corfiot gardens, takes a similar view: 'Often, the landscape is so beautiful in itself that all you have to do is refrain from betraying it. In practical terms, and especially for the immediate surroundings, all you need to do is provide transitions from the artificial to the natural. In other words, incorporate your garden into the landscape.'[11]

SOILS, WATER, AND WEATHER

Many of Corfu's village gardeners are farmers or come from farming families. Like their counterparts worldwide, they use inherited

10. Jennifer Gay, 'Island Life', *Garden Design*, January 2016. 11. Calí Doxiádis, 'A Mediterranean Garden in Corfu', unpublished.

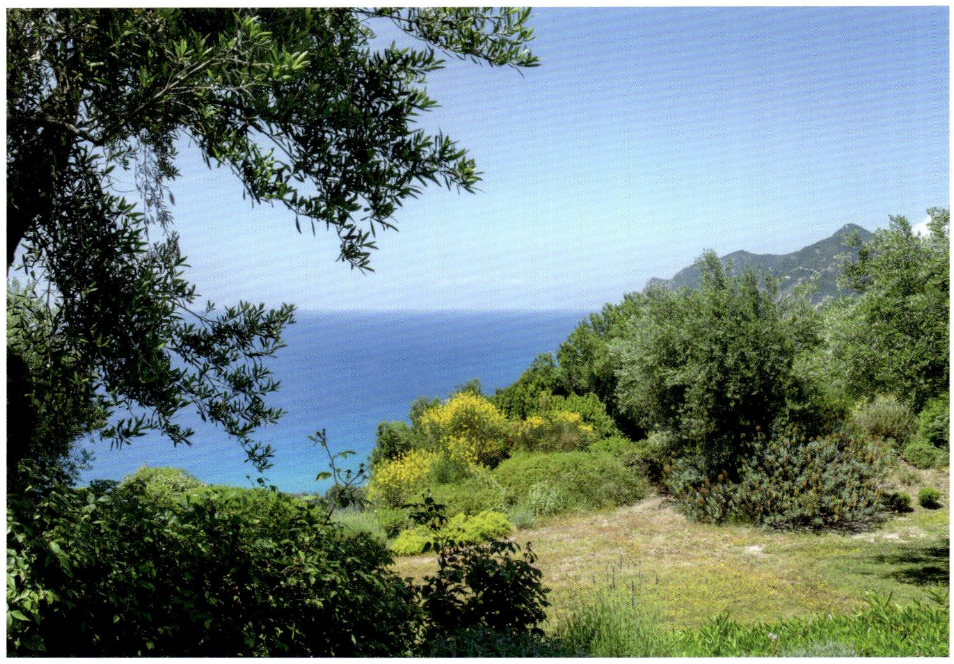

Creating this garden at Pélekas, Marílle Anargýrou added garden plants such as lavender, tree germander (*Teucrium fruticans*), and pink *Oenethera berlandieri* to the olives, wild pears, and Spanish broom (*Spartium junceum*) that she found growing on site.

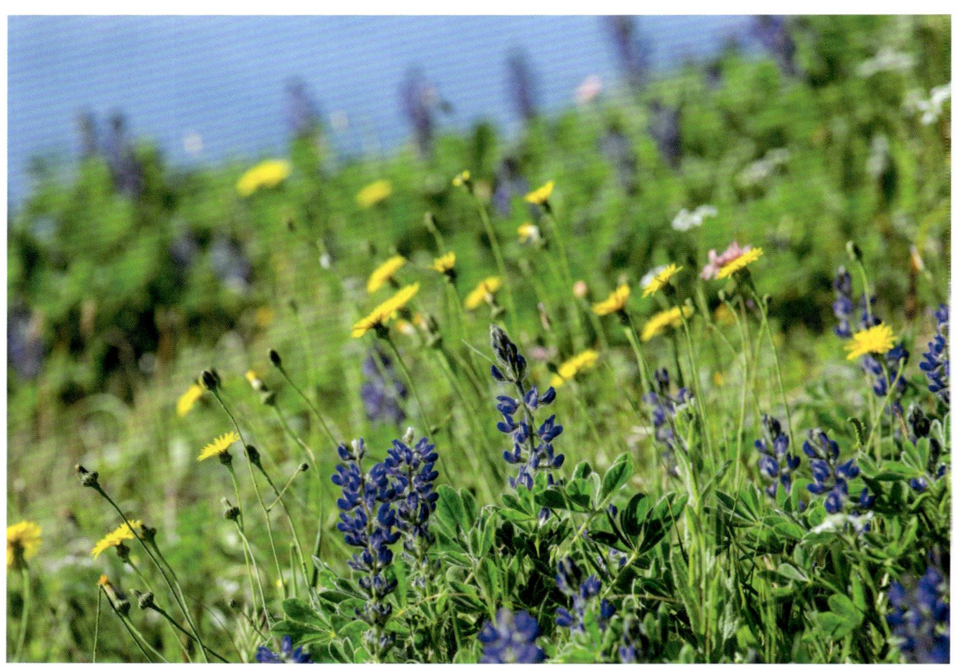

Wildflowers bloom on a headland. Mindful of such scenes, landscape architect Thomas Doxiádis has said, 'We treat all our work as didactic to help people see the importance of the native landscapes and plants, the beauty of the land, and our common responsibility to be their good stewards.'[12]

knowledge and personal experiments to match what they grow, and how they grow it, to the dictates of soil, water, and weather.

People with contemporary gardens often face more difficult physical challenges than their traditional counterparts, partly because many of them lack local gardening knowhow but also because their demands put them more in conflict with topography and climate than is normal in older settlements. Many of the new gardens are on steep hillside and exposed coastal sites, chosen for the dramatic views

12. *Financial Times*, 5 November, 2017.

these offer, but often the soils on steep slopes are so thin they may be best left alone with their wild vegetation. Exposure to wind, harsh rainfall, and unremitting sunlight are other challenges that village gardeners avoid but contemporary garden designers must contend with.

Soils and terracing. Soils in Corfu are mostly calcareous and poor but are very varied. Around the island's mountainous limestone backbone, with its shallow alkaline soil, are areas with clay, mudstone, and sandy soils that are still highly alkaline but deeper and easier to work. Alluvial plains, notably in the central Rópa Valley, the northern coast, and around the Korissión Lagoon, have friable humus-rich soil, good for cultivation. A very few areas have acidic, neutral sandy, or silty soil. Many of the island's contemporary gardens are on heavy alkaline clay.

To protect the soil from erosion, hillsides used for farming have been hand-terraced for centuries. Most of the hillside gardens have followed the traditional approach of manual terracing along the land's existing contours. But a few take a more engineered approach, regrading the land to allow straight lines, parallel walls, wide flat spaces, and right-angle corners—and in the process creating formality and drama. At historical properties, long straight terraces would have underlined the owners' power, among rural people familiar with the weight of soil and stones and the effort of moving them under a hot sun.

Rain and water supply. Corfu's annual rainfall is double that of Madeira or Sicily, and forty-four percent higher than London's, but almost all the rain falls between late September and mid-April (Figure 1). Much of the island aches with drought by late June.

OVERLEAF
Dramatic summer thunderstorms occur from time to time. Falling on dry earth, their rain quickly accumulates on the surface, forming torrents of water that carry everything—plants, rocks, topsoil—in their path in a rush to the sea.

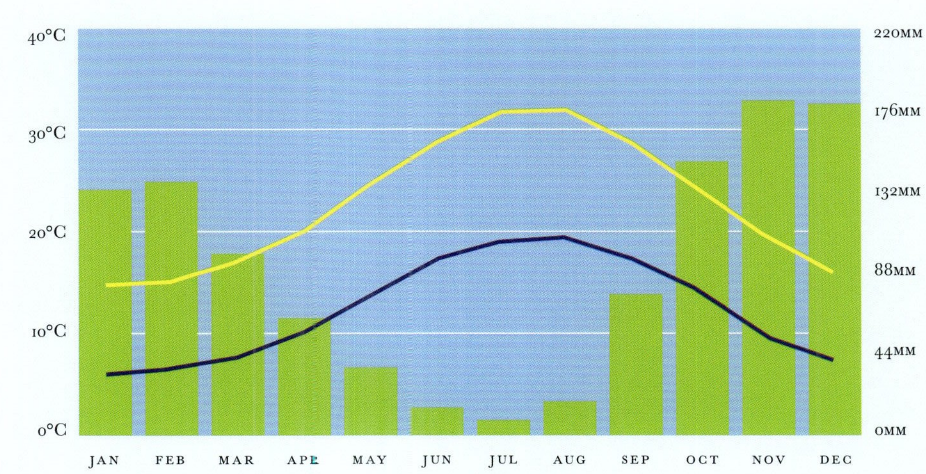

SOURCE: http://www.climatedata.eu/climate.php?loc=grxx0068&lang=en

FIG. 1 CLIMATE DATA FOR CORFU

LOW
HIGH
PRECIP.

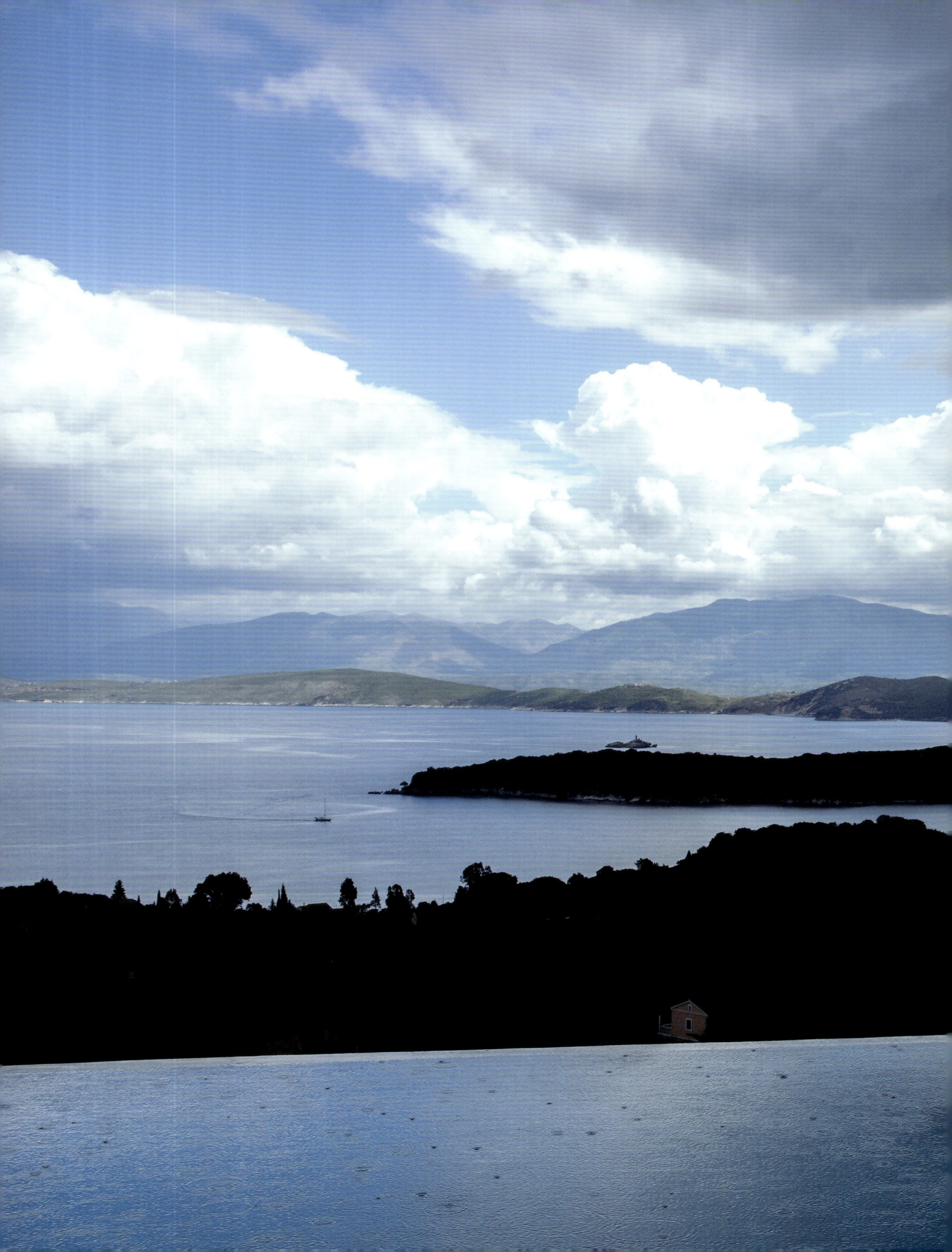

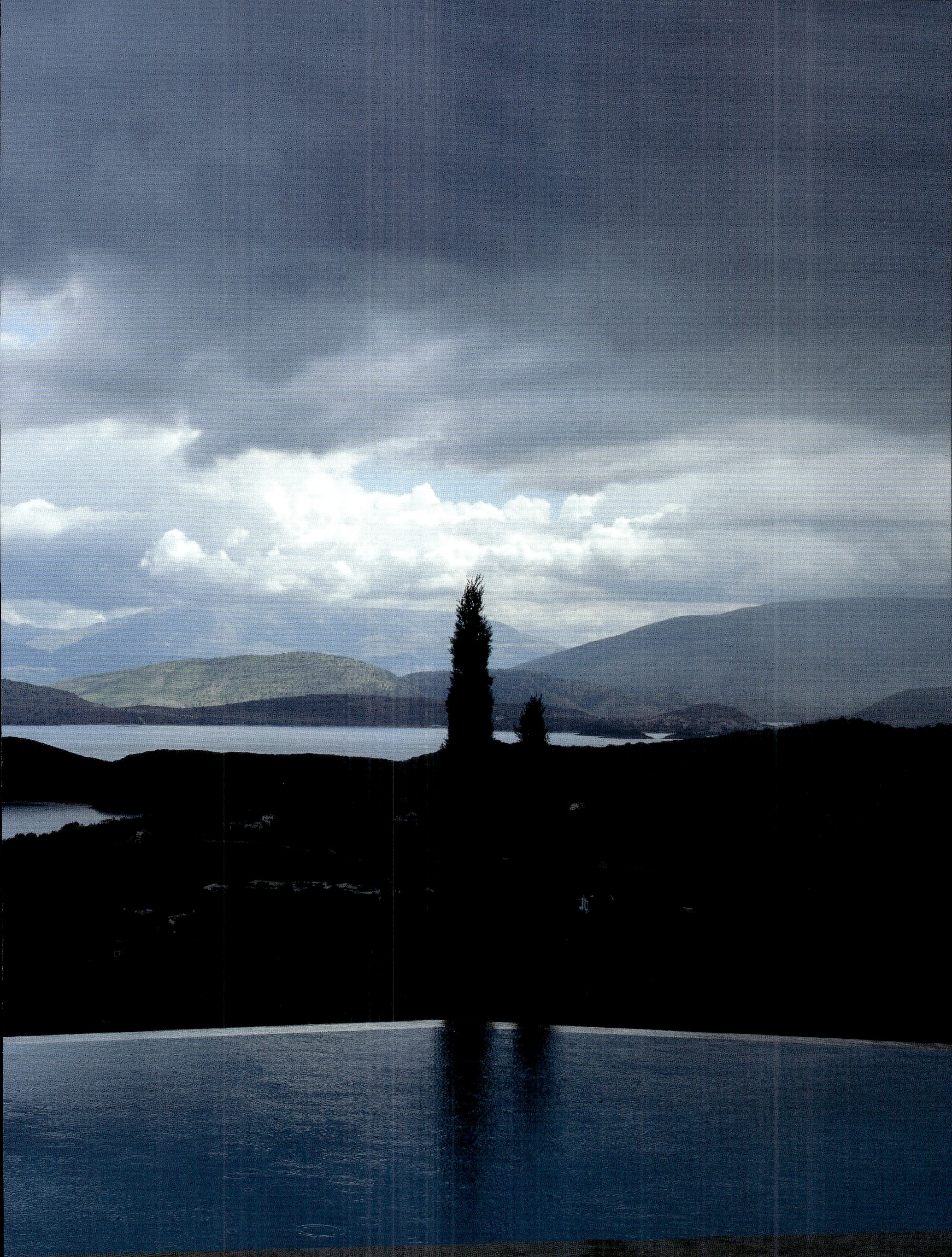

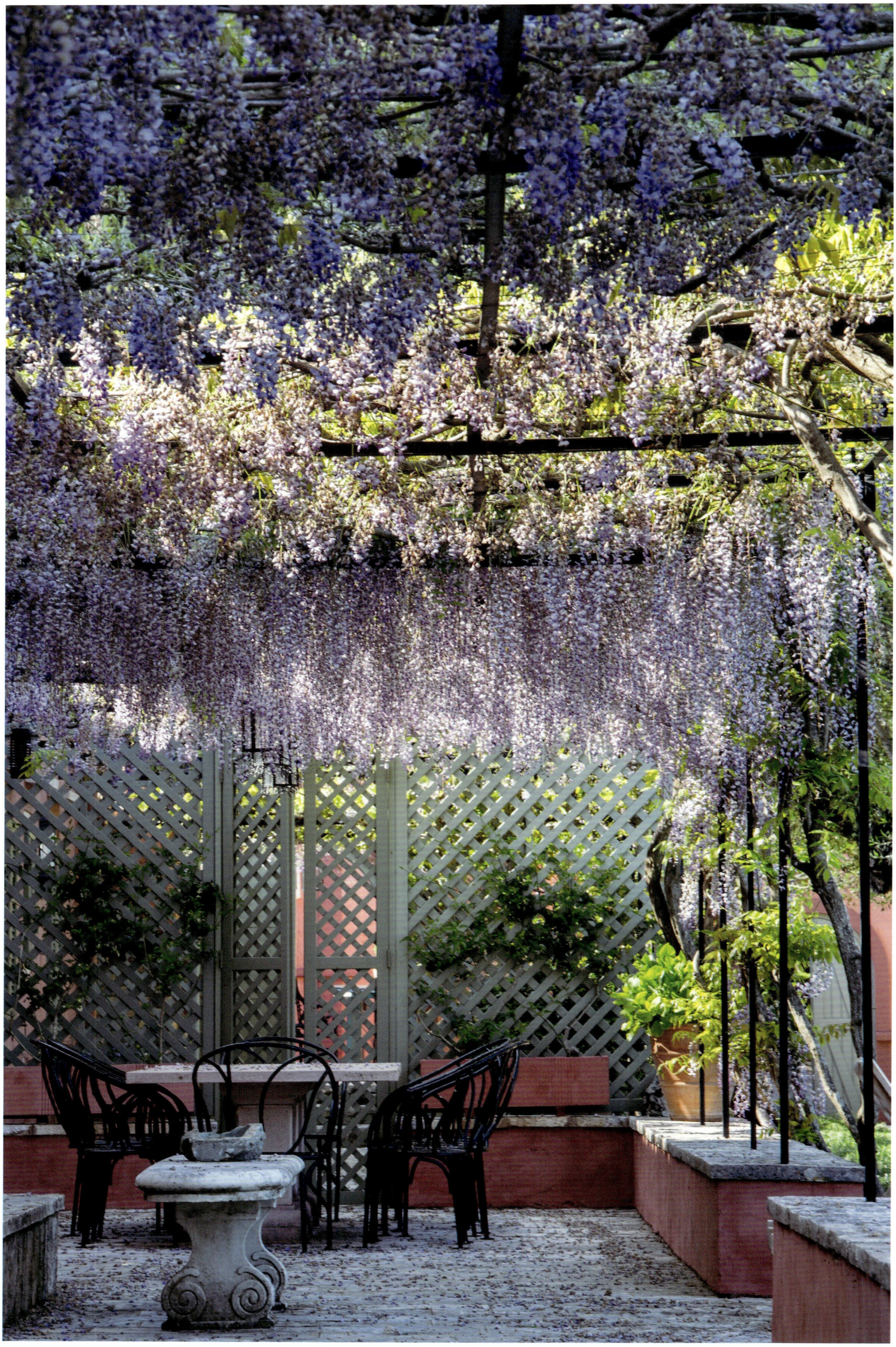

OPPOSITE
At Kanónas, an elegant version of a traditional outdoor sitting area.

Gardeners take a range of measures to cope with drought, such as mainly growing native plants and their cultivated derivatives, collecting and storing rainwater, mulching their planting beds with gravel or organic matter, or using drought-tolerant trees and shrubs to create shade and shelter from drying winds for more tender plants. Even so, those with high consumption of water for swimming pools and irrigation compete directly with the day-to-day needs of less wealthy households. Boring private wells drains the aquifers for all, and encourages the infiltration of sea water in summer—making the water lethal for irrigation and impossible to drink.

Weather. Corfu's summers are milder than those in mainland Greece but they are hot enough for most native plants to stop growing. Temperatures vary greatly by location, with implications for a gardener's choice of plants. While northern gardens are dusted by winter snow, fragrant frangipani (*Plumeria rubra*) and tall basil 'trees' survive from year to year in sheltered courtyards in Lefkímmi. Spring comes earlier on the coast than in the hills, and all through the summer, gardens at sea level are notably warmer than those higher up.

Island winters are damp, sometimes with full weeks of unremitting rain. Clayey soils become too soggy to cultivate and gardens are lashed by winds. Yet winter is a period of active growth. A few colourful flowers can always be found even on the shortest days. The greens of trees and shrubs glow as at no other time of year, and in sunny episodes under a washed sky, the whole land is radiant with the sparkles of water drops.

Especially in coastal gardens, planning for wind often needs as much care as planning for soil retention, drainage, or shade. The *Maïstros* (mistral) arises out of the northwest almost every summer afternoon, whipping up white-horse waves on the sea and sand on the beaches, sending sunbathers scuttling for cover; the same wind brings some of the worst winter storms. The *Sorókos* (sirocco, from the southeast) and the *Ostría* (from the south) blow hot blasts out of the Sahara, even in winter, desiccating the greenery and dumping gritty red dust over everything. The *Garbís* (from the southwest) normally brings rain.

SUNLIGHT AND SHADE

Corfu's fierce summer noonday light clearly calls for areas of shade. It also affects garden makers' choice of shapes and colours and limits the range of plants that can be grown.

Traditional local builders and garden makers are masters of shade, whether it is the deep shade afforded by verandas, the dappled shade under pergolas for leafy vines or wisteria, or the cool green light of secluded areas shaded by big trees. Favourite large shade trees in streets, public squares, and gardens traditionally include plane, linden, black locust (*Robinia pseudoacacia*), nettle tree (*Celtis australis*), silk tree (*Albizia julibrissin*), fruitless mulberry, paper mulberry, Canary palm, and—at higher altitudes—elm, of which an enormous old specimen (*Ulmus minor*) covers the village square at Strinílas. Gardens with large old olive trees rely on these for dappled shade and filtered sunlight, whether for sitting areas or for under-planting with shrubs or other plants. In small gardens, shade trees do double duty: they include walnut and cherry, citrus, apricot, and pear.

Unlike old houses, whose builders sheltered their outdoor sitting areas from the sun and wind, new ones often give primacy to facing the sea and getting good views—though, to the extent possible, their builders also add shaded patios in sheltered places. And most contemporary gardens also incorporate swimming pools and associated open spaces for sunbathing.

In gardens intended as art, strong sunlight calls for sharply delineated shapes. Bright light wipes out subtle details of both shape and colour, and it creates black shadows that reproduce and accentuate strong lines and sharp angles. Recognising this, many contemporary designers create a clear underlying 'bone structure': they incorporate straight lines, sharp angles, changes in level, or simple decisive curves in their hard landscaping, and they combine the resulting clear, definite shapes with almost equally strong ones contributed by planting and sometimes by urns or sculpture.

While brilliant sunlight calls for clearly defined shapes, it washes out all but the brightest flower colours. Corfu's historical gardens in the Italianate tradition make relatively little use of colour. And native Corfiot plants, so useful to gardeners otherwise, provide barely any summer flowers. Today different Corfu gardeners have different thoughts on the use of colour. Those who have chosen a muted plant palette favouring greens, greys, and silvers point out that colour is already conjured up around them by the island's extraordinary dawns and dusks reflected in the surrounding sea. Others opt for brightly flowering climbers such as Chinese trumpet vine (*Campsis grandiflora*) and *Bougainvillea* and for brilliant arrays of tender flowering plants, either in a favoured flower bed or in pots that are watered daily through the summer.

OPPOSITE TOP
A combination of drought-resistant groundcover plants for summer colour at Petróti, with blue *Convolvulus sabatius* and orange *Bulbine frutescens* along with *Agave attenuata*. Design by Julie Toll and Alithea Johns.

OPPOSITE BOTTOM
Spaces for sun-lounging never featured in traditional gardens but are crucial elements in contemporary ones, as at Velanídi, Alithea Johns' personal garden.

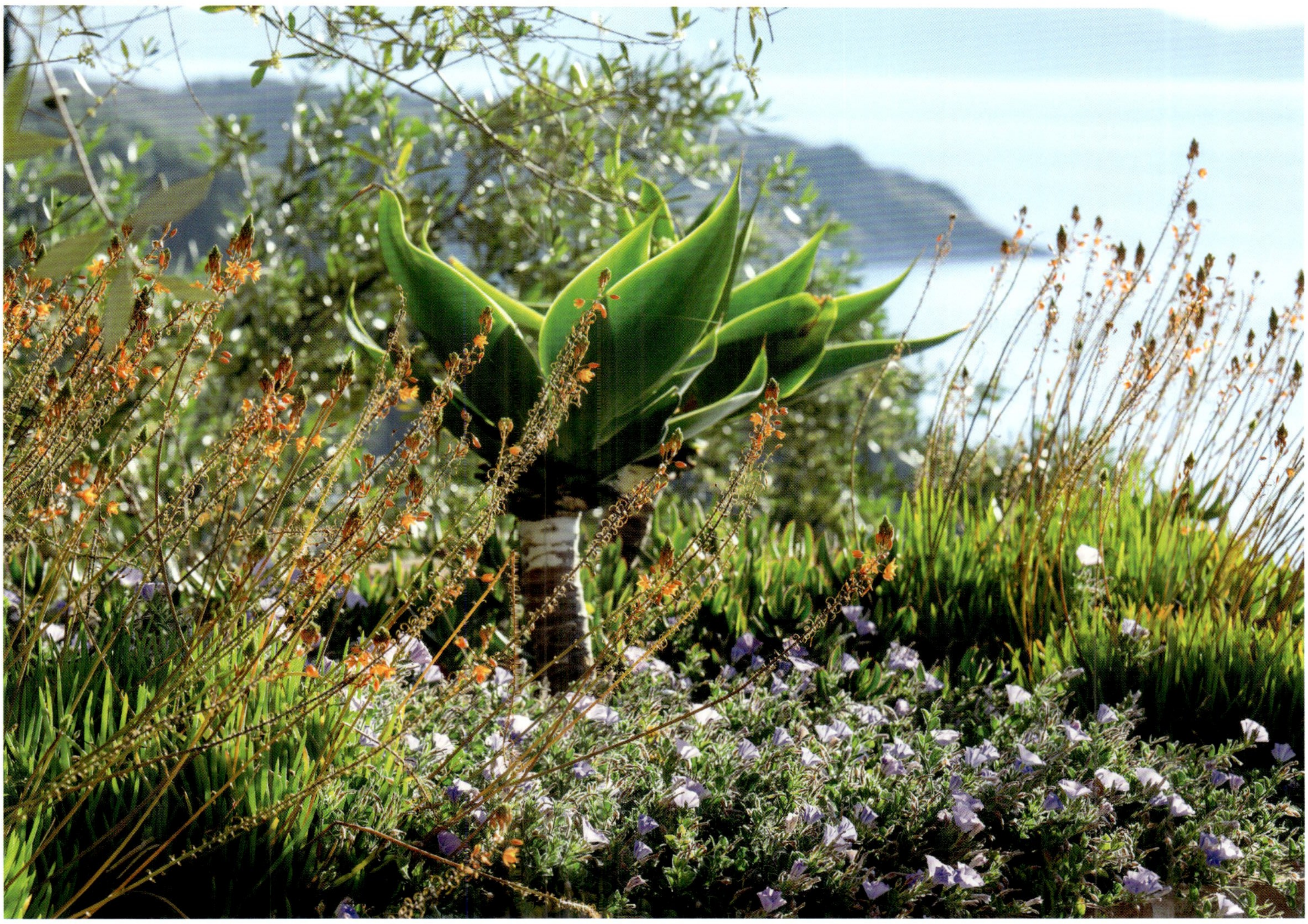

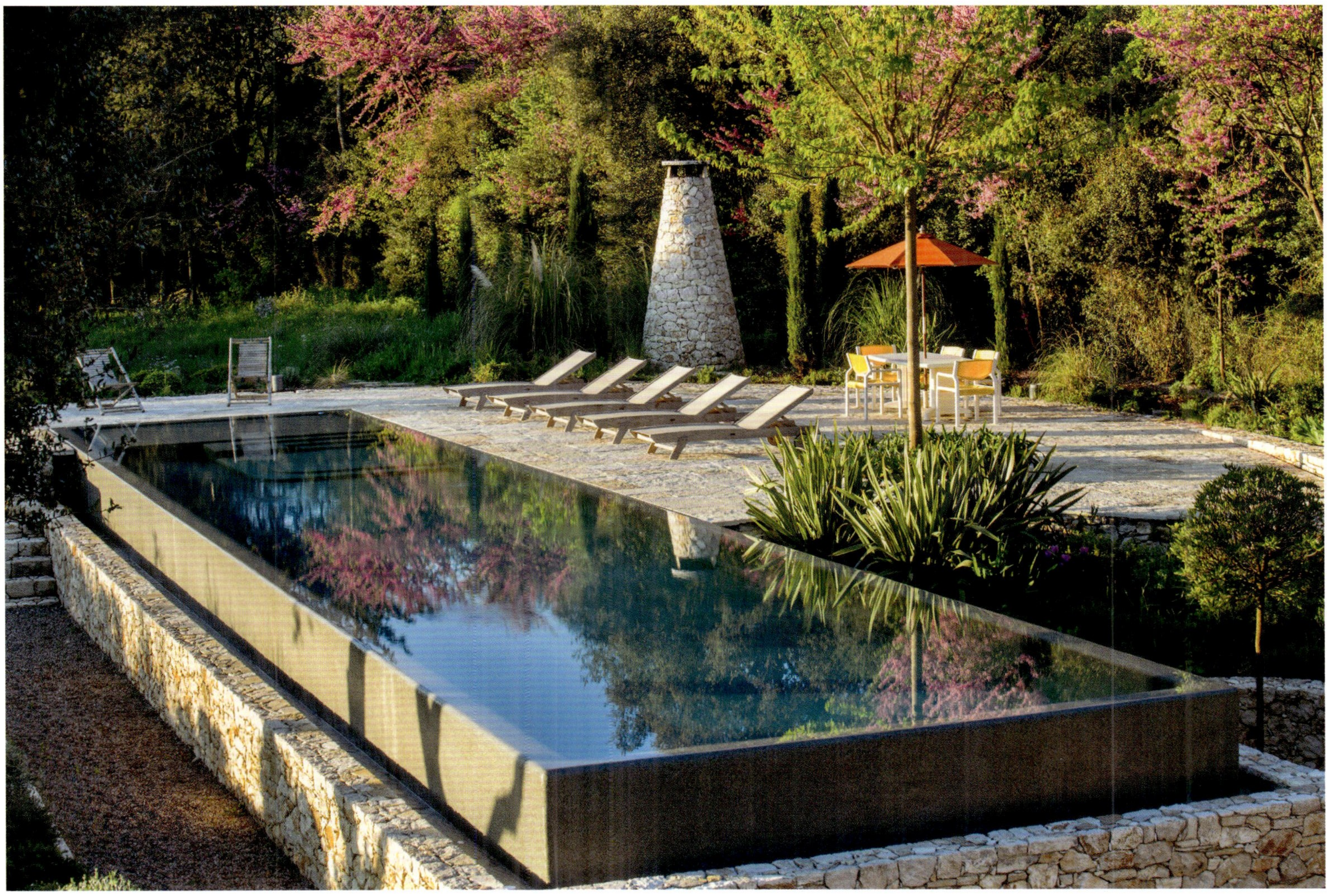

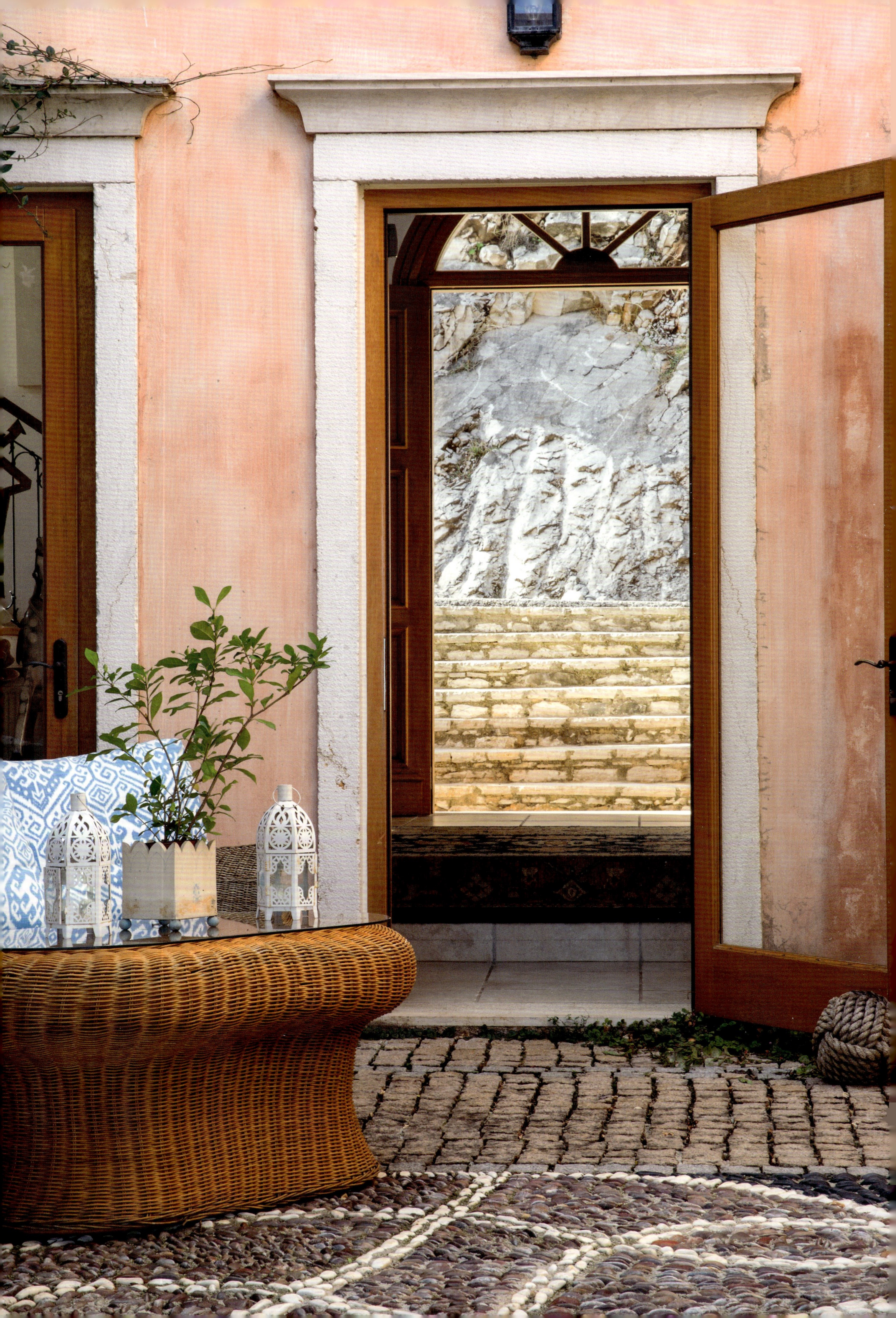

OPPOSITE
At several properties, elegant homes and garden elements are juxtaposed with brute rock, with the contrast highlighting the sophistication of the one and the rough, elemental nature of the other. This outdoor room at Linamia, home of Timothy and Victoria Chadwick, is open to the sea, while on the other side the house faces a sheer rock wall.

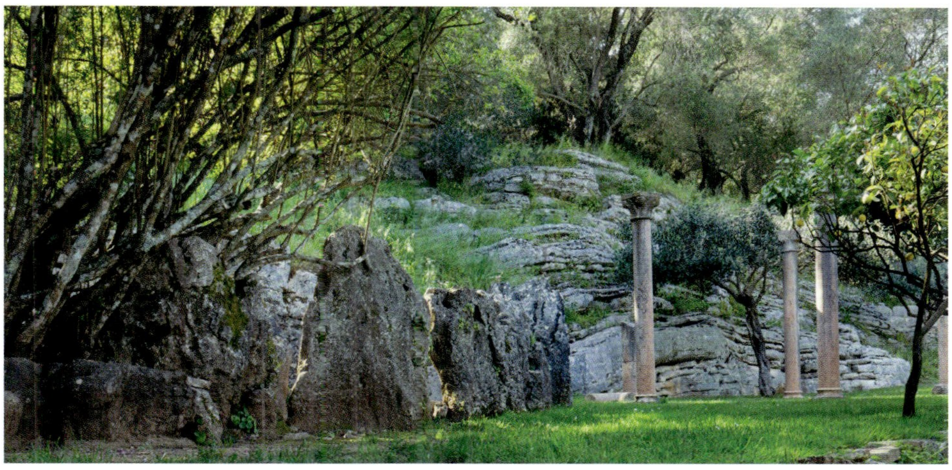

These Classical stone columns seem perfectly in place against the wild crags at Kanónas on the Rothschild estate.

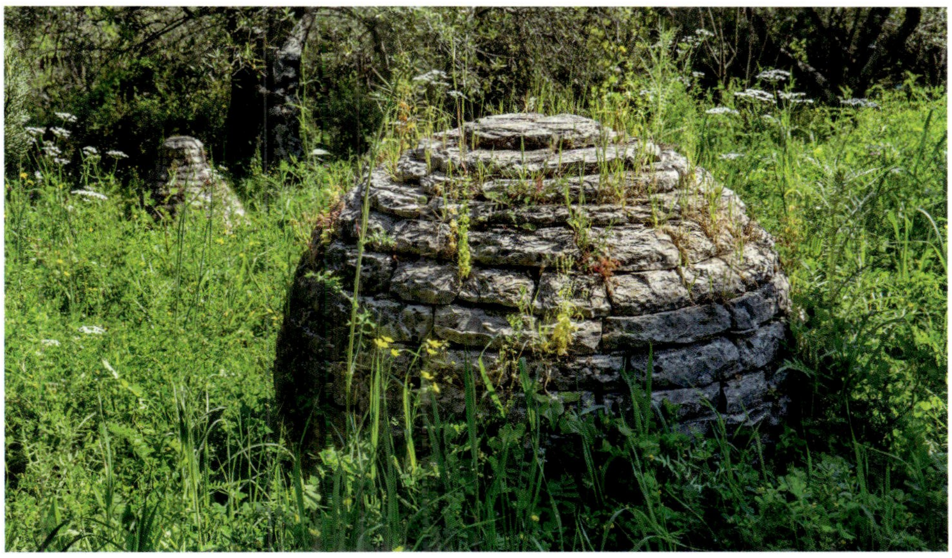

Cairn sculptures by a local stonemason at Katsafaláta.

ELEMENTS OF CORFIOT STYLE

What makes a garden 'Corfiot'? Across the spectrum of local gardens, certain ingredients give a characteristic local feel: stone, ironwork, terracotta urns, native plants, certain cultivated plants that are recurring favourites, and a tendency to incorporate fruit or other food crops into gardens that are mainly decorative.

Stone. Stone is practically everywhere in Corfu. Jagged shapes of pale limestone break through the ground as boulders and crags on wild hillsides, but also as untamed outcrops in gardens, where they visibly relate to carved urns, finials, and balusters worked from the same stone. The local stone appears again, smoothly cut, in city paving; roughly hewn, in rural terracing and boundary walls; and, hacked from the ground but precisely aligned, in the walls of houses old and new. Contemporary garden designers call for stone patio paving and stone walls made using traditional methods, in an effort to match the materials in the surrounding landscape.

At Sto Dásos, wisteria grows on a typical wrought-iron pergola evoking the tendrils of vines.

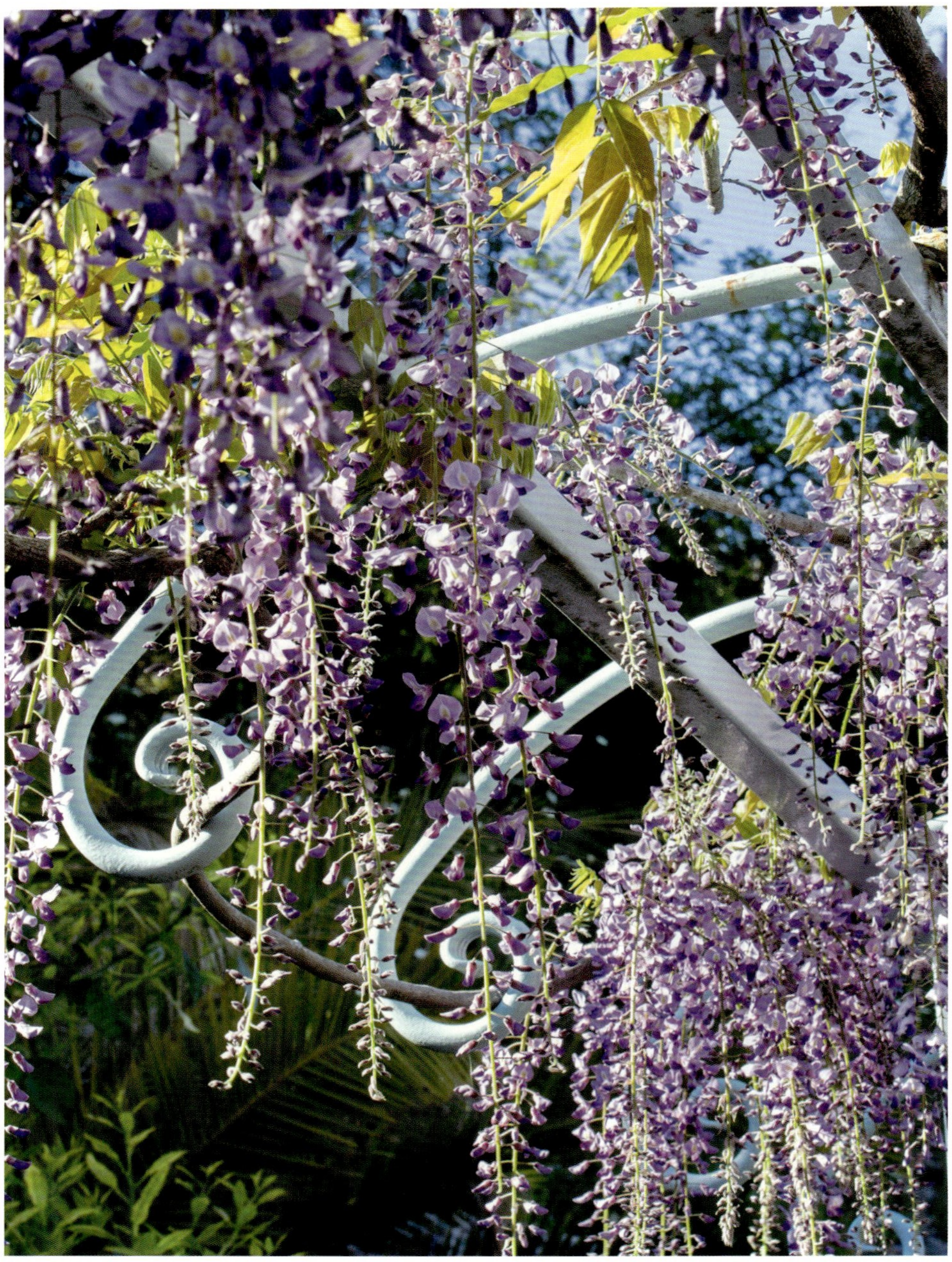

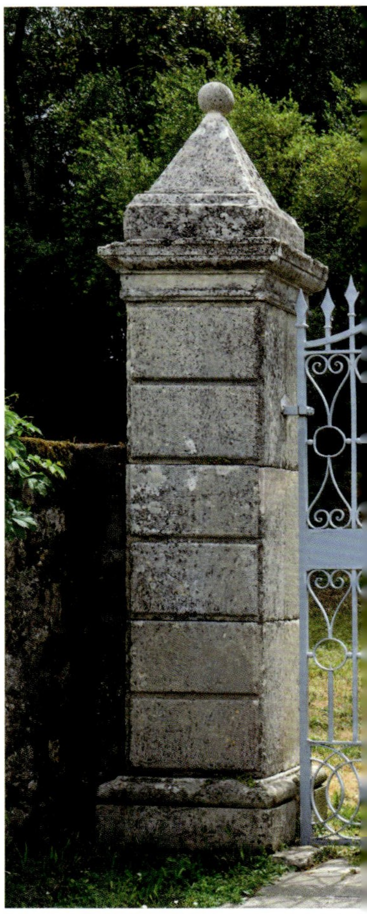

CENTRE TOP
The wrought-iron entrance gate at Doukádes.

Iron. Richly worked wrought iron is another distinctive local feature. On houses, it is seen in balcony rails, banisters, and door grilles, but it is also the material of choice for garden pergolas, gates and fences, outdoor lanterns, and garden furniture. Contemporary villas almost all have wrought-iron entrance gates, whether plain and elegant or richly worked and fanciful, as well as pergolas for flowering creepers. Curly edgings, evoking the tendrils of vines, appear equally on the pergolas of village houses and those of costly modern villas. Ironworking is still a widely distributed skill in the island. Local blacksmiths use old Venetian patterns that have become part of the Corfiot vernacular over the centuries, as well as designing their own.

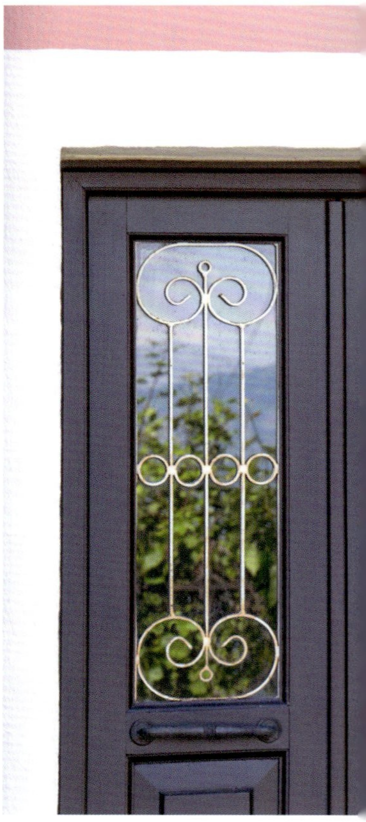

Traditional Corfiot front doors typically have glass panes with decorative wrought-iron grilles, such as this one at Siniés.

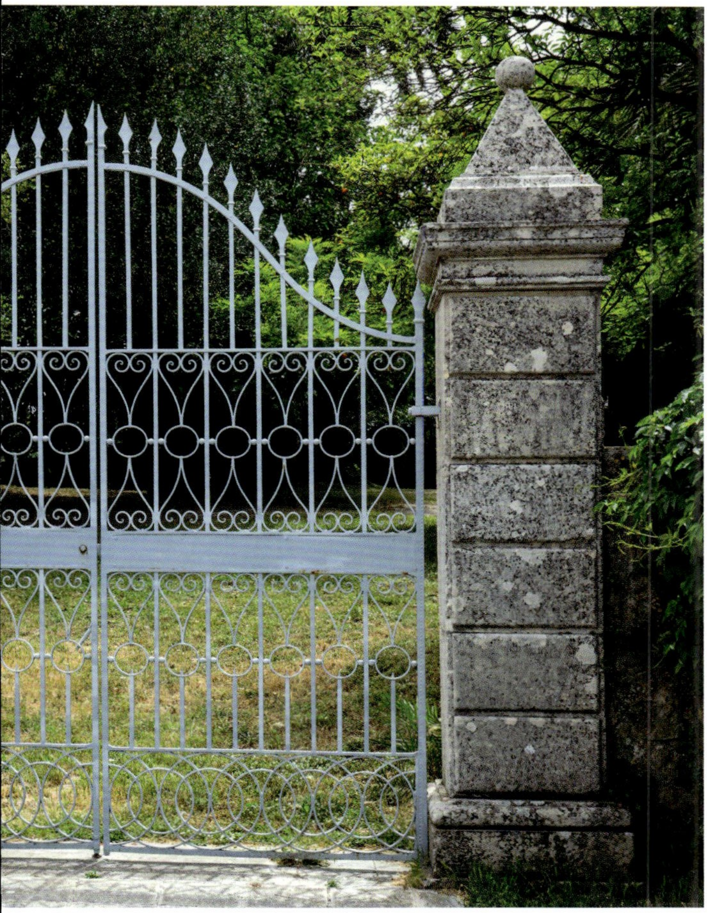

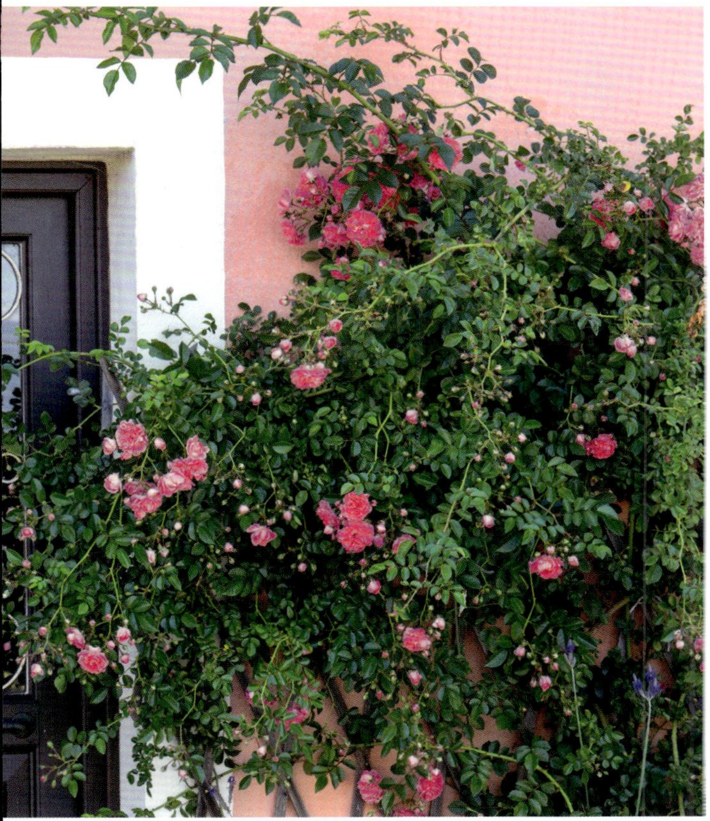

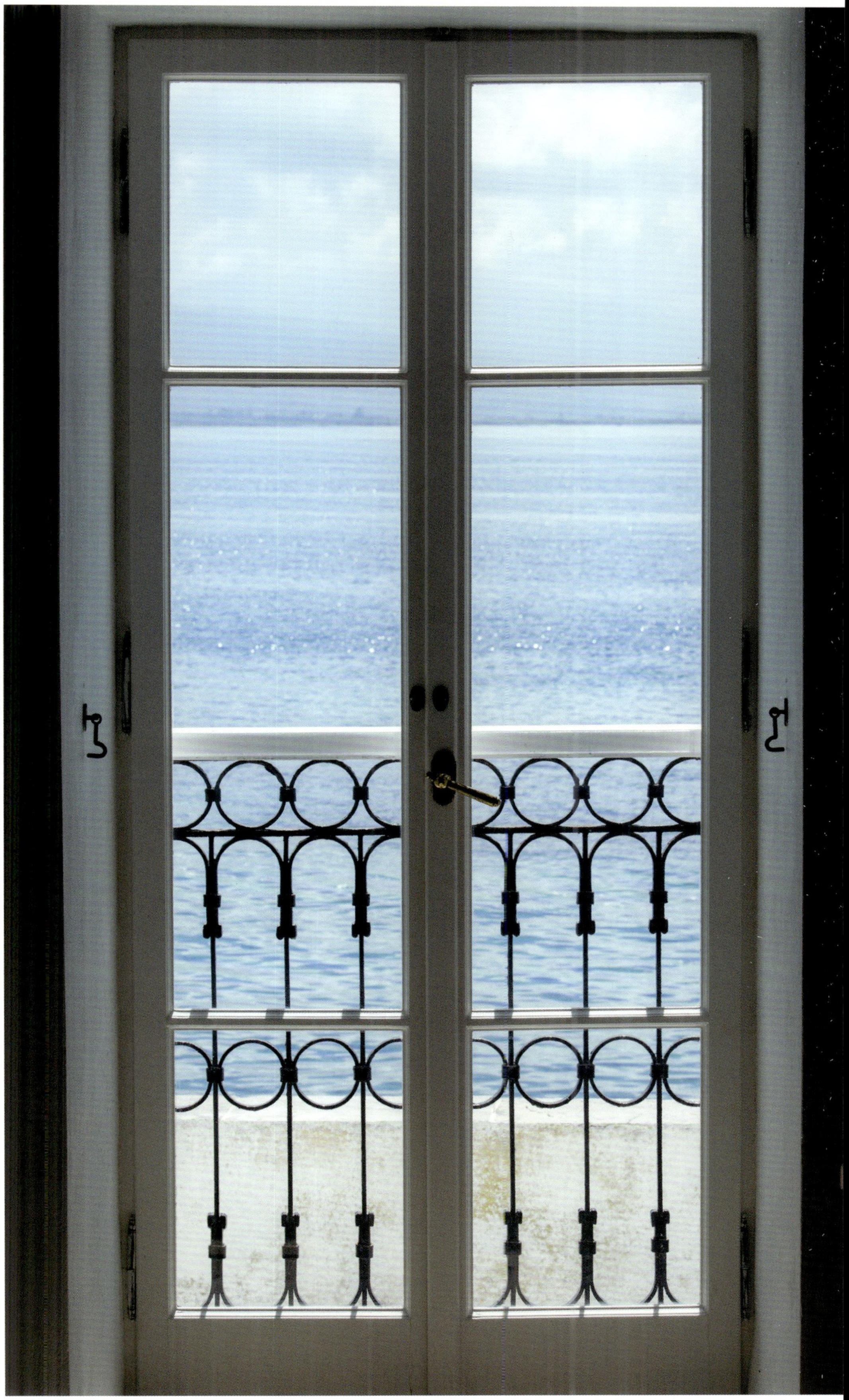

A wrought-iron balcony overlooking the sea at Kouloúra.

OVERLEAF
A wrought-iron pergola shades a terrace at the home of Jehanne Legrand Theódotou at Kastaniá.

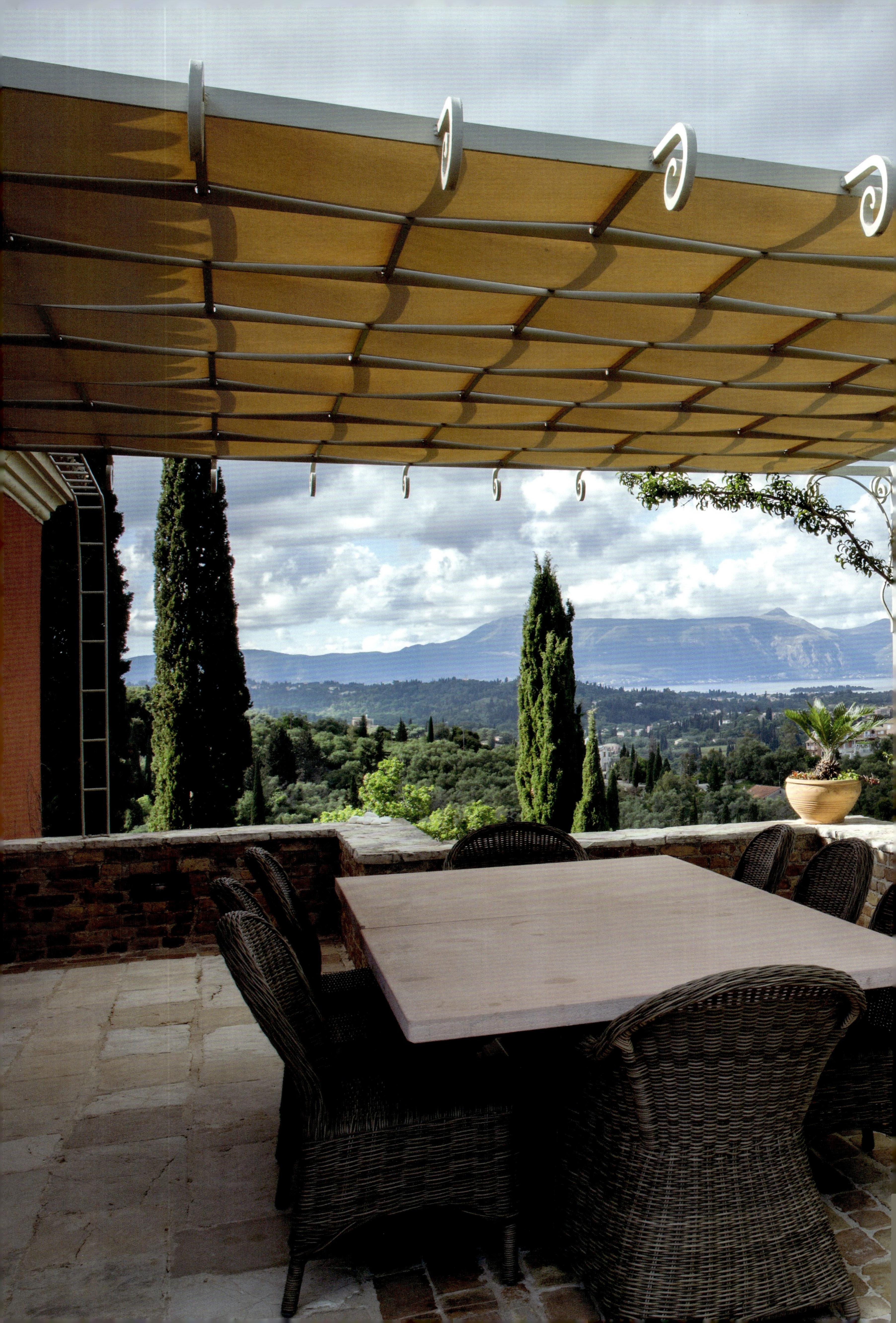

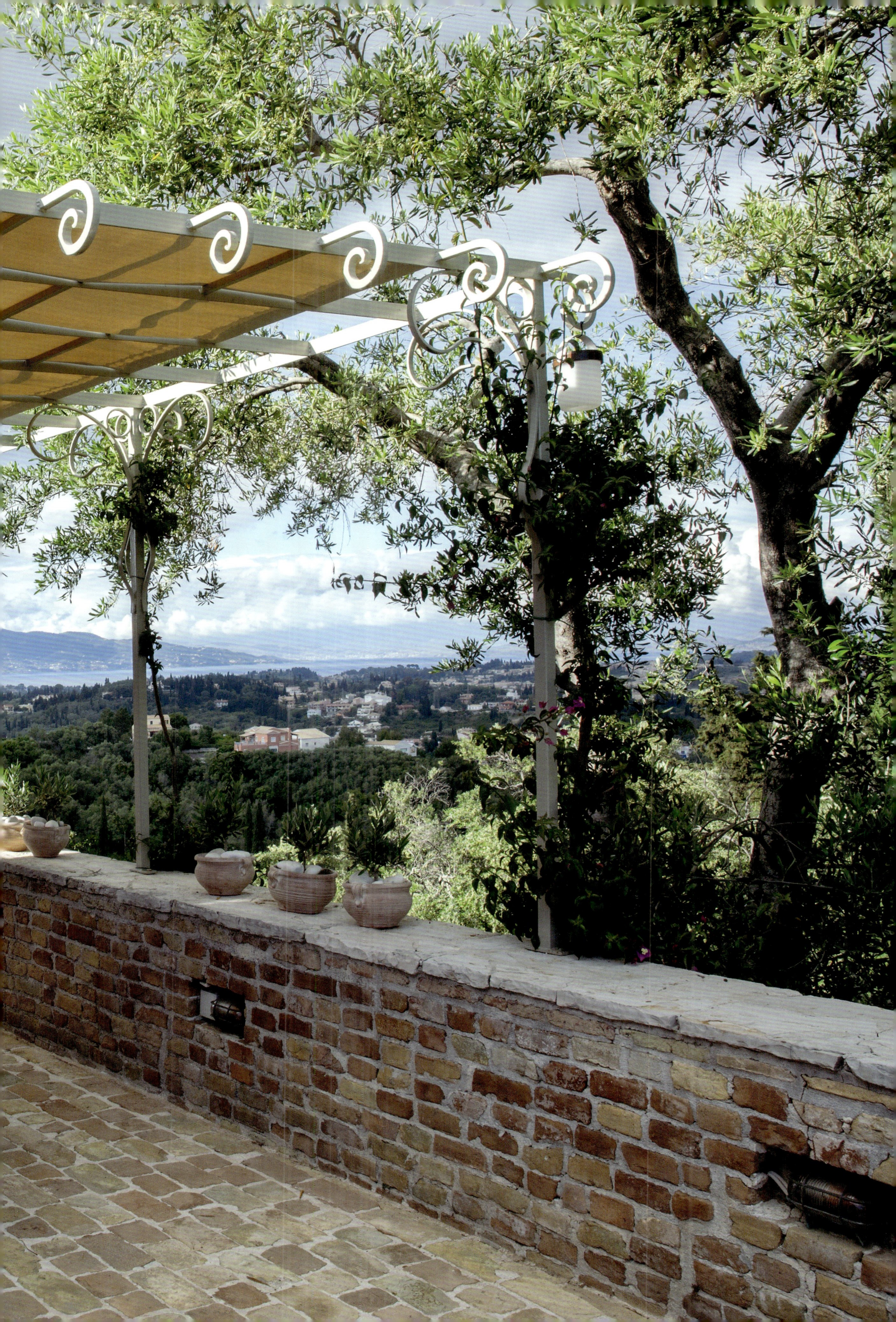

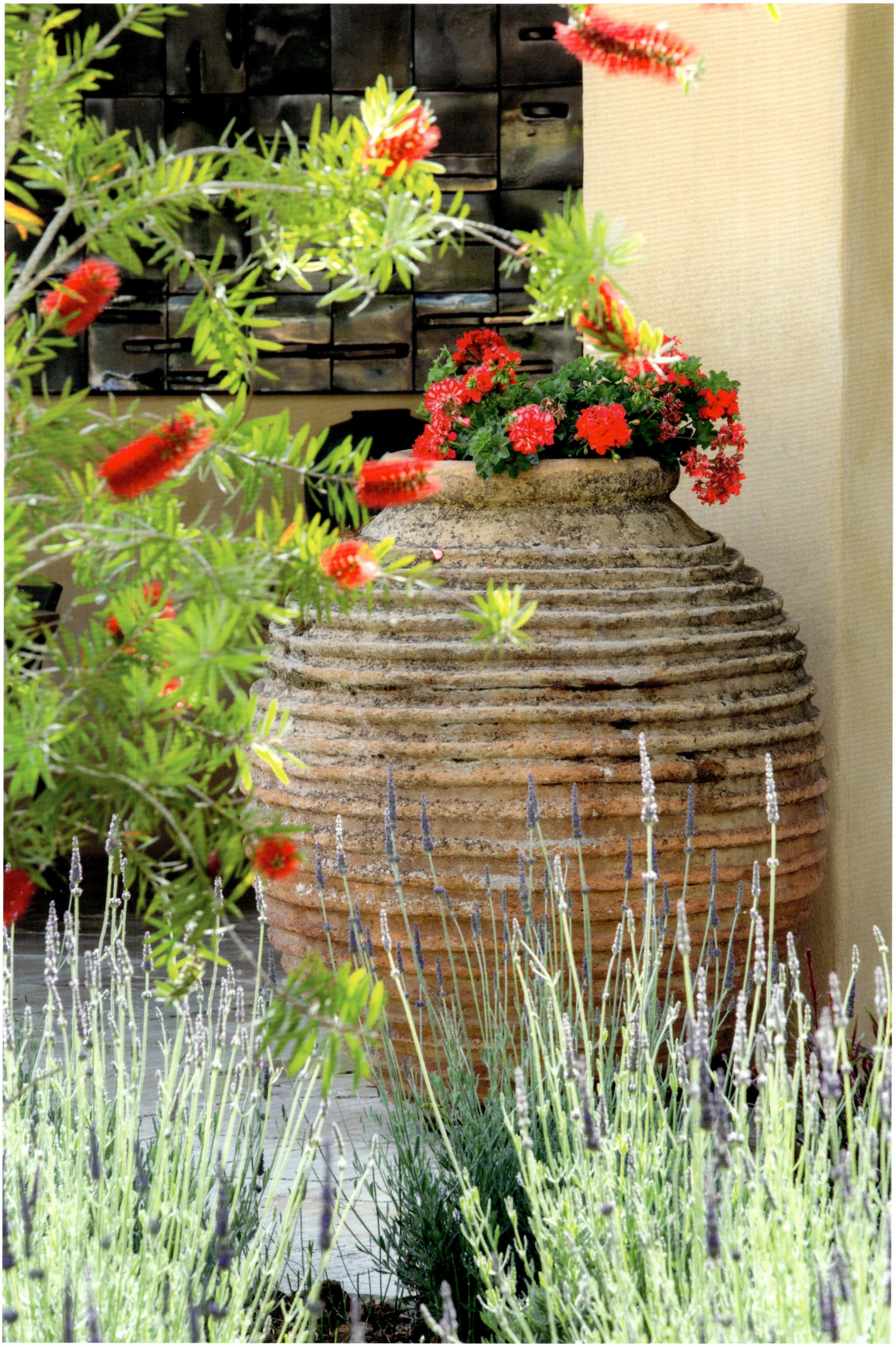

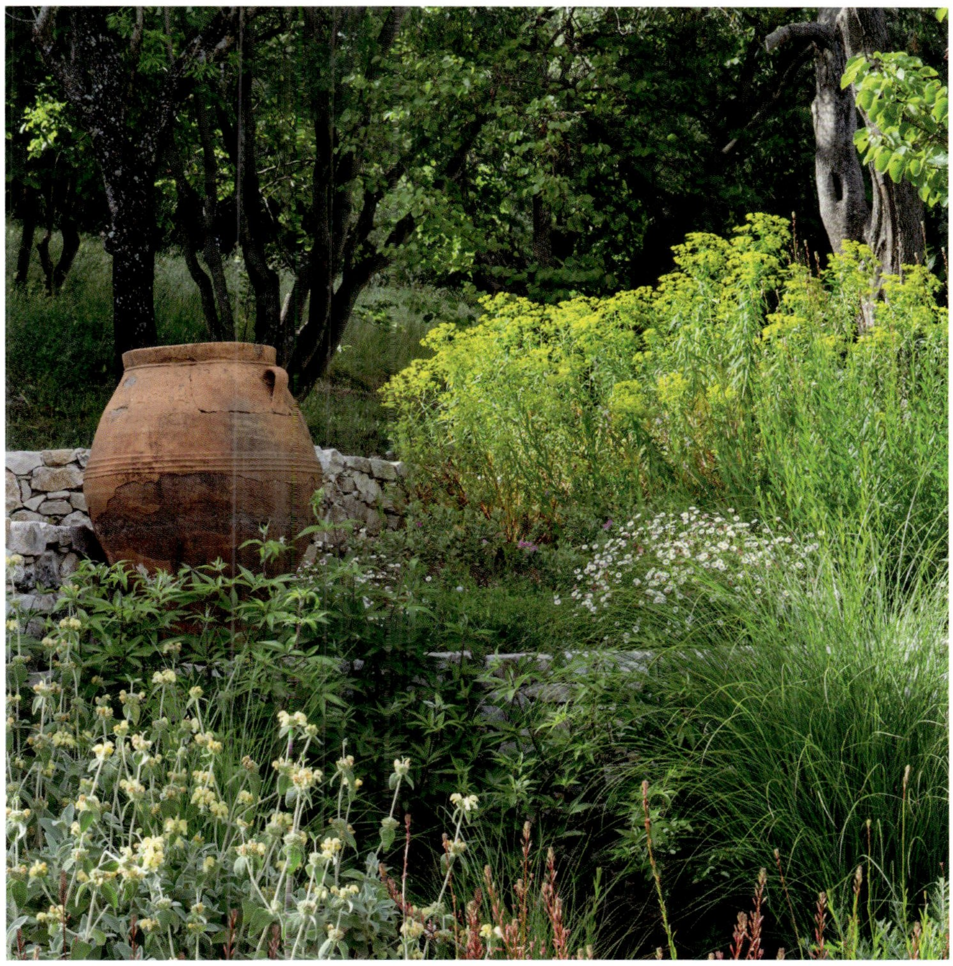

At Agnos House, the placement of this old urn draws attention to the transition zone between the planted garden and the wild trees found on the hillside. Design by Jennifer Gay.

Terracotta urns. Often large enough to hold a man, these urns are distinctively Greek. In Corfu they evoke the past, when they were widely used for storage and for exporting olive oil. Placed in a flower bed, in the angle of a walkway, or at the corner of a patio, battered and chipped in places and sometimes left sticky with the oil they used to hold, these urns ground the attention and supply local atmosphere as few other garden 'props' can. They appear equally in the gardens of old noble houses and in contemporary and village counterparts. Village gardeners usually use them as flower containers, in company with the recycled feta tins that are often considered just as decorative and need less soil to fill.

Some urns still in use are hundreds of years old. The best have the same pale colour as the old local clay roof tiles and bricks, which are no longer made and are highly sought-after for decoration of both houses and gardens. The darker urns evoke the ubiquitous modern terracotta roof tiles. The best urns readily available in Corfu today come from Crete but can often be bought from the backs of trucks that travel the local lanes in summer.

OPPOSITE
Backed by a contemporary ceramic sculpture and combined with lavender and bottlebrush—a far-from-traditional plant in Corfu—an old urn at historic Krevatsoúla has adapted perfectly to changing times. Design by Eléni Georgiádis.

Roses, a perennial favourite in Corfu, abound in the front garden of Vassílis Katékis in Chrisída.

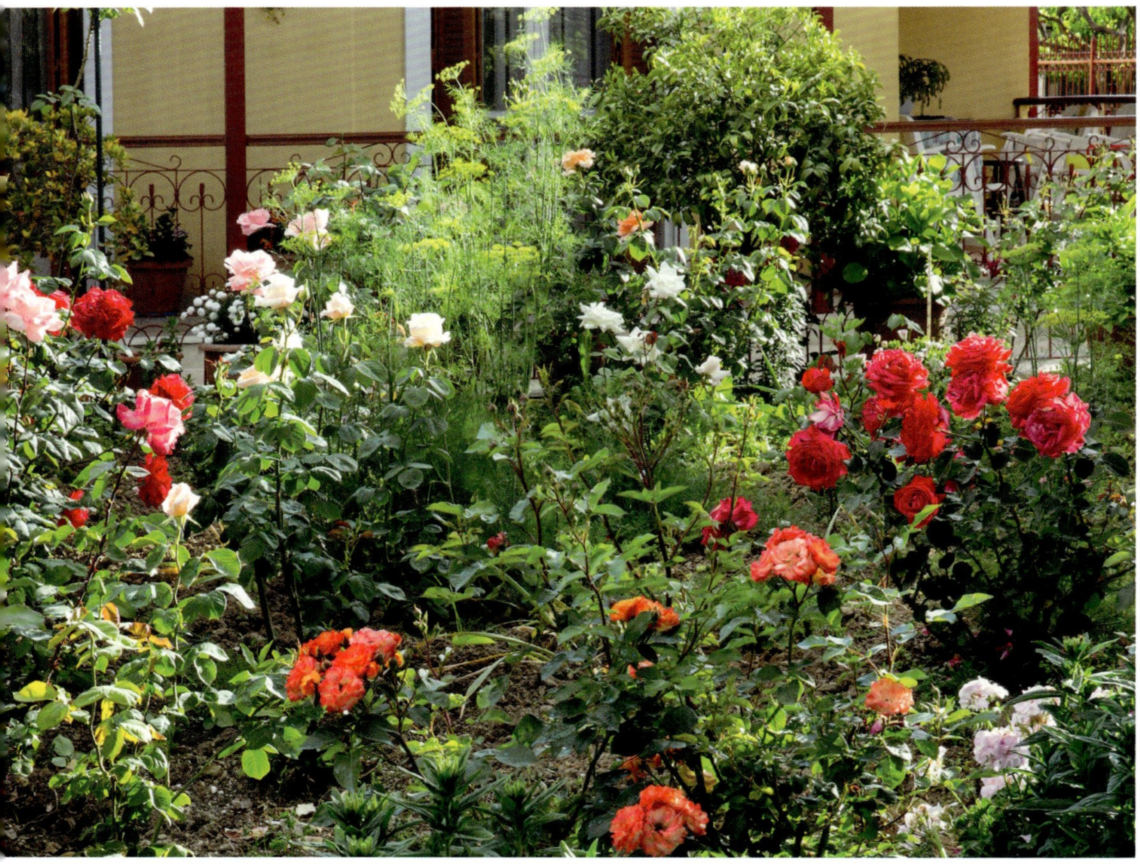

Two aromatic drought-resistant favourites, creeping rosemary (*Rosmarinus officinalis* 'Prostratus') and *Santolina chamaecyparissus*.

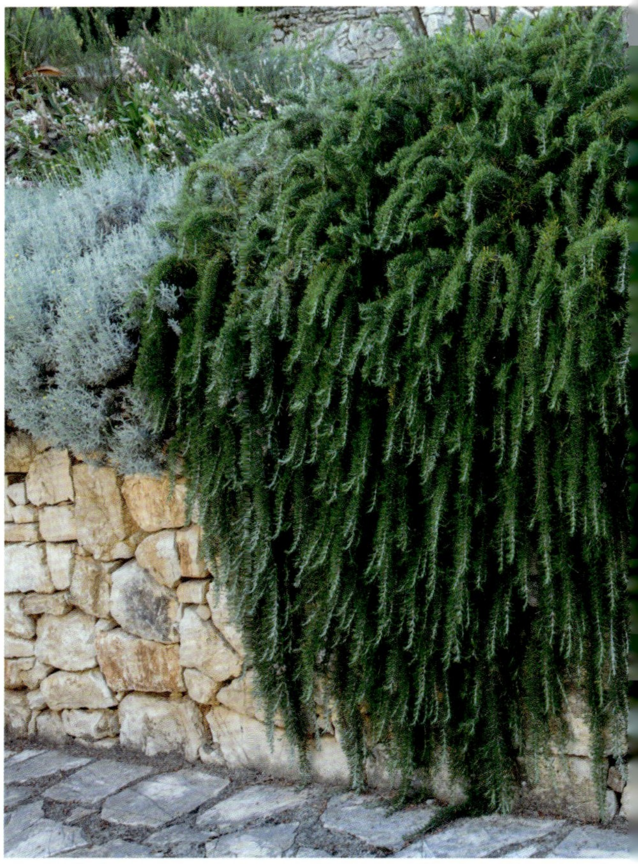

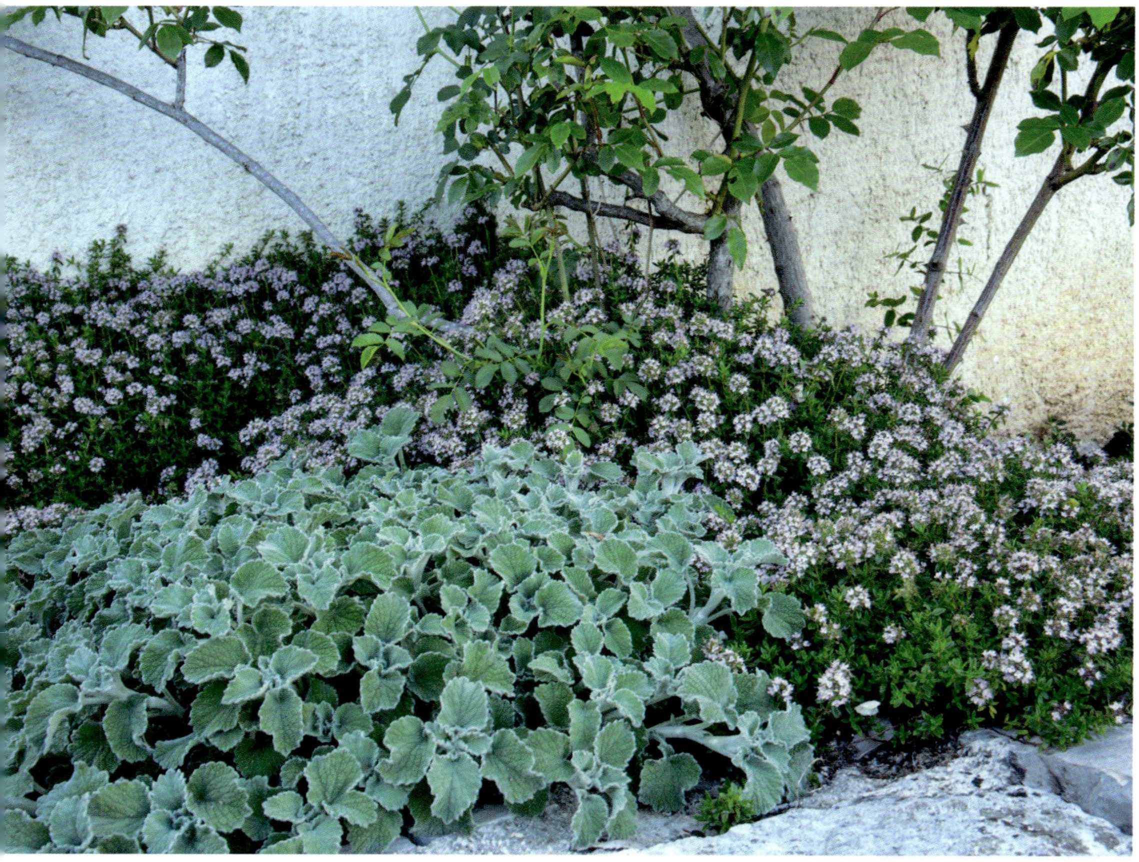

Aromatic thyme (*Thymus serpyllum*) and *Marrubium incanum* in a private garden at Rou.

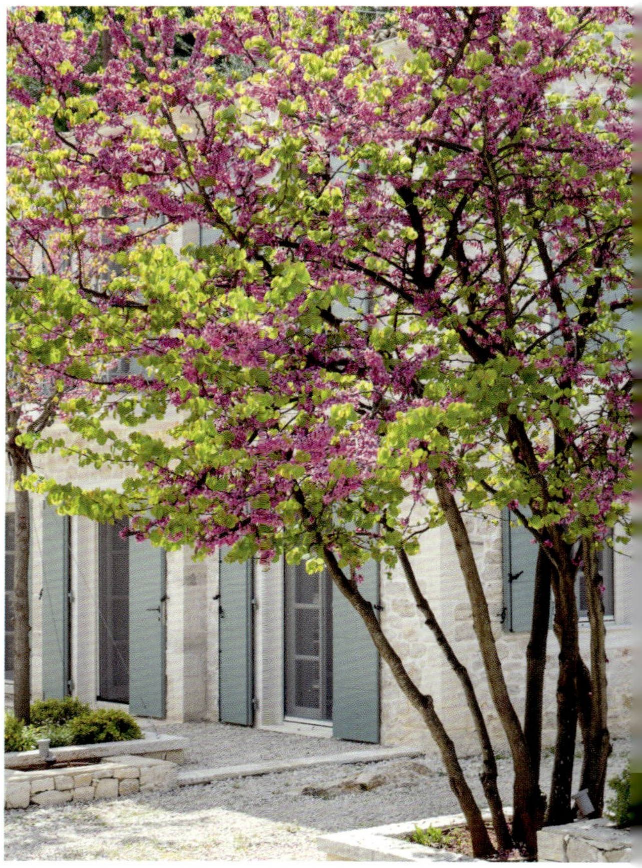

Native Judas trees (*Cercis siliquastrum*) are an important feature of the garden at Caliden, where new trees have been planted to complement those found on site and on the surrounding hillside. Design by Jennifer Gay.

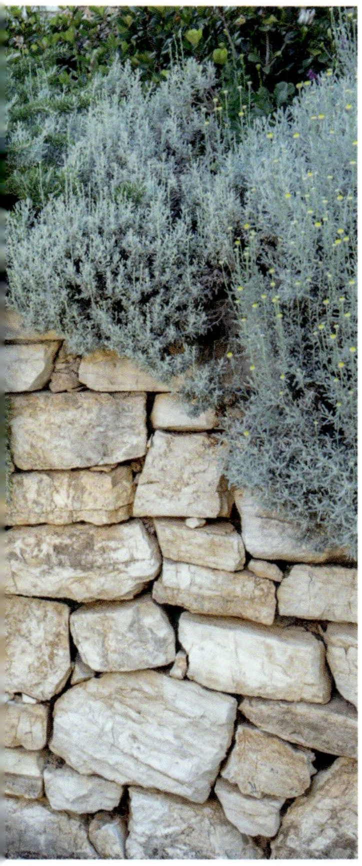

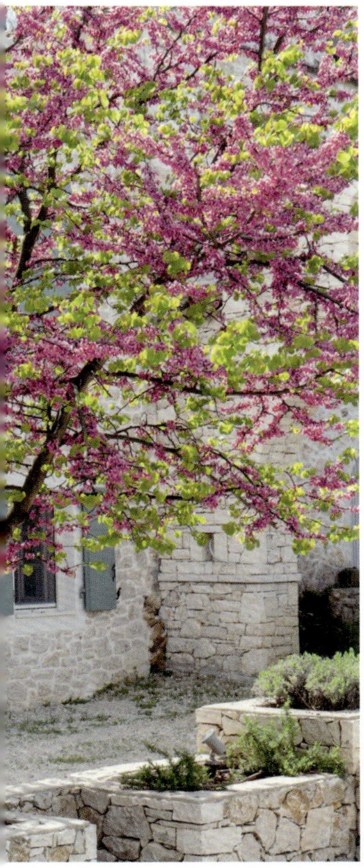

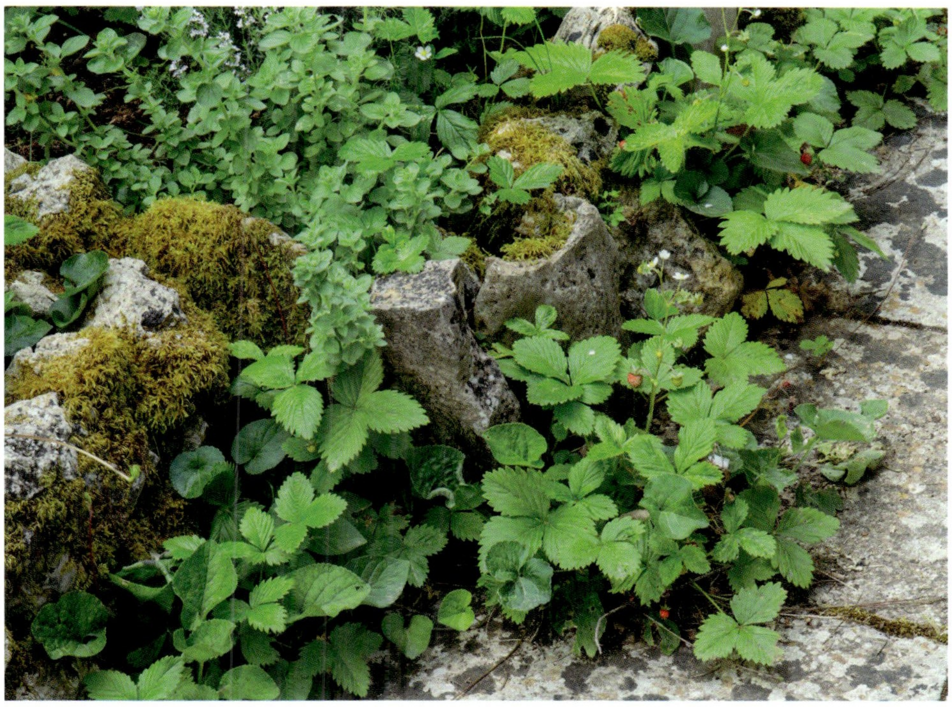

At Gastoúri, mint, thyme, marjoram, and fennel crowd into this herb bed edged with wild strawberries.

Typical plants. Drought-resistant and beautiful, olive, citrus, and native pencil cypress trees (*Cupressus sempervirens* var. *pyramidalis*) are recurrent favourites in Corfu gardens, as are Chinese trumpet vine and oleander, with their joyous colours. And, in the island's always-humid air, gardeners noticeably choose plants for scent. Jasmine and star jasmine (*Trachelospermum jasminoides*), wisteria, roses, *Cestrum nocturnum*, and gardenia are favoured, as are freesias and lilies, petunias, carnations, and winter-flowering stocks, as well as aromatic herbs and shrubs such as rosemary, lavender, myrtle (*Myrtus communis*), and bay. This predilection for scented plants ties in with Corfiots' strong appreciation for scents in the wild landscape, for example from broom, wild roses, honeysuckle, and fragrant clematis (*Clematis flammula*), as well as from native aromatic herbs.

Mediterranean native trees and shrubs are now widely used in local gardens. Designers appreciate these plants for their drought resistance as well as their decorative value, using not just cypresses and pines, as their nineteenth-century predecessors did, but also broadleaved evergreen native trees and shrubs to provide the backbone of a garden's planting. With them are often planted shrubs native to mediterranean climates beyond Corfu, such as rosemary and a range of grey-leaved shrubs including *Westringia fruticosa*, *Atriplex halimus*, lavender, and tree germander (*Teucrium fruticans*). Typically, such shrub plantings are kept pruned, both to achieve sculptural effects and to prevent them breaking apart in wet windy weather.

A shady veranda at Afiónas with grapes and decorative plants.

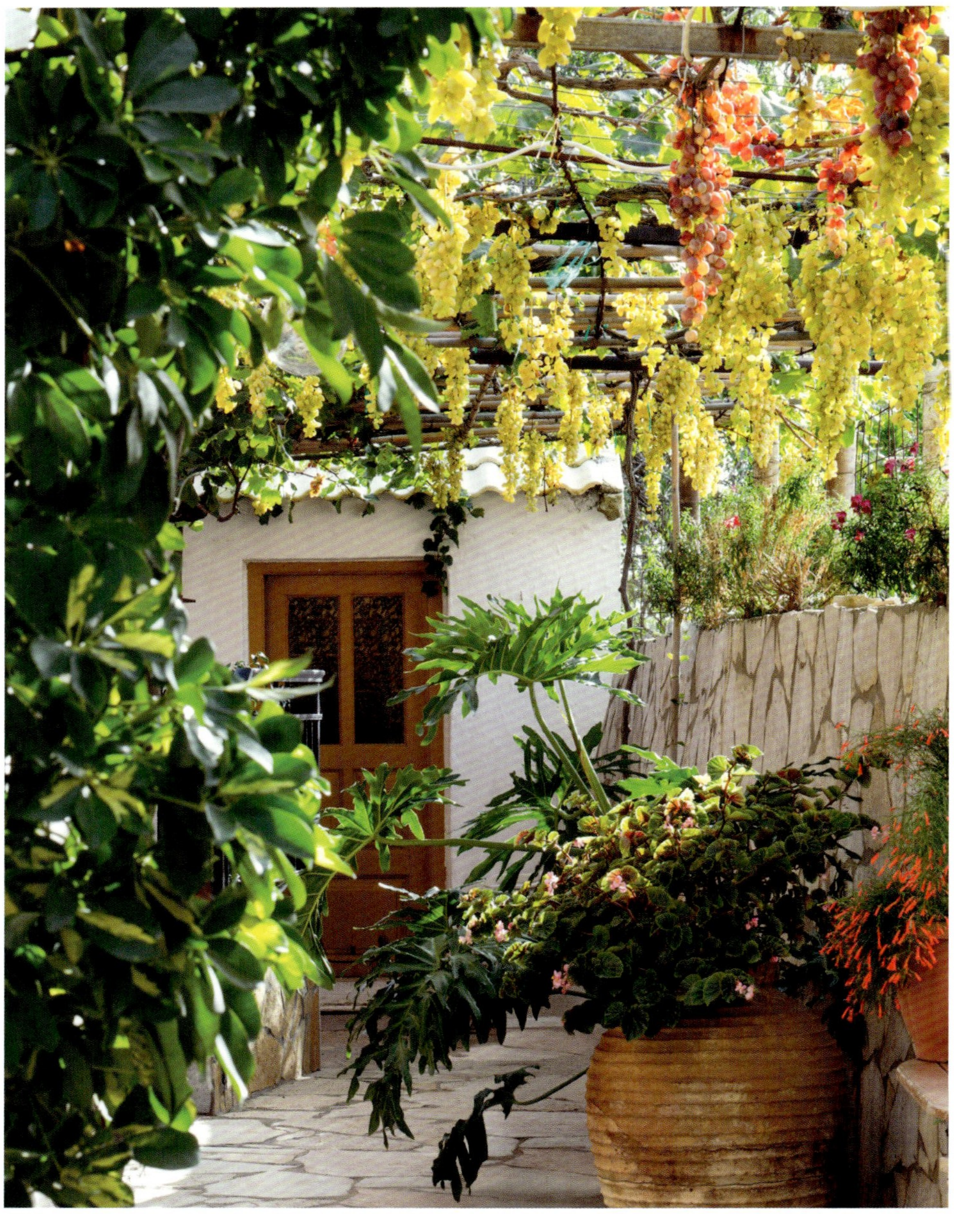

OPPOSITE
White irises are grown under orange trees at Katsafaláta.

Combining useful with ornamental plants. In this island where the working countryside is never far away, gardens tend to mix the edible with the decorative. Village gardens and old estates have always done so, and Corfu shares with the rest of Greece the tradition of the *avlí*: a courtyard garden that combines fruit and flowers—even small urban gardens and balconies usually feature at least a lemon tree and a pot of tiny-leaved Greek basil. Though contemporary villa gardens tend to be mainly ornamental, many of them feature planting that evokes the former agricultural uses of the land. Often, too, garden owners with urban backgrounds take pride in growing fruit and vegetables, harvesting the olives or other fruits from their trees, providing hives for bees, and making wine from their patio grapes.

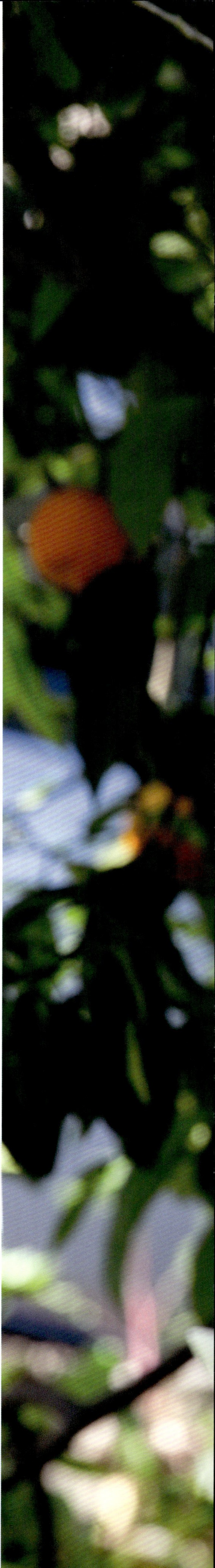

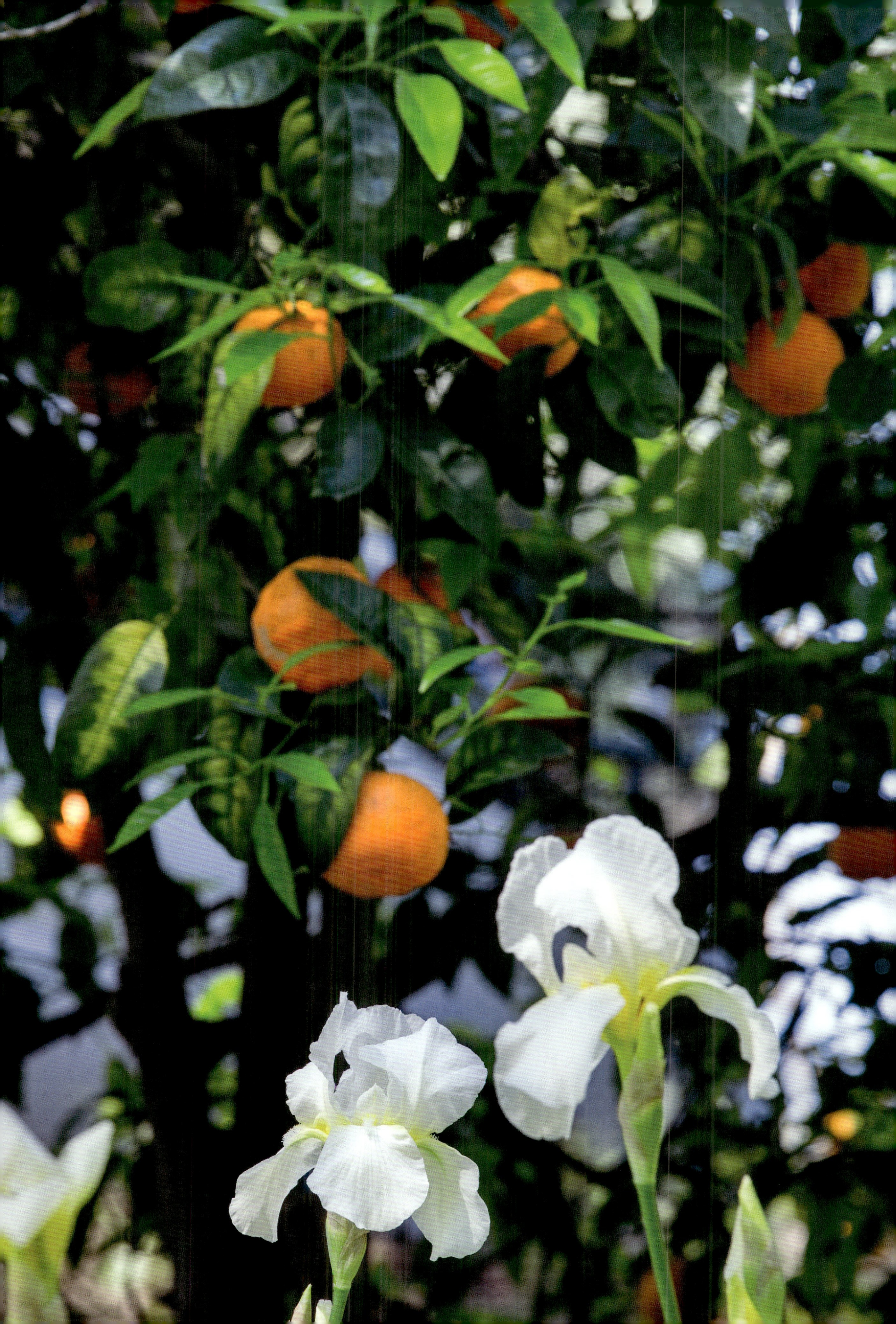

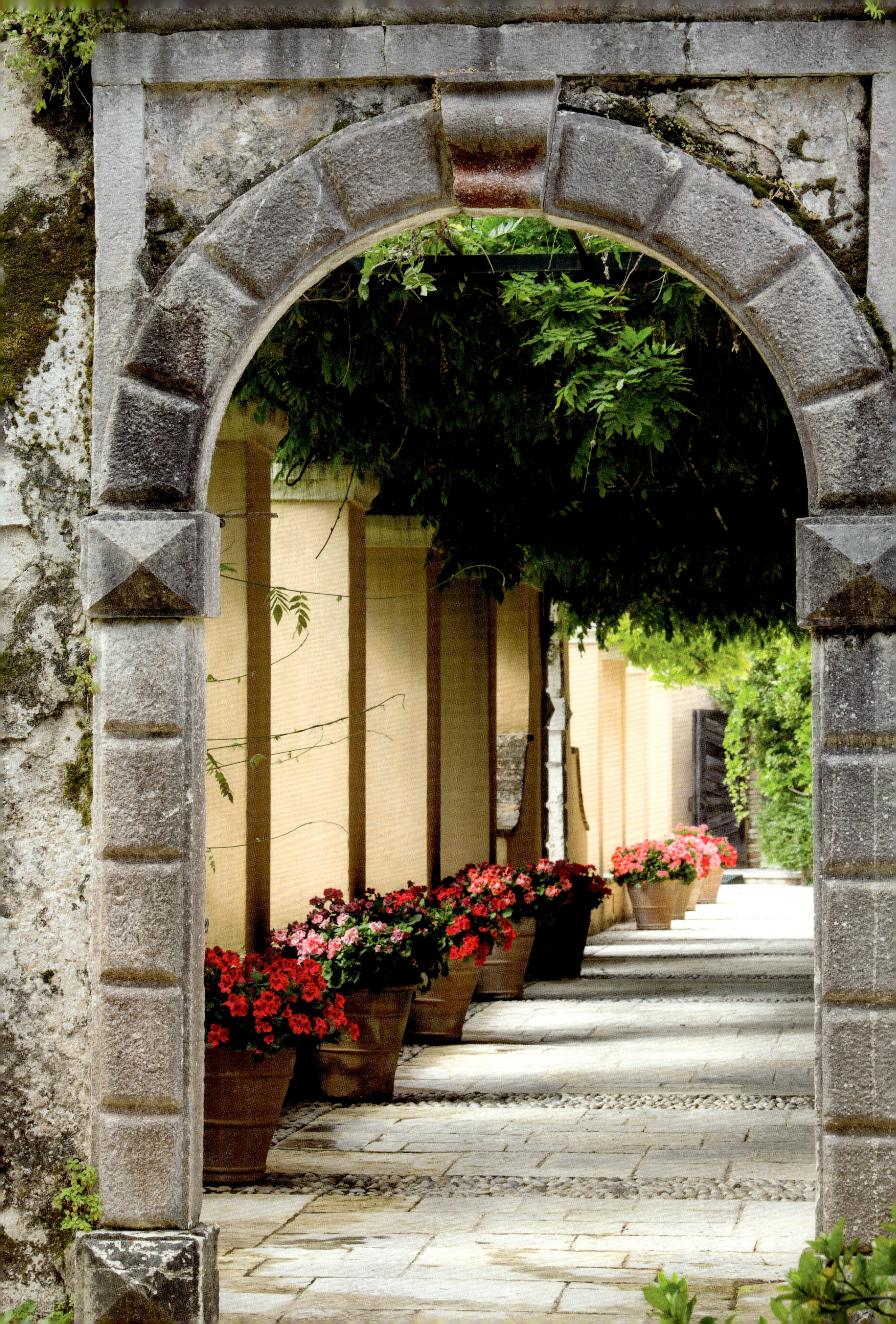

CHAPTER THREE

Heritage Gardens

OPPOSITE
A walkway shaded by wisteria at Krevatsoúla, whose name means 'little pergola'.

Corfu's garden heritage gives us insights into local cultural and economic history. The old gardens suggest what people valued and enjoyed, what they used for garden making and maintenance, and what plants they could get hold of.

Botanically, too, the old gardens are of interest: grand gardens established by people of wealth and privilege contain beautiful big specimen trees from distant continents and historical varieties of roses and other shrubs, while village gardens preserve heirloom varieties of grapevines, fruit trees, vegetables, and flowers, prized for their adaptation to specific growing conditions or simply for reasons of family or village tradition.

Not only are they beautiful and full of atmosphere, but the old gardens also provide ideas for modern gardeners about what can be grown, and how, under various local conditions. This chapter first features gardens at a selection of the island's historical properties[13] and then portrays some characteristic townscapes and village gardens.

HISTORICAL GARDENS

Corfu's country estate houses were built by the island's noble families who—as late as the nineteenth century—ran their estates on the basis of a medieval feudal system.[14] Though their incomes came mainly from farming, these families lived for much of the year in the island capital, Corfu Town, where they could pursue a sophisticated cosmopolitan lifestyle. They used their country houses '... as a base from which to oversee the gathering of agricultural produce and to supervise the labourers... These buildings, manor houses in essence, were used as temporary residences at harvest time'.[15] That said, the grand old shade trees at these properties, along with other survivors such as rambling roses, wisteria, and citrus, nut, and fig trees close to the houses, suggest that the owners kept gardens for beauty as well as for the useful products they yielded.

After Corfu's union with Greece in 1864, the noble families saw

13. For an encyclopaedic illustrated account of Corfu's manor houses and estates, see K. D. Karamoútsos, *Archontikes Agrikíes Kerkyraïkés* [Manor Houses of Corfu] (Athens: Ekdóseis Papazísi, 2010). 14. This was established by the Angevin lords, who ruled Corfu from 1267–1386; elements of the system are said to have persisted in some areas until Wold War II. 15. Déspina Paisídou, *Noble Houses of Corfu* (Thessaloniki: Altintzis, 1997).

their wealth and status decline. Many abandoned their town homes and moved permanently to the countryside. Estates that survived the land reform of 1912 were broken up after World War II, and several of the mansions decayed and were abandoned, their gardens left to run wild.[16]

What were the old gardens originally like? Paintings from a century ago give us insights. Matching what we know about the lifestyle of the garden owners, they suggest the influence of foreign gardens rather than a typical local style. They show Italianate stone architecture and decorative elements, combined with highly romantic plantings for colour and scent, against the typical Corfiot background of dark evergreens and spectacular views of the sea and mountains. Sargent's paintings from the Villa Sotiriótissa depict lush gardens with formal staircases, stone balustrades, and urns, with orange trees and white roses against a background of olives; in the distance they show a sparkling sea and the play of violet shadows on the distant mountains. Wilfrid De Glehn's painting, *Jane Reading in the Garden, Corfu* (1909), portrays his wife against a background of blue plumbago that tumbles down a high stone wall. In *Garden in Corfu,* a delicate watercolour by Giállinas (1857–1939), a stone staircase is flanked by carved stone urns and beds of flowering tree peonies and geraniums; the same artist's *Cypress Trees* shows blue irises and plumbago against the dark shapes of the cypresses. One of his later watercolours, *Corfu,* depicts a stately pleasure garden planted with palm trees and brightly coloured flowers bedded out in the English Victorian style. Parthenís (1878–1967) painted the garden of Castello Mibélli (near Dassiá); in muted colours, he shows a driveway flanked by topiary parterres full of flowers, backed with exuberantly growing trees.

Old trees in some of the estate gardens attest to Corfu's long-standing links to world trade routes and to fashion trends in other parts of Europe. At Mon Repos, on the path to the Doric temple ruins, are some huge specimens of Moreton Bay fig (*Ficus macrophylla*), native to Australia, whose aerial roots call to mind scenes from the Australian rainforest or the Cambodian jungle. This species was brought to Europe in the eighteenth century and soon became popular across the cities of Italy, Portugal, and Spain. Other eighteenth-century introductions favoured at many of the old estates are southern magnolia (*Magnolia grandiflora*), from North America, and eucalyptus and cabbage-tree palms (*Livistona australis*), from Australia. Majestic eu-

16. Hilary Paipéti, 2005, 'Rise and Fall of Corfu's Mansions', at: http://www.allcorfu.com/we-corfiot-0507.html

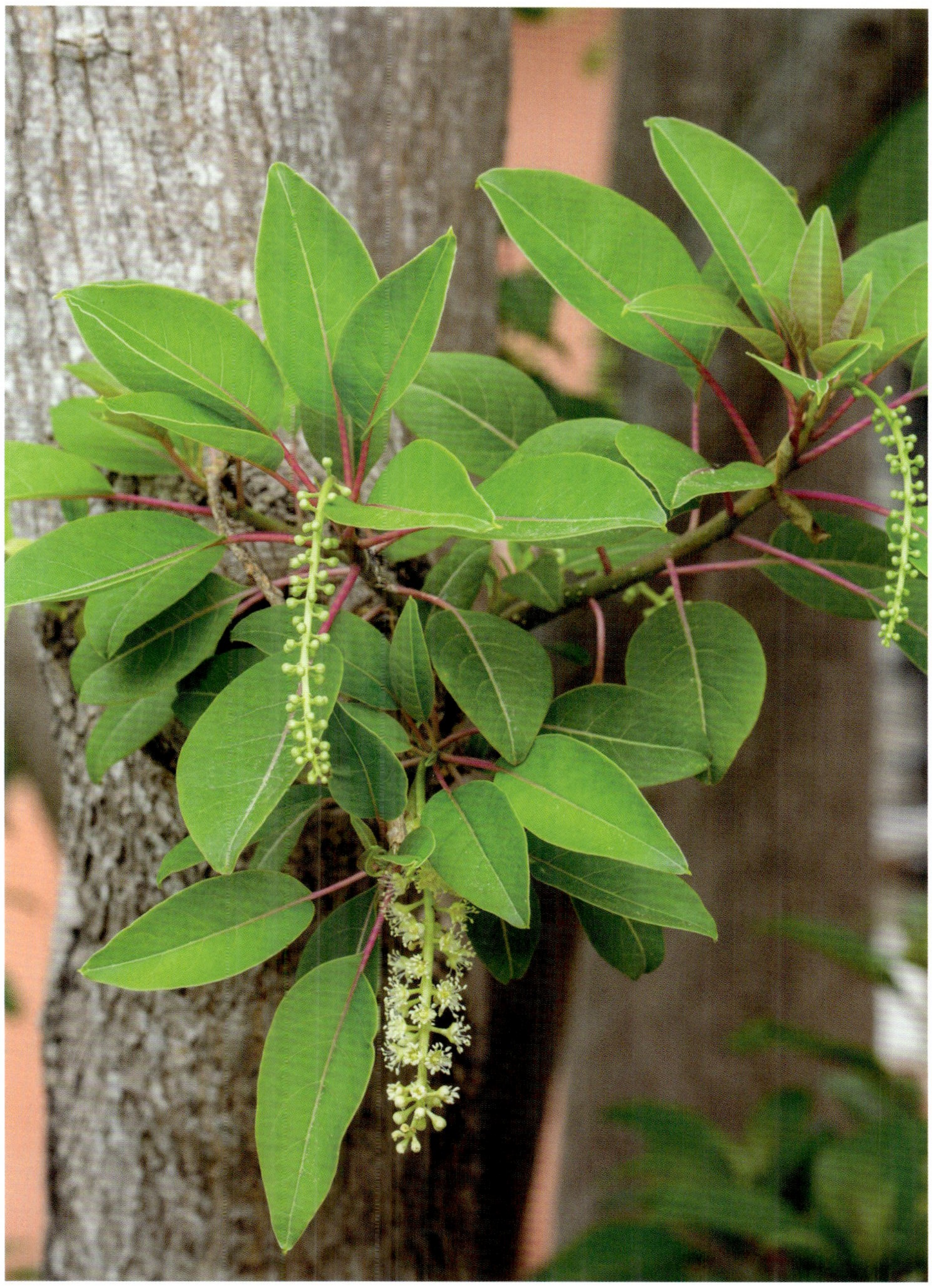

Phytolacca dioeca, sometimes called *bella sombra*, came to Europe in the late eighteenth century from Argentina. With its strangely shaped multiple trunks, it was a status symbol when it first arrived. Large old specimens can be seen today at Doukádes, Krevatsoúla, and the Palace of St. Michael and St. George; another is in the former royal gardens in Athens.

calyptus trees can be seen in the grounds at Afra and at Kouloúra; eucalypts came to be widely valued in Corfu because their thirsty roots drained marshy ground that hosted malarial mosquitoes.[17] Cabbage-tree palms were introduced to Europe in 1771 by naturalist Joseph Banks who sailed with Captain Cook on the ship Endeavour.[18]

17. The first eucalyptus in Europe was planted in the greenhouses of the Royal Botanic Gardens, Kew in 1774. See F. J. Silva-Pando and R. Pino-Pérez, 'Introduction of Eucalyptus into Europe', *Journal of Australian Forestry* 79 (4), 2016 and R. H. Groves and F. Di Castri, eds., *Biogeography of Mediterranean Invasions* (Cambridge, UK: Cambridge University Press, 1991).
18. John Leslie Dowe, *Australian Palms: Biogeography, Ecology, and Systematics* (Collingwood, Australia: CSIRO, 2010), p. 7.

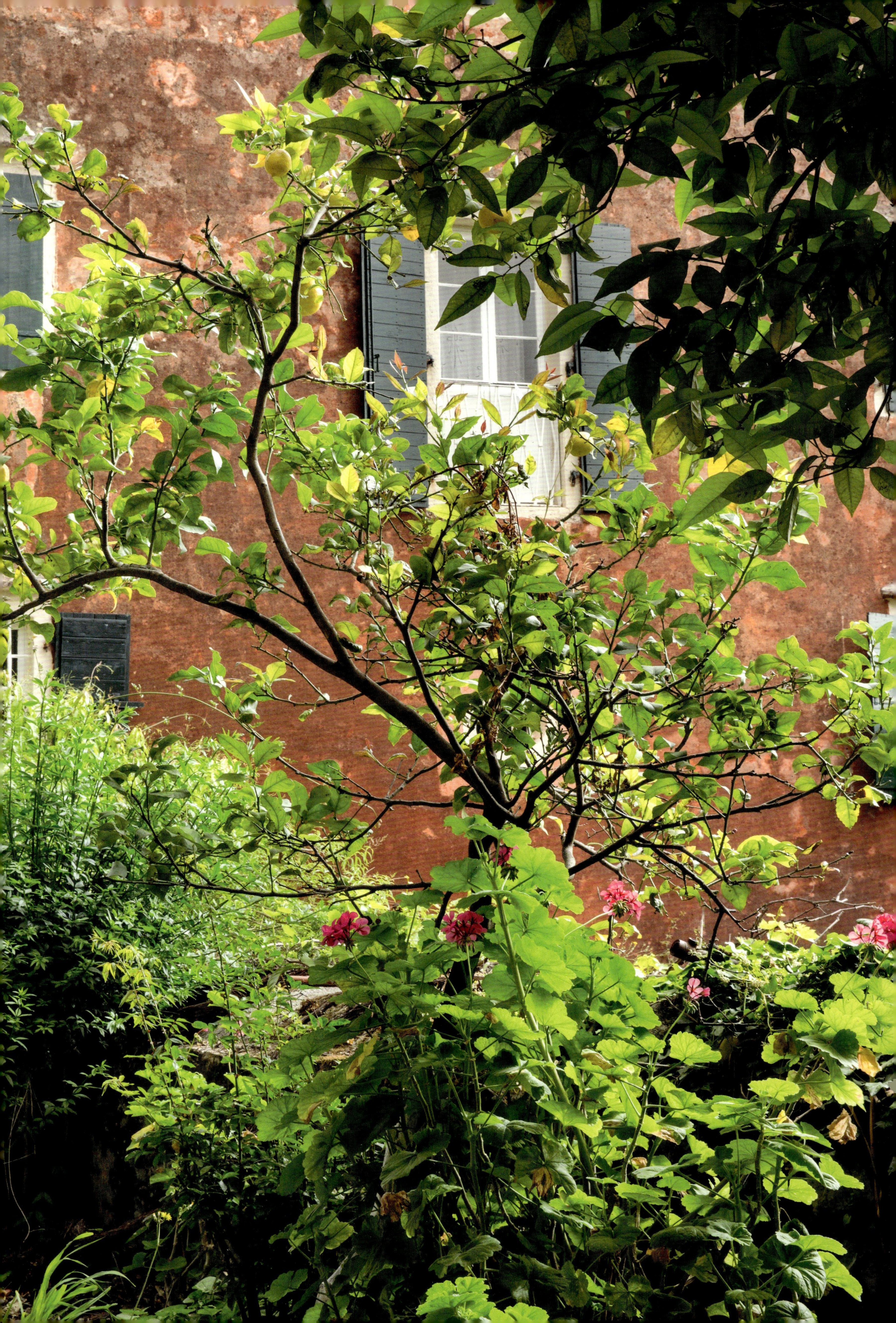

San Stefano

OPPOSITE
The courtyard garden at San Stefano combines fruit trees with flowering plants.

This famous house near Benitses passed into the family of the current owners, the Mánessis, as a marriage dowry in the late nineteenth century. Built in the early 1780s by a member of the Venetian Justiniani family, it was once the centre of a thriving agricultural estate with thousands of vines and citrus trees. Today it has survived the sale of much of the surrounding land and still sits within a romantically planted garden perched high above the Corfu Straits.

The house occupies a natural horizontal ledge in the middle of an almost vertical crag. The site cannot have been easy to build on, but it promised safety from pirates and other marauders; indeed, Jan Mánessi discovered a few years ago that a tunnel built for emergencies runs under the entrance courtyard. A mighty wisteria clambers over the huge rock that rises above the courtyard. The back of the house faces the sea, and running along its whole length is a wide veranda. Below this, the rock plunges sharply thirty metres down to a small bare rock *plateía* in front of the family's Church of St. Stephen. The church, with its free-standing bell tower so characteristic of Corfu, is backed by large old oaks and cypresses and, further down the hill, a cedar of Lebanon (*Cedrus libani*).

The garden is laid out on a series of long, engineered terraces facing the sea. Approaching the house after climbing the steep driveway from the coast, one rounds a bend by a group of cypress and eucalyptus trees and comes out on the main terrace, richly bordered with old plantings of *Magnolia* x *soulangeana*, Japanese quince (*Chaenomeles japonica*), lilac (*Syringa vulgaris*), plum, mulberry, lemon and orange trees, and snowy-white *Spiraea* 'Bridal Wreath'. Here and there are new introductions of bottlebrush (*Callistemon* varieties), one of the owner's favourite types of shrubs. Partly shaded by a large avocado tree, an intimate garden on the south side of the house is planted with *Agapanthus* and *Strelitzia regina*.

The widest of the garden terraces is level with the entrance to the house. Narrower parallel terraces continue up the slope above it, the first of them planted with regular rows of orange trees among meadow grass, its wall edged with old roses. The mood becomes progressively wilder as the land rises, eventually giving way to almost vertical rocky crags and native shrubs. Buzzards mew, circling, in the air above.

The view over the Corfu Straits from the veranda, with the family church of Saint Stephen in the foreground.

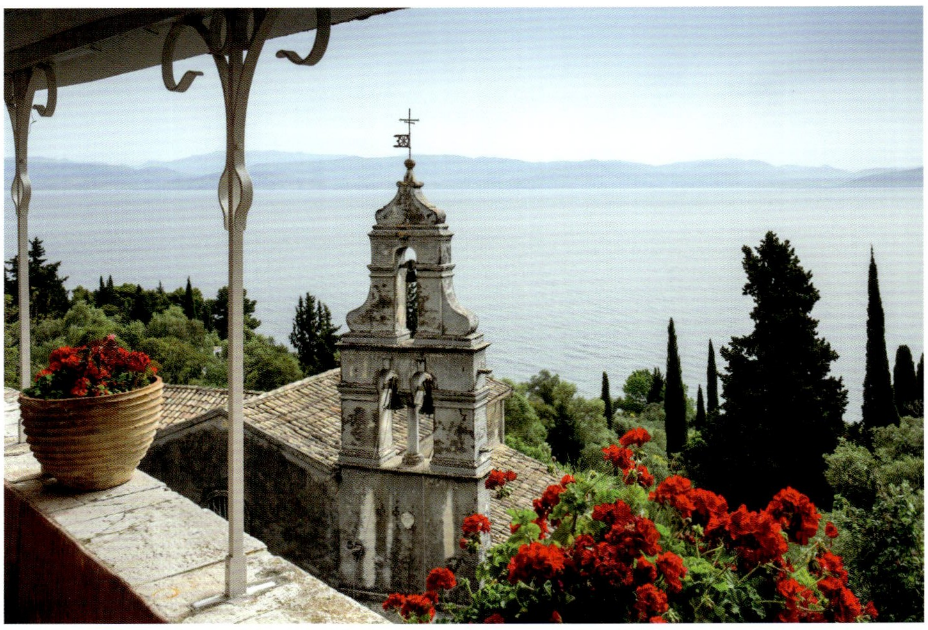

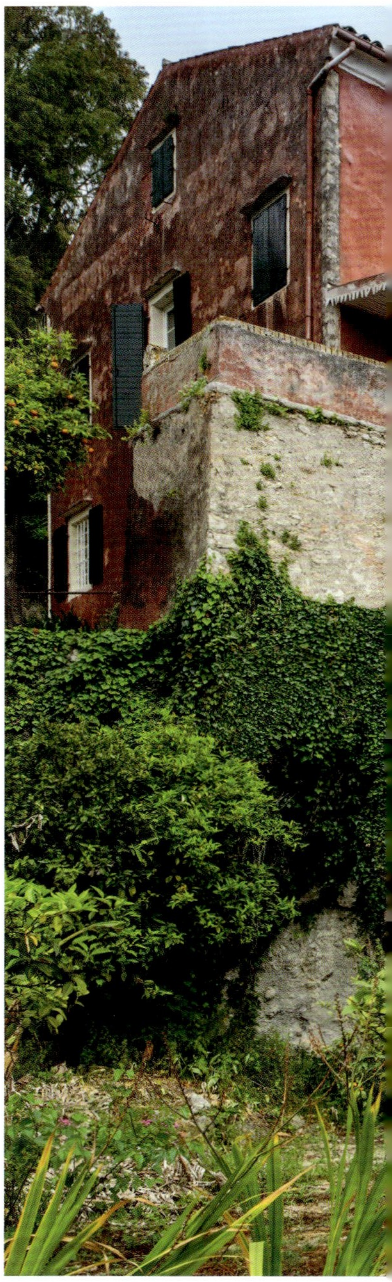

The approach to the house. One of the wellheads on the property, painted in characteristic Corfiot style, can be seen in the distance.

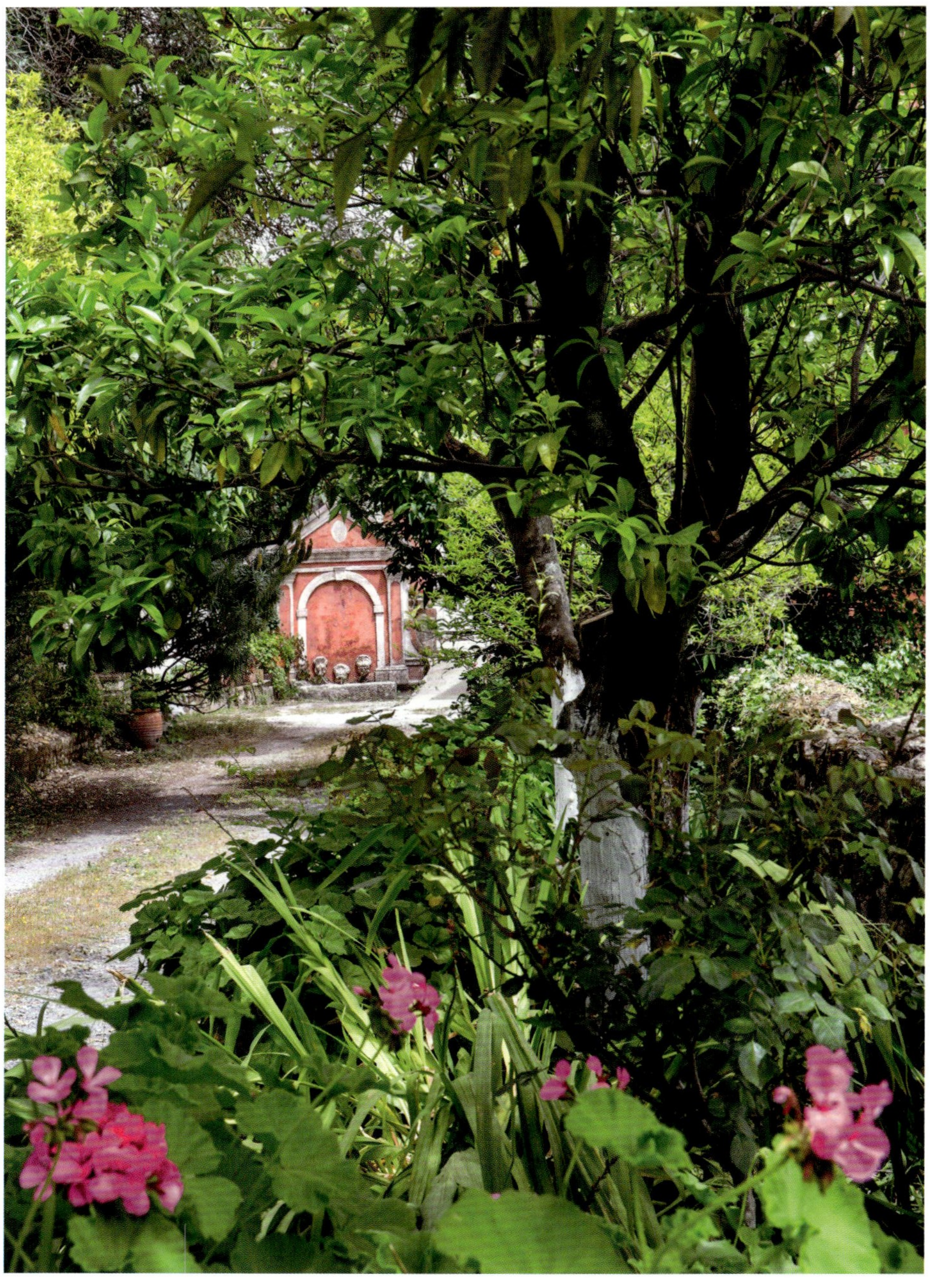

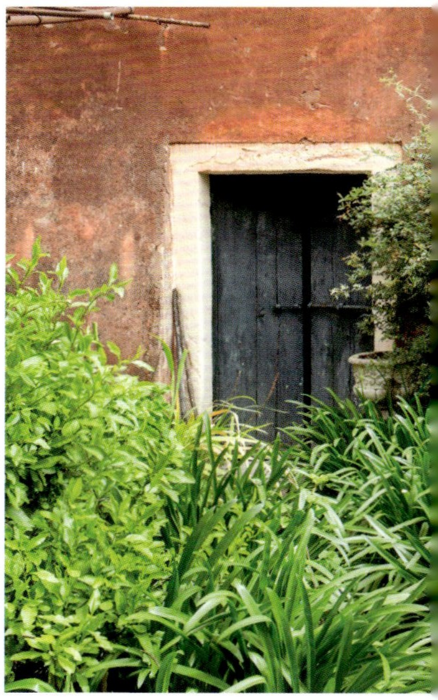

Clumps of naturalised *Agapanthus* grow with a Banks' rose.

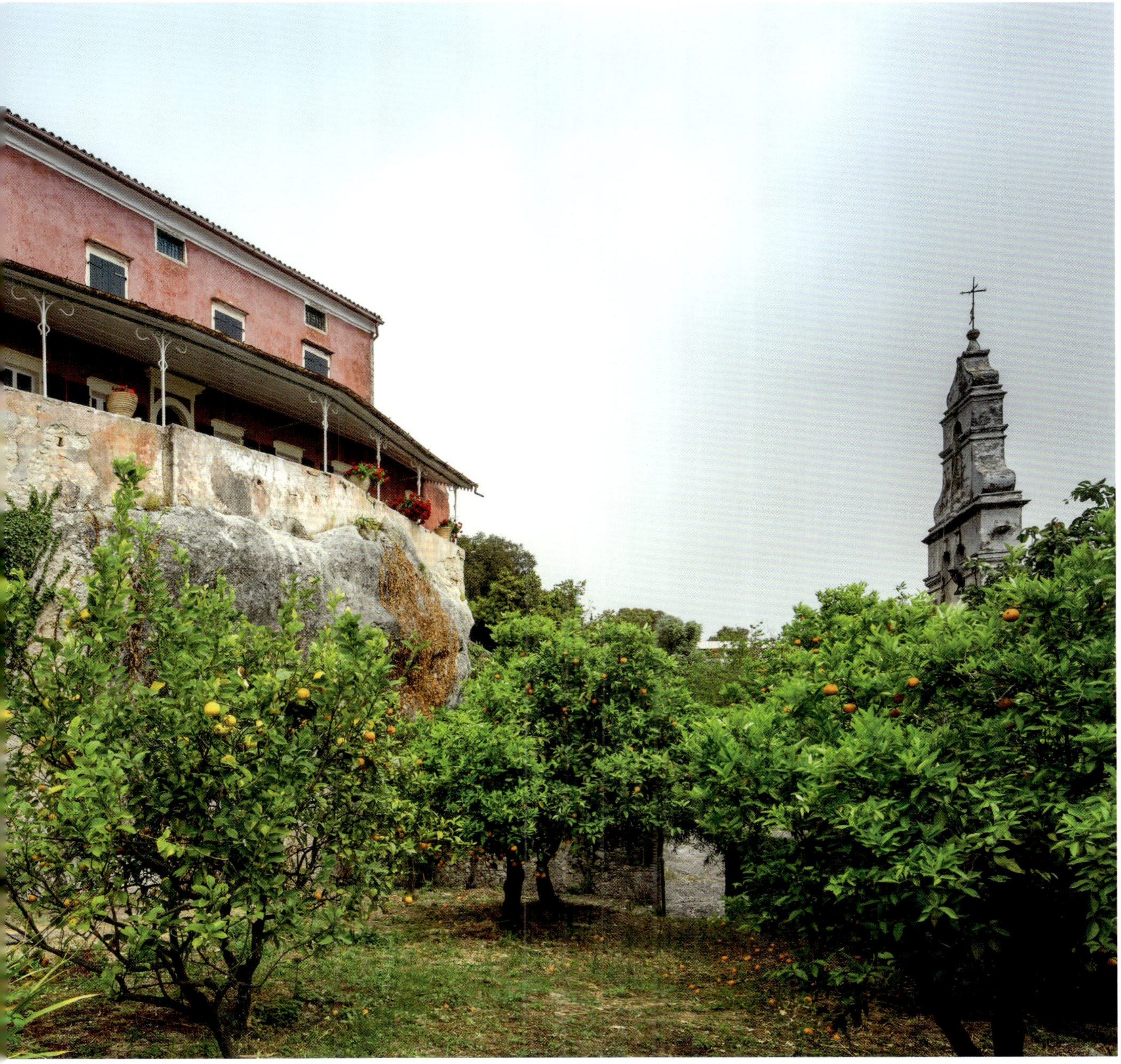

Perched on the rock, the house is seen here from the orange grove.

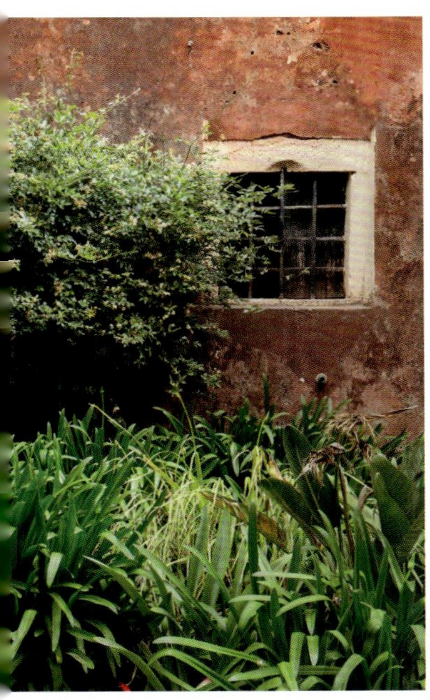

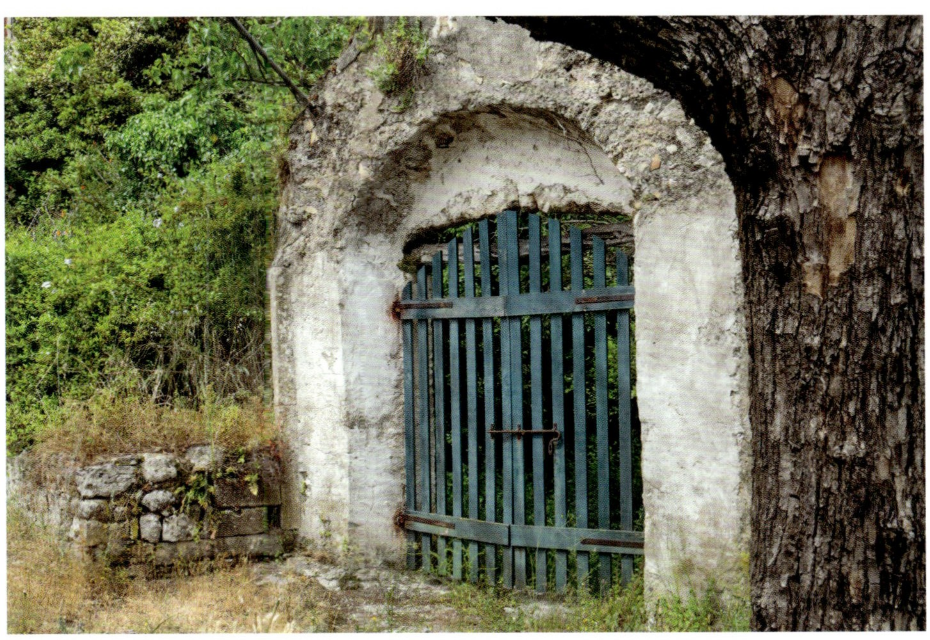

Beyond this gate, an old footpath leads to the village below.

The orange grove below the house. Along with vines, citrus trees once provided the livelihood of the estate.

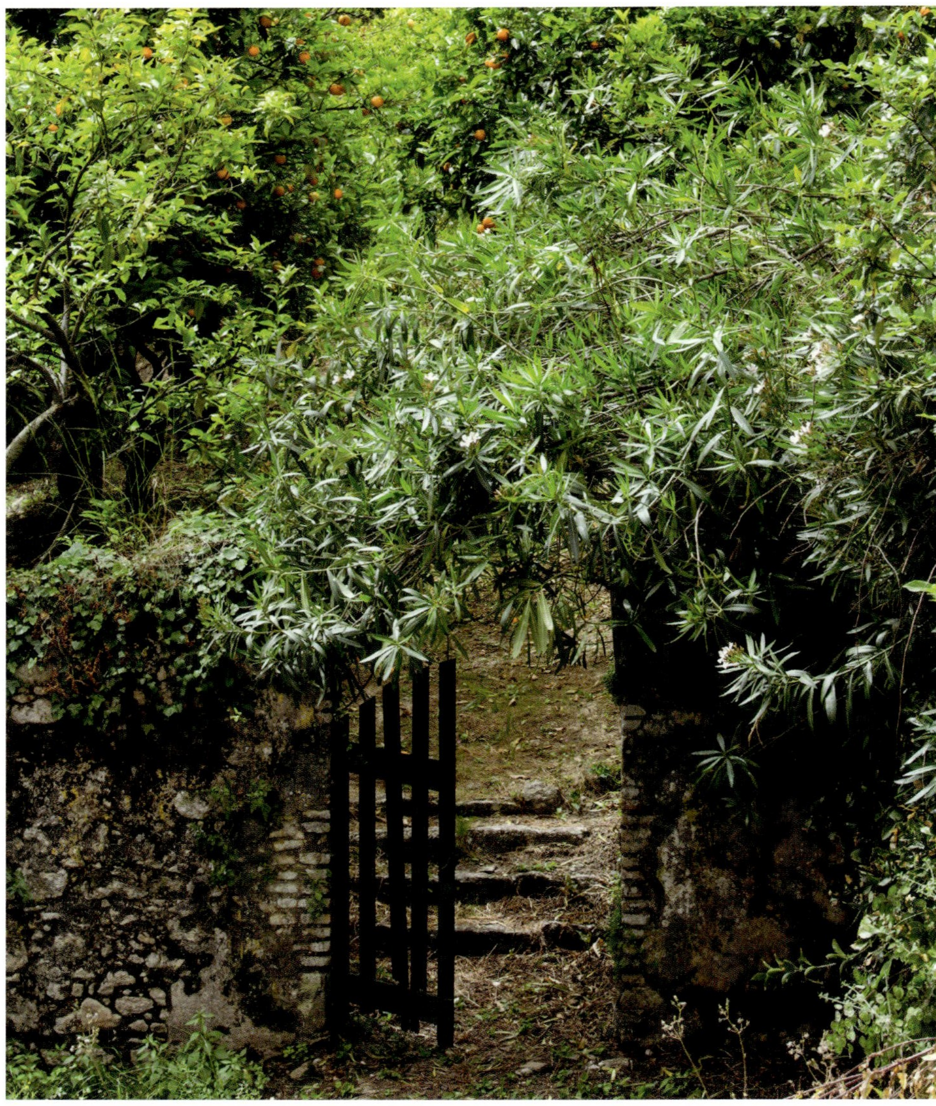

OPPOSITE TOP
The eighteenth-century house is built on a narrow rock platform with crags above and below. Below the front yard is a secret cellar that was built to allow the residents to hide from pirates.

Below the widest terrace, the land drops steeply away, with plantings of oleander, quince, mulberry, and citrus, including an unusual sweet lemon tree (*Citrus limon* 'Limetta') and even a thriving clump of banana trees. The swimming pool, a modern-day addition at some distance to the house, has a full open view over the sea below, and is bordered on the hill side by summery plantings of ornamental grasses, lavender, and *Agapanthus*. Next to it, a grid of orange trees remains.

Given its size and steepness, this is an expensive garden to maintain. One consolation is its abundant supply of groundwater. Taking advantage of natural springs, there are multiple old wellheads on the property. Several plants that normally need a damper summer climate than Corfu offers—including *Ligularia stenocephala*, with its luxuriant green leaves and yellow flower spikes, and snowball bush (*Viburnum opulus*)—survive with no summer watering.

OPPOSITE BOTTOM
A long straight terrace carries the driveway to the house. Here, lemons and oranges, native pines and cypresses are underplanted with flowering pelargoniums.

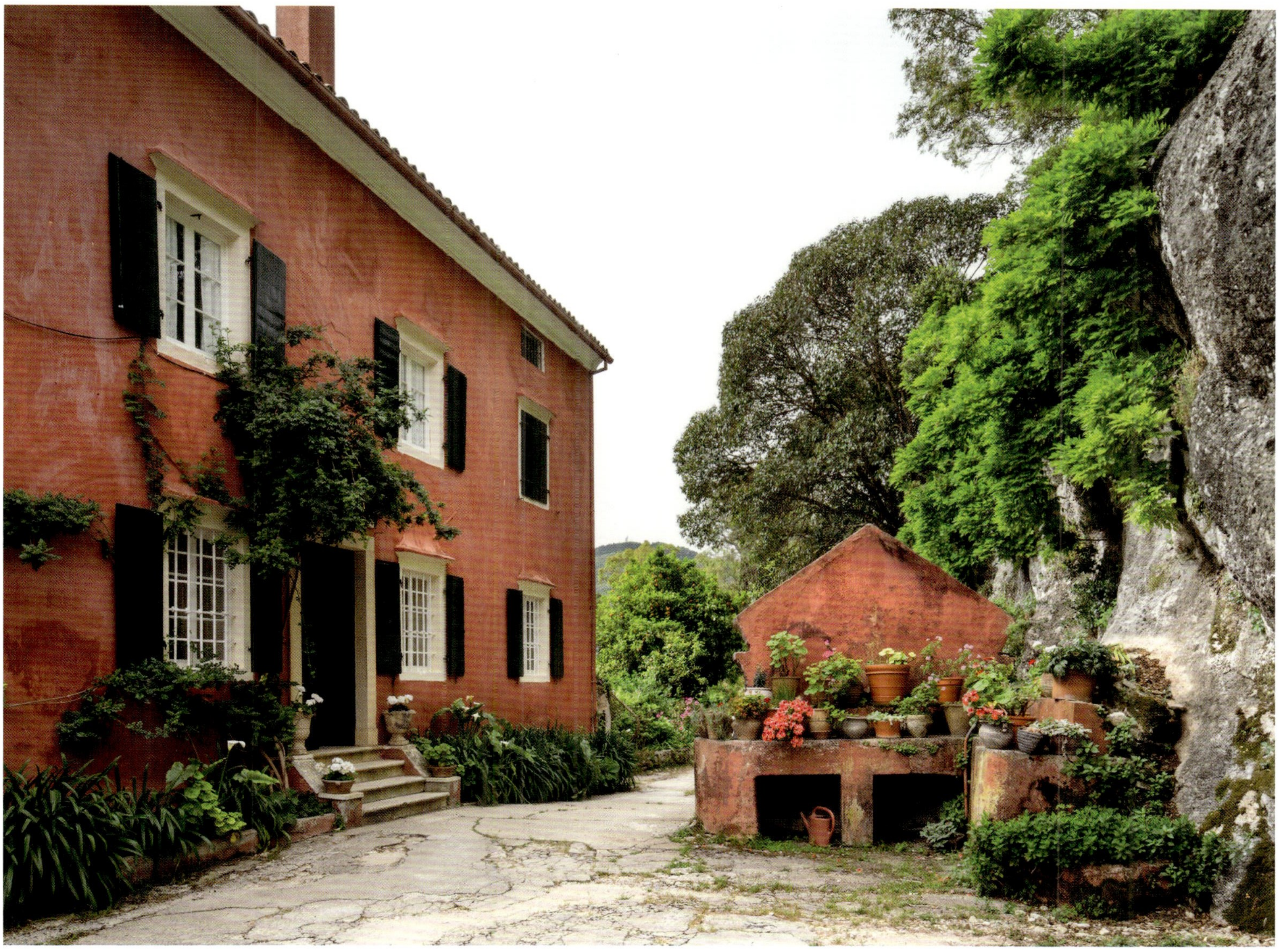

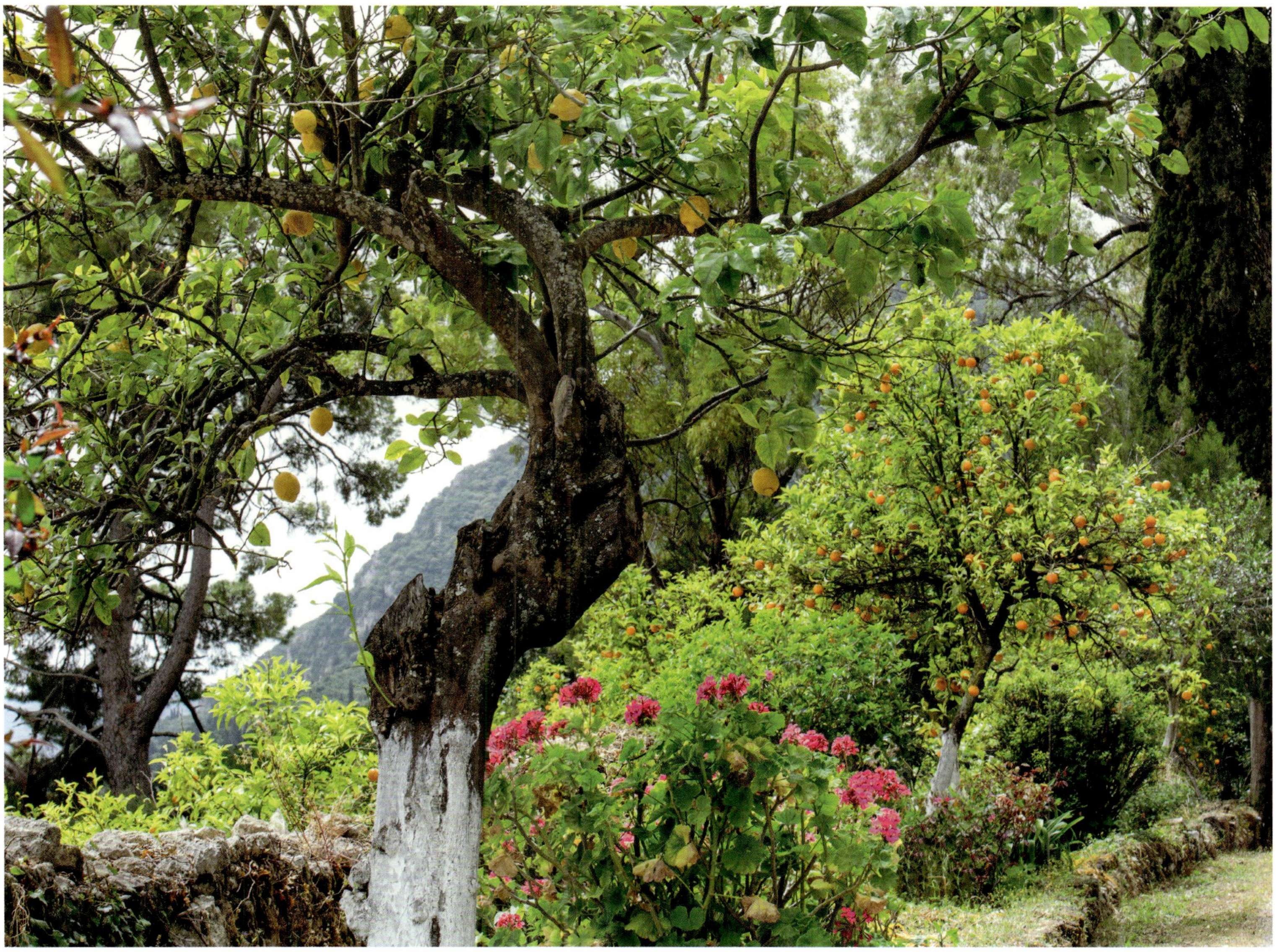

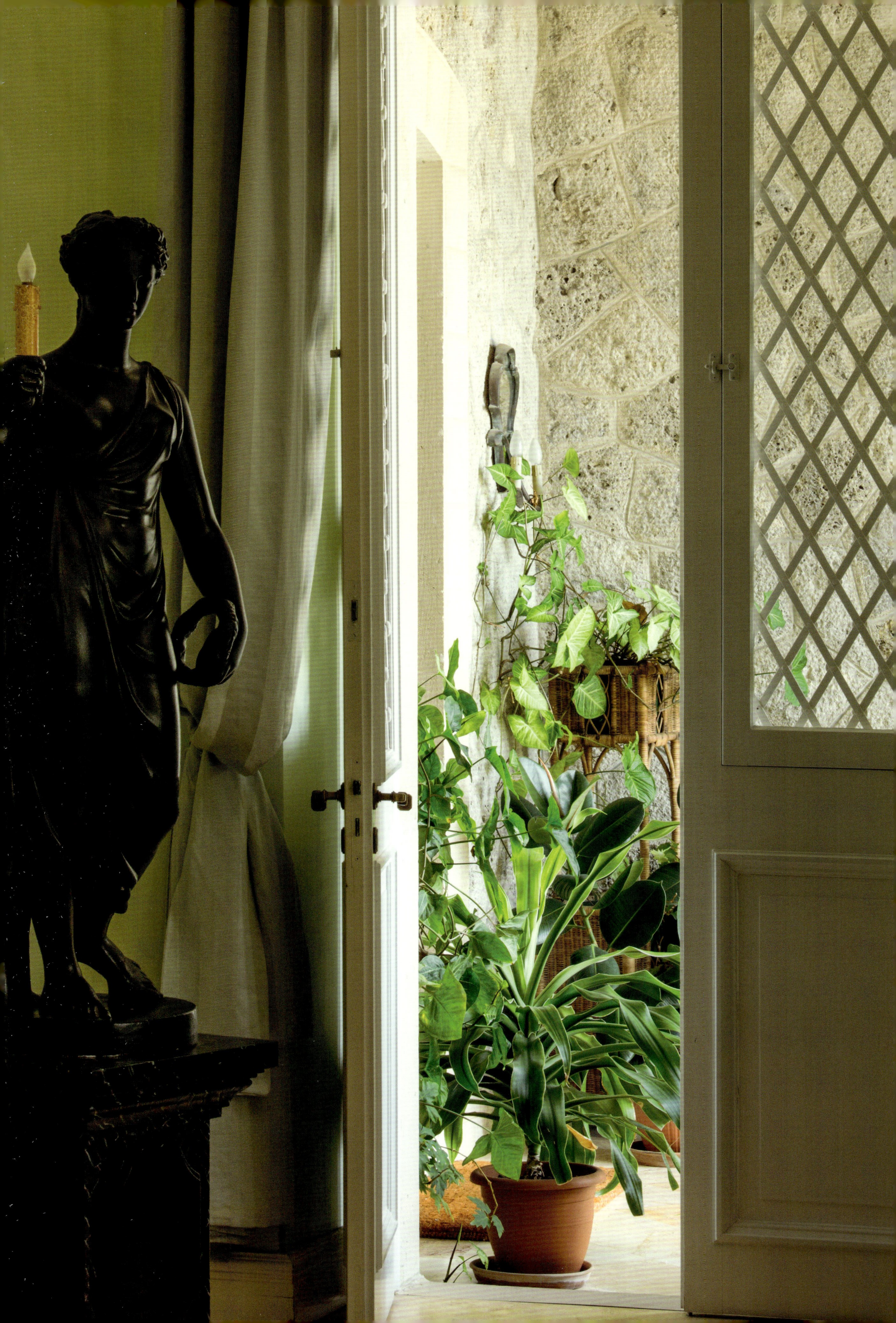

The Theotóky garden in Doukádes

OPPOSITE
A doorway leads through the conservatory to the terrace overlooking the garden.

The Theotóky family, one of the oldest in Greece, first established themselves in Corfu when they fled the fall of Constantinople in the fifteenth century. Through the ages, the family built up a long tradition of public service—and also of organic wine and organic olive oil production, which continues today at their family estate in the Rópa Valley. In a commanding position over the Doukádes valley, the Doukádes mansion was built at the turn of the twentieth century by the present owner's grandfather, George Theotóky, who served as Prime Minister of Greece from 1899 to 1909. With its massive architecture evoking ancient castles, it is an imposing presence, and today gives no hint that for years it lay abandoned. Troops who were billeted there during World War II so badly damaged the property that for decades afterwards a restoration project seemed too daunting.

But about seventeen years ago Claudia Theotóky, an artist born in Brazil of Italian descent, took on the renovation to honour her husband George Theotóky's family traditions and make the house and garden live again. In the process she made bold decisions about what to leave and what to change. The wide paved terrace running the width of the housefront looks as if it has always been there, but has been re-engineered to conceal a parking area added on the level below. With a touch of humour, next to the lawn the top of a circular underground cistern has had stone seats added around its edge to suggest an ancient amphitheatre. Across the lawn in a clearing among the trees, clipped box hedges have been preserved from an original maze. George Theotóky recalls how much he enjoyed playing here with his siblings and cousins when he was a boy.

What makes the restored garden so haunting is the drama it creates between light and shade. The centenarian Canary palms, pines, and cypresses contribute the deep shade that is a rare luxury in Corfu summers. On wide gravel walkways, pools of dappled shade from oak trees are interspersed with patches of white light and with the black arcs and stripes of shade cast by palm branches. Black starburst shadows are cast by yuccas. The garden's great exuberance of shapes is held in balance by a strong restraint in plant choices and colours.

The garden is at its most vibrant in May, when the vivid green of the trees has not been dulled by heat. Except in the rose garden, the

Through this decorative grille, one looks out over a terrace with potted *Cymbidium* orchids to the village of Doukádes and the valley below.

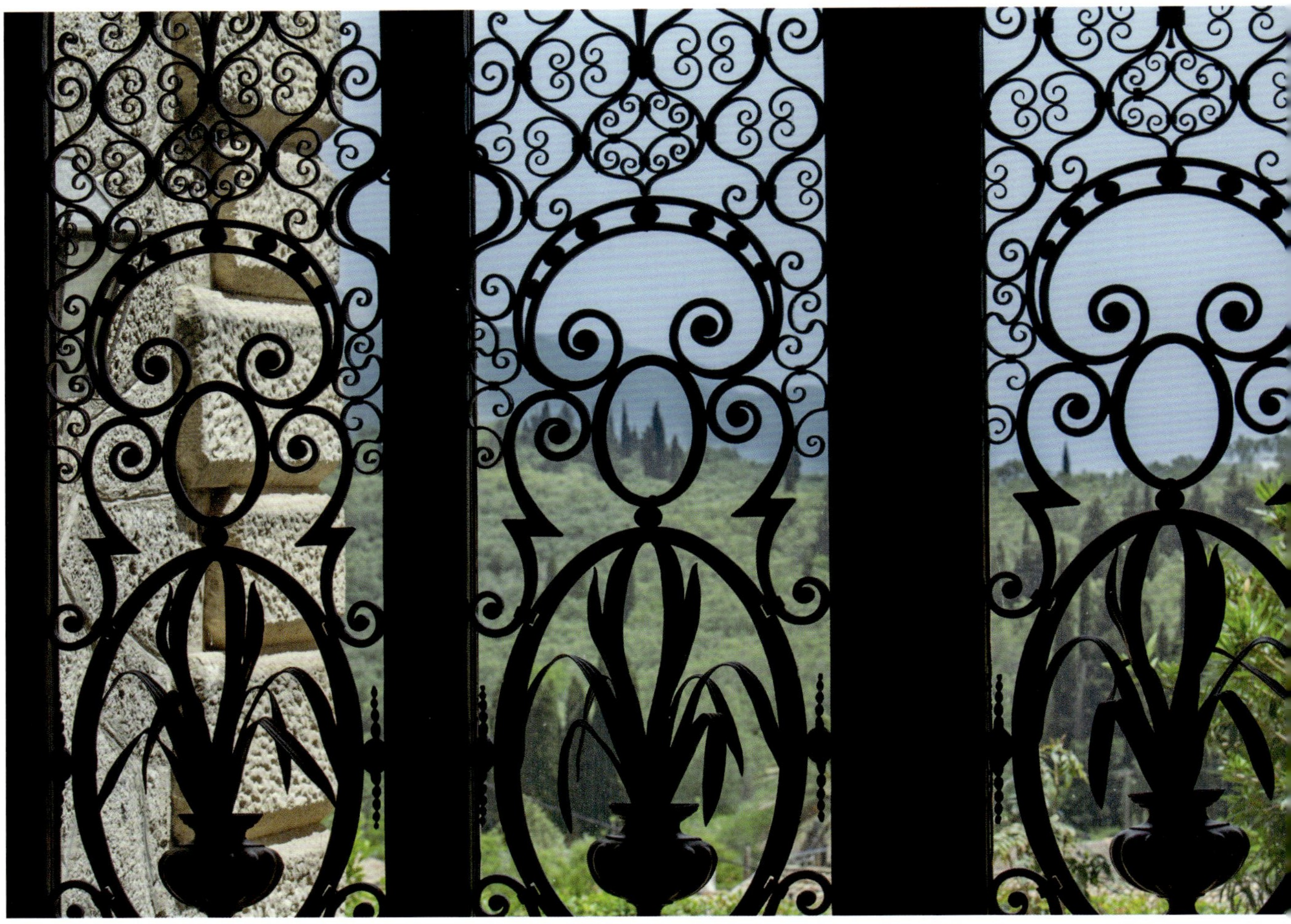

Light and shade play on a path. Because of its tall trees, this inland garden remains a cool oasis even in high summer.

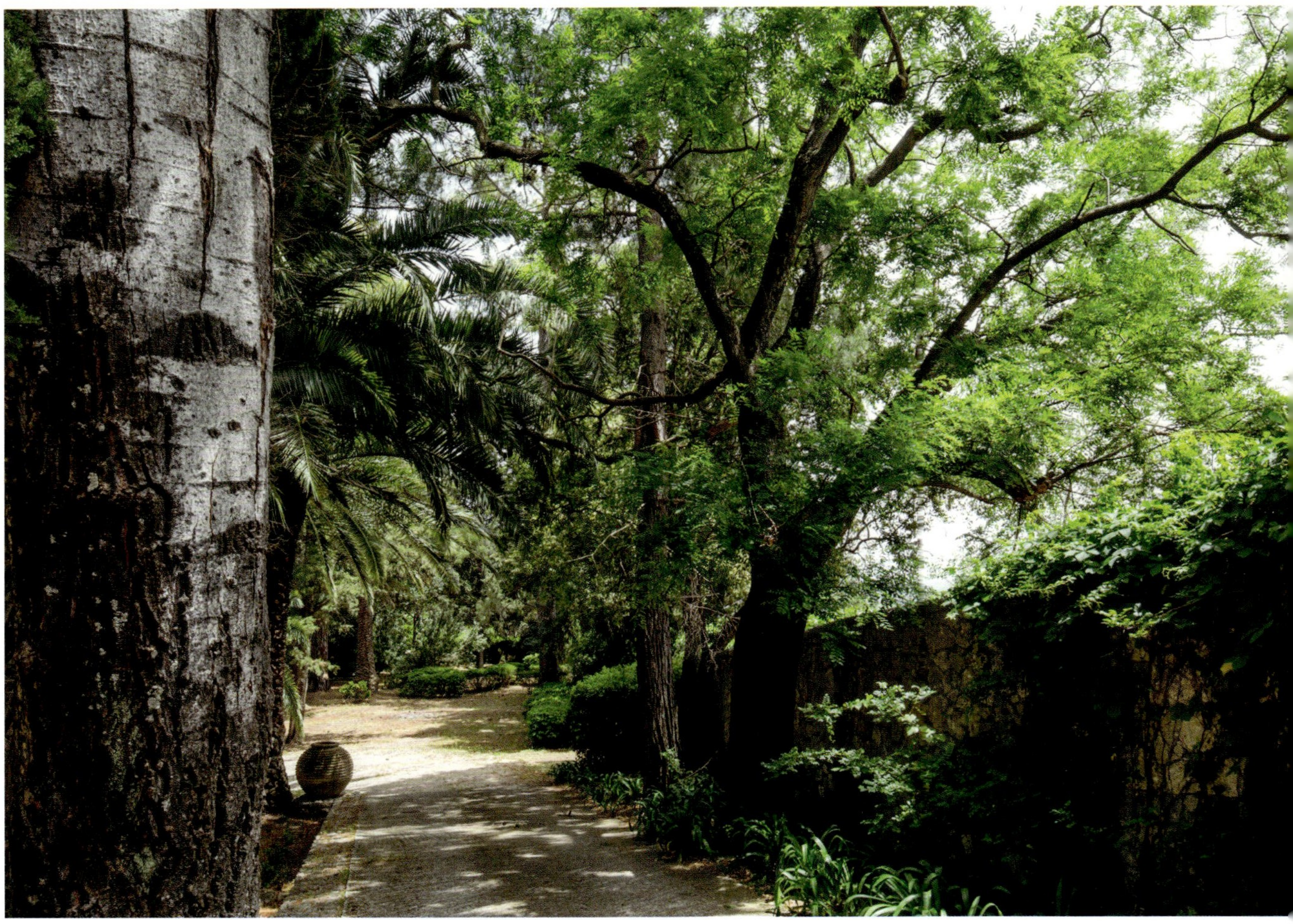

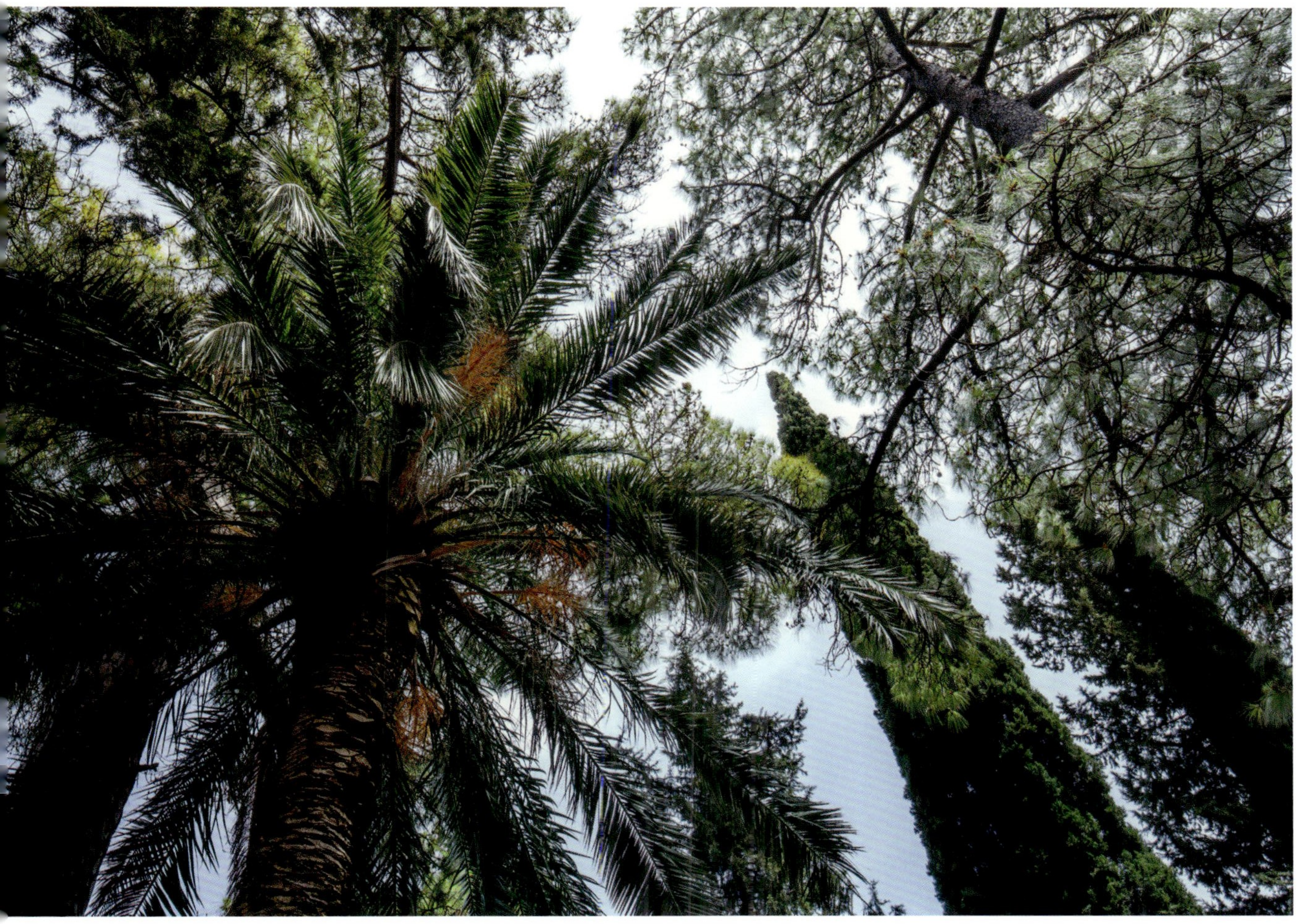

The garden is remarkable for its centenarian palms, pines, and cypresses.

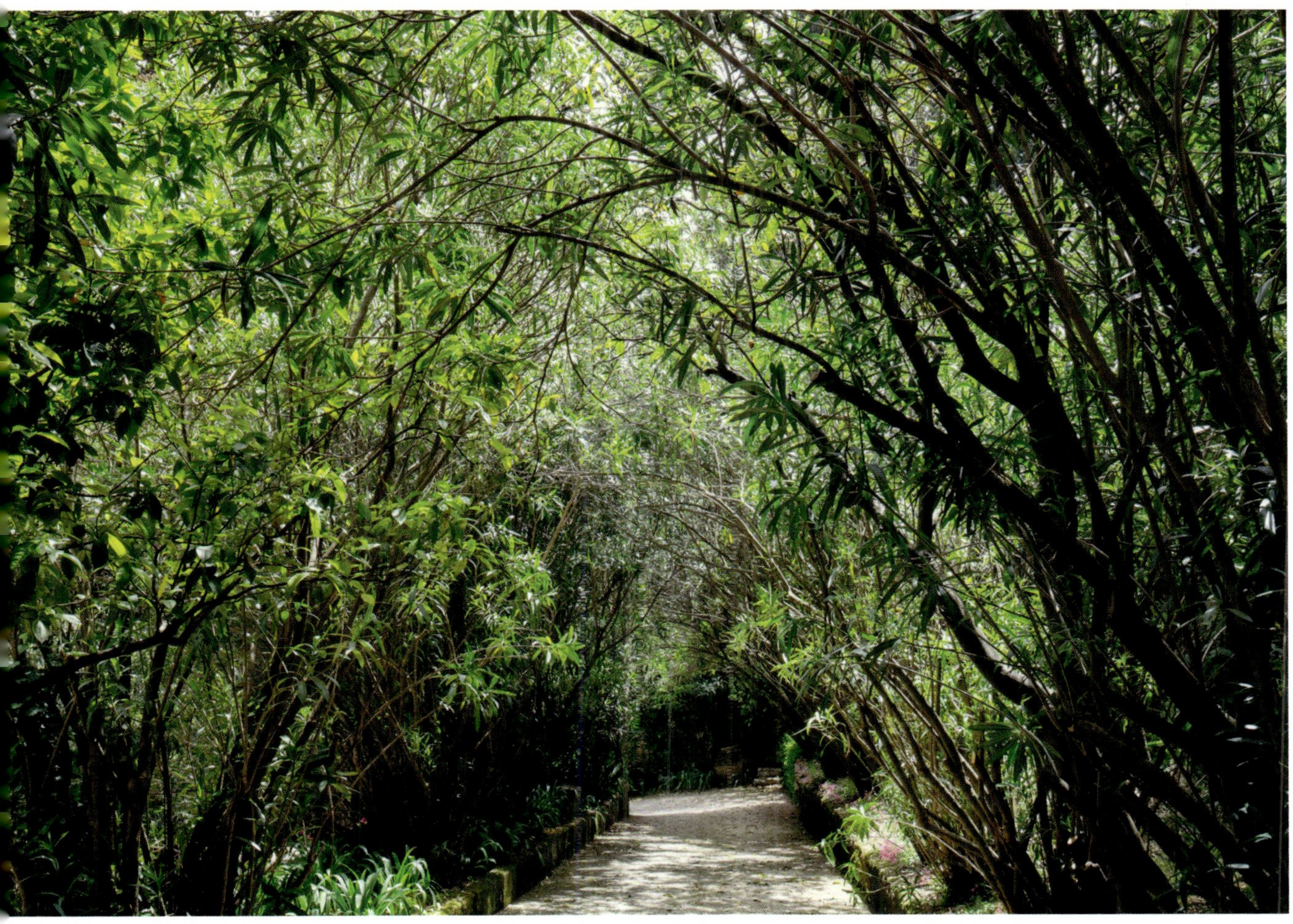

Oleanders line an alley. In the words of a young Dutch visitor, 'you step through the gateway and the fairy-tale begins'.

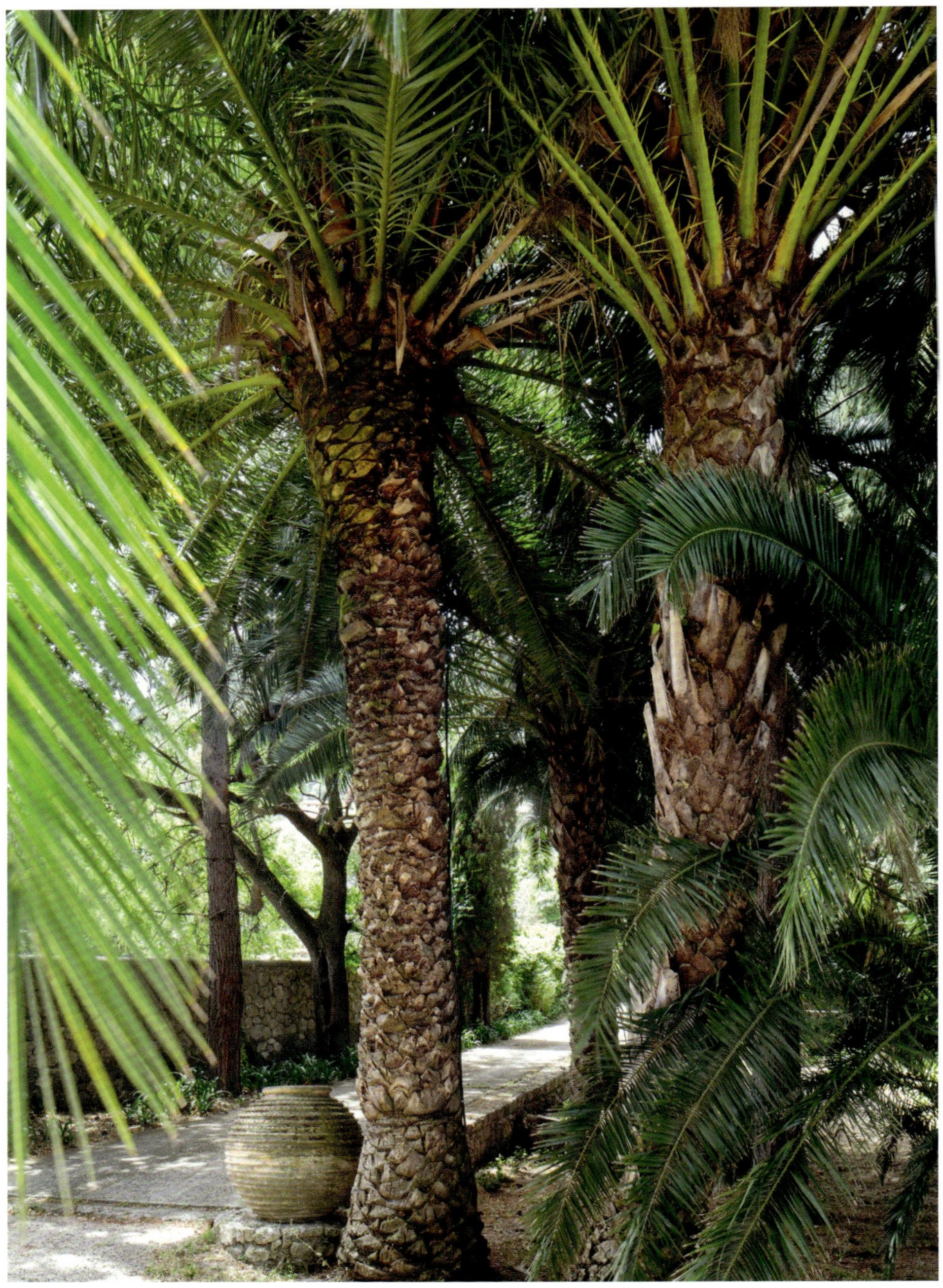

Some of the garden's Canary palms fell victim to the recent epidemic of red palm weevil *(Rhynchophorus ferrugineus)* but active protective measures have allowed most to be saved.

few flowers chosen for this season are pink, the softness and vibrancy of their colour warming up the austere stone of the terraces and staircases and the mainly dark green leaves of the planting. Brilliant pink wood sorrel is planted at regular intervals down the sides of the stone staircases; pink ivy-leafed pelargoniums overflow from stone urns. Later, the plantings of rose-coloured oleanders and hydrangeas—and, in the autumn, masses of pink belladonna lilies (*Amaryllis belladonna*)—will come into their own. A pale grey-blue that Claudia calls 'the Corfiot colour' is used for the lovely traditional wrought-iron entrance gate and for details on the exterior of the house.

OPPOSITE
Colour is used very sparingly in this garden. Here, pink wood sorrel (*Oxalis auriculata*) brightens the shade under an old *bella sombra* tree.

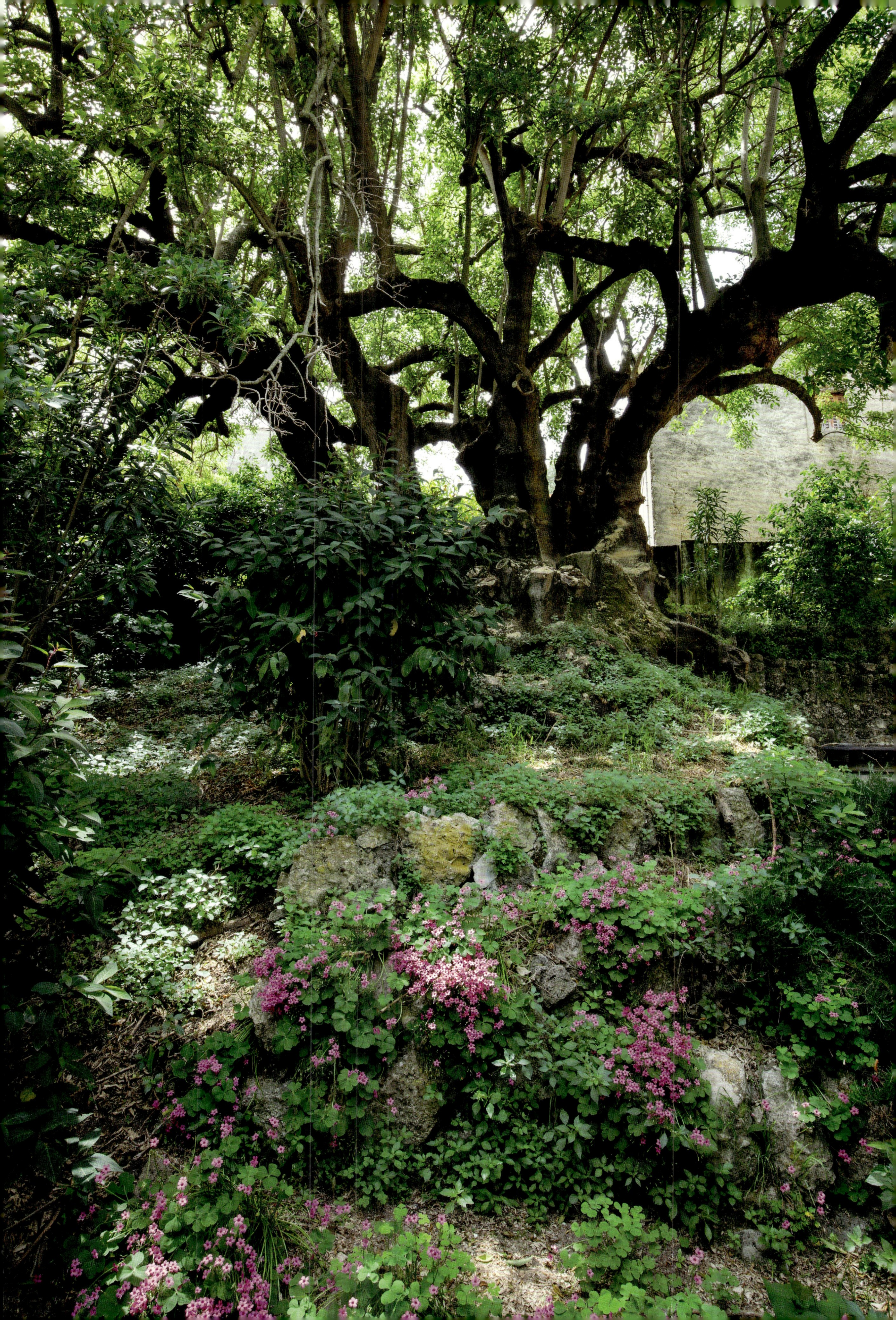

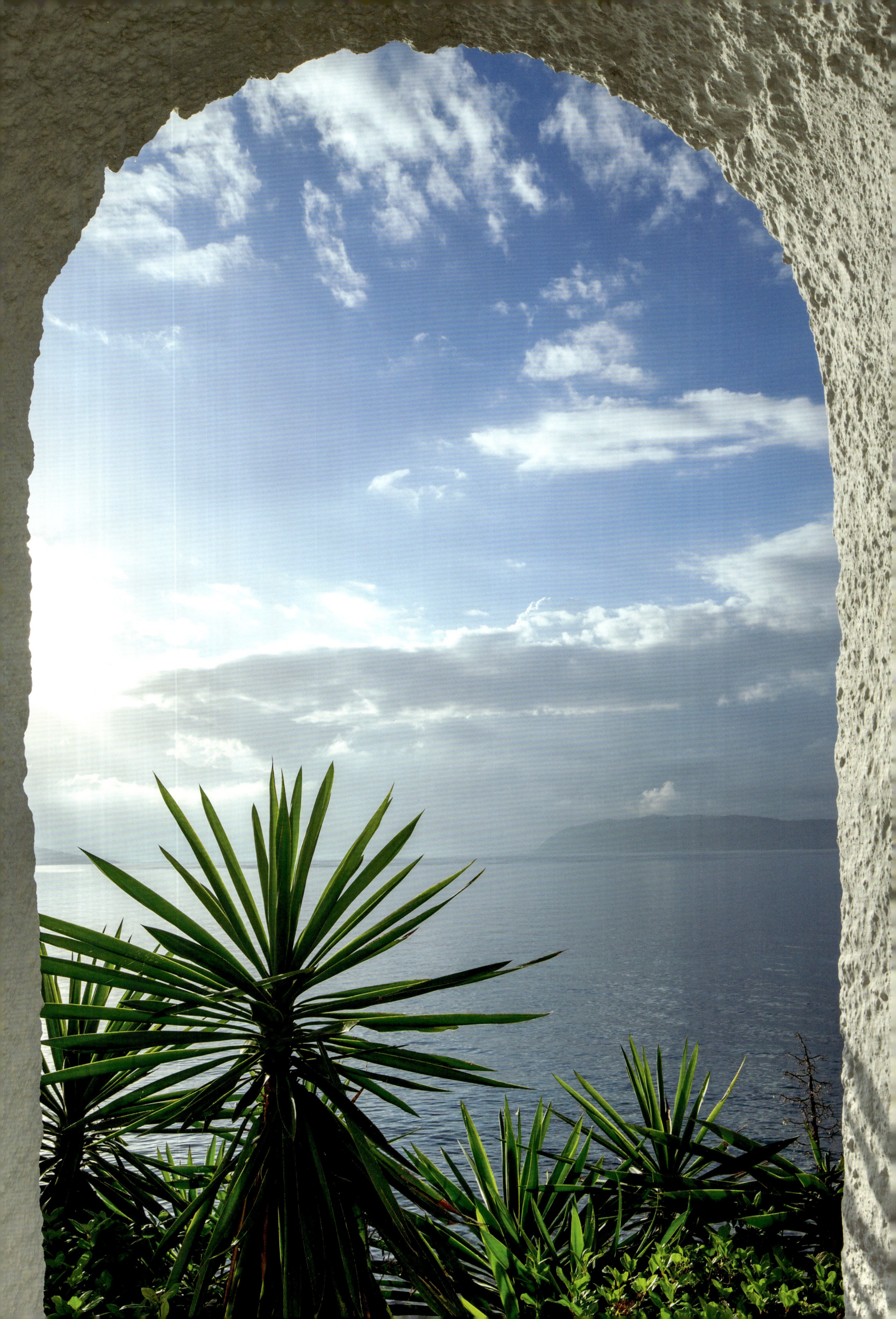

Kouloúra

Writing a century ago, Sophie Atkinson recalled that 'At Kouloúra… is a charming old fortified house just a few yards above the waves, on a rocky point from which the land runs steeply up. Cascades of geraniums fell from walls to waves, and the landing is at a most beautiful little circular basin, a tiny natural harbour, at the very gate… The old part of the house is most solidly vaulted, and has four round corner turrets, but later safer years have added verandahed rooms to catch the breezes and the vistas of the Straits. Altogether a charming place.'[19]

The charm and grace that are still here in abundance belie the fact that the house began life as a fortress. Built early in the sixteenth century by the Quartano family, who came from Venice, the property remained in the family until 1986, when it was acquired by the present owner's parents.

Dominique Bernier designed the garden in the late 1980s, and though his planting designs have all been updated the layout that he put in place remains. On the steep hillside beside the house he set out a series of narrow parallel terraces running from the entrance courtyard up to a large rectangular pond with fountain and papyrus. Connected by flights of stone steps at either end, the terraces nowadays are planted with aromatic and colourful ornamental plants combined with fruit trees—apricots, citrus, loquat, and pomegranate—and the occasional pencil cypress.

On the lowest terrace, frothy white-flowered Mexican fleabane (*Erigeron karvinskianus*) lines a playfully curving path, and silvery *Santolina chamaecyparissus* and white gaura under the lemon trees give an airy, inviting feeling. Along a higher terrace, *Agapanthus* clumps alternate with graceful *Tulbaghia violacea*, their blue and mauve flower colours complementing those of the lavender and irises across the path. Roses and bright pelargoniums in pots entice one to the top of the garden to see the magical view over the harbour. Behind this vantage point, the native cypresses under-planted with glossy evergreen shrubs provide a dark and slightly mysterious foil to the soft textures and happy colours of the plantings below.

OPPOSITE
The iconic house at Kouloúra, with its white walls, open arches, and turrets, is one of the best-known landmarks seen from the sea off Corfu's eastern coast. Below it on the narrow rocky cliff, yuccas have gained a foothold.

19. Sophie Atkinson, *An Artist in Corfu* (London: Herbert and Daniel; Boston: Dana Estes, 1911), p. 214.

A view over the harbour from the top of the garden.

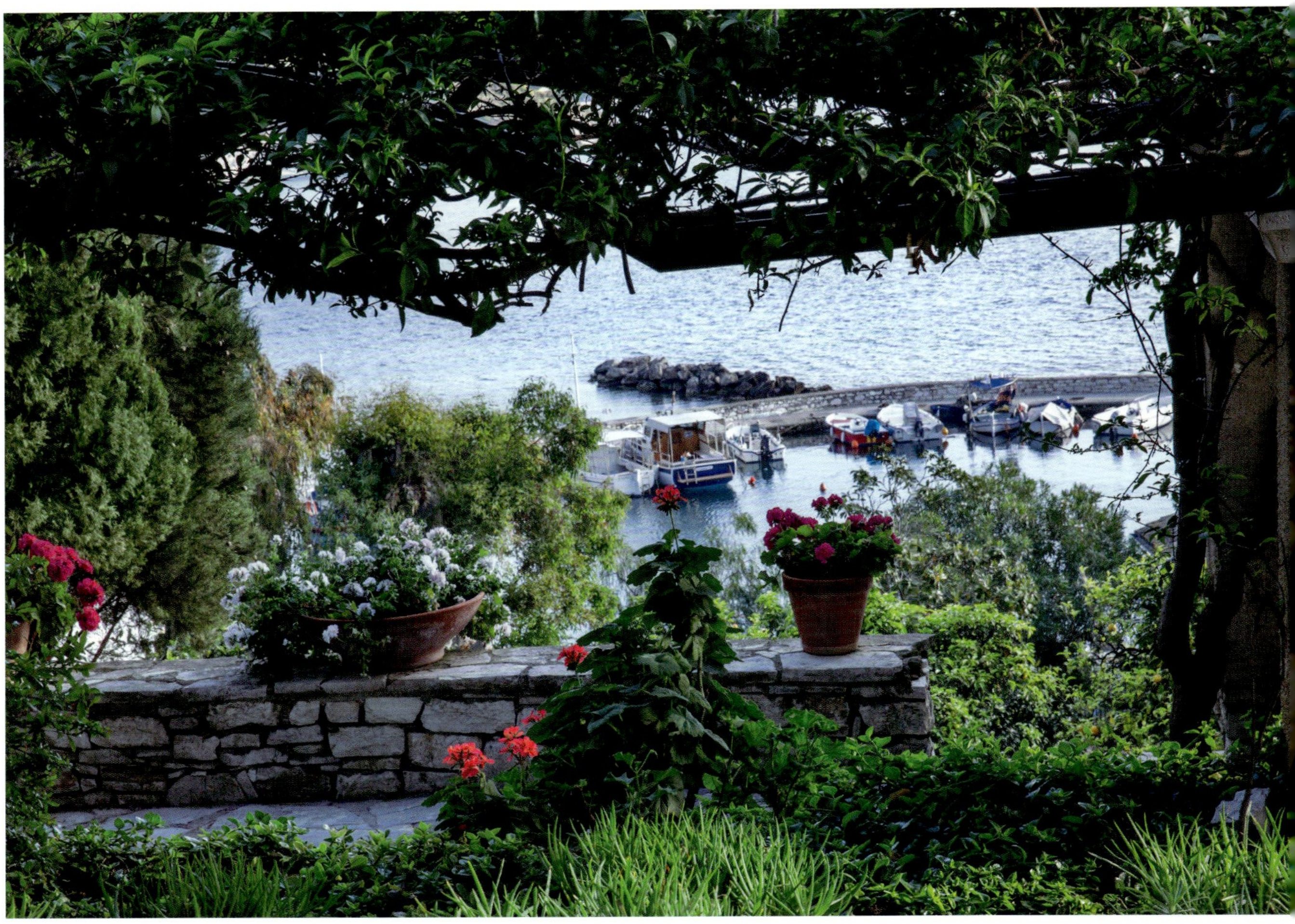

Bright *Bougainvillea* and pelargoniums contribute to the happy atmosphere in the entrance courtyard.

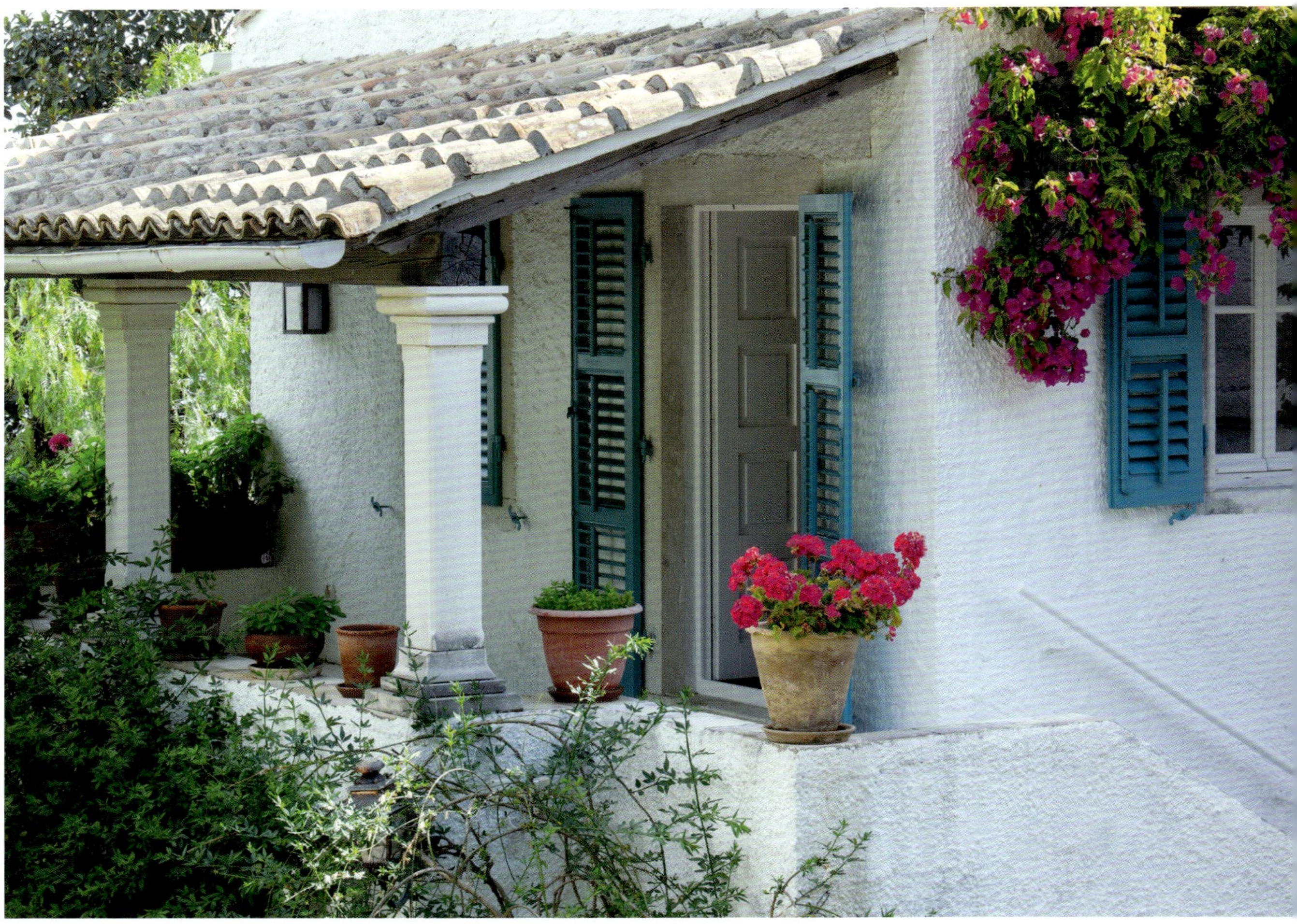

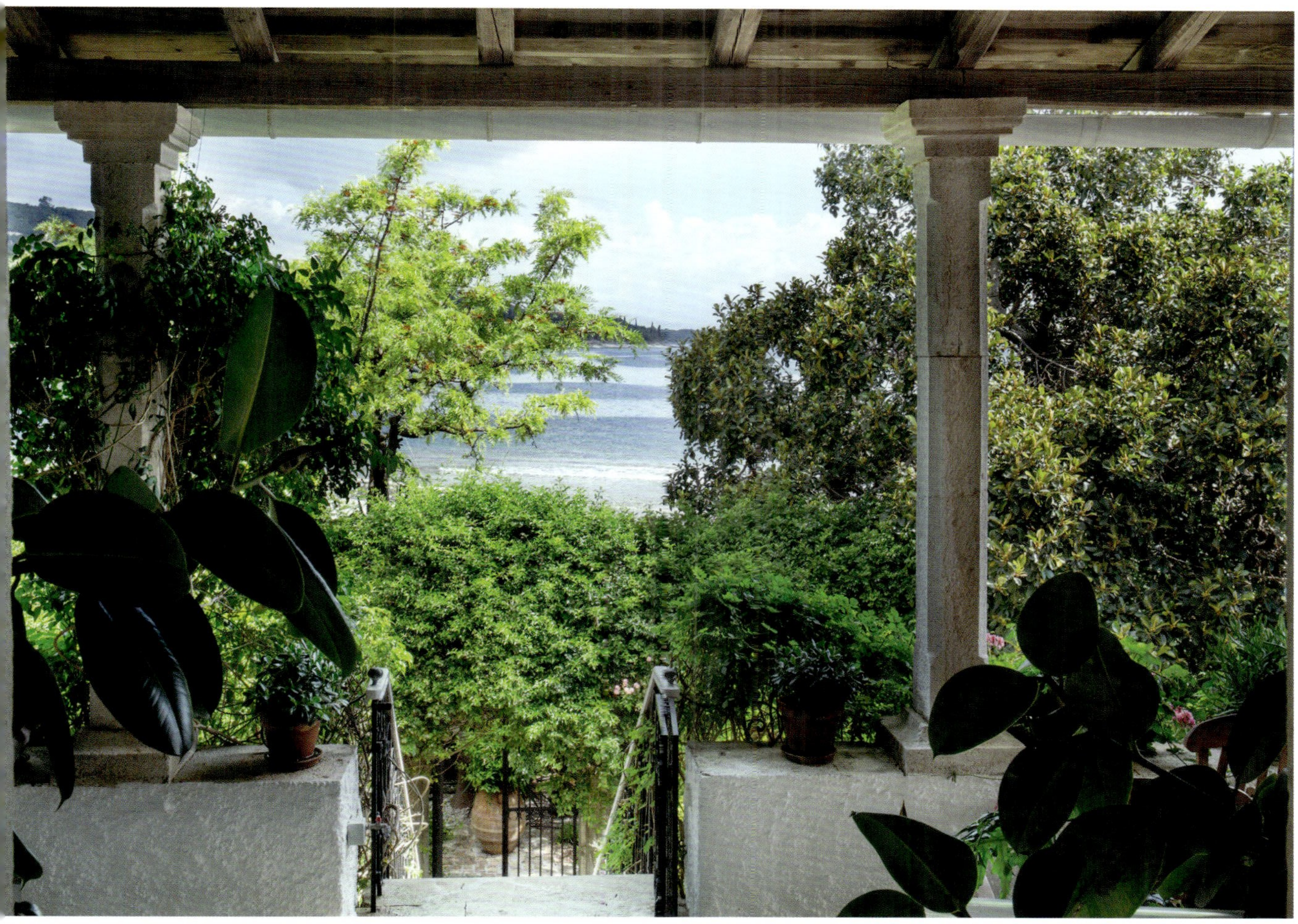

The veranda on the house's northern side typifies local tradition: in summer, Corfiot family life takes place mostly on shady verandas that span the width of the house fronts, with high wooden-beamed roofs and cool stone floors. And, as at Kouloúra, many traditional houses also have a pergola to the side or the back for a grapevine or flowering creepers.

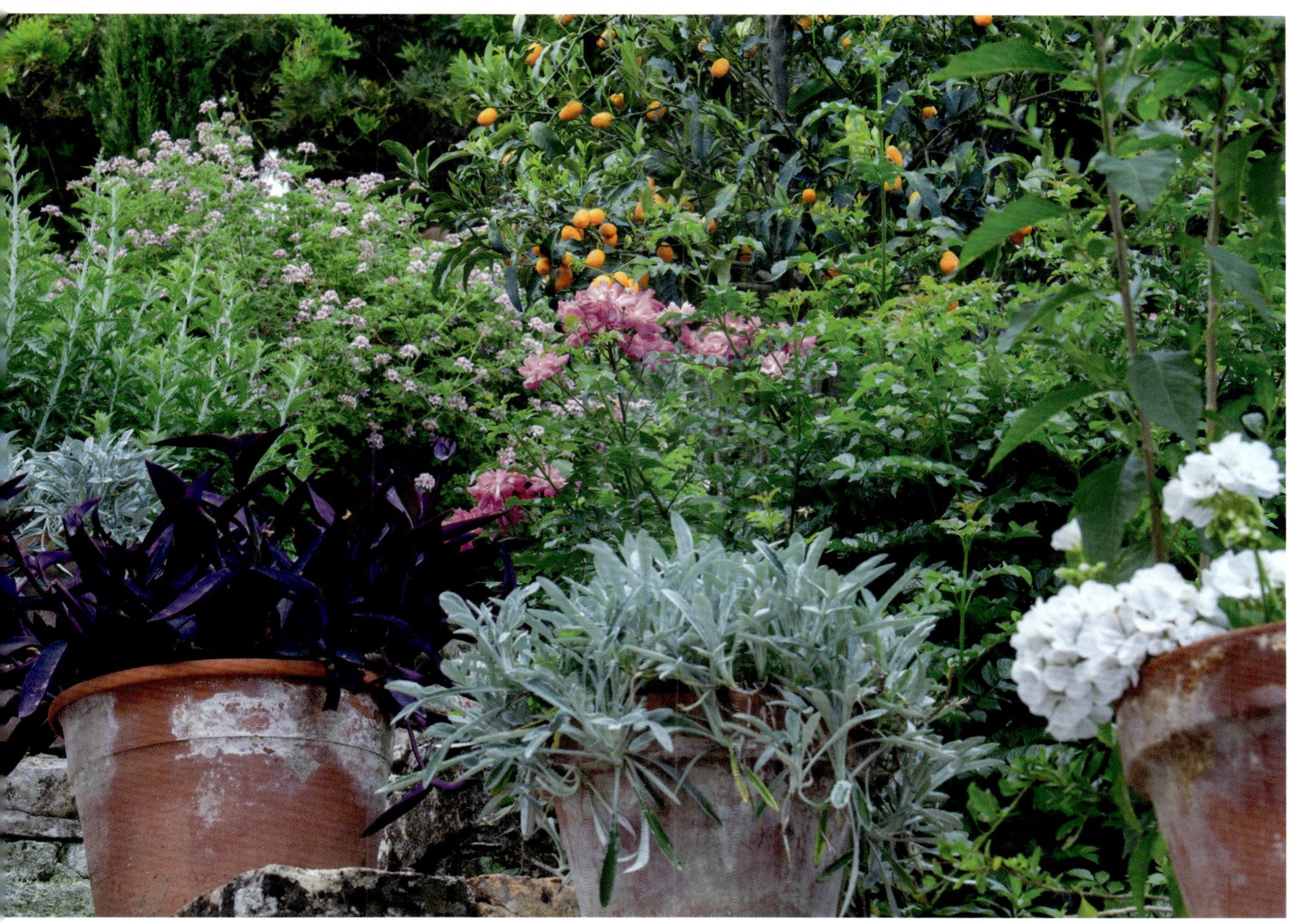

Oranges are combined with scented pelargoniums (reputed to discourage mosquitoes), roses, and ornamental plants in pots.

OPPOSITE
The name Kouloúra, meaning a coil or circle, derives from the circular shape of the harbour overlooked by the house and garden.

The several courtyards in this garden provide intriguing contrasts in atmosphere. The entrance courtyard is an expansive sunlit space, patterned in flagstones with old brick; brightly flowering oleanders and *Bougainvillea* add to its welcoming, joyous atmosphere. The trees here include a massive old eucalyptus, a southern magnolia in a round central bed, and a blue-flowering *Jacaranda mimosifolia* that spreads its ample branches over a bed of *Agapanthus*. On the north side of the house, a smaller courtyard is entered directly from the harbour through an iron gate. Almost always in shade, this space has a remarkable old Moreton Bay fig with aerial roots, and beds of *Agapanthus* and *Tulbaghia violacea*.[20] From here, a stone archway leads into an inner courtyard planted with lemon trees and perfumed by the starry white flowers of a lemon-scented jasmine (*Jasminum azoricum*) on the wall.

Steps lead up to a shady veranda—arranged with comfortable chairs for surveying the comings and goings in the harbour and the shipping in the Corfu Straits. The Quartano family coat of arms above the main entrance door to the house shows a sprig with a bunch of grapes, a blade of wheat, and a single flower. According to historian Dimitris Zymáris, it refers to the seasons of spring, summer, and autumn, 'representing only the mild seasons of the year, meaning that the family does not experience winter'.[21] Lady Silvia le Marchant, daughter of the owner Francesca Frua de Angeli, explains that despite its military origins the house once commanded large plantations of olives, grapes, and other crops.

Up the hill, the south side of the house backs on to another exquisite courtyard, topped by a grapevine on a wrought-iron pergola and with open views to the sea. From here, steps lead to the pool terrace stretched out parallel to the shoreline below it. The artist duo Anne and Patrick Poirier, friends of the family, advised on the design of this terrace, placing four single pencil cypresses in the large horizontal space in a way that evokes ancient columns. Above the pool terrace, Silvia's favourite part of the garden is a woodland path under the wild cypress trees, with views over the sea below and with the smell of the *maquis* wafting on the wind.

20. A plaque here commemorates the kidnapping in 1537 of the Quartanos' seven-year old daughter by Turkish raiders under Barbarossa Hayreddin Pasha. Sourtzinos writes that 'Because of her beauty and her intelligence [she] was educated like a princess. Later she was married to Sultan Selim II and became his adviser.' See Giorgos Sourtzinos, *Corfu: A Journey through the Ages* (Corfu: Historical Folklore Society of Corfu, 1998), p. 132. 21. Dimitris Zymáris, personal communication.

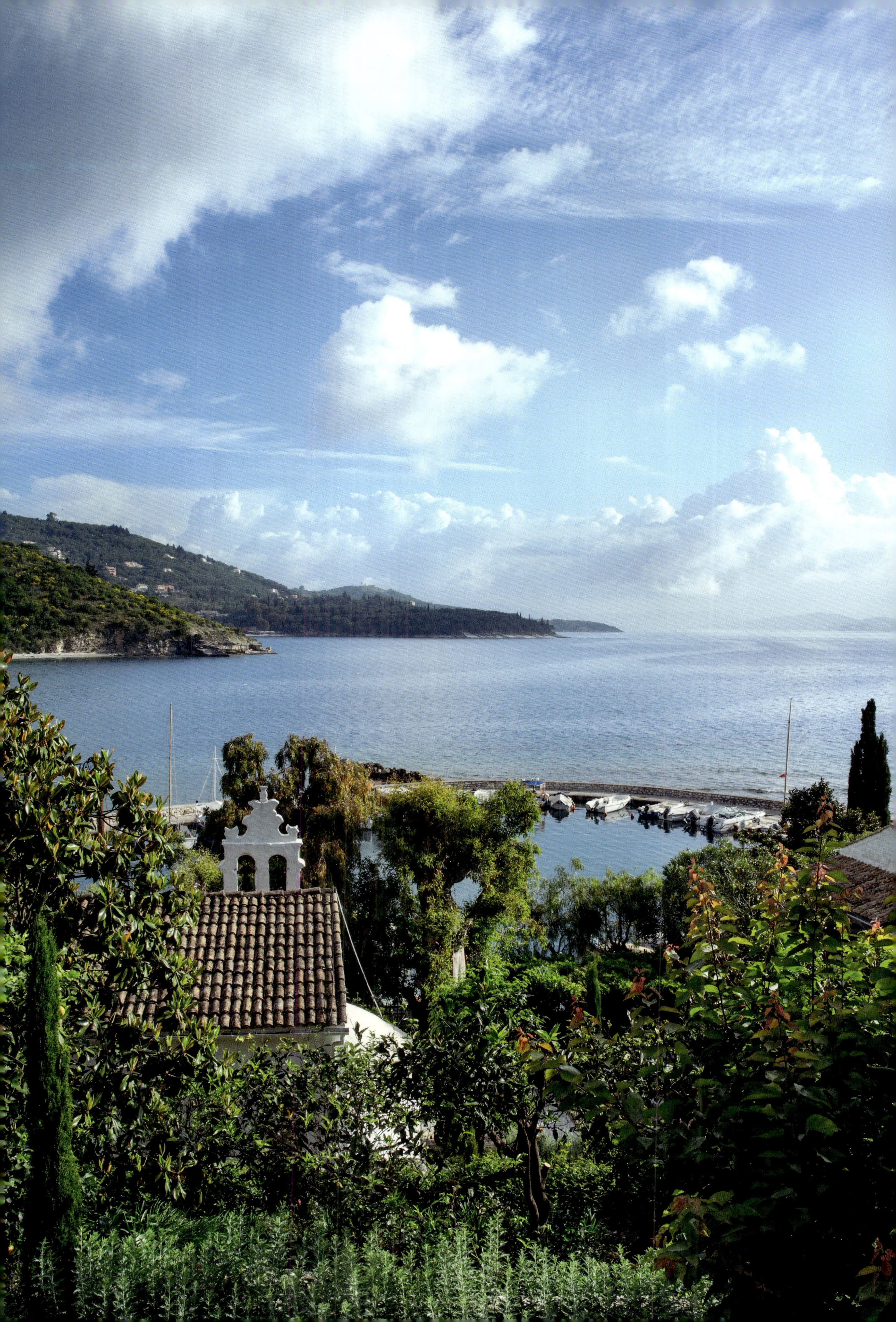

Viewed from below, the focal point at the top of the garden is this rectangular pond with fountain and papyrus (*Cyperus papyrus*).

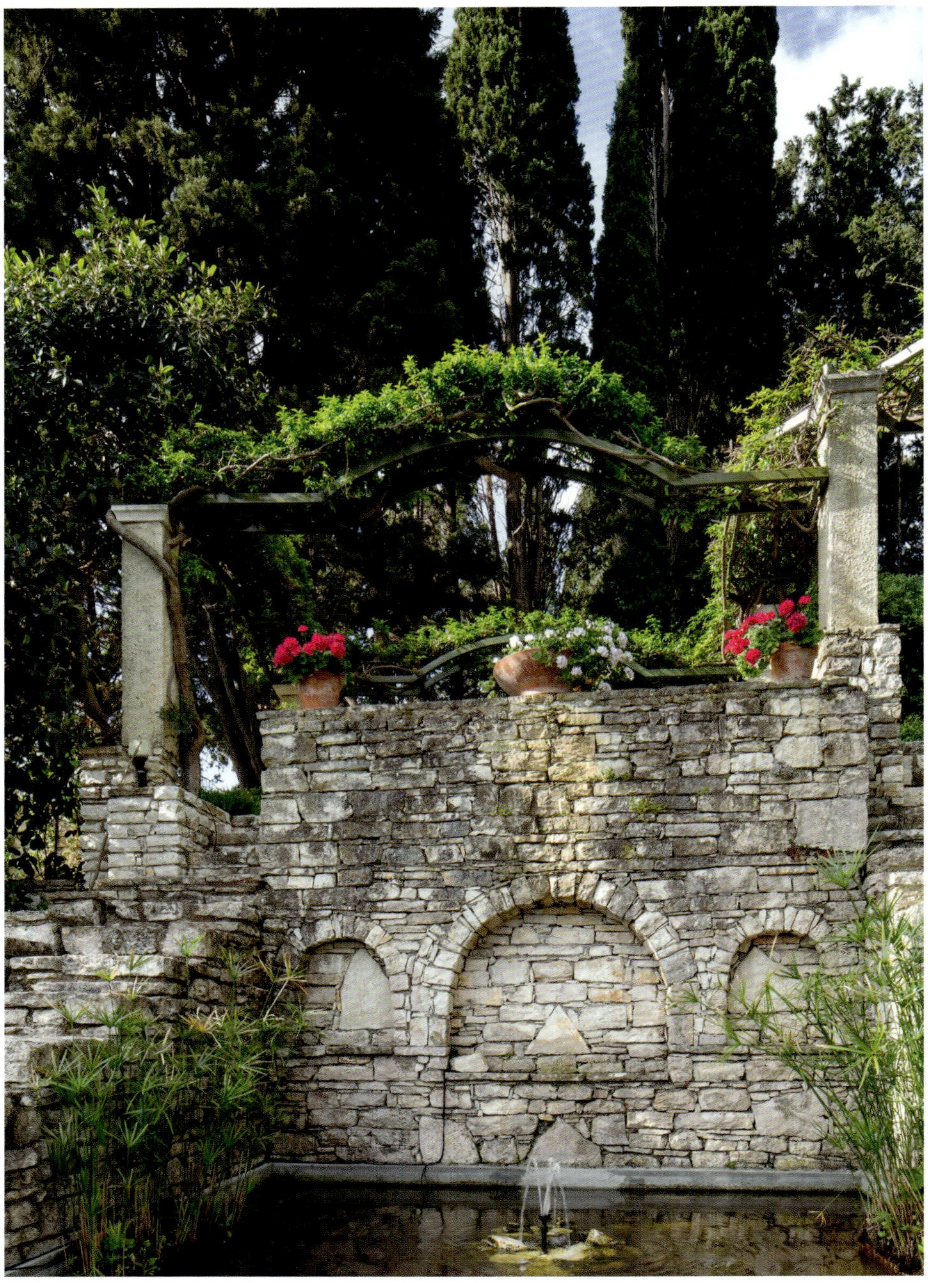

CENTRE TOP
The view from above the pond towards the sea.

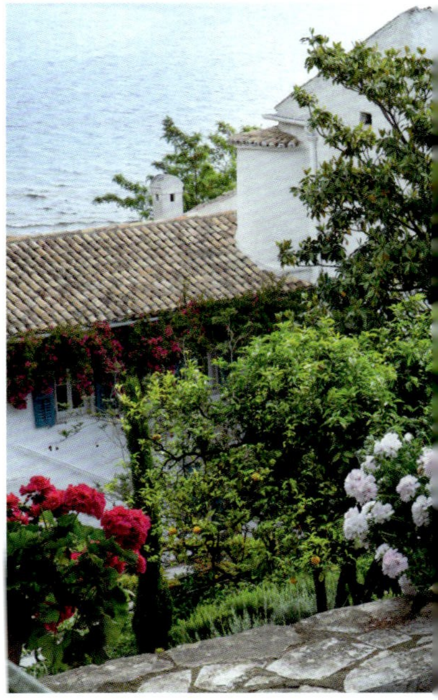

Parallel terraces ascend the hill, planted with a mixture of fruit and flowers.

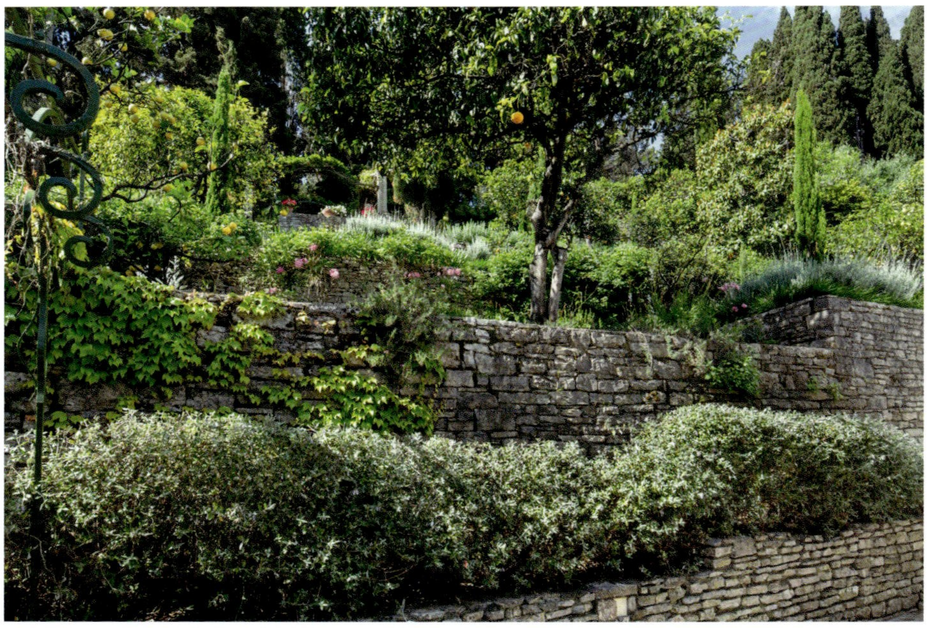

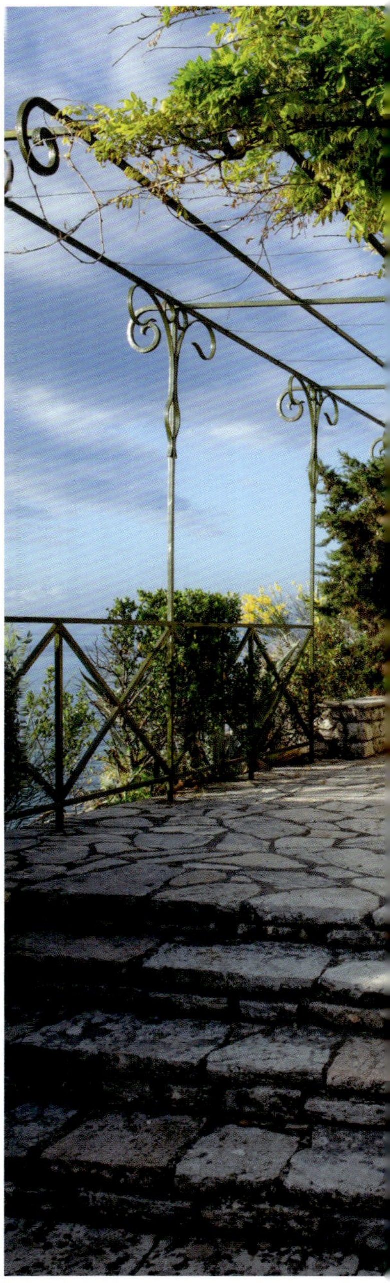

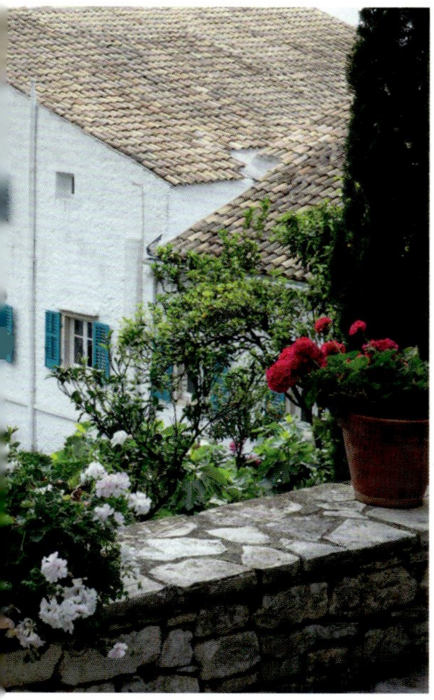

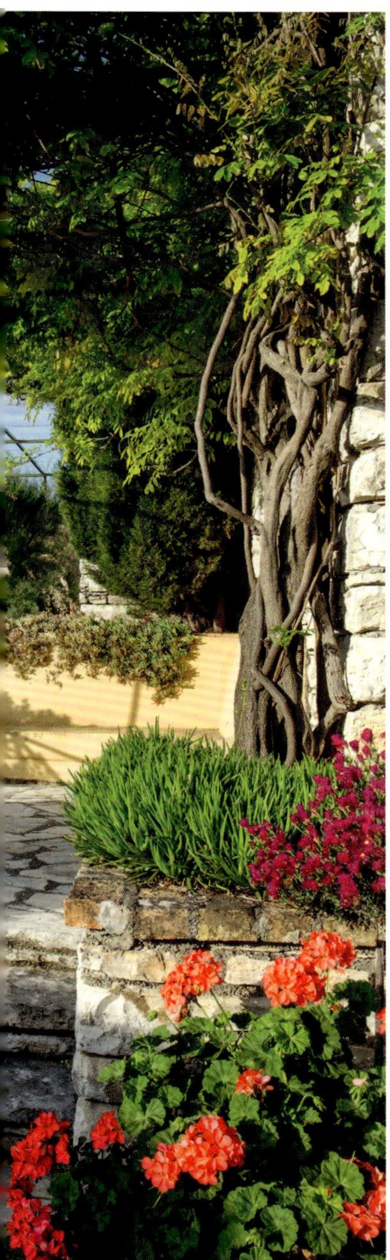

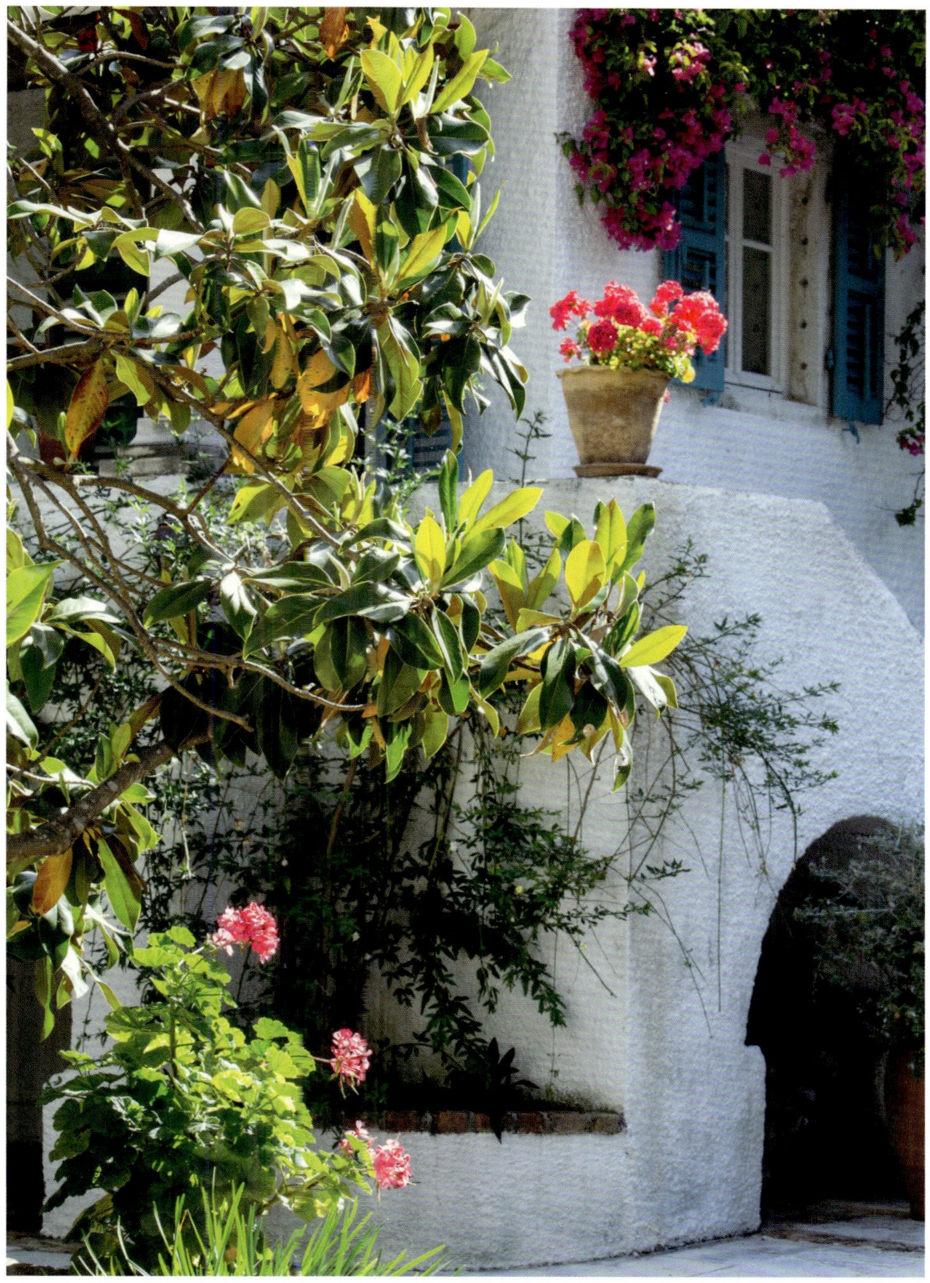

For most of each day the entrance courtyard is bathed in sunlight.

CENTRE BOTTOM
The path to the swimming pool leads under one of the garden's many distinctive wrought-iron pergolas.

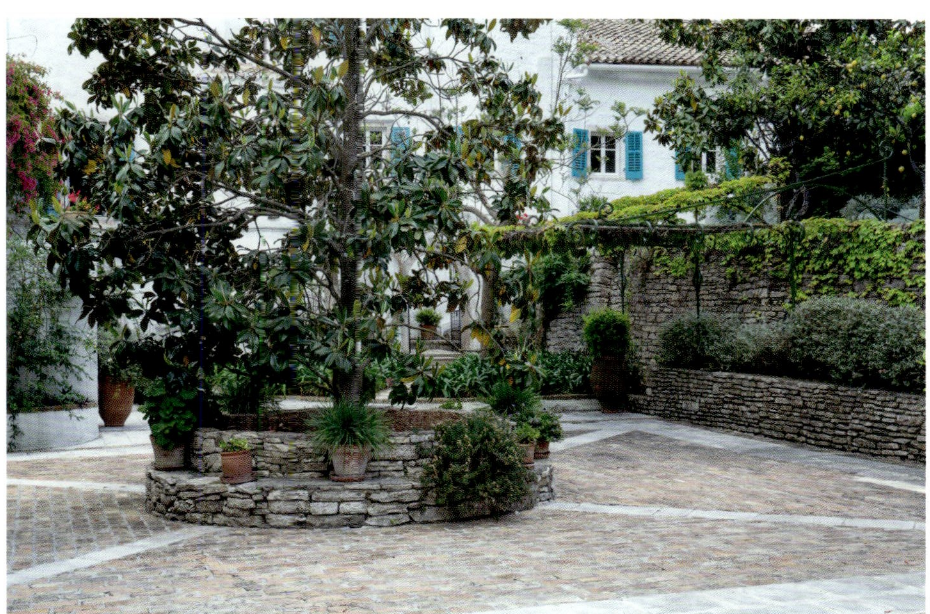

Southern magnolia trees (*Magnolia grandiflora*) feature in the entrance courtyard and on one of the hillside terraces.

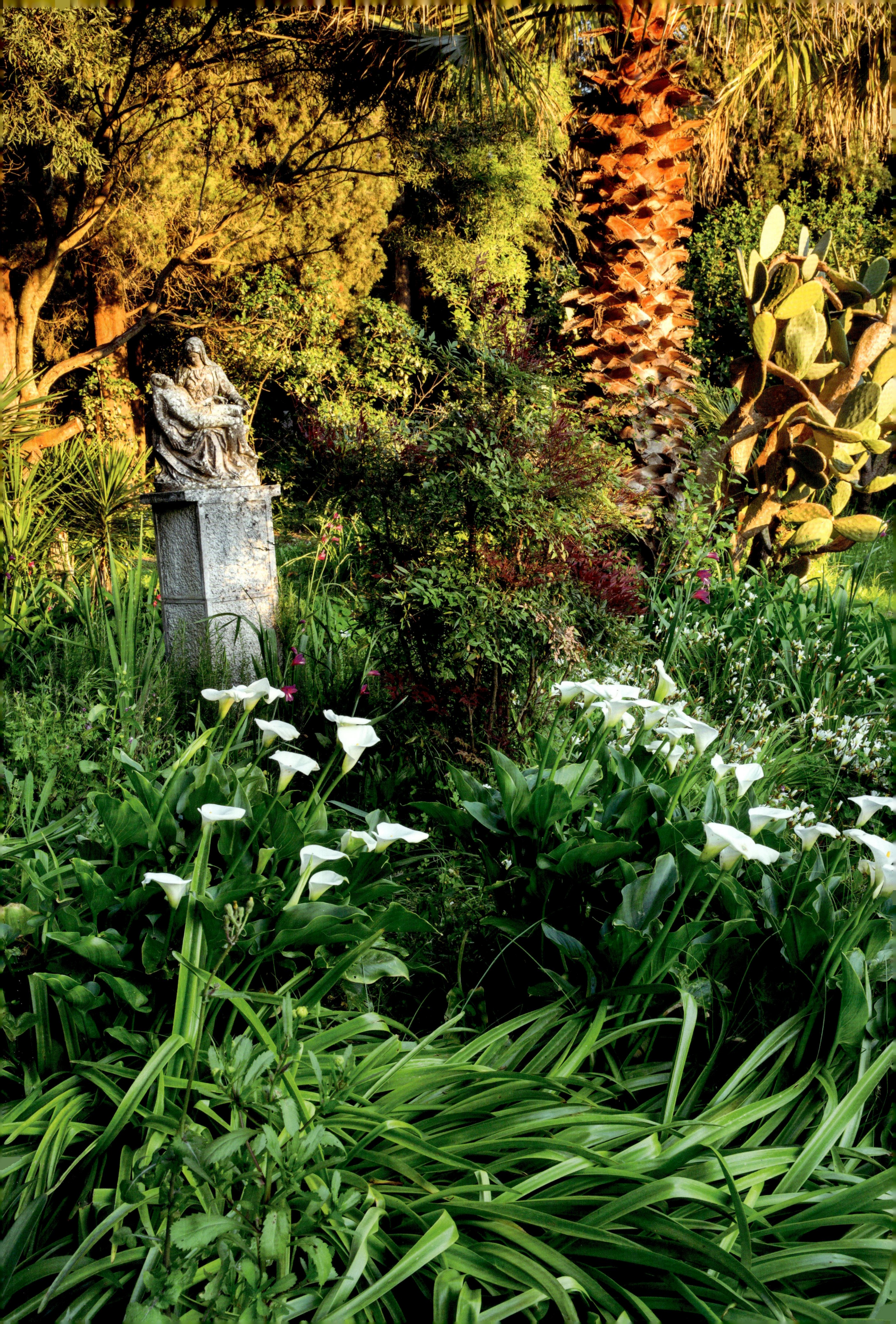

The British Cemetery

Threading one's way through the traffic on dusty Kolokotróni Street on the way from Corfu Town's bustling hub, one might easily miss the entrance to this enchanting garden. In April, the first sign of something unusual is a cloud of white roses tumbling over a high stone wall. A wrought-iron gate in the wall has been left just a little open and, when it is pushed, rings a bell which brings the caretaker and garden manager, George Psaíla, darting from his house to welcome visitors. Established in 1814 while Corfu was under British rule, this secret garden of rest is not just a haven in the midst of the busy city, but also a conservation site for wild orchids and for many exquisite old varieties of garden plants.

OPPOSITE
White arum lilies mingle with heavenly bamboo (*Nandina domestica*); in the background, a Chinese windmill palm (*Trachycarpus fortunei*) and a prickly pear (*Opuntia ficus-carica*) catch the evening sunlight.

Inside the garden, a broad grass alley leading directly from the entrance is flanked by cypress trees and, in spring, hundreds of white arum lilies in bloom. Narrow paths off the alley thread their way among stately evergreen trees including southern magnolia—some obviously dating from close to the cemetery's founding. Several towering redwood trees (*Sequoia sempervirens*) are said to have arrived as seedlings in a suitcase from California, carried by a friend of the cemetery about a hundred years ago.

The atmosphere in the open spaces of this garden is one of intense peace, but also the intense excitement of luxuriant growth just barely kept in check. Rambling roses and wisteria pierce and thread their way through old trees and wrought-iron structures, and crowds of self-seeded flower bulbs and perennials shoulder their way through dense grass, creating patches of meadowland full of spectacular colours and shapes.

In early April, these spaces are thronged with purple and white bearded irises, graceful carmine Byzantine gladiolus, and red and yellow harlequin flower (*Sparaxis tricolor*). On the edges of the wooded areas are Judas trees, fragrant *Philadelphus*, orange-flowered *Kerria*, snowball bush, and old varieties of tree peony. Wisteria sends perfume drifting on the wind. By late April, the roses are in full swing, including old shrub roses in many shades of peach, pink, and white.

In spring come the wild orchids: thirty of the fifty species endemic to Corfu can be found in the cemetery. First is the giant orchid (*Barlia robertiana*), late in February, followed by drifts of rich purple

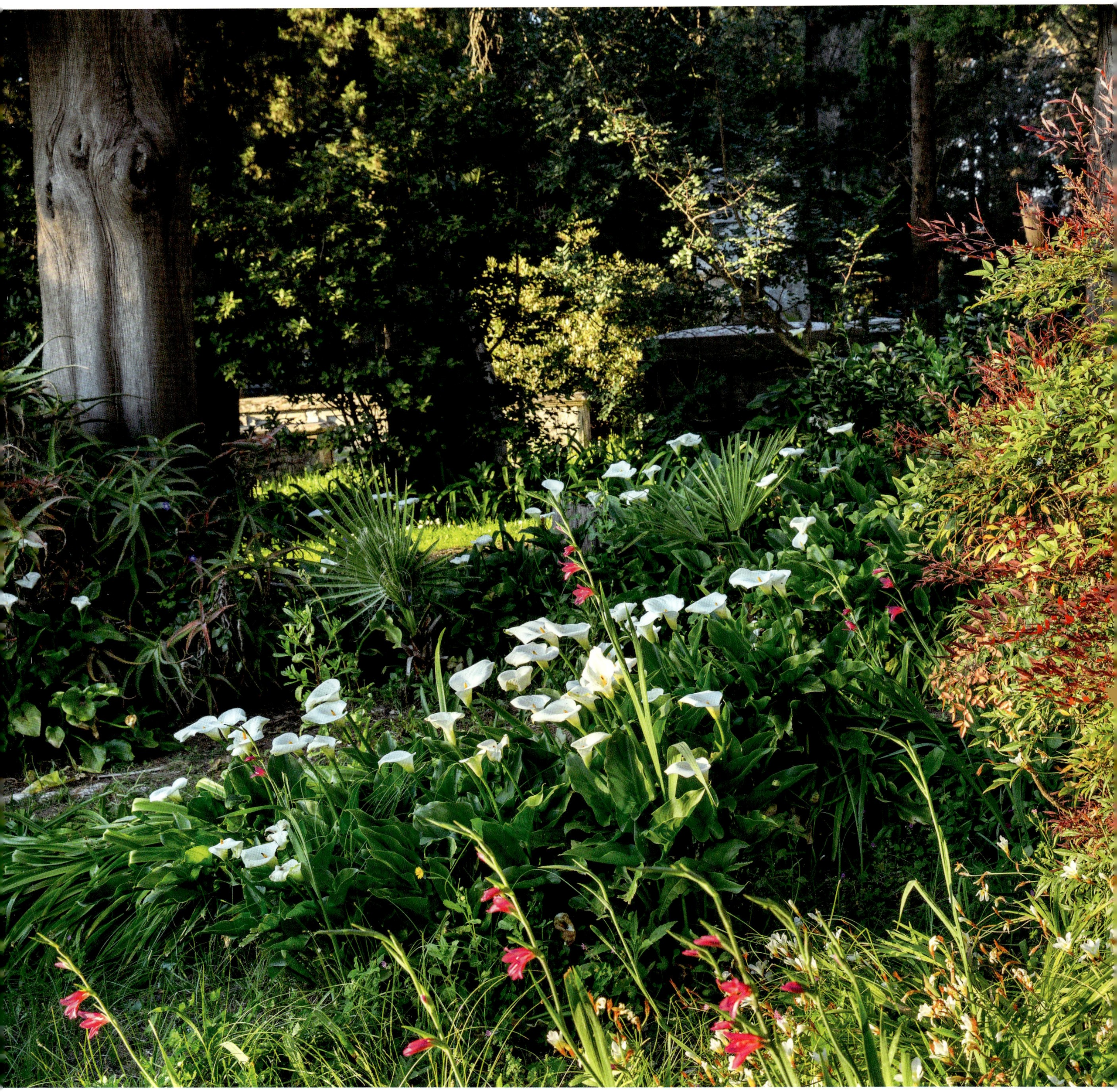

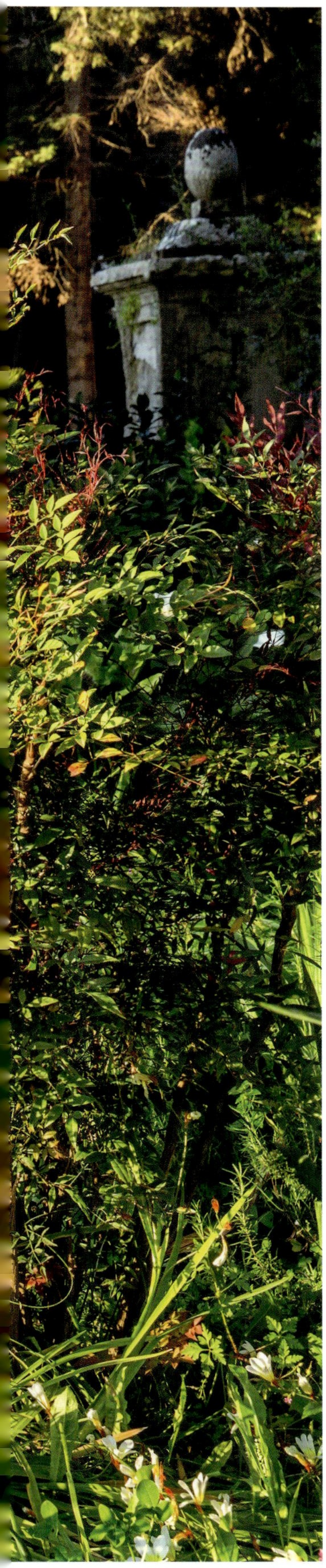

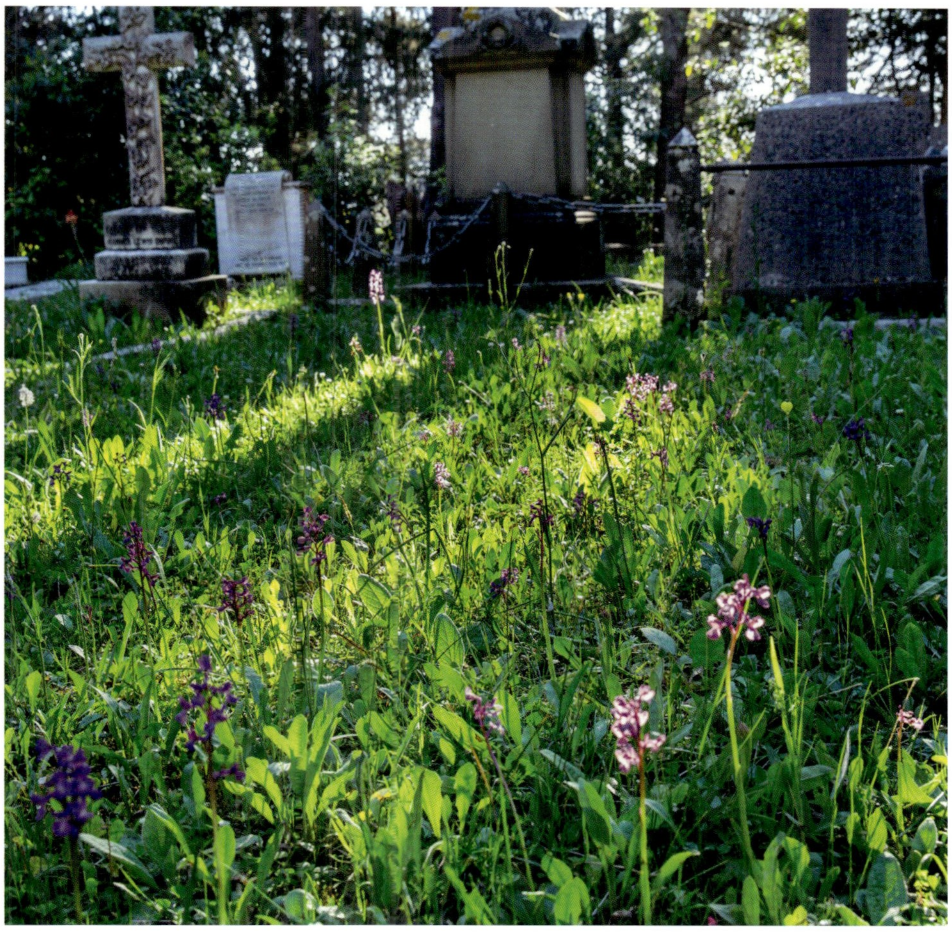

The cemetery is renowned for its preservation of wild orchids. Here, loose-flowered orchid (*Orchis laxiflora*).

loose-flowered orchid and a whole parade of *Ophrys* species with their velvety bee-like flowers, tongue orchids (*Serapias lingua*), and—to finish the season by the middle of May—pyramidal orchids (*Anacamptis pyramidalis*) both white and pink. An orchid lover all his life, George leaves the grass unmown until the season is finished.

The oldest gravestones (the earliest legible one dates from 1817) speak of the rigours of life in the early years of the nineteenth century, with tiny headstones for infants and many graves for people dead from typhus. Also buried here are members of Corfu's German community, who did not have their own cemetery, as well as crew members from nearby marine disasters, and prominent Corfu residents of several other nationalities.

When George was a boy the cemetery was a better-known part of the town landscape. He recounts that before Corfu had flower shops, families who were planning weddings and funerals used to come to the cemetery to ask him for bunches of cannas, zinnias, and dahlias, which he was happy to supply. Extremely knowledgeable about plants and the wild flora of the island, he was awarded the British Empire Medal in 1988 for his services to the cemetery.

OPPOSITE
Paths lead past open areas filled with flowers and under the deep shade of cypresses. Crimson *Gladiolus byzantinus* have seeded themselves among the arum lilies (*Zantedeschia aethiopica*).

OVERLEAF
In this peaceful scene, the sunlight catches the last flowers of African flag (*Chasmanthe floribunda*).

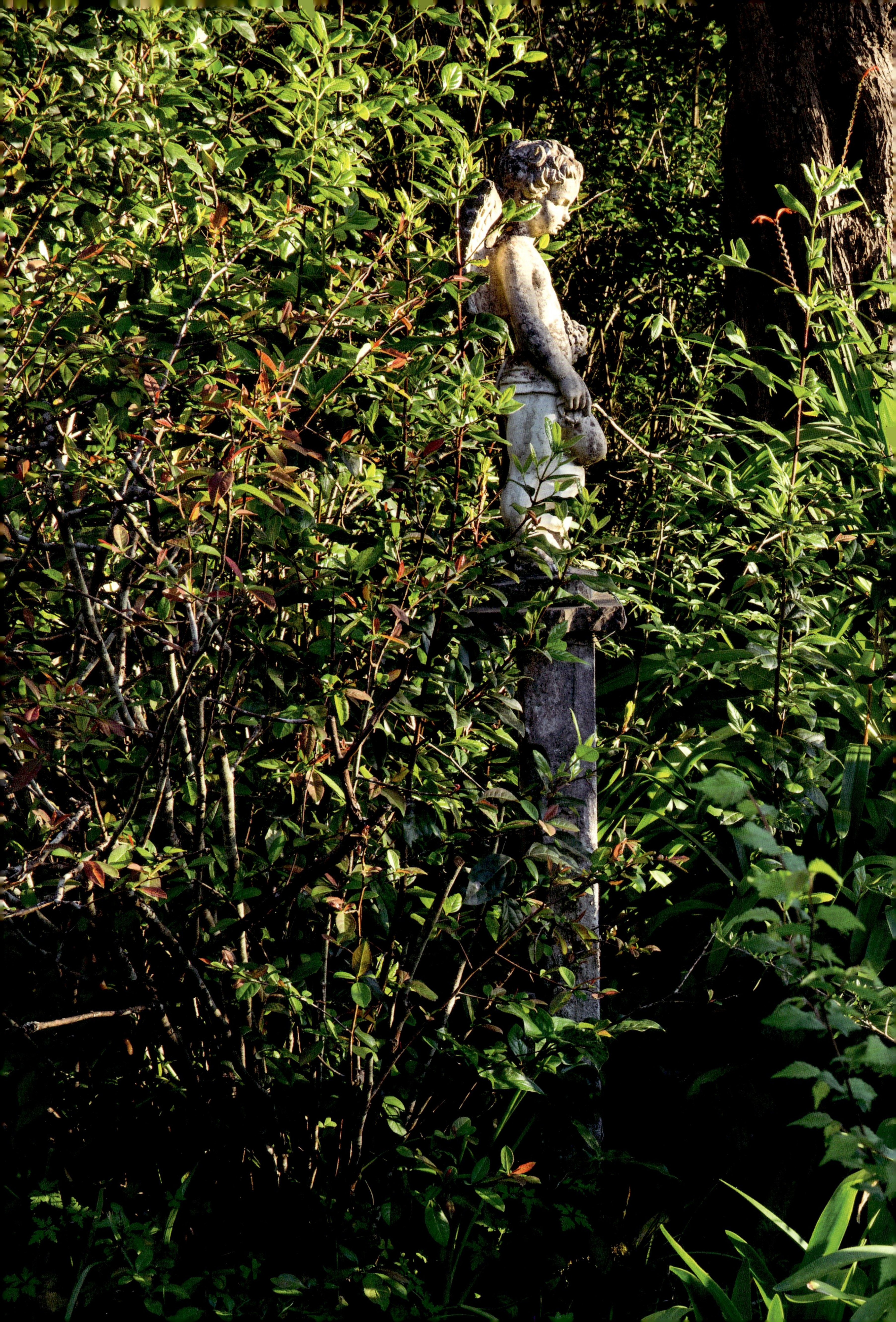

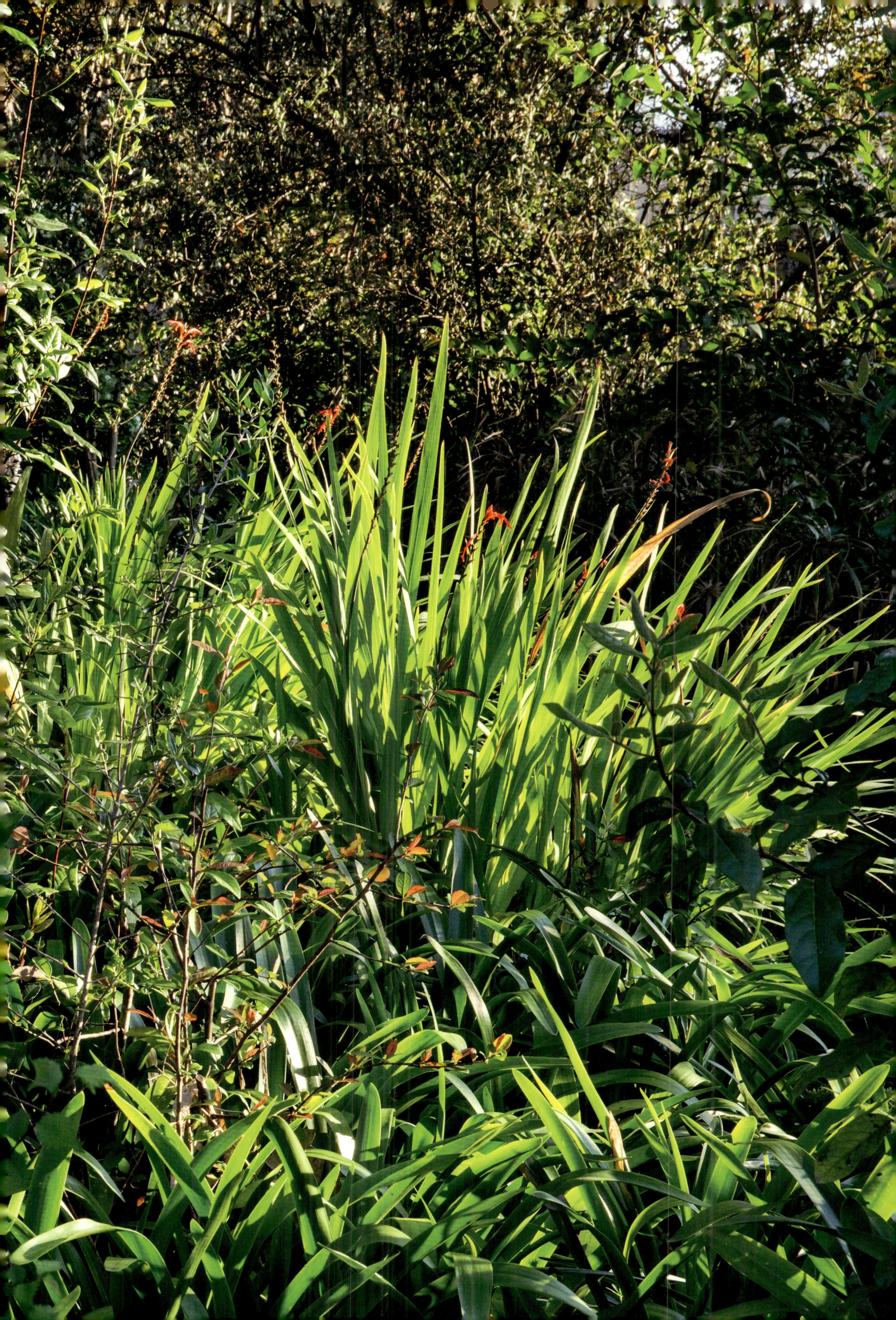

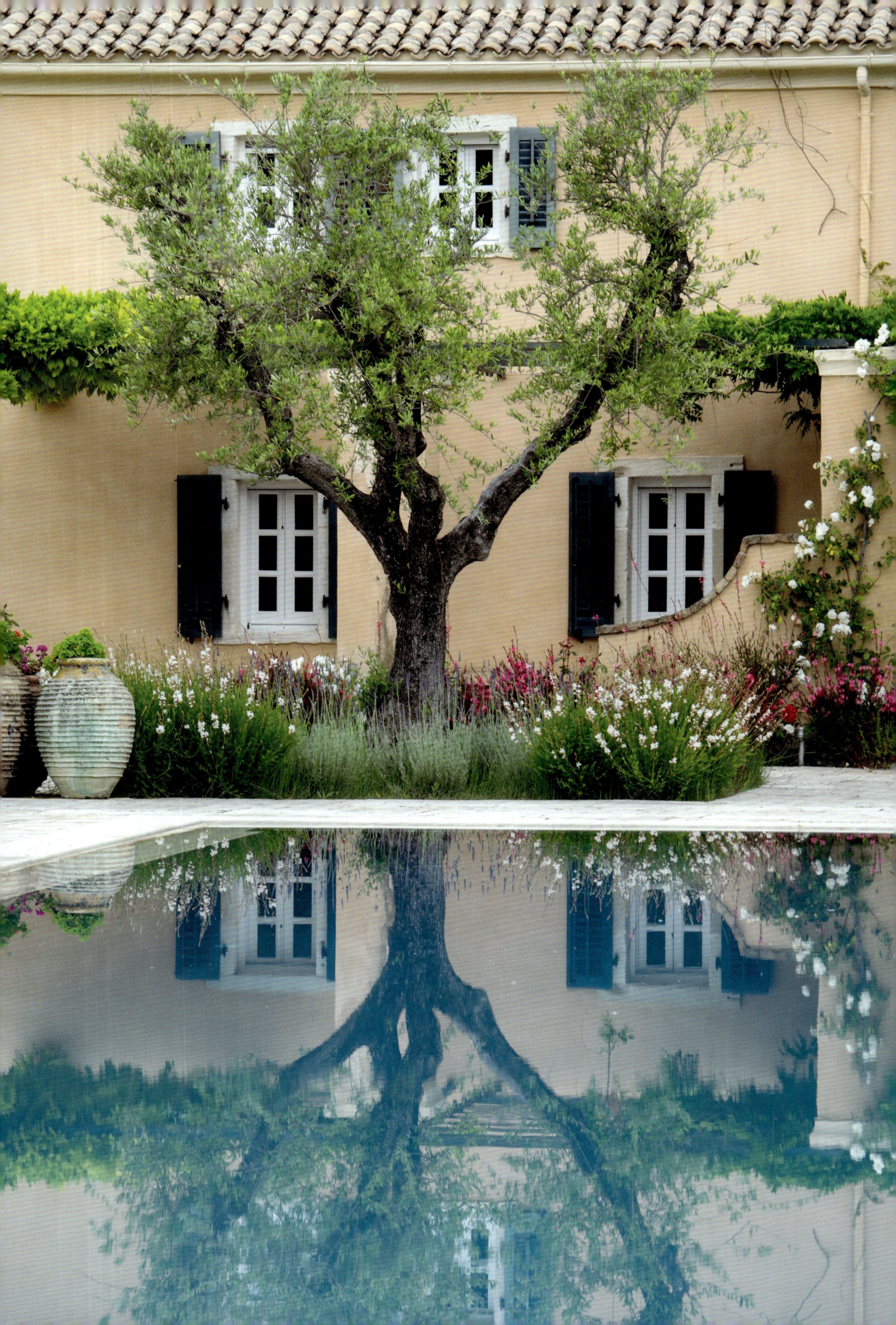

Krevatsoúla

As did many distinguished old houses in Corfu, Krevatsoúla fell upon hard times during the twentieth century. For visitors who walked its corridors then, side-stepping the panes of precious Venetian glass lying shattered on the floors, or contemplated its trees engulfed by wild vines, its restoration and rebirth seems a miraculous thing. Strategically located—facing on to Ipsos Bay and Albania—the house began as a Venetian artillery post. In the fifteenth century it was acquired by a branch of the Theotóky family, who developed it into an estate of nearly five hundred hectares, growing oranges and lemons, vines, and some three thousand olive trees.[22] Old records also mention hayfields, potato cultivation, and hay making. And, according to Paisídou, "Four hundred rose bushes filled the air with their scent and in summertime bees swarmed to the arbour…"[23]

OPPOSITE
Reflections in a corner of the pool.

The present owners acquired the property about a decade ago and have restored it with integrity and care, working with Zege Architects. Today the property is a romantic secluded world with views open only to the sea. As well as its gardens and orchards, it contains a private golf course, whose reed-lined pond is home to white geese and swans.

OVERLEAF
In the pool garden, the lively forms of the olive and whitewashed lemon-tree trunks, and the waves of gaura planted under them, emphasise the stillness of the long rectangular sheet of water.

In summer, the mood at Krevatsoúla—heady, slightly intoxicating—begins its seduction as soon as one comes through the entrance gate: this is a place arranged for the appreciation of beauty, for relaxation, restoration, play, and renewed inspiration to face the world outside. Perfume from roses and lavender wafts from the pool garden. A rill carries mountain spring water in a stone channel. Venerable poplars and pines, like the house itself, provide continuity with earlier days. A thriving orchard has rows of pomegranate trees, traditional symbol of fertility and good luck. Big hospitable spaces around the pool house include a barbecue area and outdoor kitchen. In the wooded play area to the east of the garden are tables for games and a climbing frame. The jetty that once served to unload military supplies and then to load the estate's produce for export is now adapted for pleasure boating.

Designed by Eléni Georgiádis of Zege Architects, the pool garden at the heart of Krevatsoúla is bounded by the two wings of the house on the north and west, the old protective wall on the sea side to the east, and the pool house to the south. Contemporary in design, with

22. Paisídou, *Noble Houses of Corfu*, p. 60. 23. Ibid.

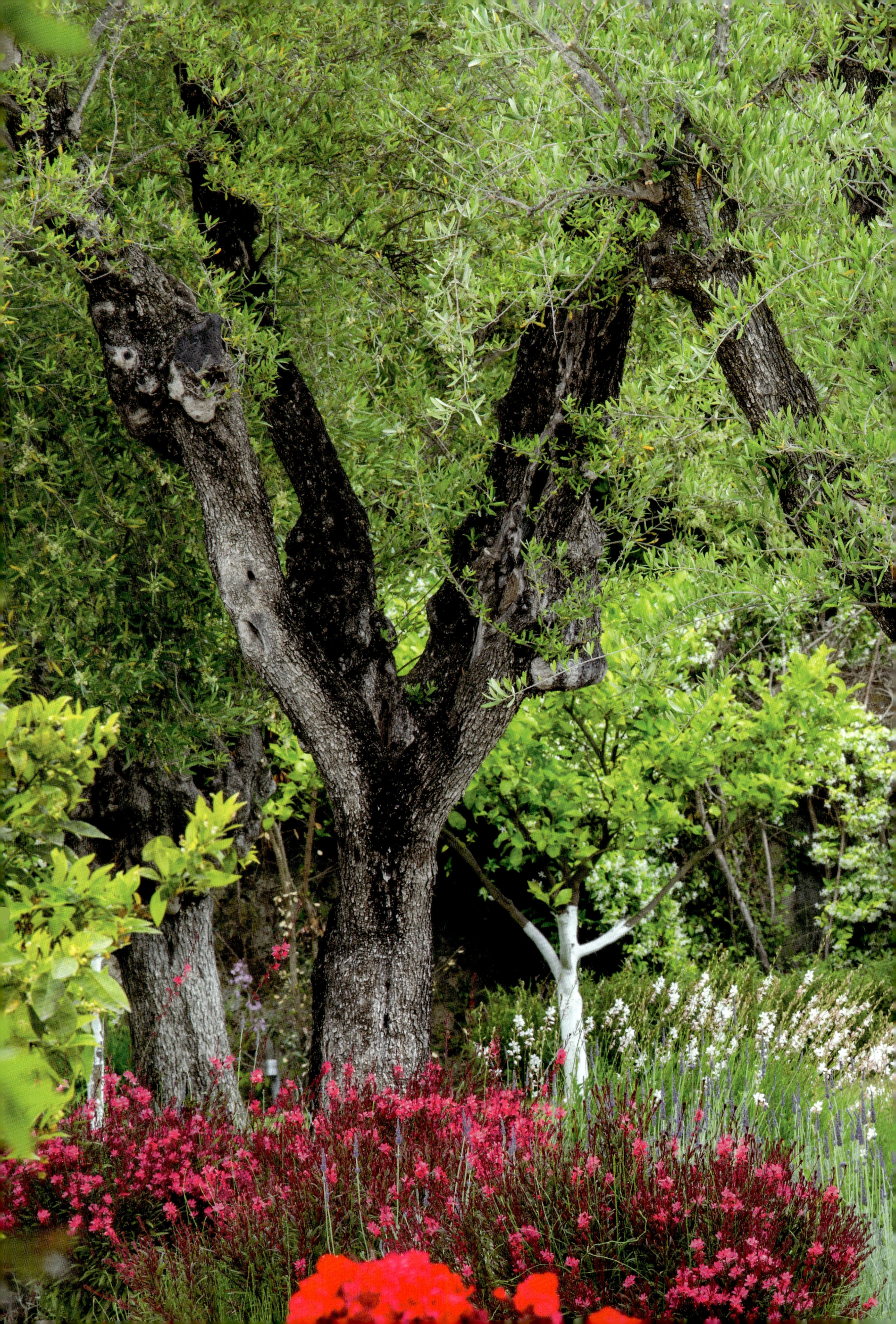

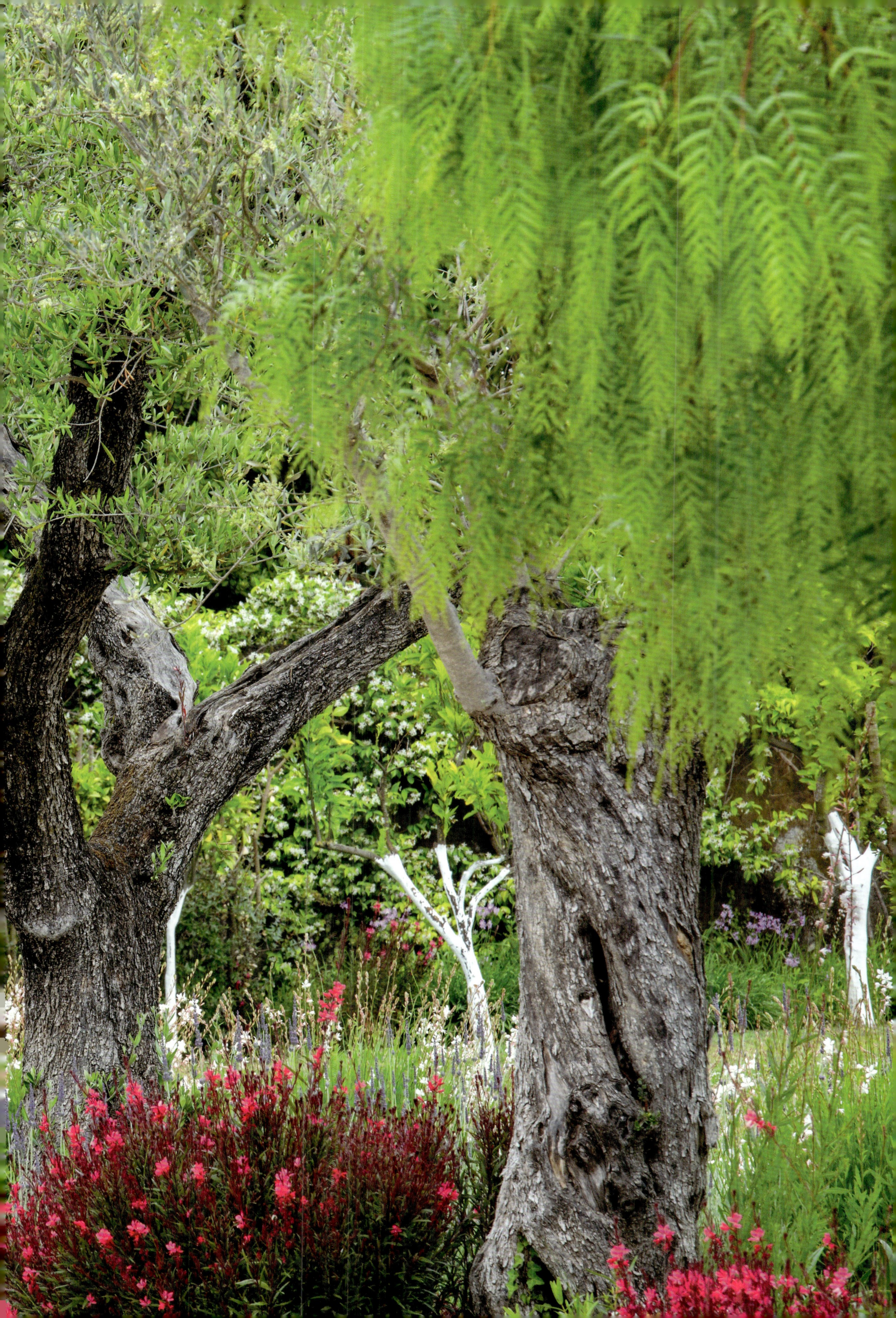

An old stone gateway leads through the sea wall to the children's play area next to the sea.

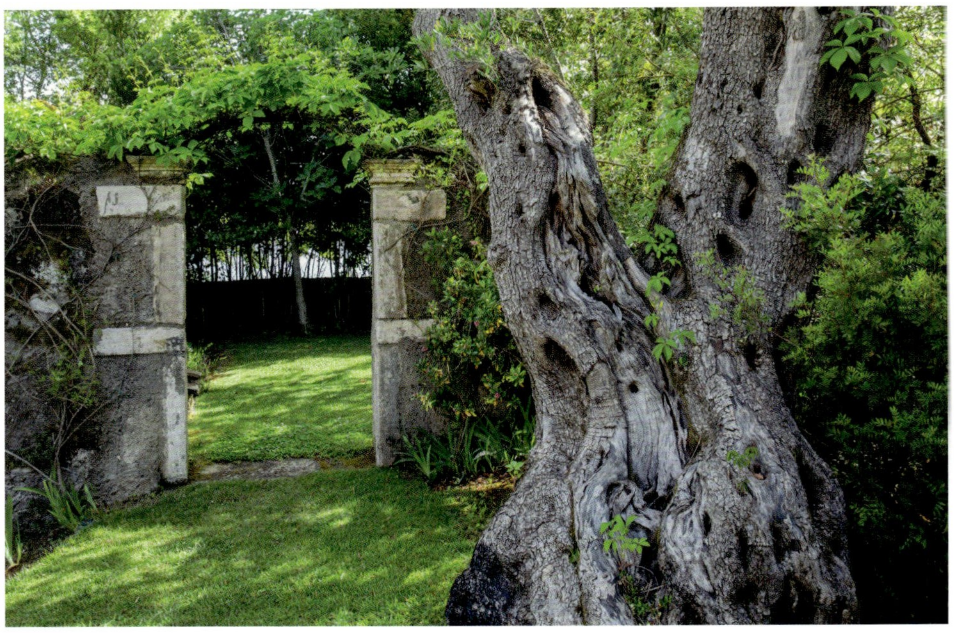

sensual plant forms contained within a strong 'bone structure', it is a perfect complement to the restored buildings. Its central feature, the long rectangular pool, is a lovely dark colour, surrounded by rectangular paving stones in pale limestone. A strong axis, cleverly placed, links the entrance pergola through the house to the pool and pool house beyond. A wide verdant lawn planted with a group of lemon trees runs the length of the pool on the eastern side; with their whitened trunks and branches, the trees call to mind a group of ballet dancers on the grass. On the pool's western side, areas of lawn alternate with planting beds and paving in a diagonal pattern; under old olive trees, glossy abelia (*Abelia* x *grandiflora*) and native lentisc bushes are combined with flowering perennials.

Within this strongly delineated layout, the garden planting is highly romantic. In April, purple and mauve wisteria blooms on the pergolas, its colours echoed by those of pansies and petunias planted in urns beneath. In May, the profusion of flowers—all in pinks, crimson, and white—includes clouds of blossoming roses, airy pink and white gaura, and pink and white pelargoniums.

For all its sophistication, the pool garden has elements of the traditional Greek *avlí*—the courtyard garden that contains both fruit and flowers. Pepper (*Schinus molle*) and olive trees are combined with pomegranate and flowering crape myrtle (*Lagerstroemia*), and their carefully pruned trunks and branches provide structure among the soft shapes of lavender, gaura, Russian sage (*Perovskia atriplicifolia*), and roses.

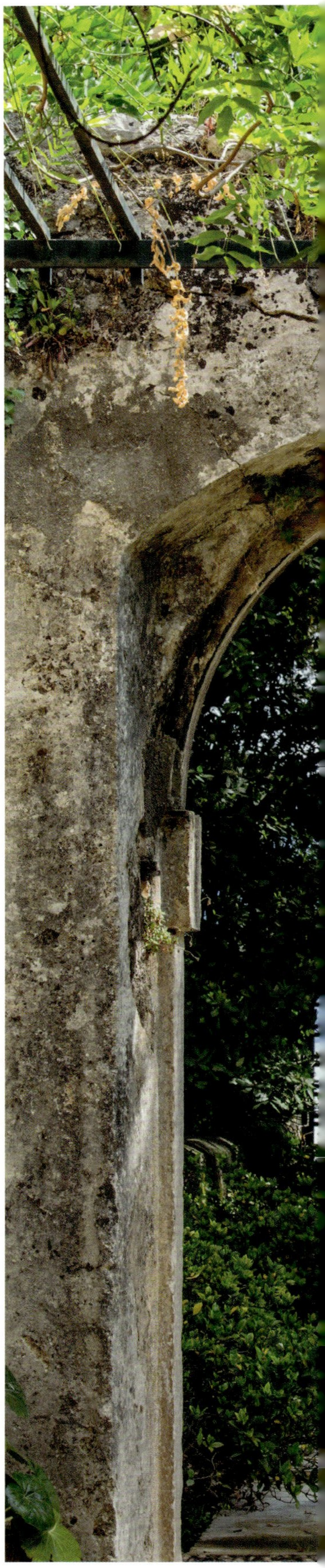

One of the entrance gates; the sea is beyond.

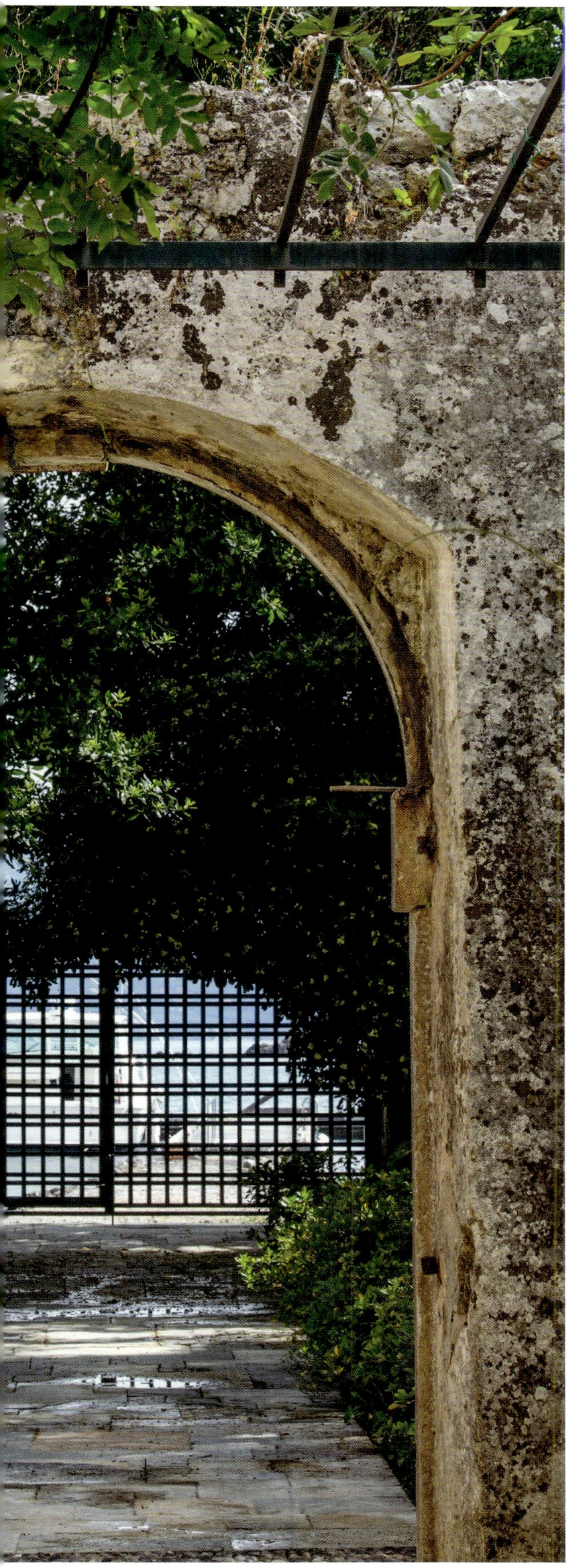

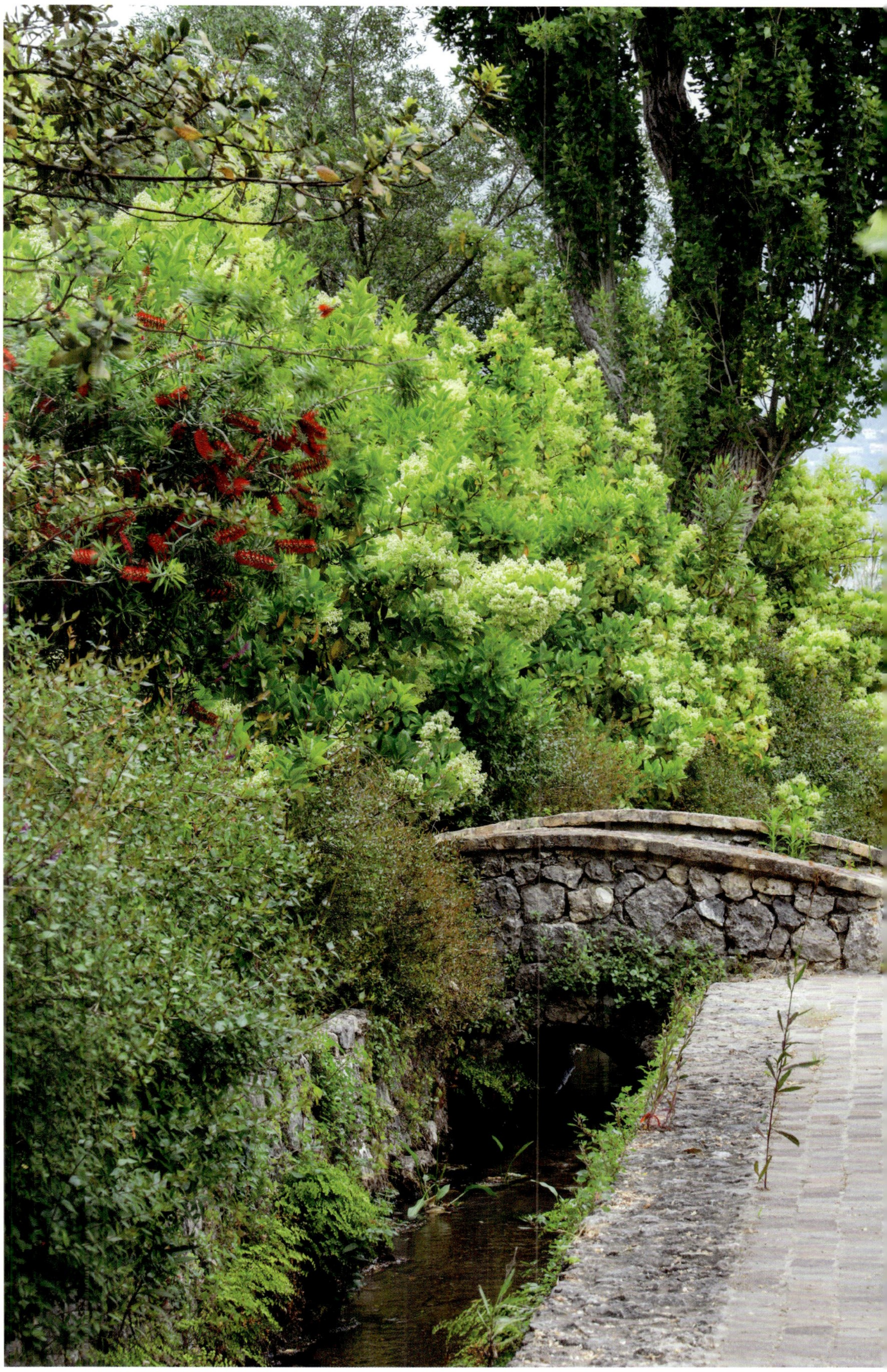

A stone-lined rill with bridges runs all around the property; according to the gardener, the supply comes from a mountain spring above Dassiá.

Groupings of old urns planted with bright flowers enhance the atmosphere at this historic house.

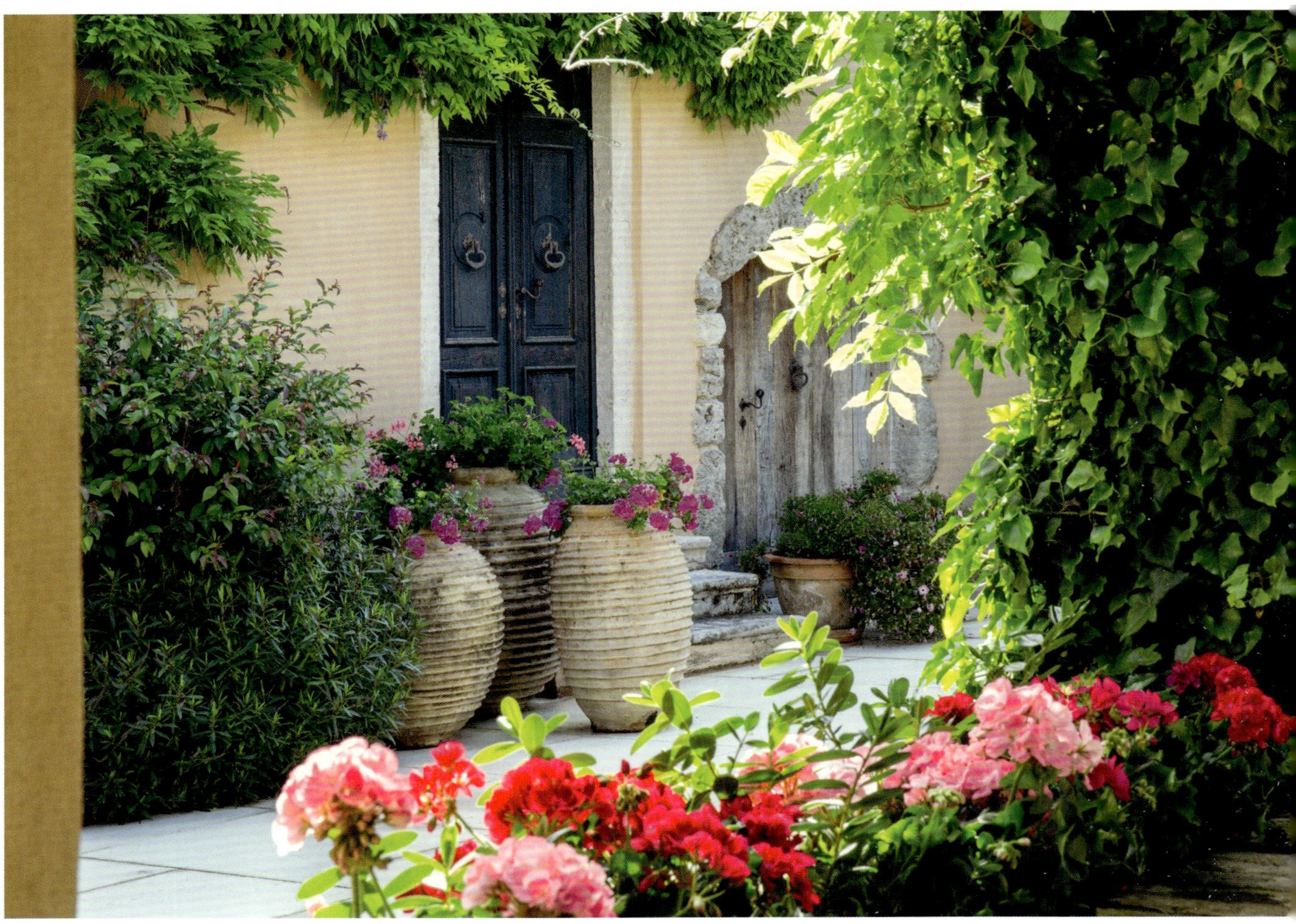

Krevatsoúla has two long pergolas unique in Corfu: one that runs from the entrance door through the main house and its courtyards to the pool garden; and another that bifurcates it, running from the sea to the far side of the family church.

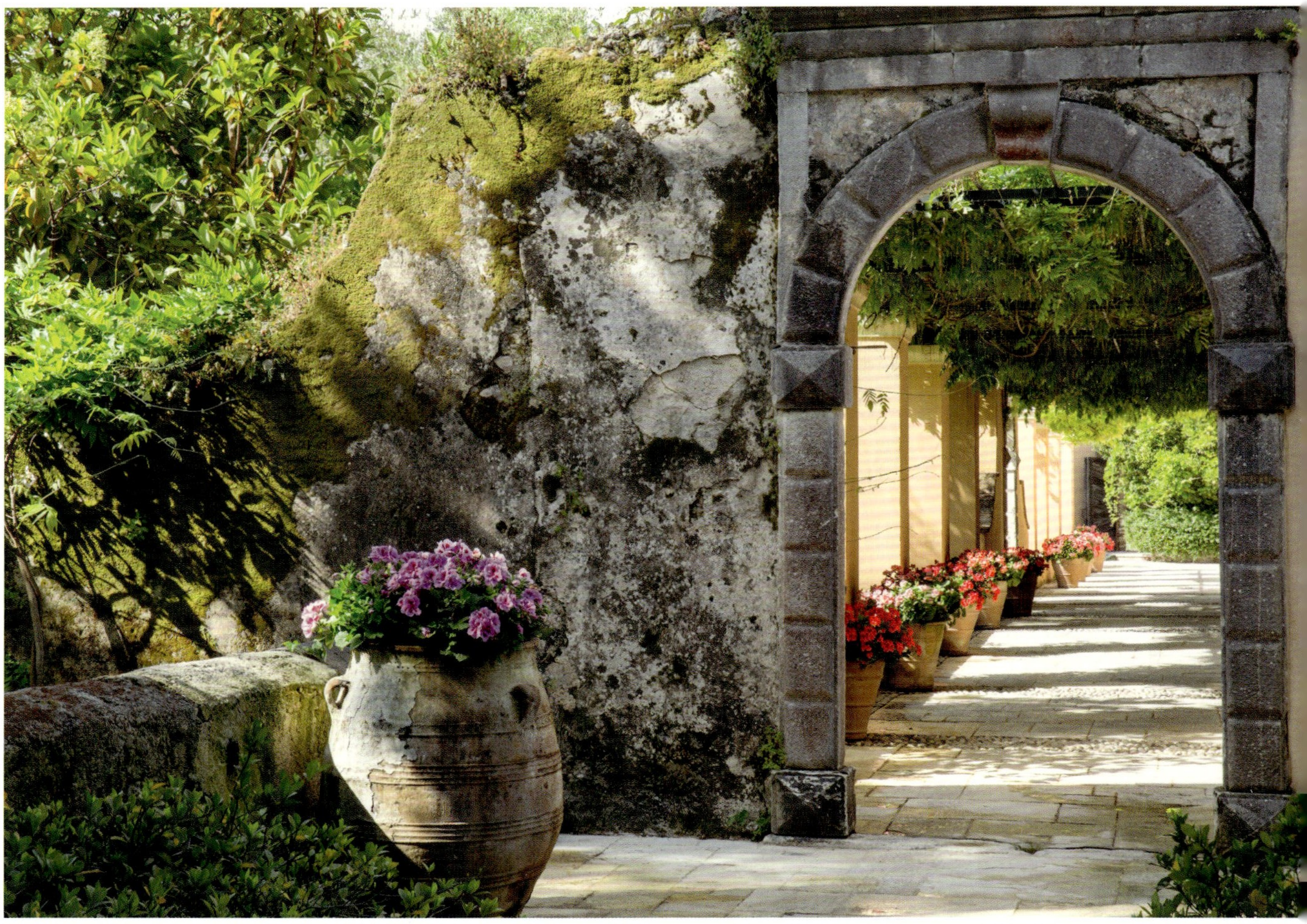

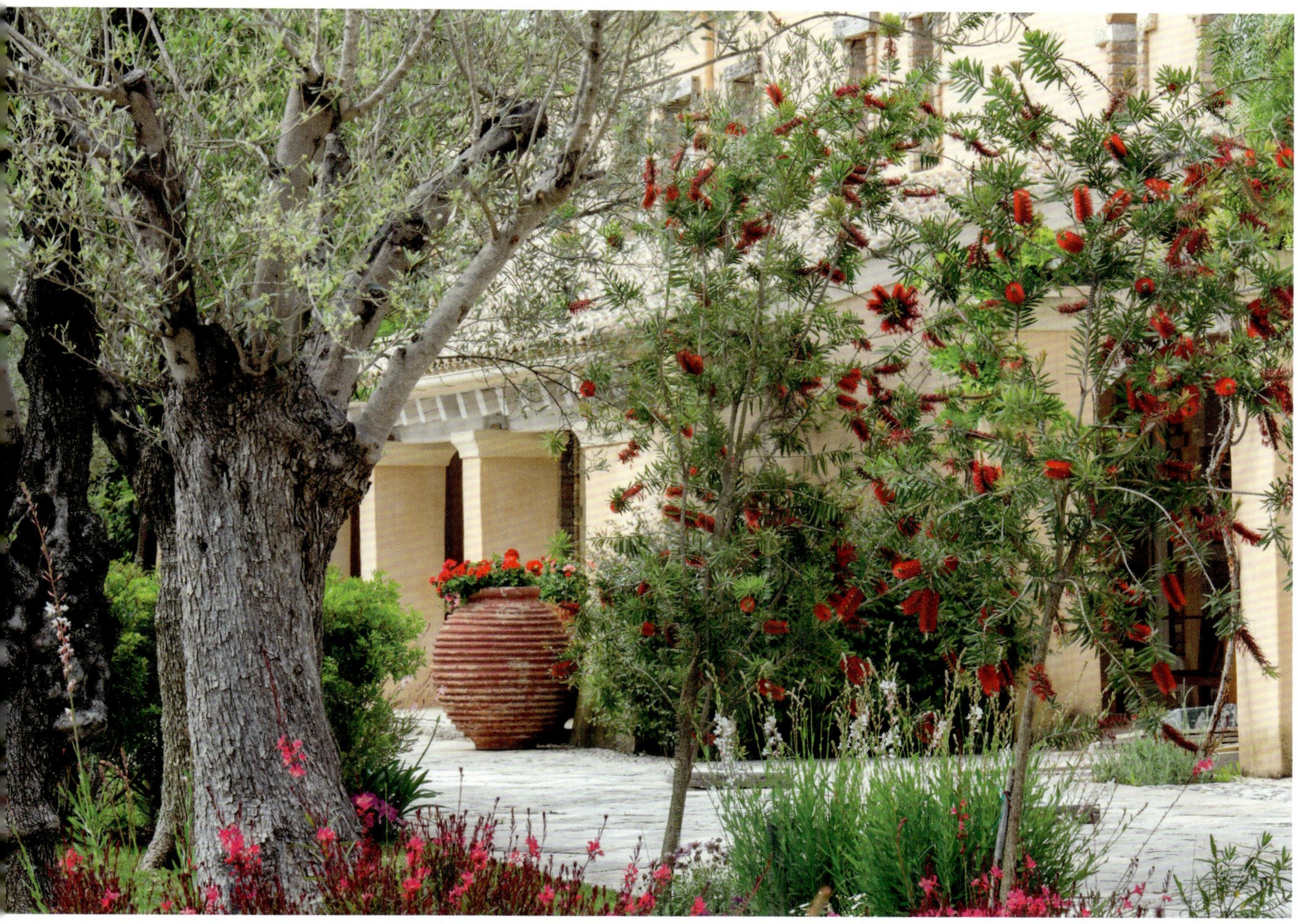

In the pool garden, old olive trees provide structure. The bright colours of gaura and bottlebrush (*Callistemon citrinus*) are picked up by those of the potted pelargoniums.

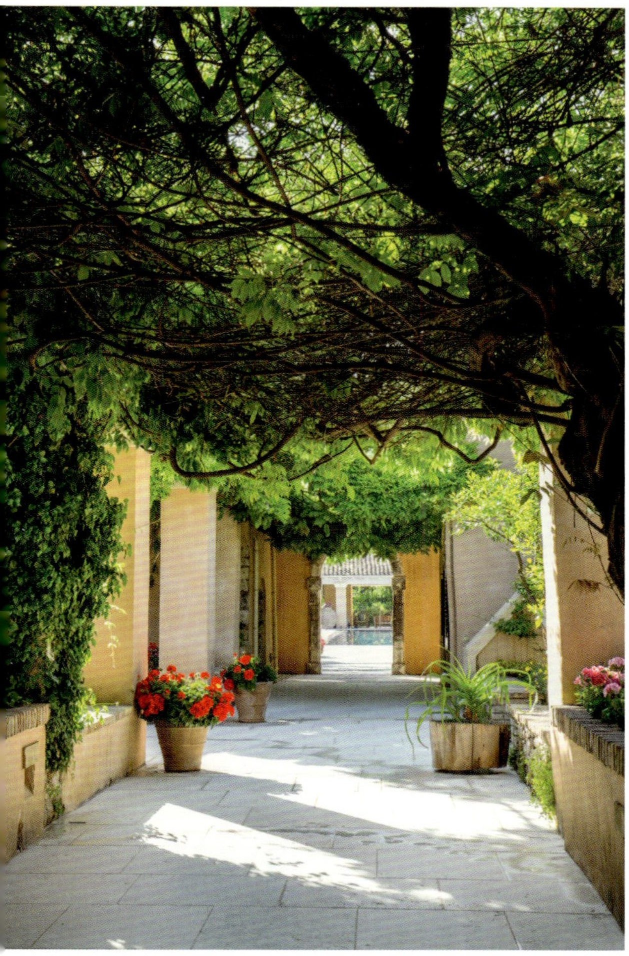

The wisteria that provides deep shade in summer abounds with blue and mauve blossom in April.

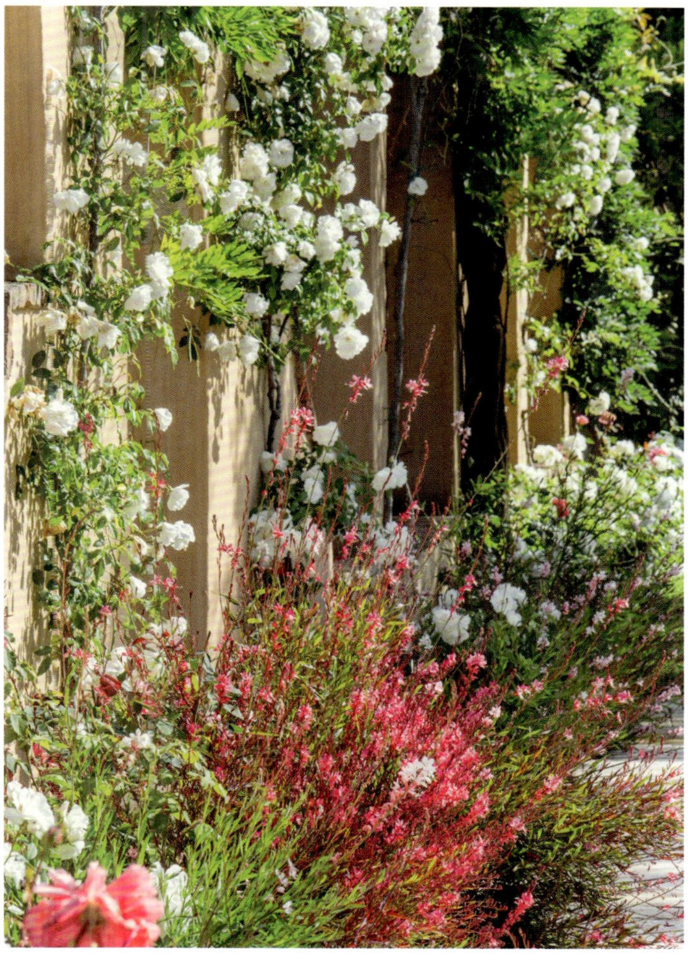

The romantic planting in the pool garden features pink, red, and white fragrant roses with crimson and white gaura.

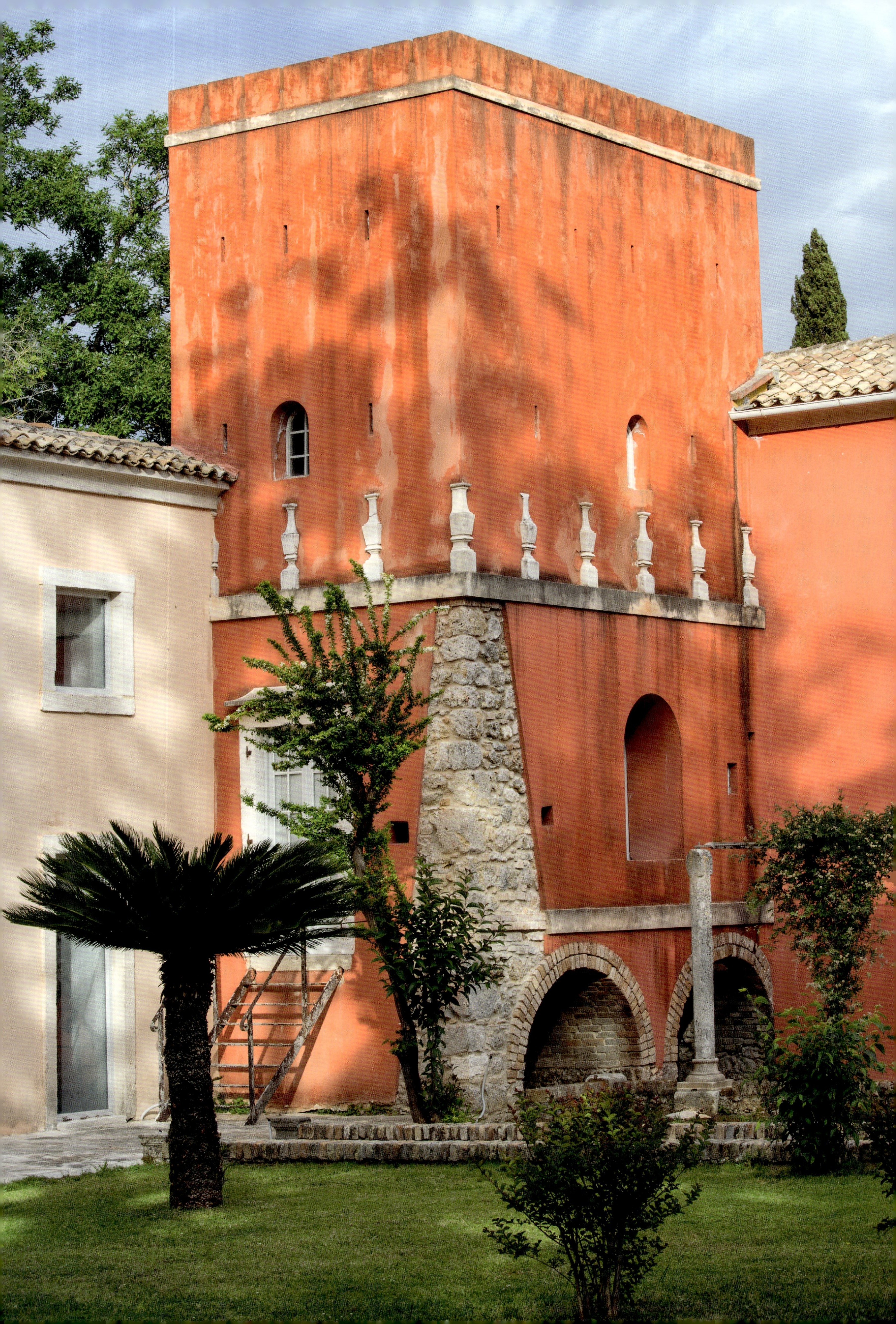

Afra

OPPOSITE
A view across the quadrangle to the tower.

Afra—a local legend for its age, the erstwhile prosperity of its estate, and its dark Venetian red façade—was built on the foundations of a thirteenth-century monastery whose presence can still be felt today. After a period of decline, the property is now being restored by a new owner.

The way to the heart of this highly atmospheric place leads through dense woodland with oaks, pines, elms, and cypresses, and opens out to a broad forecourt with a pergola and tall ornamental trees. An old moss-covered wall has iron rings for tethering horses. Rampant wisteria has broken loose and swings triumphantly from a tall cypress tree. Crossing from the forecourt through the entrance doorway and a vaulted passage, one emerges on what might well be a movie set: a large open quadrangle, planted with lawns and tall palm trees, at whose opposite end is the freshly painted neoclassical face of the house in its characteristic Venetian red, its portico restored, its white columns intact. And at one corner stands a formidable defensive tower, with crenellated battlements and slits for arrows in its walls.

Pétros Kourkouméli, who built the earliest version of the house, is said to have arrived in Corfu around 1550. One can speculate that he used the monks' cloister to shape the four-square dimensions of the building as it is today. As the hub of a feudal estate, Afra housed the owner's family but also the processing and storage of crops: the left side of the quadrangle was used for wine production (today, it houses an indoor swimming pool, discreetly hidden from outside view); the right side provided storage for timber and produce; and the fourth side, facing the house, was used for stables and storage of equipment.

Over generations Afra's estate expanded, to cover more than two thousand hectares at its peak. Some fifteen hundred were planted with vines, producing about seventy-three thousand litres of wine each year. Other products included olive oil, grain, mulberries, and silk.[24] Edward Lear, the British poet and artist, lodged with the Kourkouméli family when he first came to Corfu, and remarked, '… just about Kourkouméli's house the country is too cultivated to be very picturesque, but half a mile off there are very wild scenes of olive groves—great spreading trees, with the hills of Aghios Yiorgos

24. Paisídou, *Noble Houses of Corfu*, p. 53.

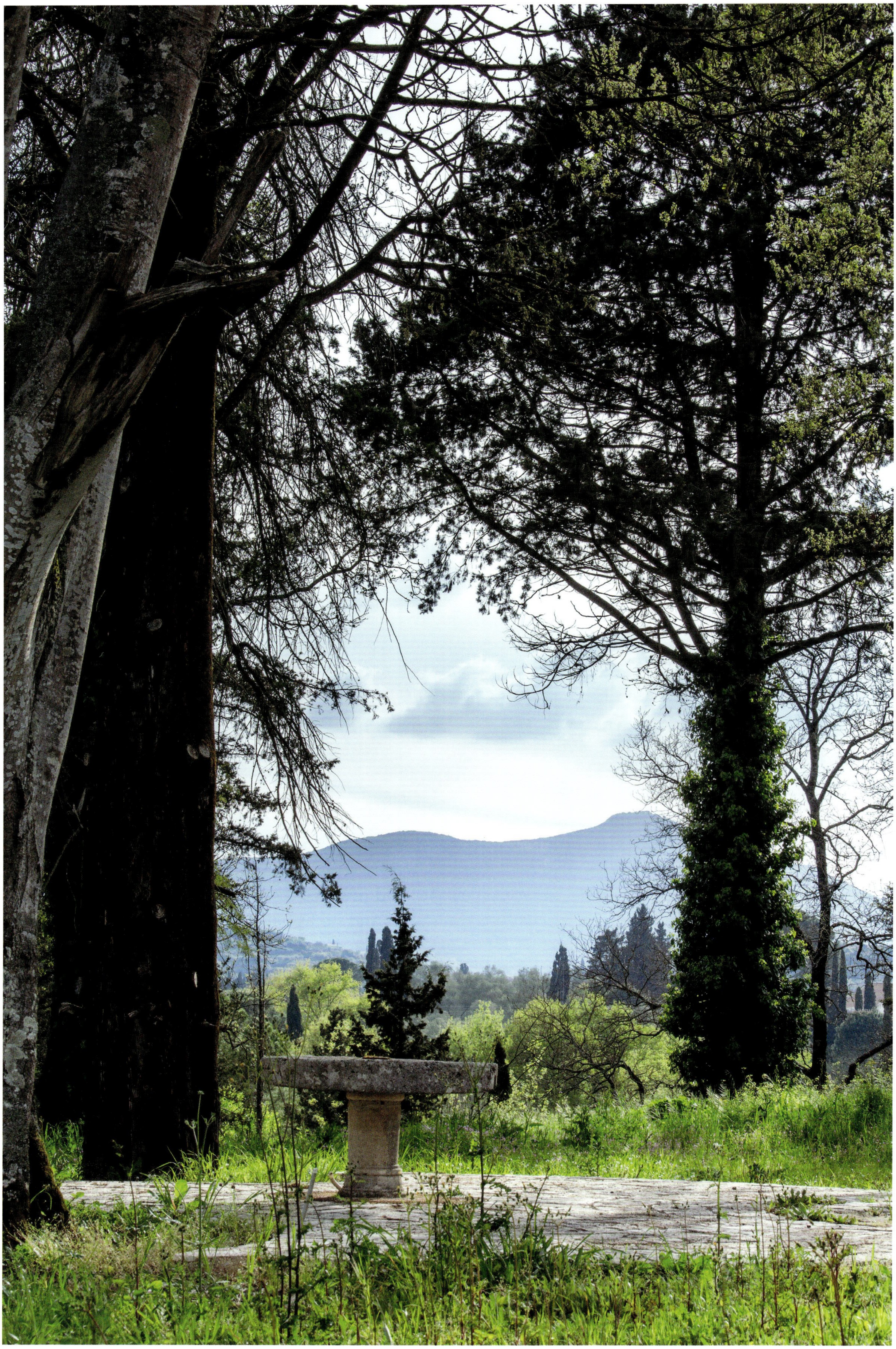

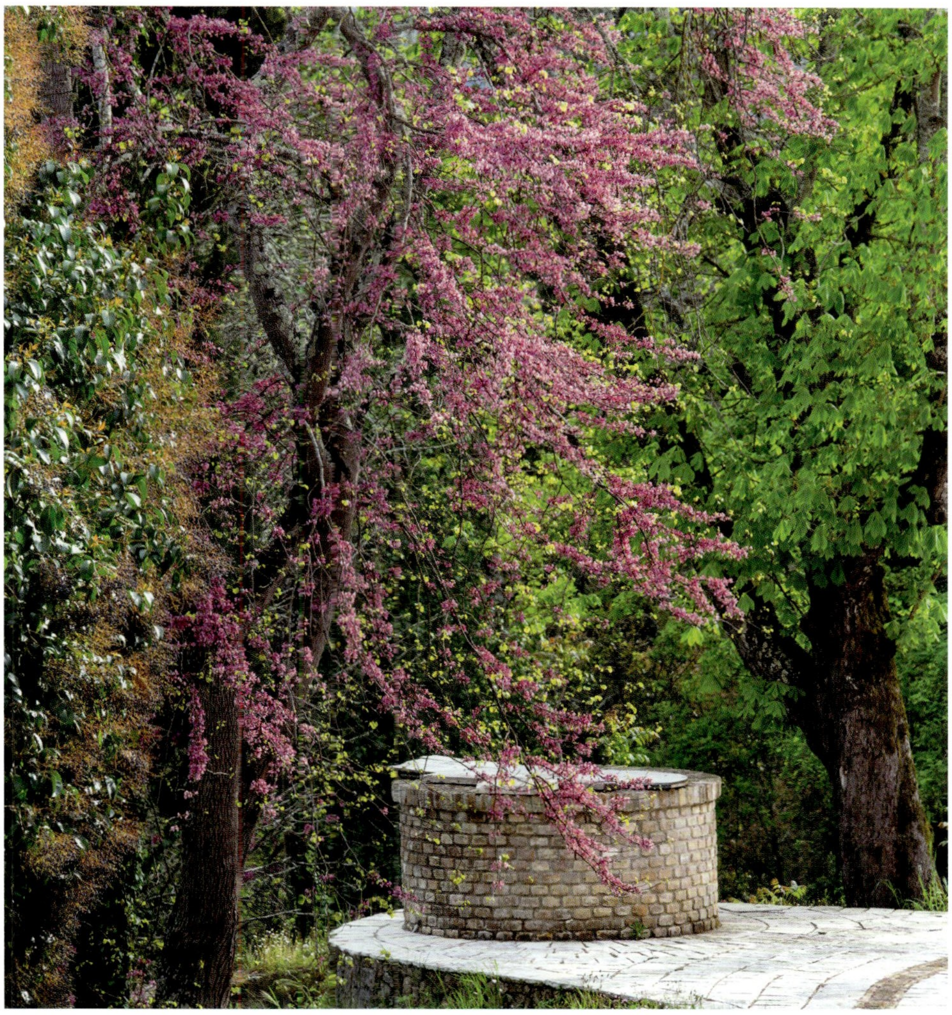

At the back of the house with its old well, horse-chestnut (*Aesculus hippocastanum*) and Chinese privet (*Ligustrum lucidum*) mingle with Judas trees.

peeping between. Early yesterday morning I had a very nice ride; the ground was covered with rose-coloured cistus, and pink everlasting peas besides innumerable large white convolvuluses.'[25]

On a May evening with lengthening shadows, the silence here is palpable. Light slants through the trees, and blossom from the horse-chestnut trees spirals slowly to the ground. Occasionally, collared doves call and answer one another from the woodland.

In the early years of the twentieth century, 'The inner garden was faithfully tended by the mother of Pétros Kourkoumélis and the air would be heavy with the scent of roses, jasmine, carnations, peonies... Almond trees at the close of winter, cherry trees in spring, apricot, pear, and apple trees in their turn.'[26] Now the inner garden, with its lawns, palms, and southern magnolia trees, is a peaceful green space, inviting reflection and contemplation as perhaps it did in the days of the cloistered monks who once lived here.

OPPOSITE
Tall pine trees frame a view west across the Rópa Valley from the grounds at Afra.

25. Letter of May 24, 1856, as quoted in Philip Sherrard, *Edward Lear: The Corfu Years* (Evia: Denise Harvey, 1988), p. 71. 26. Paisídou, *Noble Houses of Corfu*, p. 56.

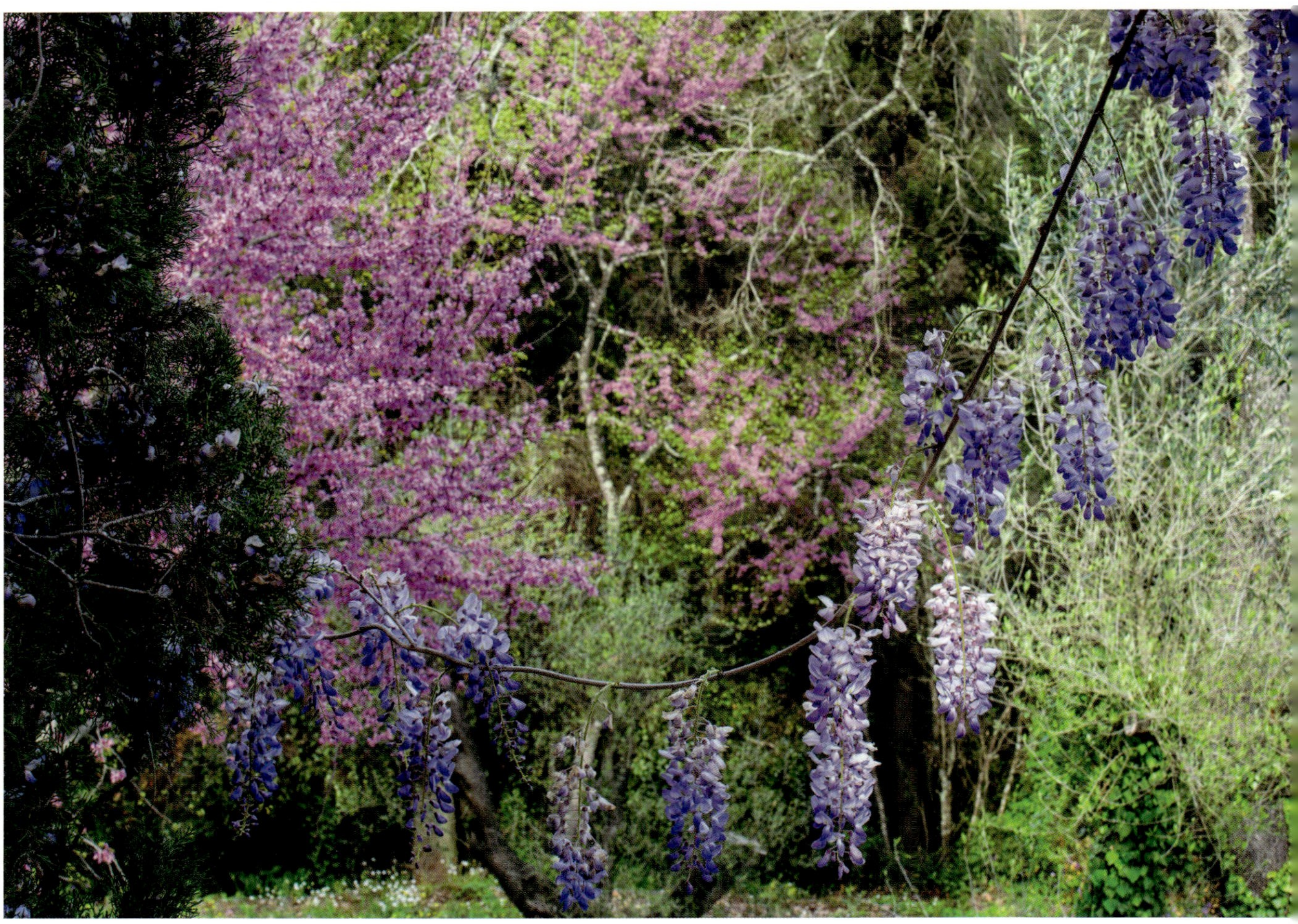

The wisteria here is more than a hundred years old. On the edges of the surrounding woodland it combines with wild Judas trees, making something of an enchanted forest.

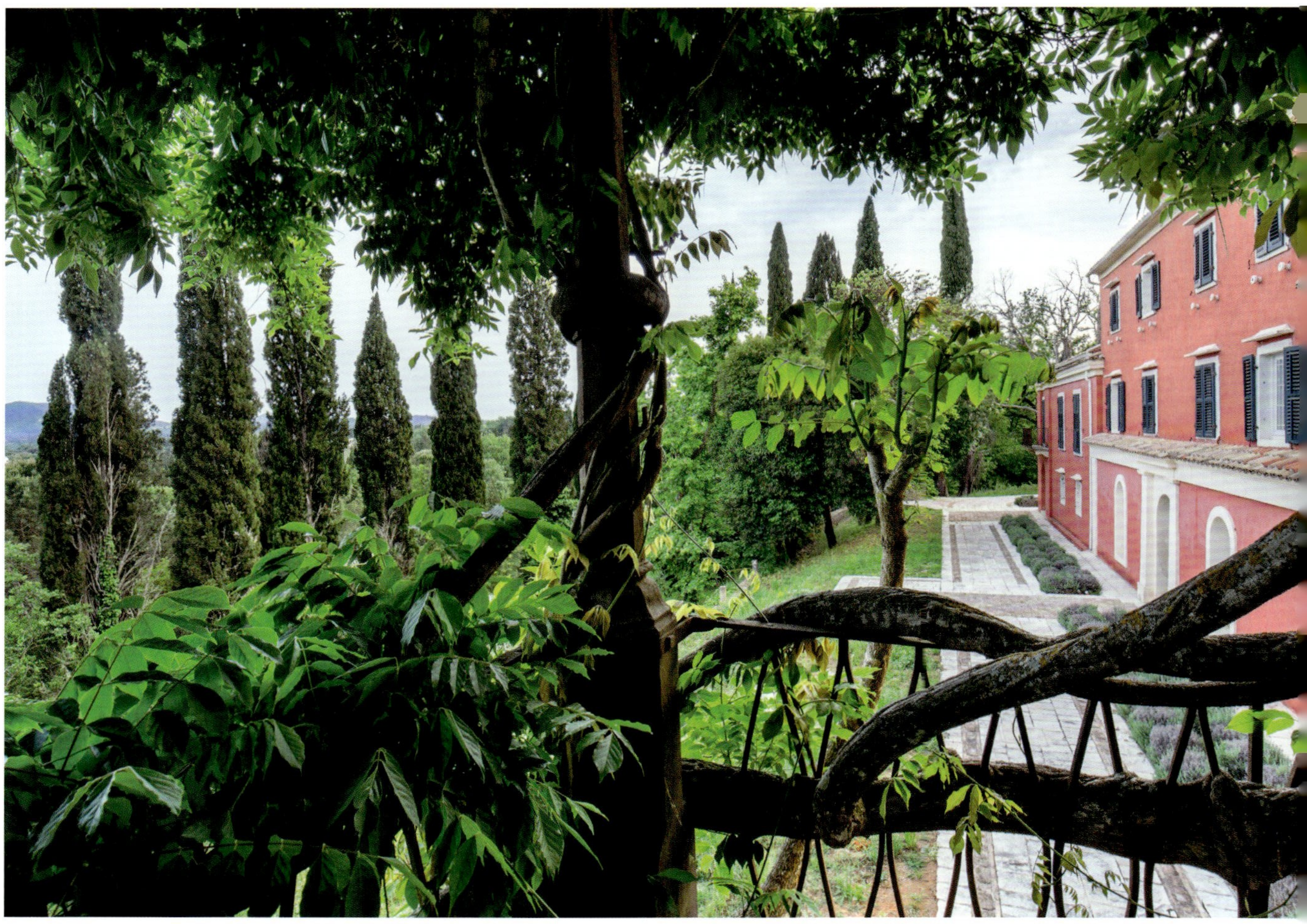

The back of the house seen from the wisteria balcony.

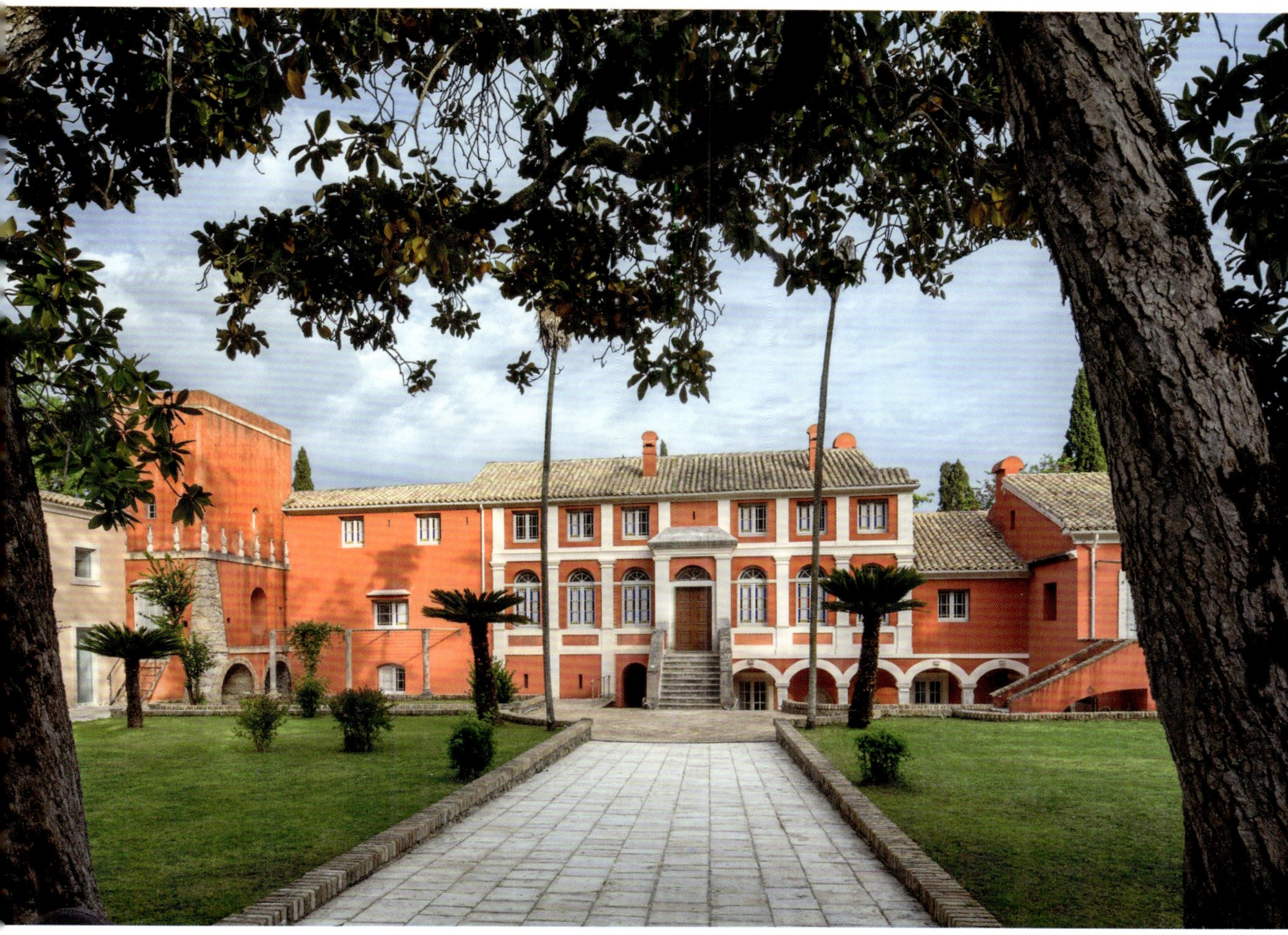

The quadrangle at Afra, with its symmetrically placed palms and cycads. Some of the old arches of the monastery can be seen next to the staircase leading to the front door. In the foreground, *Magnolia grandiflora*.

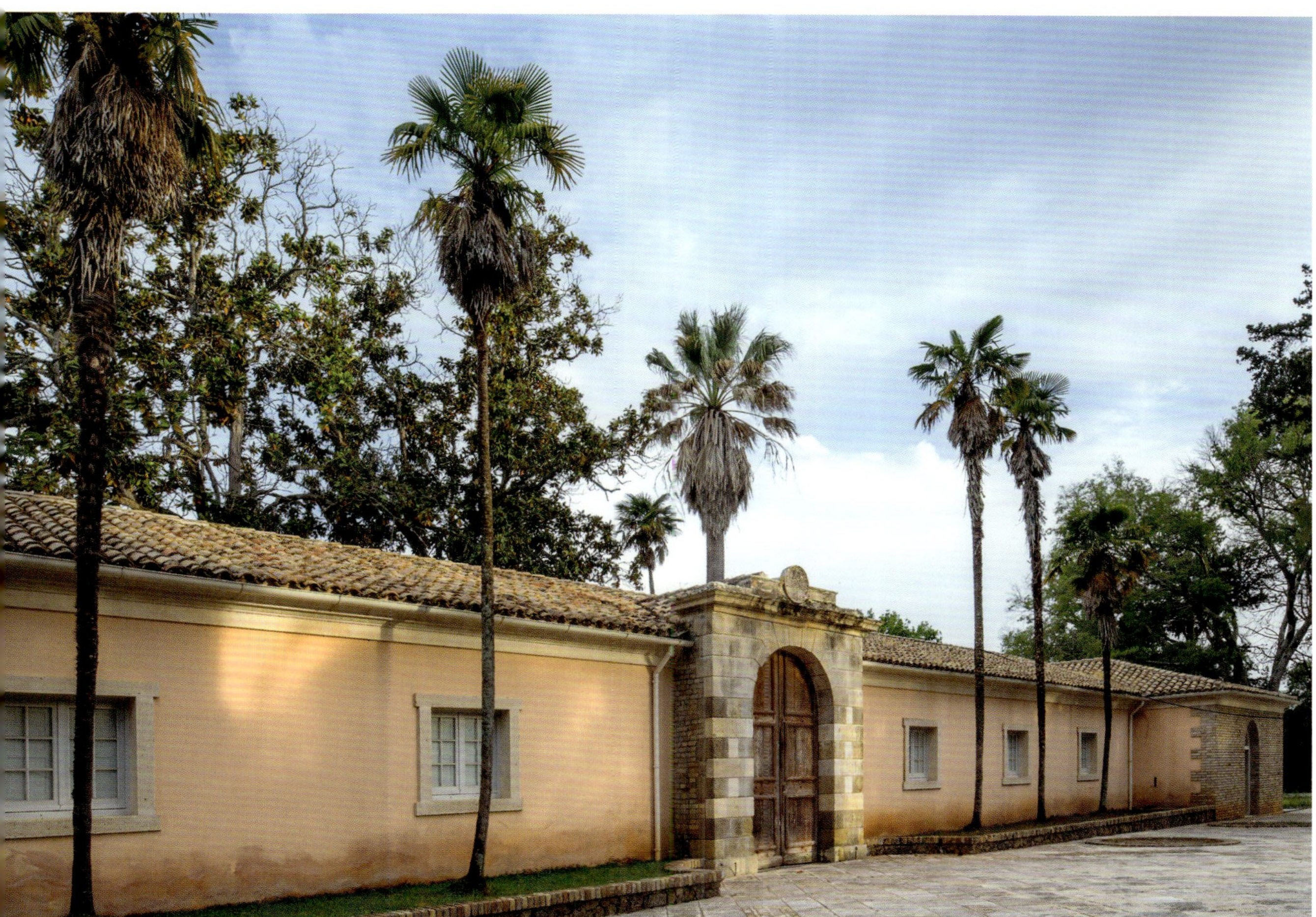

For the modern visitor, the tall cabbage-tree palms (*Livistona australis*) and the architecture of the forecourt create a sense of displacement from the local milieu and a readiness to be surprised by the architecture inside.

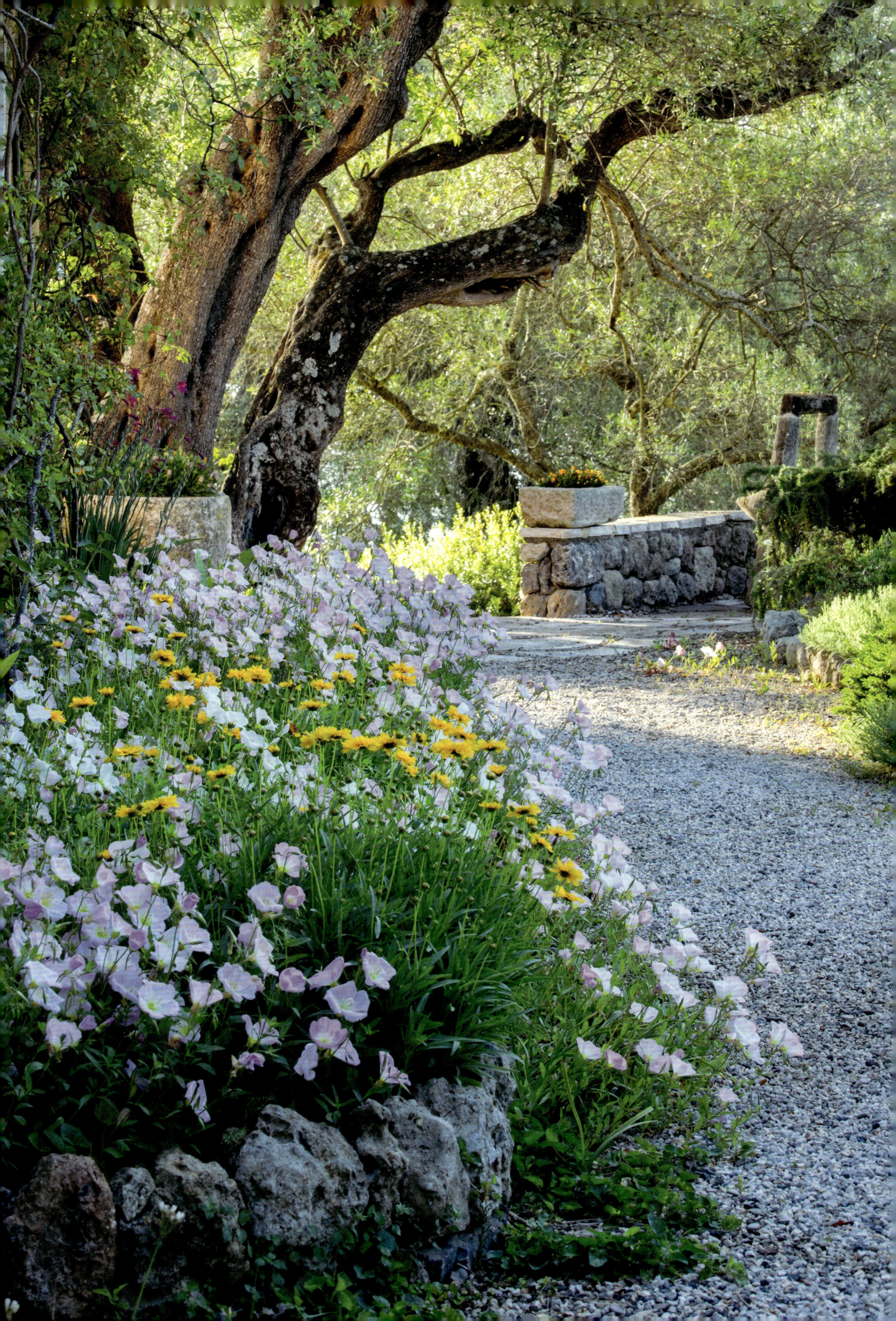

A Gastoúri estate

This historic five-hectare estate in central Corfu bridges the old and the new, the cultivated and the wild. Owned by Calí Doxiádis, it celebrates Corfu's garden and farming heritage but also embodies new trends in garden-design philosophy and water conservation. And though in this book we have grouped it among the island's heritage gardens, it justly provides inspiration to contemporary designers.

Originally dependent on its vineyards, the estate has had a mixed history. Established by the Mántzaros, a Corfiot landowning family ennobled by the Venetians,[27] it was sold to the Doúsmani family late in the nineteenth century. Over the ensuing years of land reform, war, and social change, it declined into ruin, until the 1970s when Calí fell in love with it: 'Forty-one years ago I bought a ruined 200-year old farmhouse on a hillside overlooking the sea… I walked through a rusty garden gate into a wilderness of purple irises and dripping wisteria framing a crumbling two-storey ruin in many shades of ochre. That was it.'[28]

Today, the atmosphere here is just as romantic. Native woodlands and wildflower meadows coexist with and merge into olive and citrus groves, vineyards, and gardens; rocks blend with constructed walls and steps; and cultivated plants mingle with wild. Here, by contrast with some of the other gardens in this book, the gardener's concern is less to control nature or to reveal nature's inherent grandeur than it is to assist nature's abundance: to help plants to be healthy and beautiful and to freely express themselves. The natural, often gentle beauty of the landscape is allowed to speak for itself and, with subtle enhancements such as the planting of irises under the trees by the old olive press, native woodlands and olive groves come to appear like gardens. As much as anywhere in Corfu, the place has a power to evoke emotion; it is 'a place where you are hauled across the dividing line between the mundane and the spirit world'.[29]

The walled garden in front of the house matches Louisa Jones' description of a traditional 'grandmother's garden', given its 'vital exuberance, its economy and common sense, its celebration of life in

27. One of this family, Nikolaos Mántzaros, composed the Greek National Anthem in 1865. 28. Calí Doxiádis, 'A Mediterranean Garden in Corfu', unpublished. 29. Mary Keen, Part I of 'My favourite gardens and why they work' at http://thinkingardens.co.uk/articles/otherworldly-gardens-by-mary-keen/

OPPOSITE
Pink *Oenethera berlandieri* mingles with yellow tickseed (*Coreopsis grandiflora*) under the olive trees close to the house.

For centuries, vines provided the livelihood of the estate. Today in this small vineyard Calí grows *kakotrígi* grapes, from which she makes a fragrant slightly sweet white wine.

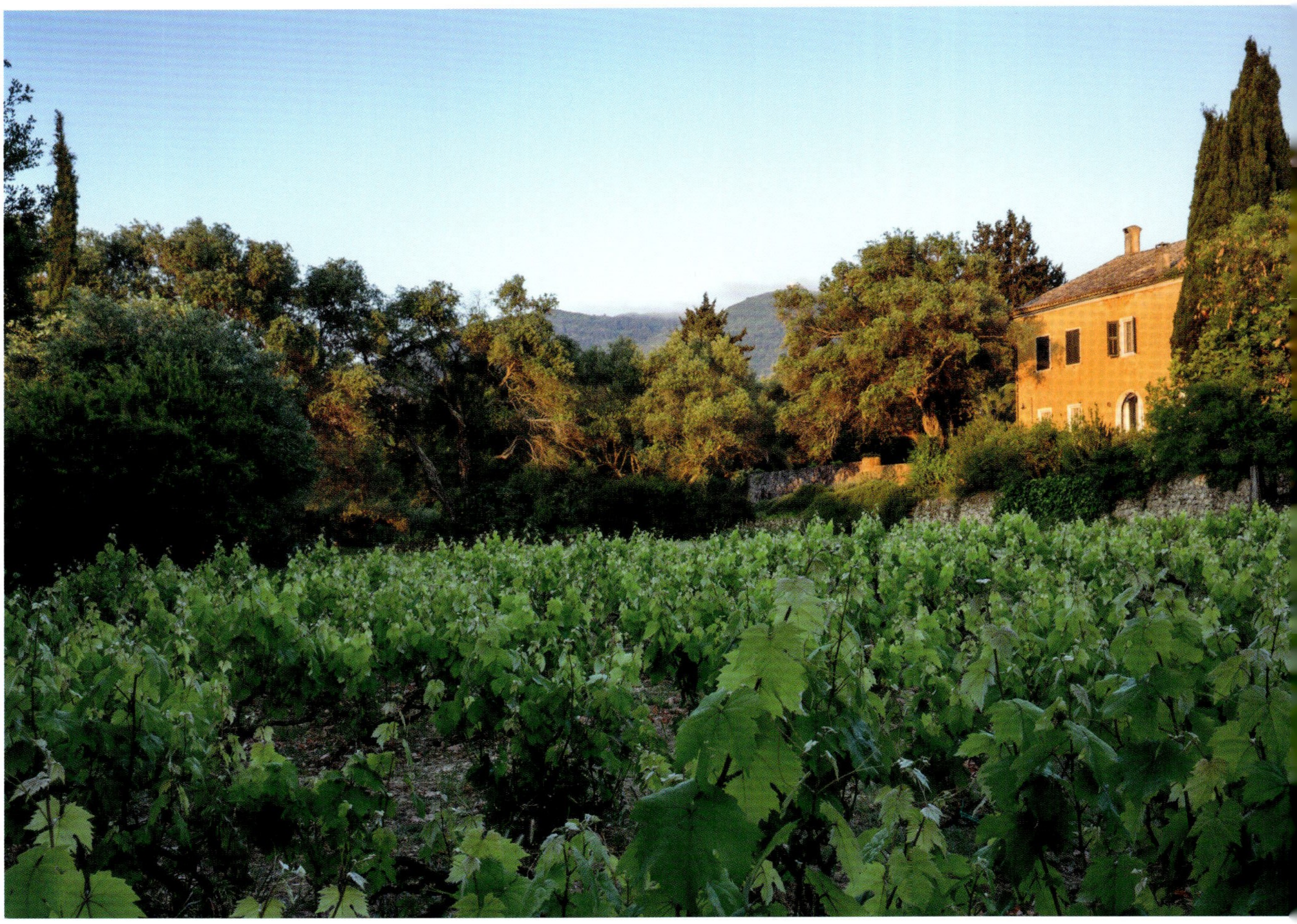

The rising sun feels its way into one of the old olive groves on the estate. Wild garlic (*Allium neapolitanum*) carpets the ground.

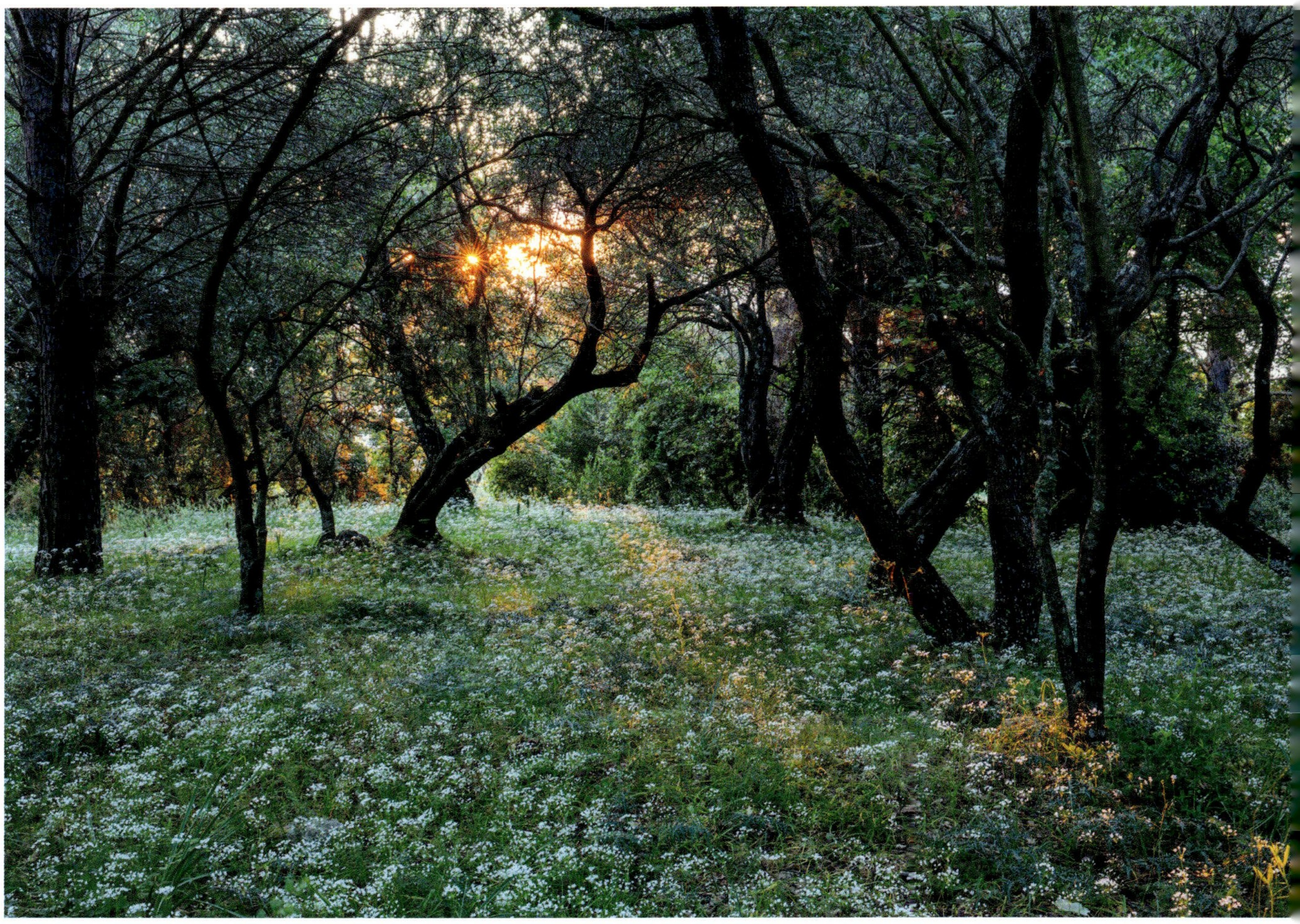

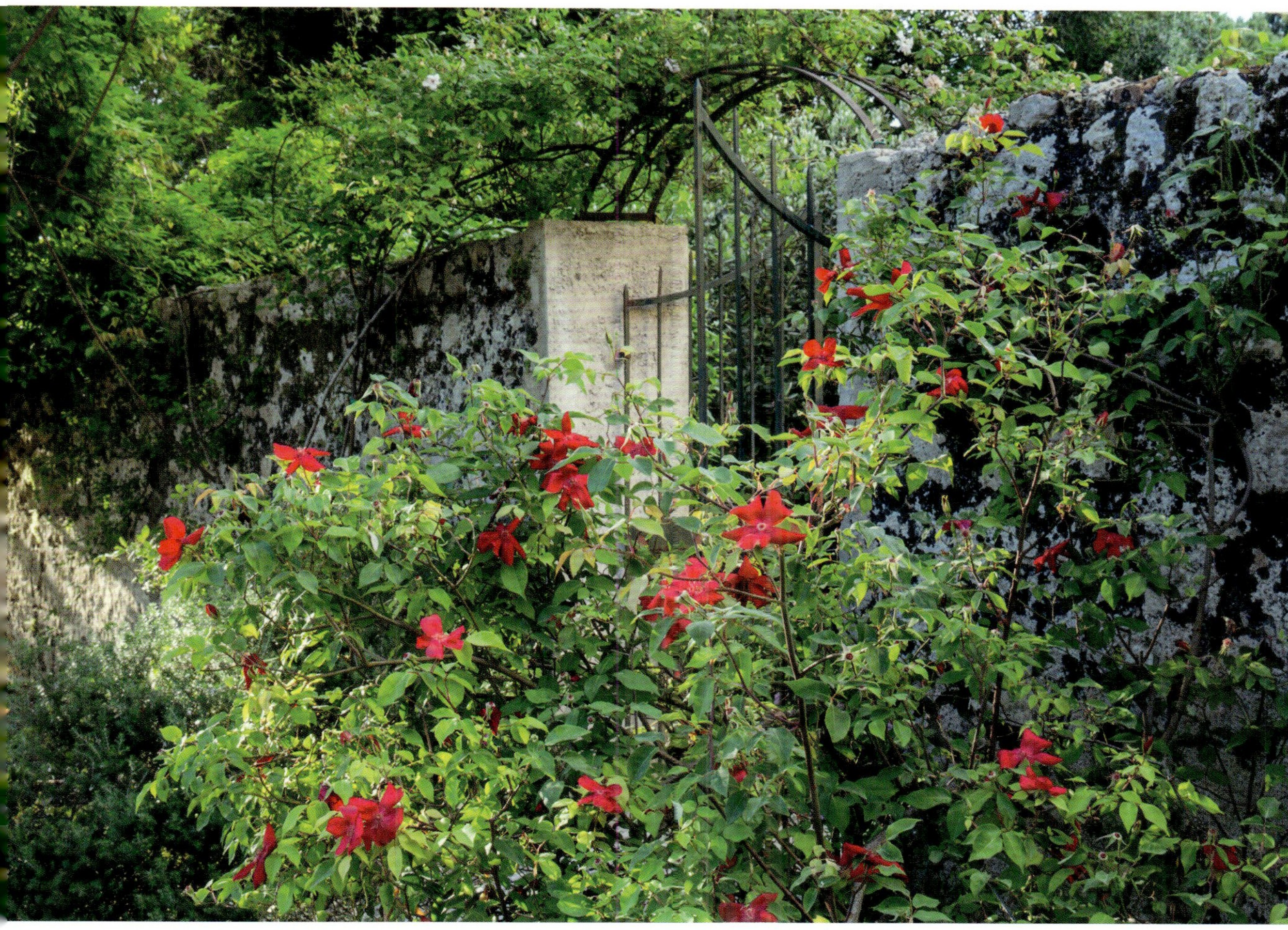

Blood-red *Rosa chinensis* 'Sanguinea' thrives on a south-facing wall.

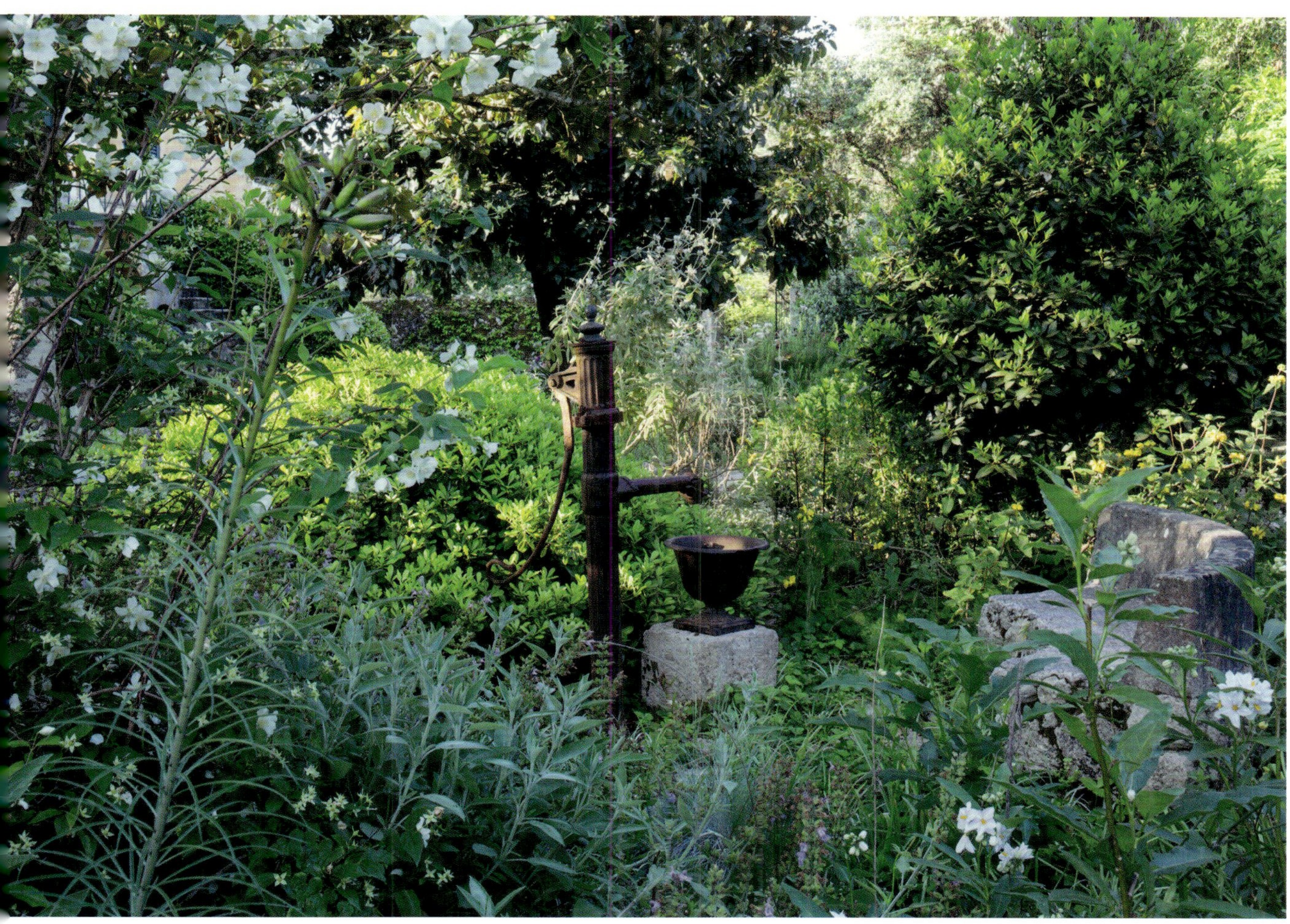

An old iron pump in a corner of the walled garden. White *Philadelphus* perfumes the air here.

small spaces, its sensuous satisfactions, its harmony with the natural world, and its scope for creative invention'.[30] Colourful combinations of flowering plants in pots, and of annuals and flowering perennials and bulbs, attest to the owner's creativity and sheer love of plants. And, says Calí, 'I'm one of those gardeners who allow themselves to be bullied by self-sowers. I seldom find it in me to stop a plant from growing where it wants to grow.'[31]

These 'grandmother's garden' virtues are combined with a fierce modern practicality. A former President of the Mediterranean Garden Society, Calí has long championed the trend to waterwise gardening that was pioneered by Heidi Gildemeister.[32] In summer, most of the garden survives without water. She writes that, 'I had come to see that I'd be betraying the aesthetics of our landscape as well as challenging the realities of our climate if I tried to create and maintain a garden that required frequent and regular watering throughout the summer. Still, ... some colour and some lushness was necessary. [So]... I made one defined space that would get daily summer watering and placed it in the most central and sunniest part of the walled garden... The Annual bed and the pots are the only parts of the garden that get watered every day in the hot months.'[33]

Several plants are of special interest. They include the old roses, *Rosa chinensis* 'Mutabilis' and *Rosa chinensis* 'Sanguinea', which flower almost all year against a south-facing wall; Mediterranean native tree spurge (*Euphorbia dendroides*); a pineapple guava (*Acca sellowiana*), native to Brazil and with pretty red-stamened flowers; and an avocado tree planted in the walled garden in the 1970s by the author Mirabel Osler, a former resident of the house. The largest tree on the estate is a majestic stone pine (*Pinus pinea*) about one hundred and fifty years old; from top to bottom its trunk bears the scar of a lightning strike five years ago.

Another important feature of the garden is the bulbs, corms, and tubers that Calí has introduced from across the world. 'Even in midwinter there are the always-spreading *Narcissi*, the wild Algerian irises, then in spring the bearded irises, species tulips, wild jonquils, grape hyacinths, as well as many different *Alliums*.' Blooms of *Agapanthus* fill the walled garden in early summer, and September brings the pink lily flowers of *Amaryllis belladonna*, followed by ivy-leaved cyclamen.

OPPOSITE
In summer, family meals are taken on this shaded patio behind the house.

30. Louisa Jones, *The French Country Garden* (London, Thames and Hudson, 2000). 31. Calí Doxiádis, 'A Mediterranean Garden in Corfu'. 32. See Heidi Gildemeister, *Mediterranean Gardening: A Waterwise Approach* (Gruibingen: Moll, 1995). 33. Calí Doxiádis, 'A Mediterranean Garden in Corfu'.

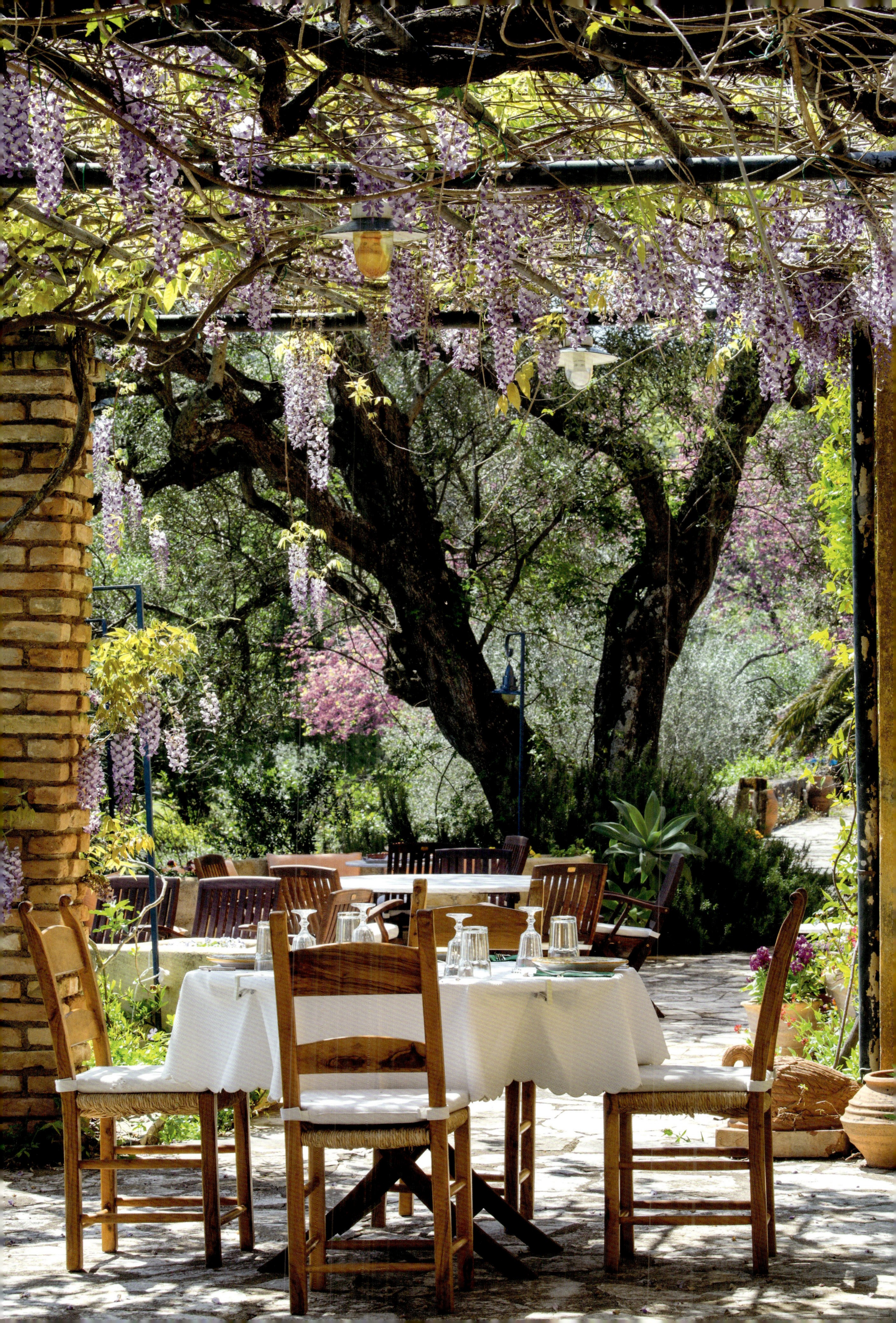

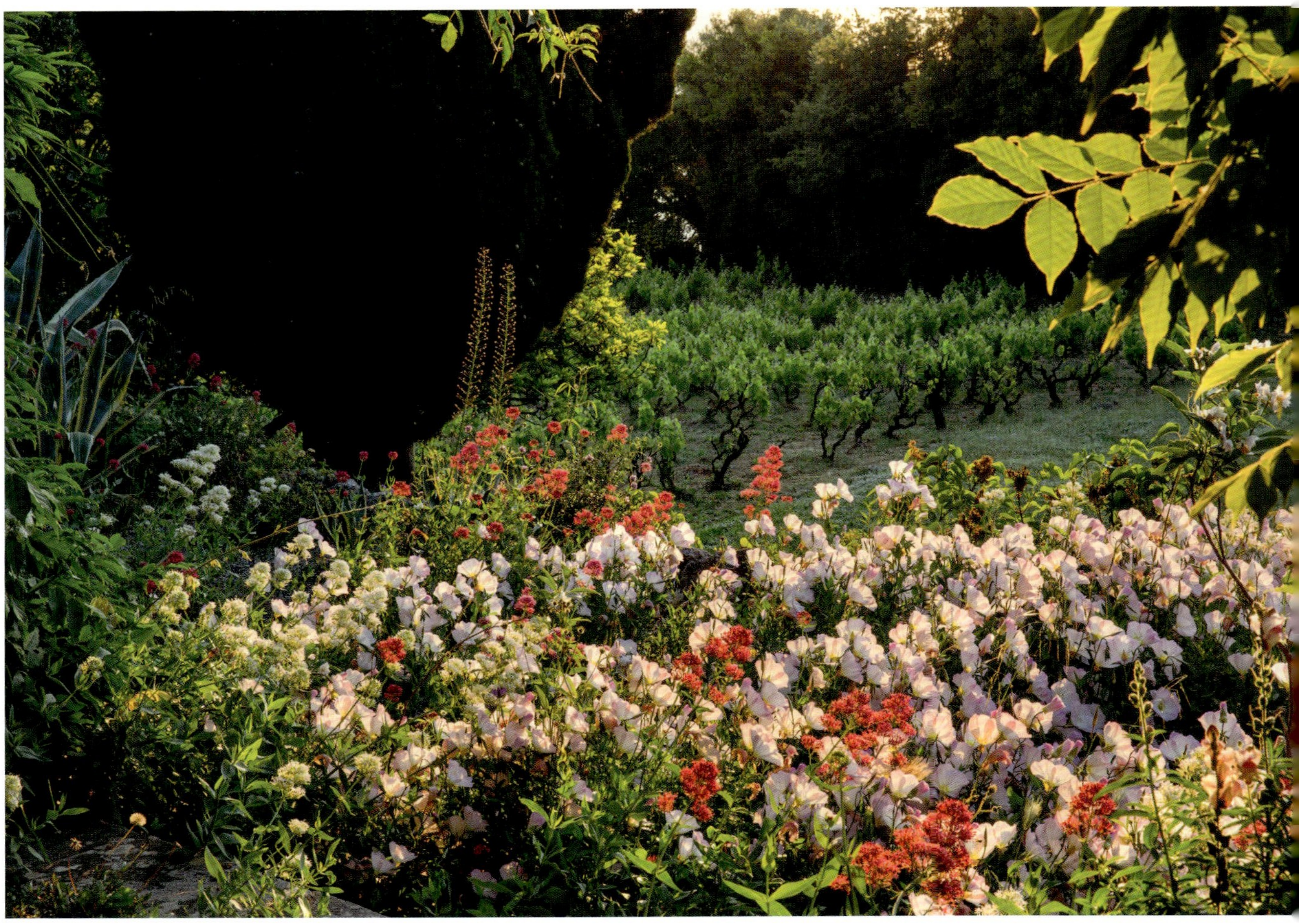

A corner of the vineyard, seen from the terrace. Pink evening primrose (*Oenethera berlandieri*) and red and white *Centranthus ruber* catch the early morning light.

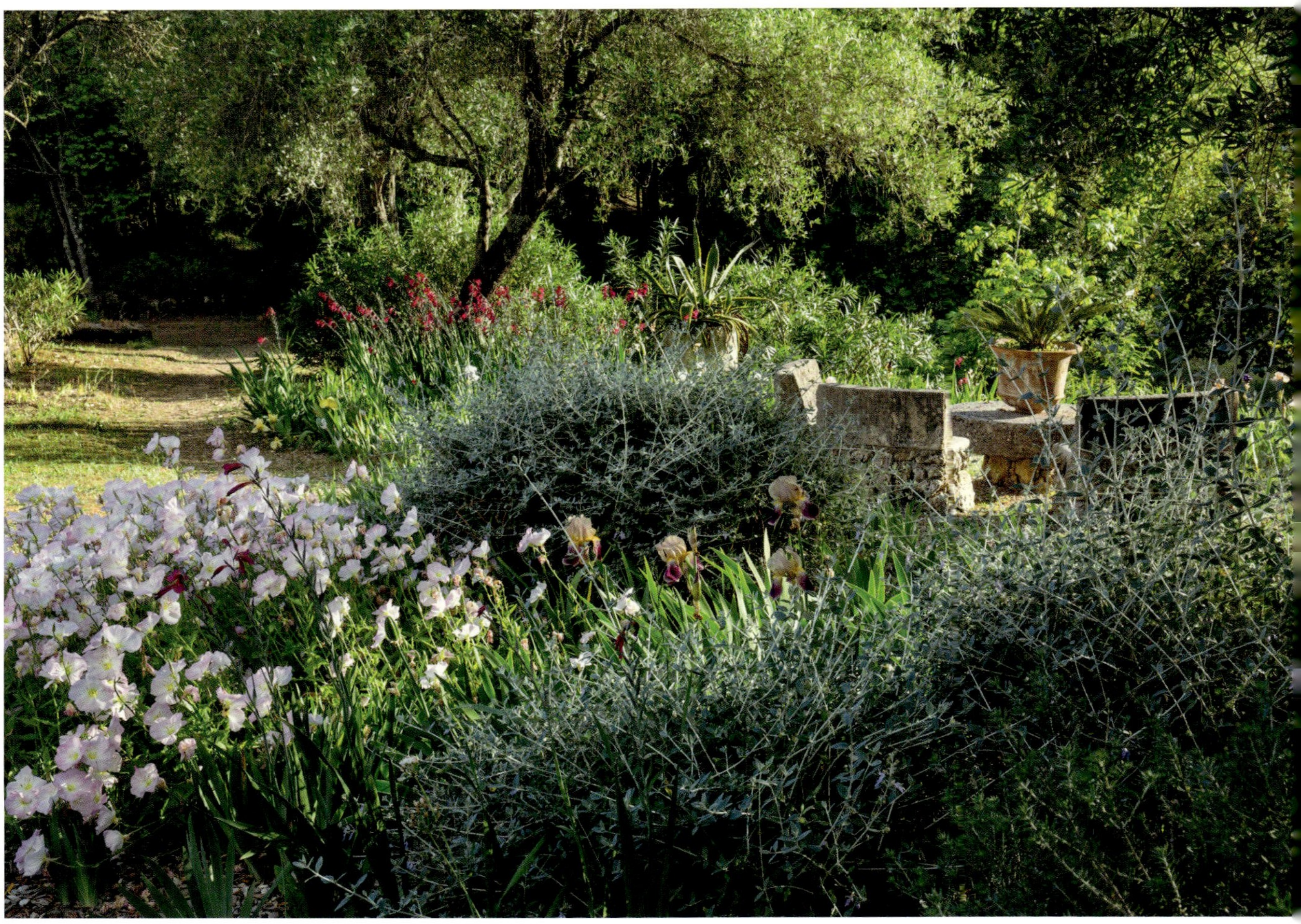

A profusion of spring growth in a part of the garden that gets no summer water. Of the carmine gladioli, Calí says that the garden variety, *Gladiolus byzantinus*, 'seems to have mated with the local *Gladiolus italicus*'.

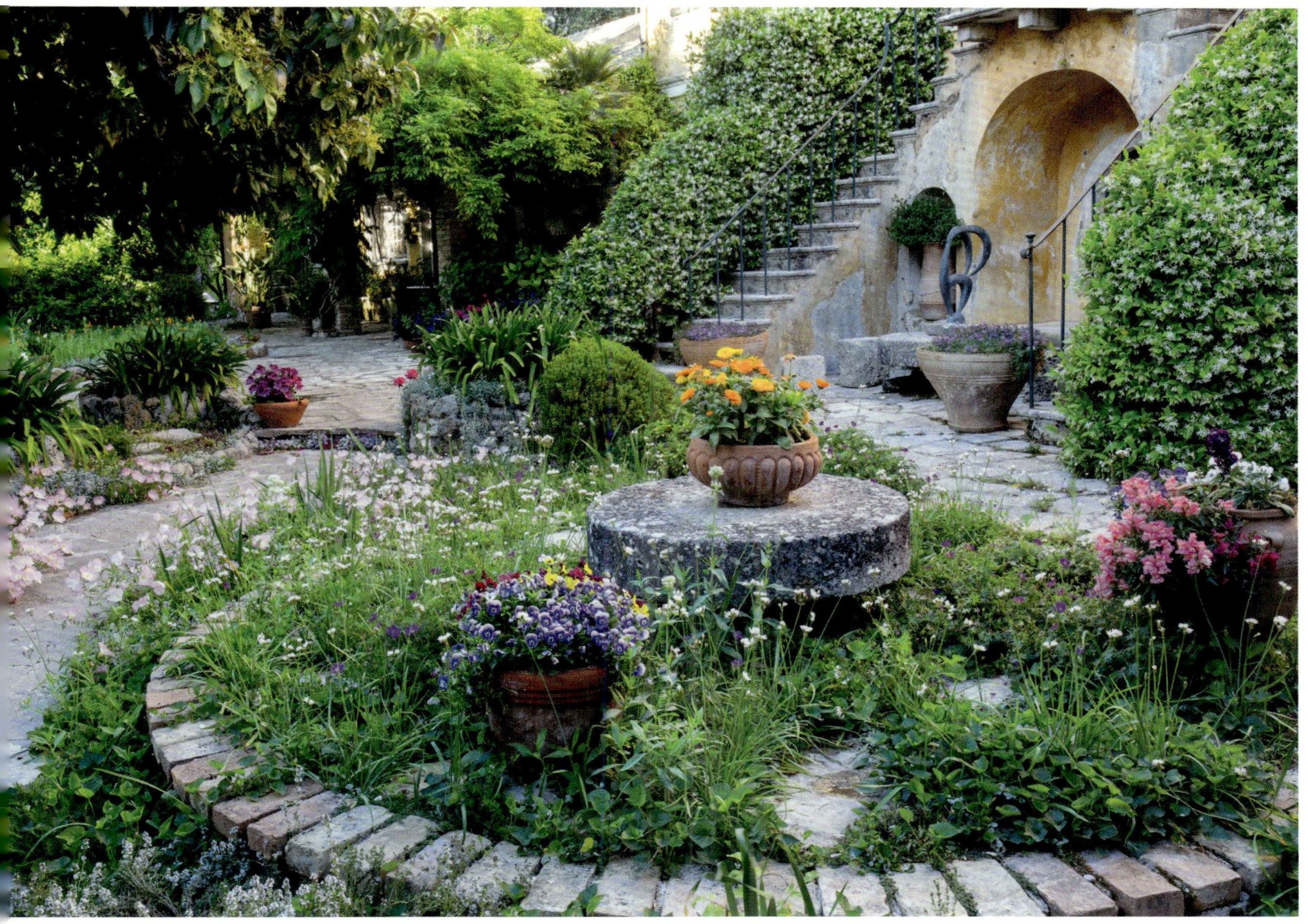

The walled garden in front of the house.

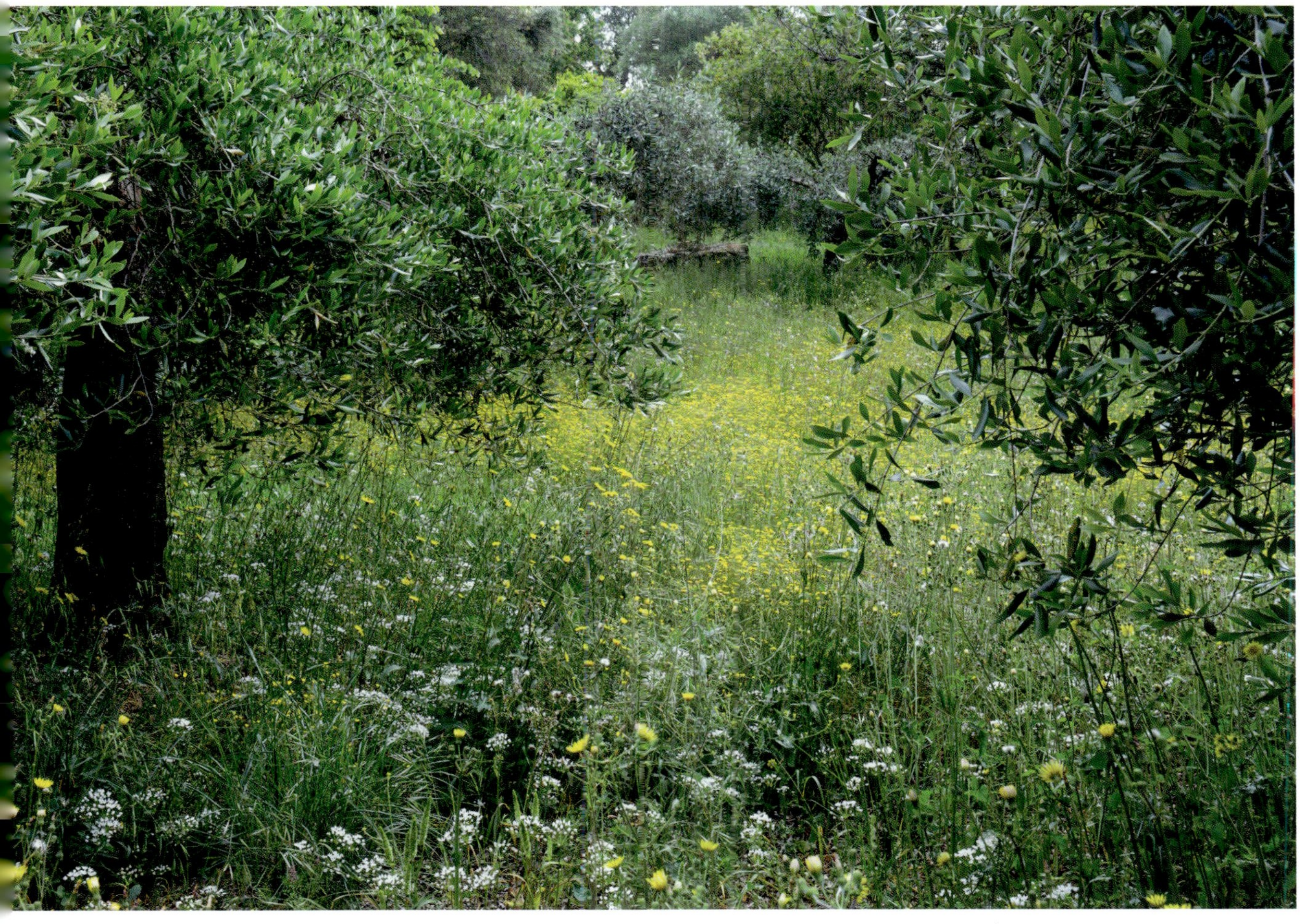

Typical meadow flowers carpet an open olive grove in May.

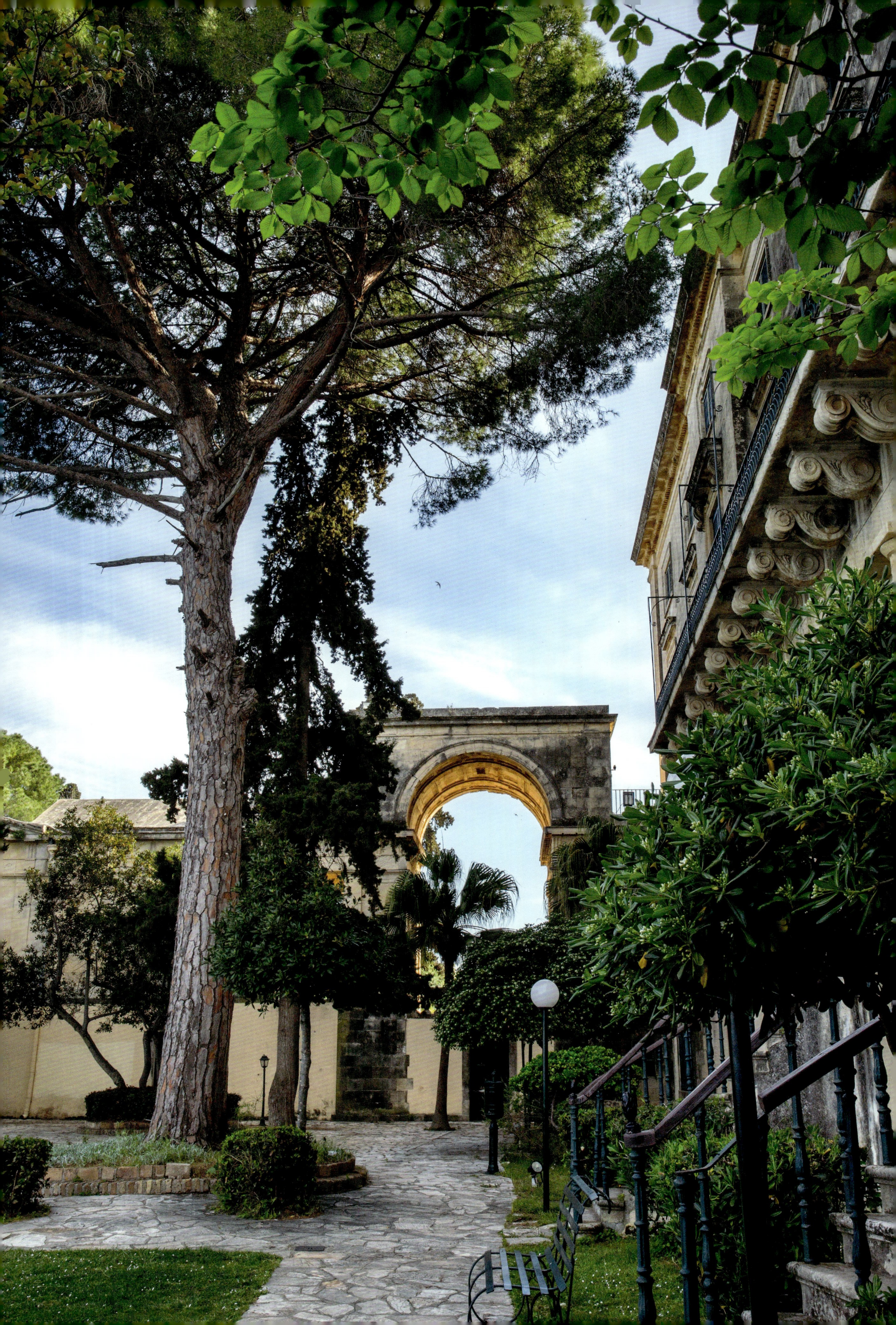

GREEN SPACES IN CORFU TOWN

The island capital Corfu Town is a UNESCO World Heritage Site and a grand collage of different architectural styles. Ancient Greek and Roman remains, Byzantine churches, Venetian villas and fountains, gracious French arcaded streets, and British neoclassical buildings built by Maltese stonemasons stand side by side, protected by massive Byzantine-Venetian fortifications. Arcaded streets with tall, peeling, pastel-painted facades and wrought-iron balconies are interlaced with hidden squares and narrow alleyways that offer tantalising glimpses of secluded gardens. Palm fronds cast shadows in noonday sun and splashes of *Bougainvillea* tumble from the tops of walls.

The town first grew up on the narrow peninsula that was the easiest place to protect from invaders. Land was so scarce within the city walls that the houses of the early Venetian period were built three and four storeys high, on plots with ninety-five percent coverage. There is no room for private gardens here, but window boxes are plentiful and within the web of narrow alleys many small squares bring in light and air.

Residential avenues added in the nineteenth century are lined with enormous trees. Through the elaborate wrought-iron gates of the villas of this period can be seen gardens with tall palms, orange and lemon trees, and shaded courtyards for sitting, typically with pots of scented pelargonium, basil, gardenia, and a range of colourful flowers.

One popular gathering place is Dimarcheío Square, in front of what is now the Town Hall. This baroque building of local limestone was built in the seventeenth century as a club for the Venetian nobility, before being converted into a theatre in the eighteenth century and later into the Town Hall.

Overlooking the Spianáda—a wide green area that houses a park with bandstand and cricket ground and divides the town from the Old Fort—are elegant nineteenth-century buildings in contrasting styles. The French modelled the long arcade of the Liston (built in 1809) on the Rue de Rivoli then being constructed in Paris. The British used Palladian precepts to design the neoclassical Palace of St. Michael and St. George; built in 1819–23 out of golden Maltese stone, it has a Doric colonnade flanked by majestic arched gates. Other neoclassical buildings constructed during the British rule include the Ionian Bank, the Ionian Parliament, the family residence of Ioánnis Capodístrias (the first Prime Minister of Greece), and Mon Repos.

As the town buildings attest, the centuries of occupation by the Venetians, French, and British meant that urban Corfu became much

OPPOSITE
The gardens of the Palace of St. Michael and St. George, overlooking the sea and deeply shaded by tall stone pines, holm oaks, and palms, are a popular gathering place offering cool shade on a hot day.

A view to the sea with statue of Ioánnis Capodístrias. Born in Corfu, he was the first head of state of independent Greece.

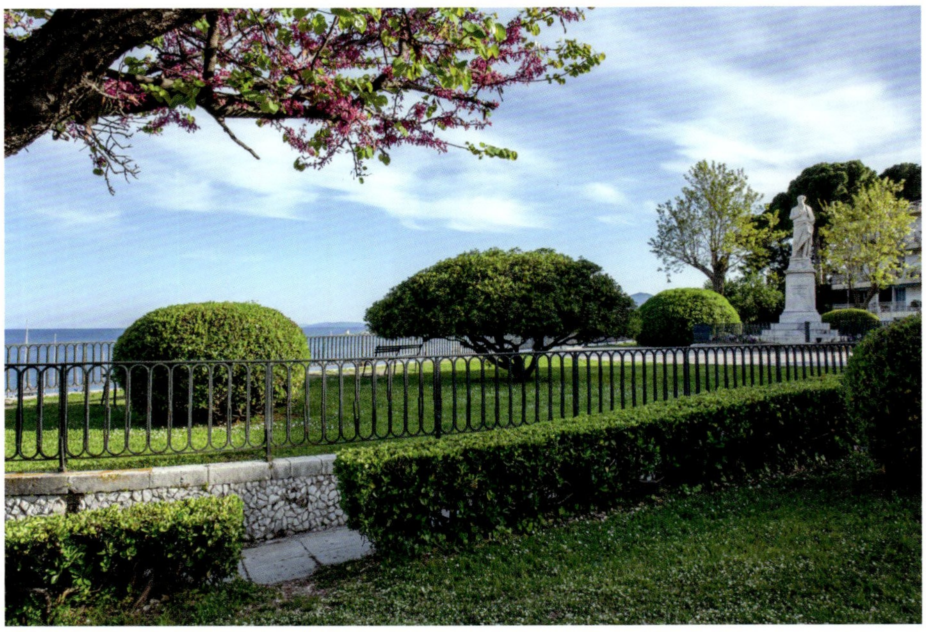

Pots on the wall at the Franciscan Monastery on Palaiokastrítsa Road.

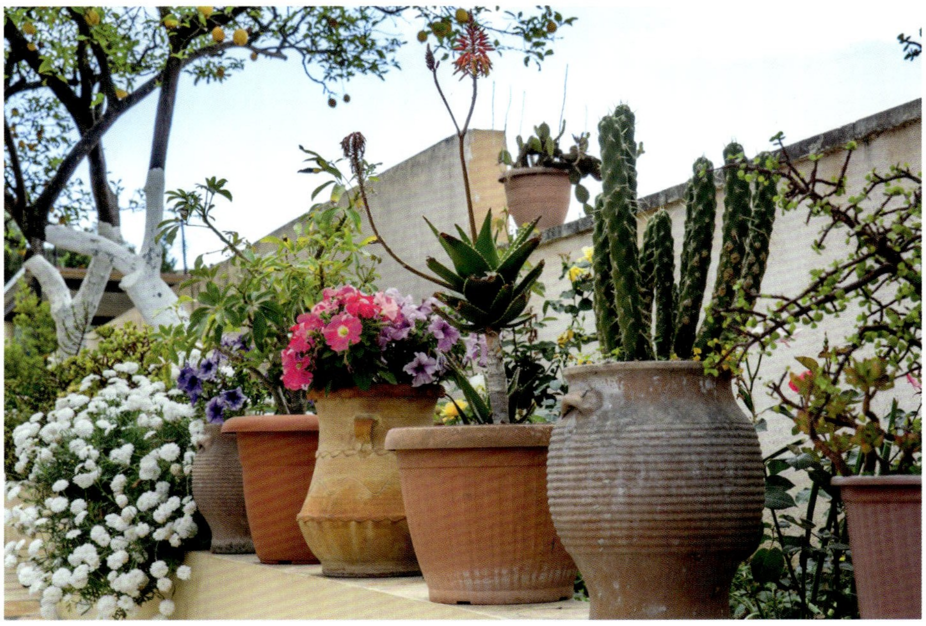

In summer, Dimarcheío Square, with its lively outdoor restaurants, is filled with colour from flowering jacaranda and *Bougainvillea*.

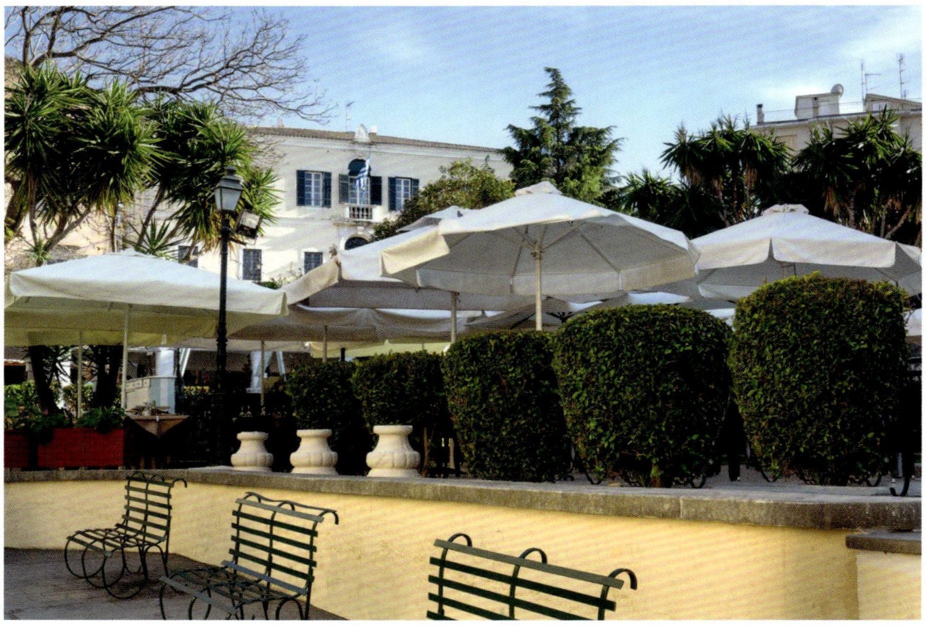

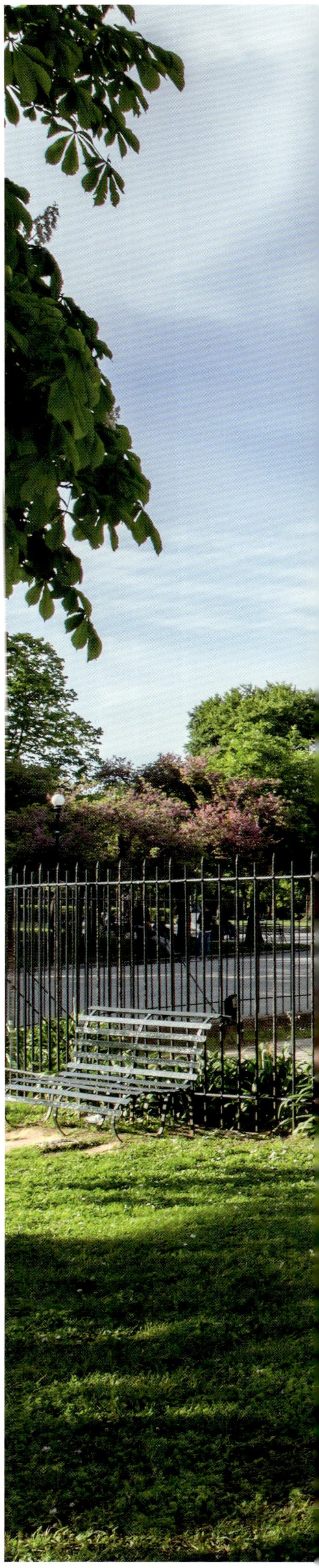

The Classically inspired memorial to Thomas Maitland, first British High Commissioner for the Ionian Islands.

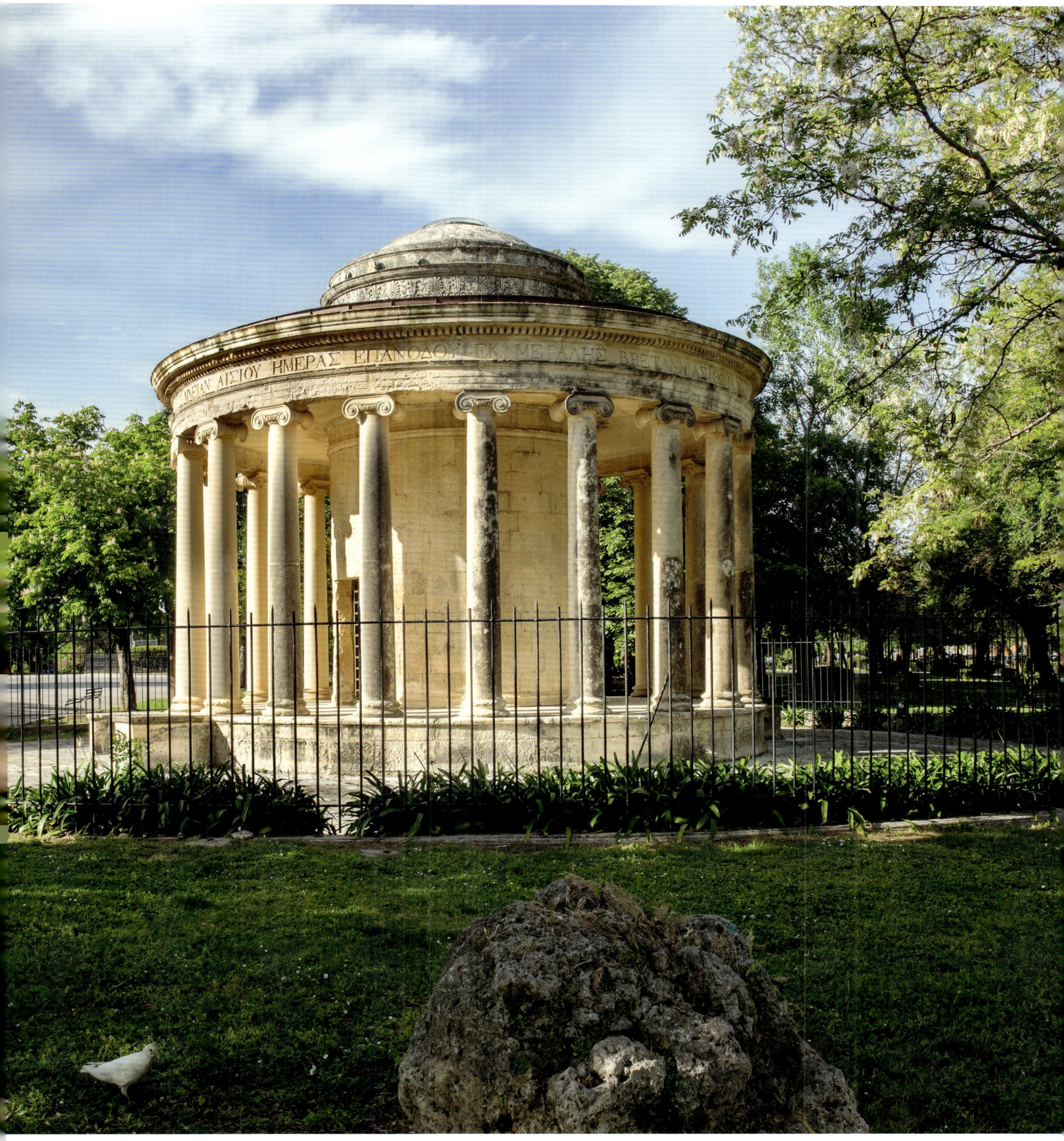
ΑΙΣΙΟΥ ΗΜΕΡΑΣ ΕΠΑΝΟΔΟΥ ΕΚ ΜΕΓΑΛΗΣ

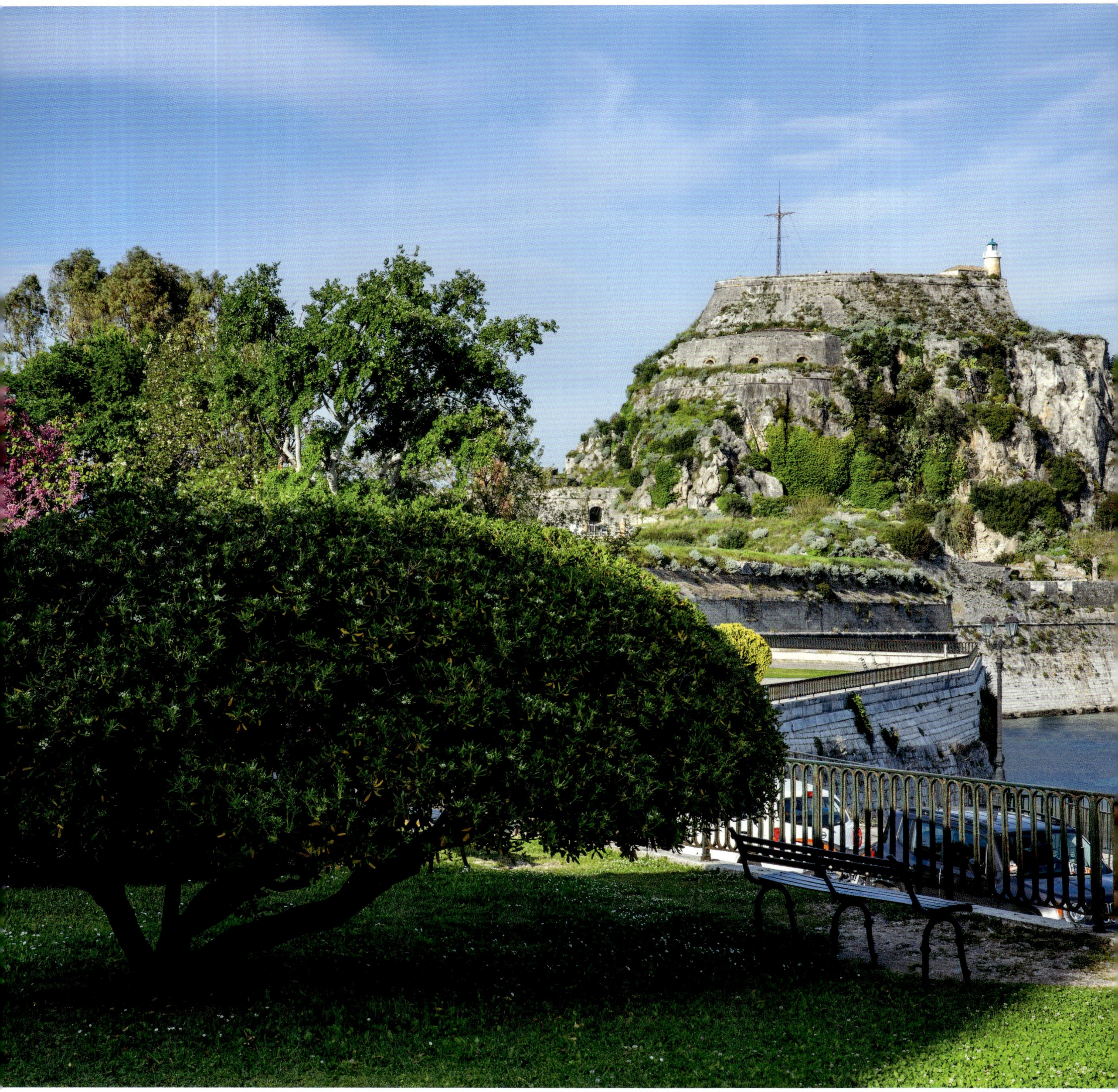

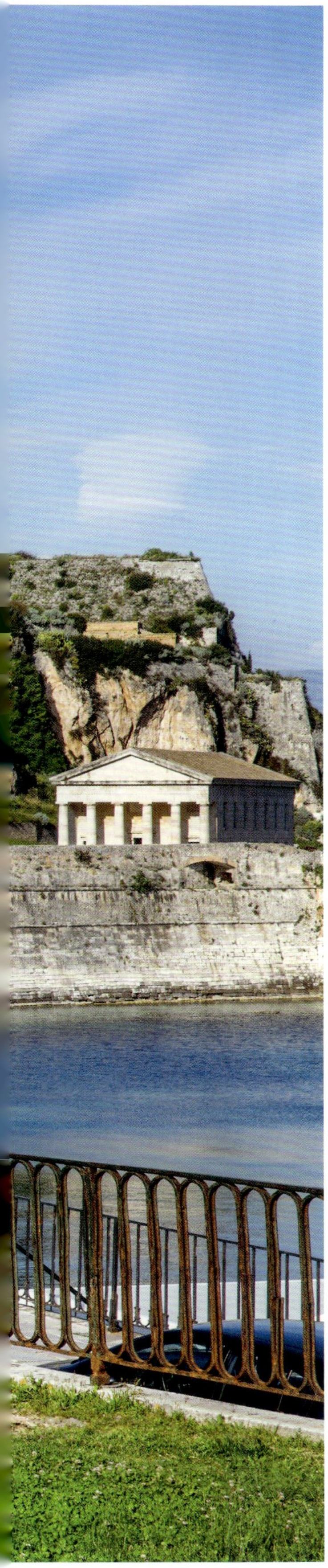

more Western than Levantine. Cosmopolitan and cultured, Corfu Town in the nineteenth century attracted travellers, artists, and musicians from Western Europe, and literary and artistic figures settled there from other parts of Greece. It was here that Greece's first university (the Ionian Academy), first philharmonic orchestra, first school of fine arts, and first botanical garden were founded.[34] Records of the theatre, opera, and music seasons show that in the mid-nineteenth century, Corfu's cultural life matched that of Europe's most sophisticated cities.[35]

OPPOSITE
Corfu's Old Fort, dating from Byzantine times and strengthened during Venetian rule. In the foreground, a characteristically pruned *Pittosporum tobira*.

Today the town in summer is thronged with visitors—many of them from the cruise ships that call into the busy harbour and many others who come to the island's hotels and rental villas. With their tall trees, the green spaces around the edge of the old city provide a welcome respite from the summer heat.

VILLAGE GARDENS

Most of Corfu's two hundred-odd small towns and villages developed as farming communities in the hills, where they were safer from pirates and tax collectors but also had better water supplies, cooler summers with fewer mosquitoes, and more shelter from winds than settlements on the coast.[36] Inland wells and springs were rare, so village people cultivated mainly on small terraces along the valleys of streams. In winter, families also grew food crops on the tiny hillside terraces supporting individual olive trees. In Venetian times, subsistence food crops were grown in secret so they would not be taxed. Well into the twentieth century, beans and lentils were the main food crops in summer, and grain in winter. Flocks of sheep and goats were grazed in olive groves and on common land. Where families had a choice, girls inherited land on the coast, and boys land in the hills.

Sophie Atkinson, writing a century ago, paints a colourful picture of the local autumn produce in those days: '...peaches and apricots, green honey-sweet figs, grapes of every degree, apples, pears, lemons, sacks of walnuts, almonds, chestnuts, donkey-loads of reddest tomatoes, all acting as chorus to the main theme of yellow melons... Monster long yellow fellows they are. It took three of us five days to eat one.'[37]

34. Paisídou, *Noble Houses of Corfu*, p. 27. 35. Elena Matheópoulos, 'Music', in Giles, *Corfu: The Garden Isle*, p. 184. 36. 'During the Venetian period, Corfu suffered repeated attacks by Genoese pirates and Turks, who razed villages and devastated the countryside. Most notably, in 1537 Ottoman Turks ... seized 20,000 men to sell as slaves in Constantinople and Egypt.' http://terrakerkyra.gr/v1/www.terrakerkyra.gr/history/en/history01.html. For centuries in northeast Corfu, malarial mosquitoes from the Butrint marshes across the channel in Albania restricted activities, particularly cultivation, near the coast. 37. Sophie Atkinson, *An Artist in Corfu*, p. 133.

A house front in Pérama with pink pelargoniums and orange nasturtiums. Not only crops but ornamental plants are key features of village life. Neighbours and relatives share cuttings and extra tubers, bulbs, and seeds, often safeguarding traditional plant varieties for generations.

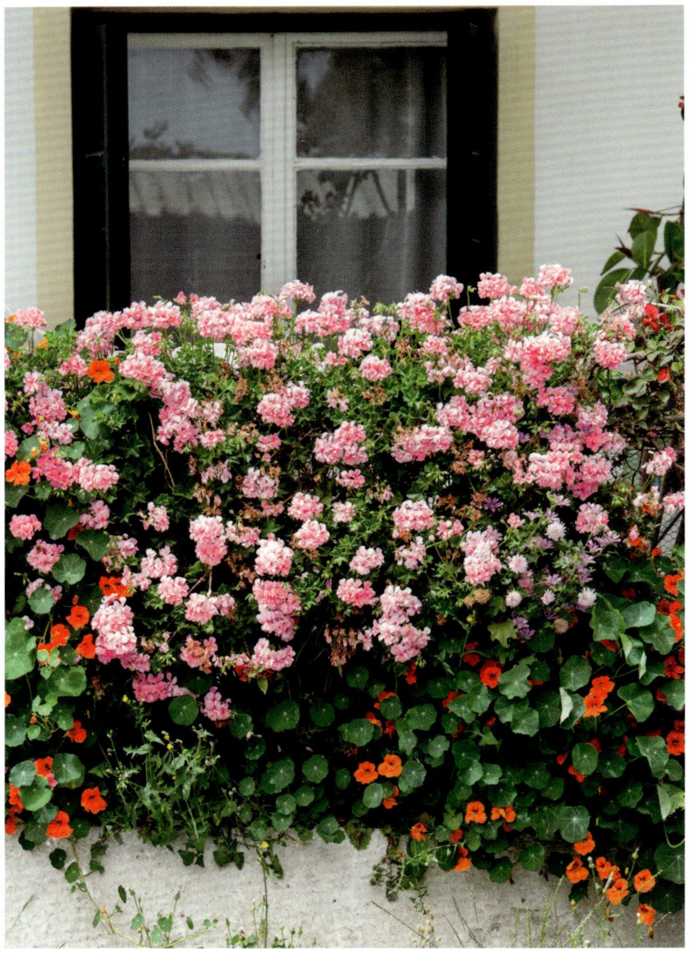

Wine-making expertise is passed from parents to children and, where family members can come together, the picking and crushing of wine grapes is a joyful annual ritual. On this pergola in Afiónas are two traditional varieties, *Rhodítis* (pink) and the eponymously named *Aidonighi*—Eagle's Claw—(white).

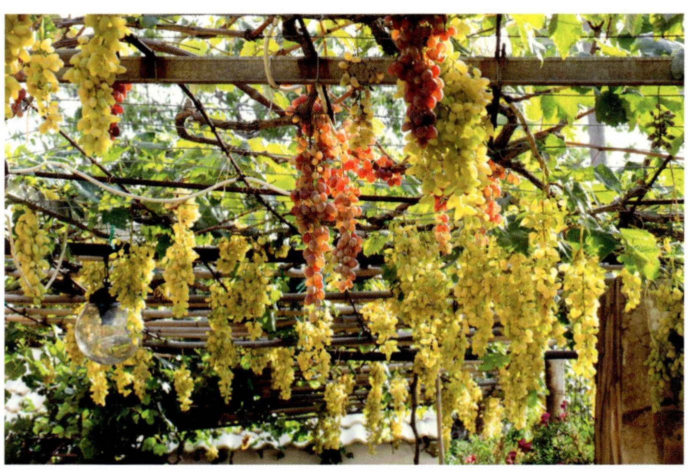

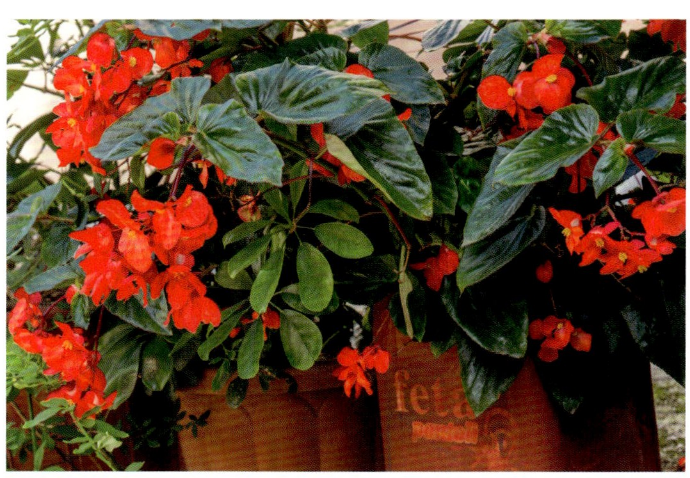

Like village gardeners in much of the world, those in Corfu make resourceful use of everyday materials. Here, begonias thrive in recycled feta cheese tins.

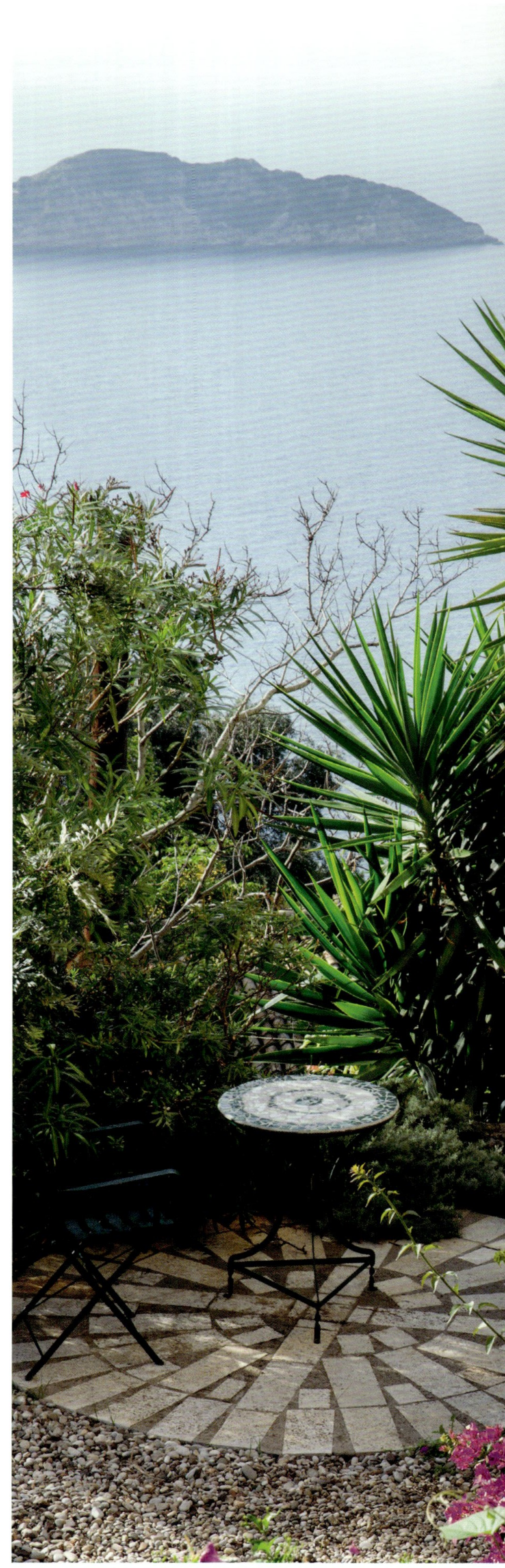

Bougainvillea and Spanish dagger yucca (*Yucca gloriosa*) surround this patio. Corfu's outer islands can be seen in the distance.

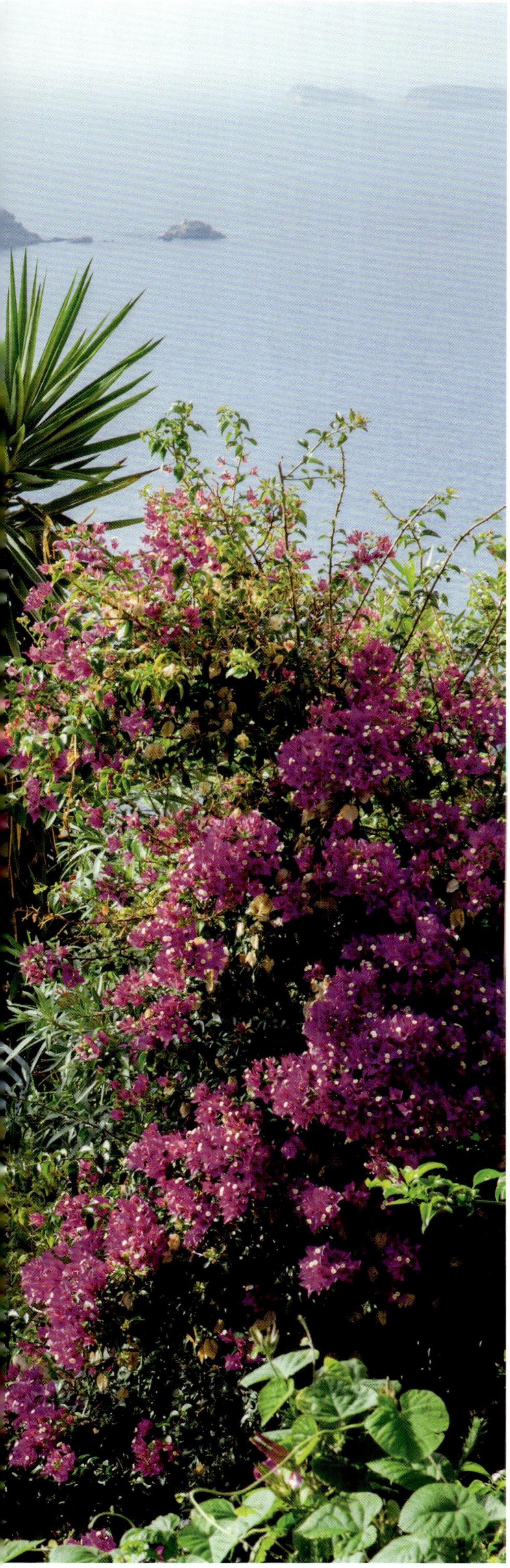

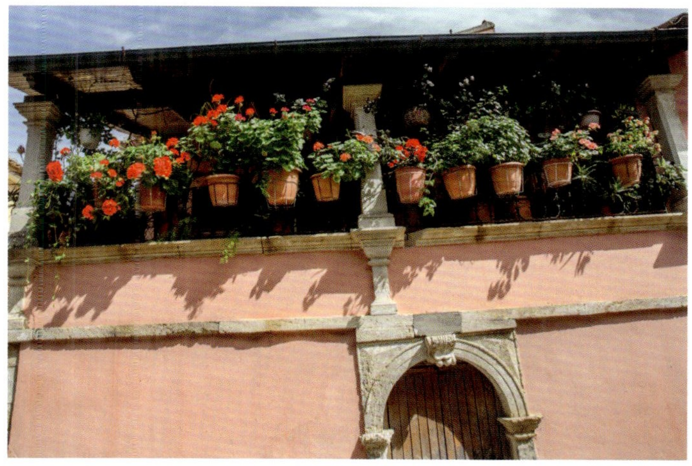

Pots line a balcony wall in the village of Doukádes.

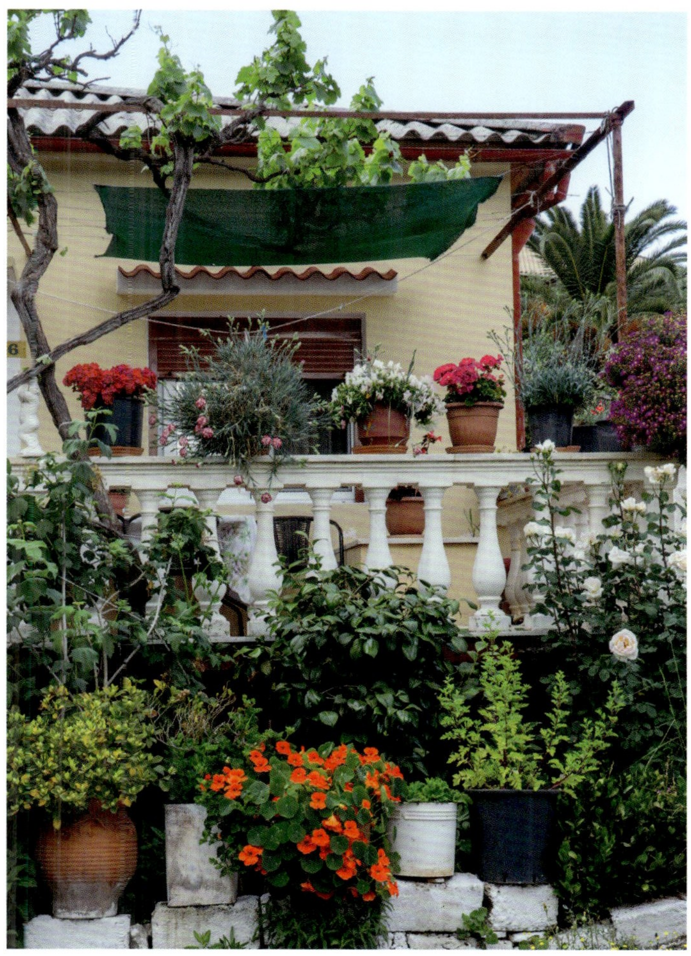

A housefront in Kassiópi. Along with the grapevine are roses and carnations for scent, and camellias, nasturtiums, and pelargoniums for colour.

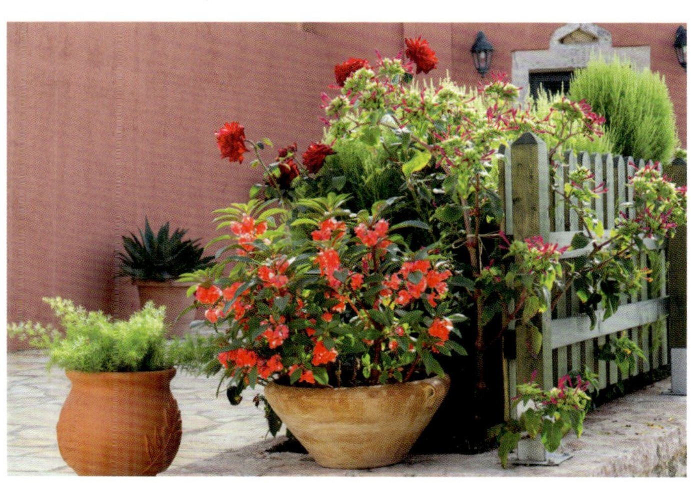

Pots in a village garden at Afiónas showcase the red flowers of *Impatiens balsamina*, roses, and marvel of Peru (*Mirabilis jalapa*).

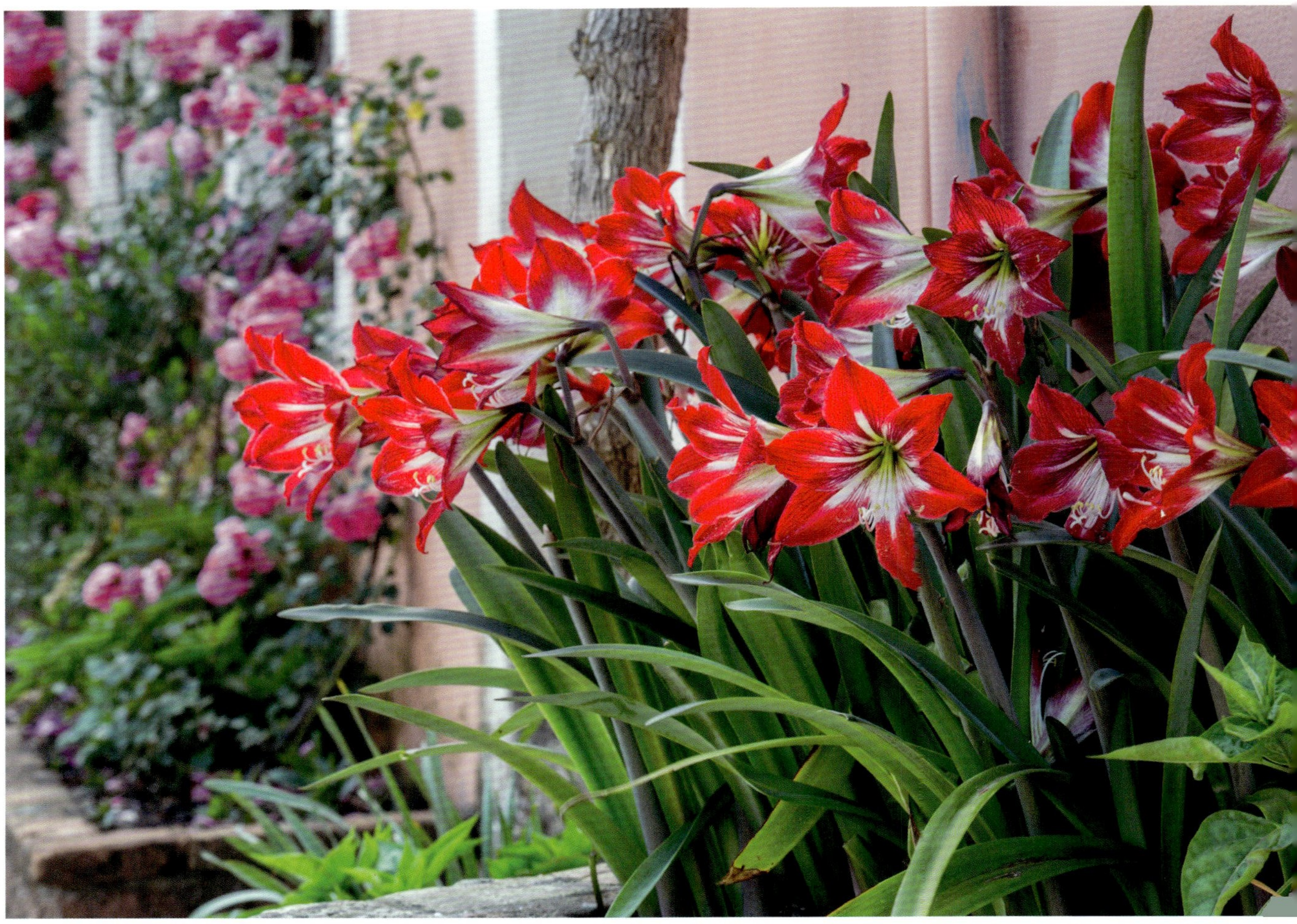

Red and white *Hippeastrum* bloom outside the hardware store in Siniés.

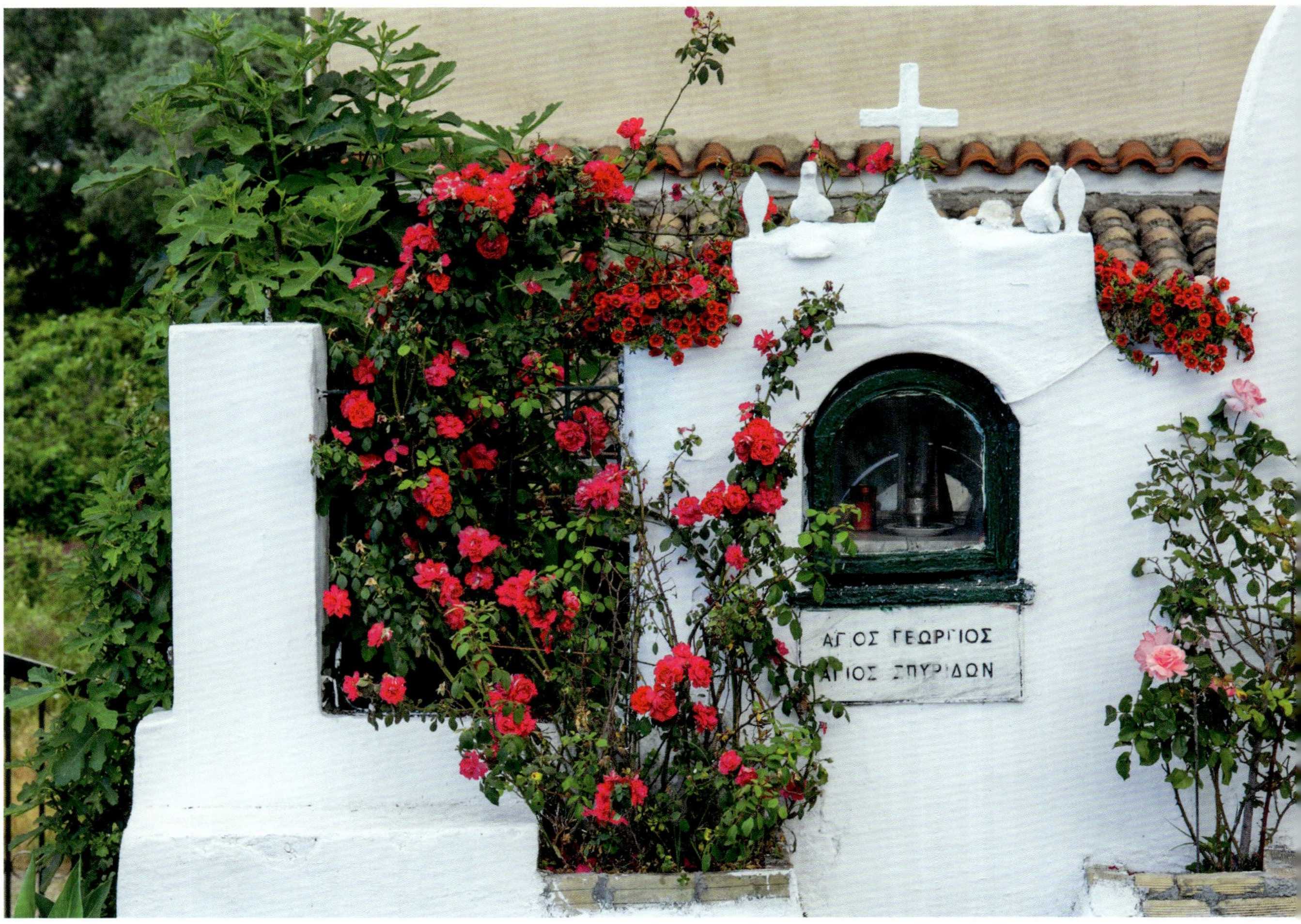

Roses decorate a roadside shrine in Kanáli.

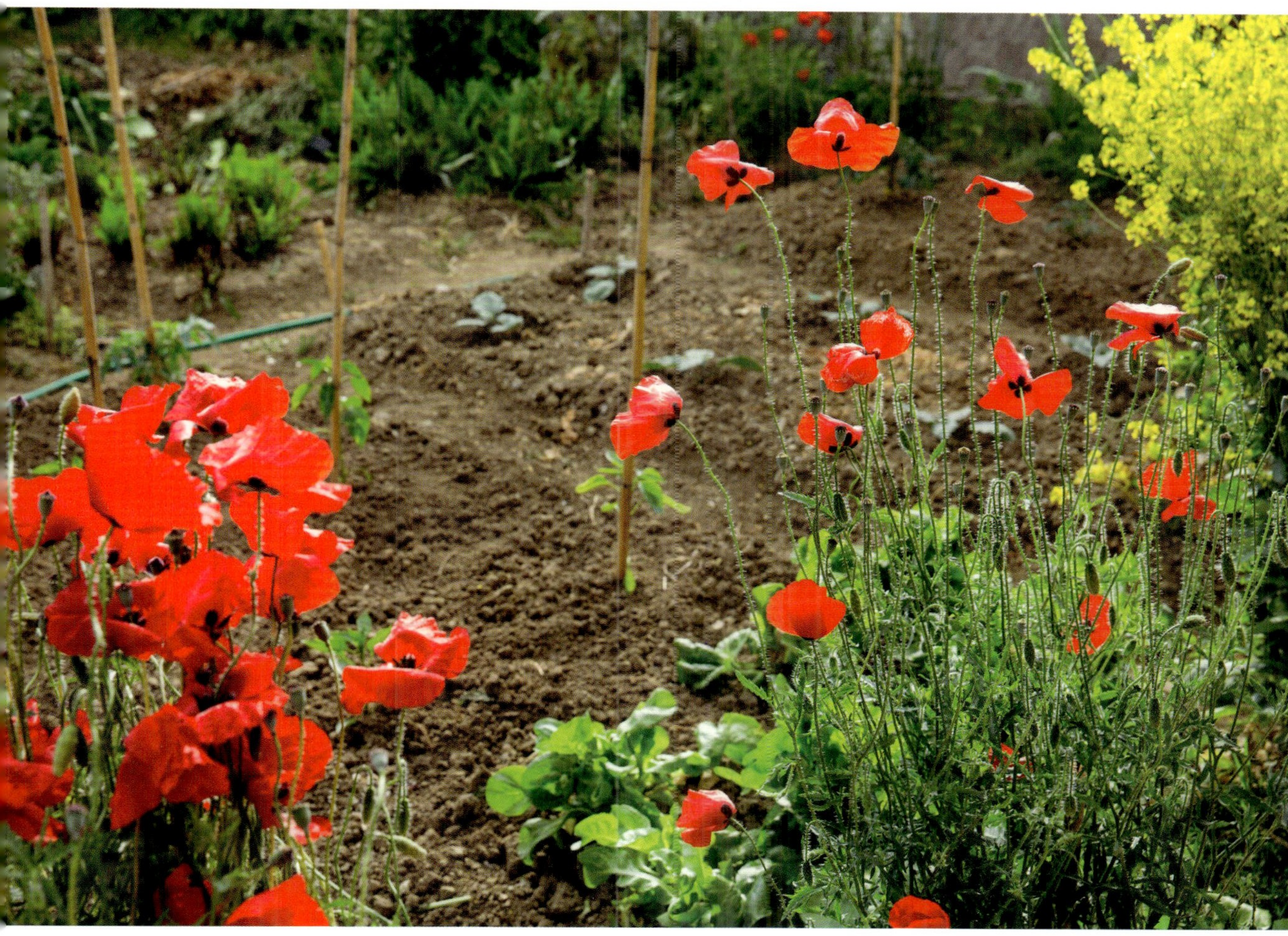

Self-seeded wild poppies (*Papaver rhoeas*) are allowed to share the ground in the Katékis vegetable garden in Chrisída.

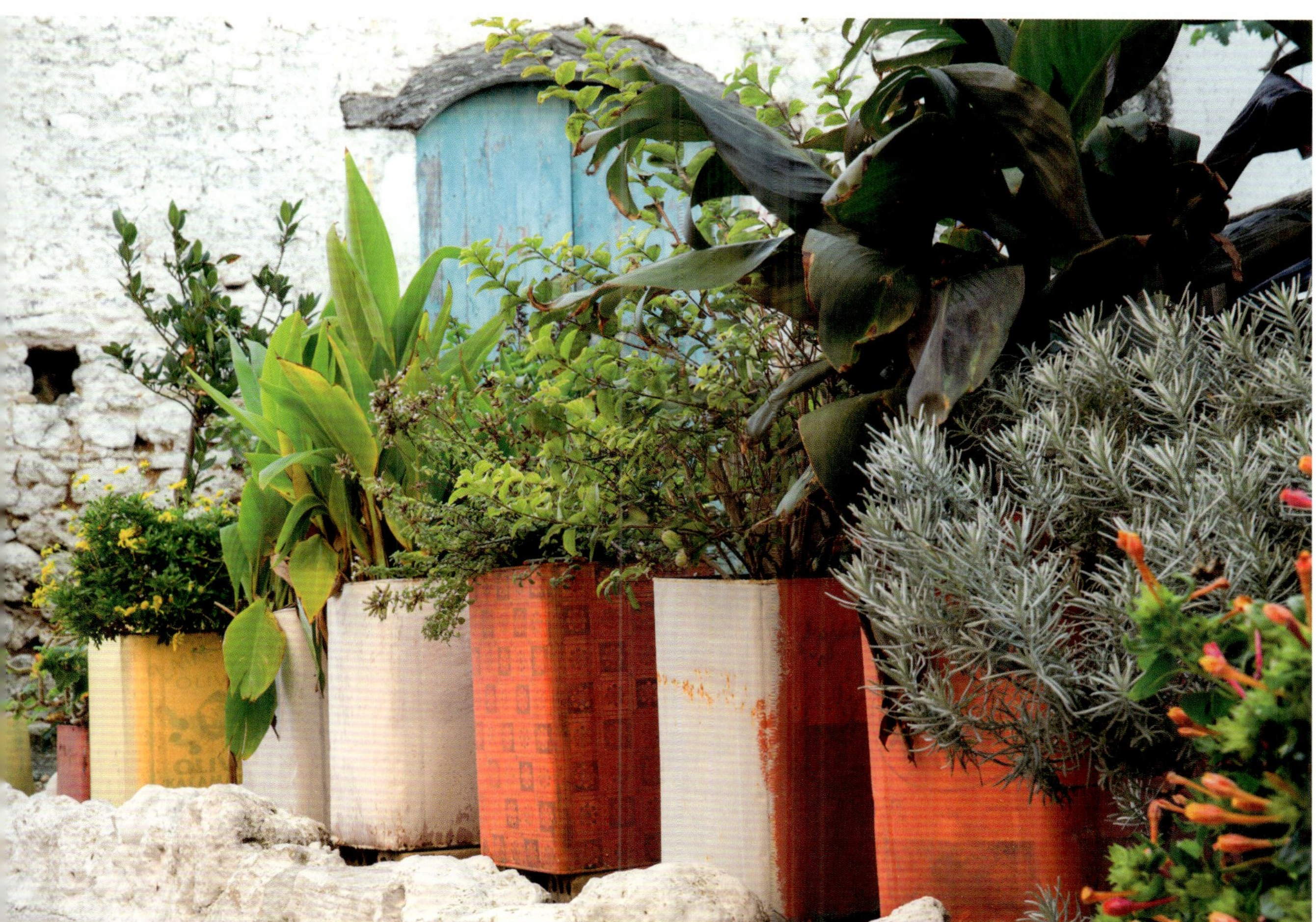

Where gardening space is short, every ledge is crammed with pots.

OPPOSITE
Pomegranates ripen in a garden at Aghios Doúli.

Modern times have seen shifts in land use and cultivation. As the population grew, farming could not provide a good livelihood for all. Increasingly, men became fishermen or joined the merchant marine, and, with the growth of tourism since the 1960s, much of the rural population moved to the coast. Some remote villages are now eerily quiet, with many of their houses falling into ruin.

But most villages still hum with life and colour. What people grow depends on their gardening conditions, including the soil, altitude, and aspect, but almost every village household has a grapevine pergola, along with a pot of basil on a doorstep or a windowsill. Where families have space for trees, lemon and orange are favourites, along with walnut, apricot, loquat, and pear. In even small household gardens, roses are crowded in alongside lilac, hibiscus, *Cestrum nocturnum*, and angel's trumpet (*Brugmansia arborea*). Cabbages and salad greens and, later in the year, bean and tomato plants, are interspersed with dahlias and chrysanthemums. Traditional urns, other terracotta pots, recycled feta tins—or even plastic water bottles sliced in half and filled with earth—hold a profusion of begonias, carnations, hydrangeas, gardenias, lilies, winter-flowering stocks, and herbs.

Many people also maintain vegetable plots and orchards (*perivóles*) and olive groves that are quite distant from their houses, often as the result of the fragmentation of land ownership over generations. Quite commonly, families now based on the coast still work their old smallholdings inland, visiting them to grow vegetables, raise livestock, and manage olives and vines.

Most village families grow grapes to make wine for their own use. One highly prized variety is *Manzaví*—an exceptionally dark red grape no longer cultivated commercially, which yields richly coloured and flavoured wine. Two favourite white varieties for domestic wine making are *Moscháto* and *Kakotrígi* (meaning 'difficult to cut', or harvest, though it is relatively easy to grow). The old dark red Isabella grape remains popular and is often referred to as *Fráoula* (strawberry), because of the perfumed fruit flavour of the resulting wine.

Citrus orchards are a feature of the southern landscape, in particular, but citrus trees appear in gardens throughout the island. Lemons are traditionally harvested in March/April—though increasingly people grow the Californian ever-bearing lemon, 'Eureka'. Among the popular oranges, *Kalokairiná* fruits once, in summer; *Omalofóro*, the navel orange, ripens around Christmas and into spring; and *Sanguiní*, the blood orange, is ready for harvest in March and April. Tangerines normally ripen in time for Christmas.

OVERLEAF
A vegetable garden in spring on the slopes of Mount Pantocrátor. This has a typical row of artichokes planted as a windbreak along the boundary. The broad beans (*Vicia fava*) and spring onions will be ready soon; potatoes have been planted for later.

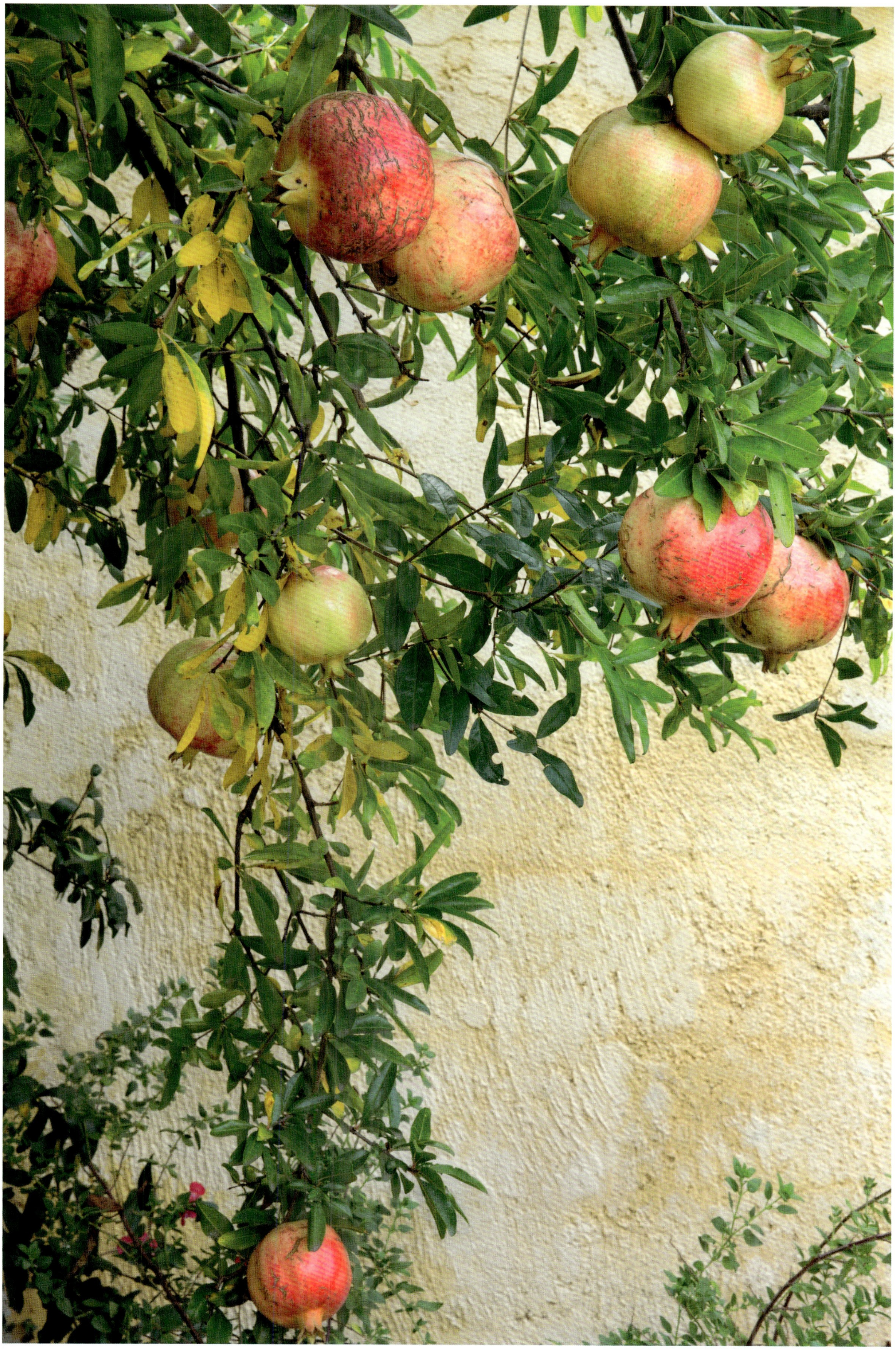

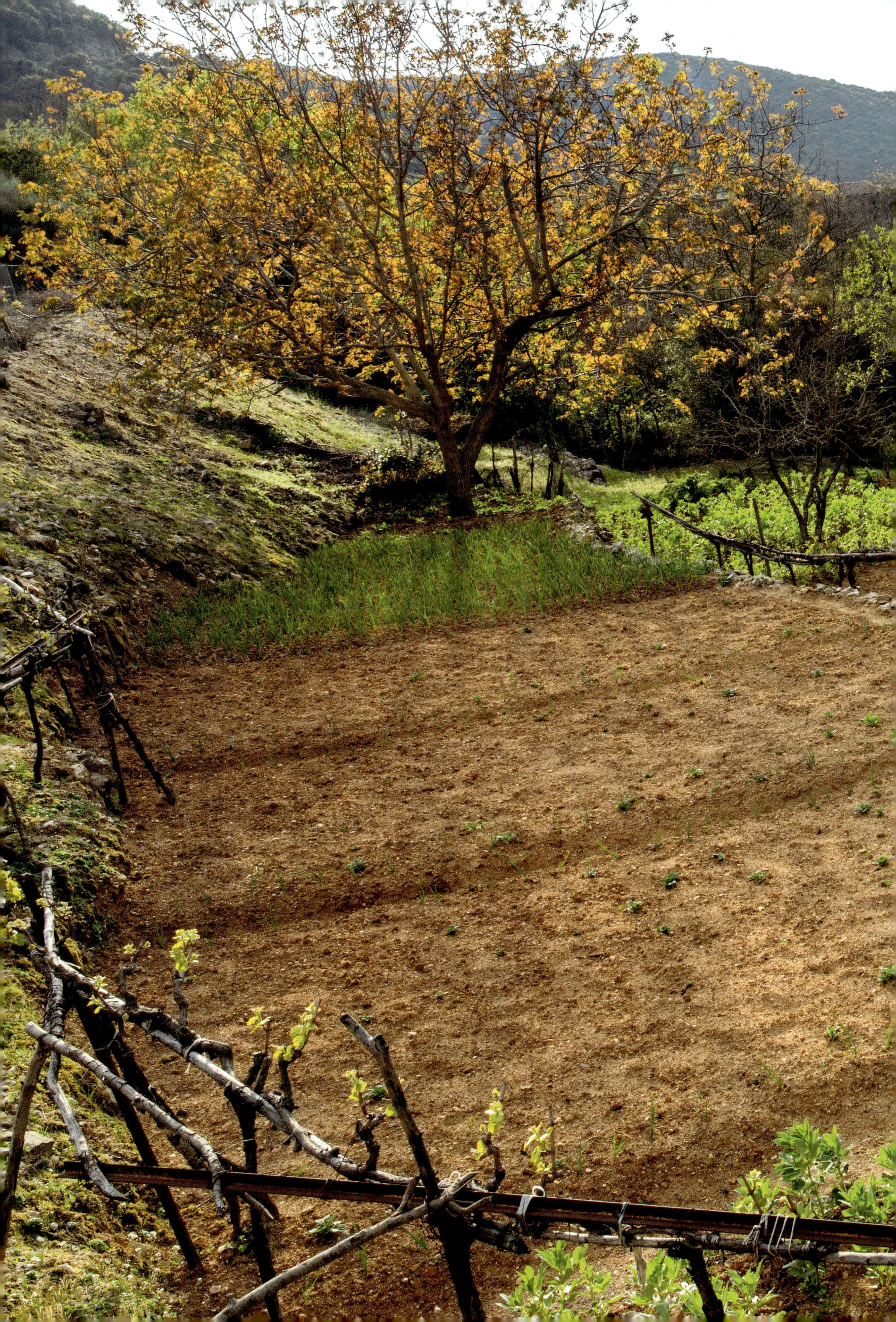

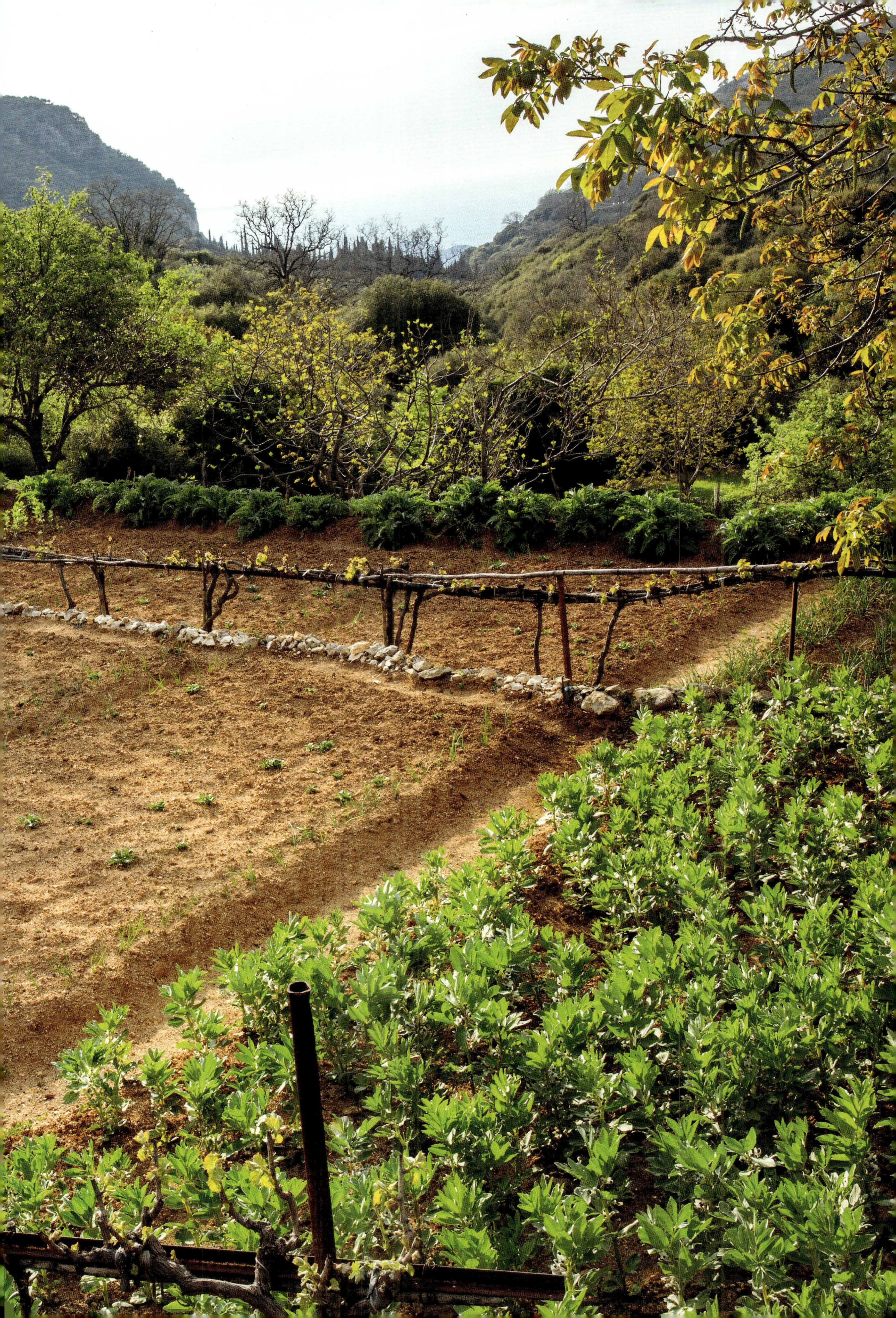

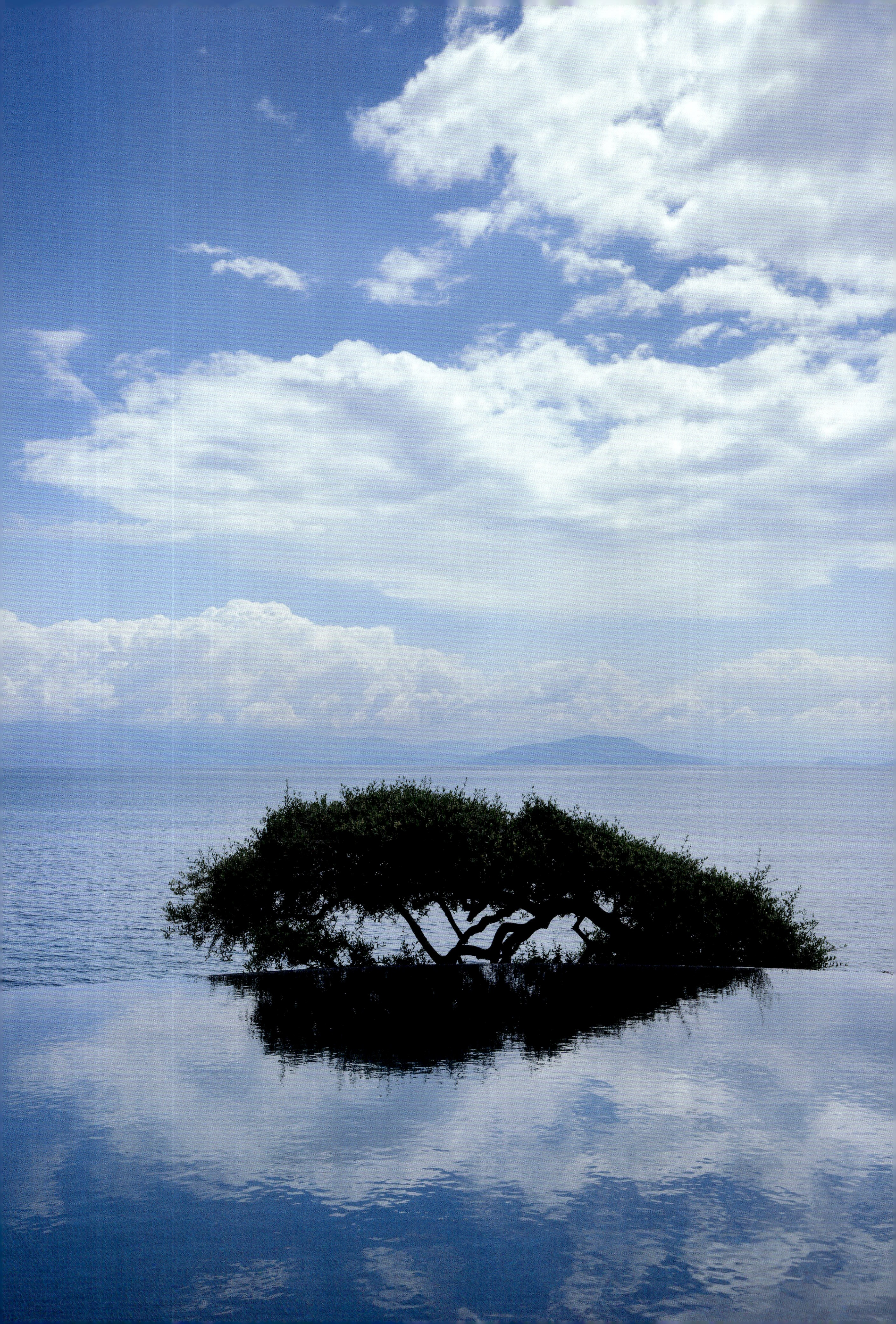

CHAPTER FOUR

Contemporary Gardens

OPPOSITE
The curved edge of the pool at Villa Principessa juts out over the sea. Design by Haim Kohen.

All the varied gardens featured in this chapter have been created or substantially augmented in the past twenty-five years. Some are breathtaking in the scale of their conception and in their designers' mastery of volume and space and understanding of the effects of light and shade. Others are enchantingly intimate, with intricate planting and intensely personal choices of decoration. Others are showcases for sculpture, whether Classical or contemporary, and still others are memorable simply for their joyous celebration of the pleasures of summer life outdoors.

But all have several key features in common. They reflect their owners' access to international designers and ability to source plants from outside Corfu. Embracing the contemporary pan-mediterranean design trend, they show a clear desire to be locally rooted and ecologically sustainable.[38] Many of them take a deliberately 'site-generated' approach, incorporating aspects of the found landscape such as rocky outcrops, patches of woodland, olive groves, or individual trees. Many preserve or replicate old stone terracing, both to prevent erosion and to acknowledge the land's agricultural history. Several that are sited in former olive groves take their structure from their inherited rows of trees, and some gardens evoke old agricultural patterns in new planting. All are designed to be explored, not just looked at from the house or the pool terrace; they have sections offering different types of planting, different moods, and different views, and they are planned with visual surprises and secret spaces awaiting around corners. To be locally authentic—and also, vitally, to conserve water—they depart from tradition by making extensive use of native plants. They also feature long-standing elements of local style: wrought iron, stone paving, terracotta urns, and fragrant plants. And, like the island's village gardens, many are not purely ornamental. Some of the urbanite owners of million-dollar homes enjoy growing their own vegetables and harvesting their own olives.

38. Pioneered by Heidi Gildemeister in the 1980s and 1990s in Majorca (see Gildemeister, 1995 and 2004), spearheaded in southern France by Nicole de Vésian (see Jones, 2011), aided and abetted by the plantsman and author Olivier Filippi (see Filippi, 2008 and 2016), and perceptively analysed by Jones (2012), the pan-mediterranean style takes its cues from the surrounding environment and the natural features of the garden site. It emphasises the use of vernacular materials and particularly of native plants, both to achieve a feeling of local authenticity and to conserve scarce water.

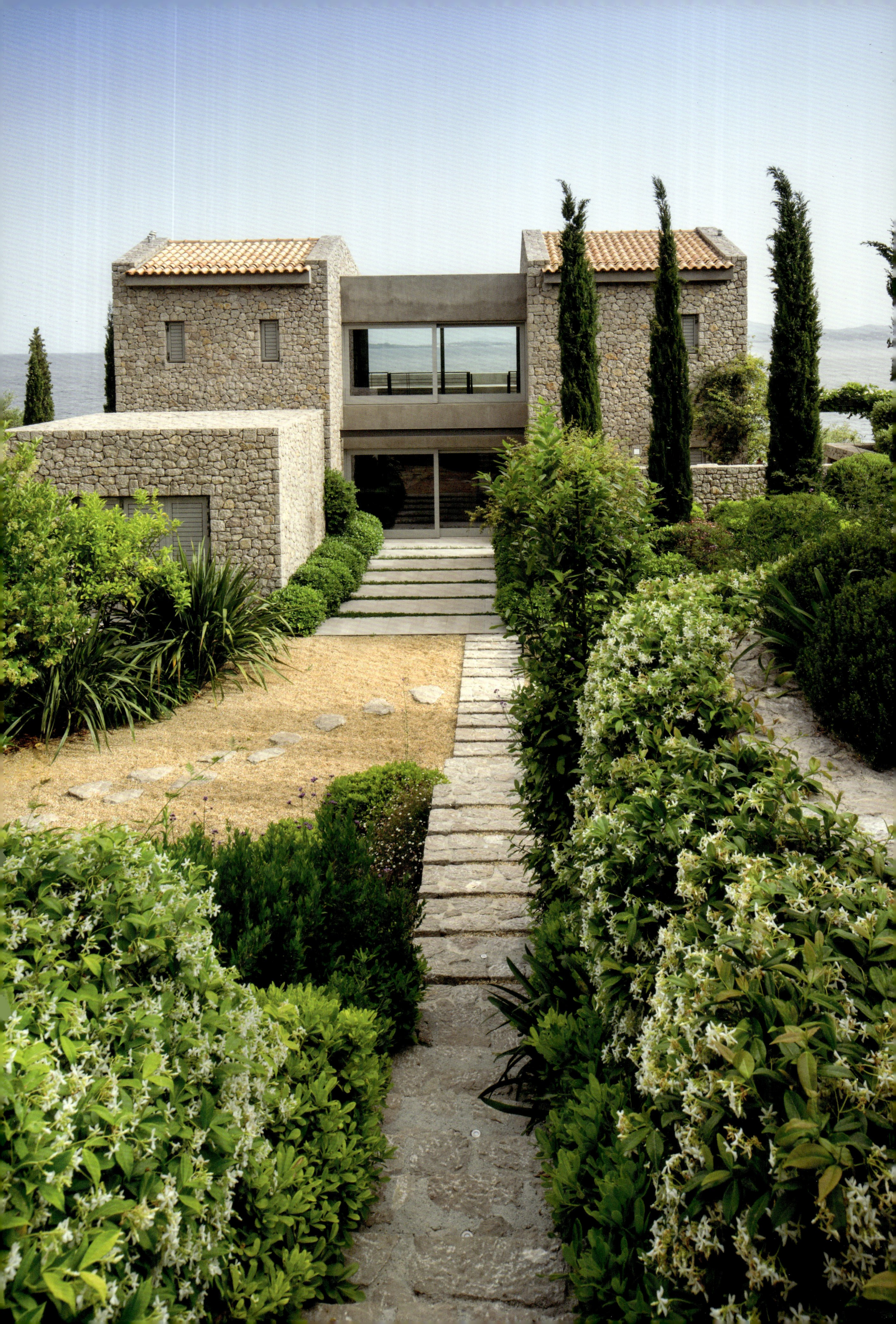

A garden in Nissáki

This serene and sophisticated but highly welcoming contemporary garden is beautiful year round, given its strong underlying structure provided by architectural elements and evergreen plants. But in summer it comes into its own: its lush growth provides a cool oasis, refreshing the senses with its colour choices—mainly dark green, white, and grey—and with its gravel 'river', mimicking water, over which one approaches the house on stepping stones.

OPPOSITE
An example of seamless collaboration between architect and garden designer. In the foreground are the white blossoms of fragrant star jasmine (*Trachelospermum jasminoides*).

The house and the beach under it face due south, with a view over the sea to Corfu Town in the distance. The owners' request to landscape architect Thomas Doxiádis was for a drought-resistant garden with 'native plants and an authentic feel', including a section that would evoke the tropical vegetation of Brazil, where one of them had spent his childhood years. Doxiádis and Dionýsia Liveri of Doxiádis+ worked closely with architect Thódoris Zoumboulákis, achieving a seamless blending of house, garden, and outdoor living spaces and an easy integration into the surrounding landscape. About one hectare in size, the garden was planted in 2011–12. On the house level and below it, the planting to the west is more mediterranean, that to the east more tropical.

The strikingly confident design is remarkable for its understanding of how light sculpts shapes—not only the masses, angles, and planes of the architecture, but also the soft mounded shapes of shrubs and the multifaceted, rough shapes of the rocks that are a presence throughout the garden. Shadows, too, are deliberately used. The spaces linking the house with the pool are dappled by geometric patterns of light that filter through the pergolas above. In a study in grey, two young olive trees, inset within the paving and paired with spiky blue fescue (*Festuca glauca*), cast sharply delineated moving shadows.

Doxiádis+ and Zoumboulákis have incorporated local traditional elements into their design but with a contemporary flair—especially in the shaded outdoor living areas adjacent to the house, with their sleek lines and smooth stone surfaces, and in the plantings for scent, notably lavender, wisteria, and copious plantings of Spanish jasmine (*Jasminum grandiflorum*) and star jasmine.

Entering the garden from the road above, the driveway follows a low curved wall covered with creeping fig (*Ficus pumila*) and garlanded with

The lively but simple planting here complements the simple shapes and intriguing texture of the building, whose warm-coloured stone comes from the Peloponnese.

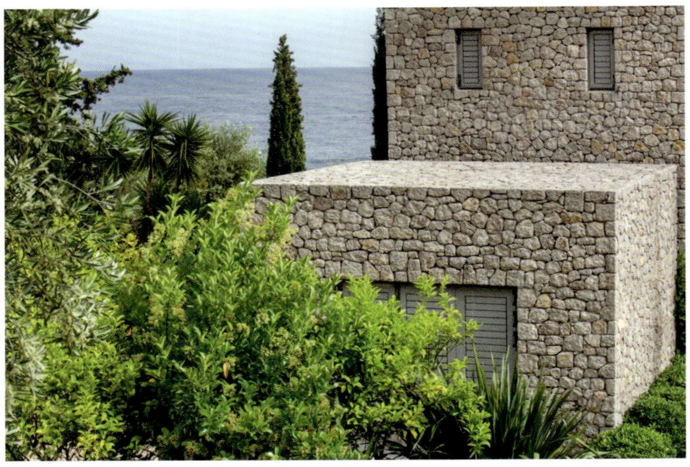

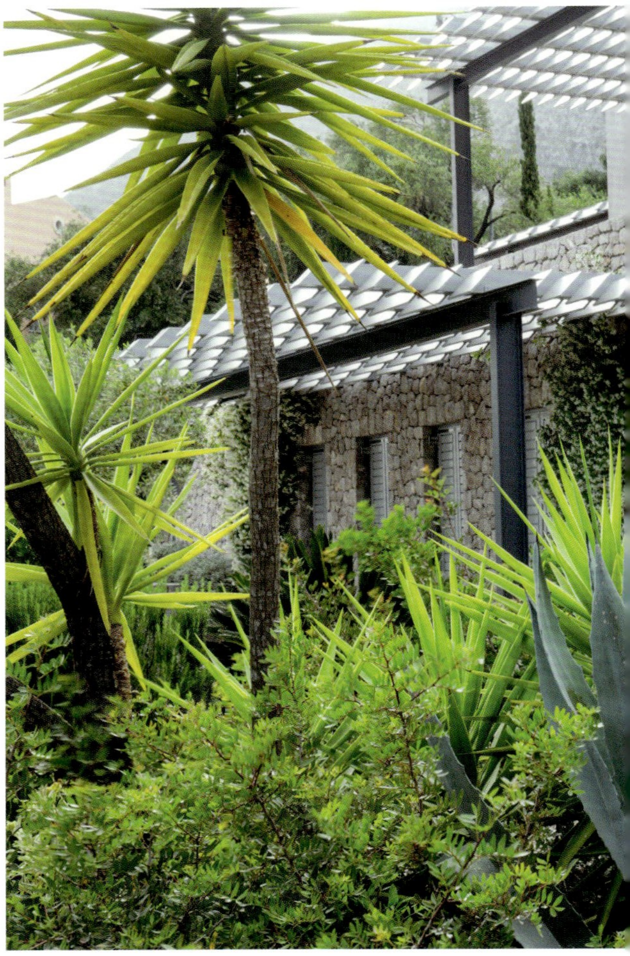

Under the grid of old olive trees on the slope in front of the house, balls of *Pittosporum tobira* 'Nana' form rhythmic patterns, punctuated by the purple flowers of *Verbena bonariensis*.

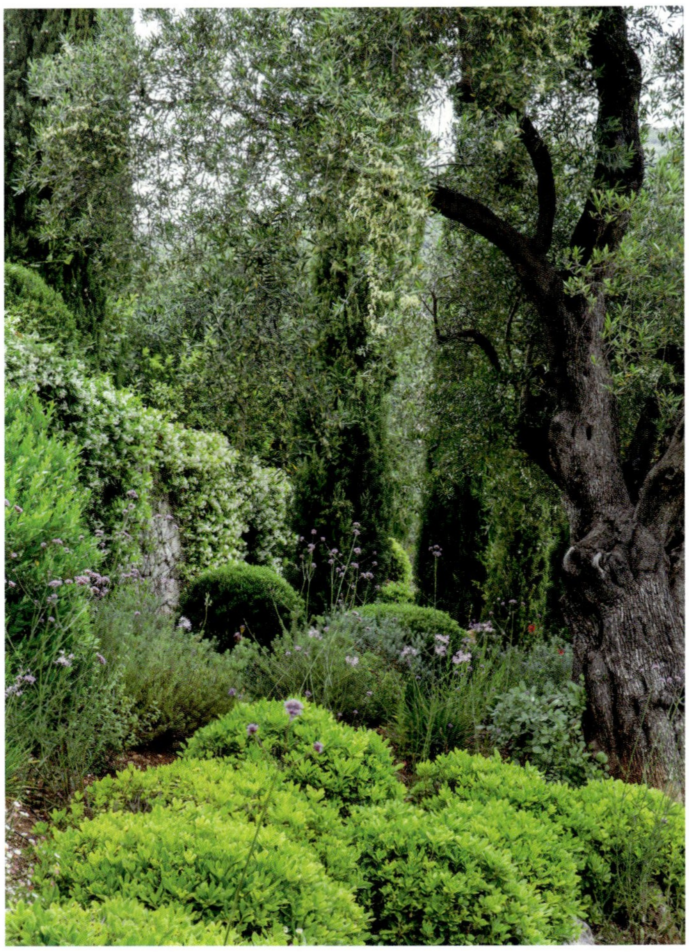

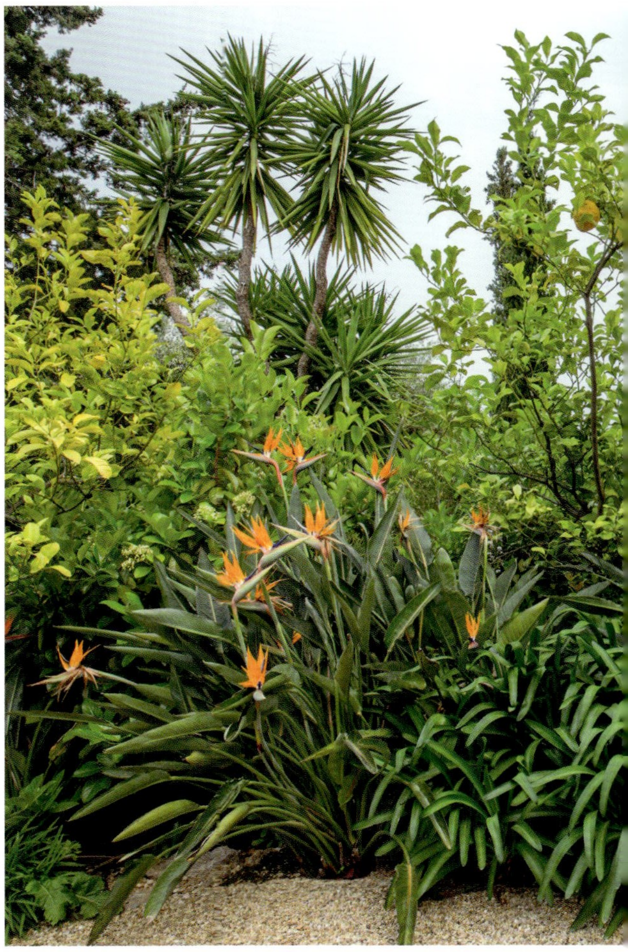

The romantic 'mediterranean' garden west of the house features a Judas tree, summer flowering perennials, and *Agapanthus*. The 'Iceberg' roses and star jasmine here provide continuity with other parts of the garden.

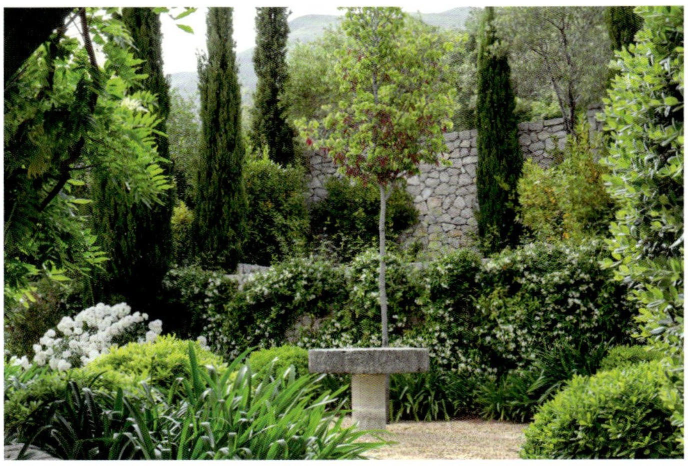

CENTRE TOP
East of the house, yuccas, agaves, and cycads help to create an exotic atmosphere on the way to the 'tropical' garden.

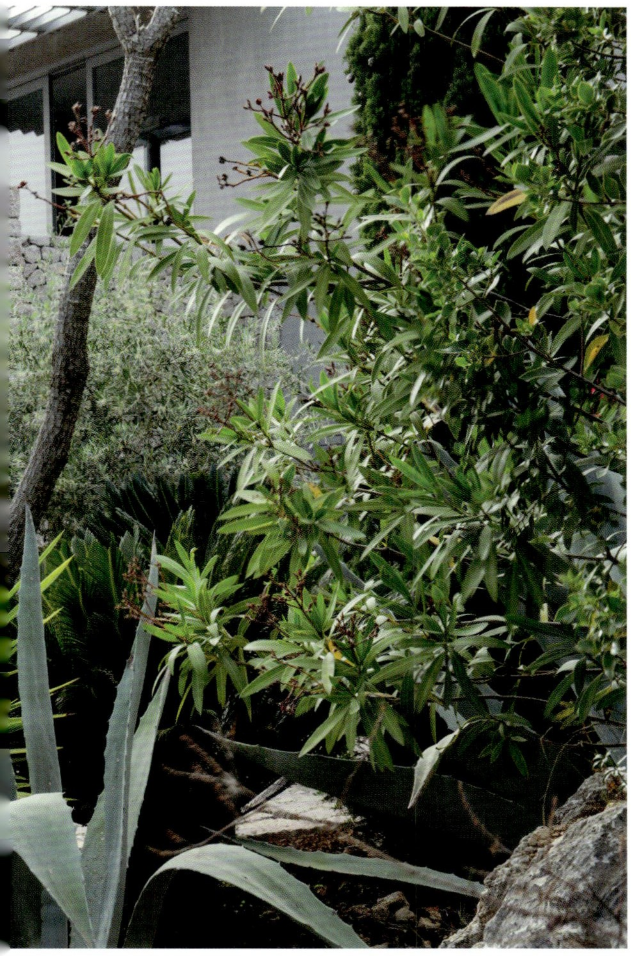

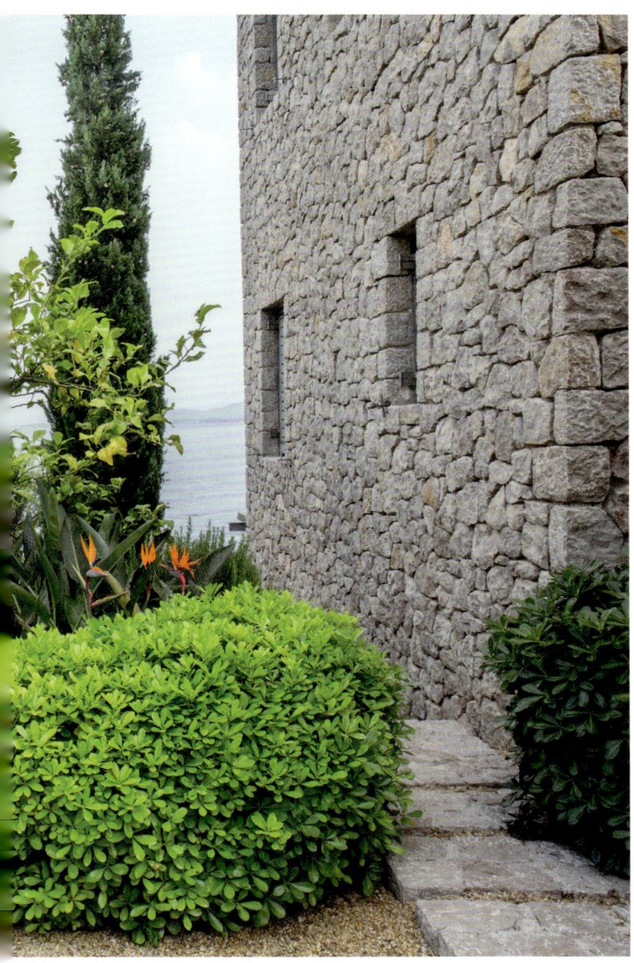

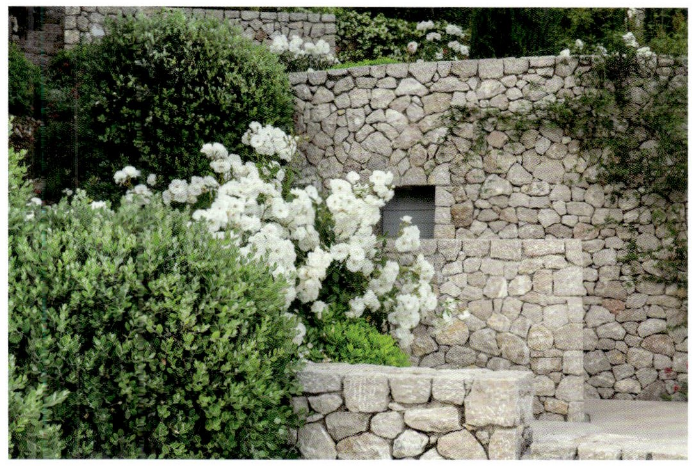

'Iceberg' roses appear in different contexts throughout the garden.

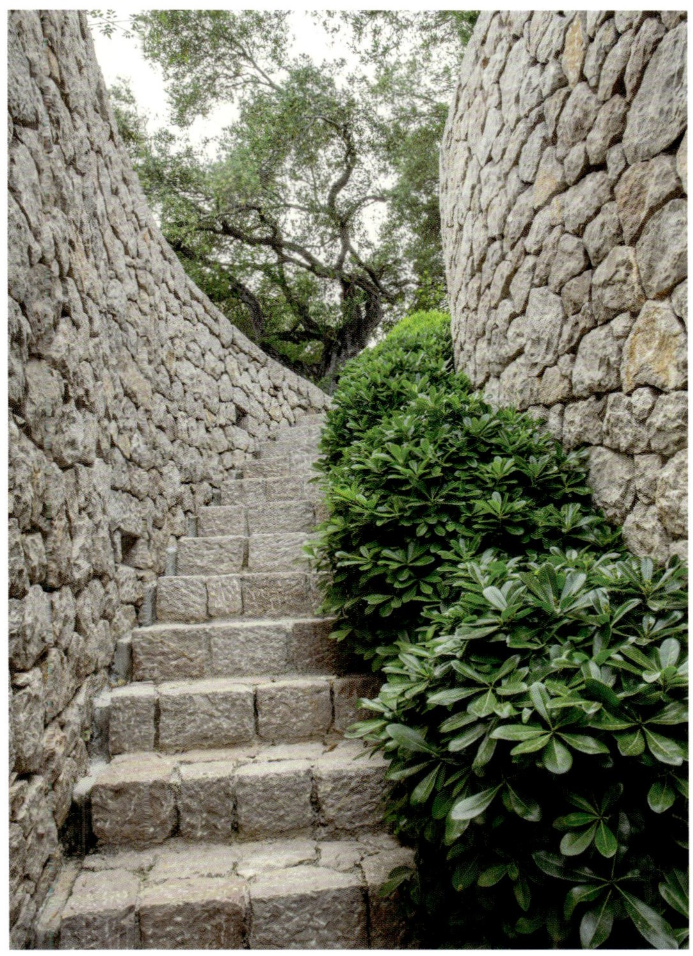

Clipped *Pittosporum tobira* 'Nana' is another plant that appears throughout much of the garden; it helps to provide a transition between the architecture and the areas of more richly textured planting.

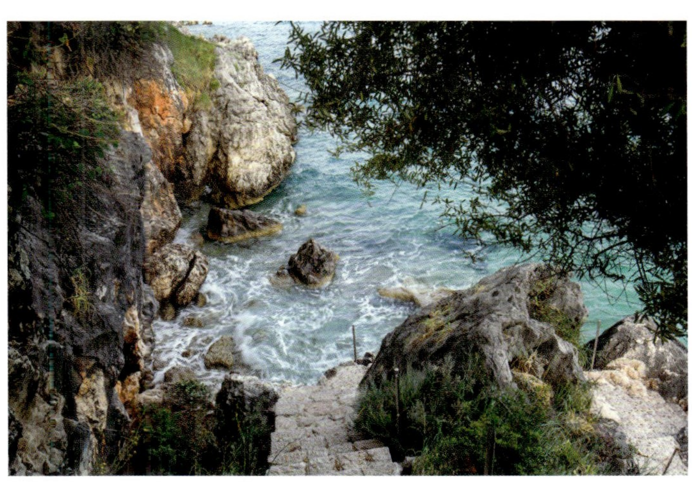

The sea is reached by paths leading through progressively freer garden planting using native mediterranean shrubs.

CENTRE BOTTOM
At the heart of the 'tropical' garden, *Strelitzia regina* and *Agapanthus* are backed by lemon trees and the spiky forms of yucca and cypress.

CENTRE TOP
The strikingly simple entrance to the house, with its view through to the sea, is lined by balls of *Pittosporum tobira* 'Nana'.

CENTRE BOTTOM
On the 'tropical' side of the garden, mediterranean rosemary, oleander, and cypress take on an exotic air in the company of cycads, yuccas, and Canary palms.

OVERLEAF
The house is approached on stepping stones over a gravel 'river' lined by balls of *Pittosporum tobira* 'Nana' and frothy-textured Mexican fleabane (*Erigeron karvinskianus*).

white-flowered swags of star jasmine growing from beneath it. Above the wall, too, the planting has a powerful rhythmic energy: under old olive trees and among the large outcrops of rock are mounds and balls of dark green *Pittosporum tobira* 'Nana' and *Rudbeckia*, interspersed with the airy dotted forms of mauve-flowering *Verbena bonariensis*. Closer to the house, the rhythm becomes more complex, with a new theme provided by the stepping stones in the gravel 'river' and their interplay with the pittosporum balls and rocks on the 'shore'. Plantings of pencil cypresses in this area add dark vertical elements.

On its eastern side, the house seems to grow out of the rock. Agave and yucca are planted here, with small pockets of dark green wall germander (*Teucrium chamaedrys*) where architecture meets bedrock. Cycads, palms, yuccas, and the brilliant pinks of flowering oleanders set a tropical, slightly otherworldly, atmosphere. Approached up a flight of steps, a secret garden—thickly encircled by lemon trees and shiny-leaved *Daphne laureola* and *Viburnum lucidum*—conjures up a Henri Rousseau jungle scene with pink, red, and orange flowers and exotic leaf shapes, and offers glimpses of the sea between the tops of cypresses and yuccas growing below.

Working together, the design team have created strong contrasts between manicured and untamed, sunlight and shade, mediterranean and tropical, contemporary and timeless, rich colour and monochrome, and between the rough textures of rock and olive wood and the smooth ones of engineered stone. Making these contrasts more poignant is the continuity of materials throughout the design. The stone for the house, garden walls, and paving all comes from a single quarry in the Peloponnese. Softer coloured and grainier than the local limestone, and hand-hewn into rounded shapes with flat faces, it perfectly complements the smooth rectangular paving stones used on the terraces. Olive trees, too, appear throughout: under-planted with clipped *Pittosporum* in the most cultivated parts close to the house and with wild native bushes on the hillside above the sea. Cypresses, thickly planted in the mediterranean beds above the house, reappear in the 'tropical' part of the garden. 'Iceberg' roses appear not only in the exquisite terrace garden to the west of the house but also lower down. The white and green colour scheme seen next to the entrance continues around the house, joined there by blue-flowering *Agapanthus* and plants in silver and grey.

The garden is impeccably maintained by Arthoúros Korakídis with guidance from Alithea Johns.

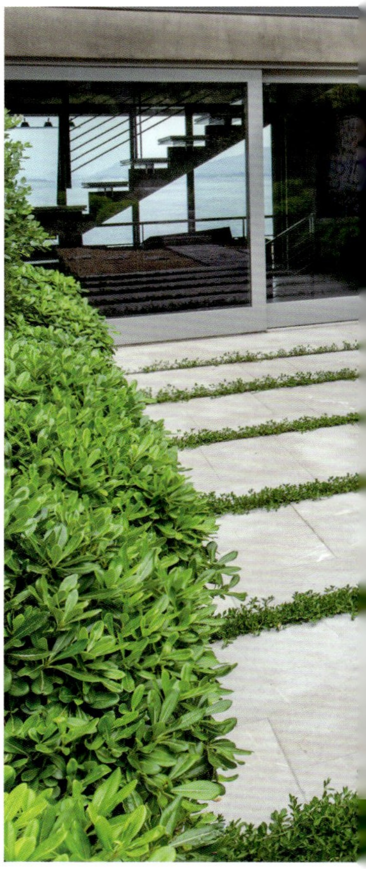

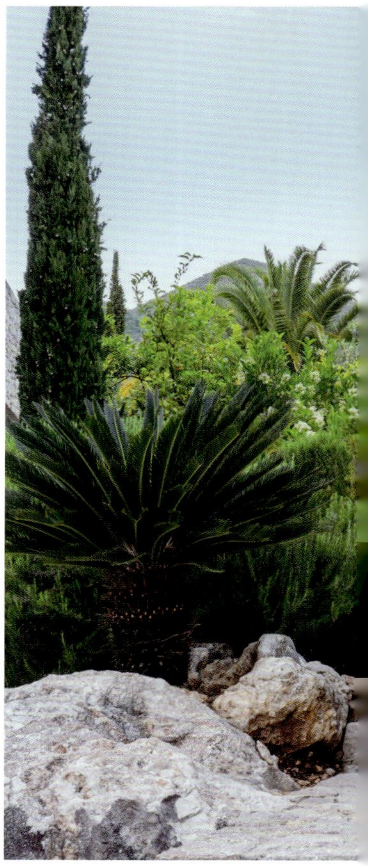

The infinity pool leaves visible the canopies of olive trees growing on the hillside beneath it.

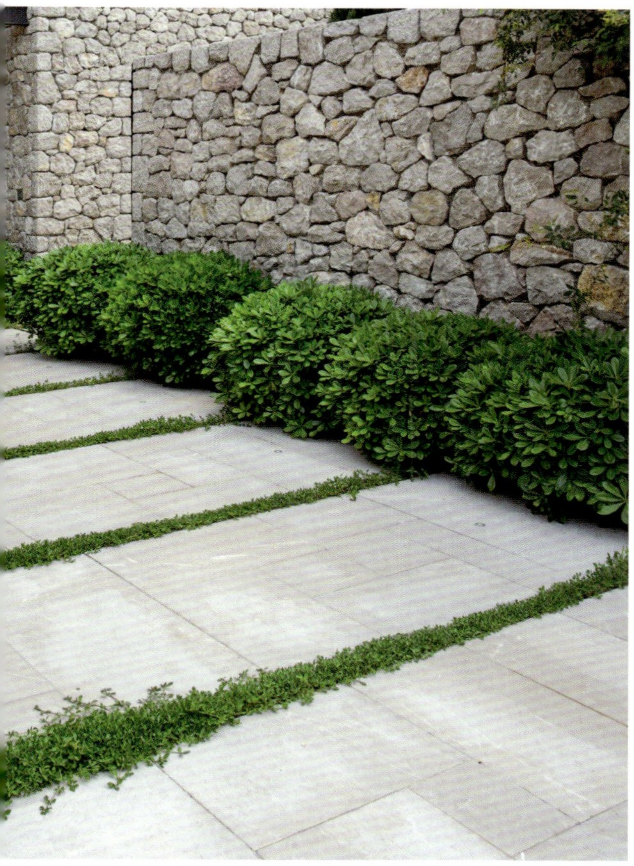

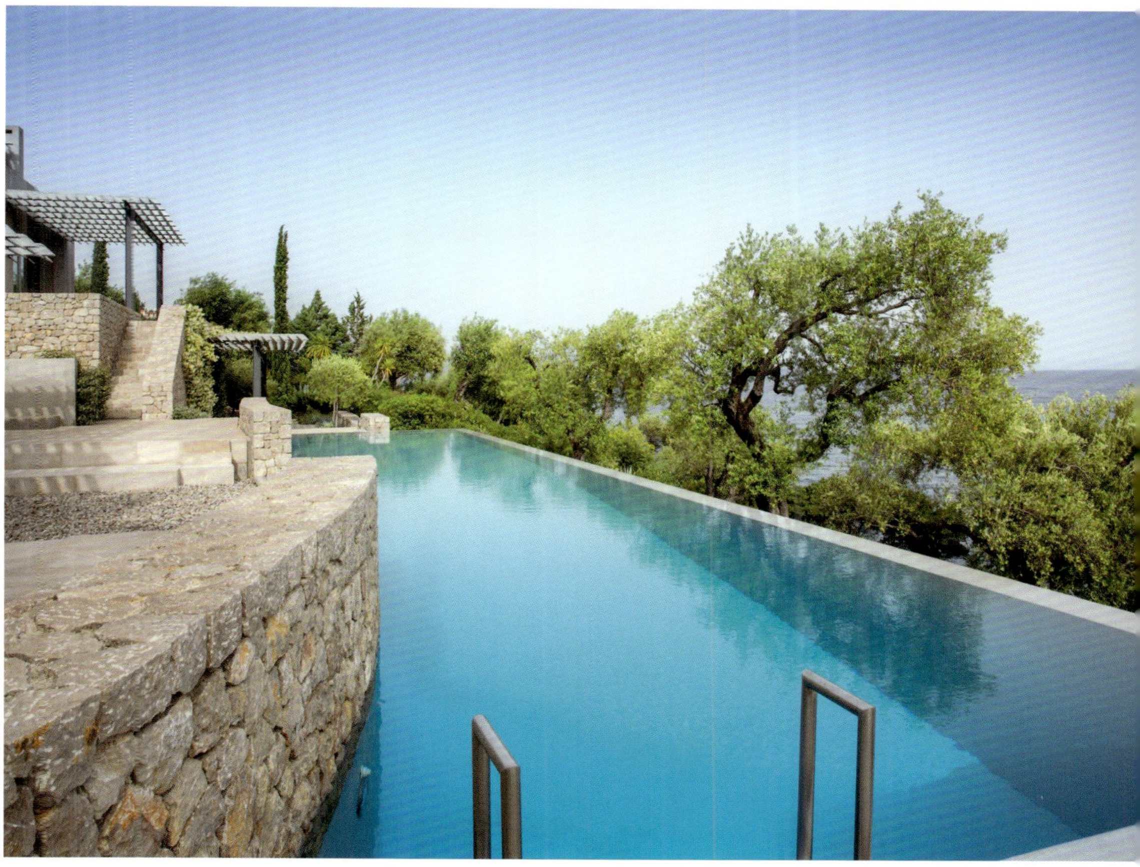

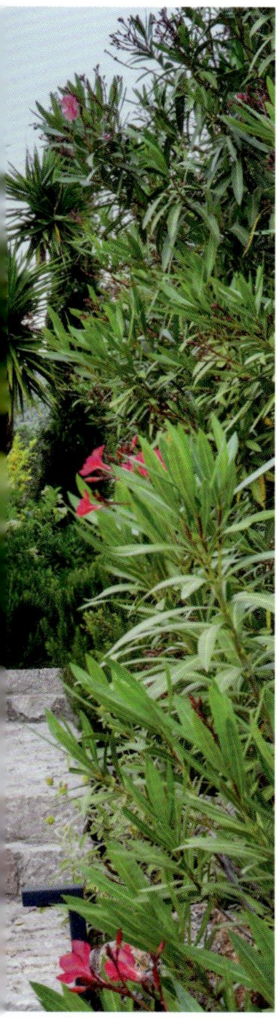

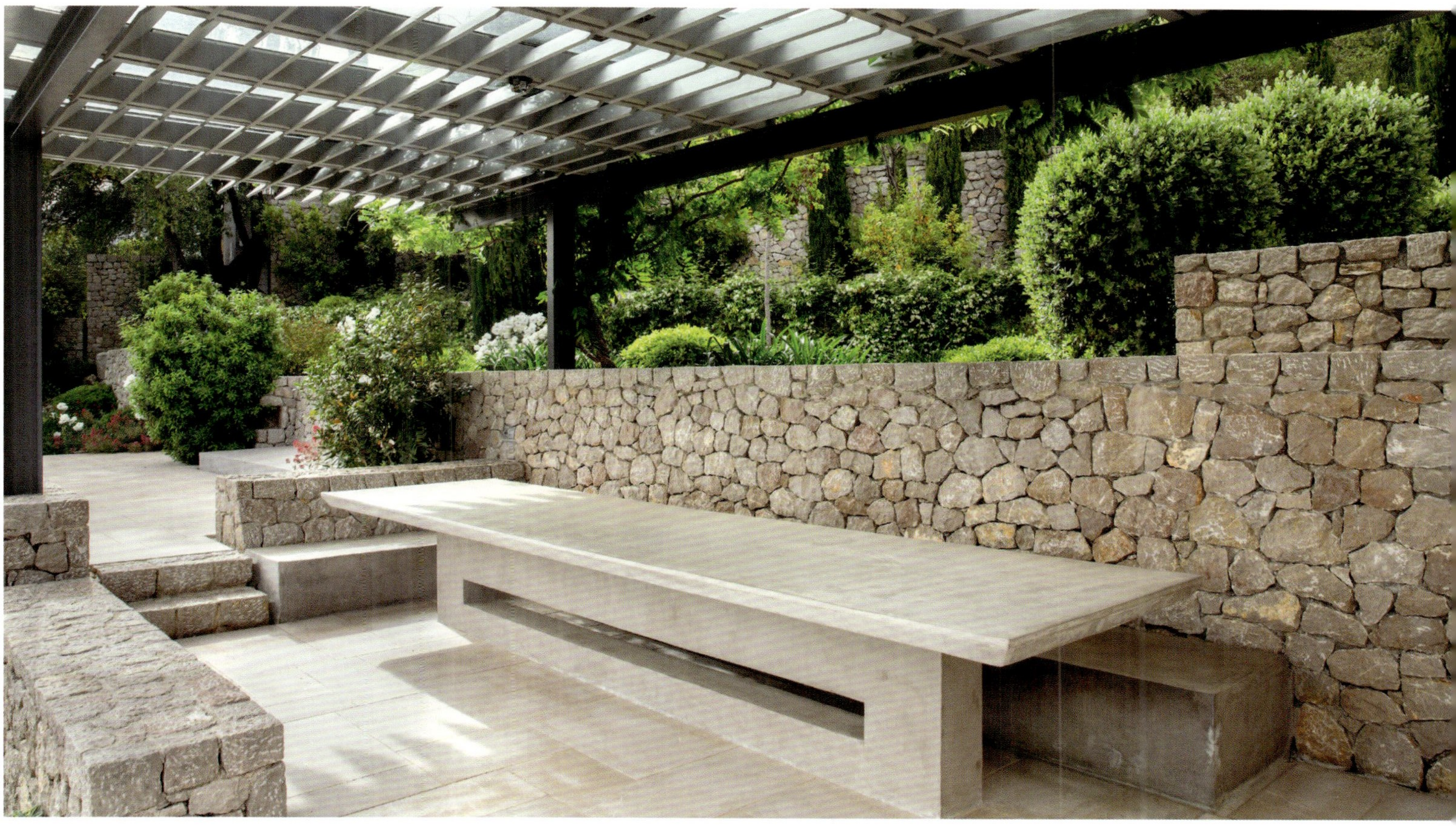

In this outdoor sitting area, the smooth stone is shaded by the angled slats of the pergola.

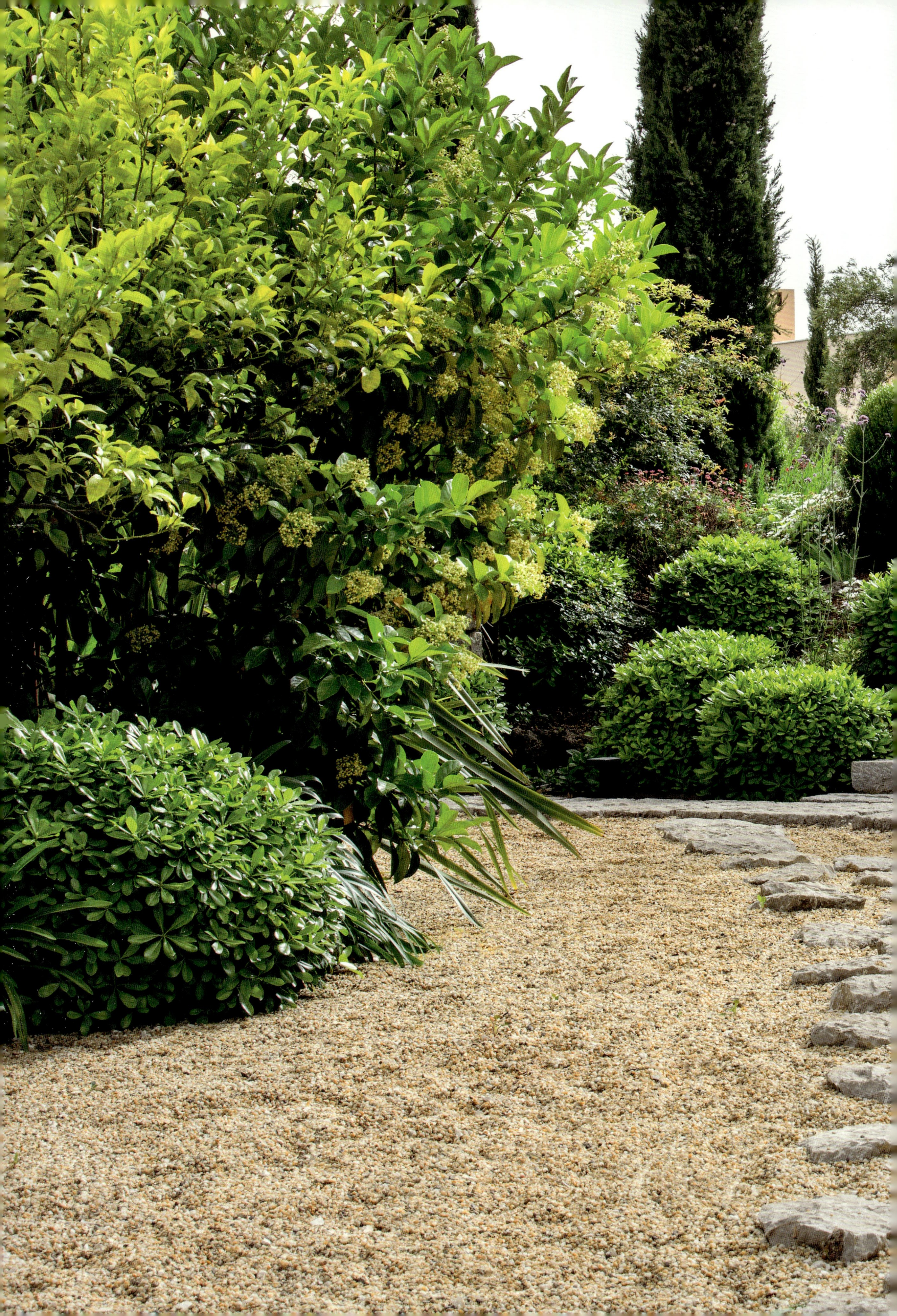

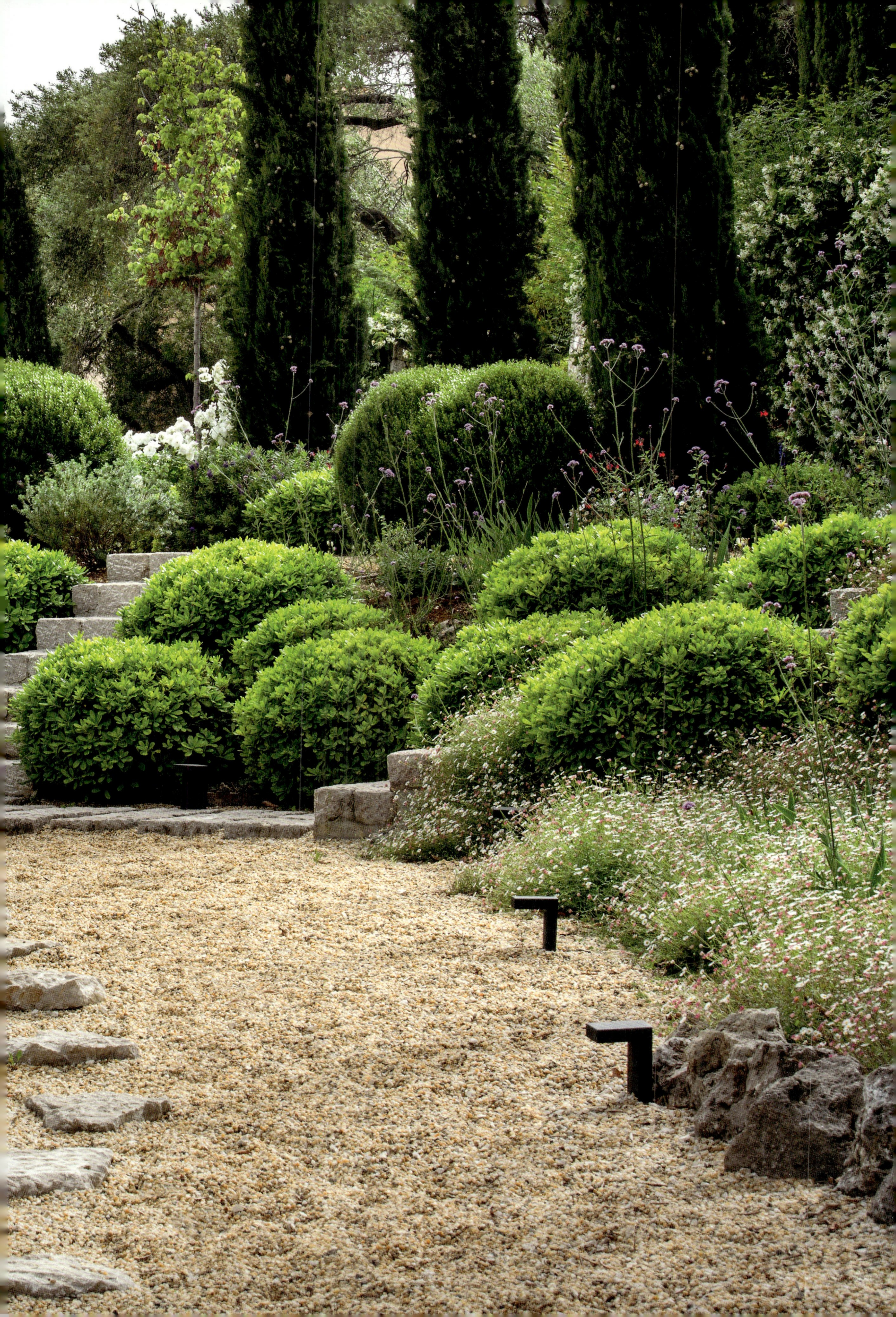

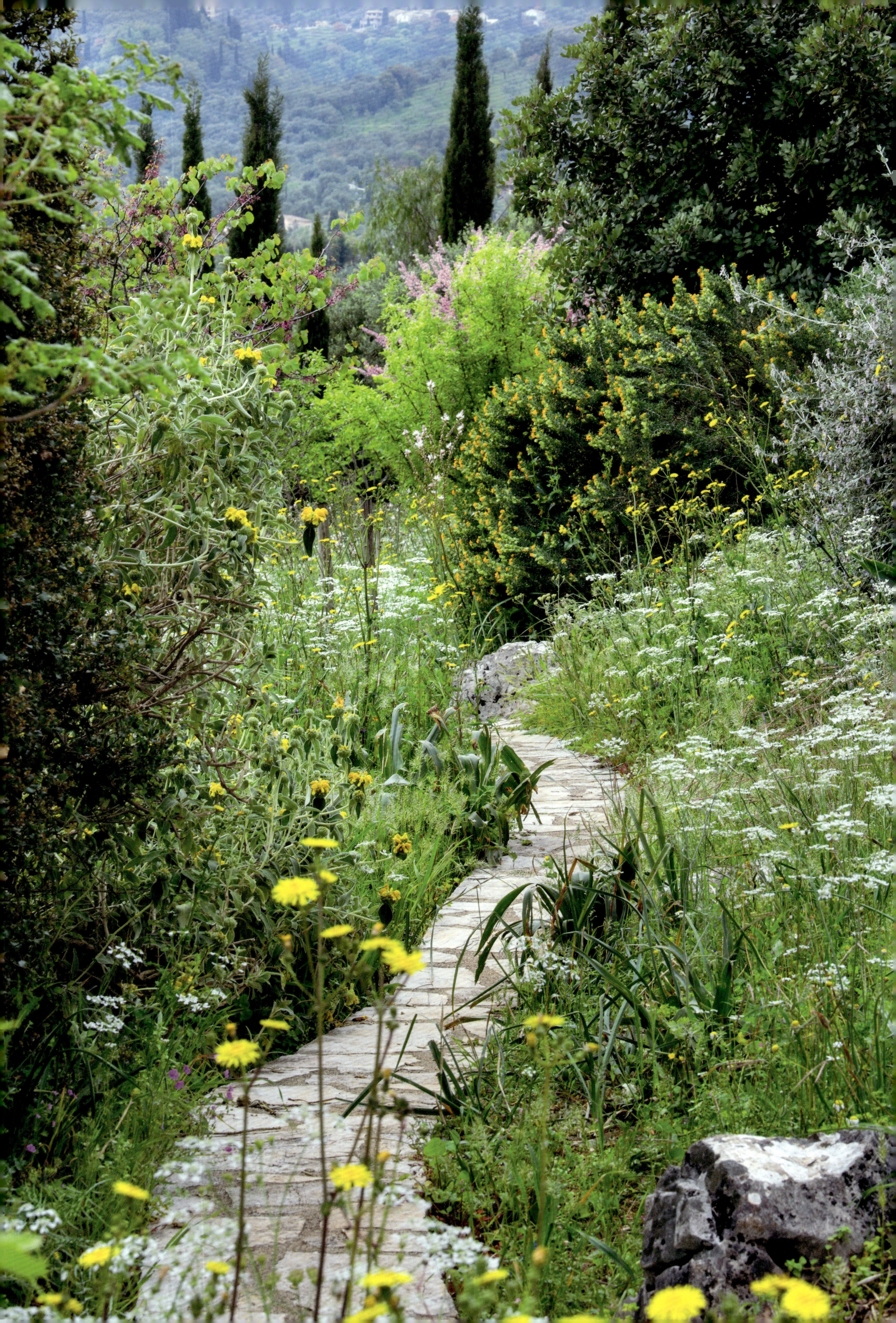

Kassiopia Estate

Overlooking the Corfu Straits, Kassiopia Estate in northeast Corfu was established in 2010 and has gardens designed and created by Jennifer Gay. The Estate's two traditional-style houses, Cassiopeia and Atolikos, have different gardens that are shaped by their contrasting environments—one rugged and open to the prevailing north wind, with winter temperatures that can fall below zero, the other sheltered and more south-facing—but flow naturally into one another. Gay's design provides simple naturalistic planting that links the houses into their surrounding environment. Large parts are site-generated, with subtle enhancements that bring out the natural emotive power of the place. The new planting makes extensive use of native species, reflecting Gay's deep understanding of the Mediterranean flora.

OPPOSITE
A path through the meadow below Atolikos. The native trees have been left in place and enhanced with silvery *Teucrium fruticans* and native shrubs.

The houses and hard landscaping were largely created with rocks quarried from the site. Gay regraded what had been steep slopes and introduced large quantities of top soil mixed with organic compost, adding gravel where needed for good drainage. An ancient fig tree predates the gardens. To it were added olive and pencil cypress trees (*Cupressus sempervirens* 'Stricta') along with Mediterranean shrubs such as myrtle and rosemary. Within the ornamental gardens are plantings of blue and white *Agapanthus*, lavenders, jasmine, *Verbena bonariensis*, Russian sage (*Perovskia atriplicifolia* 'Blue Spire'), and David Austin roses. Gay says, 'most of the plants have established themselves really well over the seven years since we installed them'.

Cassiopeia is entered through a graciously proportioned courtyard with two olive trees more than four hundred years old. Close to the house are gardens with swathes of pink gaura and culinary herbs such as the typical Greek oregano, basil, marjoram, and bay. Below the house, the planting is inspired by natural coastal plant communities but contains a much more diverse and colourful range of Mediterranean natives than might spontaneously grow together—pink- and white-flowering cistus and yellow-flowering tree medick and Jerusalem sage—interspersed with tough trees: Judas tree, pencil cypress, wild pear, turpentine tree, strawberry tree, and carob, along with pomegranate cultivars.

At the tip of the headland Gay found dense scrubby woodland with

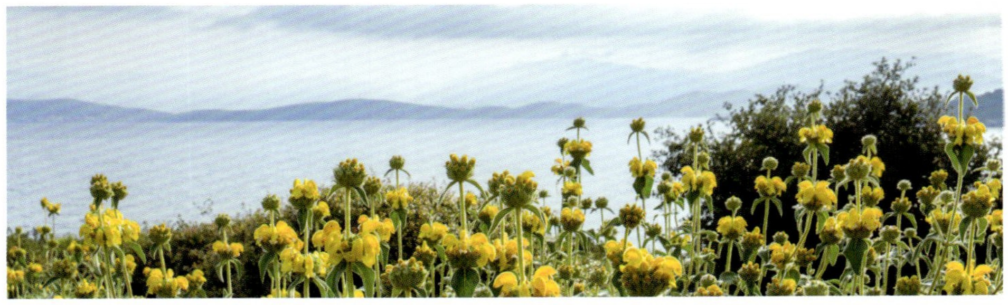

A mass planting of Jerusalem sage (*Phlomis fruticosa*) on the headland.

typical multi-trunked trees of the *maquis*: kermes oak (*Quercus coccifera*), Mediterranean buckthorn (*Rhamnus alaternus*), mock privet (*Phillyrea angustifolia*), and turpentine tree. She left these in place to form glades with views of the sea, pruning and shaping the trees, clearing away brush, and in some places adding shiny evergreen clumps of large-leaved butcher's broom (*Ruscus hypophyllum*). A carpet of wild pink ivy-leaved cyclamen blooms under these trees in autumn.

Atolikos is protected from wind and the atmosphere is gentler. Around the house are terraces with sheltered spaces for non-native plants, including *Echium fastuosum*, *Bougainvillea glabra*, and *Plumbago auriculata*. Taking advantage of the shelter are shade trees chosen for their summer flowers: black locust (*Robinia pseudoacacia*), mauve-flowering Indian bead tree (*Melia azedarach*), and—unusual in Corfu—evergreen Norfolk Island hibiscus (*Lagunaria patersonii*) with its star-shaped pink flowers. Below the pool terrace a lush meadow spreads out, shielded by thick groupings of strawberry trees and other natives on its south side. Gay worked sensitively to enhance what was already there: this began as an area of unmanaged waist-high grassland, but after it began to be mown in late spring and early winter a rich range of meadow plants re-emerged, and a procession of wildflowers now unfurls in a rainbow of colours throughout spring. The regular mowing keeps aggressive grasses from crowding out the other species; flowers are left to seed themselves and the area is allowed to dry out naturally in summer. Stone paths, some shaded by pergolas, weave through the gardens and past sitting areas, including one sheltered by a magnificent old wild pear tree, and down to the sea. Old terracotta urns, strategically placed, complement the planting. On the sheltered side of each house are small fruit orchards, whose range of trees includes oranges and lemons, tiny-fruited everbearing Mexican limes (*Citrus latifolia*), peach, apricot, cherry, and clementine.

The gardens are sensitively managed: rain and grey waste water are conserved for irrigation and garden clippings are composted. This provides a good habitat for wildlife. Birds, butterflies, lizards, and tortoises all abound.

OPPOSITE TOP
A Judas tree (*Cercis siliquastrum*) blooms in the wildflower meadow. Twice-yearly mowings keep aggressive species in check and encourage the natural diversity of flowering plants.

OPPOSITE BOTTOM
A path from the sea leads up through an old olive grove towards Cassiopeia.

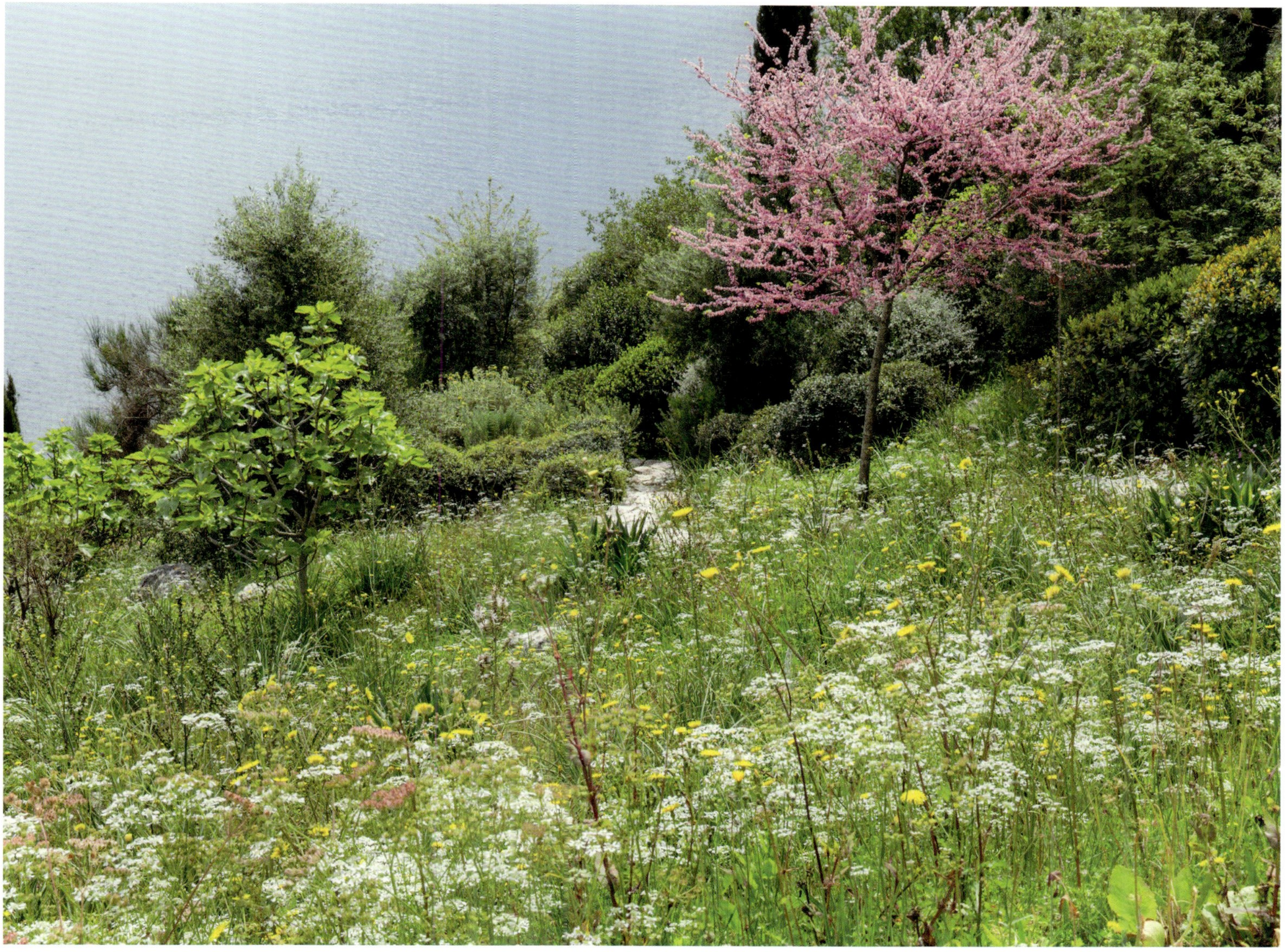
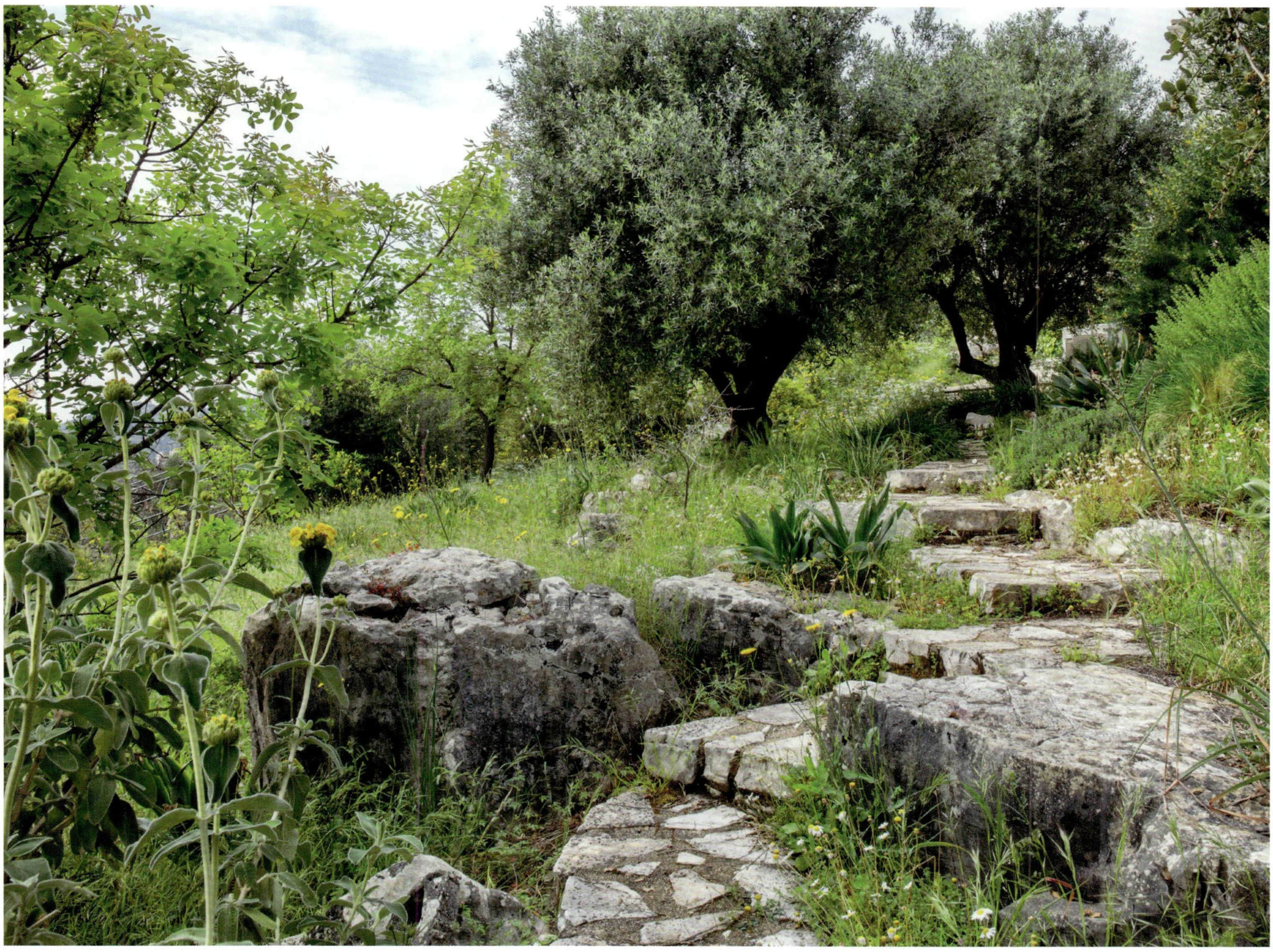

The coppery new leaves of native turpentine tree (*Pistacia terebinthus*) in spring.

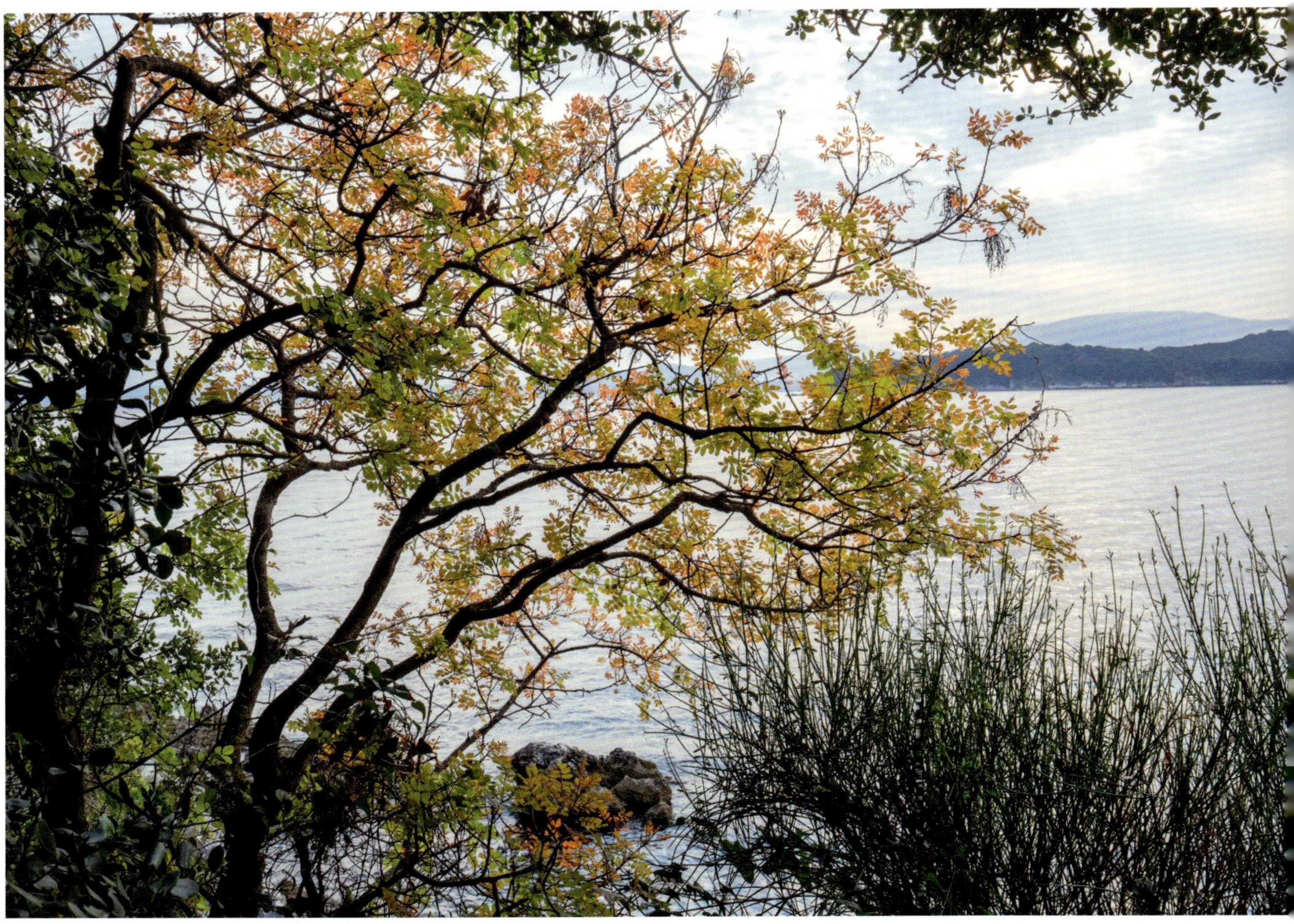

Cypresses, Judas trees, and strawberry trees (*Arbutus unedo*), along with olives.

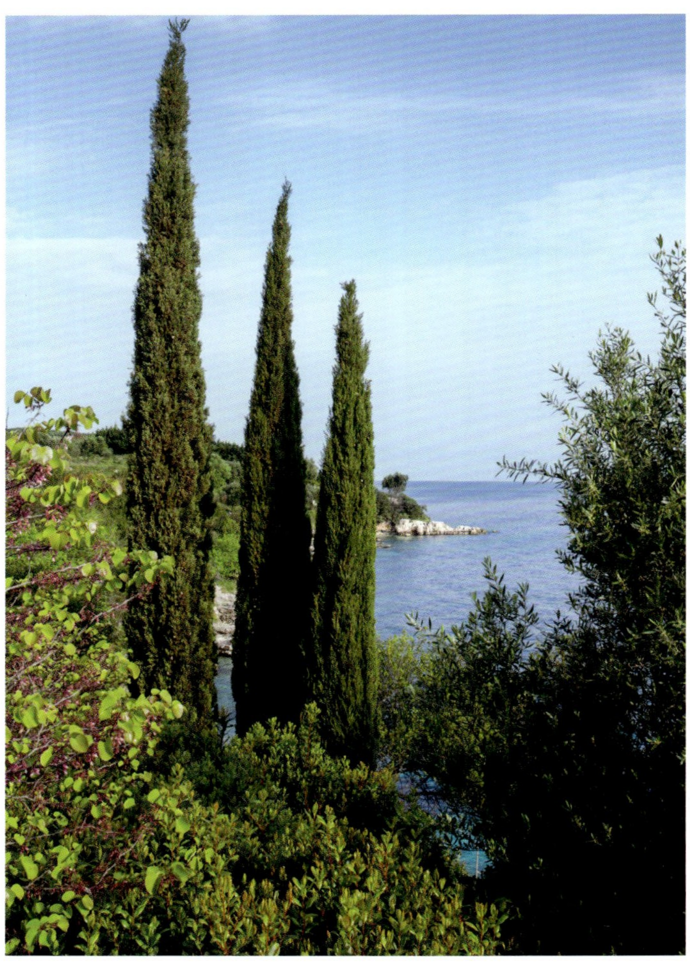

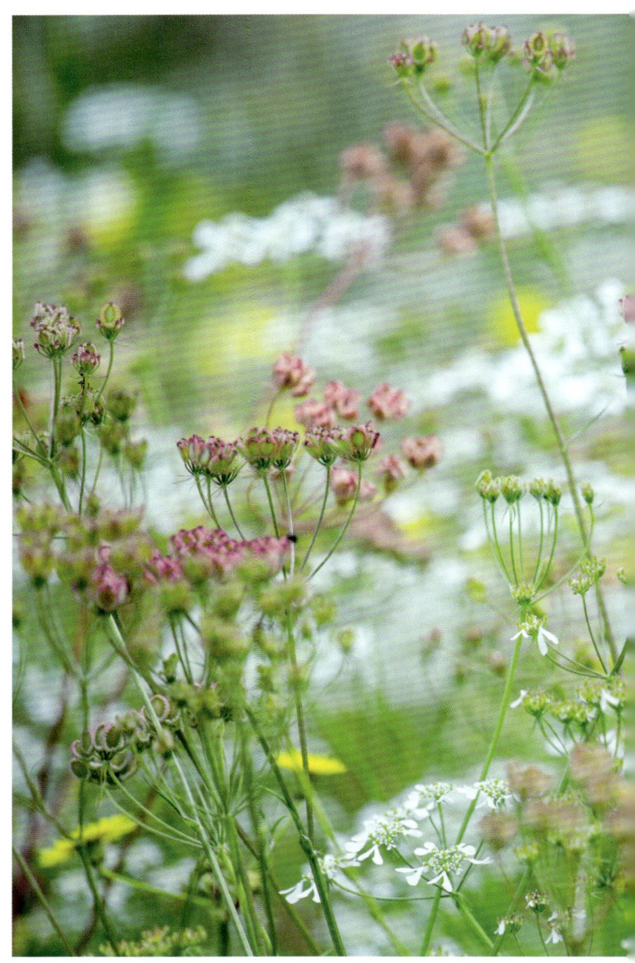

Wildflowers in the meadow in spring include *Tordylium apulum* and yellow *Sonchus oleraceus*.

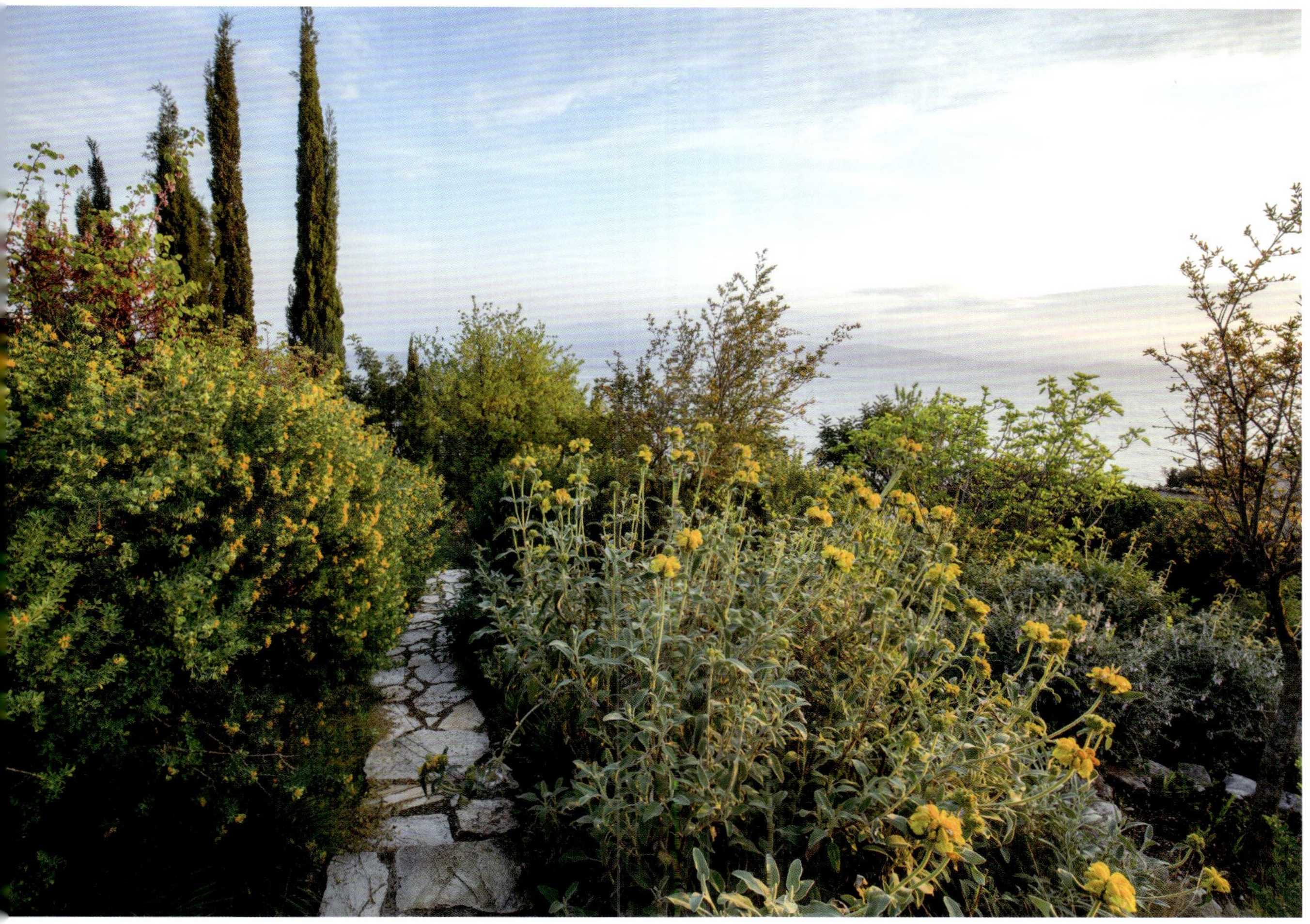

On the headland, Gay planted native flowering shrubs, including tree medick (*Medicago arborea*) and Jerusalem sage (*Phlomis fruticosa*), in groupings inspired by wild coastal plant communities and visibly related to those outside the garden.

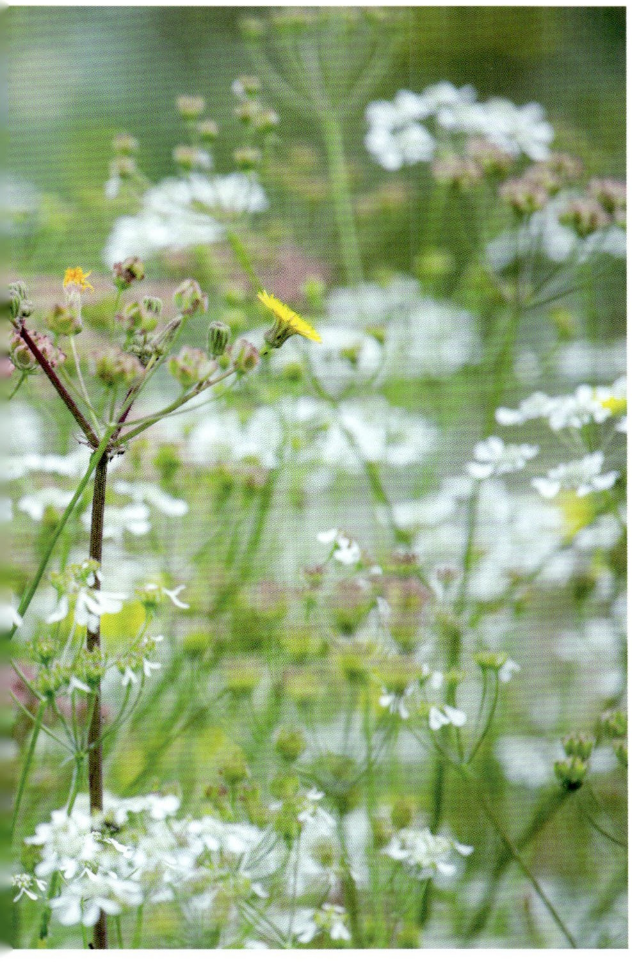

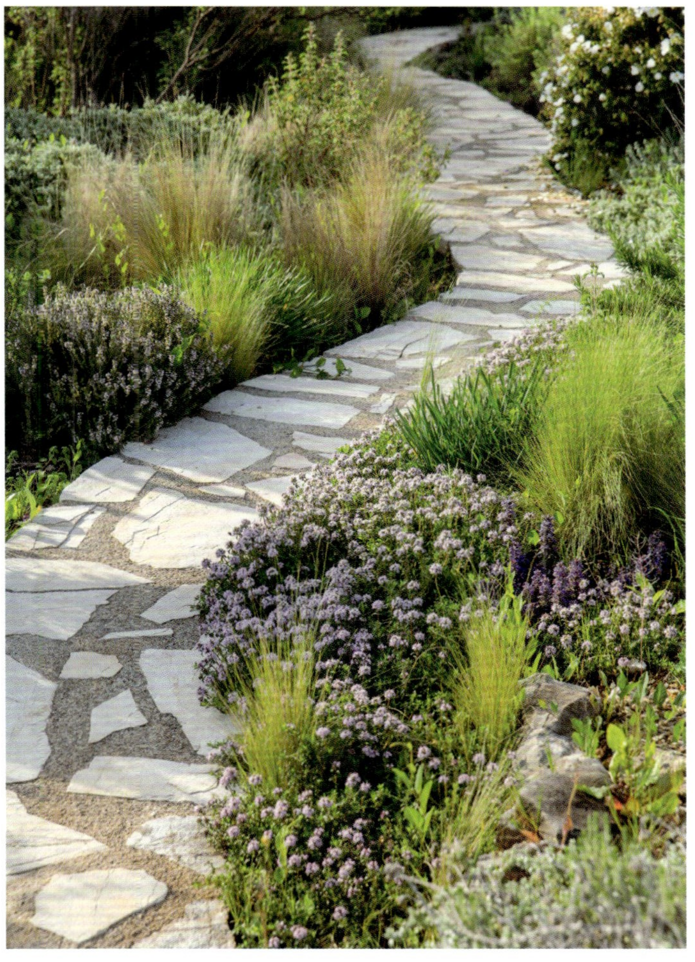

Herbaceous plants lining the stone pathways below Cassiopeia include thyme, *Ajuga reptans*, *Tulbaghia violacea*, and Mexican feathergrass (*Stipa tenuissima*), which stands up well in winter.

OVERLEAF
Sunrise over the headland at Kassiopia Estate.

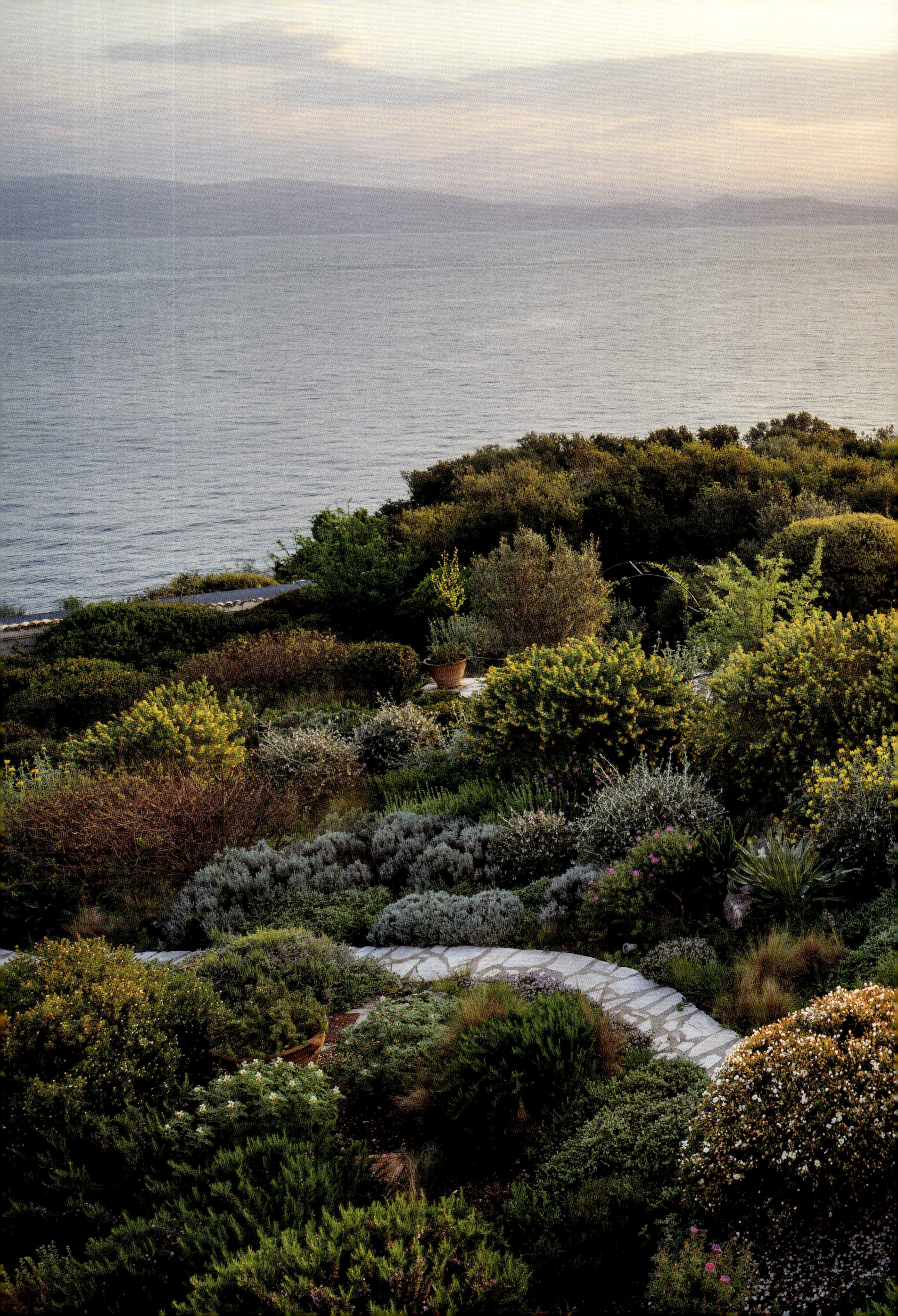

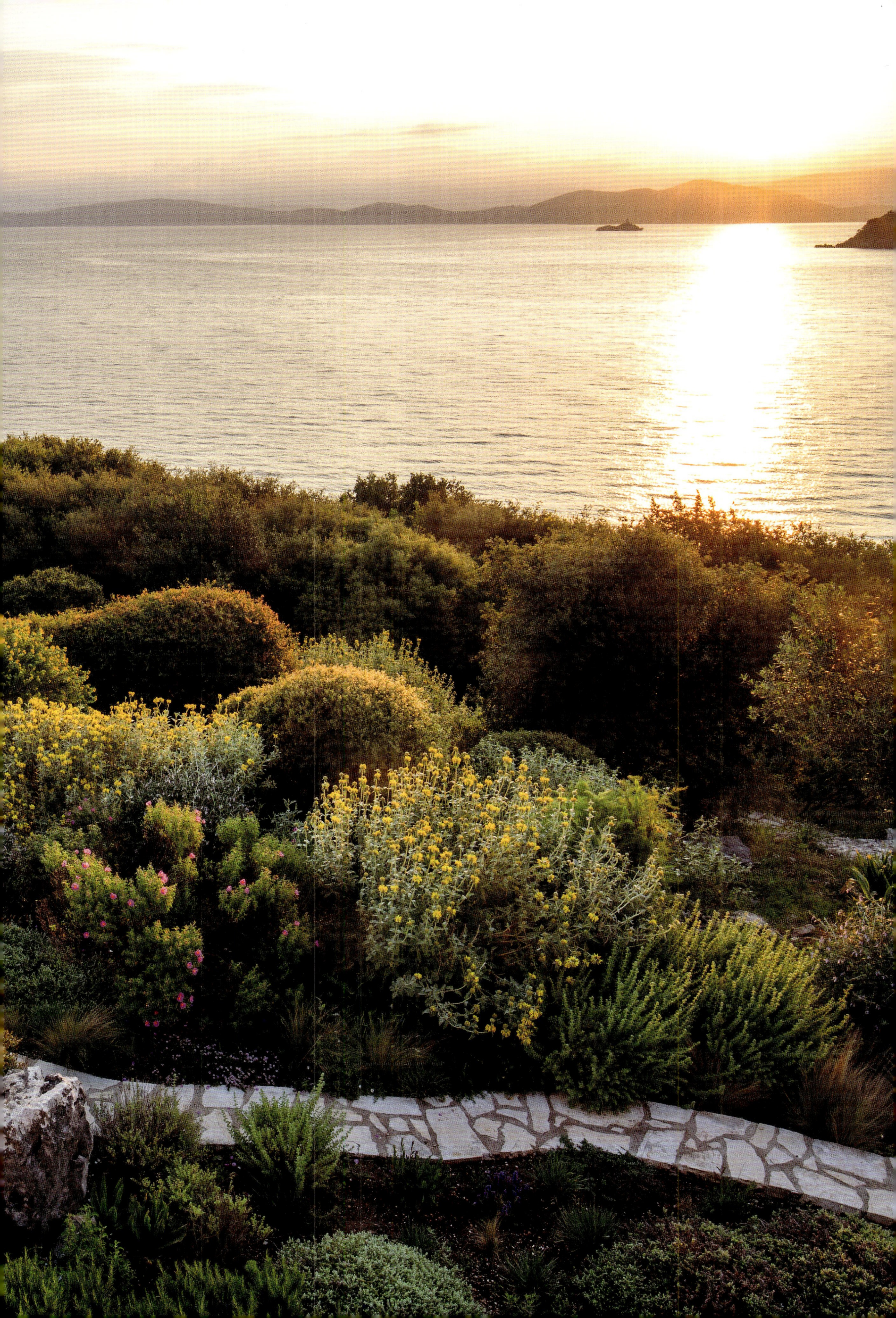

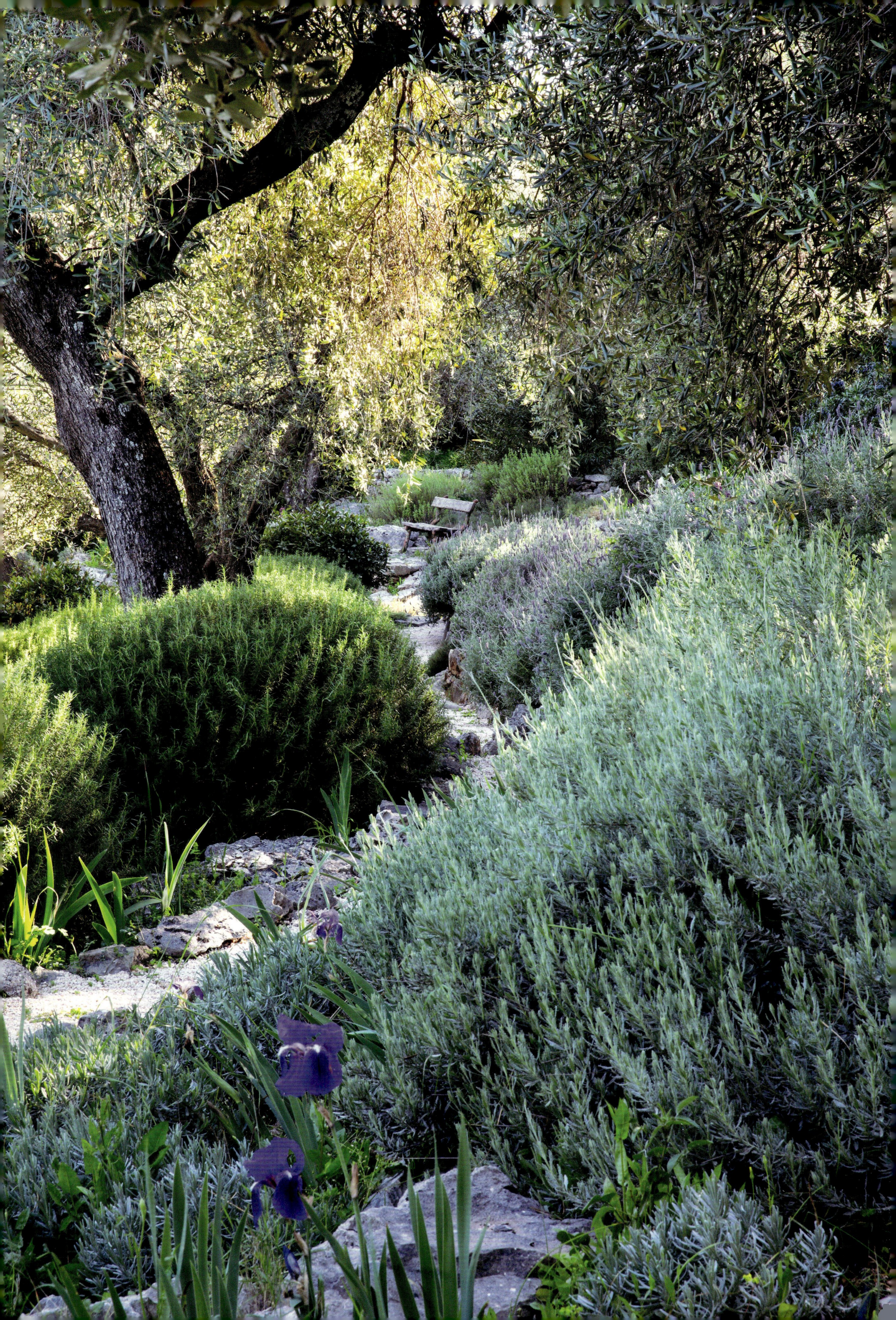

Sto Dásos

On a steep hillside at Keliá near Kassiópi, the garden at Sto Dásos was designed by Alithea Johns of Skopos Design and established about eleven years ago. From the sunny entrance courtyard, with its urbane, hospitable atmosphere, archways and staircases lead to partially hidden spaces, inviting private exploration of what is just out of view.

Above the entrance courtyard is a steep terraced bank with bearded irises that foreshadow those that are naturalised in the olive grove below. In summer, *Cestrum nocturnum*, daylilies, and purple *Verbena bonariensis* and *Tulbaghia violacea* come into their own, along with blue-flowering *Agapanthus* and Russian sage.

A series of patios, each with a different character, clusters around the house on its different levels; some offer wide open spaces for convivial groups and some are intimate shaded areas for quiet conversations—or just for watching the ever-changing views of sea, mountains, and sky. At the back of the house, the living room opens to the largest of these patios, whose key feature is the wide view of the sea and the Albanian mountains. Garden shapes and colours are kept very simple here and the edging of rosemary and glossy abelia is clipped to reflect the shape of the Cavo Bárbaro promontory in the distance.

Leaving the house, and passing the swimming pool below it, the path leads down the hill into a wilder space: an ancient olive grove, patterned mysteriously with light and shade and perfumed by plantings of lavender, rosemary, and thyme. At their edges, the planted olive terraces merge naturally into the wild landscape.

Even with its sophisticated air, this is a garden that sits naturally in its site. Above the entrance courtyard, the planting on the terraced layers gradually gives way to the wild landscape. Rock is never far from the surface, and Johns has incorporated and celebrated the naturally occurring boulders and slabs as parts of her design, while using the same stone in cut forms for walls and paving. Antique brick made of Corfiot clay is used for wall toppings and for borders in the paving that emphasise the lines and angles of the designed space. These choices help create a sure-handed balance between the surrounding landscape and Rahdy Elwan's graceful architecture of the house.

OPPOSITE
The garden embraces the old olive grove below the house. Here, paths wend along the terraces, and the wild plants have been supplemented with lavender, rosemary, and other drought-tolerant shrubs and herbs.

A view of Cavo Bárbaro and the lighthouse island of Kaparelli from one of the many inviting sitting areas around the house.

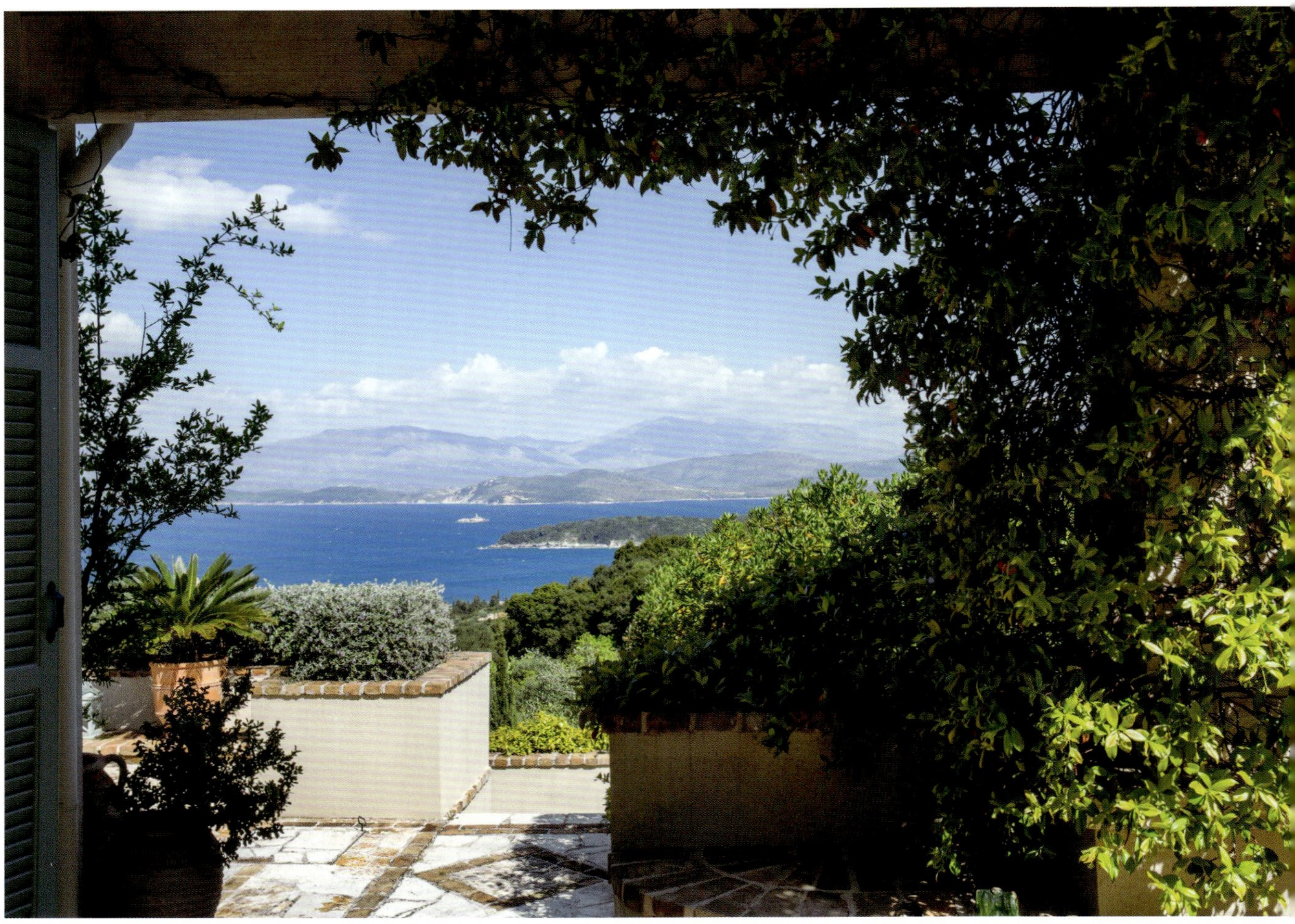

Afternoon patterns of light and shade play in the olive grove below the house.

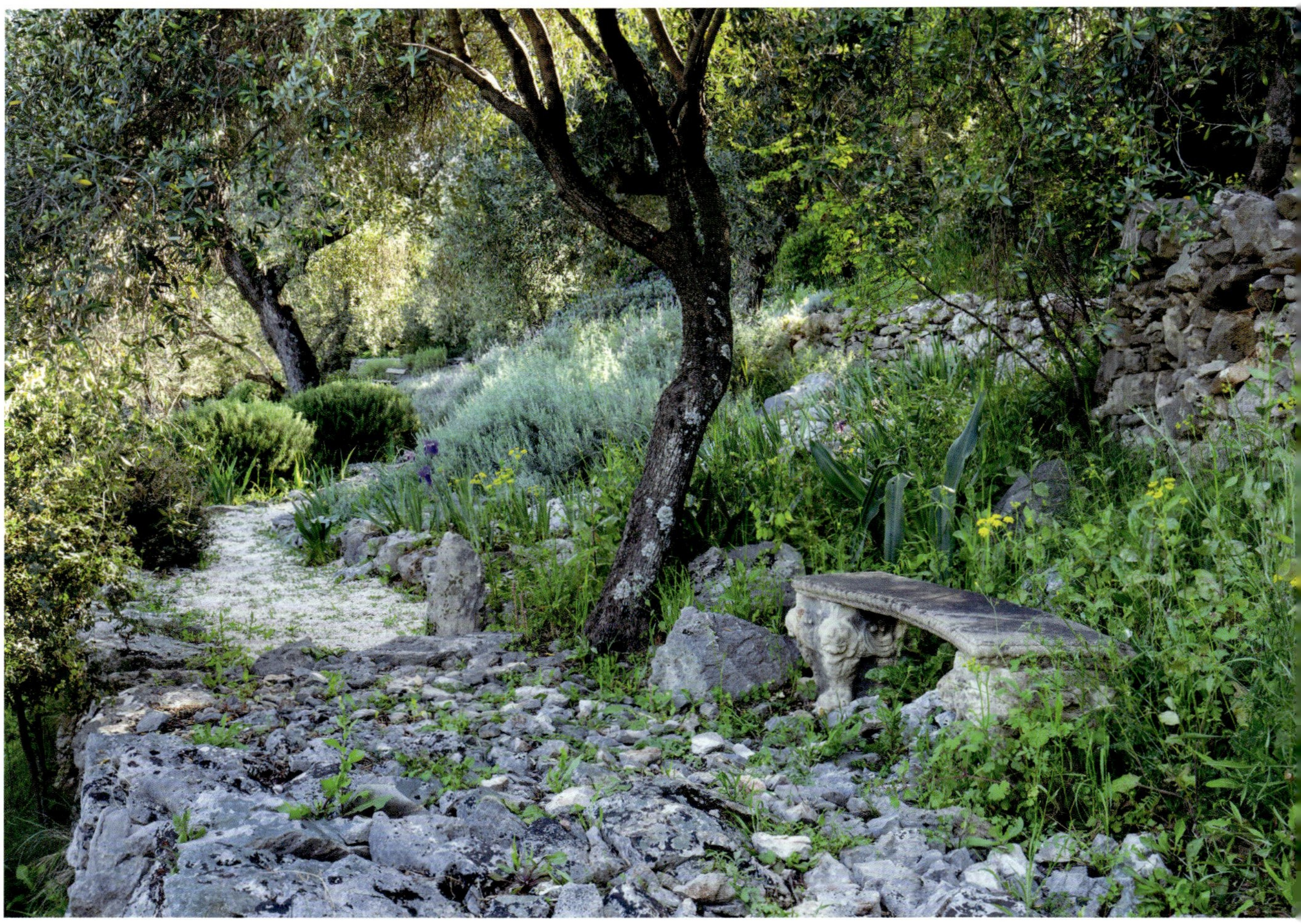

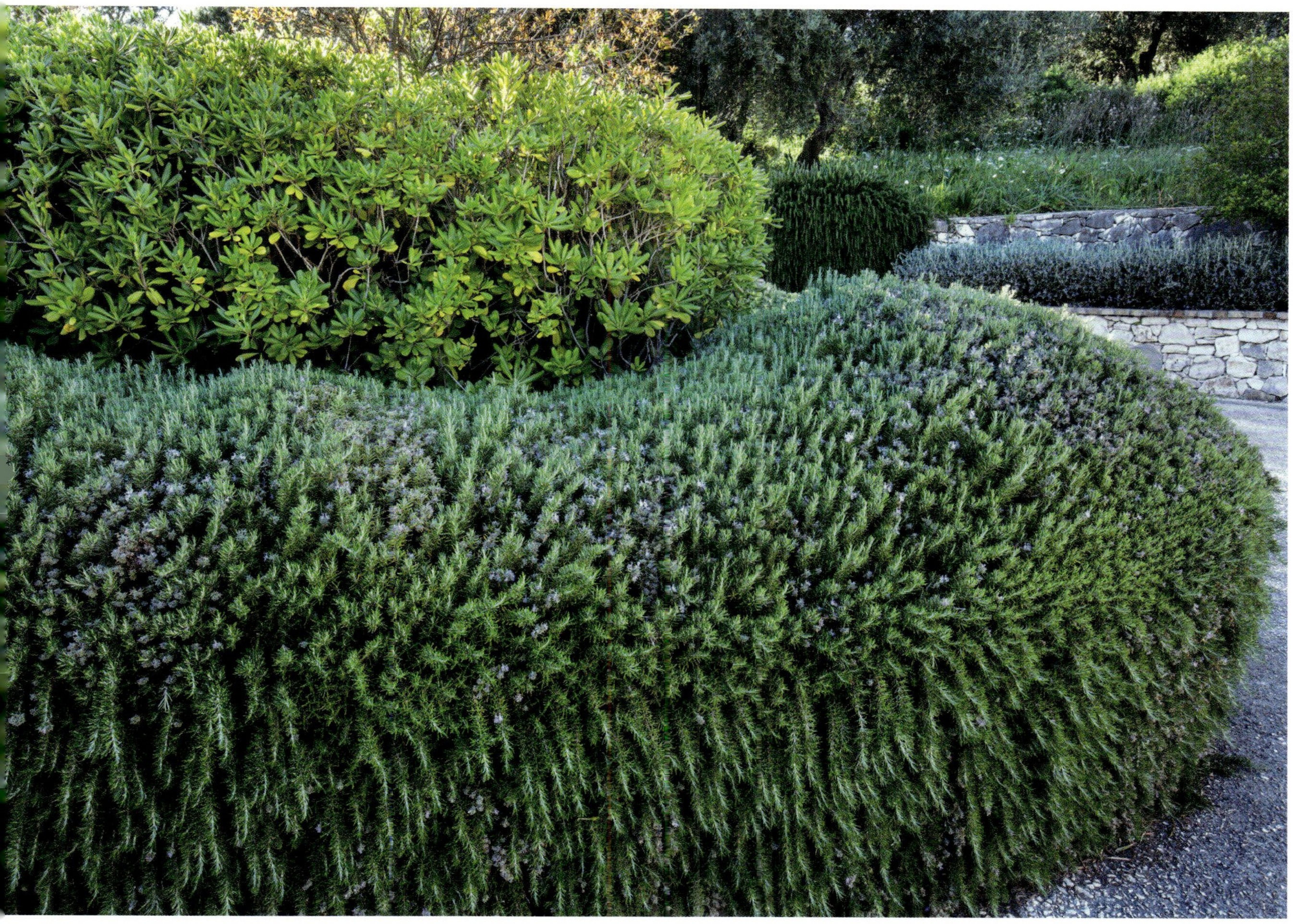

Sculptural effects are achieved with this simple planting of *Pittosporum tobira* and rosemary.

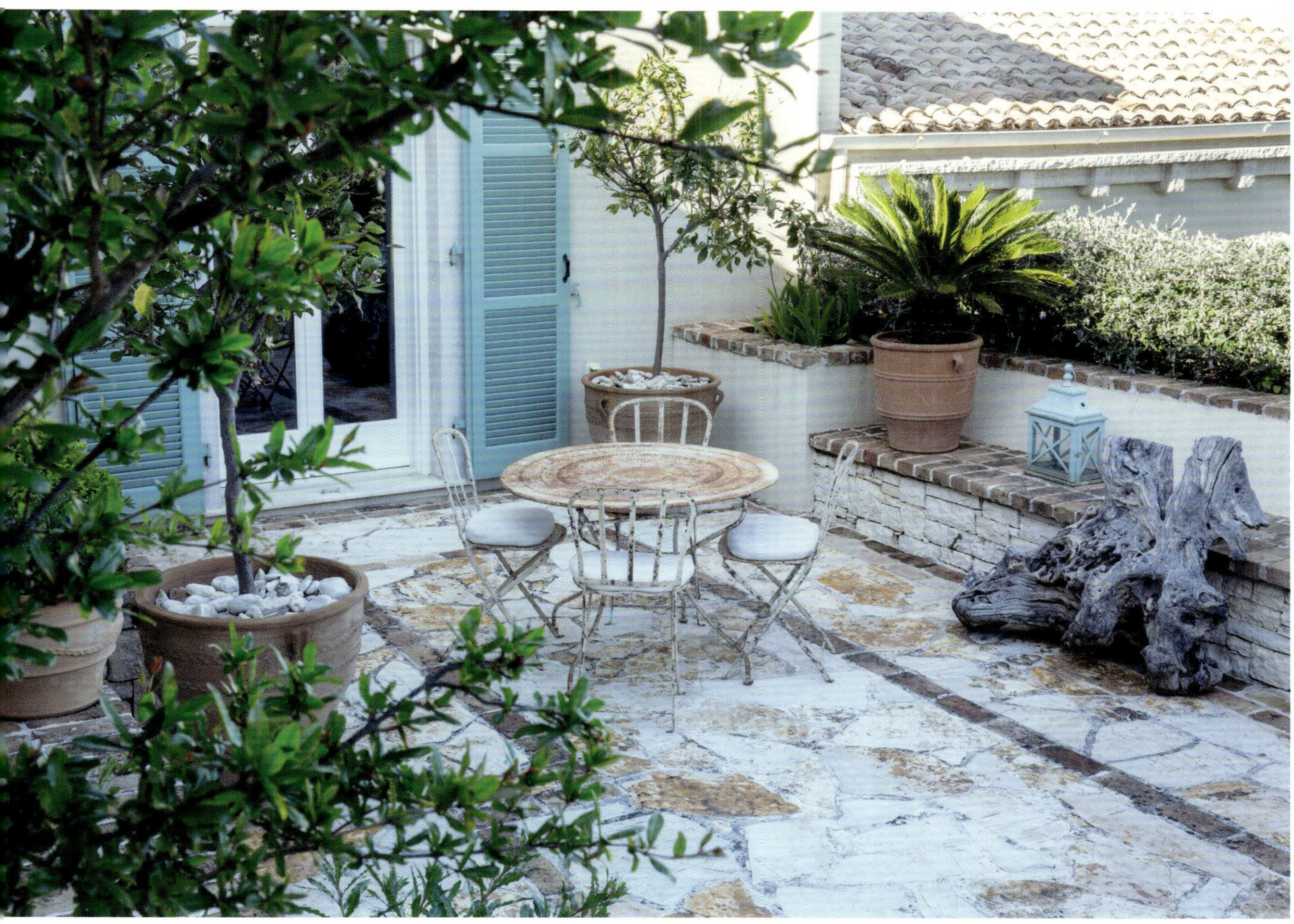

Descending the hillside, a staircase links a series of patios adjacent to the house. Here, the pots contain a pomegranate tree and a cycad *(Cycas revoluta)*.

In spring, a courtyard on the house's western side is filled with the scent of wisteria.

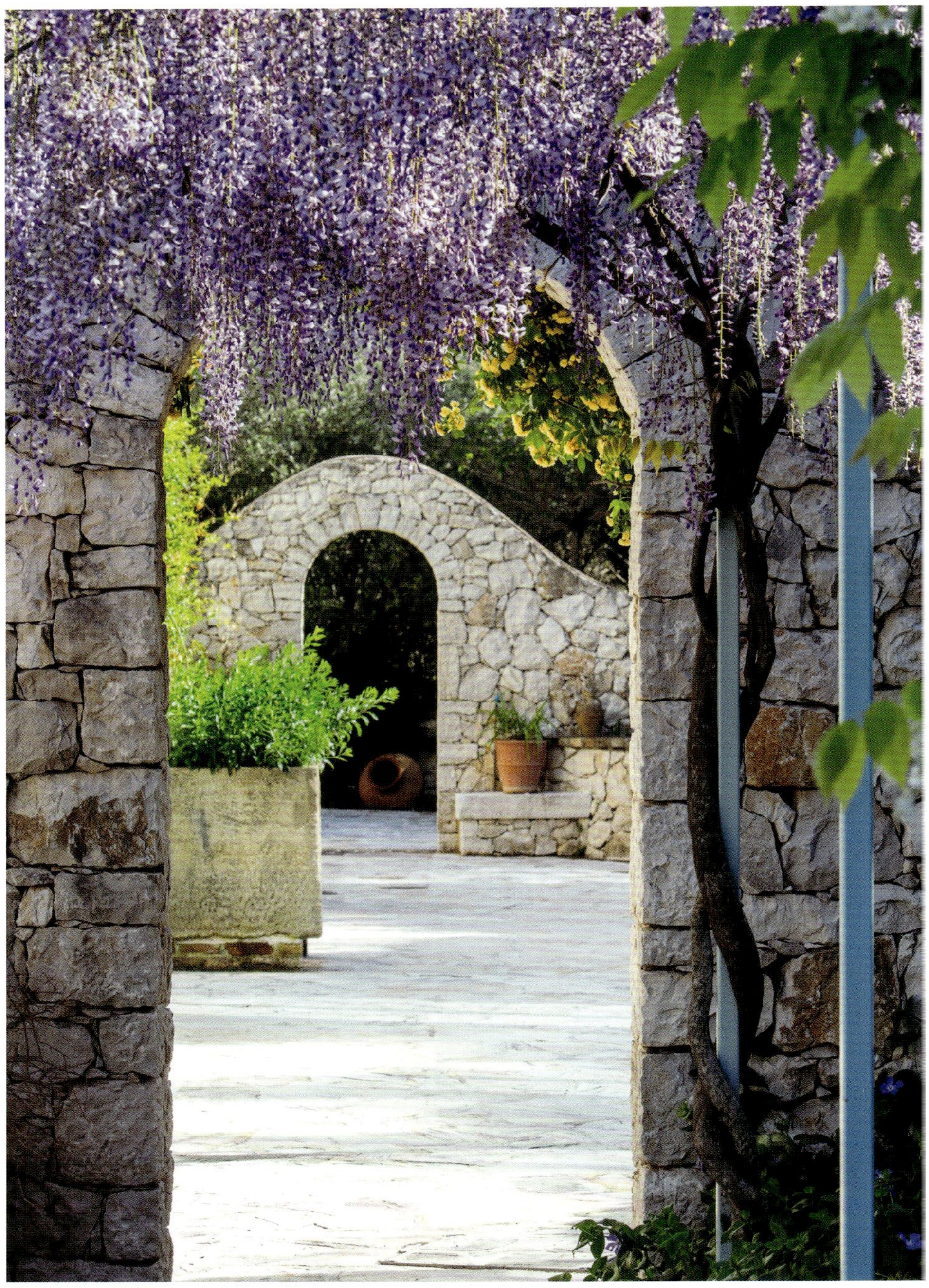

OPPOSITE TOP
In the entrance courtyard with its multiple stone arches, a yellow Banks' rose blooms in April. Here, as in much of the garden, naturally occurring boulders are incorporated into the design.

Johns' design features a restrained choice of plants, with very strong foundations of evergreens and greys that look good in all seasons, complemented by romantically flowering climbing roses, jasmine, and wisteria. Signature plants, all chosen for their drought-resistance, are grey-leaved tree germander and *Westringia fruticosa*; dark green *Pittosporum tobira* 'Nana'; sweetpea bush (*Polygala myrtifolia*), with its rich purple flowers in autumn; prostrate rosemary; glossy abelia; star jasmine; and bearded iris. Shrubs are pruned into disciplined shapes close to the house, and loosely into ball shapes in the informal lower section of the garden.

OPPOSITE BOTTOM
Next to the graceful curving staircase opposite the house is a pepper tree (*Schinus molle*), whose weeping branches respond to all but the slightest wind.

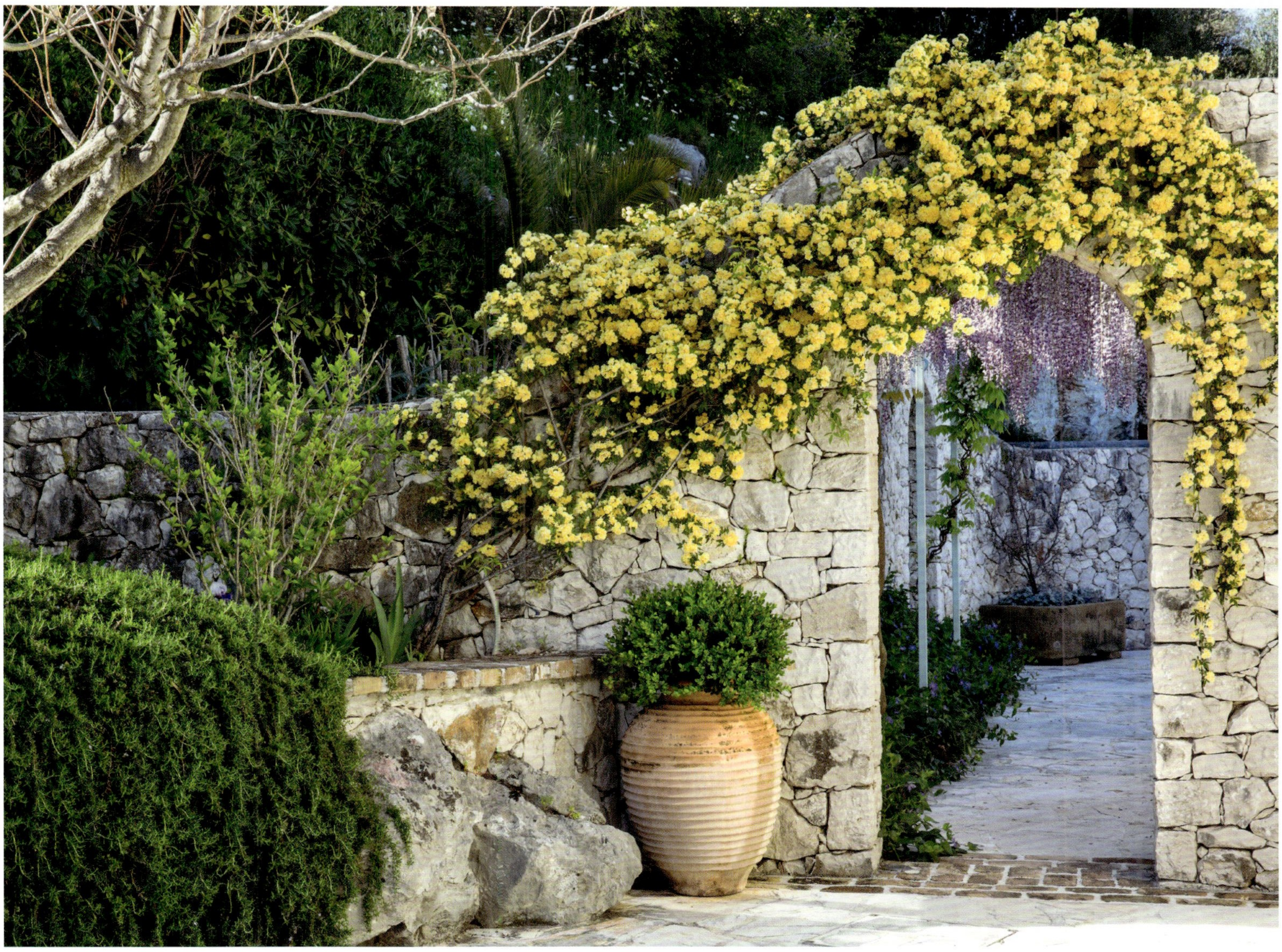

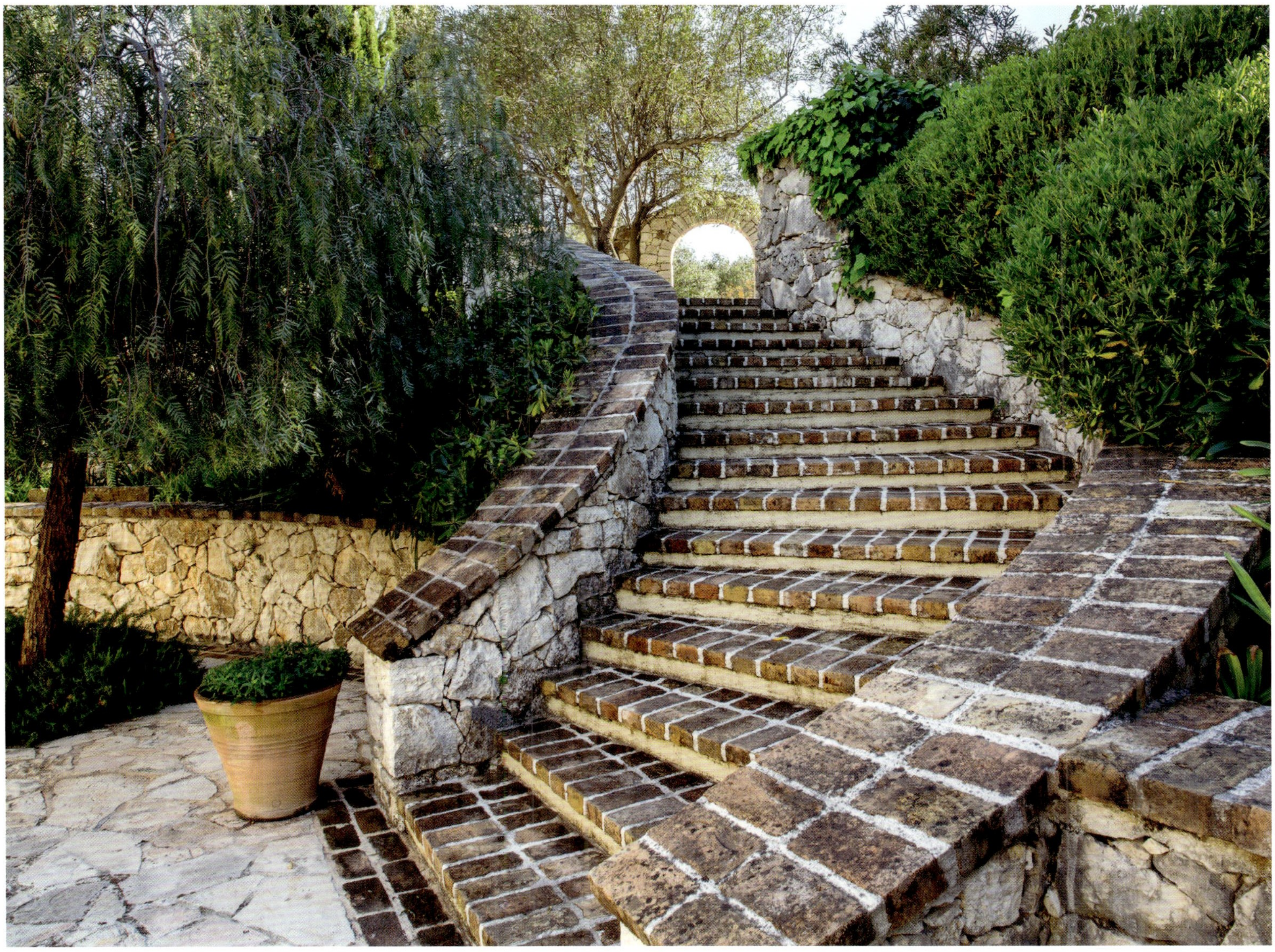

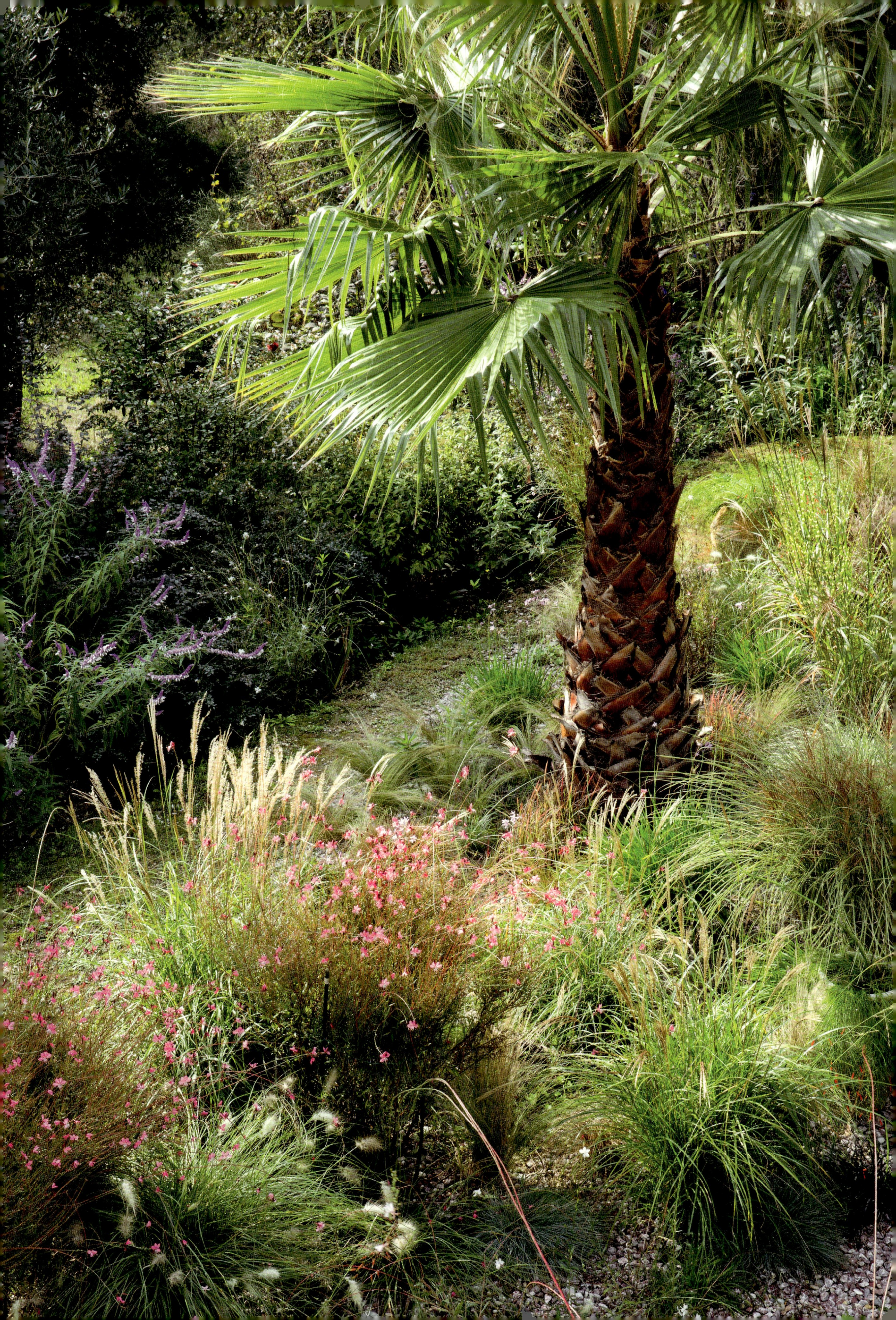

A garden in Sgombou

A huge range of plants thrives in this hillside garden of intimate spaces in central Corfu, rewarding the owner's years of hard work and reflecting her passion to find out what will grow locally, even if transposed from its normal surroundings. Designing the garden, with its great sensitivity to plant forms and colours, the owner Anne Jerram took elements of inspiration from her British gardening heroes Beth Chatto and Christopher Lloyd,[39] but deftly adapted them to the Corfiot setting. Many of her plants came from garden centres up and down the island but many others arrived as cuttings, small plants, or seeds traded with friends or brought from England.

About fifteen hundred square metres in size, the garden is sited in a sheltered hollow facing southeast over a romantic view of olive-covered hills. Large trees provide structure and vital shade in summer: old olives and pines; a huge eucalyptus on the western border; a grove of bushy native cypresses (*Cupressus sempervirens* var. *horizontalis*) through which one approaches the house; a tall Canary palm; and new fan palms that the owners have planted.

During its first seven years, each square metre of the garden received almost a truckload of compost—and in high summer Anne and her partner Bengt Bergman may spend up to four hours a day watering. The garden shows the results of this dedication, looking much more mature than its actual age of twelve years.

At the entrance to the property, the cypresses have been pruned to allow light to reach the under-planting: sunlight and shade play on the silver leaves of *Echium fastuosum*, *Miscanthus* 'Flamingo', and fleshy, fuzzy-textured *Tradescantia sillamontana*, along with dark green *Pittosporum tobira* 'Nana', yucca, and bearded irises. On the upper side of the lawn, where the planting bed began as 'just rubble over rock', Anne and Bengt hacked out holes and filled them with soil for foundation plantings of cotoneaster, other evergreen shrubs, and a group of agaves. Dramatic shadows are cast over the lawn in summer by the large Canary palm and by a whiskery young desert fan palm (*Washingtonia filifera*) in the lawn's centre, their shapes echoed by those of a range of spiky plants in pots, including *Dasylirion* and agaves.

OPPOSITE
The garden is remarkable for its lush summer growth and subtle interplay of light and colour. Here *Miscanthus sinensis*, *Salvia leucantha*, and *Gaura lindheimeri* 'Rosyjane' are planted with a Chinese windmill palm (*Trachycarpus fortunei*).

39. See, for example, Beth Chatto, *The Dry Garden* (London: Orion Press, 1978), and Christopher Lloyd, *The Well-Tempered Garden* (London: Harper Collins, 1970).

A collection of succulents, including jade plants (*Crassula ovata*), *Echeveria* varieties, and *Aeonium arboreum* 'Atropurpureum'.

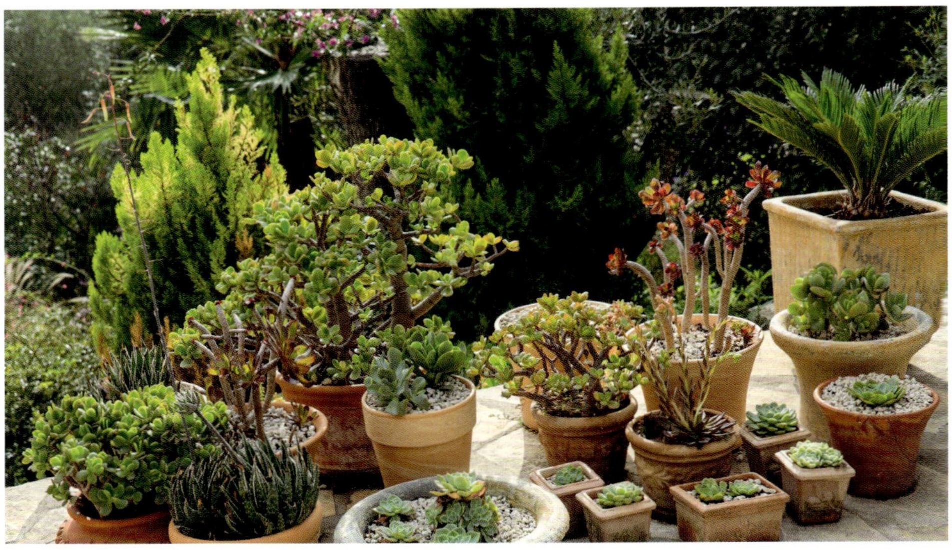

OPPOSITE
In front of an old olive tree, *Gaura lindheimeri* 'Rosyjane' mingles with *Miscanthus sinensis*, *Cortaderia selloana*, and *Pennisetum* species.

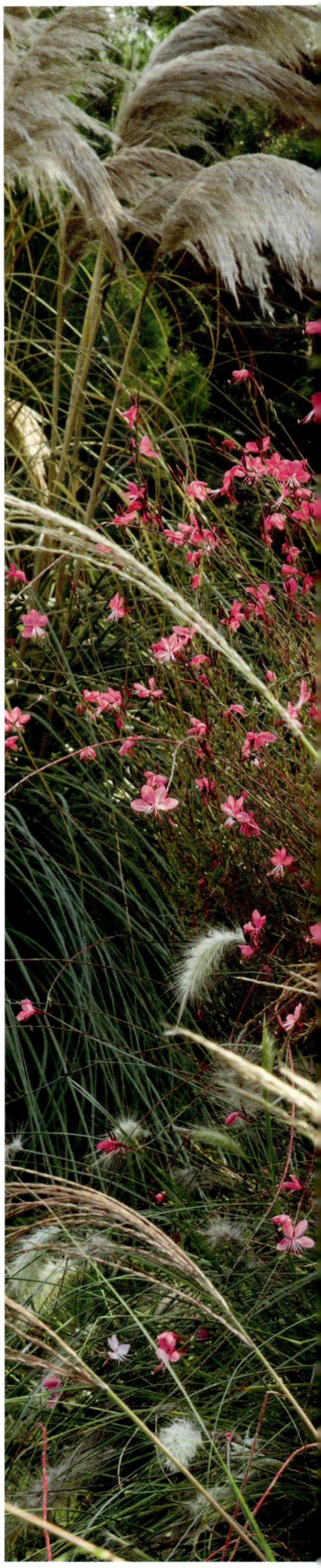

Steps lead downhill beside a rockery. Though this looks completely natural it has been dug out of solid rock, with new soil added and extra rocks strategically placed to retain it. Plants in this area are highly drought resistant, with long roots that help keep the soil in place. They include the useful groundcover *Bulbine frutescens* in both yellow- and orange-flowering varieties.

Lower down, the mood changes: a large bed anchored by an original olive tree and a Chinese windmill palm contains a spectacular range of large grasses and pink gaura, all set in a gravel mix. In this inspired combination of textures and shapes, the feathery and fluffy grasses, moving in the slightest wind, contrast with the architectural shapes of the palm and the rough dark surfaces of the olive trunk and branches.

The long herbaceous beds on this level are partly protected from the summer sun by large trees; they are mulched regularly with compost and generously watered by hand in summer. The plantings here are luxuriant, with a deep appreciation for the interplay of flower colours. They include perennials with flowers in hot colours—red, orange, and a range of purples—and deep blue, rhythmically interspersed with dark purple- and bronze-leaved shrubs. Smoke tree (*Cotinus coggygria*) and *Berberis thunbergii*, with their smouldering purple leaves, are combined with purplish-bronze hop bush (*Dodonea viscosa* 'Purpurea') and with the burgundy-flowered South American shrub, *Iochroma coccinea*. Among these shrubs are orange-flowered butterfly weed (*Asclepias tuberosa*), purple *Verbena bonariensis*, and many sages: *Salvia leucantha* with its silver leaves, deep purple bracts, and shrubby habit; crimson-flowered *S. coccinea* and shade-loving *S. elegans*; and indigo-flowered *S. guaranitica*.

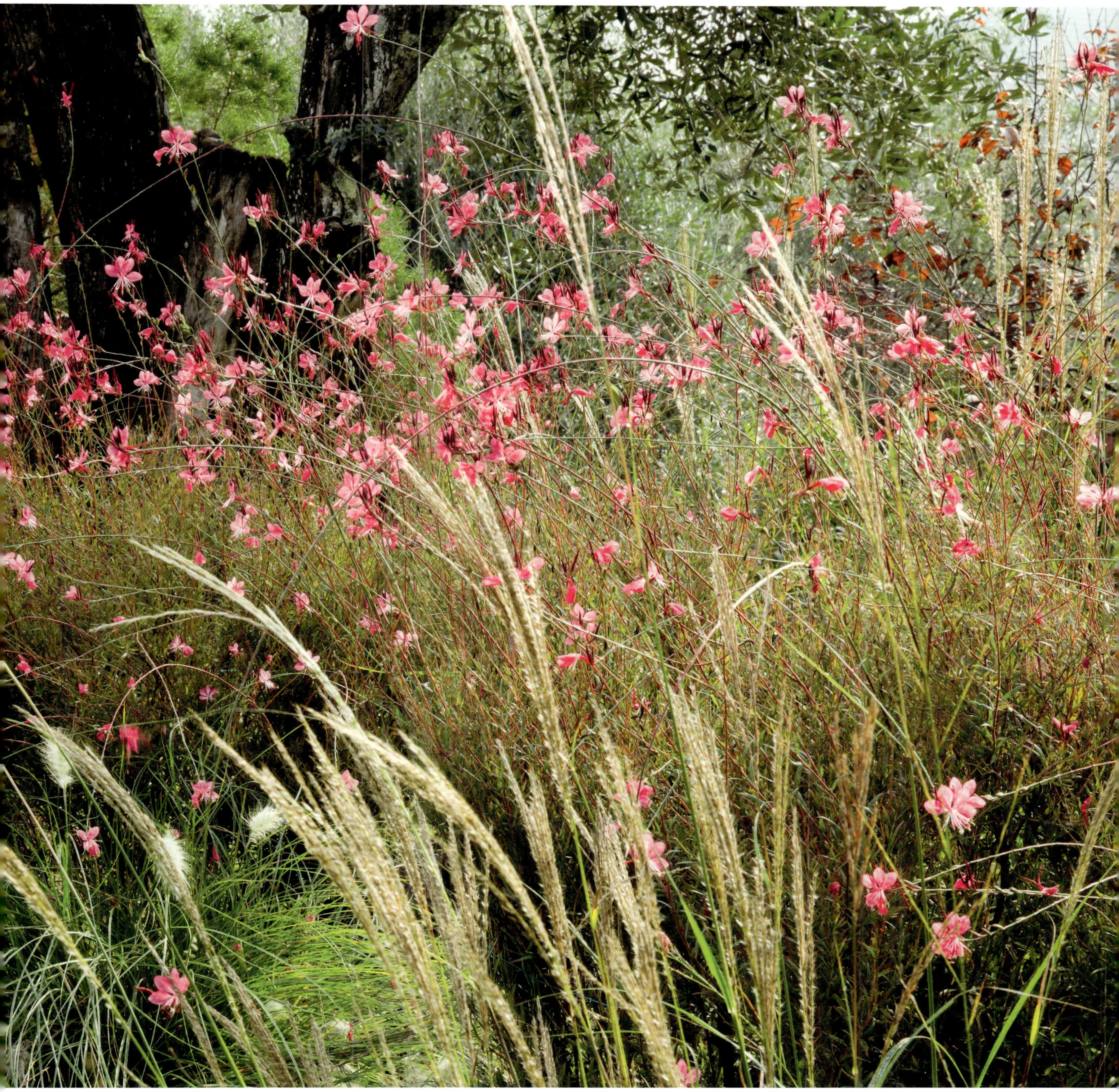

OVERLEAF
Anne finds that *Salvia guaranitica* grows well in partial shade with moderate summer water.

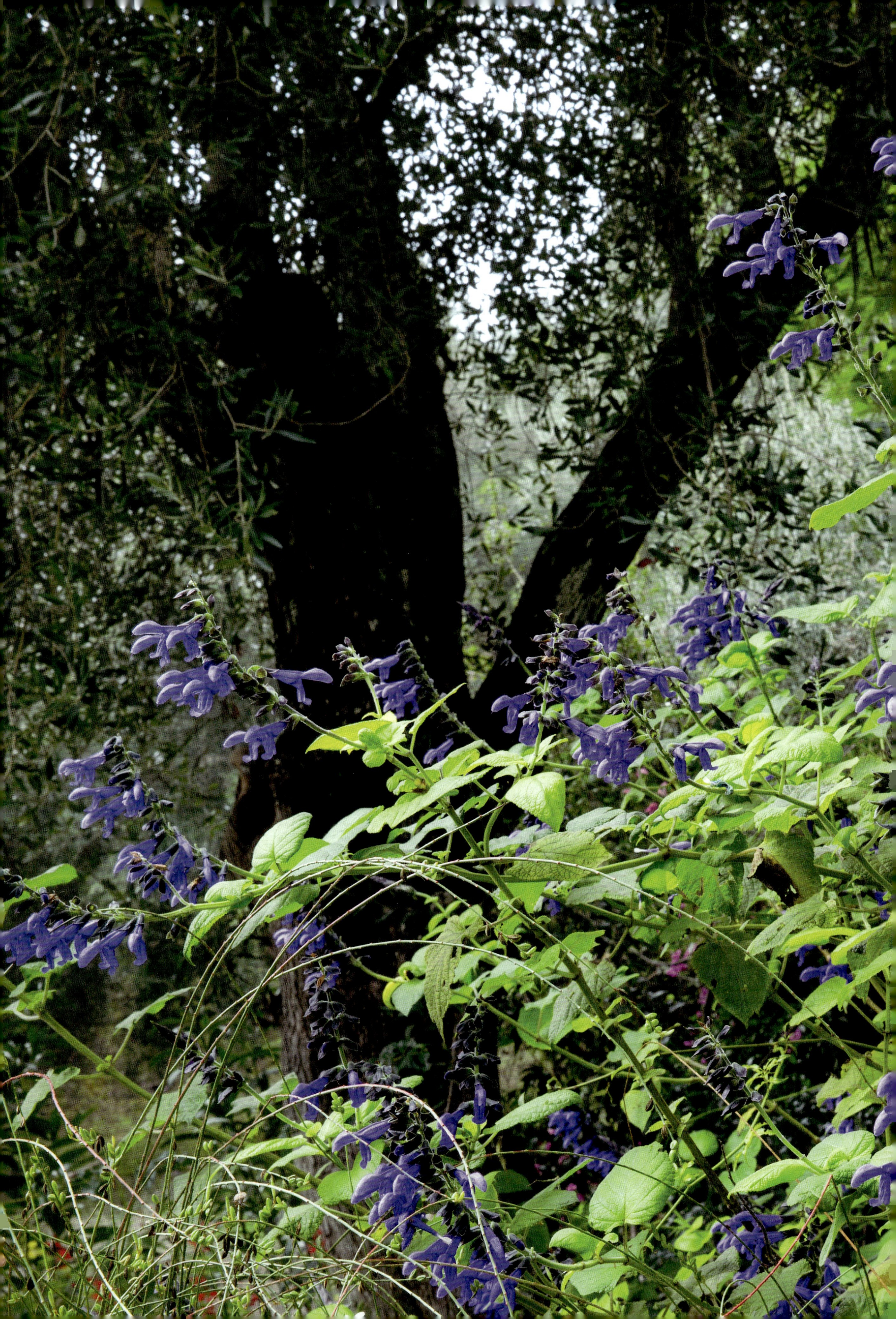

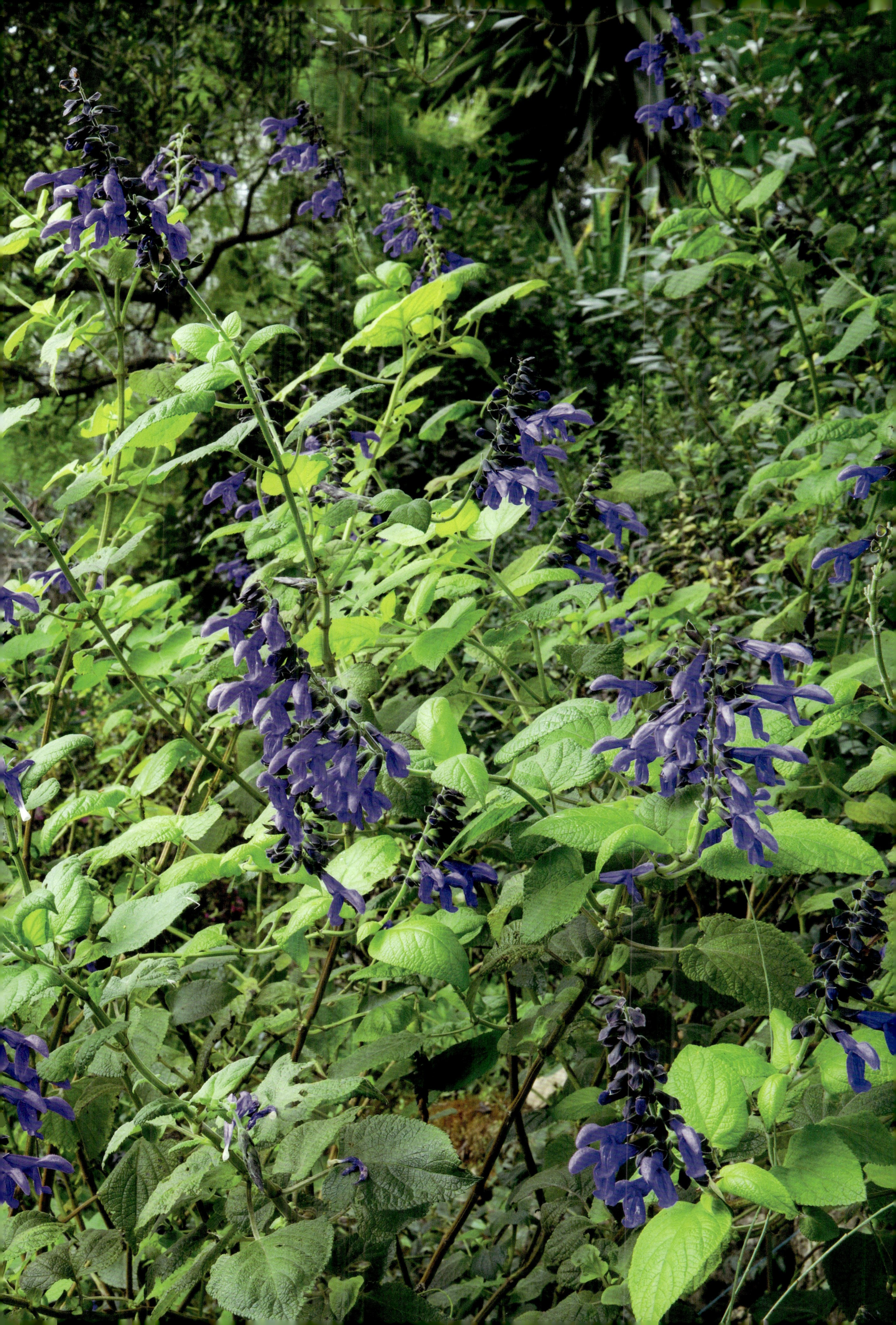

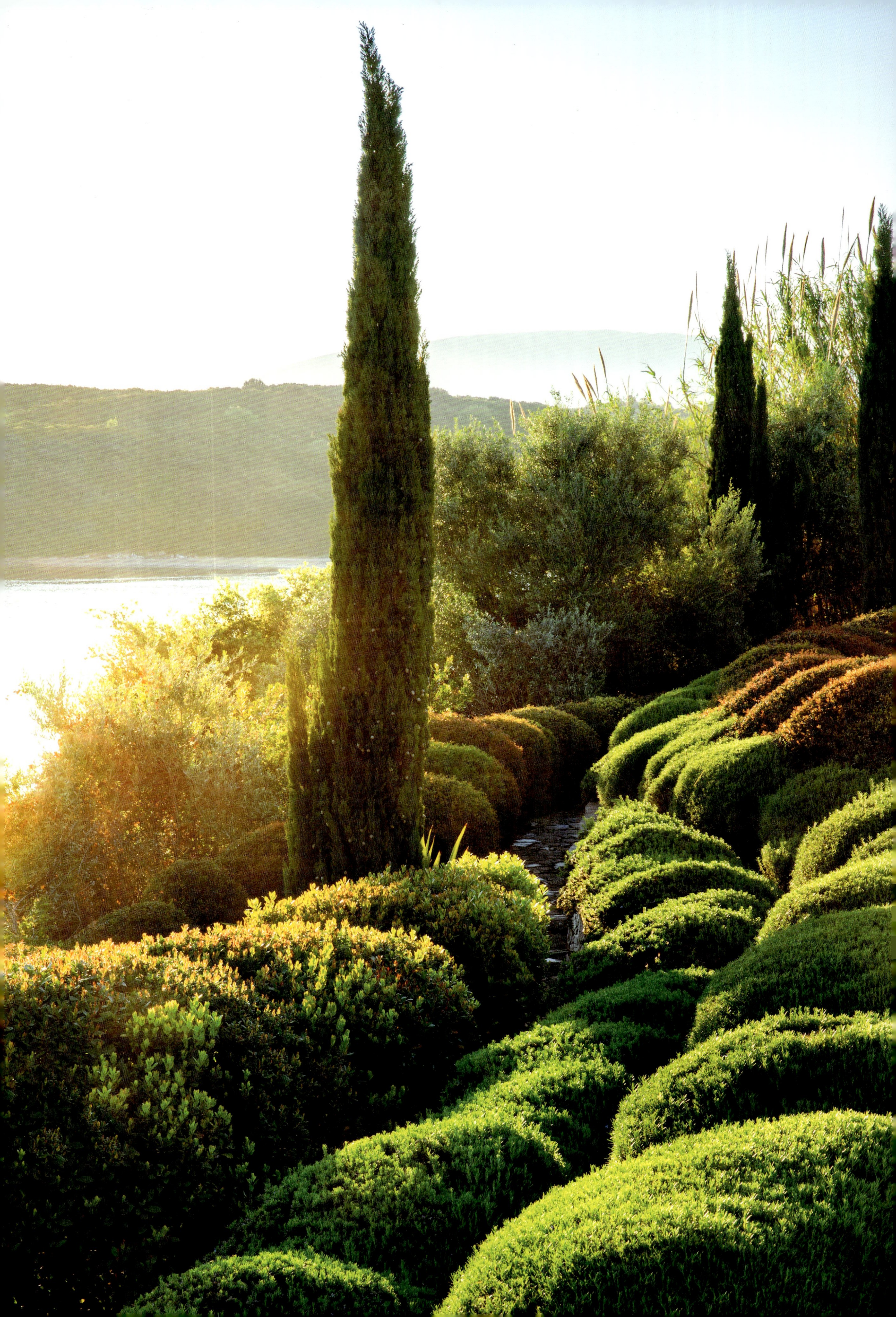

Cavo Alkyóni

The garden at Cavo Alkyóni (Kingfisher Point) is remarkable for its masterly treatment of space and scale. Its grand open spaces, with formal elements, wide views, and large sheets of water, seem all the more inspiring because of their contrast with the intimate sheltered courtyards of the two houses here, and with the narrow paths that lead between dense, sculpted shrubs, beckoning the visitor on to see what might lie beyond the next bend.

Contemporary in their design, the buildings and garden also speak of a deep understanding of local vernacular architecture and of the owner's love of the local landscape, born of long familiarity. A collaboration between the owner and his late, lamented, professional colleague and friend, architect Robert Turner, with landscaping by Alithea Johns of Skopos Design, Cavo Alkyóni interprets historical architectural themes in a modern context, respecting local building traditions while also conveying something of a pan-mediterranean atmosphere. Before starting work, Turner and the Skopos partners visited villages throughout northern Corfu, including the evocative, mainly-ruined, Old Períthia, and investigated local traditional skills in stone- and woodworking.

Today it is hard to believe that when the owner acquired the three-hectare site it had been denuded by his predecessors, who had planned to develop it as a caravan park. Construction of Amalthéa and Pelagía, the two linked houses on the estate, began in 2006 and the gardens were planted soon afterwards.

Once inside the entrance gates and up the driveway from the road, leaving the car in the sheltered forecourt, one is drawn to a pair of thick oak double doors in a wall. Inside, the path curves between high walls edged with soft shapes of tall grasses and mounded shrubs. Water falls into an old stone basin from a group of simple faucets in the wall. What lies ahead is not in view. At the end of the path a further door opens into a private world: each of the two houses has its own courtyard, enclosed, protected, secluded, yet with light and airy planting and open to the sky. Here, the carved wooden door lintels and lattice windows, like the *mashrabiya* lattices in old houses in Arab countries, may have been inspired by Turner's time working in Cairo, or perhaps by old grand houses in Epirus on the nearby Greek

OPPOSITE
Below the pool at Amalthéa, the planting makes extensive use of indigenous trees and shrubs. The sinuous lines, contrasting textures, and luxuriant rounded shapes, all in shades of green, follow the contours of the hillside and echo the landscape beyond. Cypresses provide all-important darker vertical accents.

A wild clump of giant reed in the background emphasises the stillness of the pool and the rounded forms of the shrubs that border it.

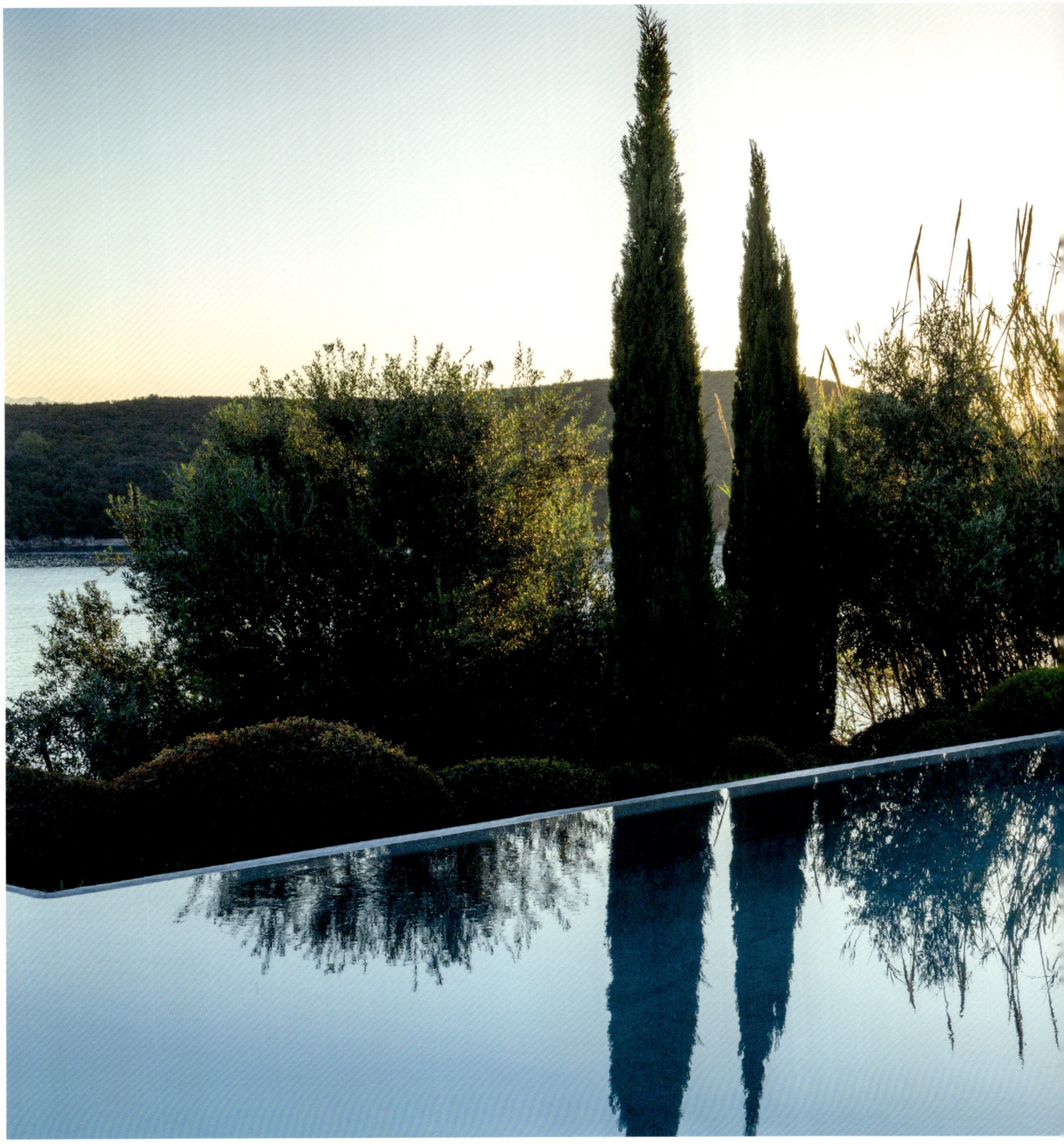

Though Pelagía is smaller, the two houses have many architectural and planting elements in common, including this tapering staircase with pots of box *(Buxus sempervirens)* on ledges.

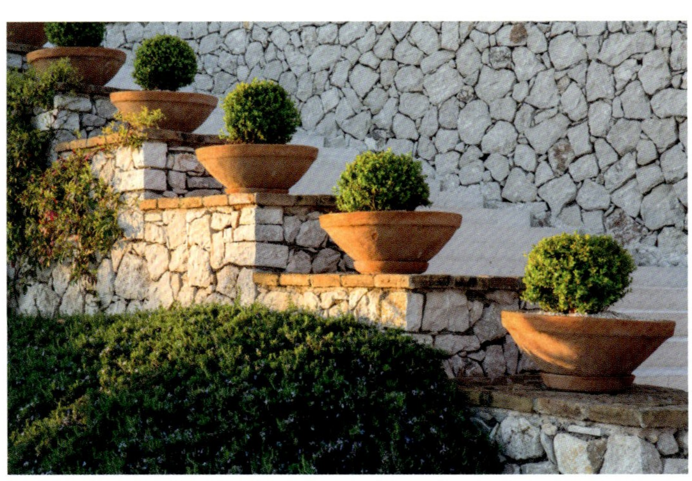

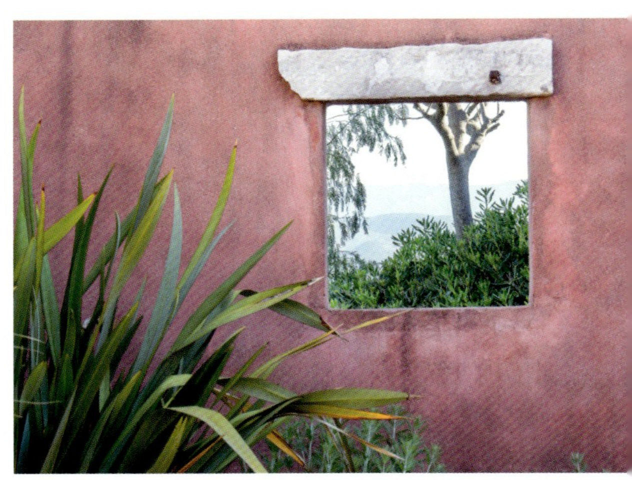

A glimpse of the world beyond the wall, with the Albanian coastline in the distance. In the foreground, New Zealand flax (*Phormium tenax*).

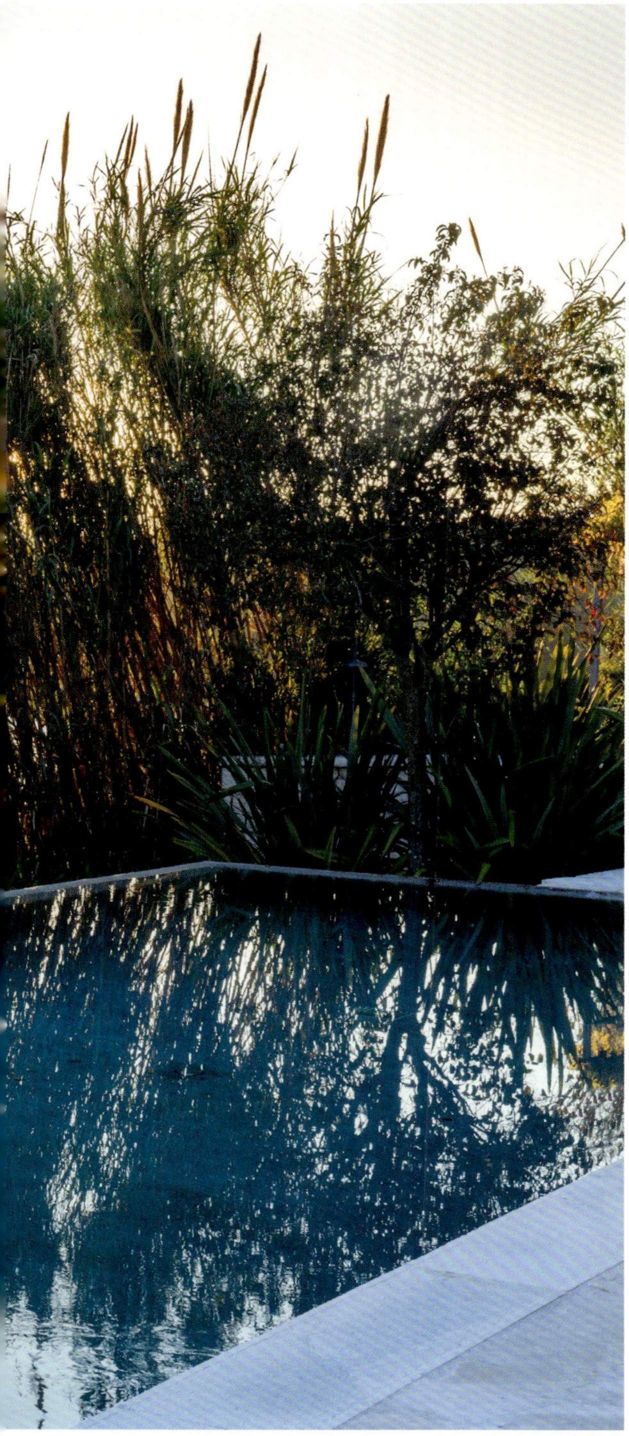

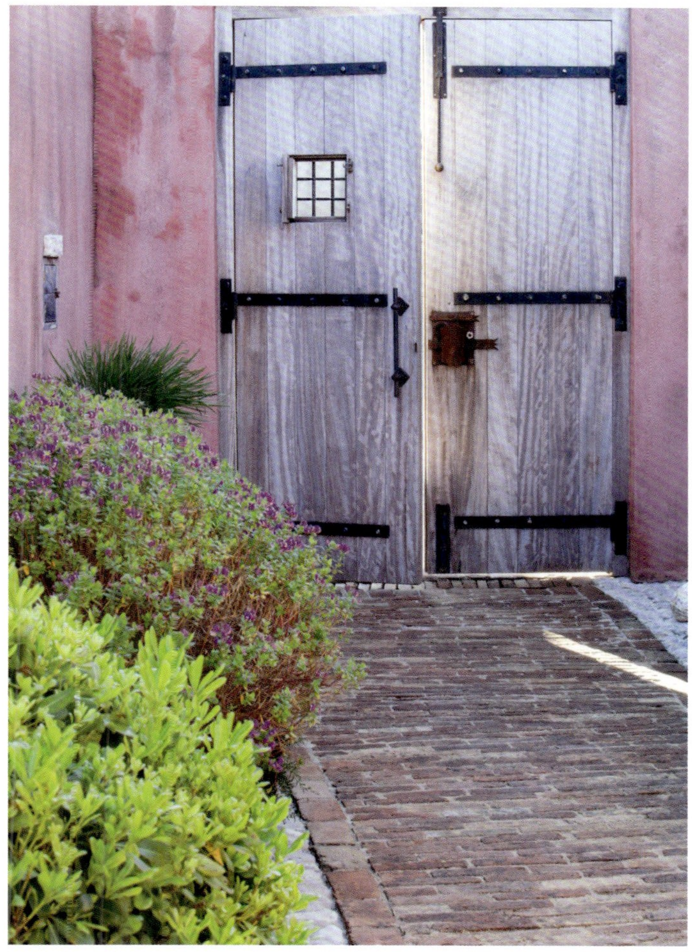

Close to the houses, simplicity in the planting draws attention to the carefully chosen details of the paving and the wooden doors and window lattices.

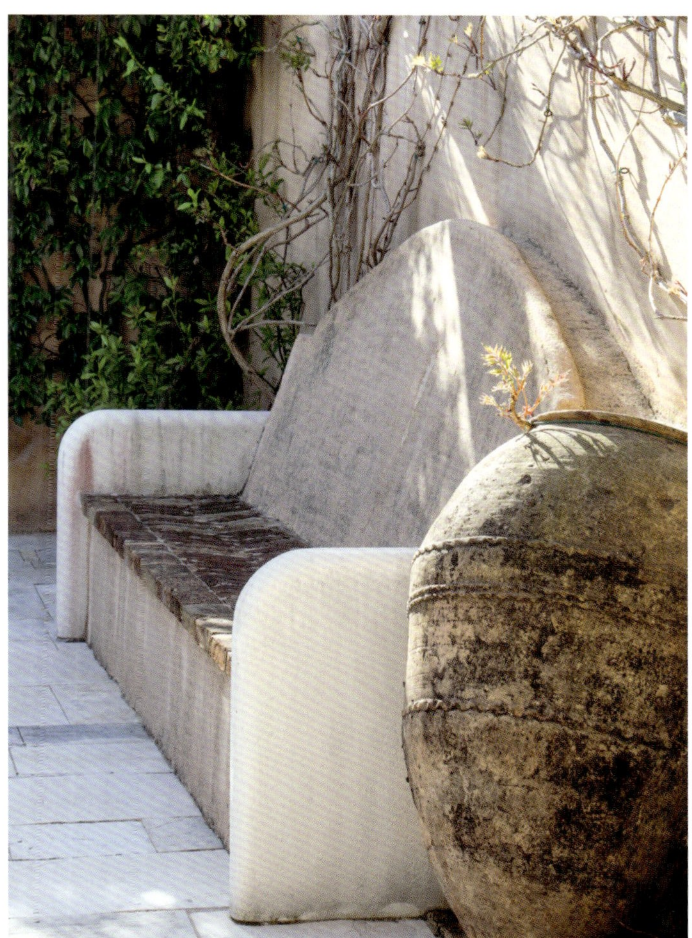

A built-in seat in the courtyard at Amalthéa.

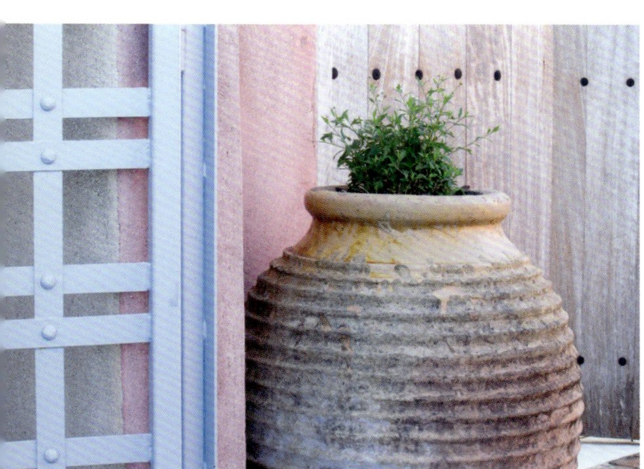

Traditional urns help ground the design within its local context.

OVERLEAF
Beyond the pool, the original native oak tree (*Quercus pubescens*) provides both a focal point for views and a destination for explorers of the garden.

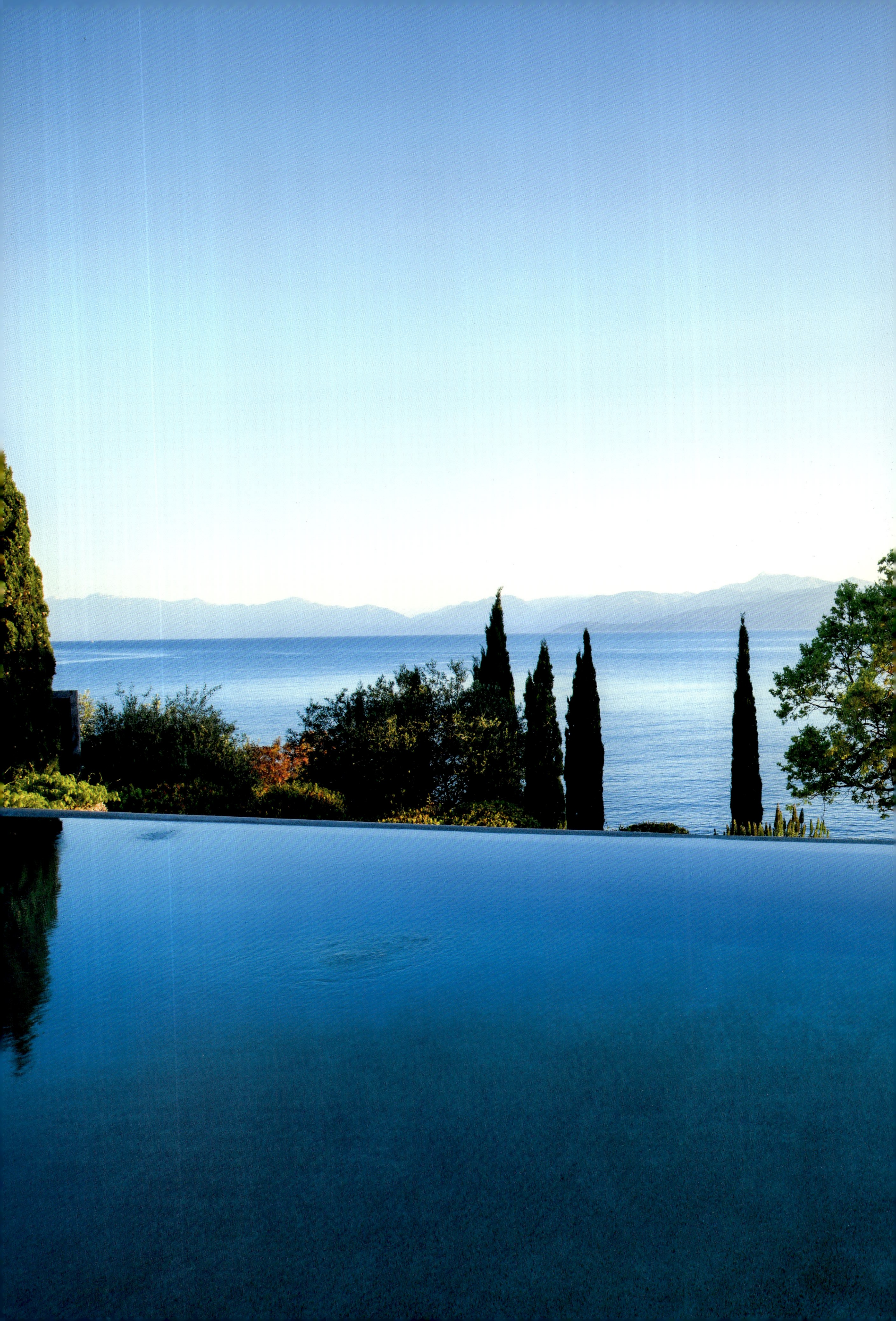

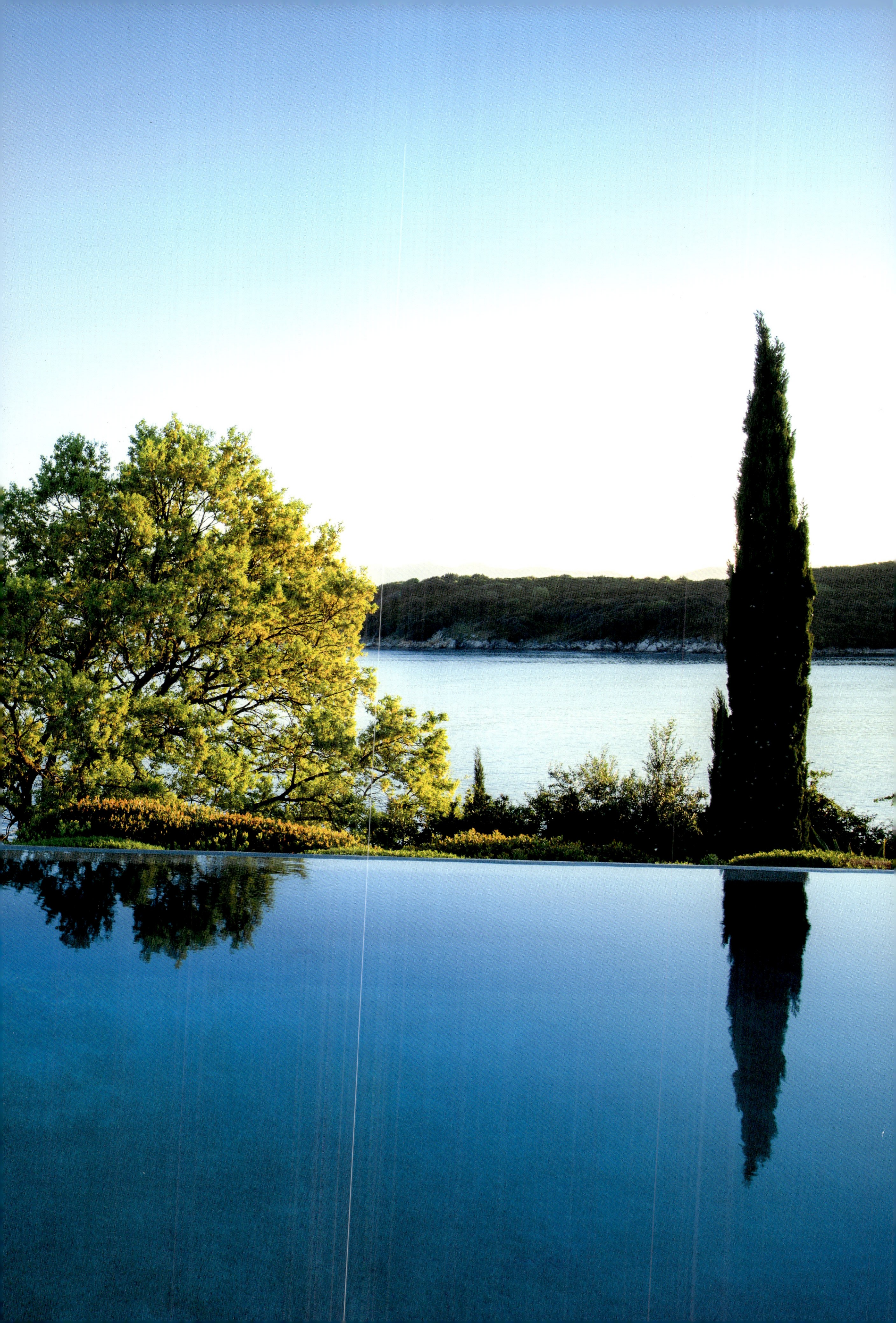

On the way down to the sea, the lush planting includes strawberry tree (*Arbutus unedo*), with its coppery-green new leaves, along with cypress, New Zealand flax (*Phormium tenax*), blue-flowered *Echium fastuosum*, and myrtle (*Myrtus communis*).

mainland. They evoke feelings of seclusion and safety, of being able to look from the inside out, without being seen. Simple wooden bridges into the houses subtly suggest the drawbridges of fortified buildings and signal that this is a place of safety where nothing will disturb the calm.

Turning a corner from the courtyard at Amalthéa, one comes out upon an open terrace overhung with wisteria and looking down into the middle zone of this private world: a breathtaking open space with a spectacular sheet of water. The rectangular swimming pool, forty metres long and parallel to the house, reflects the sky. Its colour is one with that of the sea just beyond.

Turner's assured treatment of water and light, and his perfectly proportioned spaces, called for simple, sophisticated planting, and Johns' design provides an inspired, confident foil to the architecture and roots it into the magnificent natural setting. Individual trees with finely textured airy foliage—silk tree, pepper tree, olive—complement the block-plantings of silverberry (*Elaeagnus* x *ebbingei*), bright green box, and the dark evergreen pillars of star jasmine she has placed along the fronts of both houses. In the courtyards, box balls and star jasmine foreshadow the use of these plants in areas of the garden that the arriving visitor has yet to see. Other plants that provide unifying elements throughout the garden include pencil cypresses; clipped silvery tree germander and *Westringia fruticosa*; wisteria in white, pink, and mauve; New Zealand flax (*Phormium tenax*) and pampas grass (*Cortaderia selloana*), with their fountain-like shapes; rosemary; *Agapanthus*; and climbing Banks' rose and 'Mermaid' rose.

Both the courtyards and the hillside gardens provide exquisite 'peaceful hide-away corners' much valued by the owner and his family. Between the pools and the sea, one can happily lose oneself exploring paths and staircases among the enfolding shapes of shrubs pruned in soft curves, with every now and then some drama added by a glimpse of the sea. Lower down, a path leads to a decades-old oak tree with a secluded sitting area, and down the cliff to a sandy beach. Under the long Amalthéa pool, the planting is mainly of clipped intermingled mounds of rosemary and evergreen native shrubs, interspersed with clumps of *Echium fastuosum*, New Zealand flax, and cypress. The more intricately planted garden below Pelagía, designed for summer pleasure, features white oleander and orange daylilies, mingled with the rich blues of *Agapanthus* and the hazier blue of Russian sage.

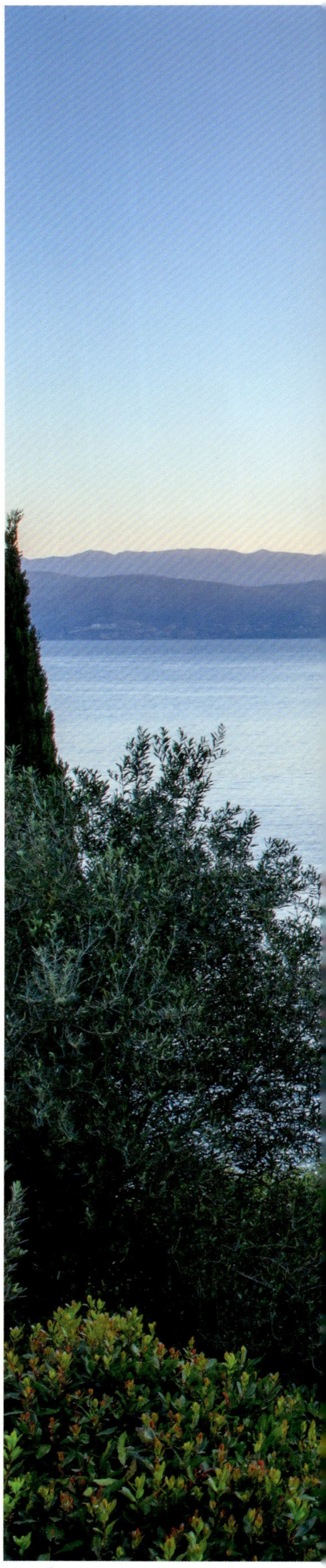

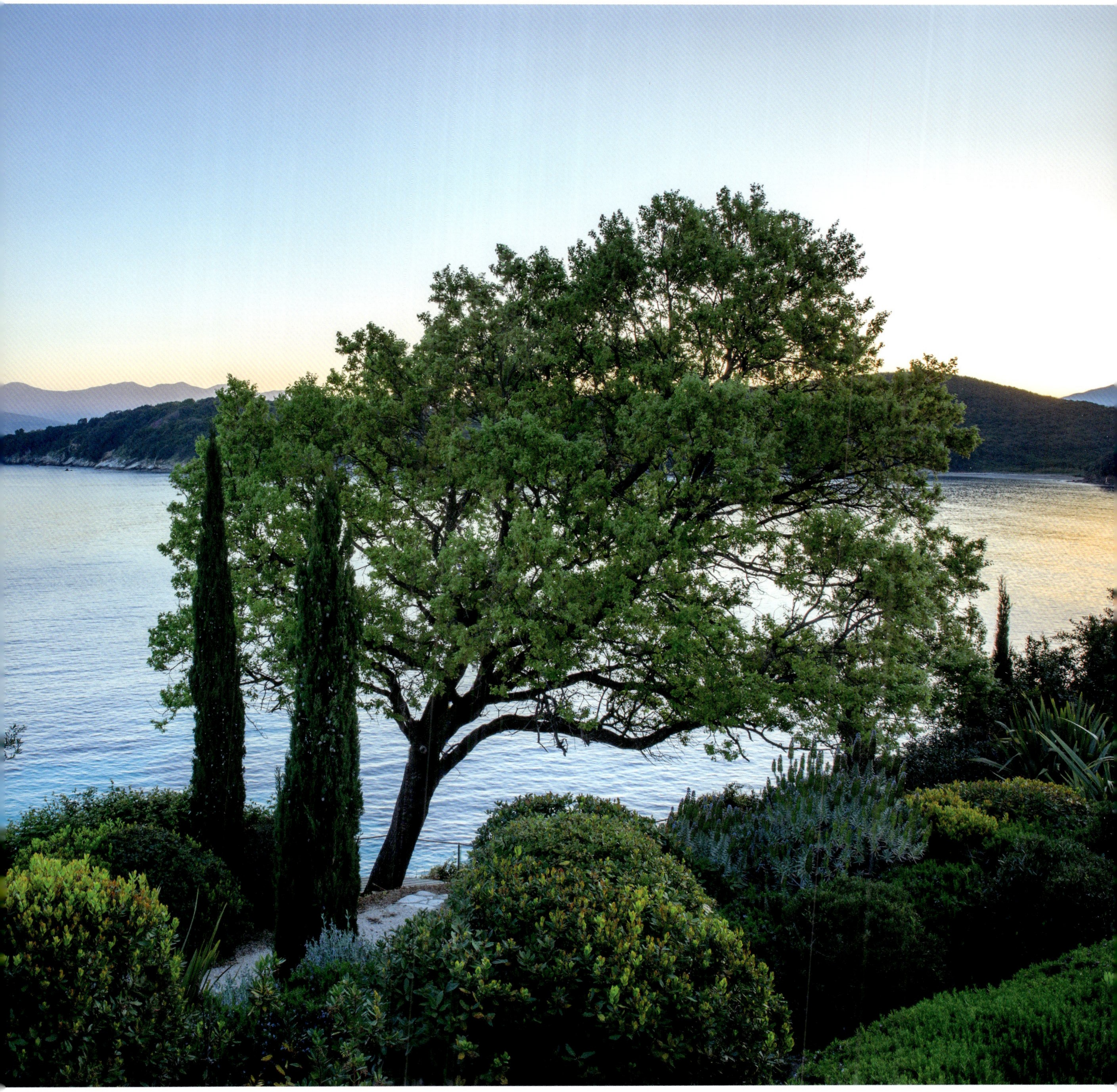

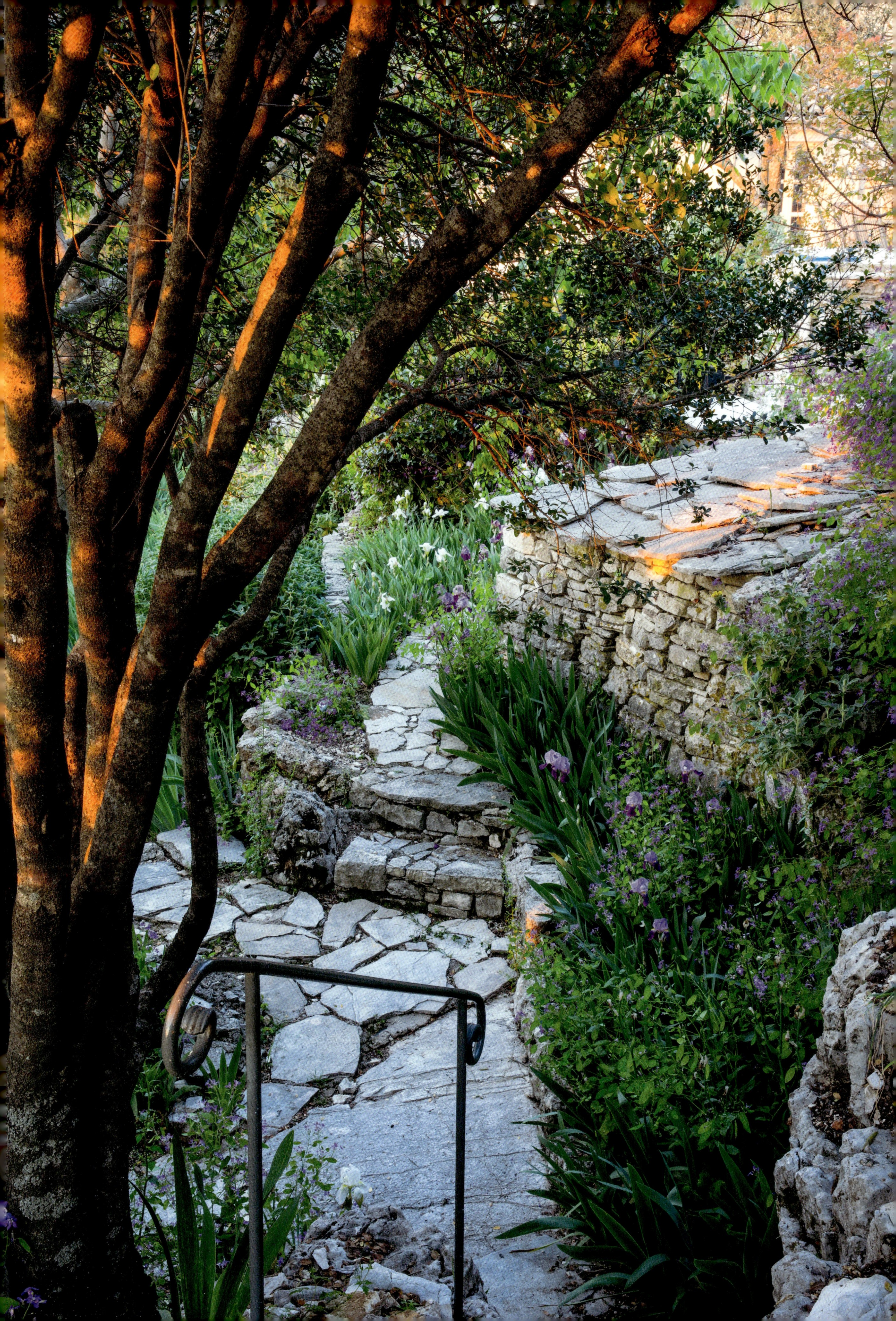

Rou

Up here in the clear air, sounds travel far. Early on a spring morning on top of the ridge at Rou, the only sounds breaking the silence are birdsong and the bells of distant sheep and goats. Cares dissolve in the peace of this place, no matter whether one looks inland across the starry shapes of wildflowers in the nearby meadow to the distant hills, or towards the sea, where miles of coastline stretch out in a hazy dawn.

OPPOSITE
A typical path between the houses at Rou. The original native trees have been left in place and native flowering plants and shrubs have been added.

The rebirth of the hilltop hamlet of Rou was a project of architect Dominic Skinner, who bought the ruined two-hundred-year-old houses and in 2005 began their authentic restoration, using local wood and stone worked by local craftsmen. Today many of the Rou houses have individual owners; all may be rented. Working with landscape designer Jennifer Gay, Skinner visualised the varied outdoor spaces here rather like stage sets, giving careful thought to how they are entered and exited and what can be seen within—and from—each. Together, the two explored different ways of achieving 'drama and serenity; natural balance and local heritage'.[40] The four-hectare property stretches down a steep hillside with old olive trees, patches of native woodland, and views over the distant sea, to an old quarry which became the site for a serene and beautiful swimming pool.

Gay has explained that 'For both architect and gardeners it was important that indoor and outdoor spaces merged almost imperceptibly into the Corfiot hillside'.[41] To achieve this, she let herself be guided by the site itself: 'Our landscaping philosophy placed great emphasis on the enhancement of existing habitats of woodland, *maquis*, and meadow. We wanted to create a place in harmony with the character and colours of the locality. We recognised that the *maquis* shrubs that were engulfing the houses would, with a little tender loving care, actually form the permanent green framework of the gardens... Beautiful but neglected trees ... simply needed pruning to become significant structural elements.'[42]

Entering the hamlet down one of its paved paths between the houses (no cars enter Rou), one comes upon a long central allée that stretches parallel to the top of the ridge and formed the original main street.

40. Dominic Skinner in conversation with the author. 41 Jennifer Gay, writing in *Athens News*: http://www.athensnews.gr/issue/13492/55011. Viewed April 2014. 42 Ibid.

CENTRE TOP
The intimacy of the public and private spaces at Rou contrasts with the wide open views. In the middle distance here the hillside is lit up with the spring colours of oak and turpentine tree.

CENTRE BOTTOM
Cistus x *purpureus* flowers beside a path.

Covered by a wisteria pergola and edged simply with blue-flowering *Agapanthus* and *Plumbago auriculata*, this still provides the structural and atmospheric heart of the village. From here, paths and staircases lead to the lower parts of the hamlet and, between them, doors lead directly into private courtyards and gardens. Mature nettle trees, mulberries, and almonds, all very typical of villages in the area, have been left in place, with new quince and pomegranate trees added. Enchanting spaces open up on the paths among the houses, some with large old trees under-planted with a mix of wild species and cultivated varieties.

Small details, such as the dark green germander (*Teucrium chamaedrys*) inset along the top of a stone wall, add to the pleasure of exploration. Ferns are left to grow in rock crevices as they have always done; big drifts of bearded irises are intermixed with Jerusalem sage and purple honesty—all plants that occur in the wild here—complementing the pruned and natural forms of evergreen native shrubs. In the woodland near the pool, under the lifted crowns of oaks, paths wend among natural outcrops of rock and past shiny-leaved *Acanthus mollis*, wild cyclamen, prickly pear (*Opuntia ficus-carica*), ferns, and both small and large-leaved species of evergreen butcher's broom (*Ruscus aculeatus* and *R. hypophyllum*).

The private gardens at Rou complement the public spaces. In some of them Gay's planting is more intricate, providing what she calls 'a natural mosaic of herbs and perennials'.[43] Herbs that the original villagers might have had—thyme, lavender, sage, oregano, and rosemary—are mingled with decorative and aromatic introductions, such as silvery *Helichrysum orientalis*, *Santolina chamaecyparissus*, and Russian sage, and with climbing 'Iceberg' roses, jasmine, and star jasmine.

Gay explains that the plants she chose for Rou had to be 'native or quintessentially mediterranean; they had to fit the character and colour of the locality both climatically and aesthetically; they had to be drought-tolerant, but able to withstand winter cold; and some key plants needed to be summer flowering when visitors to Rou would be at their peak'.[44] The colour palette overall is subtle, with much use of year-round greens and greys, enhanced by flowers in white, mauve, purple, lavender, bright yellow-green, and the occasional pink of cistus and old roses.

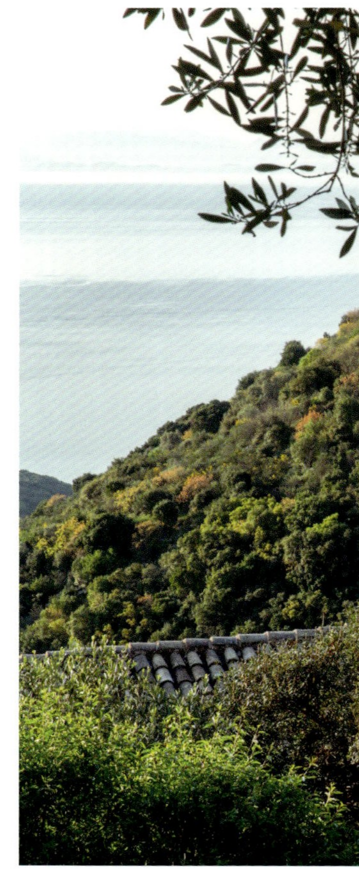

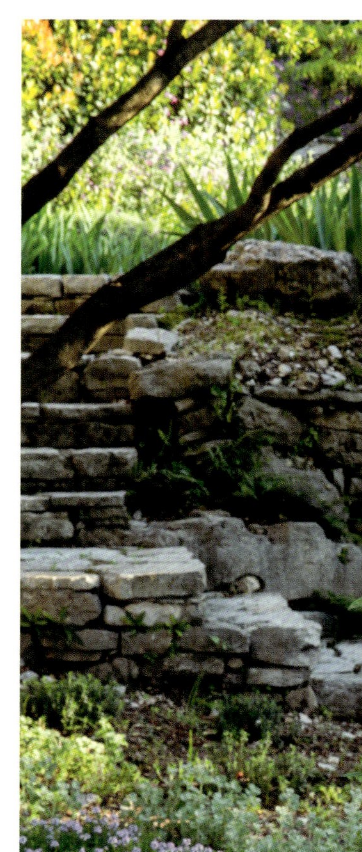

43. Ibid. 44. Ibid.

Mediterranean spurge (*Euphorbia characias* subsp. *Wulfenii*) and bearded irises, both local natives, have been encouraged to colonise this shady slope under olive trees.

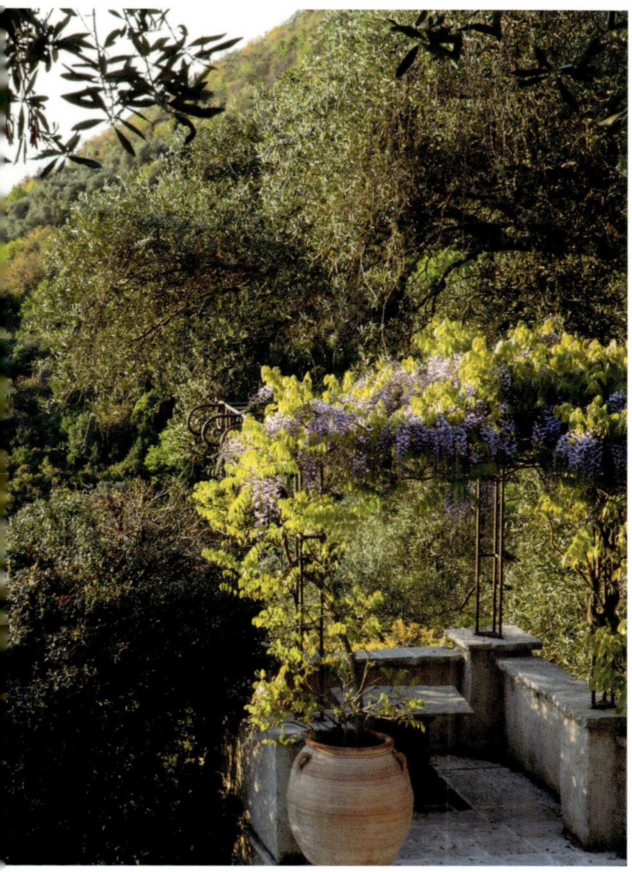

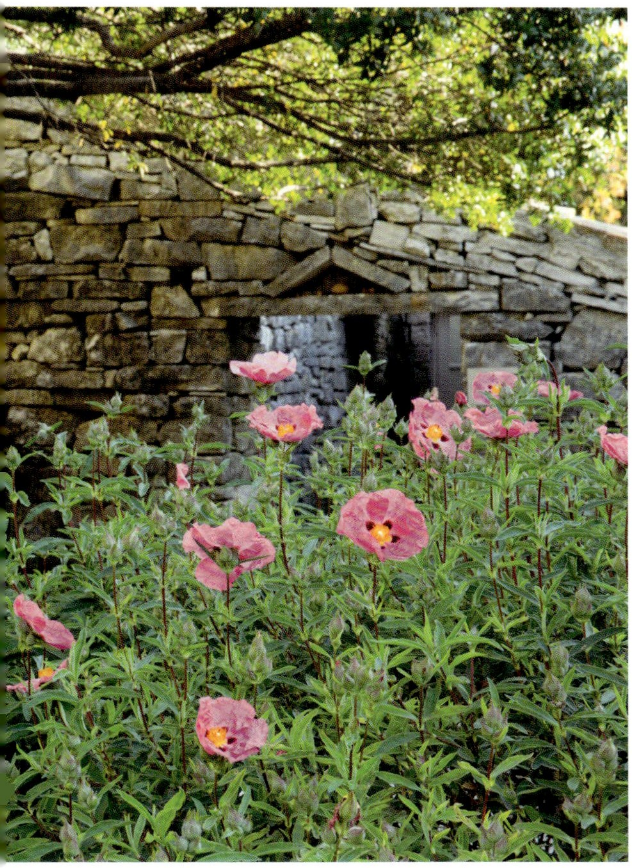

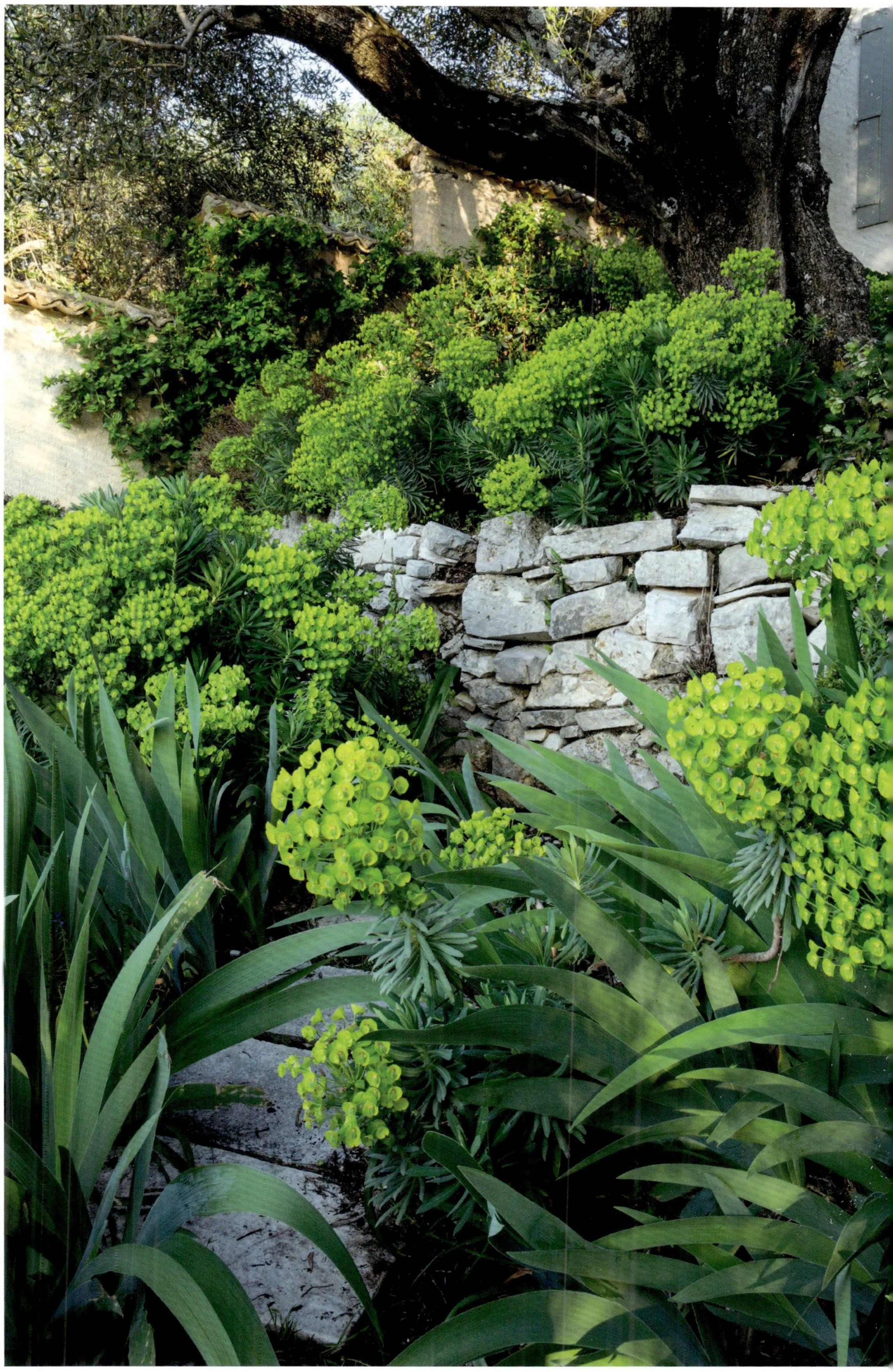

OVERLEAF
Rou is justly famous locally for its wisterias, which line the central allée of the village.

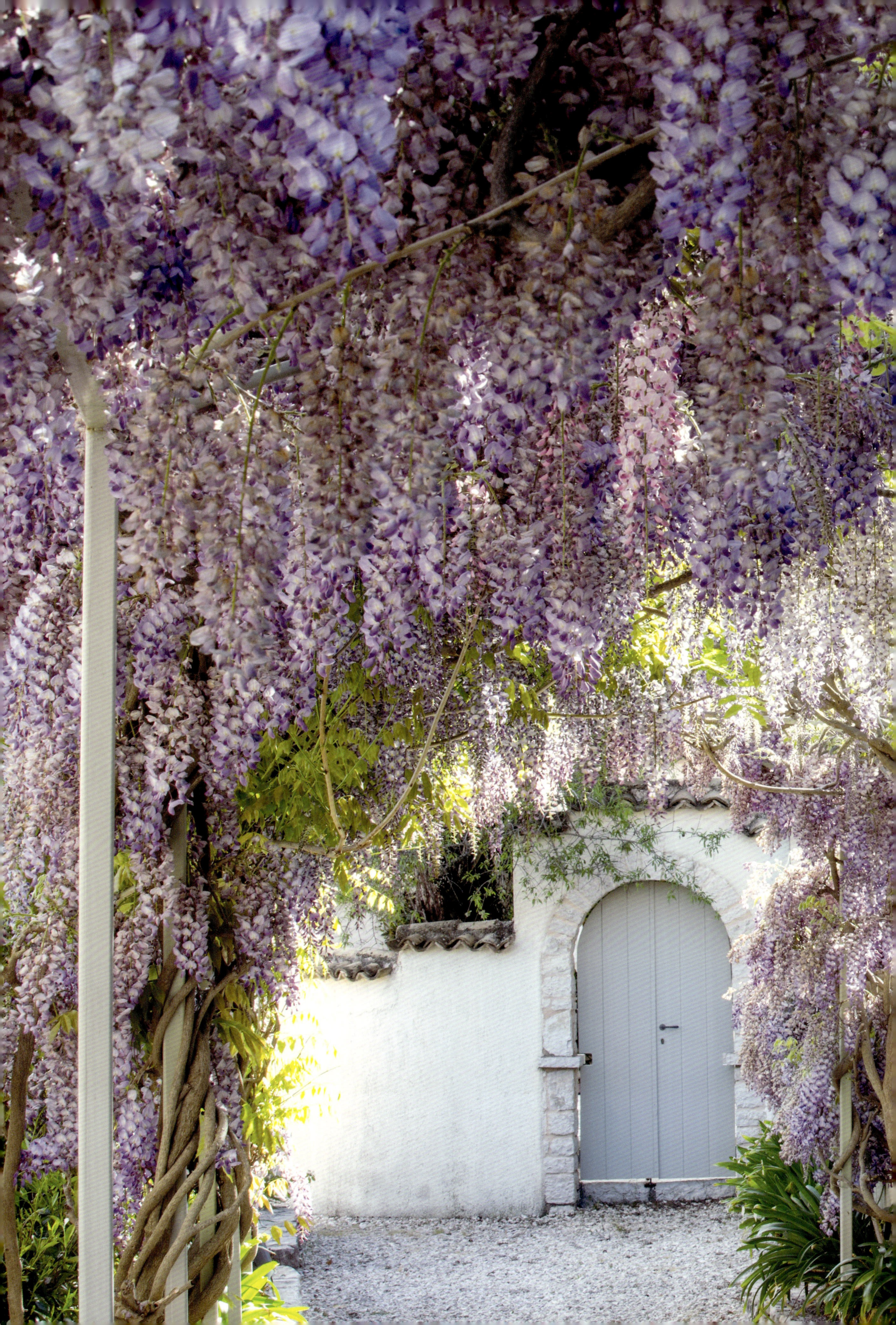

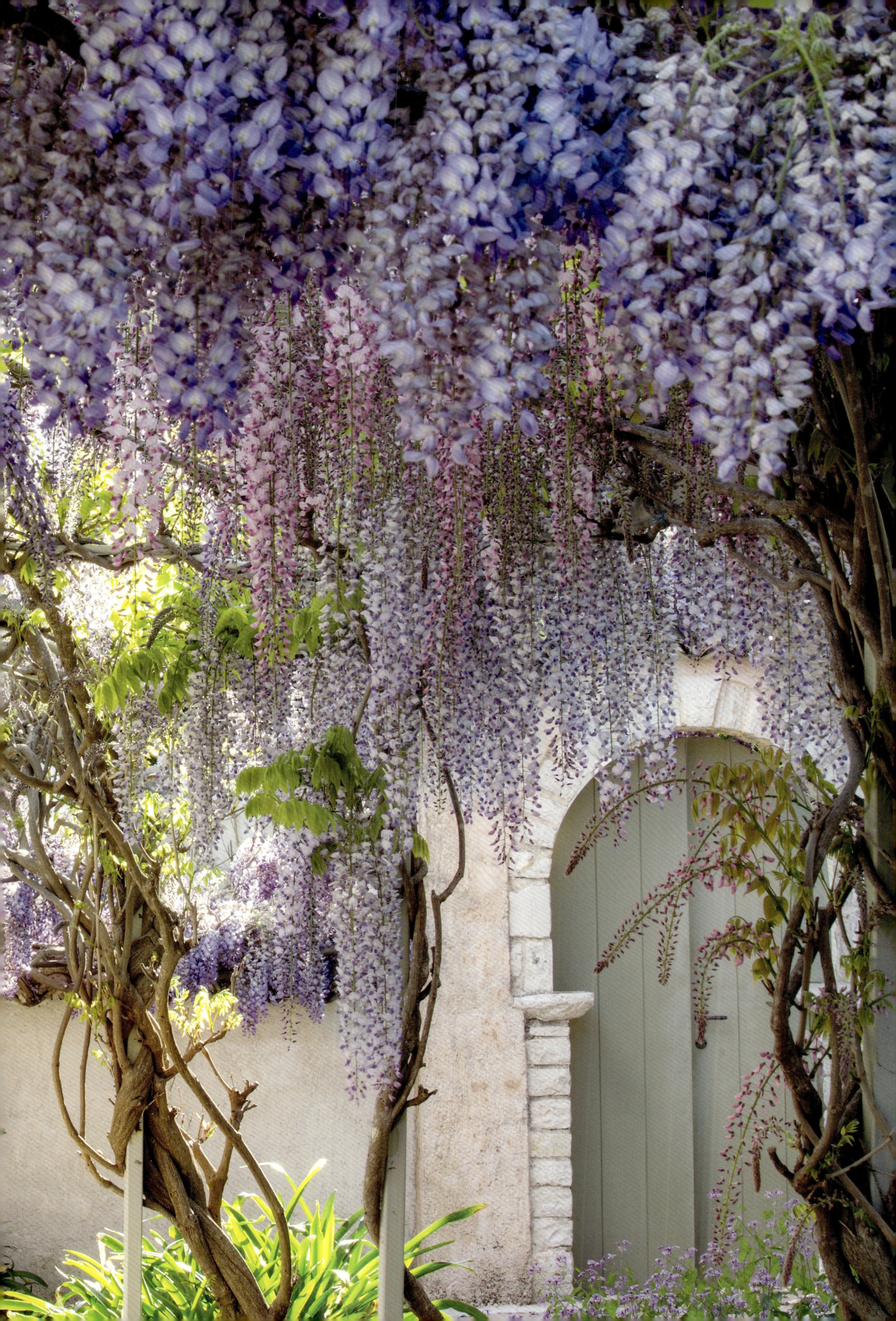

One of Rou's many exquisite sitting areas with views of the sea.

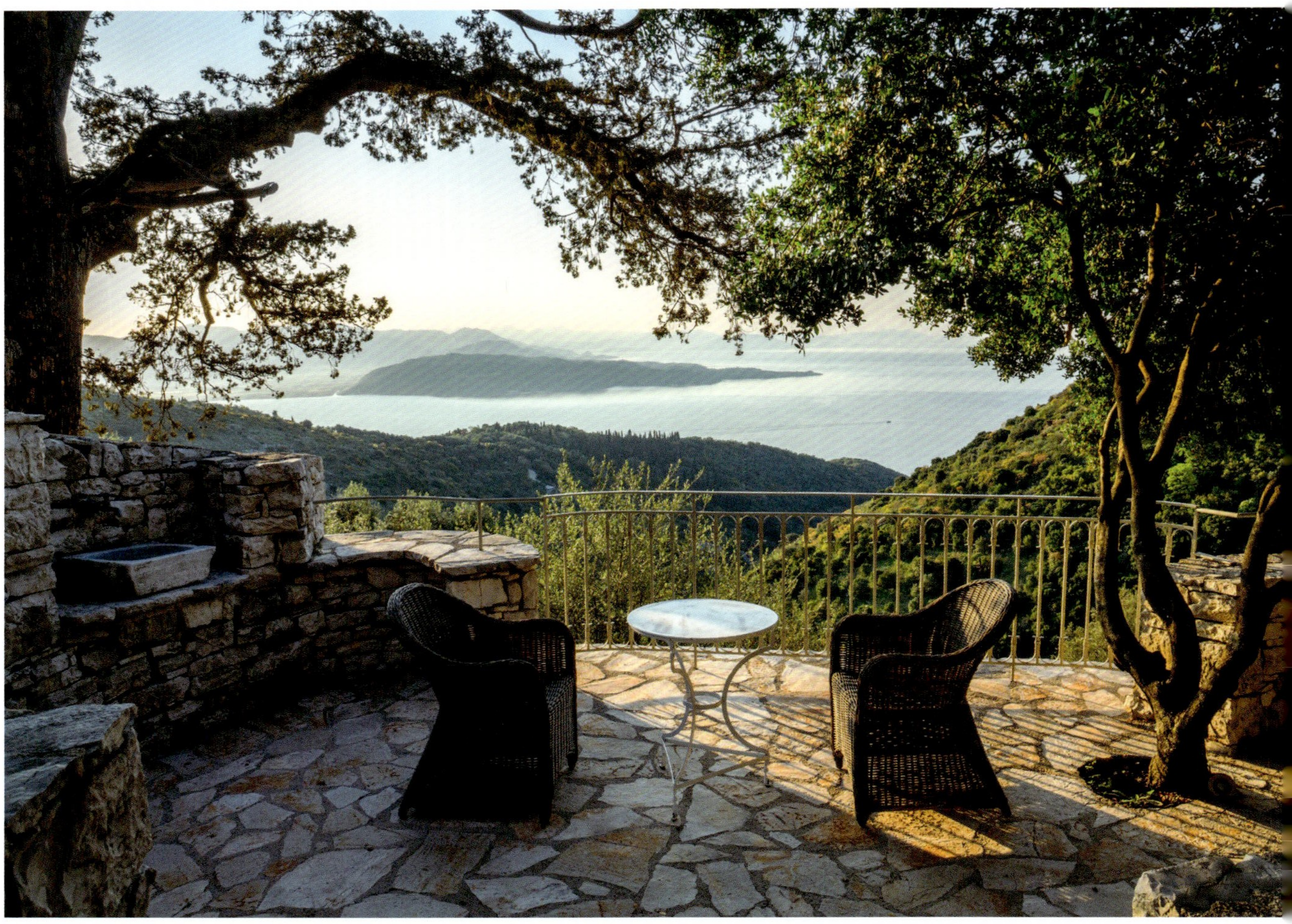

Bearded irises, naturalised in Corfu, grow with wild Jerusalem sage and honesty (*Lunaria annua* subsp. *pachyriza*) along this path.

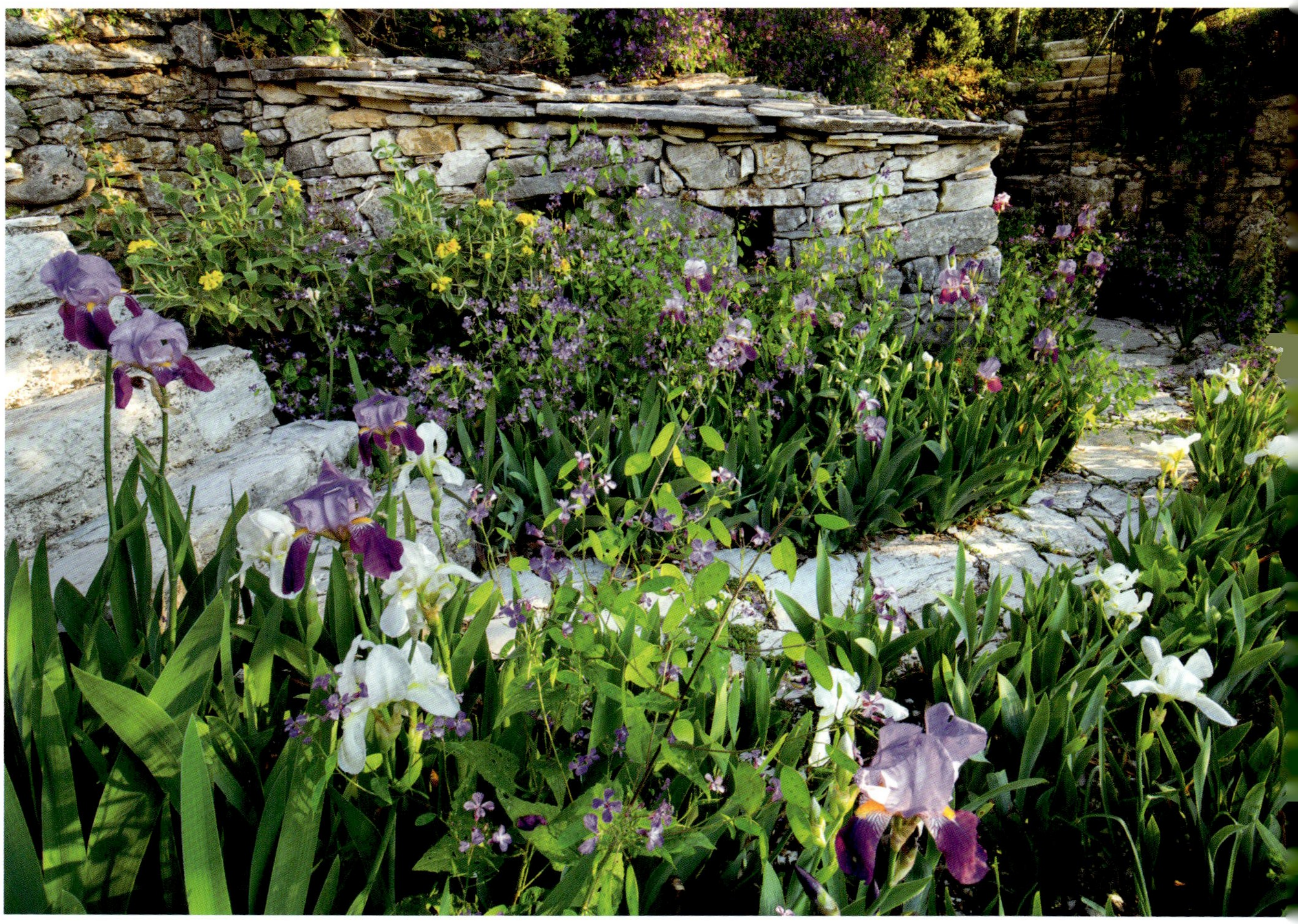

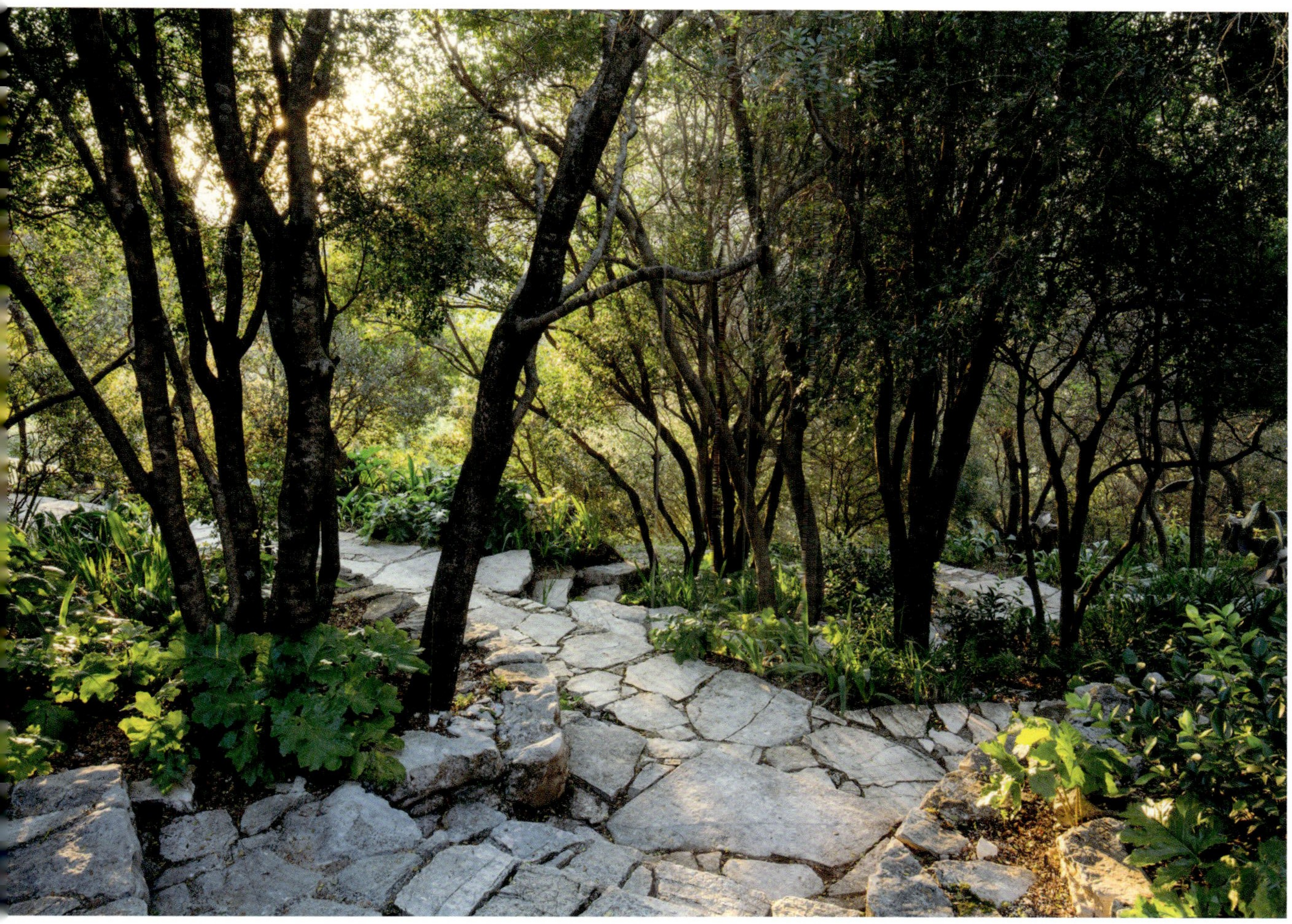

The path to the pool leads through original woodland, cleared and under-planted with *Acanthus mollis* and large-leaved butcher's broom (*Ruscus hypophyllum*).

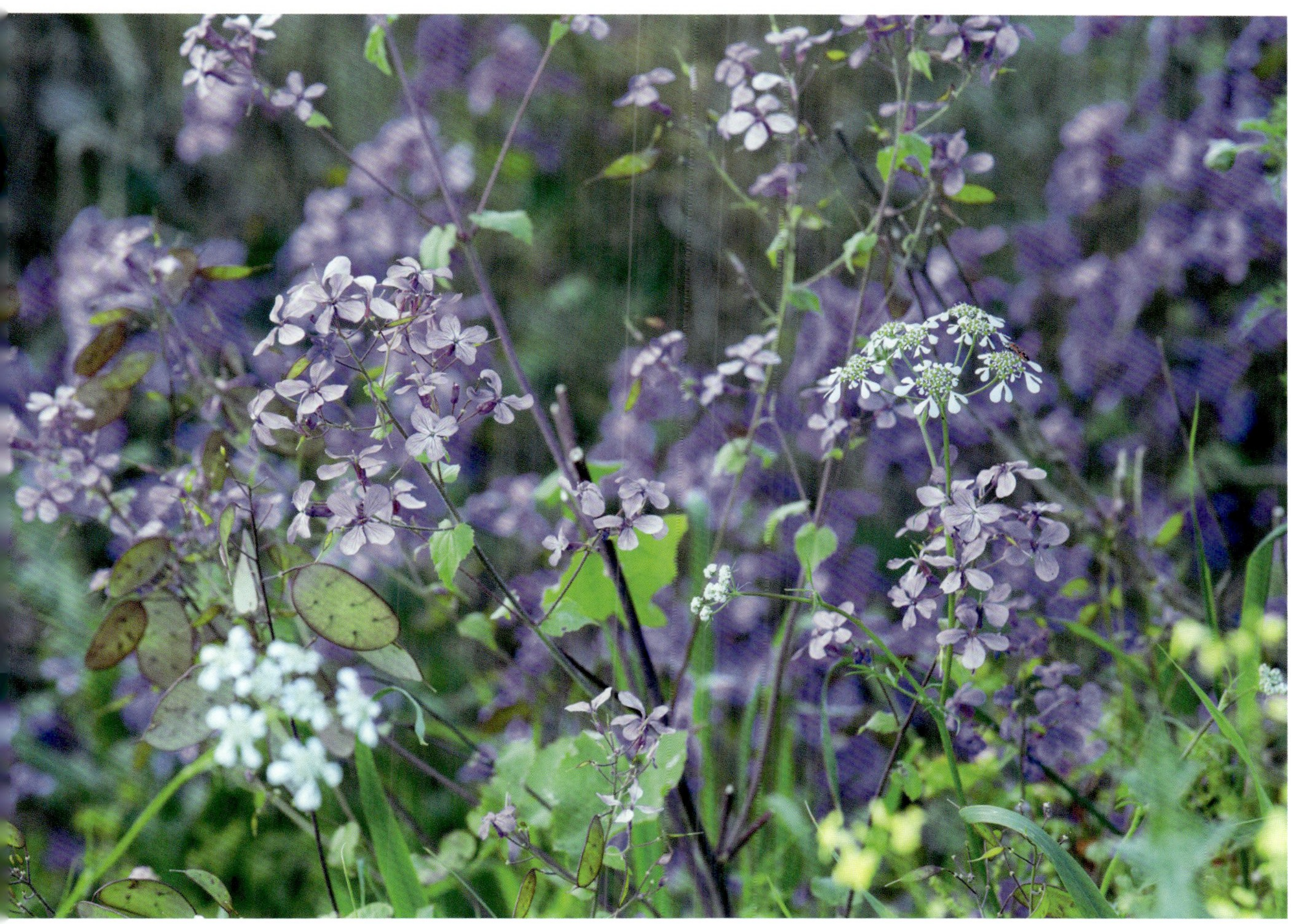

Wildflowers abound at Rou. Here, honesty grows with white *Tordylium apulum*.

OVERLEAF
A morning view from the top of the ridge at Rou, with the starry flowers of hollow-stemmed asphodel (*Asphodeline fistulosus*) and the yellow of Jerusalem sage.

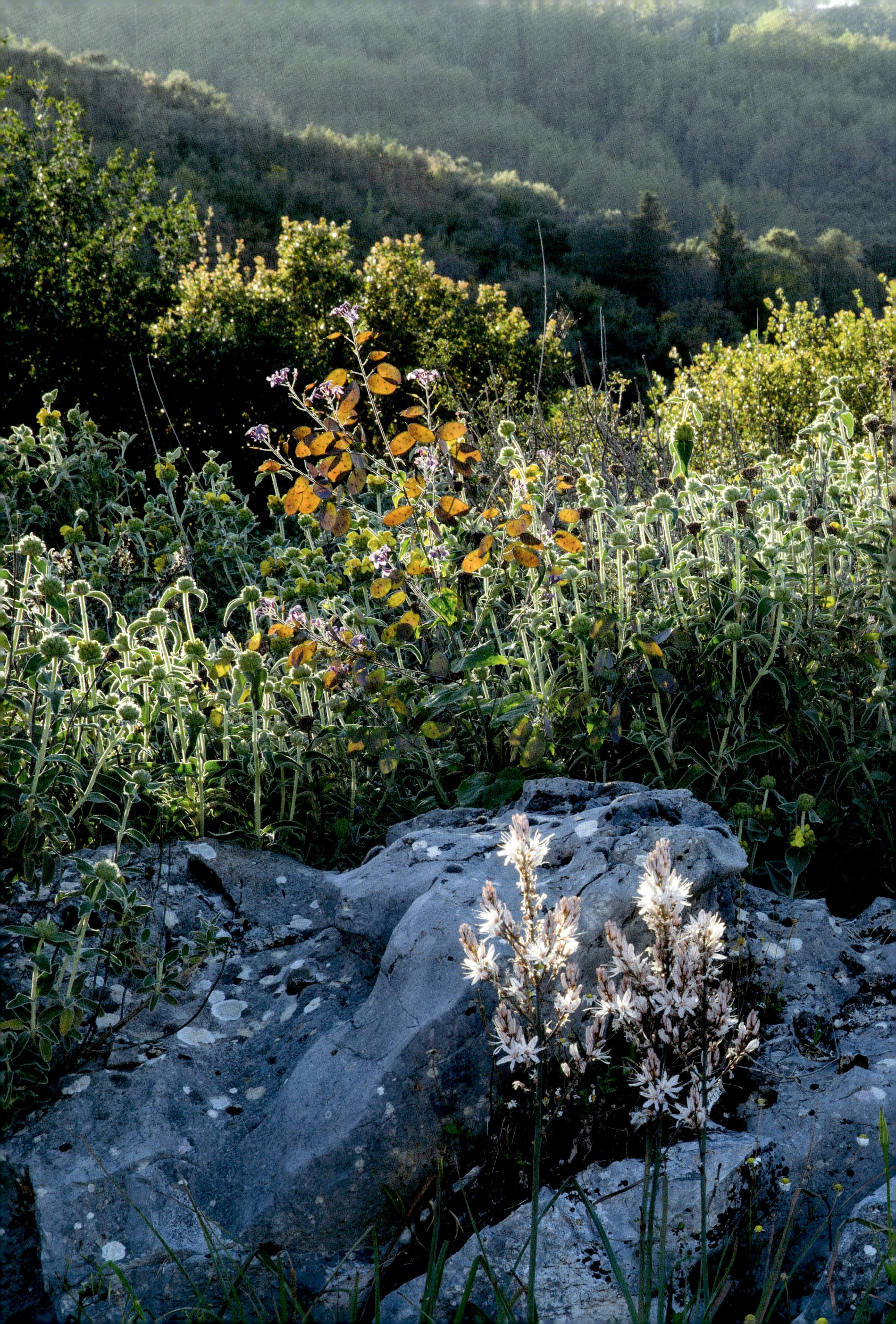

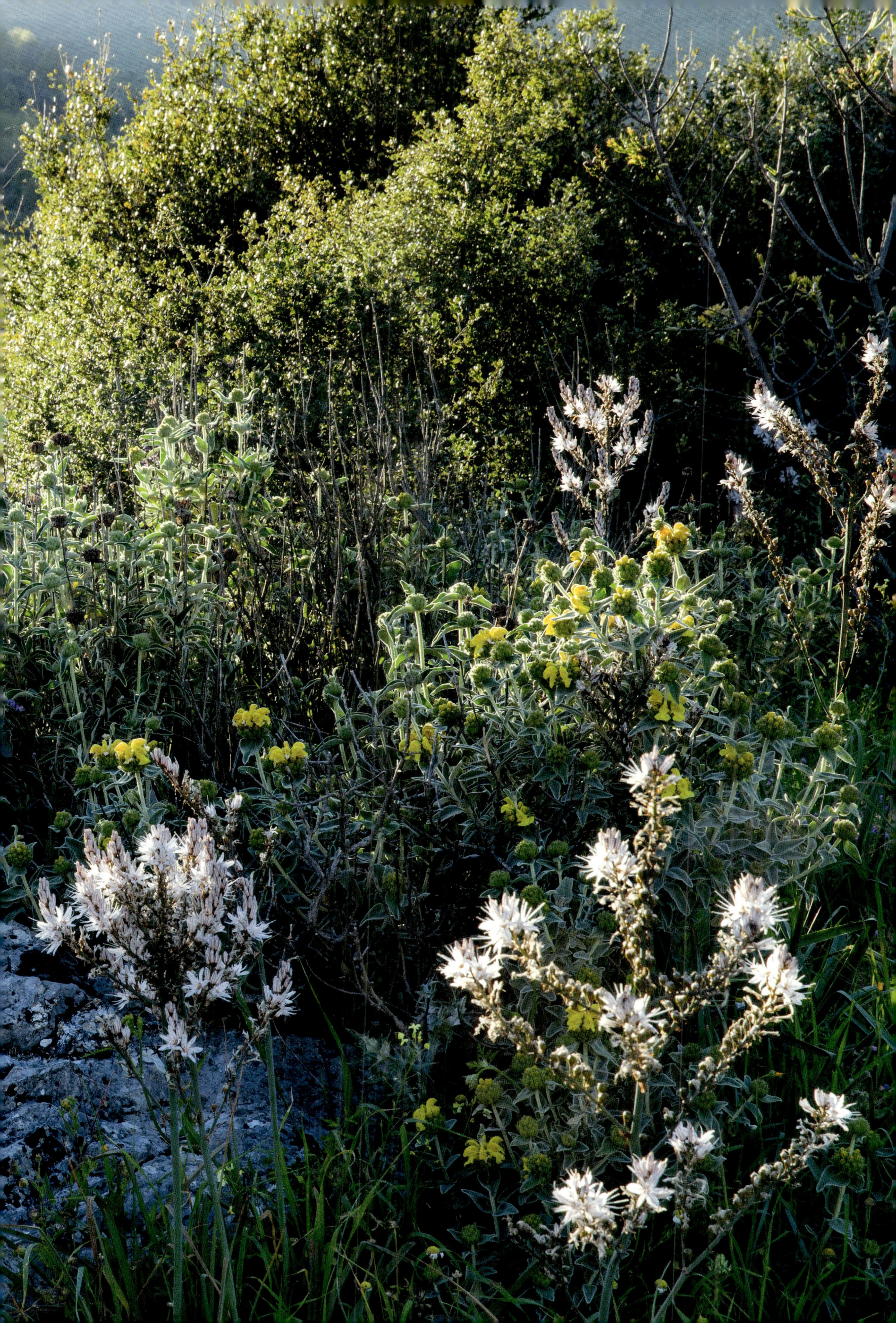

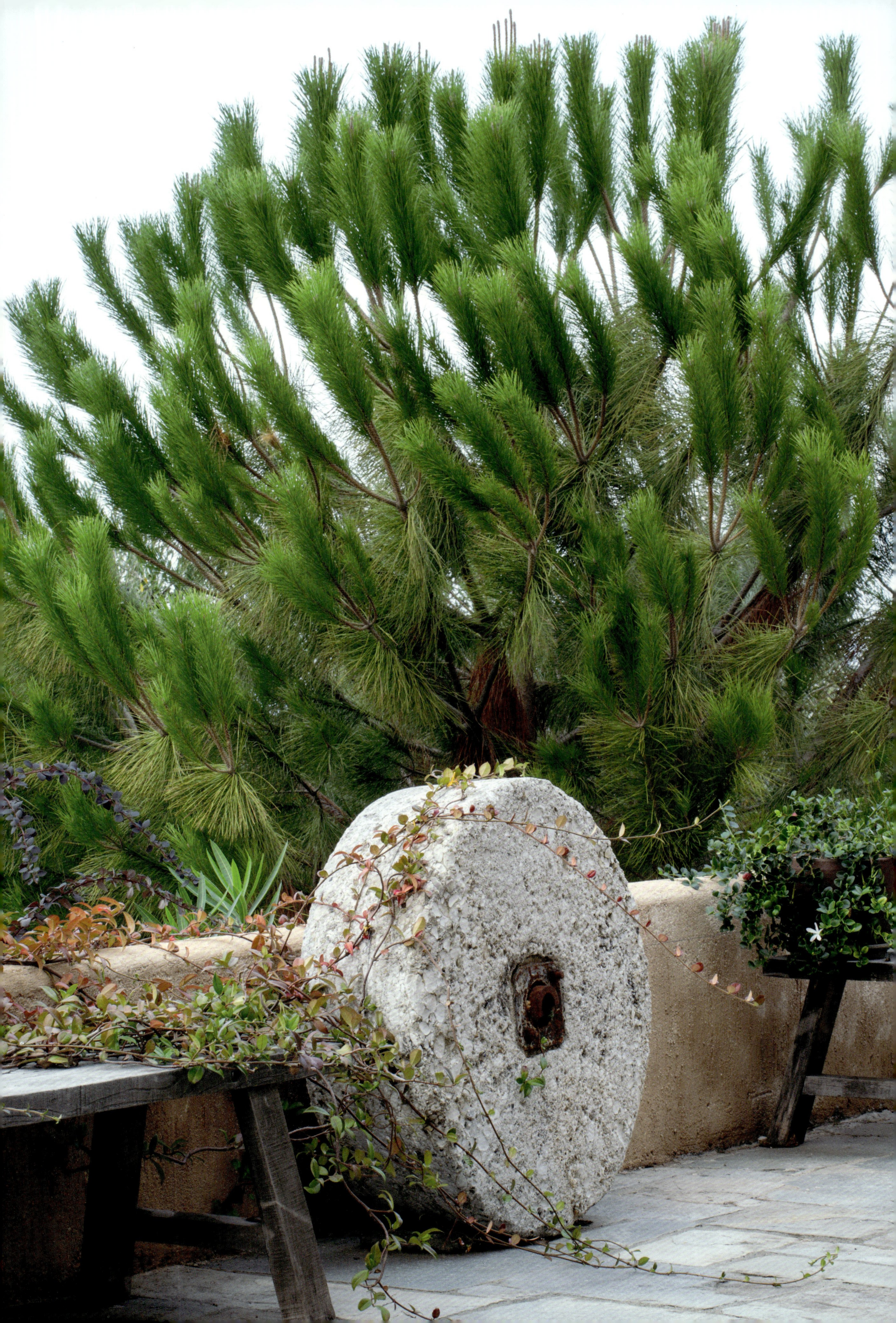

Lámari

This contemporary hillside garden not only has a spectacular view but also provides a showcase for the owner's sculptures. Sculptor Katherine Wise and her husband Richard Woods created the garden in 2008, when they restored the ruined olive press in northern Corfu that is now their home. The couple had searched for many years for a home-site from which one could see 'both the sea and the sunset'—and indeed, the garden is designed to make the most of the mesmerising view west to Corfu's outlying islands.

OPPOSITE
The house at Lámari is a converted olive press; the hilltop garden features works by the owner, an internationally known sculptor, along with salvaged millstones that acquire the qualities of art.

In converting the olive press into a home, Katherine and Richard were careful to preserve its authenticity; they restored the original stonework and used traditional local materials and craftsmanship throughout. In designing the garden, Katherine has respected the rustic but approached it with a contemporary, more international sensibility. The garden's retaining walls and arches, some finished with a smooth, honey-coloured plaster–concrete mix, divide it into 'rooms' a little like those in an indoor art gallery. Carefully sited to best advantage, large iron and stone objects salvaged from the workings of the olive press acquire the qualities of art, complementing the sculptures on display.

The garden is entered from a parking area shaded in summer by a large old nettle tree. Dark-flowered hollyhocks and silvery-green Mediterranean spurge (*Euphorbia characias*) seed themselves among gravel, and bearded irises grow against the walls. Under a gnarled olive tree, silvery-leaved *Cerastium tomentosum* carpets the ground.

To the north and west, the house opens on to an expansive paved terrace, austere with its large spaces, straight lines, sharp angles, and light-reflecting geometric shapes created by bodies of water. All these hold the eye, rather than letting it drift too quickly into the view of forest, sea, and islands beyond. Complementing the horizontal lines of the sea at the horizon and the pools in the foreground, Katherine has placed the vertical spires of a sculpture, *Towers of Time*, which is reflected in its own pool and in the swimming pool.

Throughout the garden one can see an artist's eye at work in the choice of plants for their striking shapes and contrasting textures: mop heads of Mediterranean spurge, flowering spears of *Echium fastuosum*, drifts of bearded iris, and clumps of New Zealand flax in green and

Close to the house, plants and their containers complement the varied colours of the ancient walls.

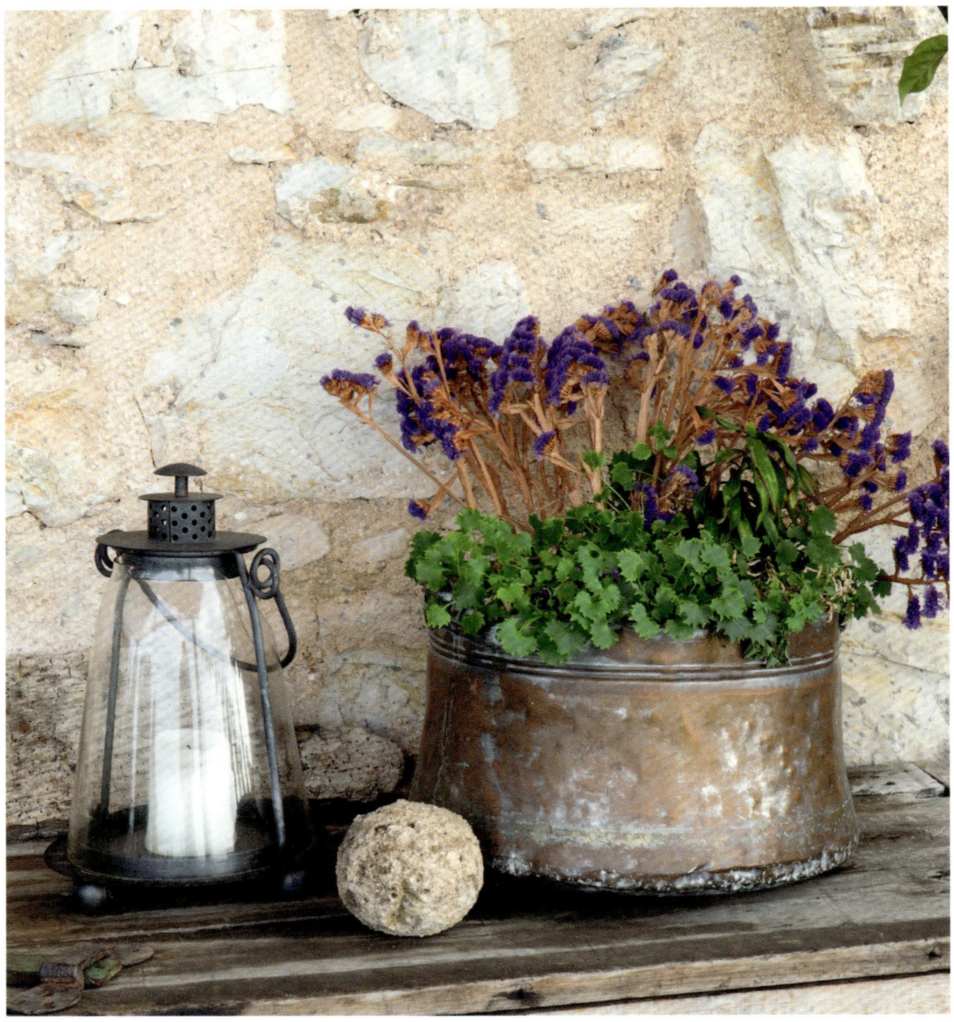

OPPOSITE TOP
A sunset view towards Cape Drástis and Corfu's outer islands. The spires of Katherine Wise's sculpture, *Towers of Time*, are echoed by cypresses on lower levels of the garden and beyond.

OVERLEAF
Autumn offers intense colours even without flowers: *Berberis thunbergii* turns a deep shade of smoky purple and the leaves of star jasmine (*Trachelospermum jasminoides*) turn scarlet. The oak sculpture is entitled *Wherever you are is called Here.*

bronze. Groupings of architectural plants such as yuccas, palms, and agaves provide a foil to the strong shapes of the sculptures and found objects. Also in use are fine-textured drought-tolerant shrubs: creeping rosemary, glossy abelia, and deep-blue flowering jagged lavender (*Lavandula multifida*).

Colour, too, has been deliberately chosen. Though no pink or yellow is allowed, there is a rich palette of bronze, silver, grey-green, dark green, purples, blues, oranges, and white. In her design, Katherine sought 'subtlety in colour hues, variety in form and texture' but she also appreciates its 'areas of raucous colour', noting that 'in the design process there is always the dilemma of deciding which aspect of one's appetite to satisfy'.

In this very open site, cool shaded areas are especially welcome. Under the deep veranda that runs around the west and north of the house is a sheltered sitting area with a lush collection of plants, including white hydrangeas, gardenias, and *Strelitzia regina*. Star jasmine on the walls wafts its fragrance into the house in early summer.

OPPOSITE BOTTOM
Walls divide the garden into rooms, much as in an indoor art gallery.

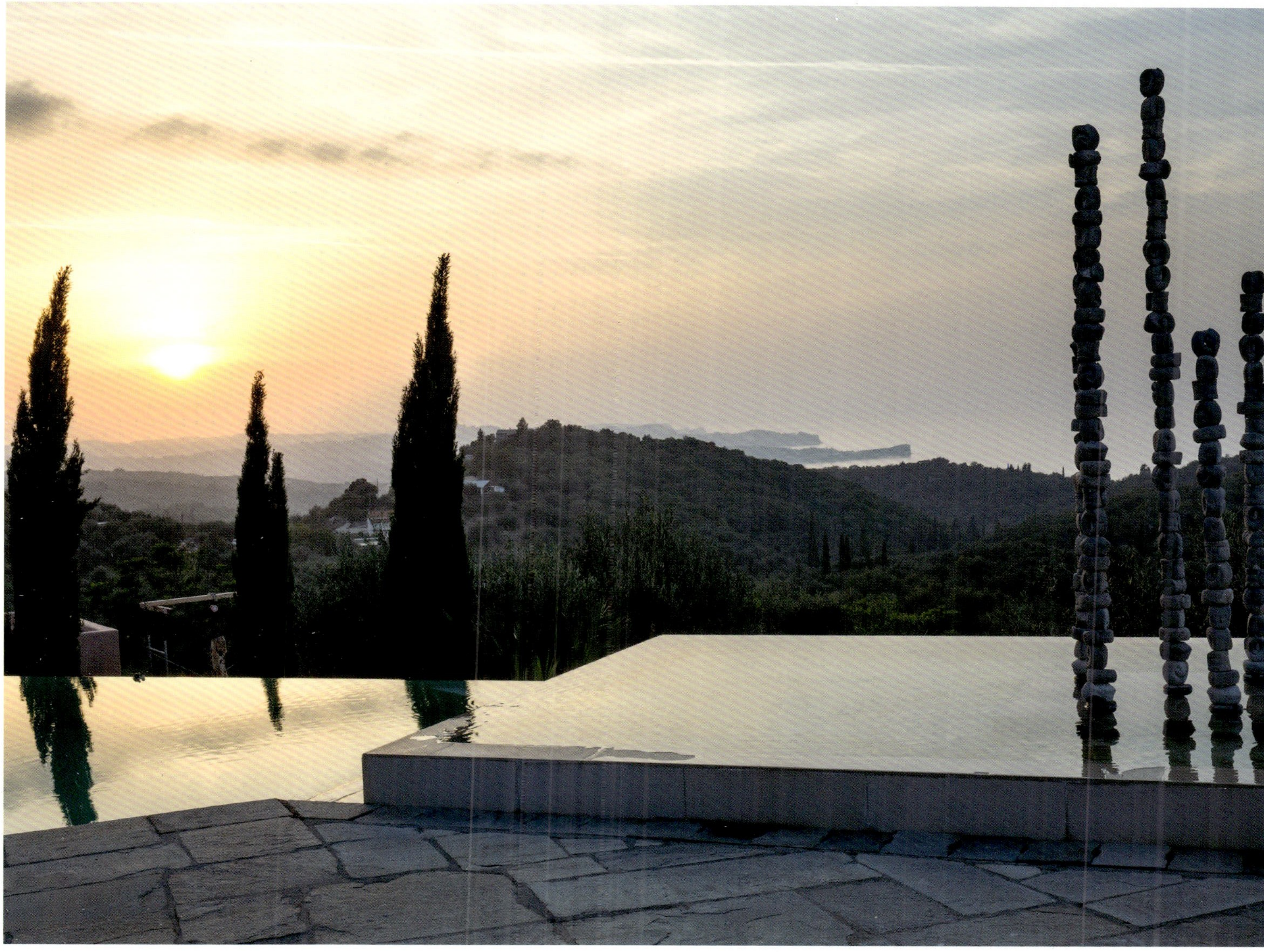

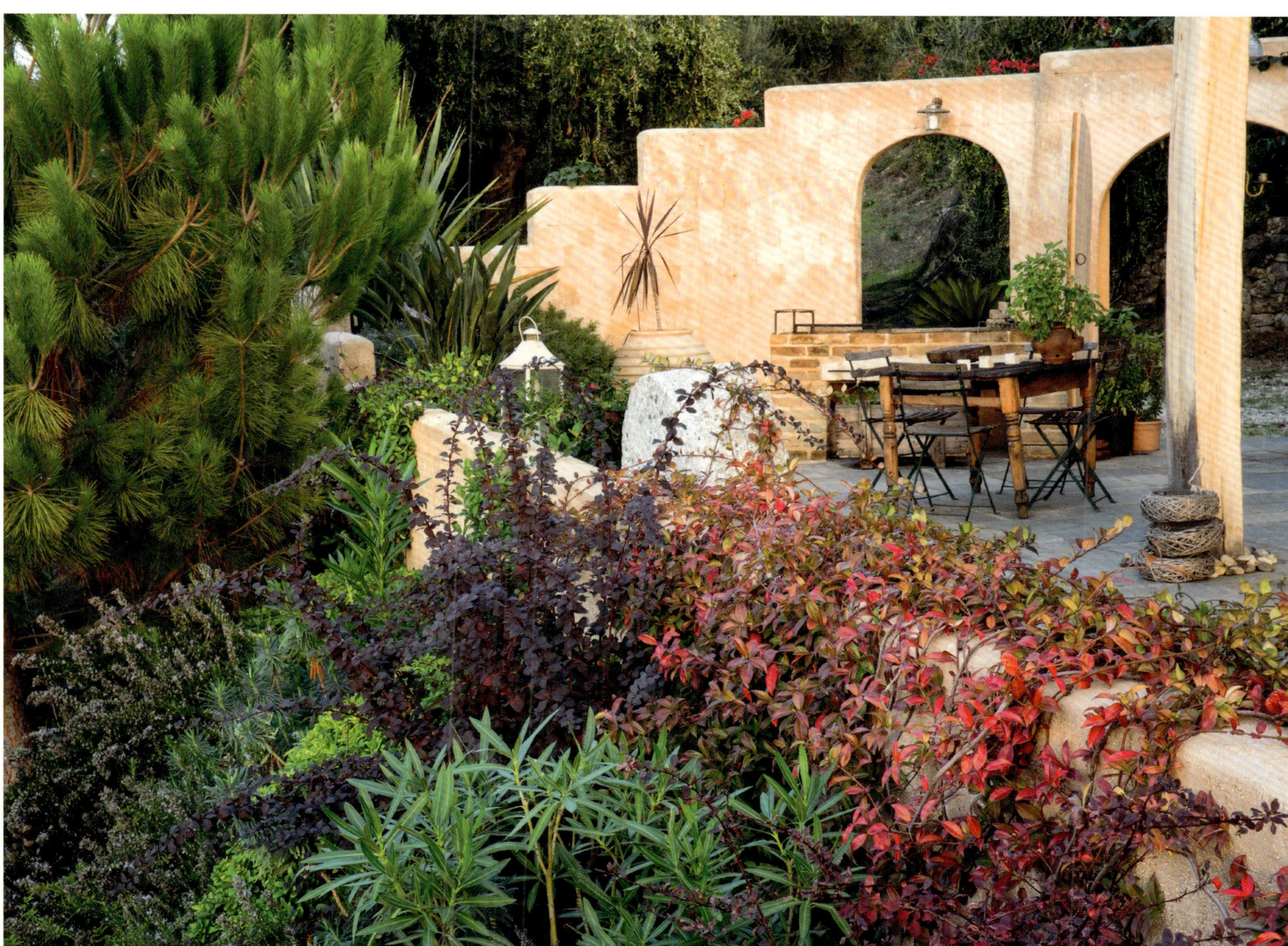

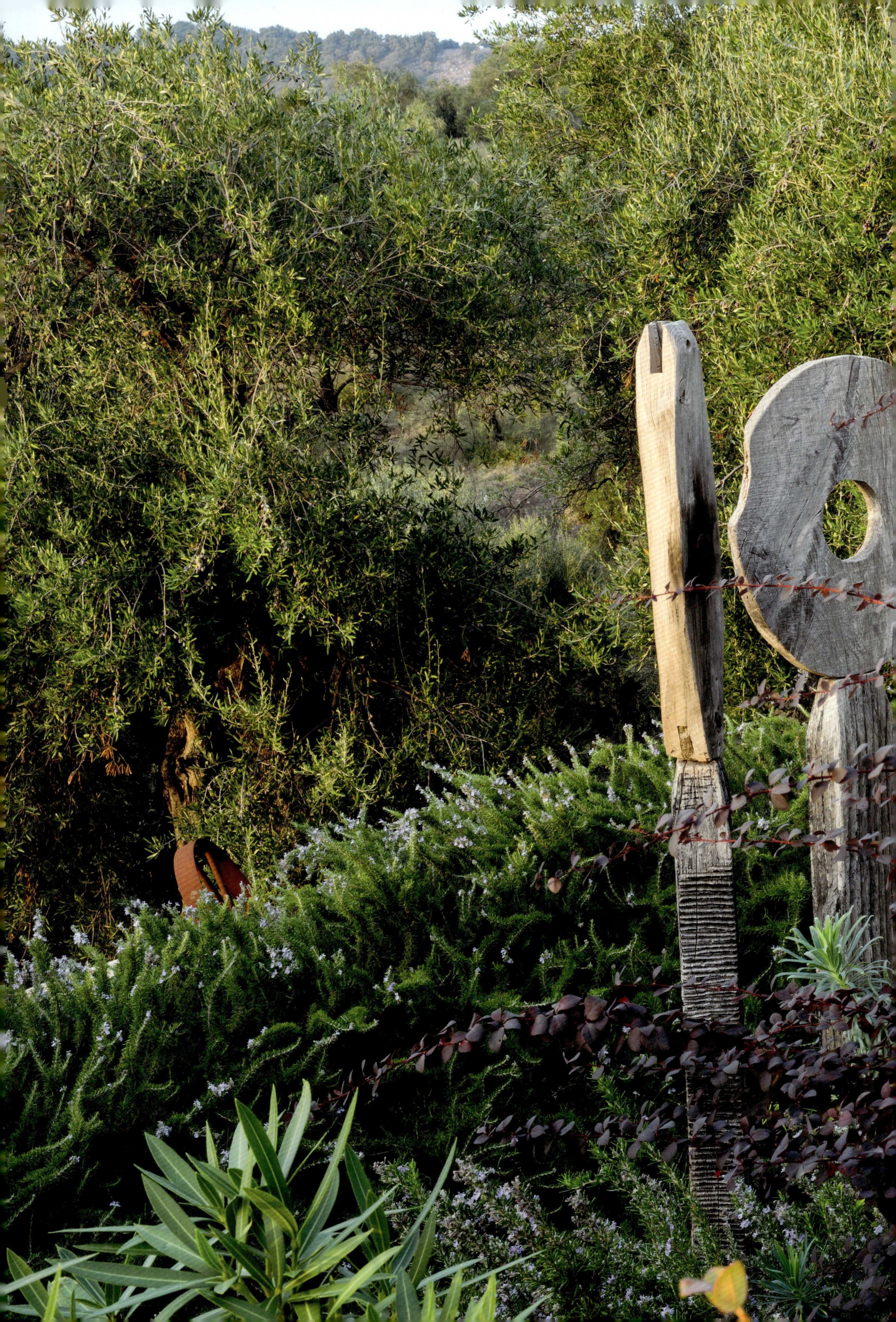

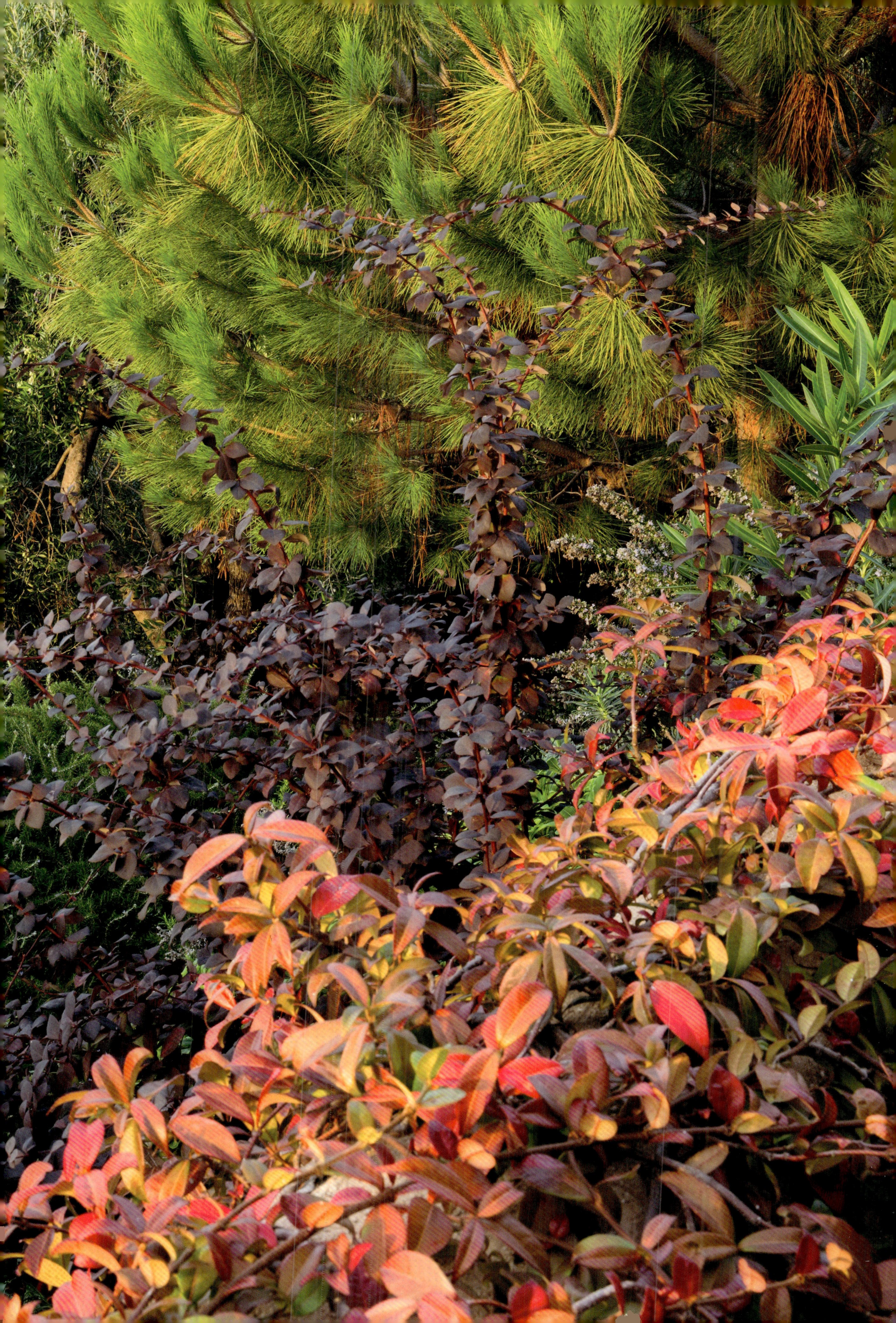

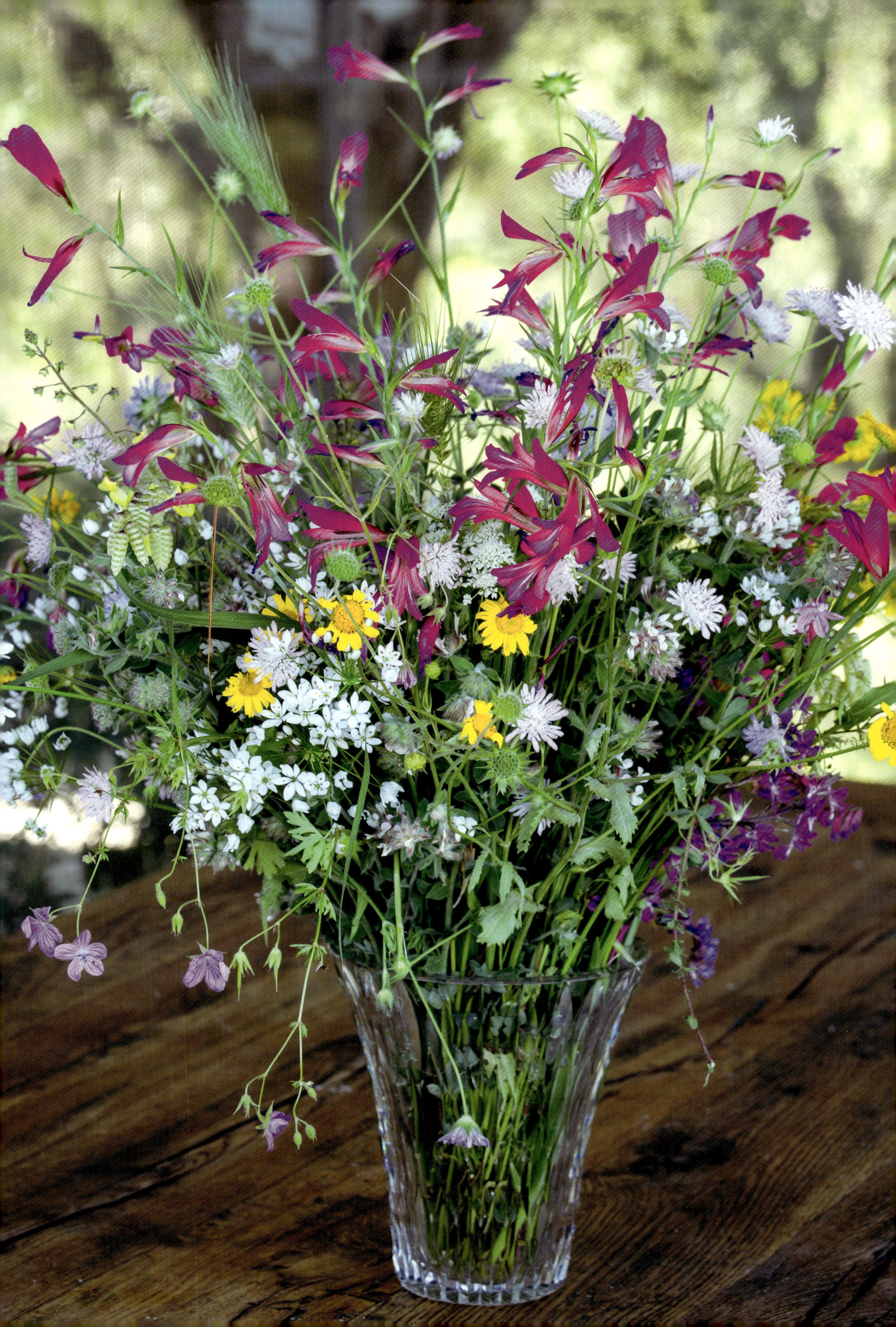

Bellerbe

OPPOSITE
May wildflowers, gathered from around the garden at Bellerbe. They include magenta *Gladiolus italicus*, white Neapolitan garlic (*Allium neapolitanum*), pale blue scabious (*Scabiosa atropurpurea*), and yellow corn marigold (*Chrysanthemum segetum*).

The name 'Bellerbe' comes from the Venetians, who called this area near Káto Korakiána 'belle erbe': the place where good and beautiful herbs grow. Bruce and Marina McAlpine's contemporary, very naturalistic garden here was designed by Alithea Johns of Skopos Design. The garden surrounds the house on the top of a conical hill that has breathtaking views: toward the sea to the east, and inland to the west over steep wooded hills and valleys. About 1.3 hectares in size, the garden was established in 2010.

An example par excellence of design based on the 'found landscape', Bellerbe is distinctive for its sculptural forms created from the trees and shrubs that were found on site. Marina comments that 'We were keen to leave the atmosphere untouched and did not want to add plants that you would not find in the surrounding land. We have used native shrubs and plants that are used to the extremes in weather, the heavy rains in winter, and the scorching sun in summer. We have taken great care not to fell or disturb any of the more than one hundred olive trees, each one a sculpture in itself, that cover the estate.'

The olive trees, centuries old and up to fifteen metres high, became a defining feature of the garden. They are carefully pruned and maintained to show their branching, spreading shapes to best advantage. Nothing is grown under them, so that their forms can be best appreciated. The other defining feature of the garden is its beautifully cloud-pruned native shrubs. Colour in the garden is mainly green and grey, with white blossoms added by star jasmine and oleander and blue by *Plumbago auriculata*.

Johns has said that her greatest inspiration as a designer comes from 'following nature', especially 'the natural vegetation of Corfu', but she also acknowledges the influence of Nicole de Vésian,[45] whose path-breaking Provençal gardens make distinctive use of sculpted native shrubs. Johns explains that with its strikingly simple choice of plants and its stylised shapes, the success of the design at Bellerbe depends crucially on good garden maintenance; nature provides the material but it is the hand of the gardener that shapes it into art. In fact, the garden is beautifully maintained, largely by Fótis Skarlátos.

45. See, for example, Louisa Jones, *Nicole de Vésian Gardens: Modern Design in Provence* (Paris: Actes Sud, 2011).

Sunlight accentuates the shapes of these sculpted bushes. In the foreground, the trunks of olive trees. Pruning by Spiros Gogas.

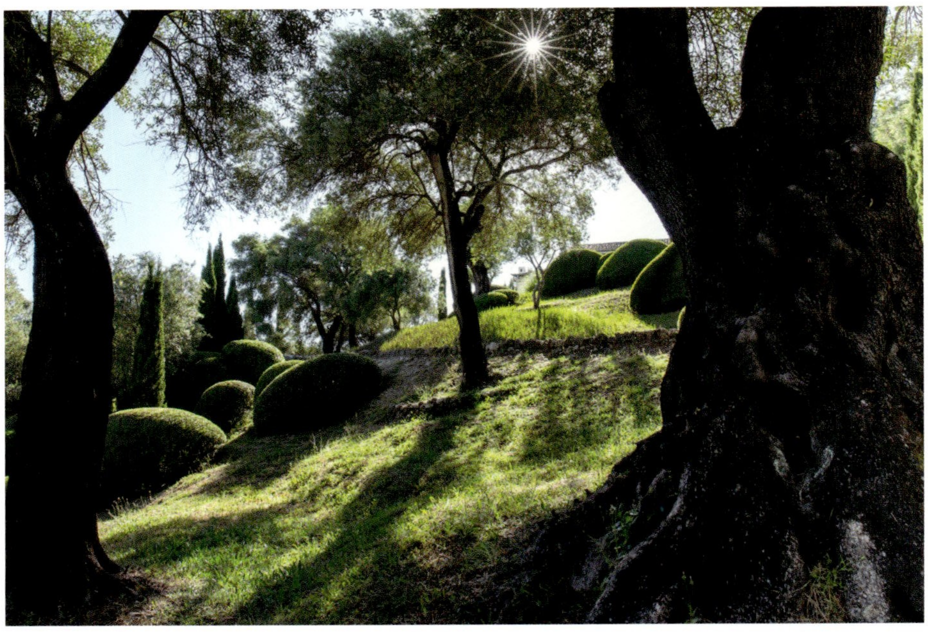

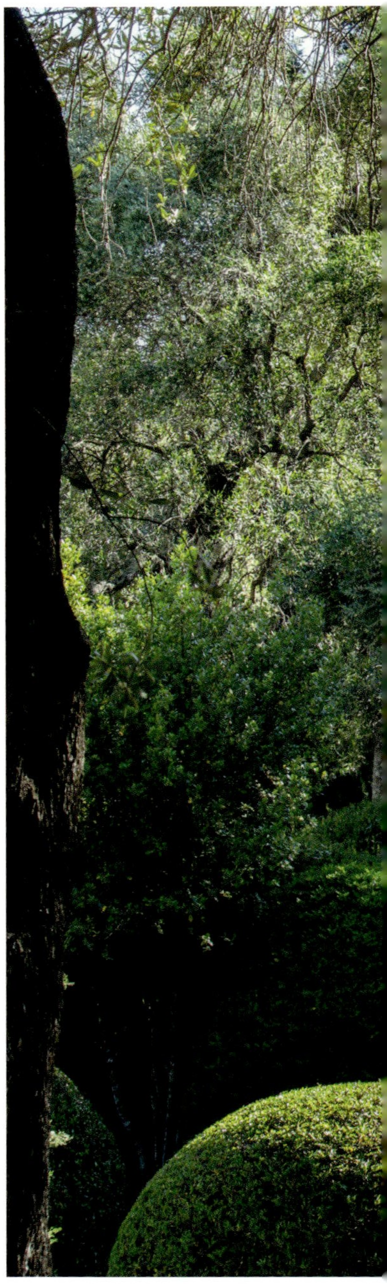

On the western side of the house, a flight of graceful steps leads down the hill to the olive grove on the way to the pool. Once into the grove the path becomes less formal, changing to stepping stones.

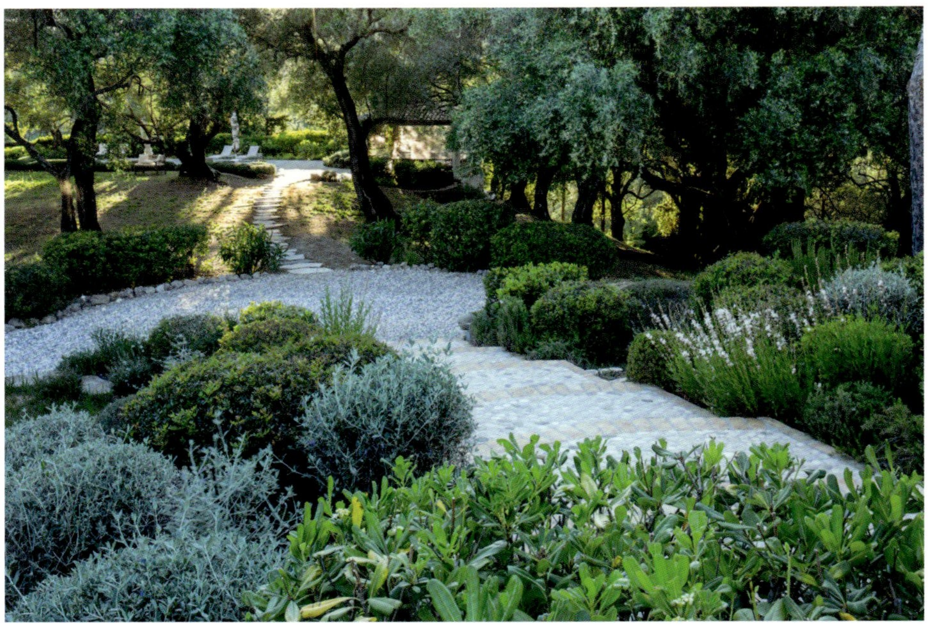

The restful veranda along the western front of the house is paved with local antique brick. The window shutters are in traditional Corfiot style.

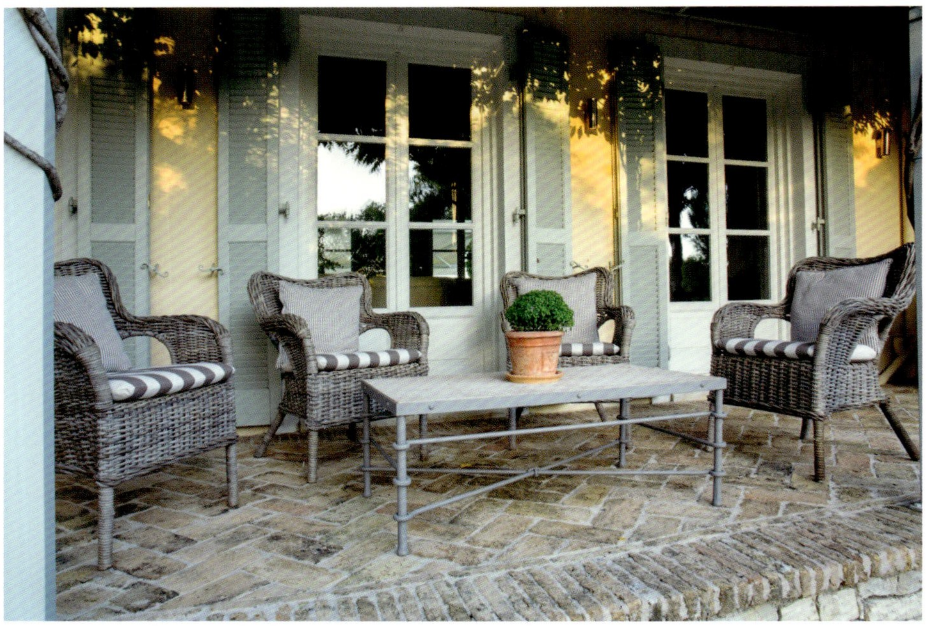

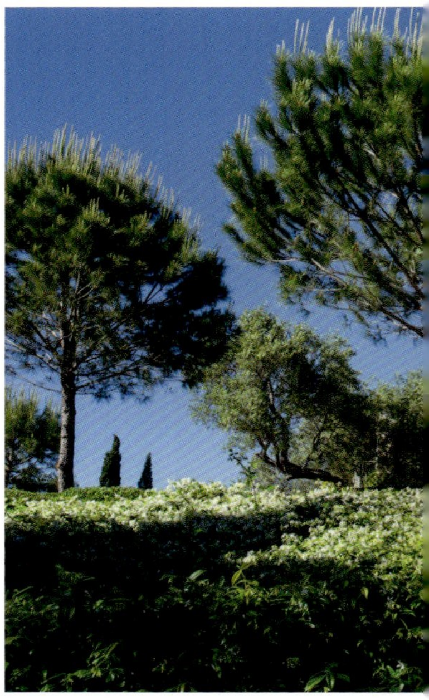

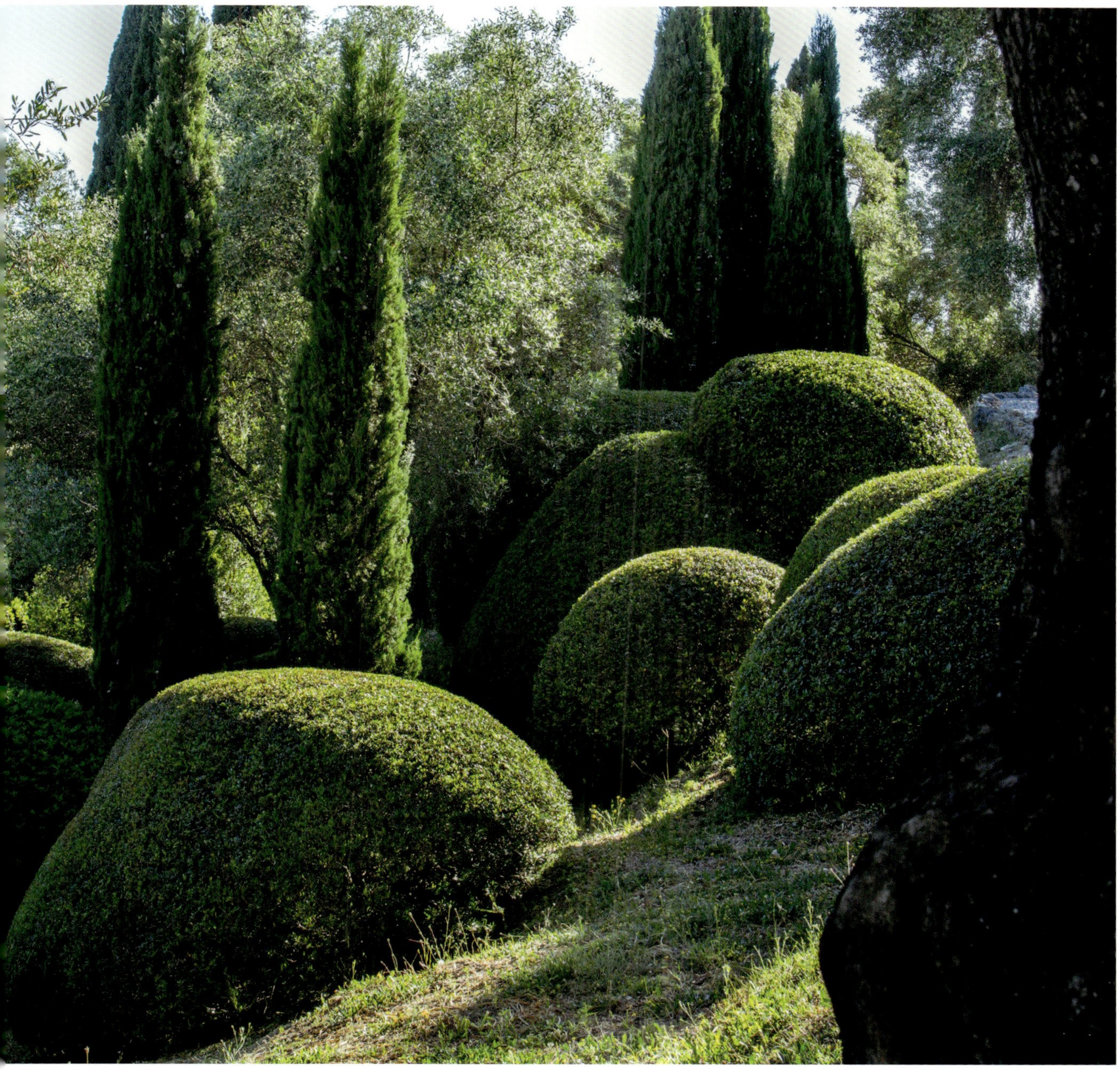

Johns planted cypresses to add drama to the shapes of the native lentiscs (*Pistacia lentiscus*) and strawberry trees (*Arbutus unedo*) found on site.

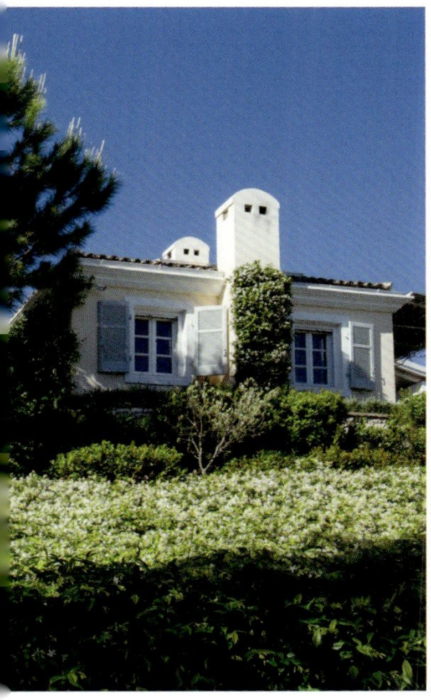

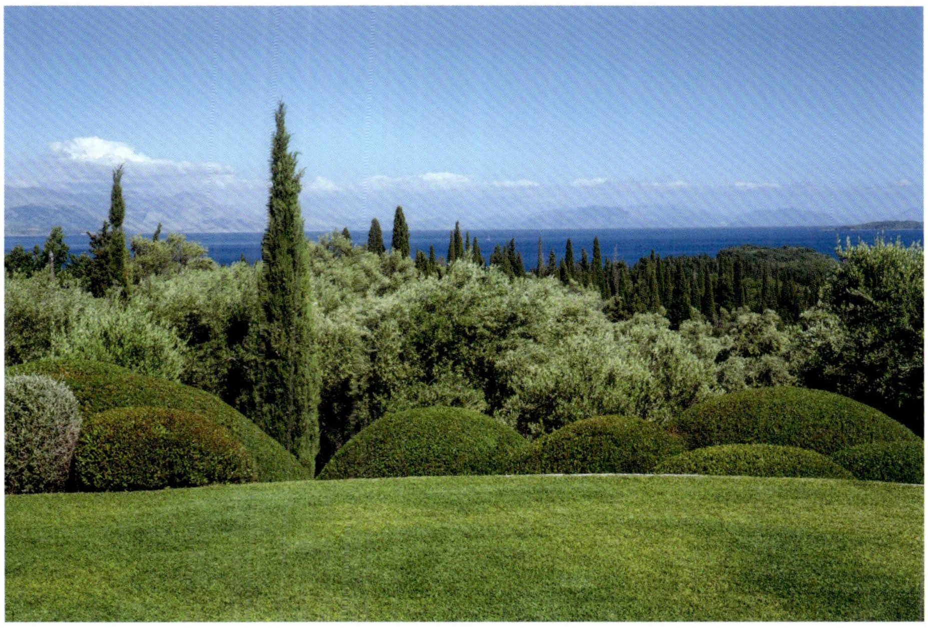

CENTRE BOTTOM
Star jasmine (*Trachelospermum jasminoides*) is used very effectively to cover a slope next to the driveway, as well as more conventionally on the chimney and the pillars of the veranda. The stone pine (*Pinus pinea*), three of which are planted in front of the house, is a favourite tree of Bruce's.

The lawn at the back of the house looks over the tops of olives and cypresses to the sea. The lentisc bushes in the foreground, now meticulously clipped, were already growing on site in their wild state.

The pool, with its dark water and beautiful proportions, sits comfortably among the old trees. The soft grey stone paving is laid diagonally, helping the pool area look less self-contained.

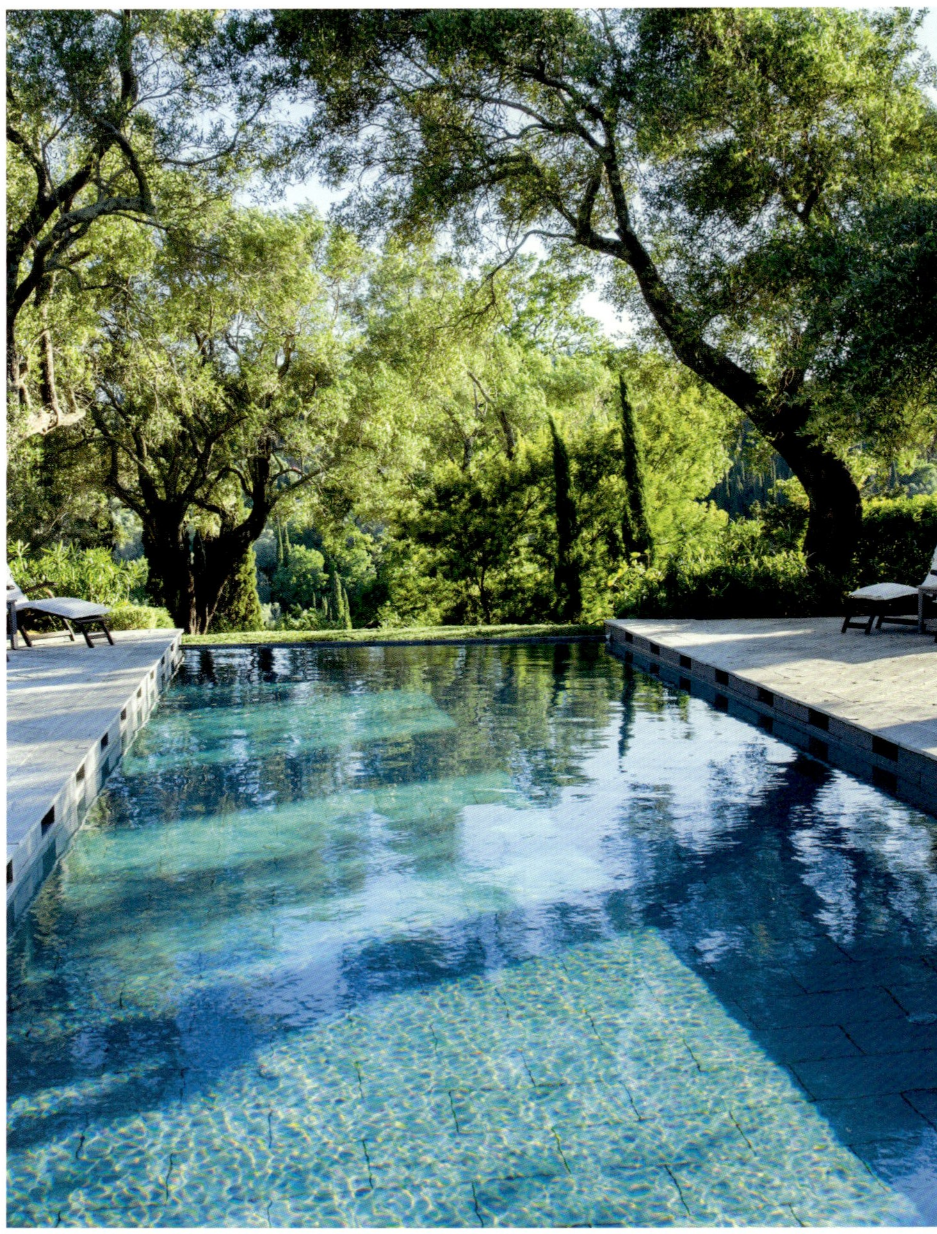

OPPOSITE
Carefully pruned and maintained, the centuries-old olive trees are a defining feature of the garden.

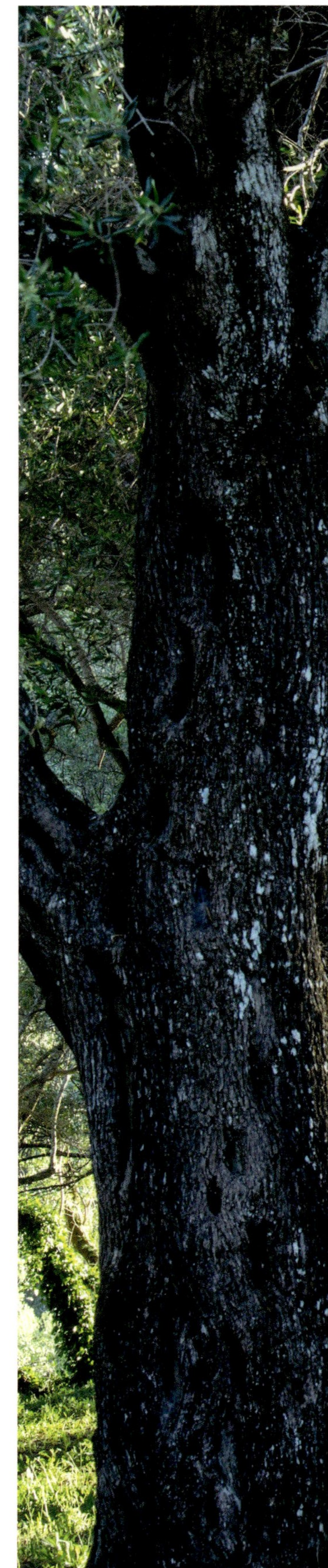

When Johns began work, the native bushes that now form sculpted masses were all in situ in their wild state. She directed their pruning by Spíros Gógas, and added cypresses among them. Beside the driveway she added tree germander and *Agapanthus* and left the existing patches of tough native pearl grass (*Melica ciliata*), with its attractive white foxtail flower spikes, to spread as a groundcover.

The back of the house, facing southeast, opens to a shaded veranda and an expanse of lawn with a spectacular view to the sea and Corfu Town beyond. Johns planted lavenders and glossy abelia at the edge of the veranda, along with climbing wisteria and star jasmine—which now thickly covers the pillars. Clumps of pampas grass add wispy shapes, catching the wind and adding movement to the view.

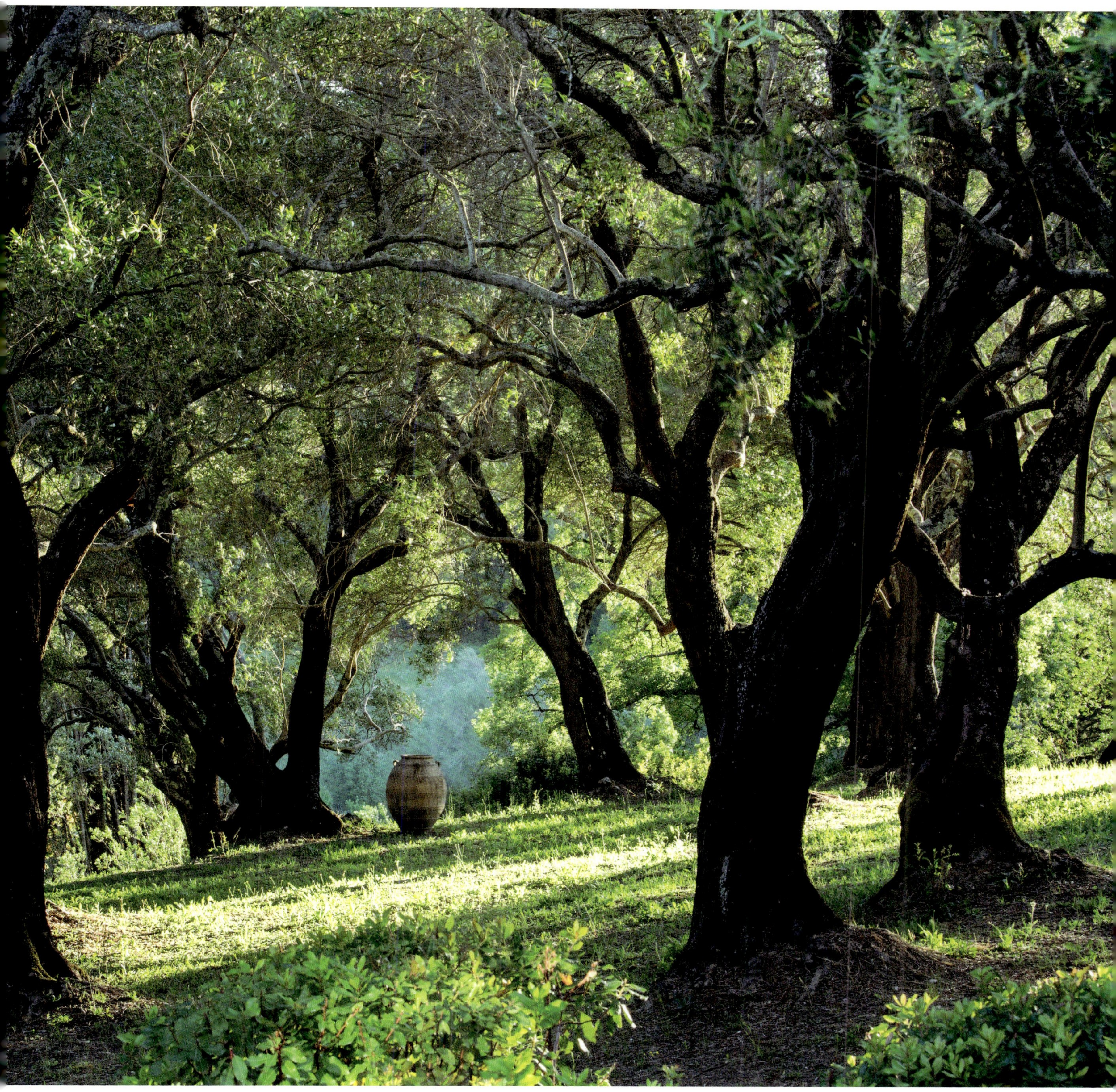

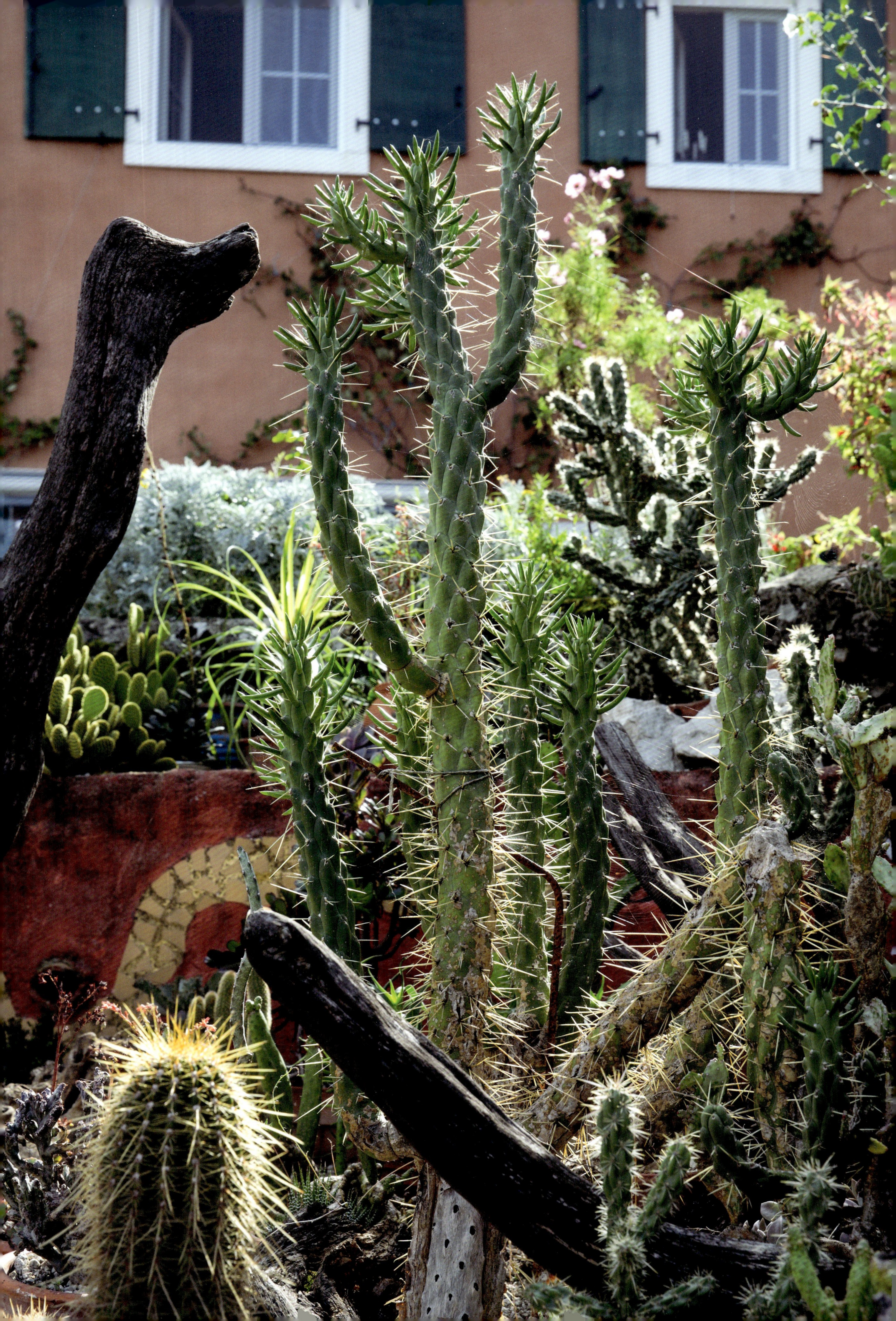

A garden in Láfki

This eclectic, highly original garden is on a steep north-facing hillside in Láfki, a mountain village with stunning views. The owner, Alyson Deléglise, now an artist in mosaics, was for many years in the travel business, and the garden showcases plants she and her husband Denis have collected on all continents of the world. One cactus came as a cutting from a volcanic mountainside in Cape Verde; another travelled in a briefcase from Mexico. An heirloom red iris from an aunt in France, and a pineapple sage from a friend in Zimbabwe, are among the many unusual plants received as swaps or gifts from relatives, friends, and neighbours. Though winter frost is a problem in exposed parts of this garden, which is at roughly five hundred metres, the relatively cool summers allow Alyson and Denis to grow a range of temperate-climate plants that would not thrive lower down.

OPPOSITE
The garden contains several varied plant collections, including spurges (*Euphorbia*), large grasses, and cactuses and succulents, seen here.

Work on the garden began some twenty years ago when the owners acquired the house and began its restoration. At that time the garden was an untended strip of land; it now extends down the steep hillside in multiple terraces linked by stone staircases and walkways to a patio with a swimming pool. Two mature oak trees and a large old nettle tree were left in place and provide valuable shade. Halfway down, paths lead to a natural-looking pond with yellow flag iris, water plantain, and water lilies—not to mention dragonflies and frogs.

Every inch of the garden is richly planted. Beds at all levels feature a wide range of flowering shrubs, colourful perennials, and bulbs. Several beds are devoted to groupings by type of plant, highlighting the dramatic variations in colour and form within the plant groups. This is also a highly productive garden, with pomegranates, peaches, soft fruit including currants and gooseberries, and raised beds that produce salad greens and a broad range of summer vegetables, including heirloom tomatoes.

The garden is always full of life and movement. The owners' cats normally accompany visitors, prowling ahead on the paths, slinking through the planting beds, and leaping into trees to survey the scene. The owners' own abundant creative energy means that there is always something just built, just made, just reaching the peak of its flowering, or just ready to be harvested.

The garden extends down the hillside on multiple terraces.

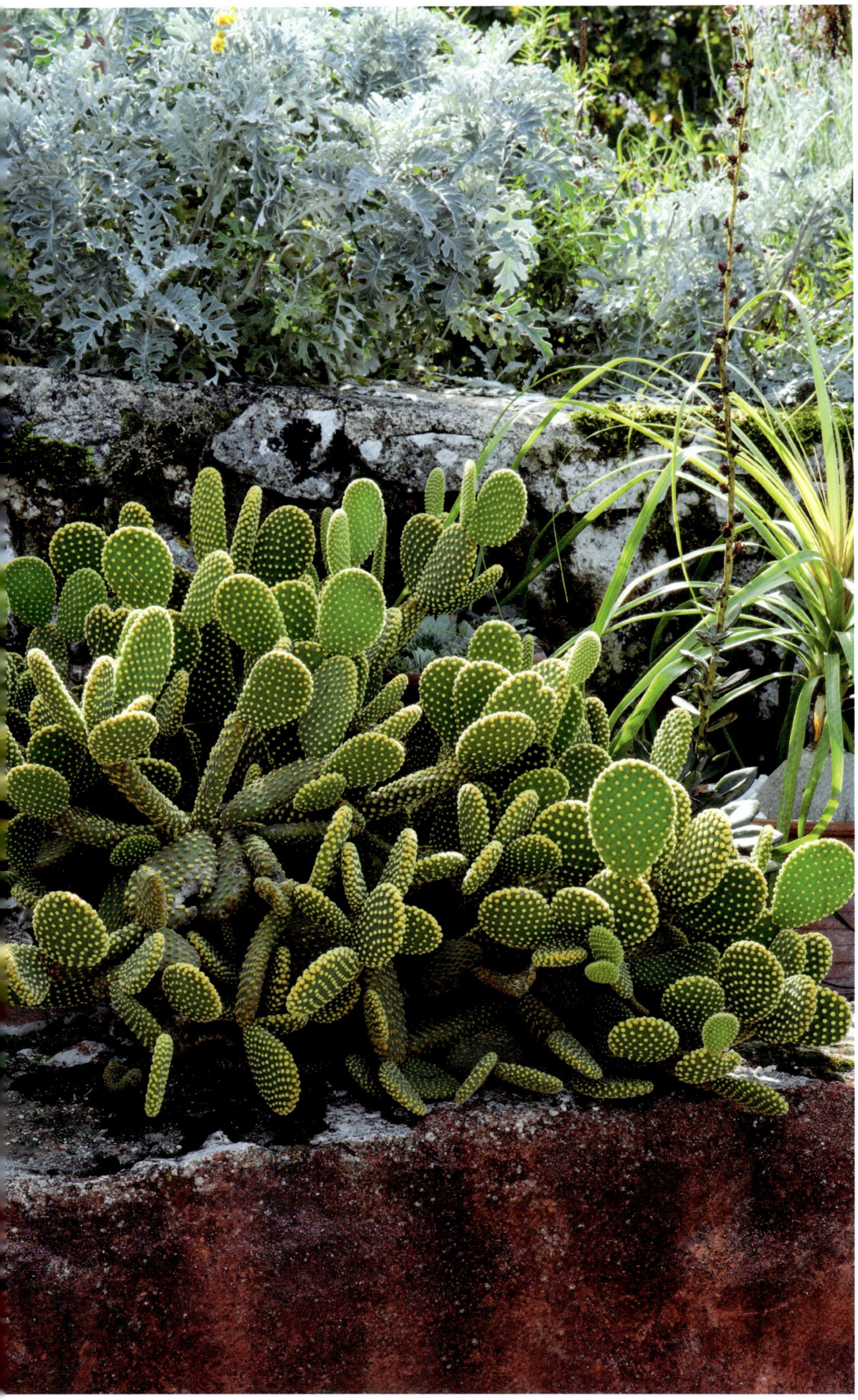

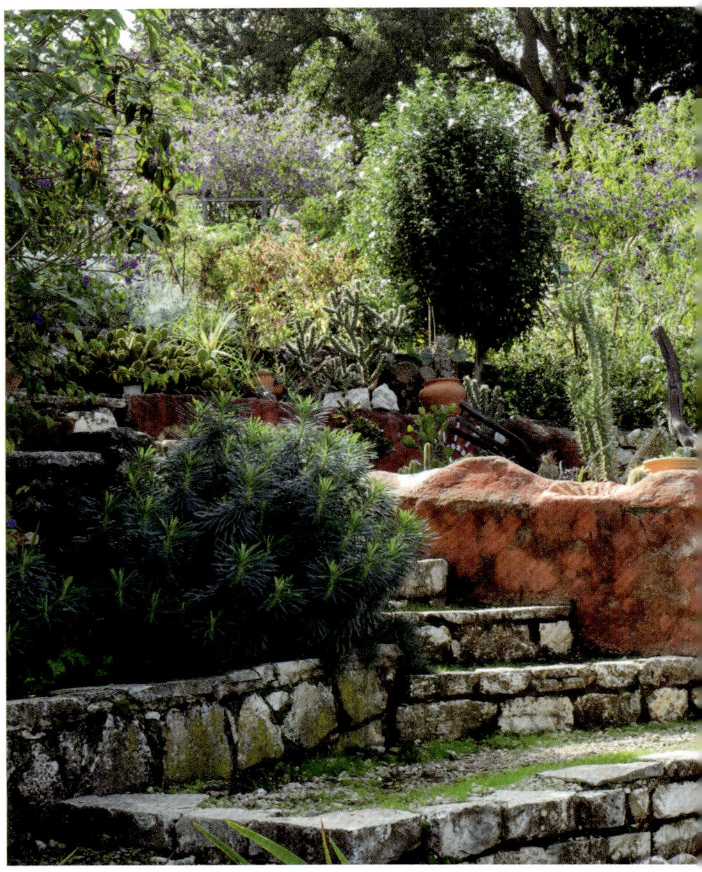

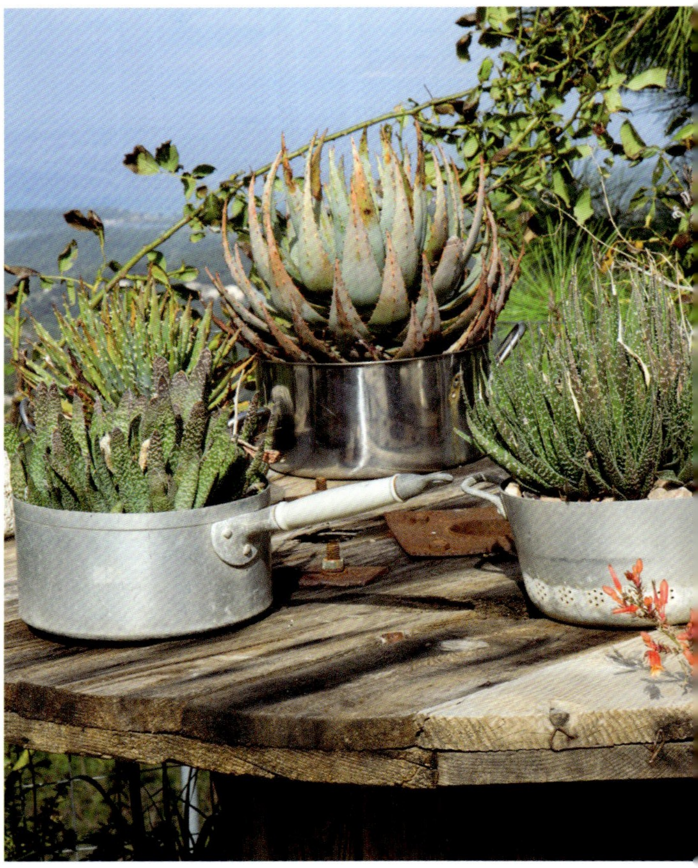

Jacobaea maritima in an effective combination with bunny ear cactus (*Opuntia microdasys*) and a young *Dracaena*.

A whimsical collection with a view to the coast below.

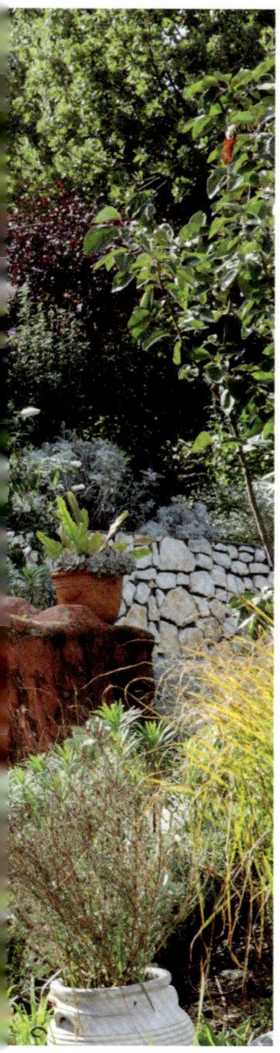

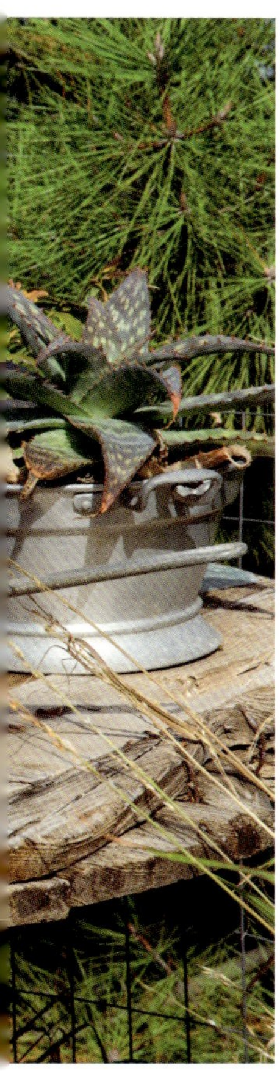

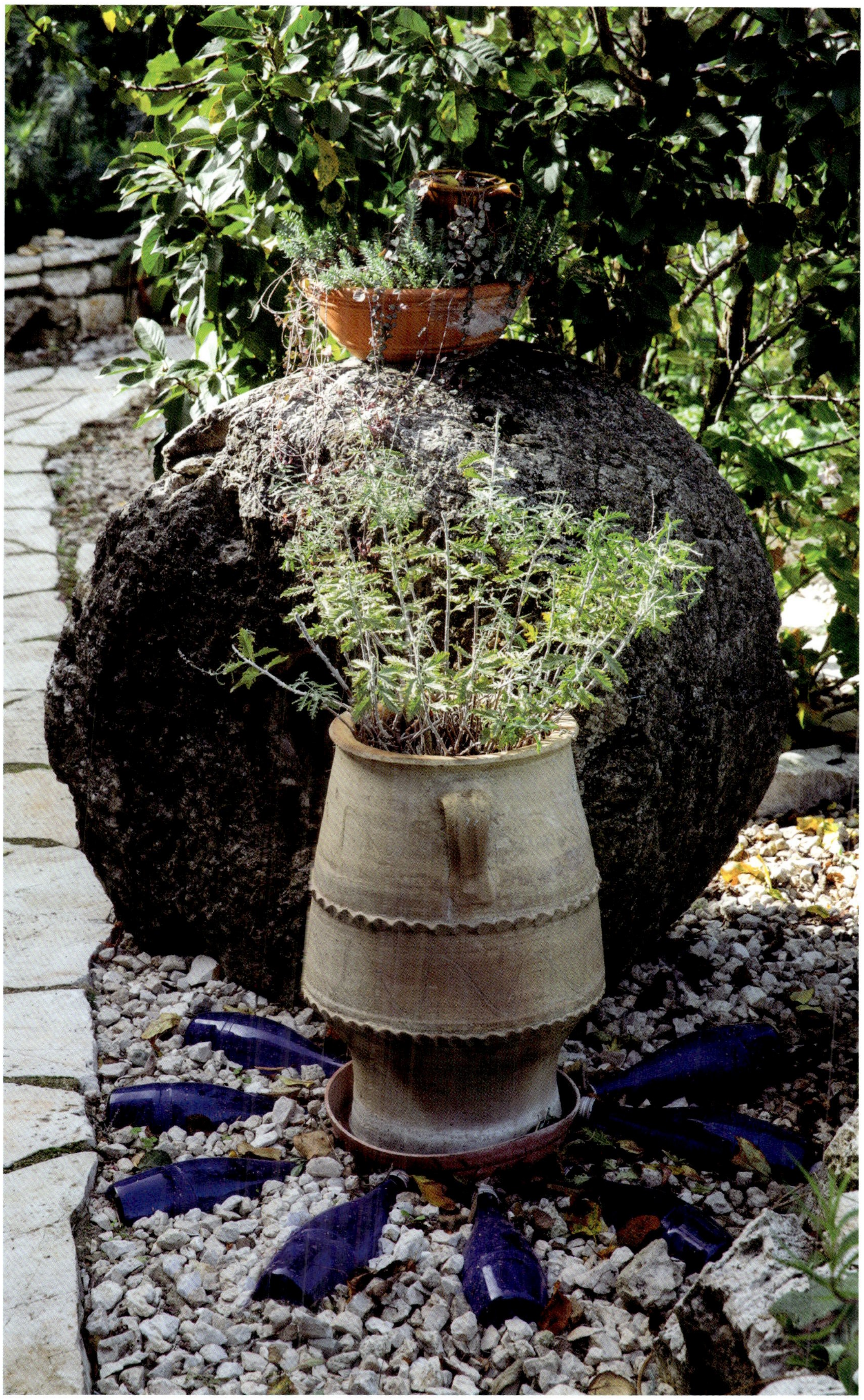

Found objects and other decorative pieces abound in this garden, along with mosaics created by the owner, adding to the sense of excitement and joy of discovery as one explores.

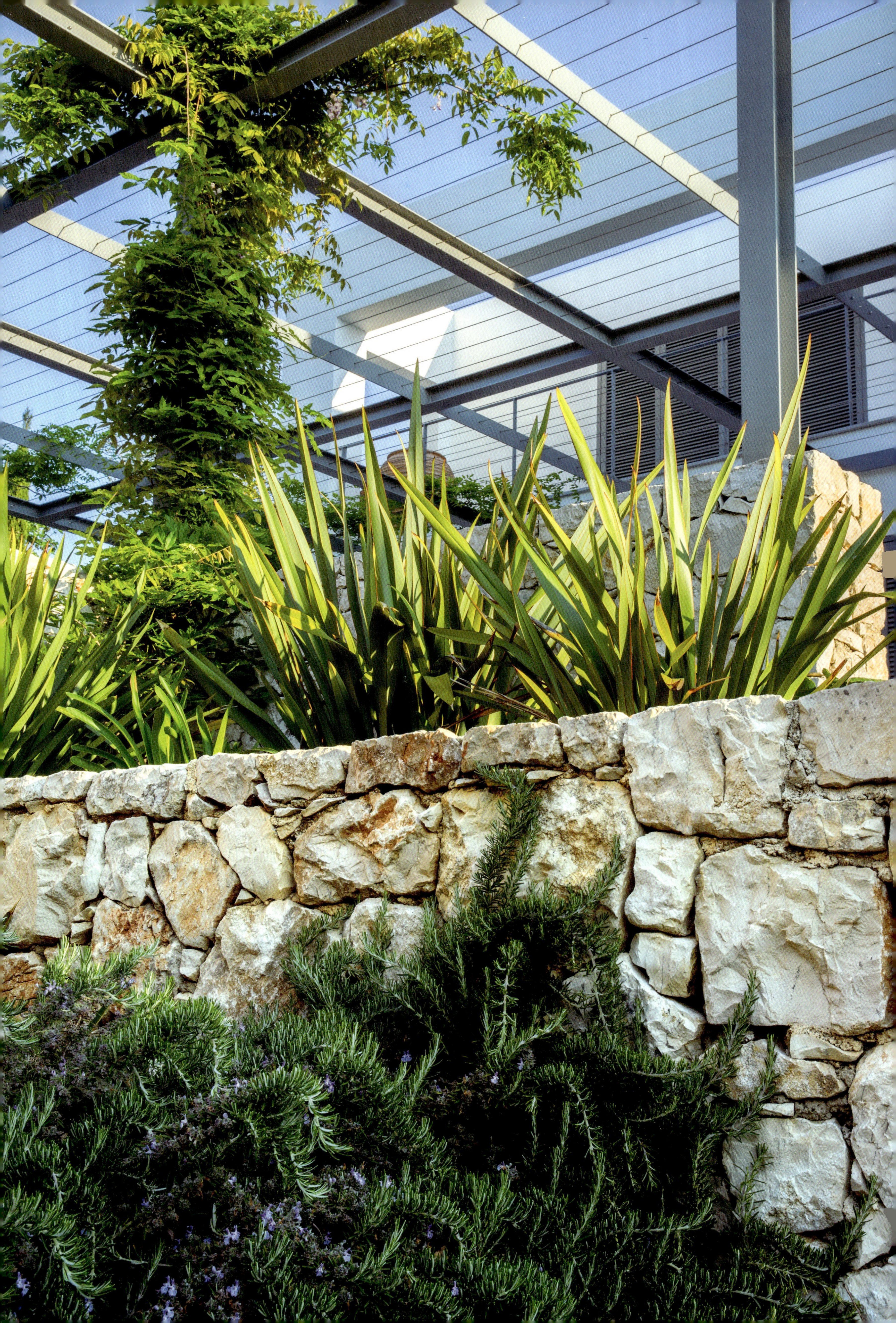

A garden in northeast Corfu

Creating this villa on a bluff overlooking the sea, architect Pitsou Kedem used the framework of a house that previously stood here, paring down the original to its most essential lines. Designing the garden on this site bathed in light from dawn to dusk, Alithea Johns and Marcus Warren of Skopos Design worked in the same contemporary minimalist idiom. Together they have created a serene and graceful place where drama is evoked by the contrasts between wide open spaces and secluded corners, between wild and controlled, and between bright sunlight and the play of dramatic shadows.

For the owners, this is a second home for relaxation and fun but also for connecting with the earth: the original almond orchard has been left in place, as have the old olive trees, and new fruit trees have been added, including modern olive varieties, cherries, plums, and loquats. The owners cure their own olives and are proud that their large vegetable garden, in a sheltered spot below the house, 'provides hundreds of kilos of vegetables' each year.

The dramatic approach to the house—a deeply shaded corridor carved through rock at the top of a steep ascent—puts one in mind of a medieval stronghold. Here, the original trees remain, including tall branching kermes oaks, bays, and holm oaks. Bright evergreen plants grow in rock pockets on either side of the path: round-leaved *Farfugium japonicum* and clumps of lily-turf (*Liriope muscari*). At the end of the corridor, a dramatic view opens over the sea below, the tops of trees in the fruit orchard, and the clean lines of the contemporary house down the hill.

Close to the house, soft billowy planting complements the angular lines of the architecture and hardscaping. Subtle in its wide range of textures and narrow range of colours, always sensual and intriguing, it features blue-, white-, and mauve-flowering plants along with grey-leaved foliage, including fuzzy *Stachys byzantina* and *Echium fastuosum* and shiny *Convolvulus cneorum*; aromatic plants such as oregano and thyme; and drifts of graceful Mexican feathergrass. Beside the curving path down from the pool are narrow channels topped with gravel and planted with grasses and aromatic herbs rhythmically interspersed with boulders.

South of the house, where the midday light is very strong, the plants

OPPOSITE
Throughout this contemporary garden, the planting provides a confident complement to the architecture. Here the strong forms of New Zealand flax (*Phormium tenax*) and creeping rosemary (*Rosmarinus officinalis* 'Prostratus') hold their own in bright sunlight.

Elegant but tough, *Tulbaghia violacea* flowers in front of a New Zealand flax.

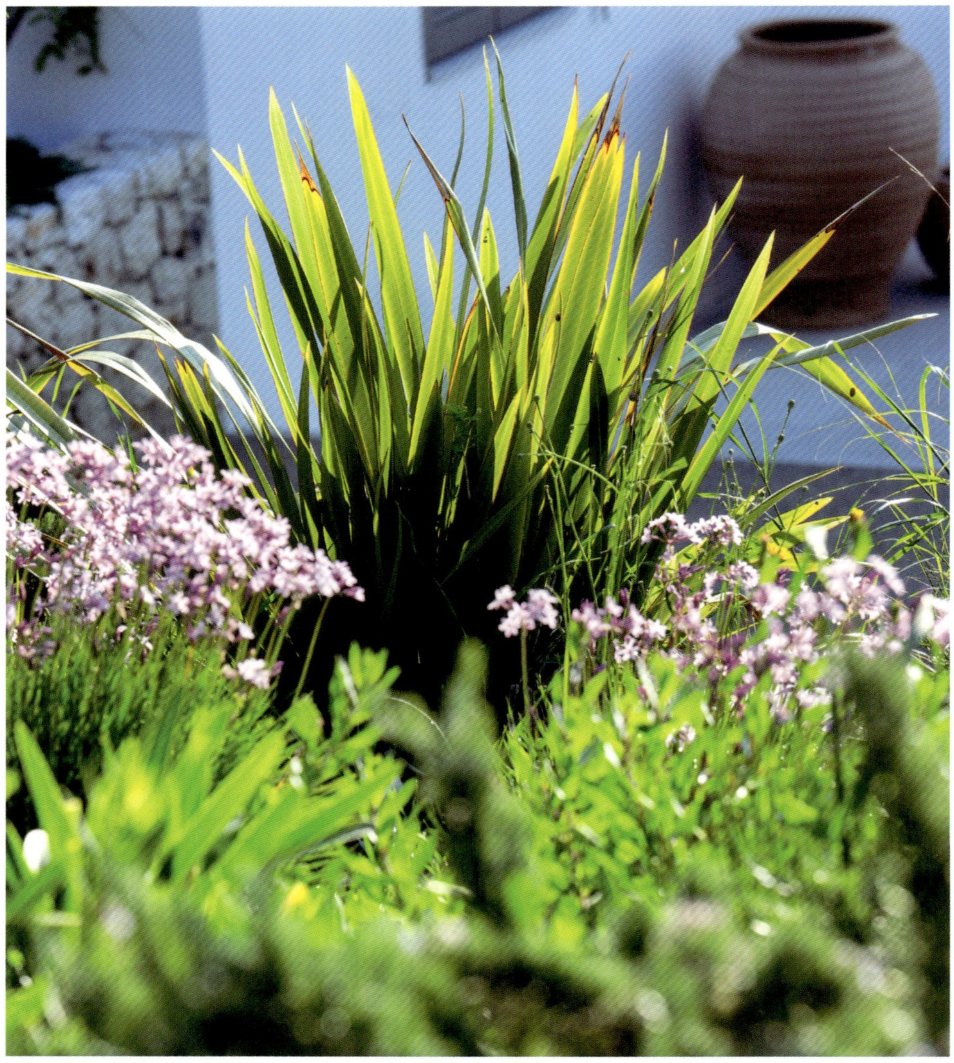

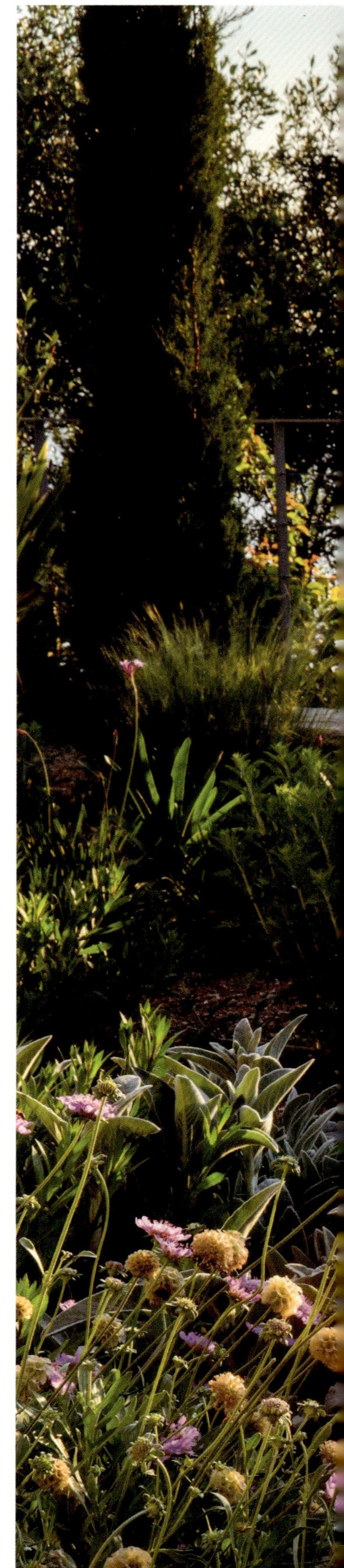

OPPOSITE
Fluffy-textured planting complements the clean lines of the architecture at the back of the house. In this corner of the herbaceous border are furry-leaved *Stachys byzantina* with *Scabiosa cretica* and Mexican feathergrass (*Stipa tenuissima*).

are mainly chosen for their architectural shapes and for their bright jewel-green colour. A large weeping willow at the corner creates intricate shadows with its almost constant movement in the sea breezes. Along with *Plumbago auriculata* and *Westringia fruticosa*, the plants here include *Farfugium japonicum*, *Agapanthus*, lily-turf, and large spiky New Zealand flax. A stone staircase leads down past a weeping pepper tree and further planting beds towards the sea.

At the water's edge, Skopos cleared away the natural scrub, including tangled thickets of spiny *Smilax aspera*, to expose the trunks of wild cypresses, Mediterranean buckthorn, and oaks, and made paved paths through the woodland down to a launching platform for swimming and water sports and a wooden deck for storing equipment. They added new pencil cypresses to the mix, and planted lily-turf to line the sides of the paved footpaths going up the hill, along with creeping fig to spread over the new stone walls.

The garden is ably maintained by Giánnis Kouloorídis.

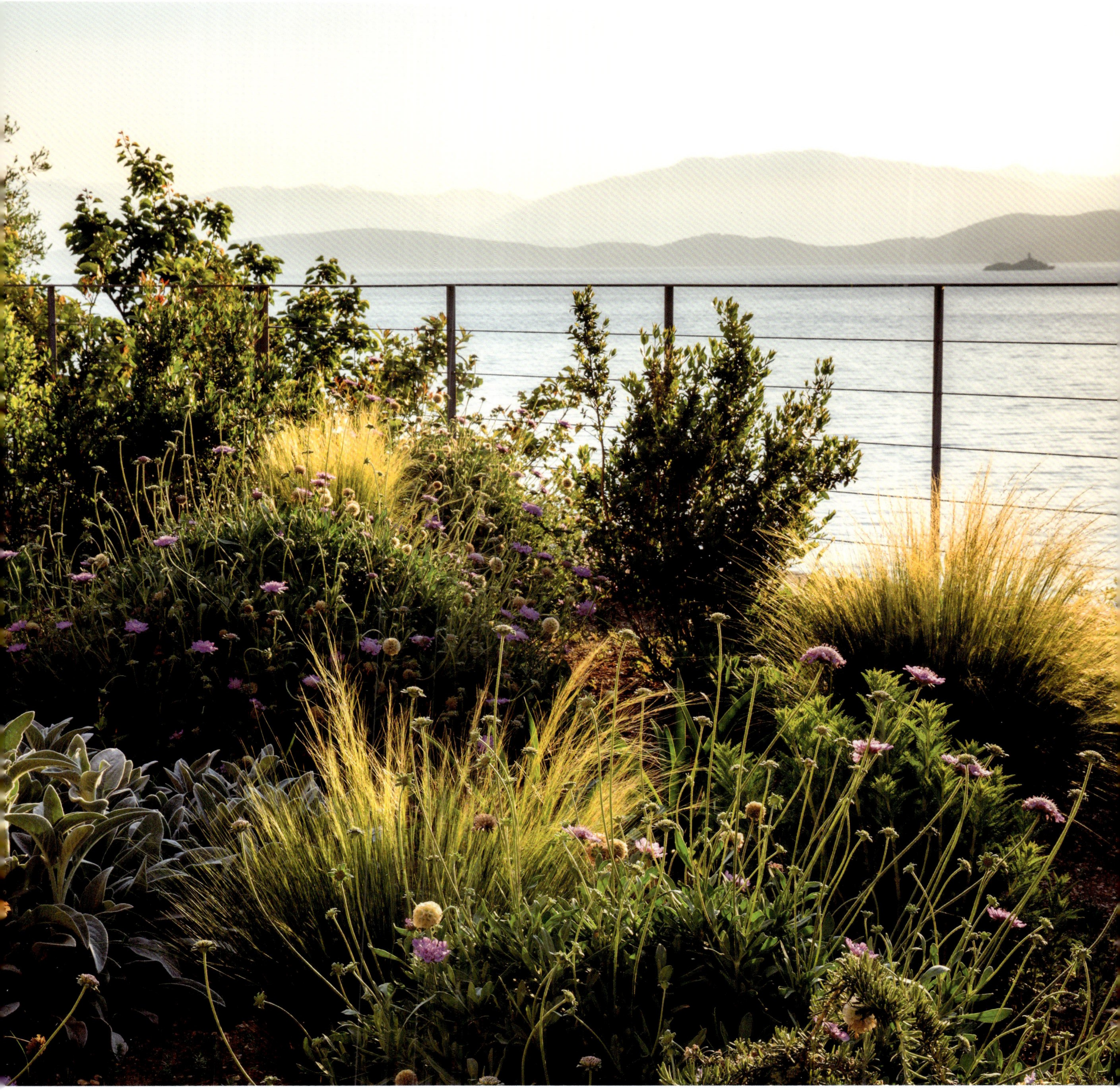

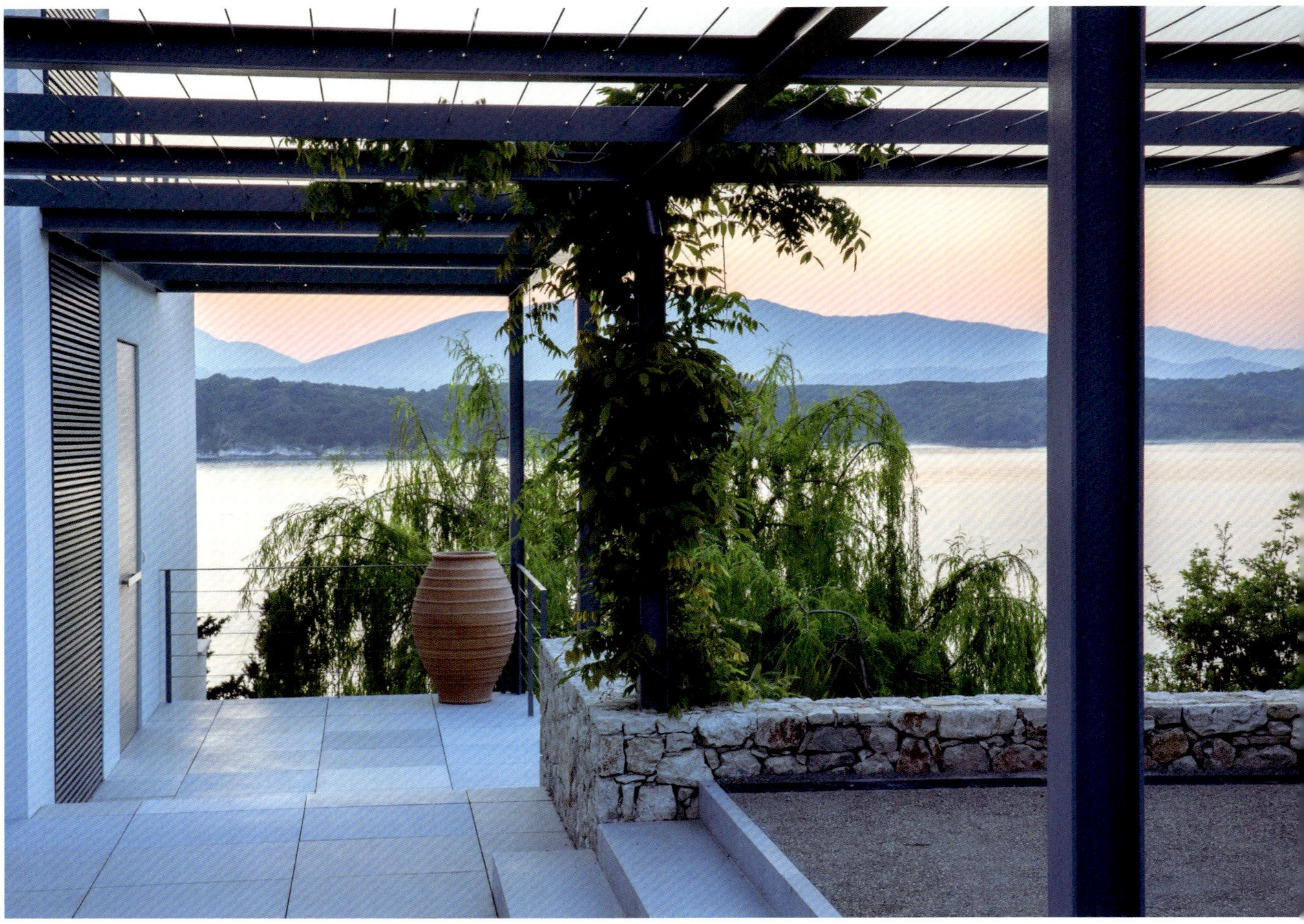

A view from the house's entrance level to the Corfu Straits and beyond.

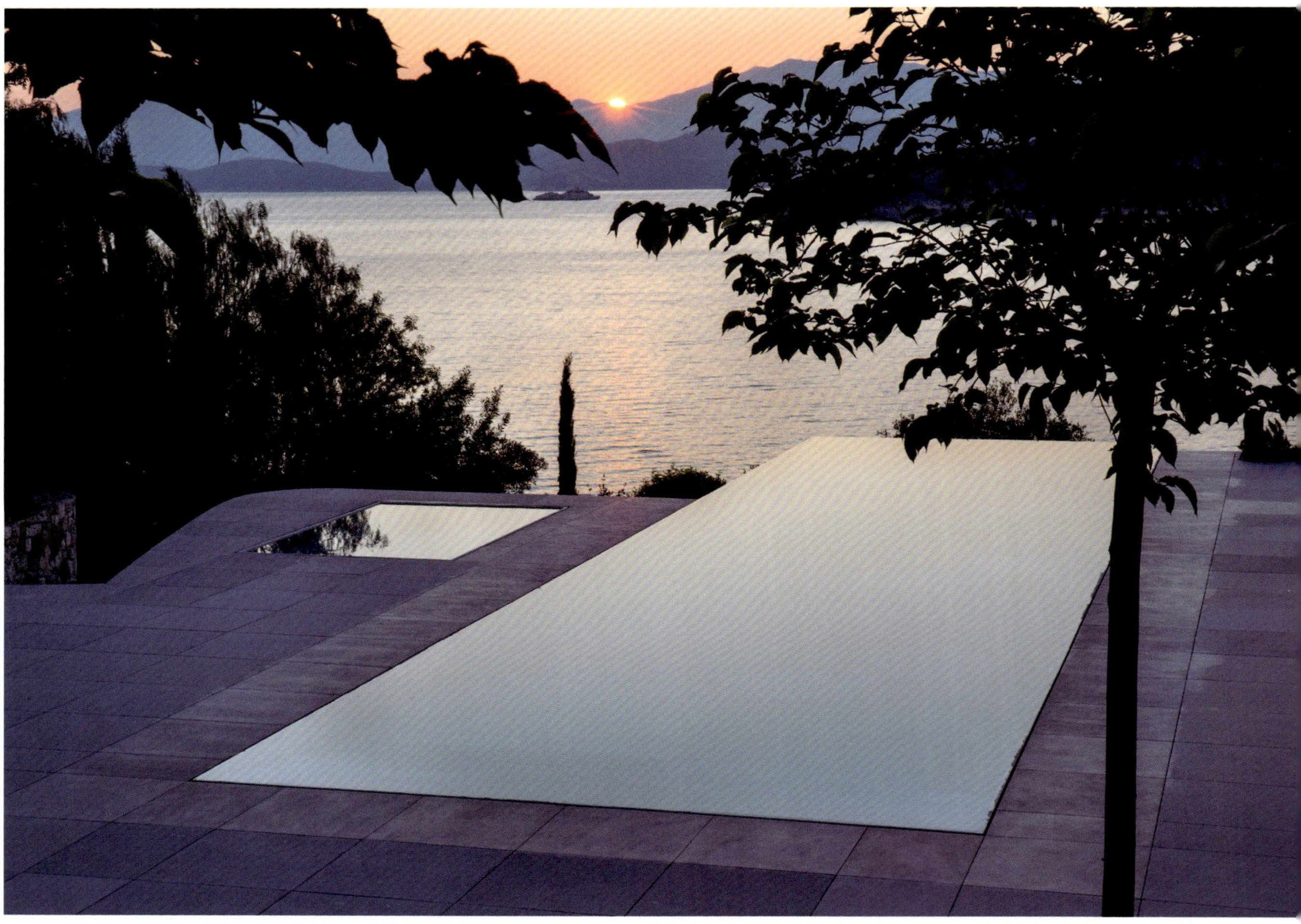

Day dawns over the pool.

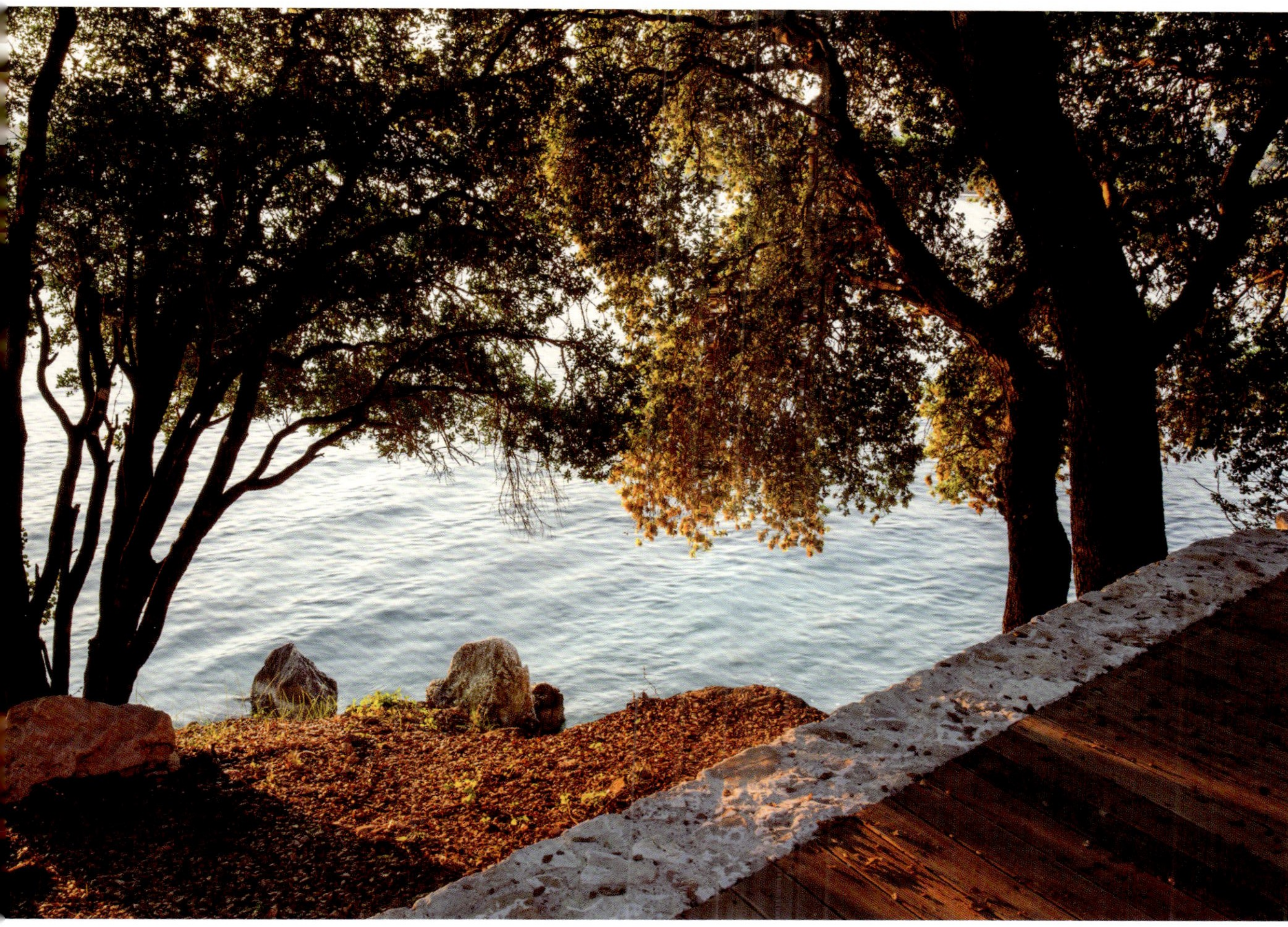

Next to the sea, the trees found on site included holm oaks (*Quercus ilex*), seen here, along with cypresses and Mediterranean buckthorn (*Rhamnus alaternus*).

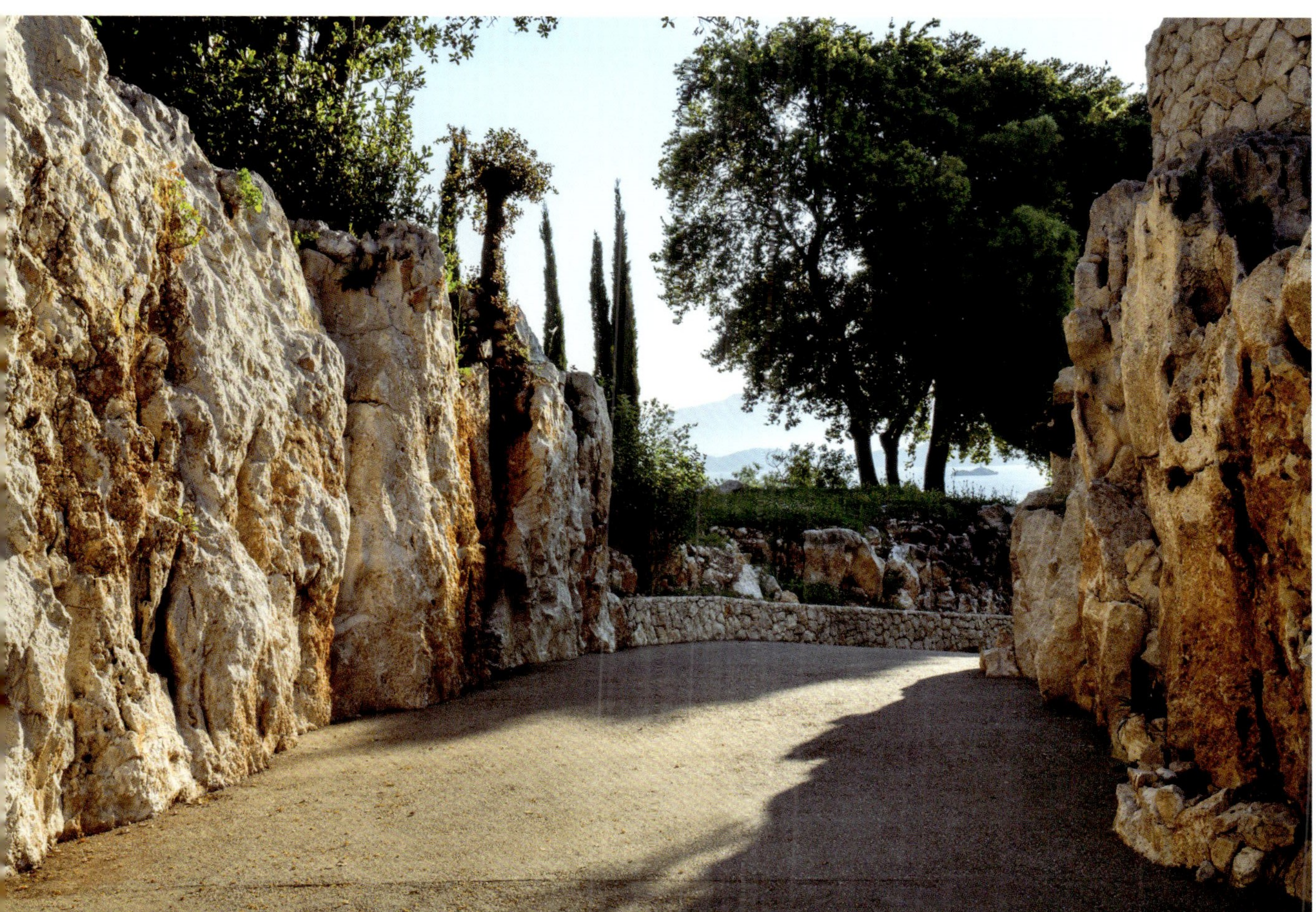

Creating the entrance corridor took three weeks of blasting through rock.

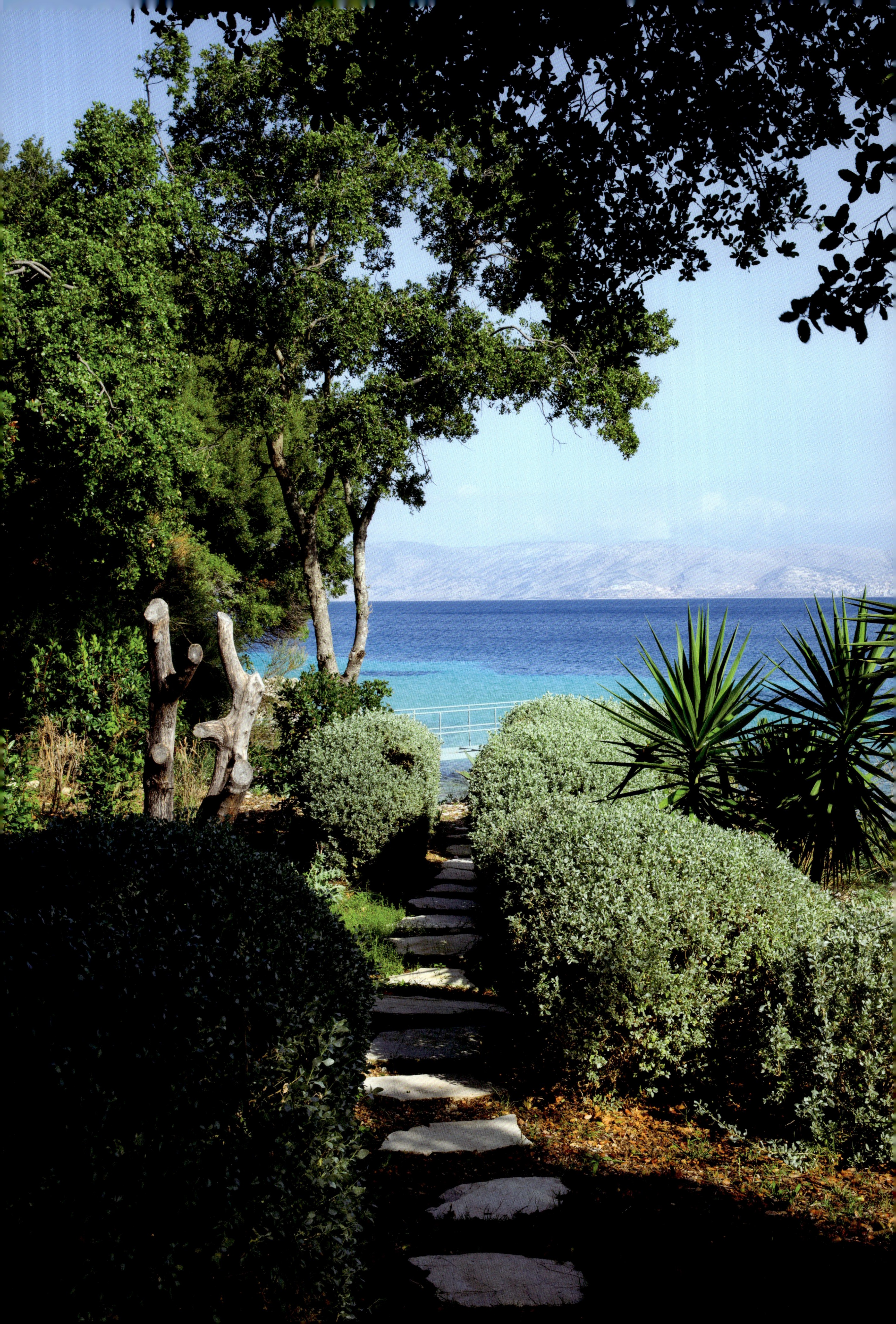

Levánta

This beachfront garden of four thousand square metres has an unusual flat site at the bottom of a shallow valley. Taking advantage of this, Alithea Johns designed the garden as a series of 'rooms' with the house at their centre, allowing the drama in these rooms to unfold for the visitor before revealing the garden's most influential feature—the sea. Established in 2007, the garden 'perfectly encloses our space, giving a sense of privacy, while overlooking the sea', says the owner Christine Yusef.

The design of this sophisticated garden plays with a tension between the wild and the formal. Elements such as the symmetrically placed matching urns and the grid pattern of trees planted in the entrance courtyard, which forms the garden's first 'room', give way gradually to wild nature, subtly assisted—as seen in the native shrubs on the terraced hillside at the property's northern border, the agaves and native yellow horned poppies planted among the pebbles at the edge of the beach, and the carefully pruned native oak trees whose slim trunks stand out like sculptures against the colours of the sea. Throughout, continuity is provided by the rounded shapes of precisely pruned bushes—rows of spheres at the beginning of the garden journey, and more naturalistic cloud and wave forms where the garden spreads out up the hill and in front of the sea.

From the road, one enters the garden down an enclosed flight of shallow stone steps between high stone walls, deeply shaded by wisteria on a pergola above. At the foot of the steps, an antique Indian wooden door opens to a sun-filled courtyard in front of the house. The courtyard harks back to the Greek *avlí*—the traditional courtyard garden combining useful and beautiful plants—though it is much larger and more open. The planting here in shades of copper and silvery grey complements the soft colours of the young olive trees, planted in a grid pattern, and of the paving in grey stone subtly bordered in antique brick and pale pebbles.

Rounding a corner, past a thriving lemon tree, one comes upon a path to the beach. Splashes of grey tree germander and coppery hop bush and glossy abelia, all very drought tolerant and resistant to salt spray, keep the original colour palette going even as the growing conditions become more difficult closer to the sea.

OPPOSITE
A stepping-stone path to the beach is lined with grey-leaved Mediterranean salt bush (*Atriplex halimus*).

OVERLEAF
On the hillside above the pool, the terraces give way to rocks. Johns left in place the original native bushes and added drought-tolerant silverberry (*Elaeagnus* x *ebbingei*) and strawberry tree (*Arbutus unedo*).

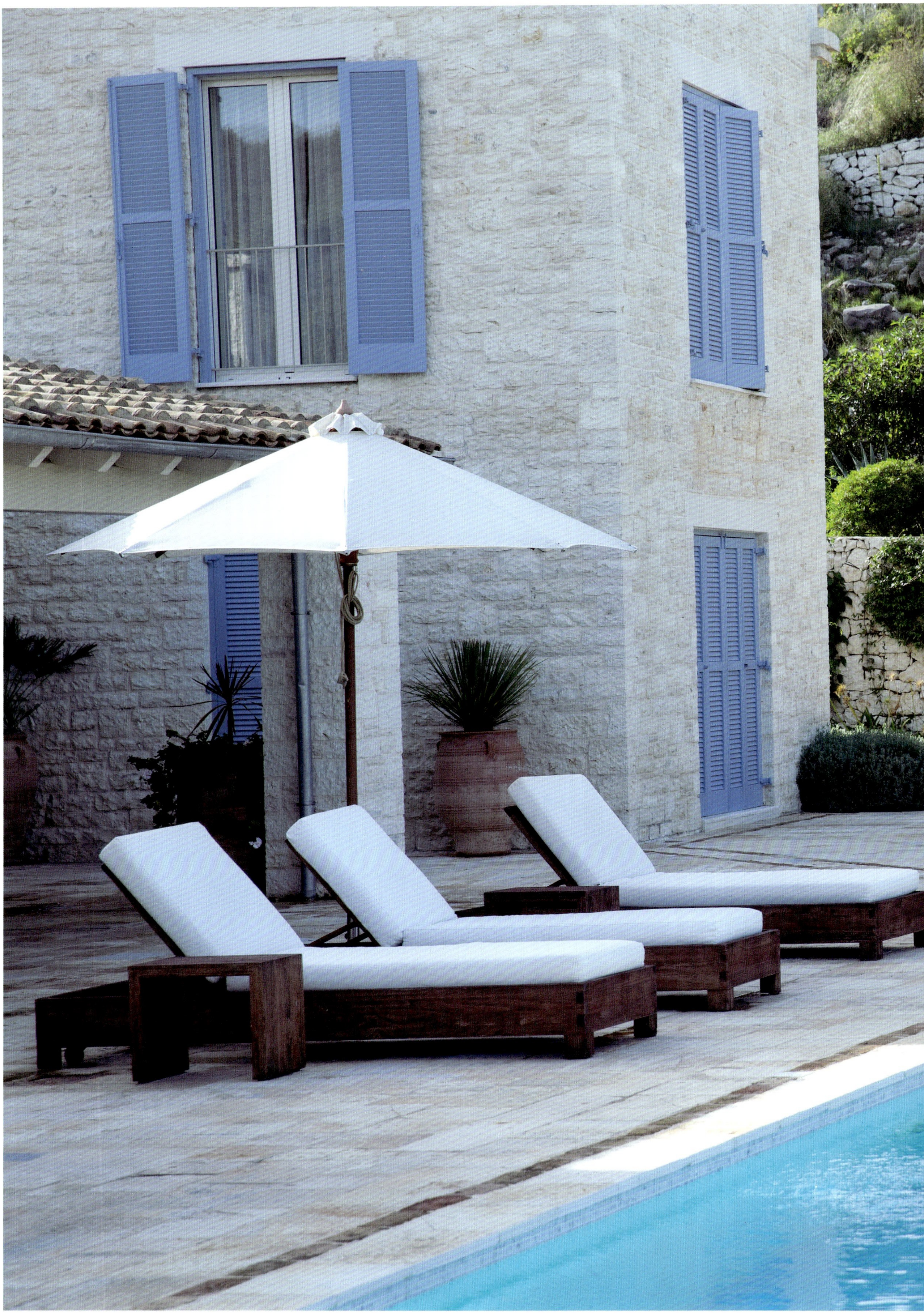

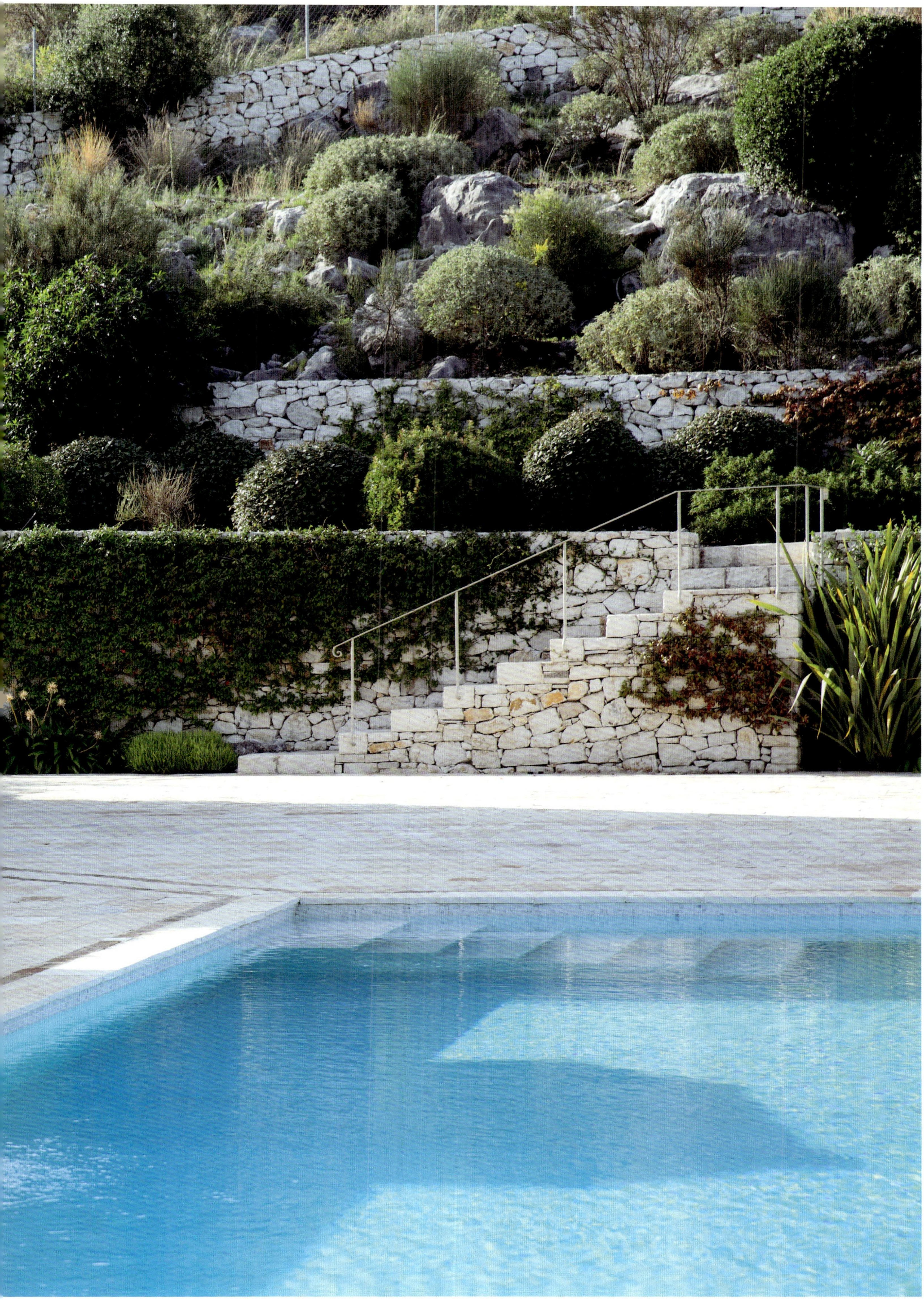

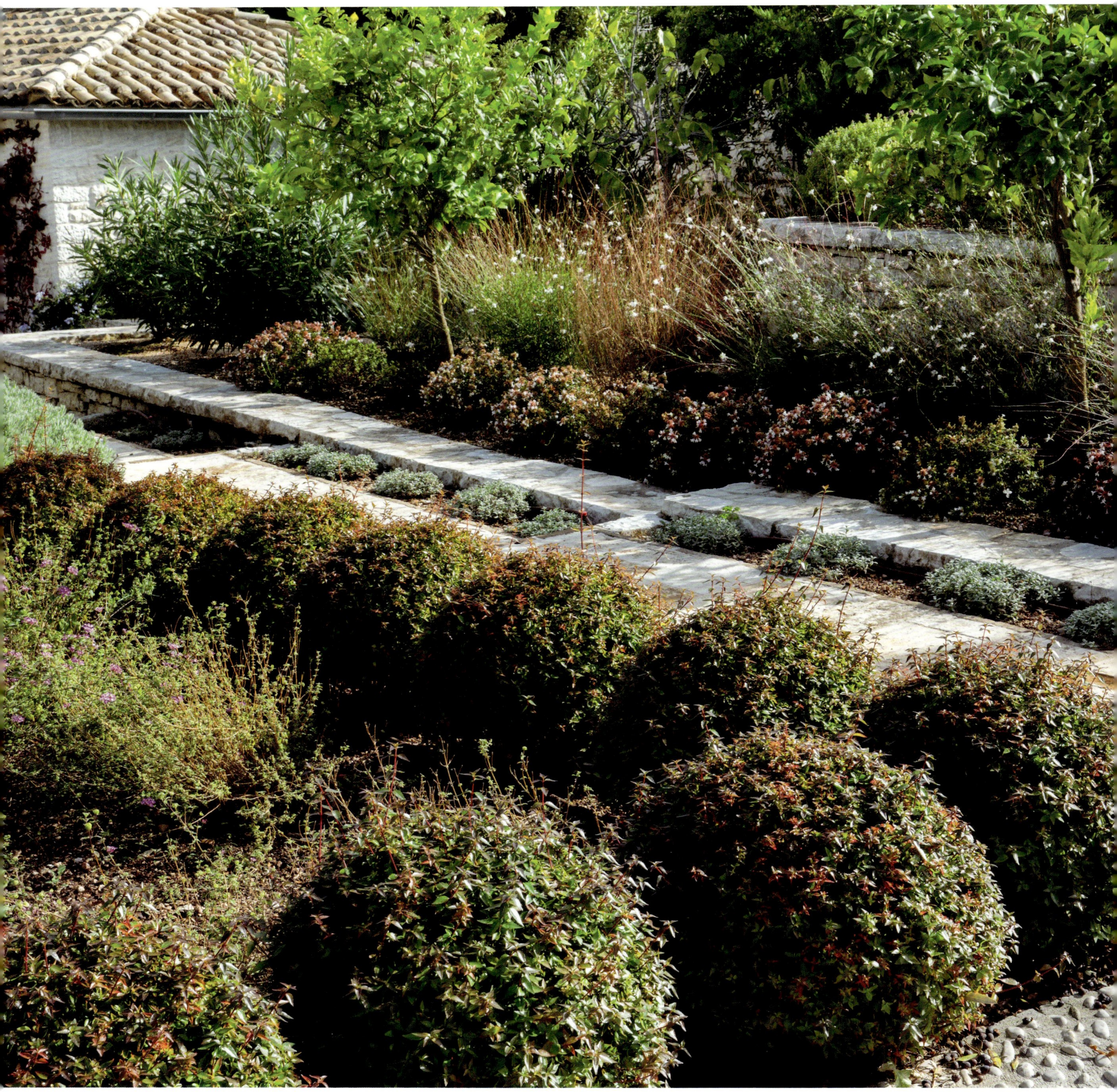

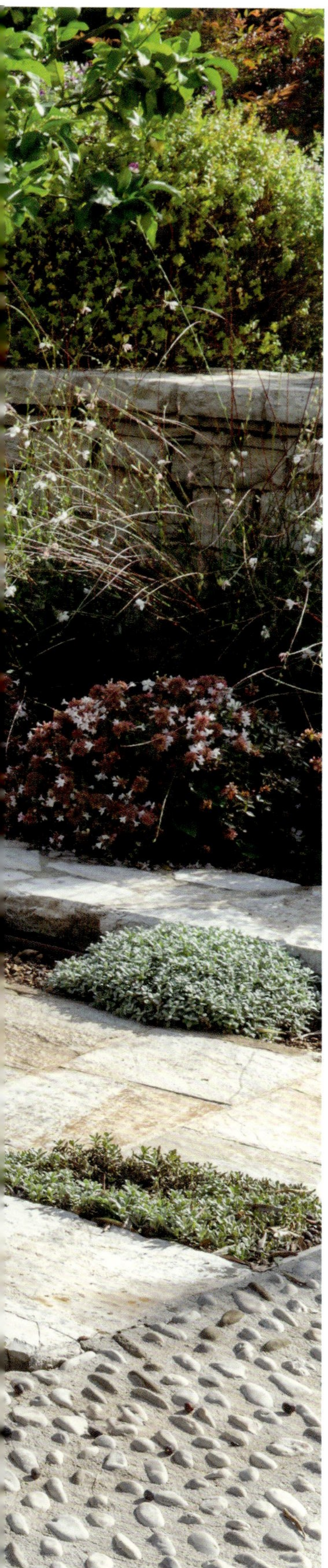

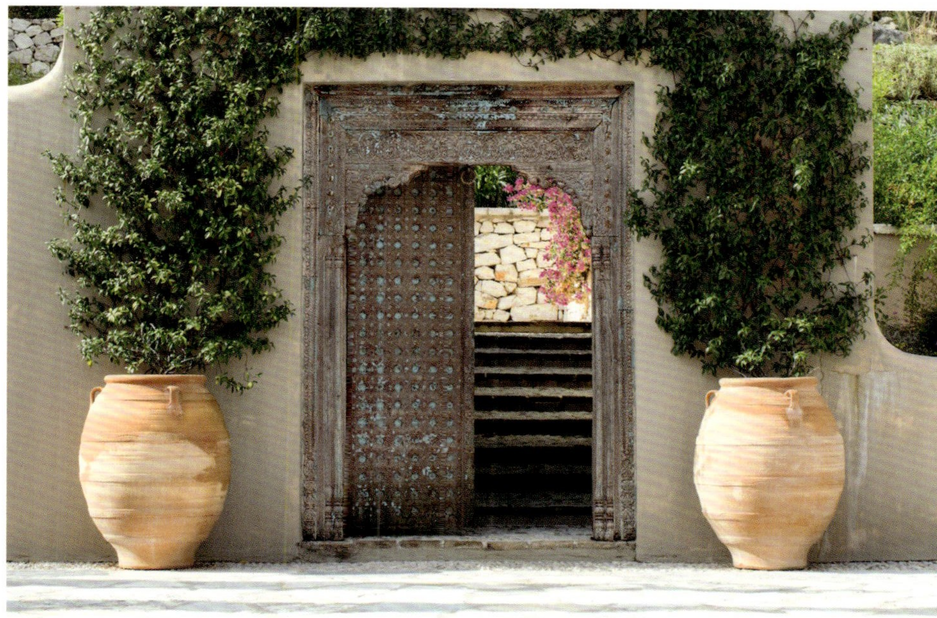

The garden's secluded entrance belies its beachfront site.

Between the house and the sea is a broad terrace and swimming pool with an 'infinity' edge, designed to provide a continuous water view from the house.

From here, a path leads up the hillside to a gazebo with a view over the treetops to the sea. Johns created terraces to retain the steeply sloping land and chose a range of native evergreen plants to supplement the wild bushes that were already in place. Clumps of smooth, silvery *Agave attenuata* also appear along the pathway and provide visual echoes of their rougher-looking relative, *Agave americana*, planted at the edge of the beach.

Exploring the other garden rooms around the house, one passes borders of *Agapanthus* and free-flowering *Tulbaghia violacea*, and turns underneath an archway into a further courtyard. Climbers here include a yellow Banks' rose and, on a sheltered southwest-facing wall, a *Bougainvillea* in a rich coppery red. Raised beds of light-textured gaura and Russian sage are edged with cascading silvery fronds of Greek horehound (*Ballota pseudodictamnus*).

Johns has made a careful limited choice of plant colours in this garden, where shape is so important and the natural light is bright throughout the year—and where, in summer, intense and ever-changing colour is provided by the sea. Moreover, the planting is designed so that its look is relatively little affected by the seasons. Drought-tolerant evergreen shrubs and perennials provide a play of textures in greens, silver-greys, and bronze. The effect of these choices is a feeling of peace, stability, and permanence—an encouragement to meditation on the ever-changing moods of the sea.

OPPOSITE
This passageway between garden 'rooms' continues the bronze and silvery theme of the entrance courtyard, with balls of glossy abelia (*Abelia* x *grandiflora*), *Gaura lindheimeri* 'Whirling Butterflies', and low-growing *Cerastium tomentosum* planted in channels within the path.

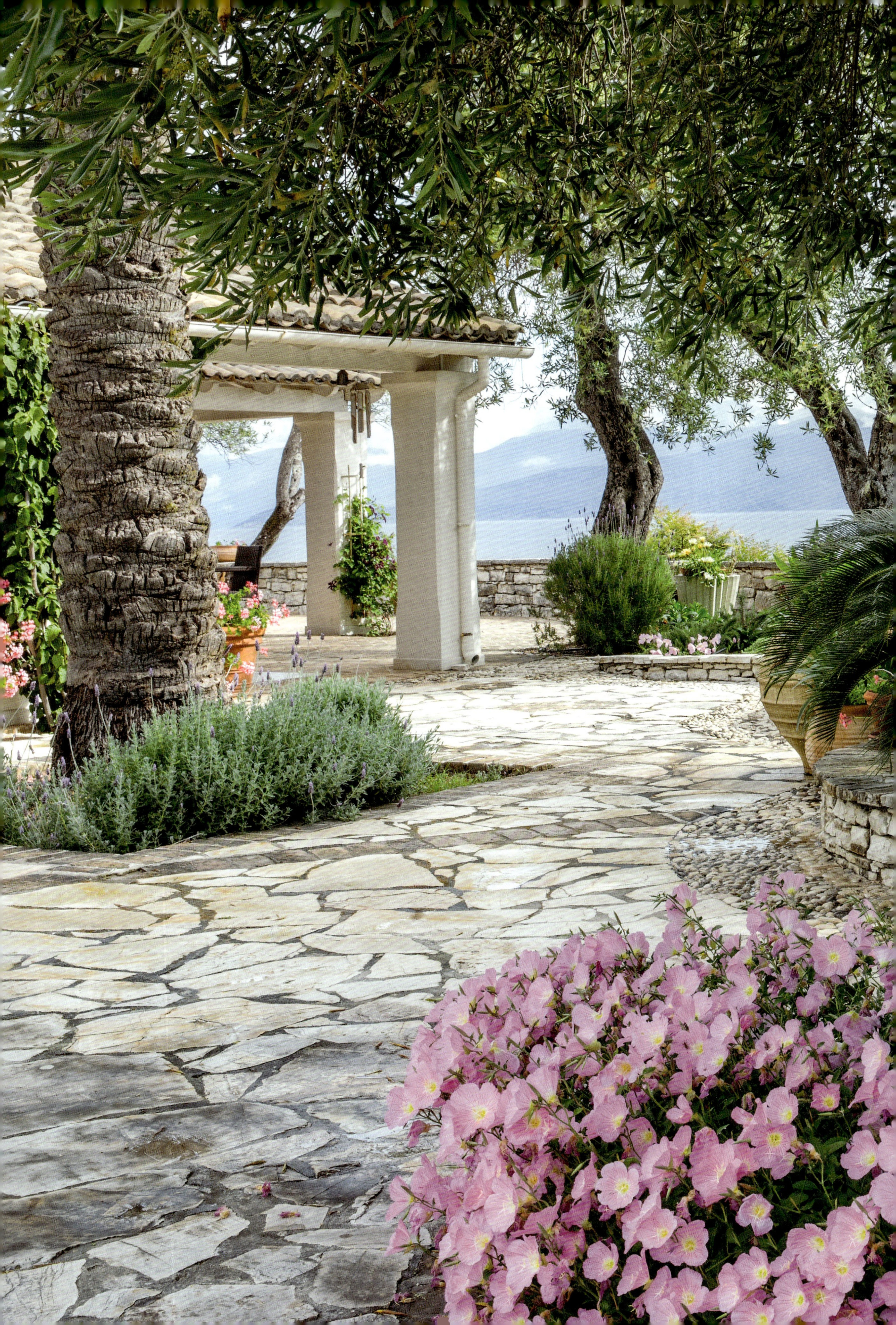

Soukiá

Soukiá, or 'fig trees', occupies a promontory facing east across the sea to Albania. One of the first villas of the modern generation to be built in northeast Corfu, the property has been dramatically remodelled by the present owners, who acquired it in 1996. The six-hundred-square-metre garden here, designed by Dominique Bernier, has a highly distinctive atmosphere, fusing local design elements and local materials with others that evoke North Africa and the Middle East. Though the garden is only about ten metres above sea level and exposed to fierce winds on its north side, clever placement of walls and trees allows it to be both sheltered and airy, protected and comfortable, in all seasons.

OPPOSITE
The original olive trees at Soukiá have been preserved from the time when the promontory was an olive grove. Now they are joined by date palms (*Phoenix dactylifera*) and a range of ornamental trees.

From the public road, a stone-paved driveway flanked with oleanders and pencil cypresses leads to the entrance gates. Inside, a large enclosed courtyard evokes the original 'Paradise gardens' of Persia[46] that inspired the Moorish rulers of southern Spain—but also, simultaneously, the Greek *avlí*, with its combination of fruit and flowers. Two mature date palms, symmetrically placed, help to set the mood here, as do the subtle Moorish patterns within the courtyard's stone paving. The palms arrived by sea as a present to the owners. Though sulky and uncertain at first about Corfu's damp winter weather, they eventually established themselves well among cypresses, olives, and pepper trees.

Along the front of the house, which faces south, is a traditional deep arcaded veranda, whose wrought-iron pergola carries two mature wisterias with long racemes of mauve and pink flowers in April. Other climbers on this side of the house provide a succession of blooms throughout the year; they include two with cheerful yellow flowers: flannel bush (*Fremontodendron* 'California Glory') and climbing groundsel (*Senecio angulatus*). South of the courtyard, the ground rises, with low terraces planted with roses backed by dark evergreen shrubs. Curved pathways lead to lower levels of the garden with lemon and fig trees, *Agapanthus*, and rose-scented pelargonium.

46. The English word paradise comes from the old Persian word *pairi-daeza*, meaning a walled space. 'In the very dry climate in most parts of Iran, it was necessary to have high walls to protect from the outside elements, and inside, it was how one imagined paradise.' Nadereh Chamlou, personal communication. See also Mehdi Khansari, M. Reza Moghtader, and Minouch Yavari, *The Persian Garden: Echoes of Paradise* (Washington, DC: Mage Publishers, 1998).

The curving walls and patterns in the paving add to the sense of movement in this garden. In the foreground is a large cycad.

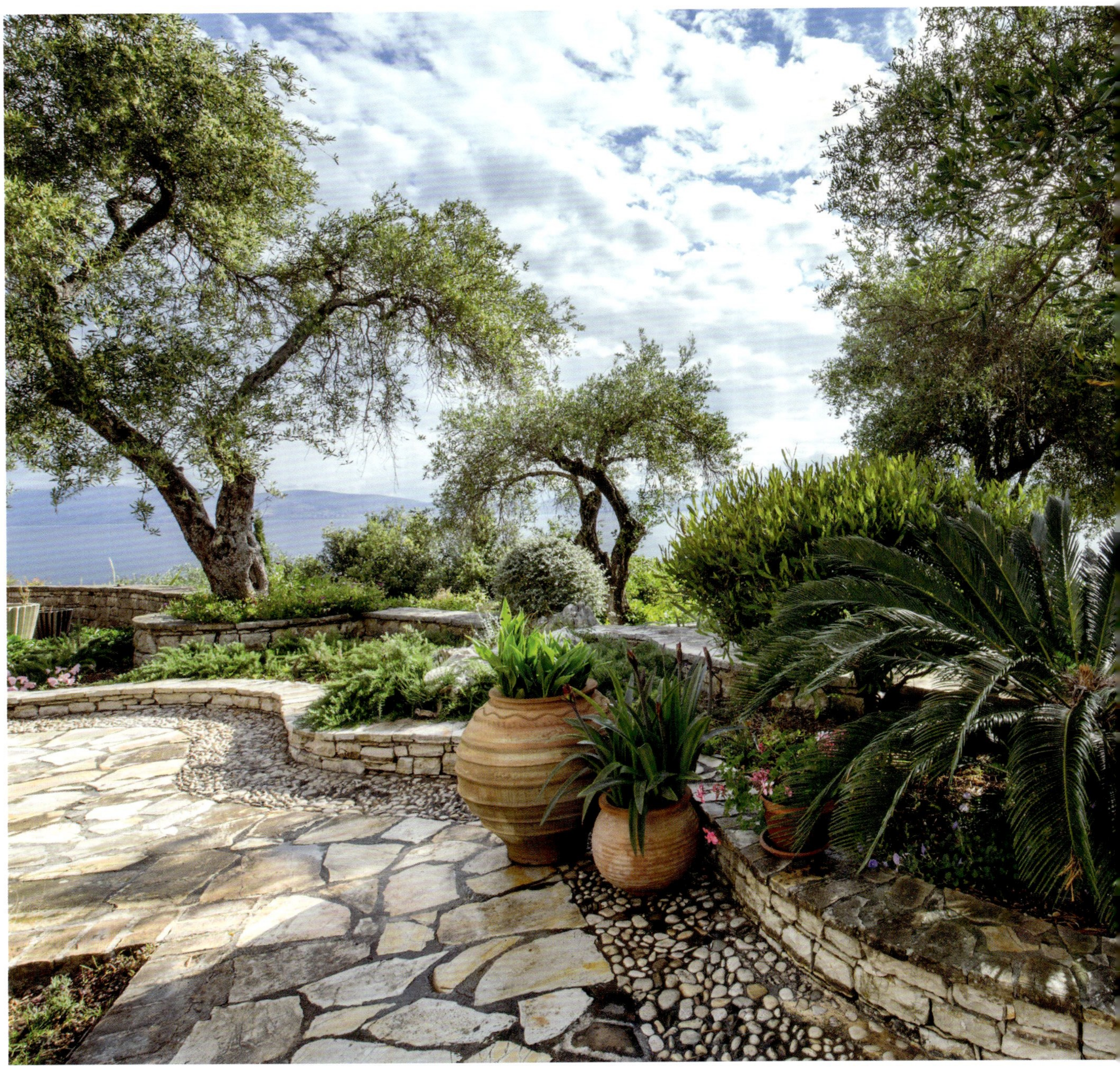

Patterns in the paving evoke those in Moorish gardens.

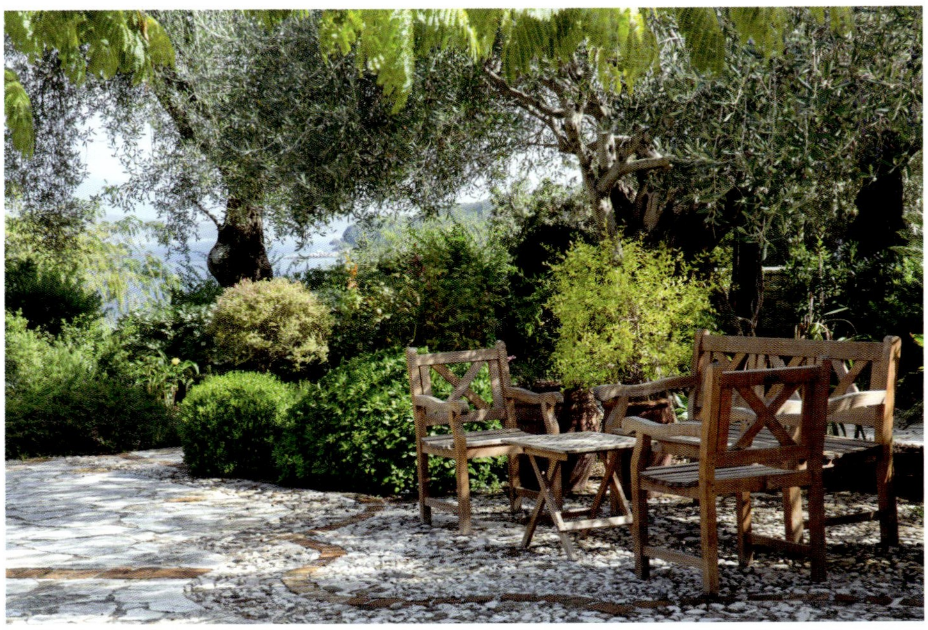

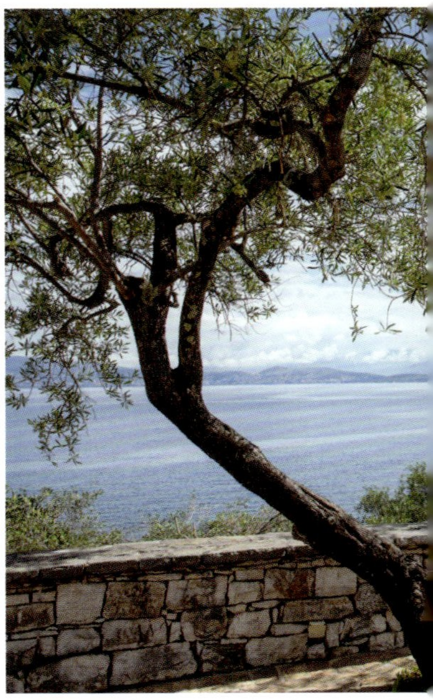

Continuing around the house to the north, the paved patio is bordered by the sea wall. Original olive trees frame the view of sea and mountains.

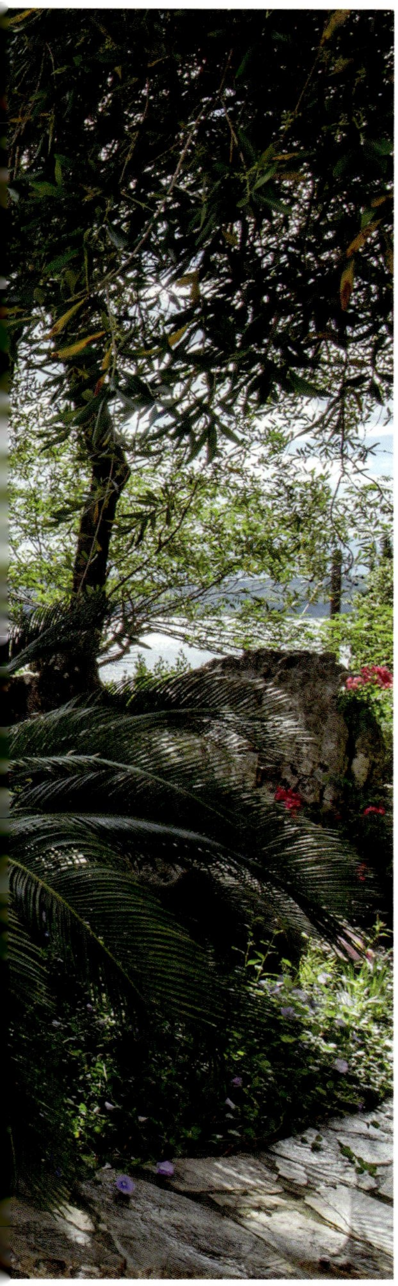

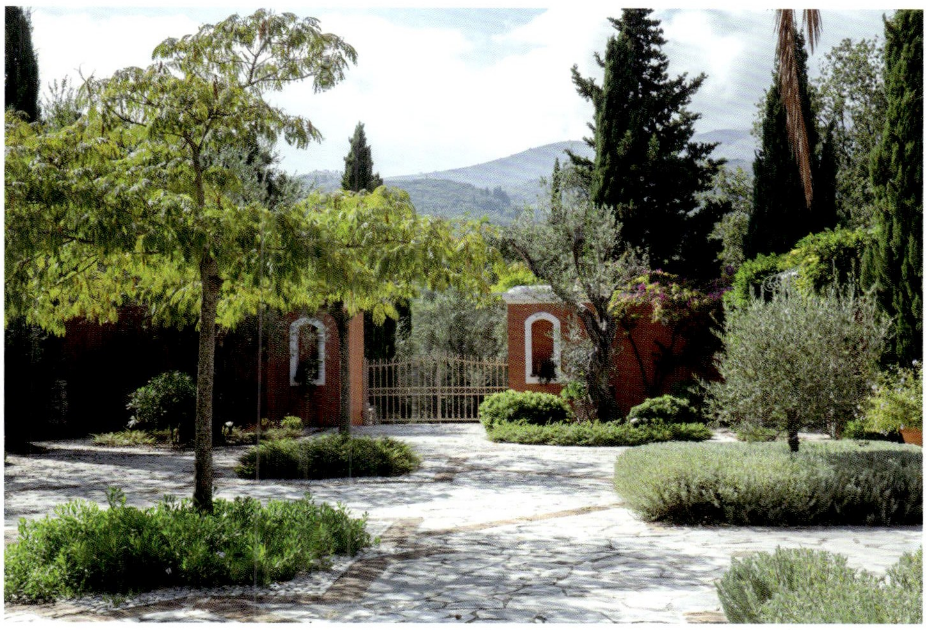

The entrance courtyard, with walls painted in typical Corfiot style.

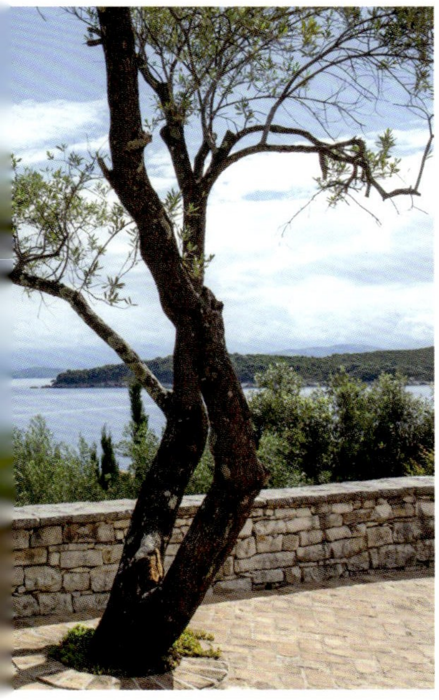

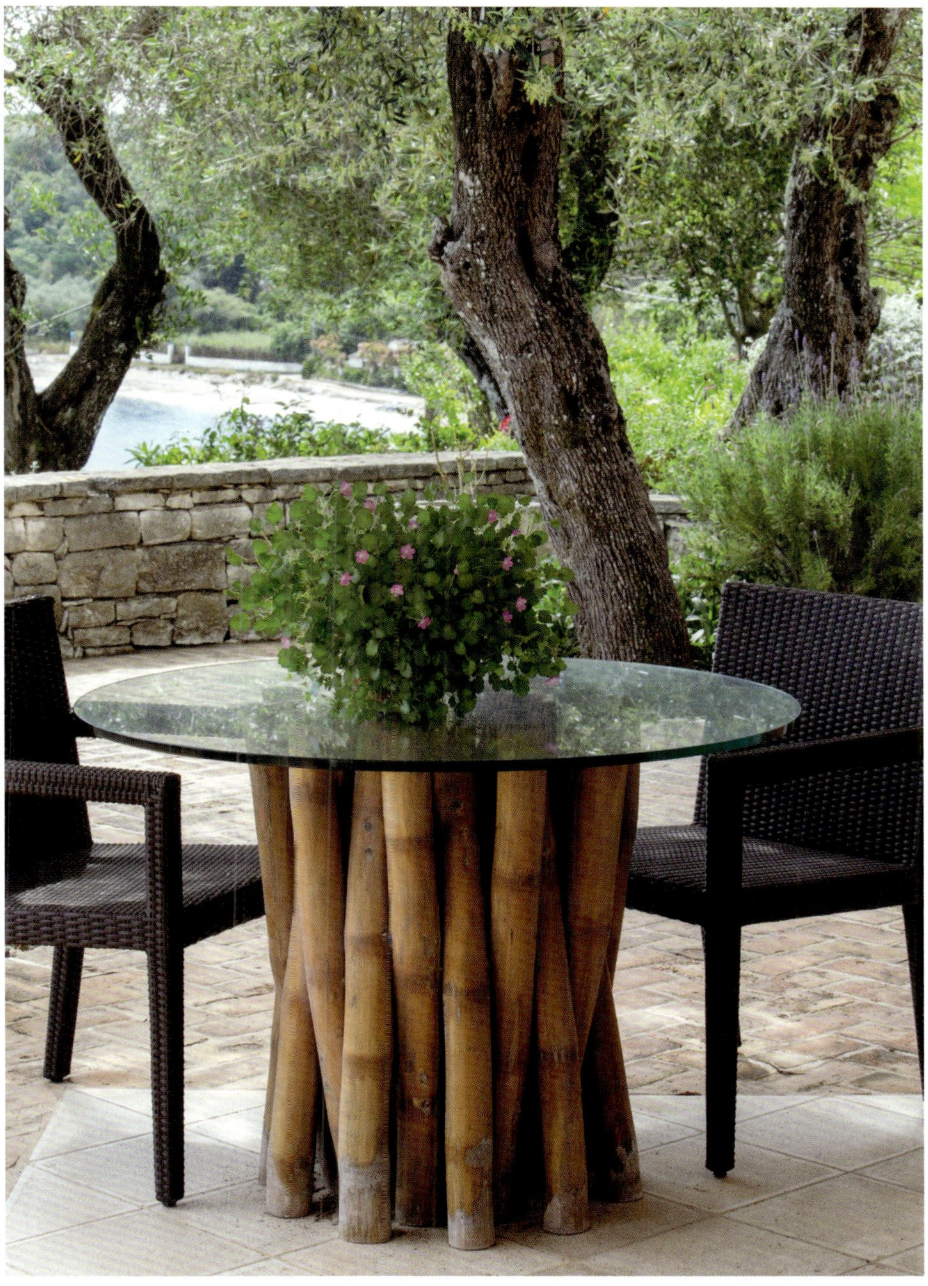

The house is sheltered on three sides by a deep arcaded veranda, where most of family activity takes place in summer. From all three sides, there are views of the sea.

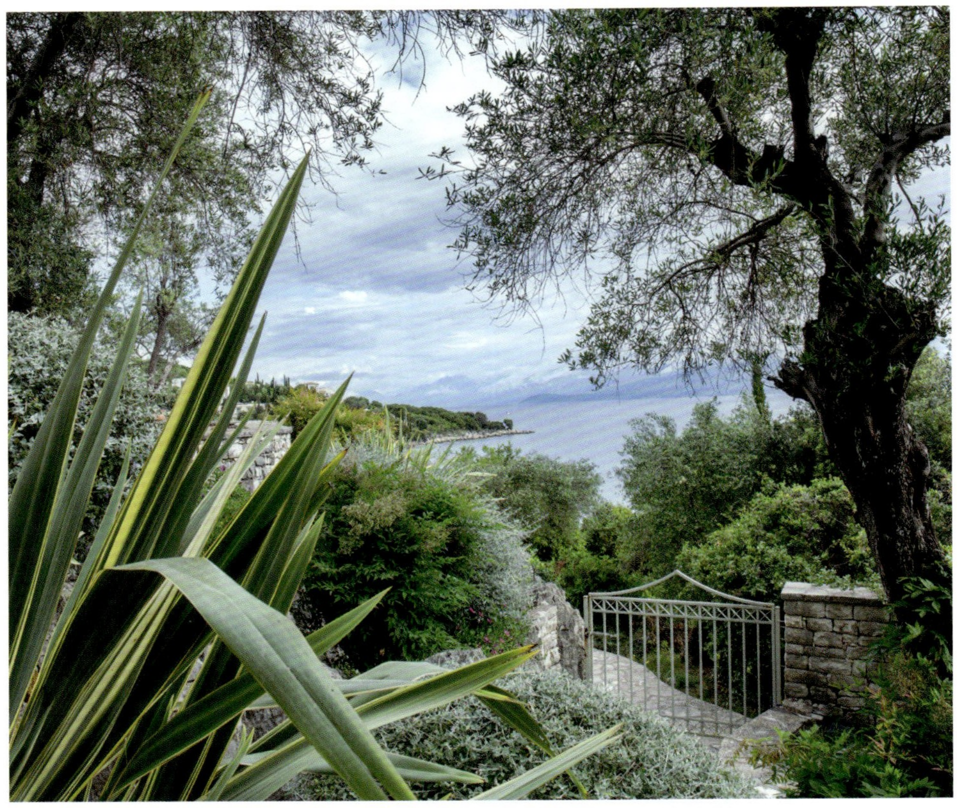

Paths lead to lower levels of the garden and thence to the olive grove and sea below.

OPPOSITE
With its shelter carefully planned, *Clematis* 'Niobe' thrives in close proximity to the sea.

The glorious views of sea and mountains from this garden can delay one from noticing its rich range of mature plants. These include camellias, purple-flowering sweetpea bush, *Westringia fruticosa*, crimson-flowering tea tree (*Leptospermum scoparium*), Indian hawthorn (*Raphiolepis indica*), bright violet-flowered *Lycianthes rantonnetii*, and *Duranta plumieri*, with its pretty clusters of mauve flowers followed by golden berries. Continuing around the house to the north, the paved patio is bordered by the sea wall. Original olive trees frame the view of sea and mountains, and large urns hold *Bougainvillea* varieties in crimson and purple and a white Banks' rose. The garden plantings on the north side of the house help provide shelter from the wind. A path leads from here down through a meadow, full of wild flowers in spring, to a copse of Mediterranean buckthorn and kermes oak and a secluded beach.

At first the soil throughout the garden was so thin, poor, and rocky that holes had to be dug with a backhoe and pickaxe to plant the trees and shrubs. But after years of dedicated digging and sieving to rid the soil of stones, and amendments with compost, the owners grow plants such as peonies and roses that were unthinkable candidates for the original soil. Vegetables and fruit are also produced: under lemon and fig trees are rectangular beds of onions and greens in winter, and sweet peppers, aubergines, tomatoes, and chili peppers in summer.

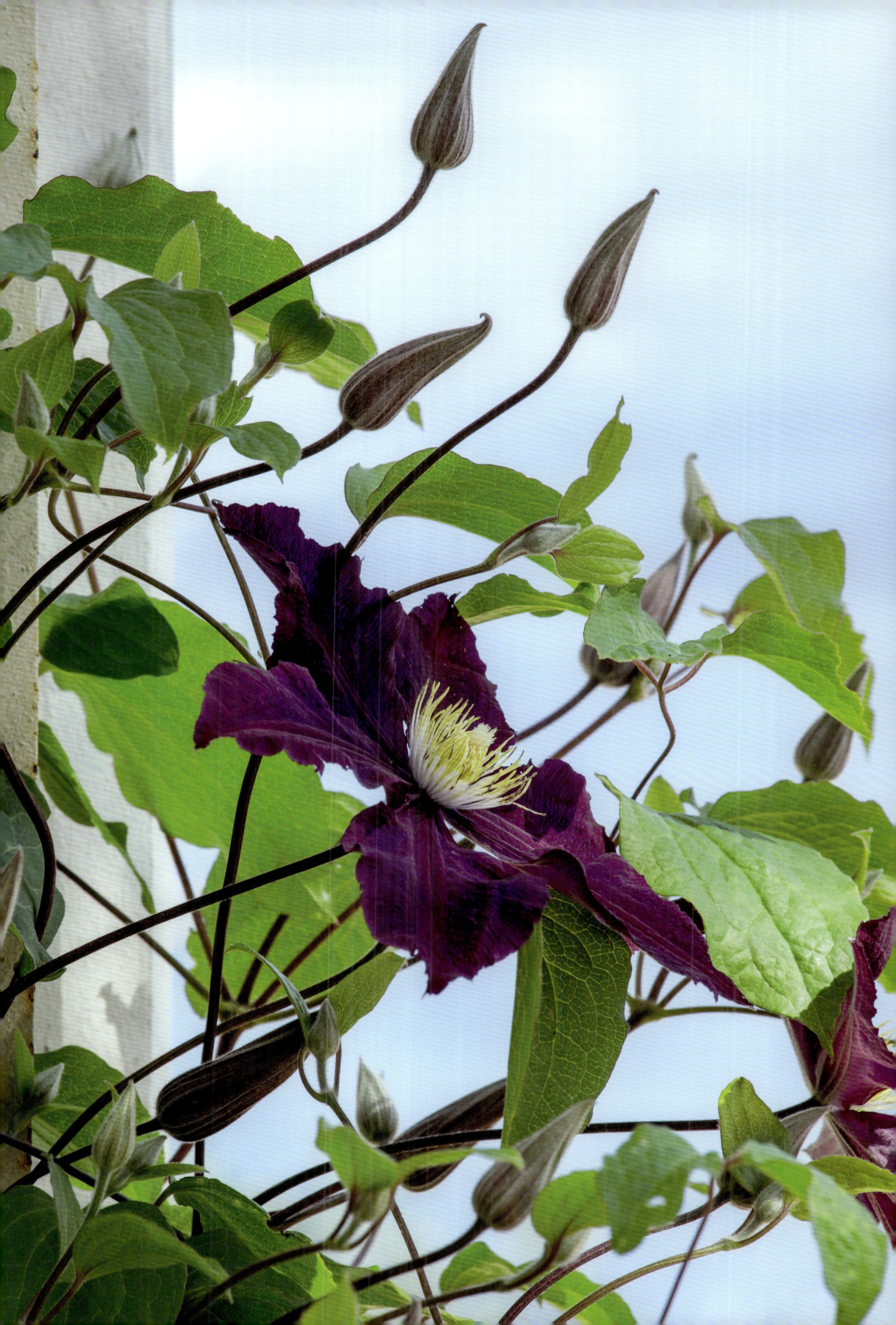

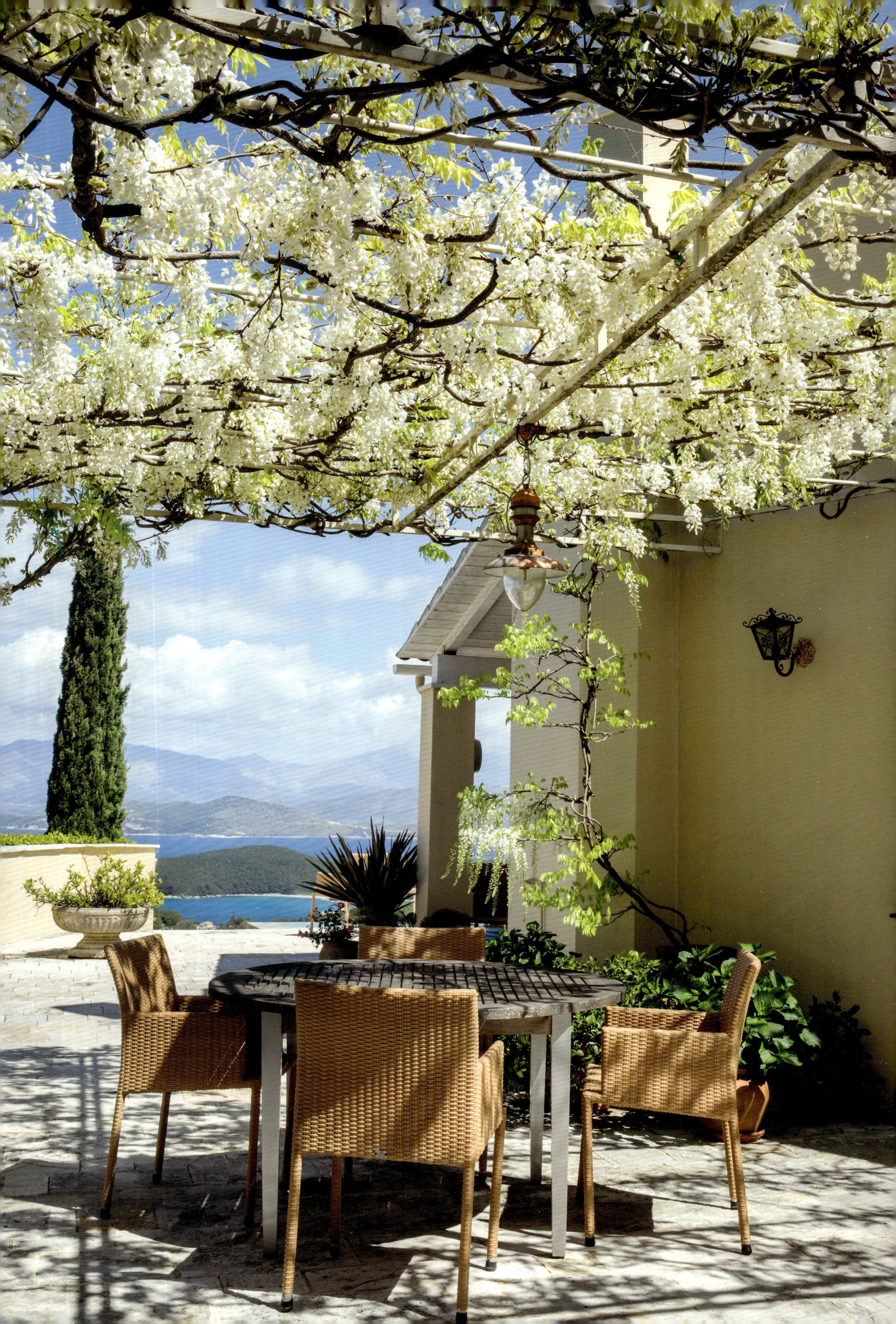

Zetouna

Most people who visit this garden are held captive at first by the view. Behind the house, designed by Rahdy Elwan, the wide terrace with its 'infinity' pool has a 180-degree perspective over the hills and village below, across the sea to the Albanian coast and mountains beyond.

OPPOSITE
Both Chinese (*Wisteria sinensis*) and Japanese wisteria (*W. floribunda*), with its longer flower clusters, are used to shade this dining area.

But for visitors who step off the pool terrace to explore, the garden reveals rich rewards. Arranged on a sequence of descending levels with contrasting moods and surrounded by olive groves hundreds of years old, it produces both fruit and flowers, incorporates local wild flowers into its planting designs, and evokes the local agricultural past.

Establishing the garden some twelve years ago on about half of this 0.7 hectare property, the owners left intact most of the olive trees that were on the land, as well as a big clump of pencil cypresses they found on the southern border. Formal planting close to the house, with a simple hedge of clipped box along the housefront, progresses to minimally managed natural growth and wild flowers where the garden meets the sparingly tended olive groves of its neighbours. Throughout the garden are plants collected on the owner's travels and plants selected for their associations with people in her life and places she has known.

The garden in summer features mainly white flowers, for their refreshing look in hot weather. But in spring, climbing roses and more than fifty varieties of bearded iris, one of the owner's favourite flowers, provide a rainbow of colour.

In front of the house, which faces uphill, a long cut-away cliff has been left exposed, allowing wild ferns and flowering plants to sprout from its crevices. Against the background of the rock are white-flowering plants of contrasting shapes—*Plumbago auriculata* 'Alba' and white gaura, 'Iceberg' roses, foxgloves, flowering tobacco, California tree poppies (*Romneya coulteri*), and regal lilies—along with mauve *Tulbaghia violacea*. In spring, the purple and carmine of wild honesty and gladiolus (from seed collected locally) add to the mix.

A paved stone terrace wraps around the north side of the house under a wrought-iron pergola, which is covered with white wisteria and used for family meals, to the pool area with its wide view. The planting here is kept minimal, and again the flowers are mainly

Ivy-leaved cyclamen (*Cyclamen hederifolium*) flower in the meadow in autumn. Once grazed regularly by sheep and goats throughout the winter, the meadow is now mown in early summer and in autumn. Starting in January, native anemones, irises, scabious, and hollyhocks appear in succession before the summer drought begins.

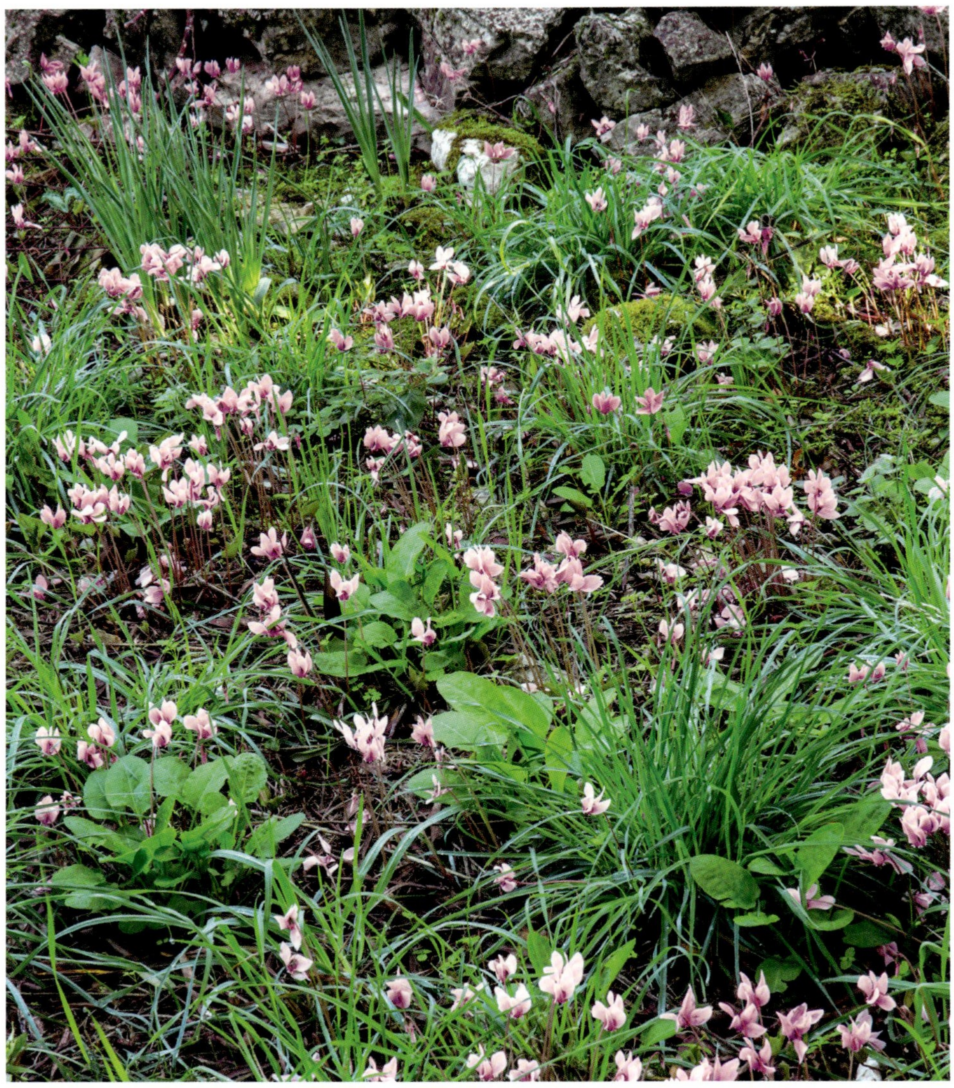

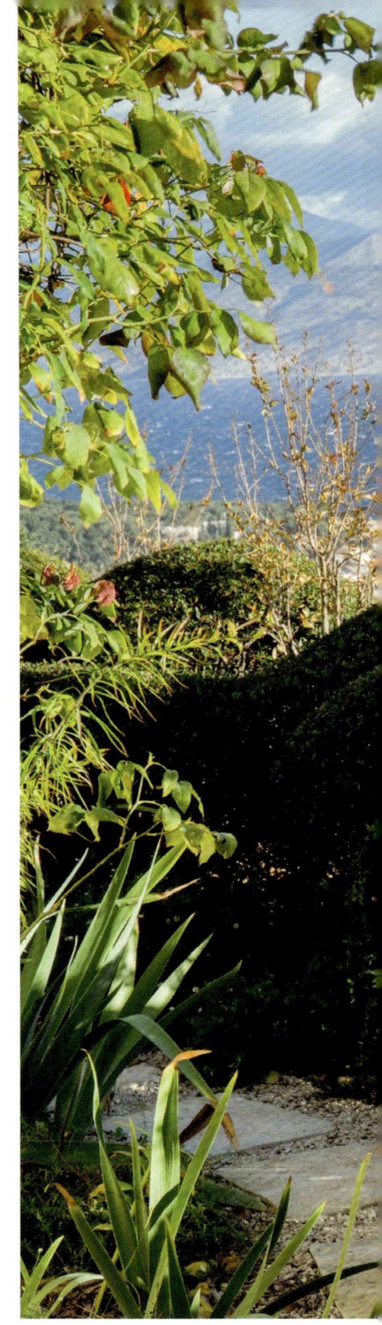

white, with star jasmine, Spanish jasmine, white hydrangeas, and 'Iceberg' roses, anchored by dark green *Pittosporum tobira* 'Nana'.

Contrasting with the openness and bright light on the pool terrace, smaller patios that adjoin the house on different levels provide shaded spaces. On the lowest of these, in deep green shade under a large olive tree, the green and white theme continues with fragrant *Cestrum nocturnum* and gardenias alongside white hydrangeas, white 'Busy Lizzy' impatiens, green and white Japanese sweet flag (*Acorus gramineus*), and the green and white striped strap-shaped leaves of *Dianella tasmanica*. A collection of hellebores flowers here in winter.

Citrus trees planted in a grid pattern on the terraces to the south of the house, and—lower down the hill—rows of lavender with fruit trees, evoke agricultural patterns but on an intimate scale. At the furthest distance above and below the house, the olive groves are mown twice yearly to encourage wildflowers.

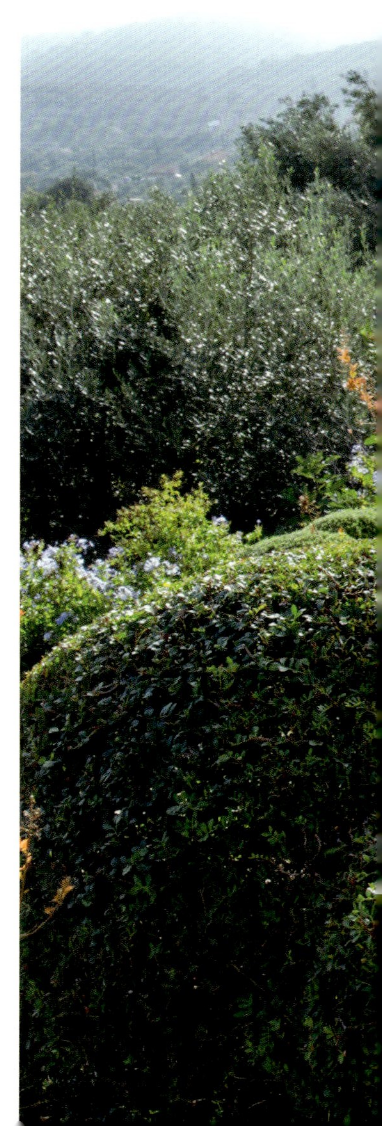

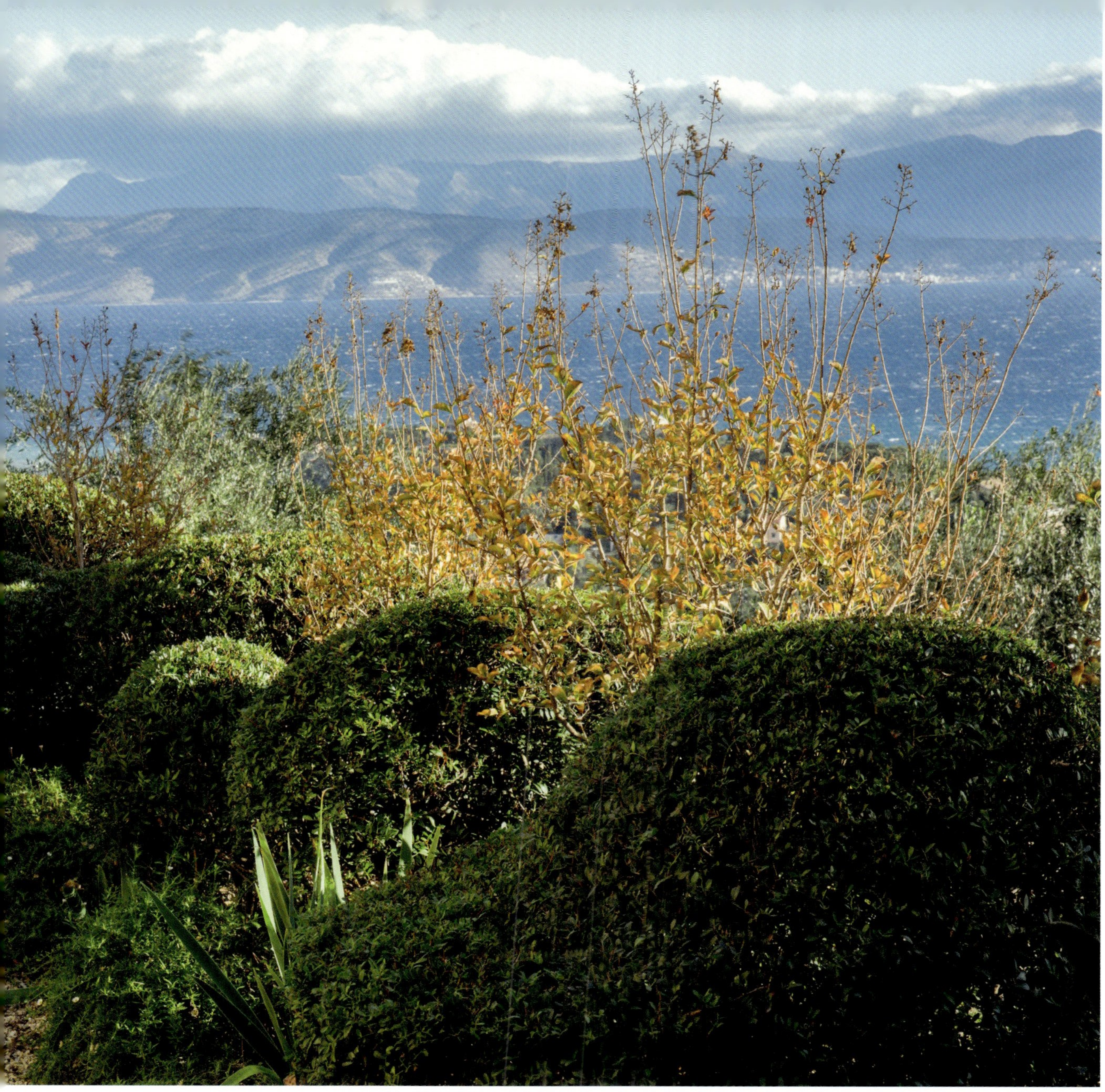

A view north towards the Albanian mountains. Above the pruned lentiscs are white-flowered crape myrtles (*Lagerstroemia*), seen here with autumn leaves.

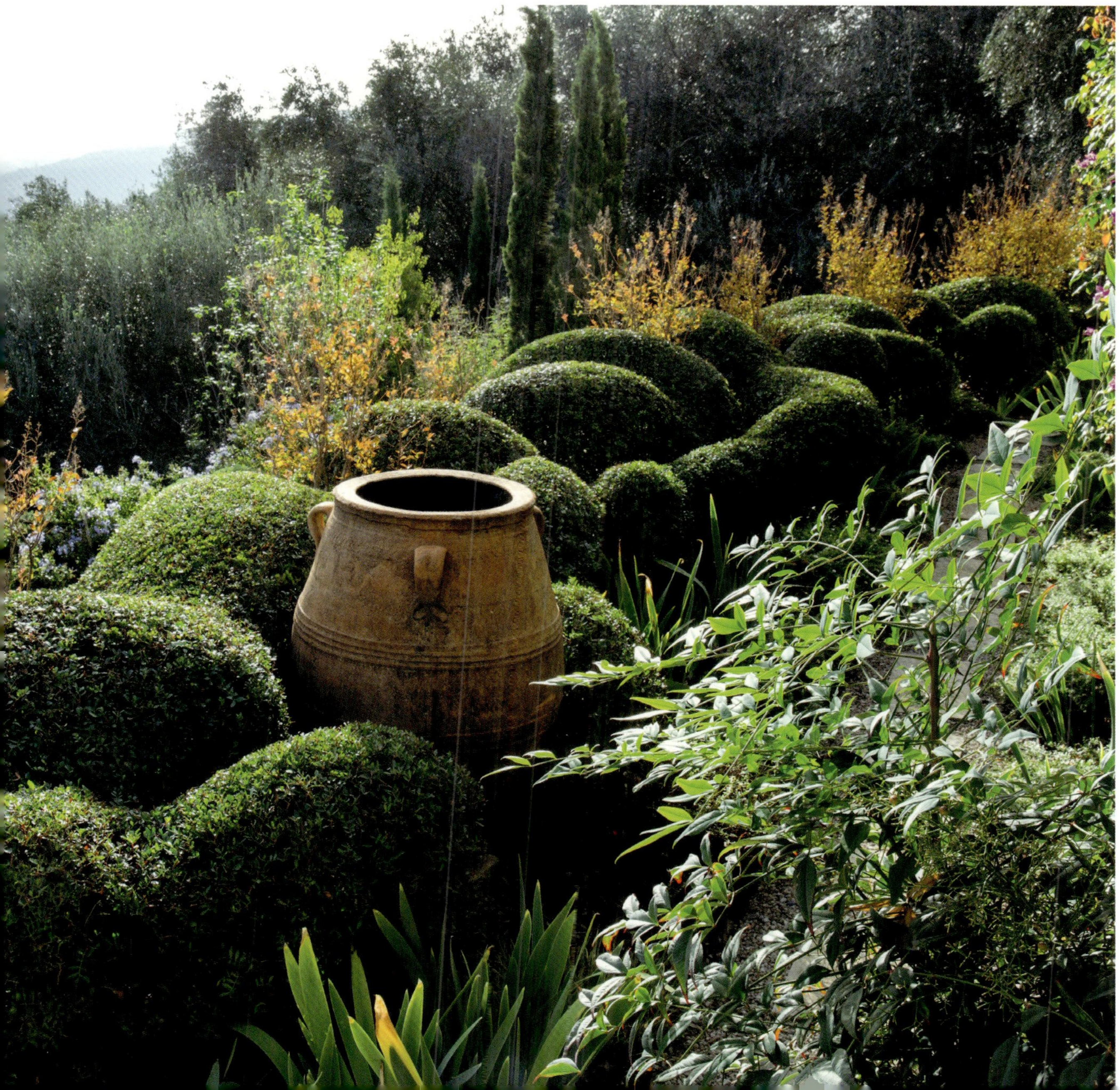

In Corfu's wild pastures and scrubland, lentisc is often whipped into shape by coastal winds or sculpted by hungry sheep and goats. For gardeners it offers a drought- and disease-resistant alternative to box.

OPPOSITE
Below the house, small 'fields' of lavender (*L. dentata*, *angustifolia*, and *stoechas*) and *Santolina chamaecyparissus* have been planted under the original olive trees.

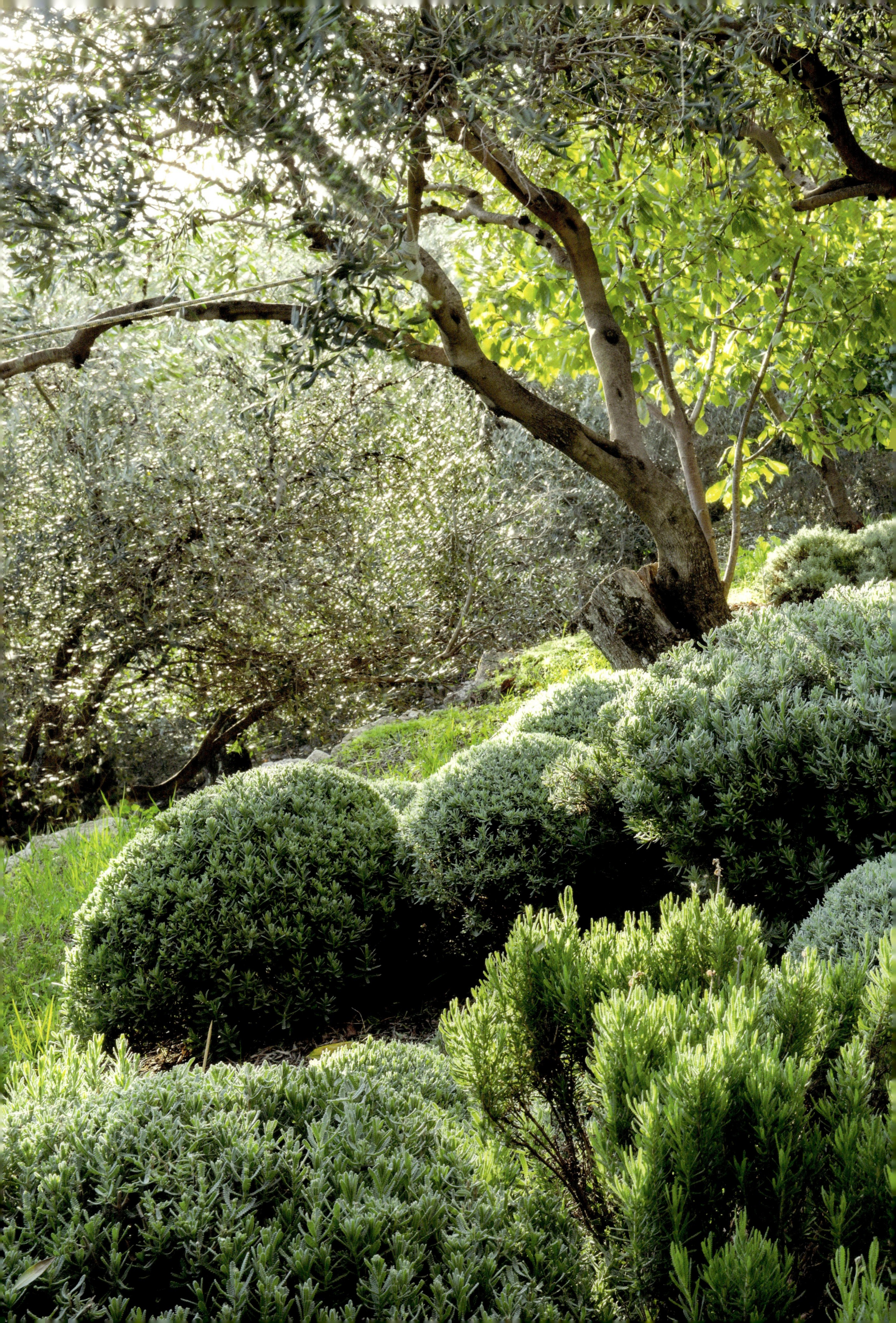

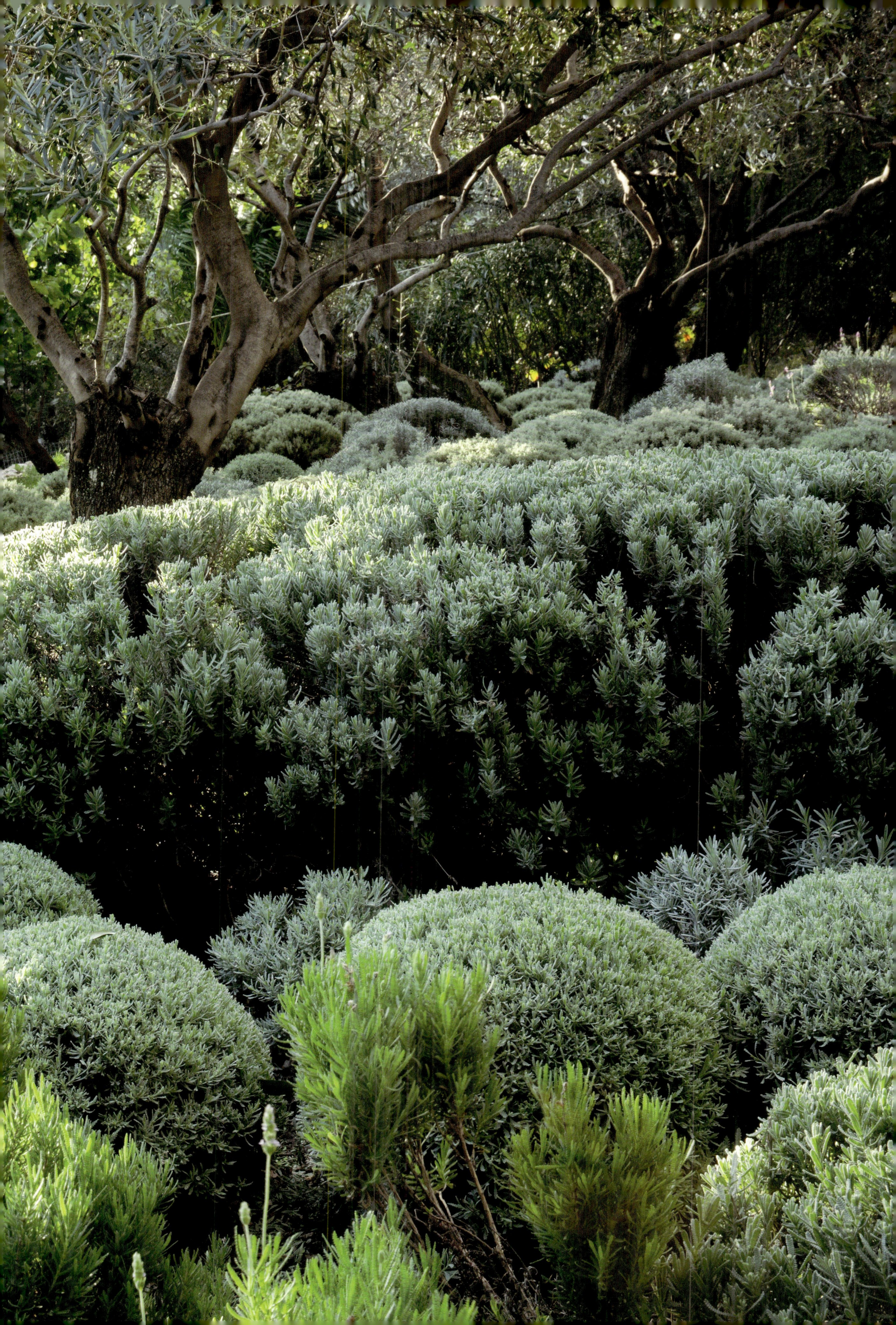

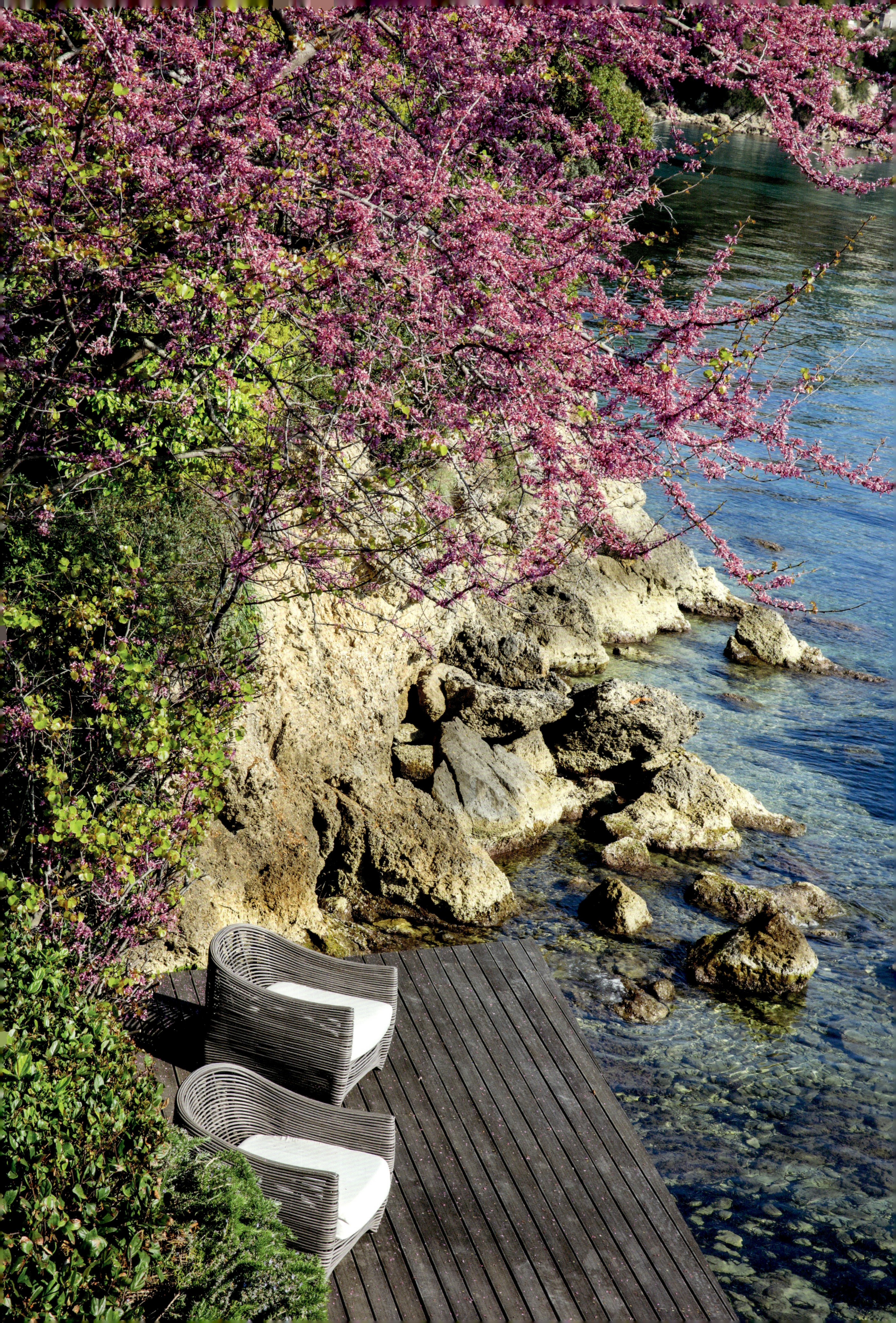

Villa Principessa

OPPOSITE
Judas trees overhang this simple platform at the edge of the sea.

This joyful garden on a dramatically steep coastal site at Pérama in central Corfu was established in 2009. The owners asked landscape architect Haim Kohen to create a garden that was 'local and wild—not pretentious' to complement their house newly designed by Erríkos Theódotos and to provide an oasis of respite from a busy life.

In early spring, the garden is a celebration of green: the deep greens of evergreen shrubs and cypresses take centre stage, contrasting with the fresh yellow green of the weeping willows that are a vital presence here. But by summer, green is playing a different role as a foil for the brilliant crimsons and pinks of hundreds of roses in bloom. Asked about her favourite features of the garden, the owner says she loves 'the weeping willow trees—my favourite tree. I love the roses, the herbs. I love it all!'

Entering the garden at the top, one is stopped in one's tracks by the glorious views across the sea to Mouse Island, Kanóni peninsula, and mainland Greece, and down to the curved sweep of the swimming pool below. The driveway wends steeply down past willows and dense evergreen shrubs planted against the tall stone walls that retain the cliff, with a view to the sea over the lower garden and house. Ledges in the retaining walls are planted with rosemary and with hedges of large-leaved native evergreens, along with Indian hawthorn, *Photinia serratifolia*, southern magnolia, and camellia.

From the end of the driveway, steps lead past a roof garden planted on the top of a stone outbuilding and down to the house. The beds are thick with roses in crimsons and pinks against a background of dark evergreens.

Next to the house, the crimson, pink, and dark green theme continues—but with more detailed planting, including crape myrtle, gardenia, sweetpea bush, and *Tulbaghia violacea*. The dark green shrubs Kohen has chosen, most of them with large shiny leaves, provide a backdrop for the lush roses but also point up the lightness and movement of the willows.

From the house and pool terrace, with its sparkling infinity pool curved breathtakingly over the sea, a path leads down to where a wooden platform on the rocks provides an idyllic secret sitting area.

OVERLEAF
Graceful willows (*Salix babylonica*), the owner's favourite tree, are planted on the sea wall of the garden and on the hillside above.

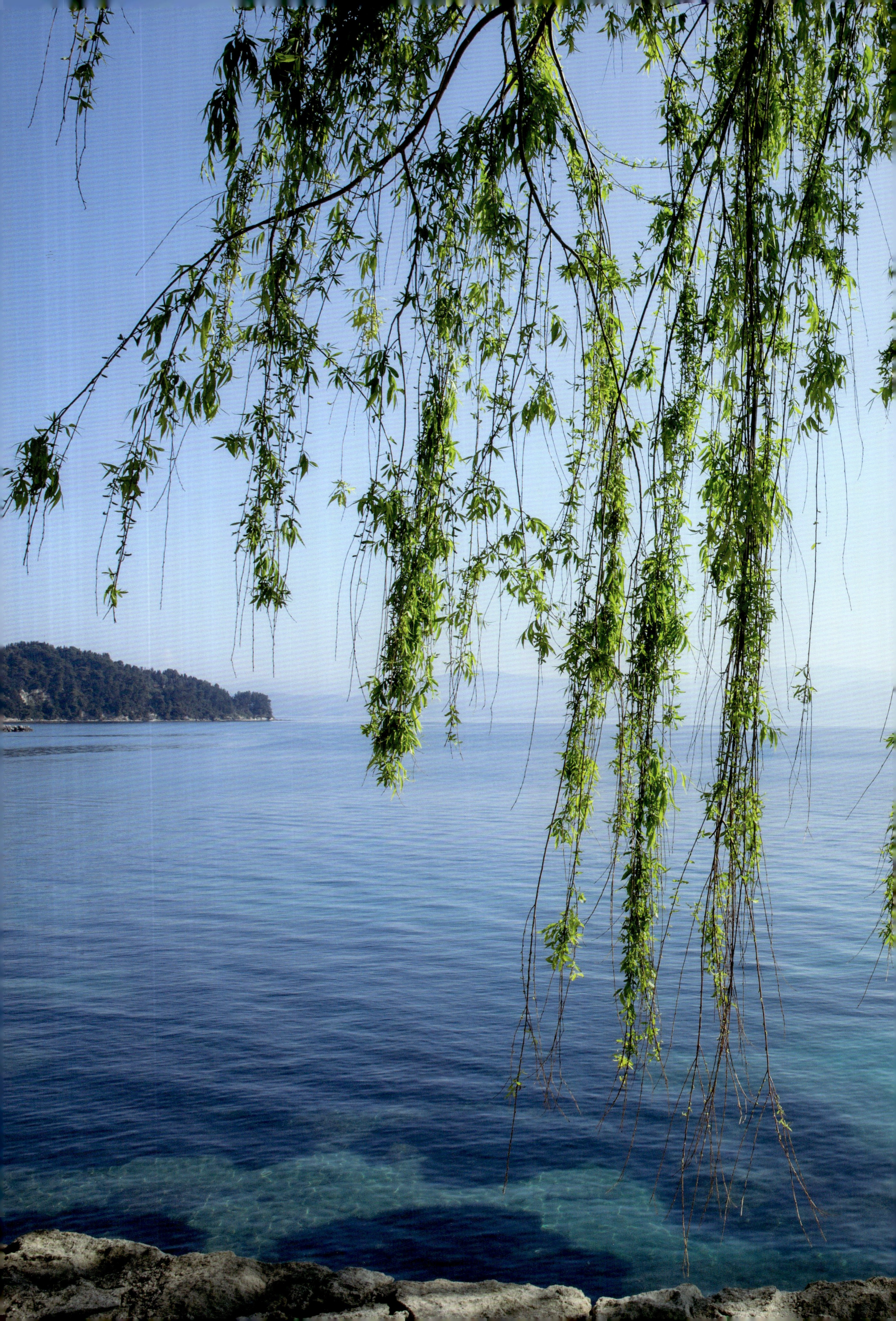

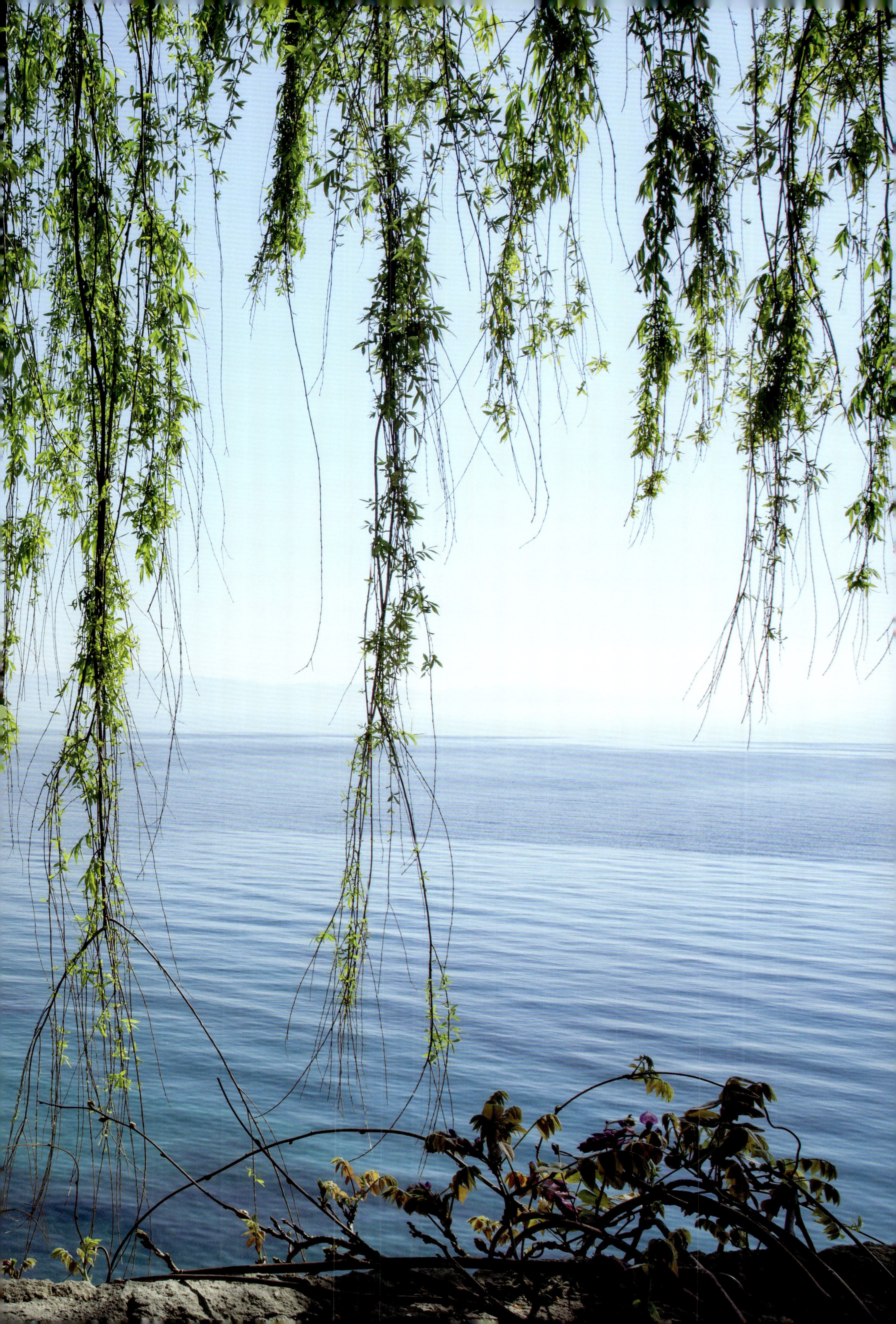

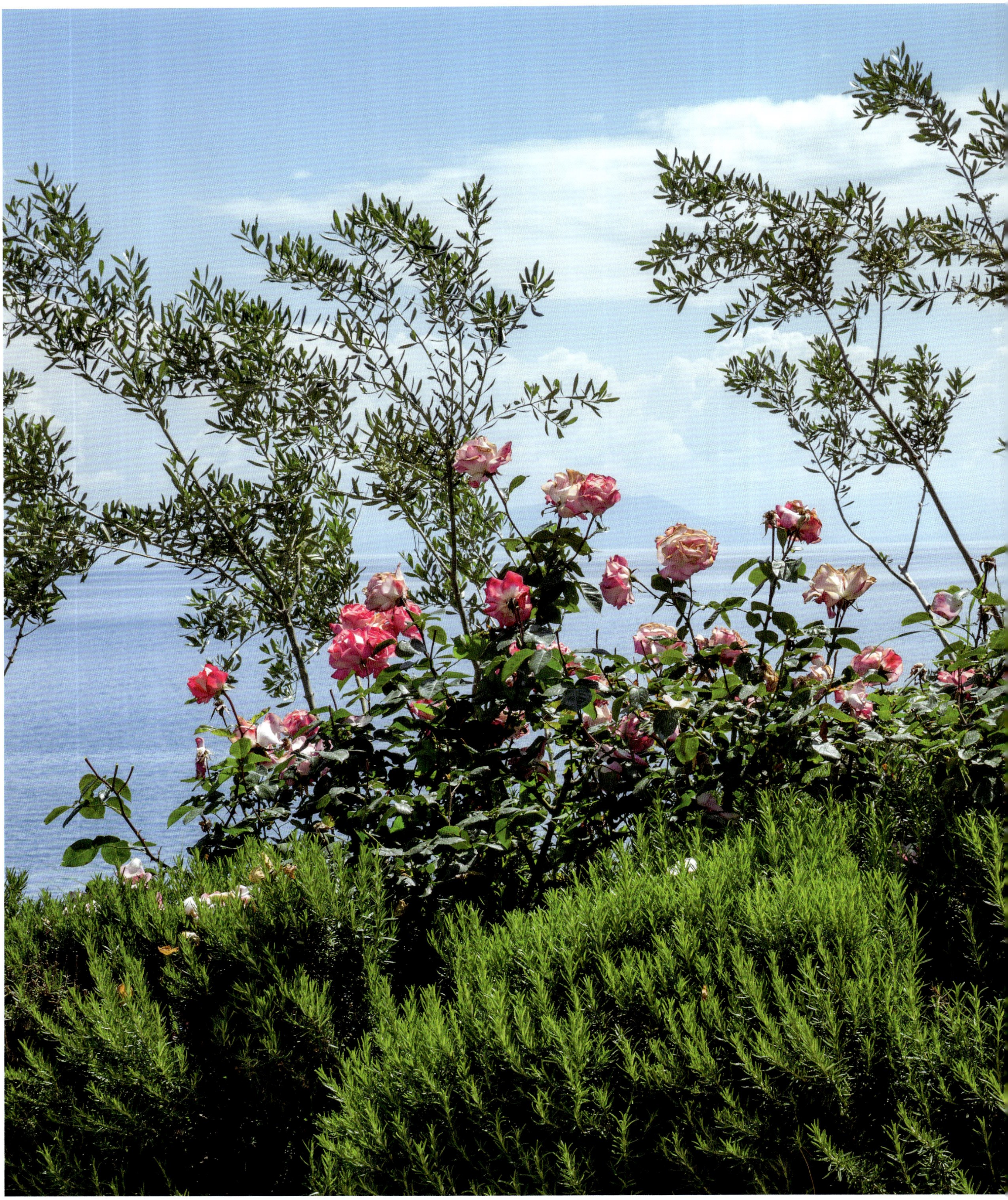

At the top of the garden, roses flower against the backdrop of the sea.

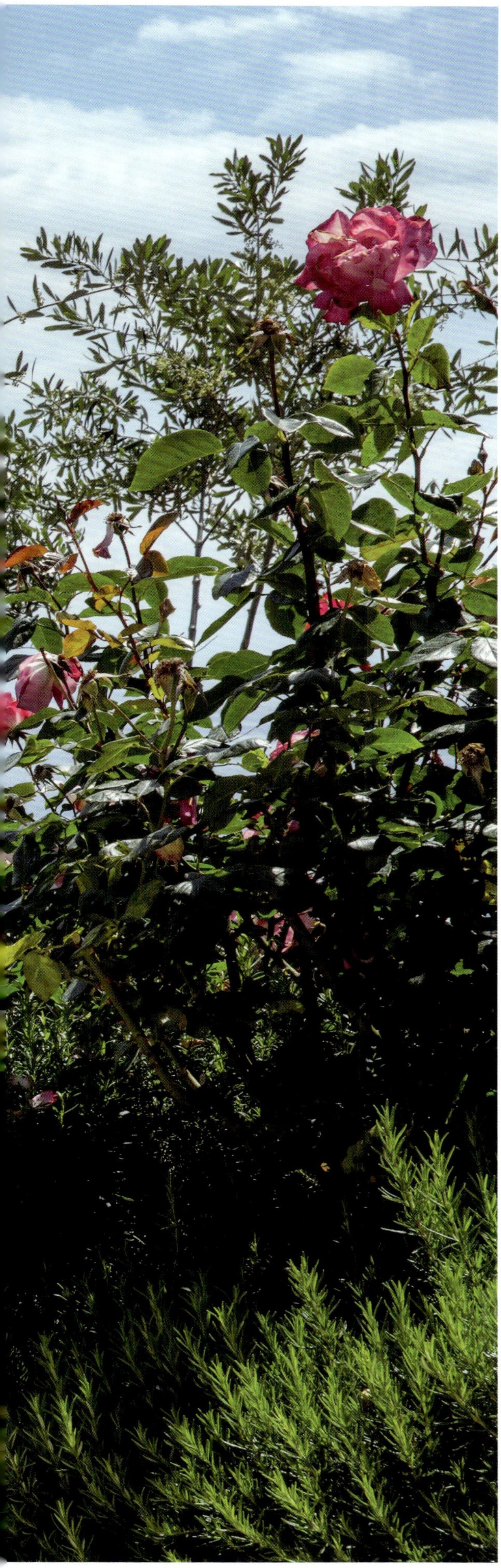

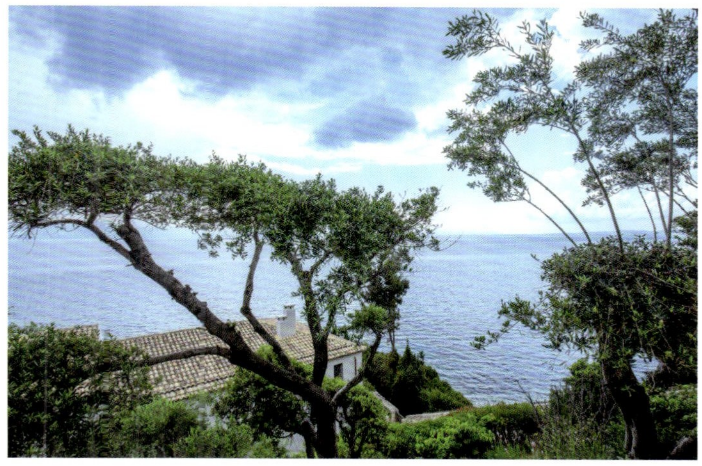

A view from the top of the driveway, under a stormy sky.

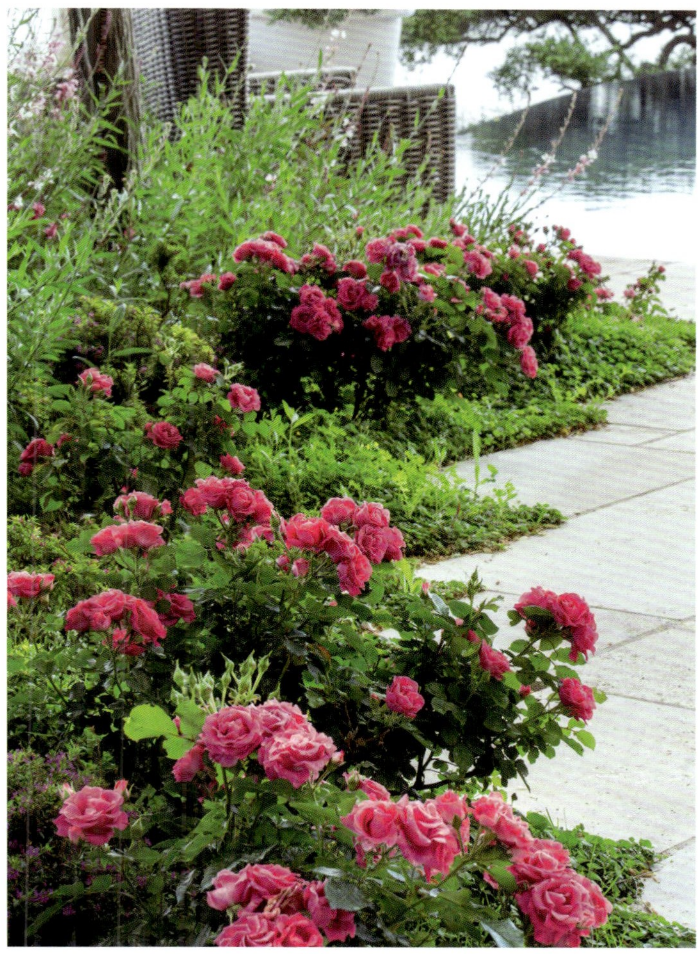

Smooth travertine paving is used around the house and for the pool terrace, and also for stepping stones within the planting beds, whose playful zigzag edges give an animated feel, complementing the movement of the willows.

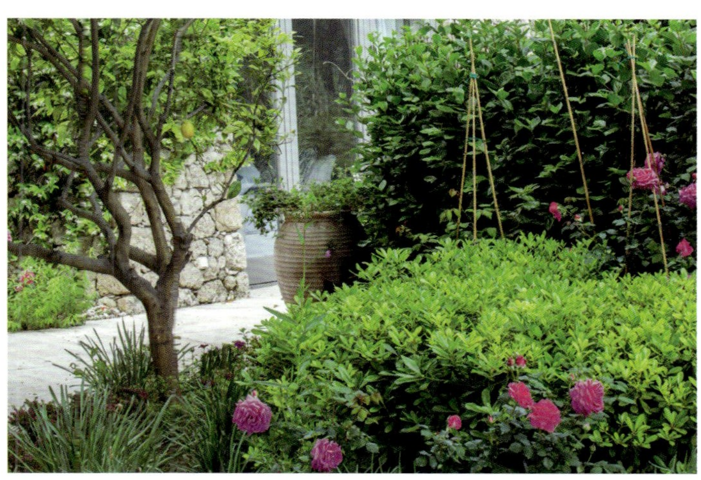

Close to the house, roses and lemon trees are combined against a lush background of dark green shrubs.

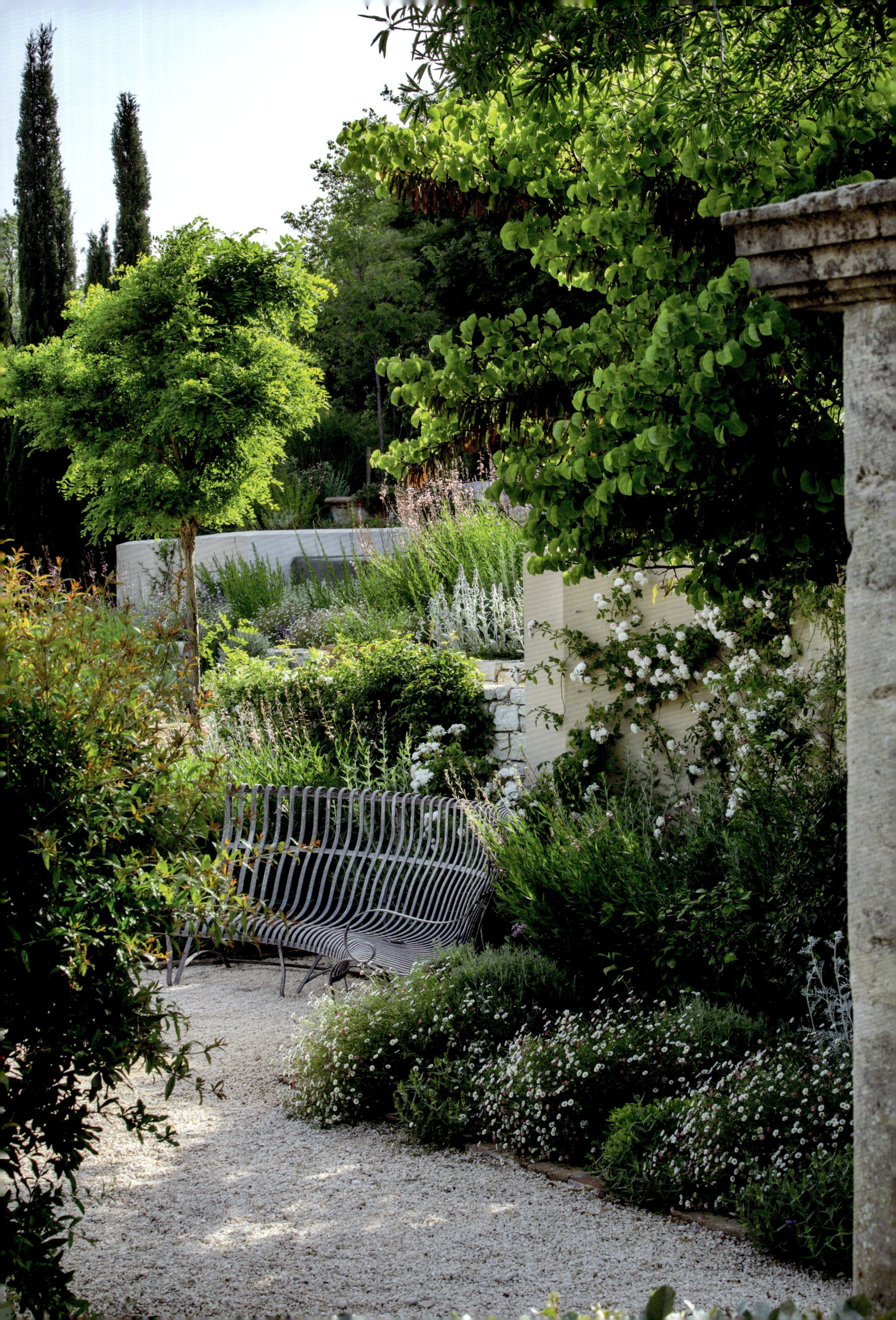

Agnos House

Refined and intricately planted, the hillside garden at Agnos House evokes happy, lazy summer days in the English countryside. The garden seems much larger than it is, both because of its detailed planting, which in some areas is so rich and complex than it invites delighted pauses at almost every step, and because of its long vistas, unusual broad flat spaces, and changes of angle that hide what is ahead and create suspense. Viewed from below, its stepped parallel terraces look wider than they are and lead the eye up and out of the cultivated garden into the woods beyond. Viewed from above, across the lawn and through breaks in the treetops to the sea, the garden merges seamlessly into the wild landscape.

OPPOSITE
In this inviting corner, the pink and white flowers of *Erigeron karvinskianus* and *Gaura lindheimeri* pick up the colours of the climbing rose, *Rosa* x *fortuneana*.

Designer Jennifer Gay explains that 'it was the owners' dream to have a house in Corfu' and that they gave her free rein to redesign the former garden to connect it better with its site, giving 'more possibilities for movement and exploration up and down, rather than just across, the hillside', and to selectively open up views to the sea. Gay created a series of low parallel terraces in local stone both above and below the pool, reducing the original steep drop from pool to lawn. She relocated the pool house, which was never used and distracted attention from the view over the Corfu Straits.

Gay's 'two biggest inspirations' are the plantsman Olivier Filippi and the garden designer Dan Pearson,[47] as perhaps one might guess from her deep knowledge of Mediterranean plants and sophisticated understanding of how to combine them for artistic effect. The varied plant combinations here look as natural as wild plant communities, but are planned for their contrasting or complementary colours and their interplay of textures and shapes. For example, groupings of plants in multiple greys and silvers call attention to differences in their leaf forms and growth habits and light-reflective properties; to highlight the subtle variations in their colour, the greys are mixed sometimes with whites and greens and at other times with plants that flower in pink, mauve, blue, or pale yellow.

From the garden's imposing entrance gate, steps lead up to the

47. See, for example, Olivier Filippi, *The Dry Gardening Handbook: Plants and Practices for a Changing Climate* (London: Thames and Hudson, 2008), and Dan Pearson's blog at http://digdelve.com/about/

The pool reflects the shapes of *Gaura lindheimeri* 'Whirling butterflies'. Gay opened up spaces between the trees to reveal views to the Corfu Straits and Albania.

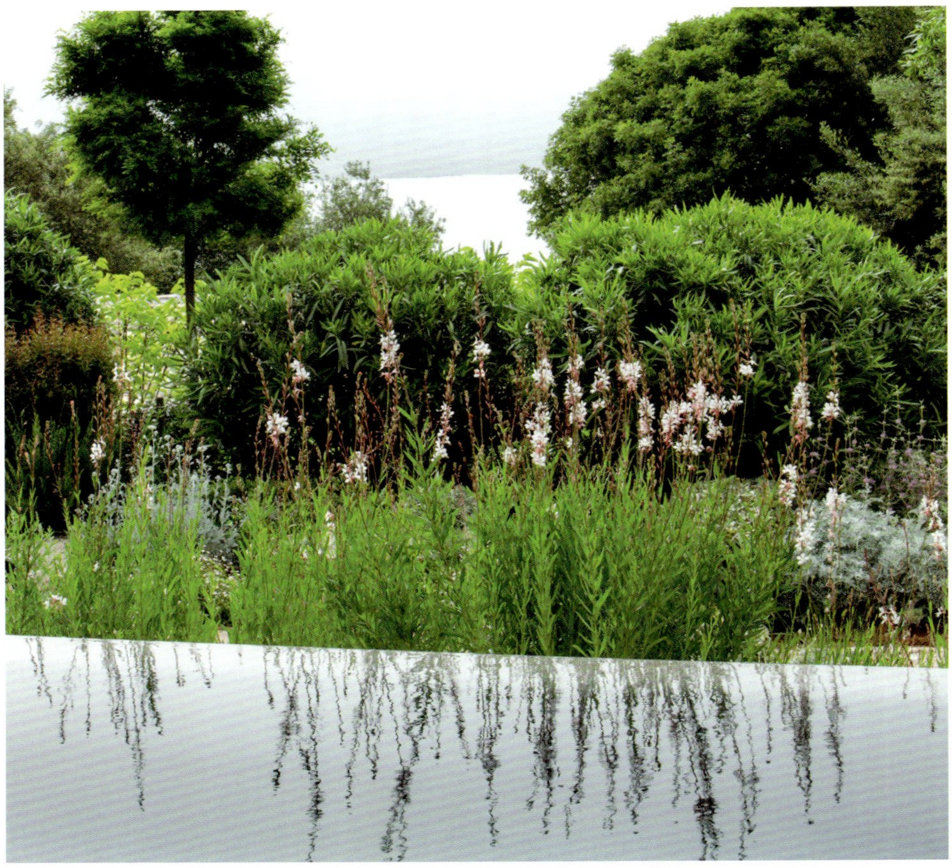

To encourage movement up and down, rather than just across, this hillside garden, Gay created low parallel terraces both above and below the pool, reducing the original steep drop from pool to lawn.

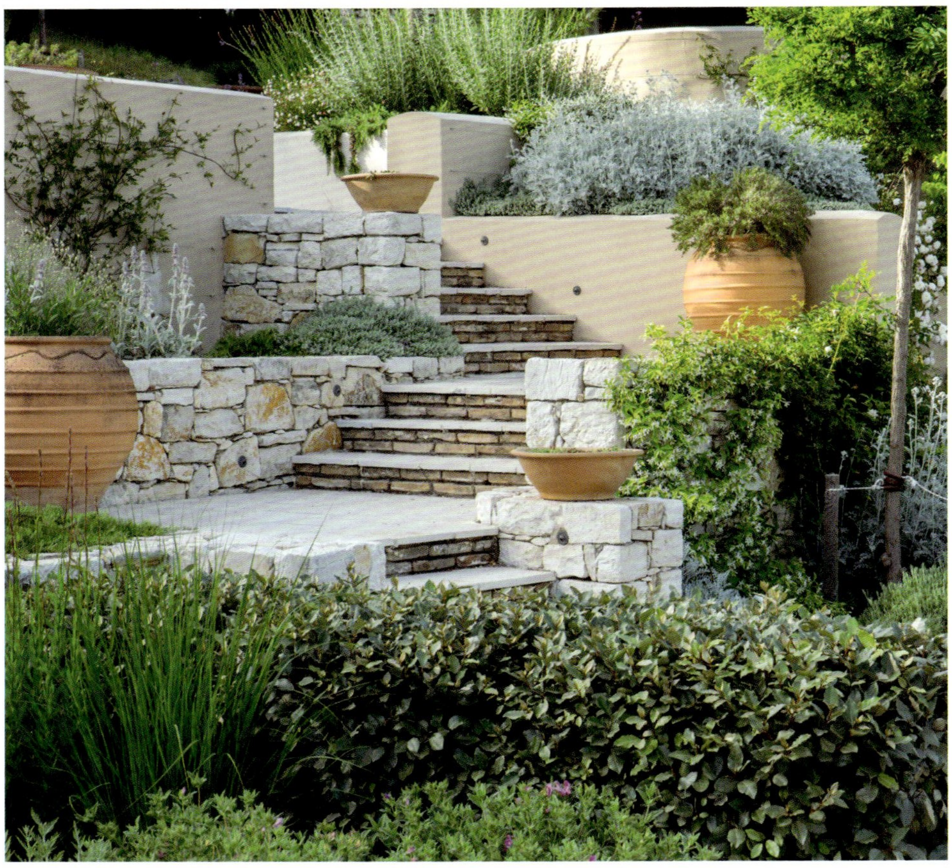

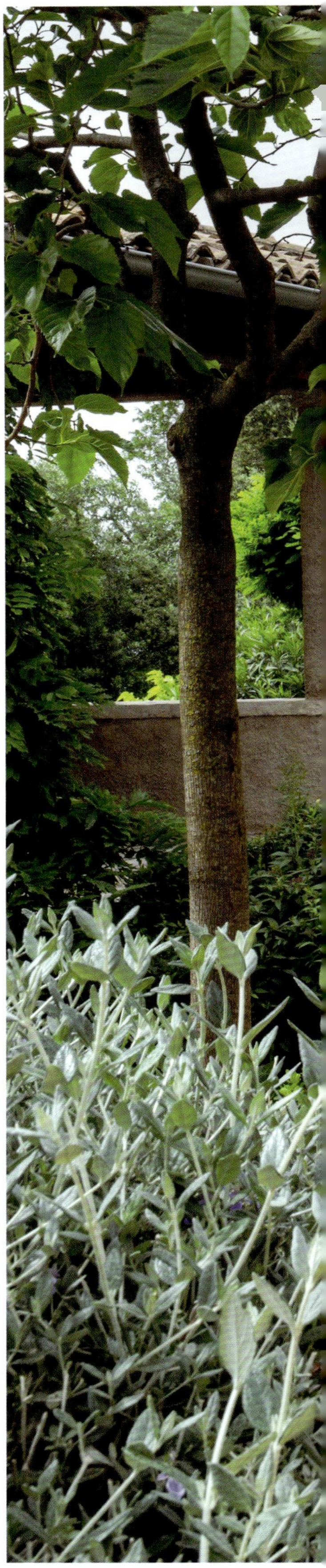

Two stone columns flank the path towards the lawn. On the left is the 'bracken building', one of several original farm buildings on the site and now a pavilion with a view over the treetops to Albania. The planting here is simple with mounds of dark green and silver-leaved shrubs and smaller mounds of lavender and *Jacobaea maritima*.

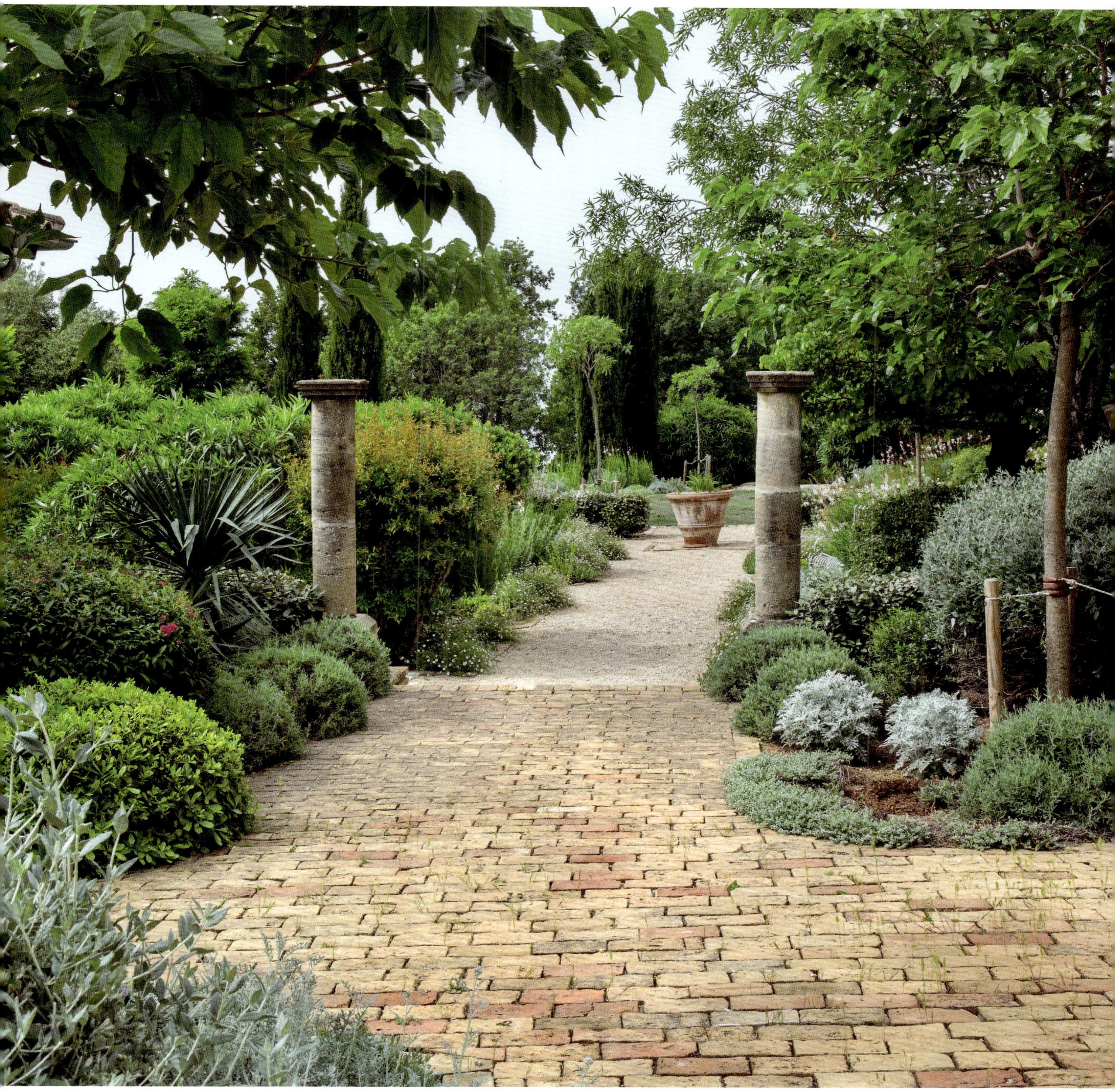

OVERLEAF

A view over the pool to the lawn below. Instead of grass, the lawn features a combination of fragrant low-growing flowering plants: *Phyla nodiflora* var. *canescens* (a tiny plant in the verbena family) along with six varieties of thyme and *Achillea crithmifolia*.

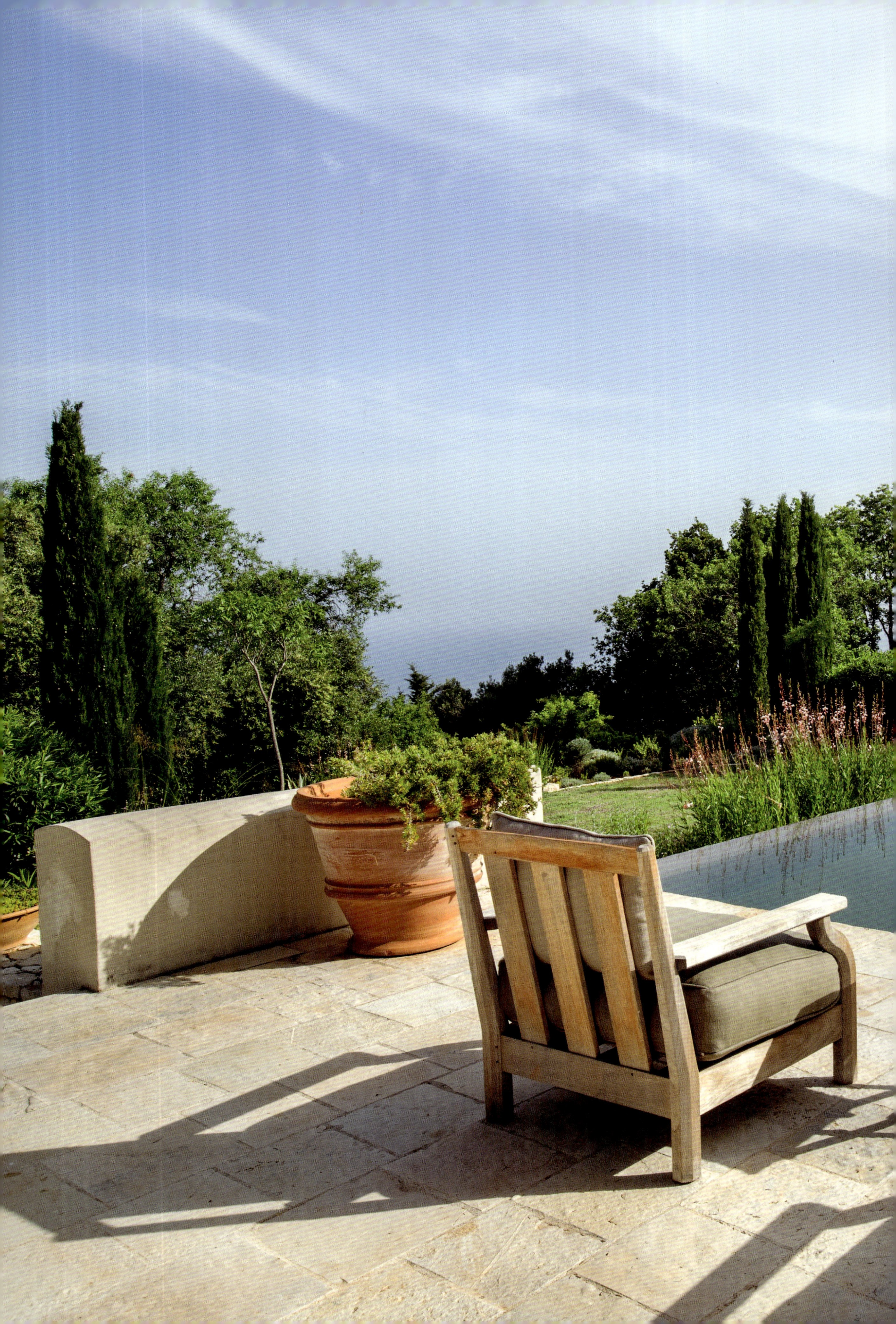

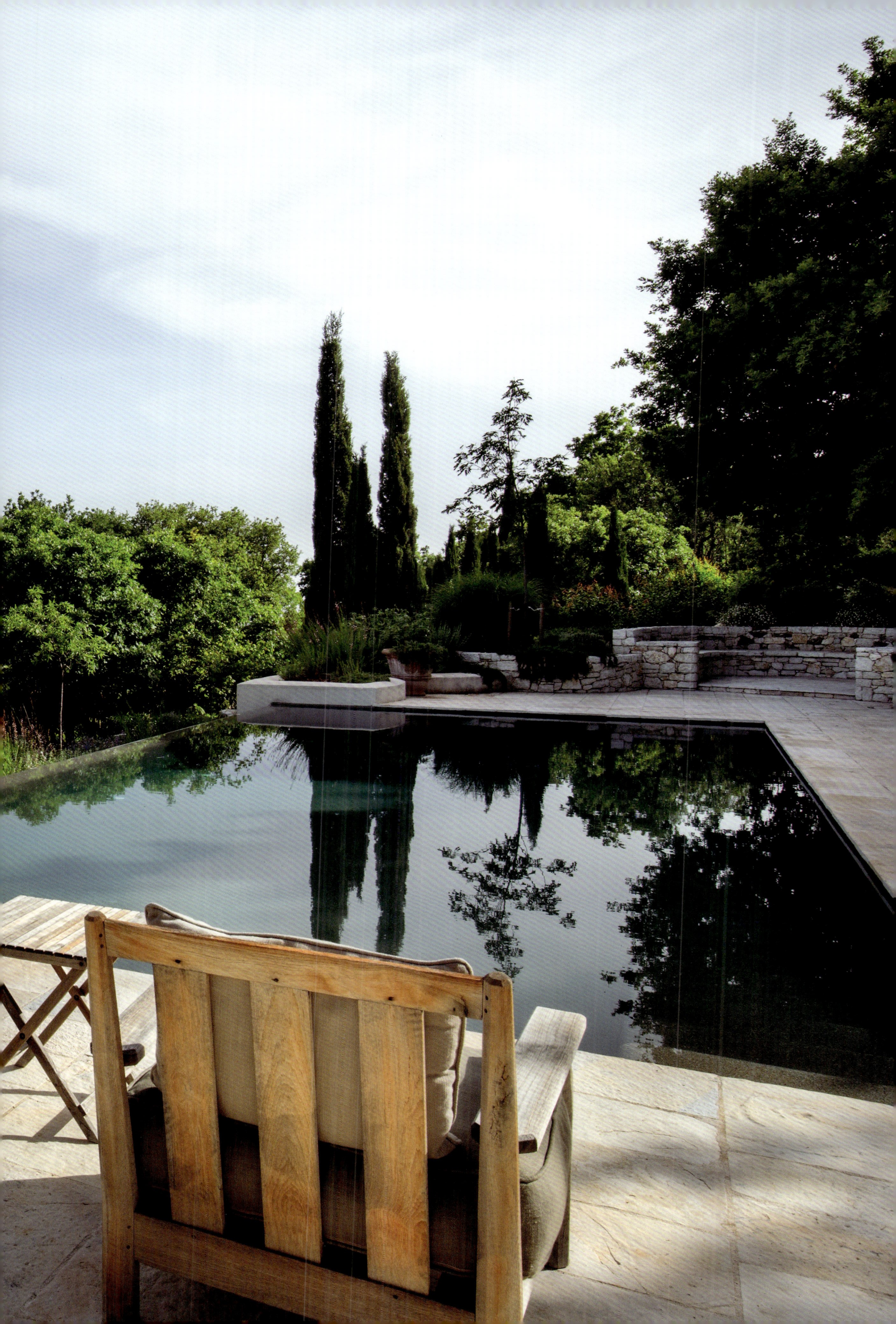

Blue-flowering *Salvia chamaedryoides* with *Erigeron karvinskianus.*

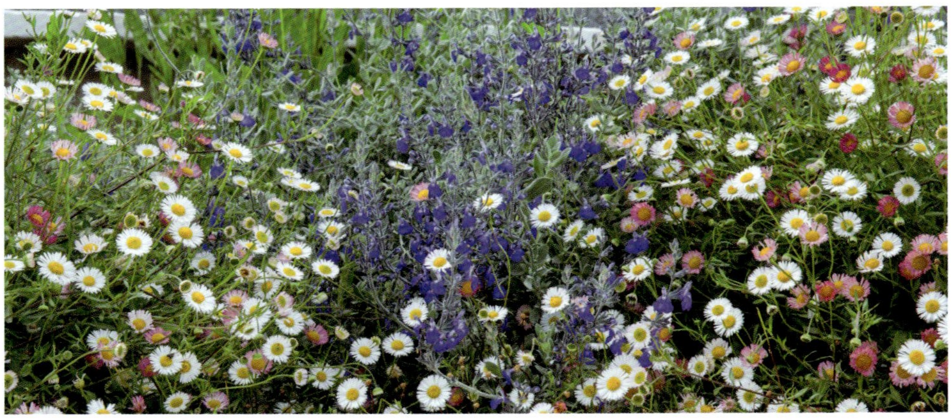

house past simple block plantings of tree germander and *Pittosporum tobira* that pre-date the recent developments. A lemon tree enjoys the shelter of a south-facing wall. At the top of the steps is a beautiful combination of fragrant white shrub- and climbing roses with star jasmine and green- and silver-leaved shrubs.

In the central area of the garden, the planting is at its most detailed and the textural contrasts and colour harmonies most fascinating. Pink cistus of multiple kinds, subtly differentiated in colour and shape, appear around the fragrant lawn, along with lavenders and a range of grey- and silver-leaved plants with mauve, pink, and blue flowers. Yellow accents are supplied by the drought-tolerant native *Euphorbia spinosa*, *Teucrium marum* from the western Mediterranean, and yellow *Teucrium luteum*, native to Tunisia. On the terraces above and below, the blues of catmints and sages enter the mixture, including the brilliant blues of *Salvia chamaedryoides*.

Along with the original almond and Judas trees, and new mulberries, manna ash (*Fraxinus ornus*), lemons, and pomegranates characteristic of nearby village gardens, Gay has chosen summer-flowering shade trees: black locust (*Robinia pseudoacacia* 'Umbraculifera') and pink-flowered Chilean desert willow tree (x *Chitalpa tashkentensis*). Little square beds set in gravel have native strawberry trees simply underplanted with white gaura, *Tulbaghia violacea*, Russian sage, and frothy pink- and white-flowered Mexican fleabane.

On the edges of this intensively designed and tended garden, Gay handles the transition perfectly between the cultivated and the wild. On the terraces immediately above the pool terrace the planting is clearly cultivated, but higher up, where decorative local wild species are combined with garden plants, it begins to give way to the wild. Not far beyond, up the hillside, the dark inviting shade of the original oak woodland provides a foil to the shimmering silvers and varied textures of the planted garden.

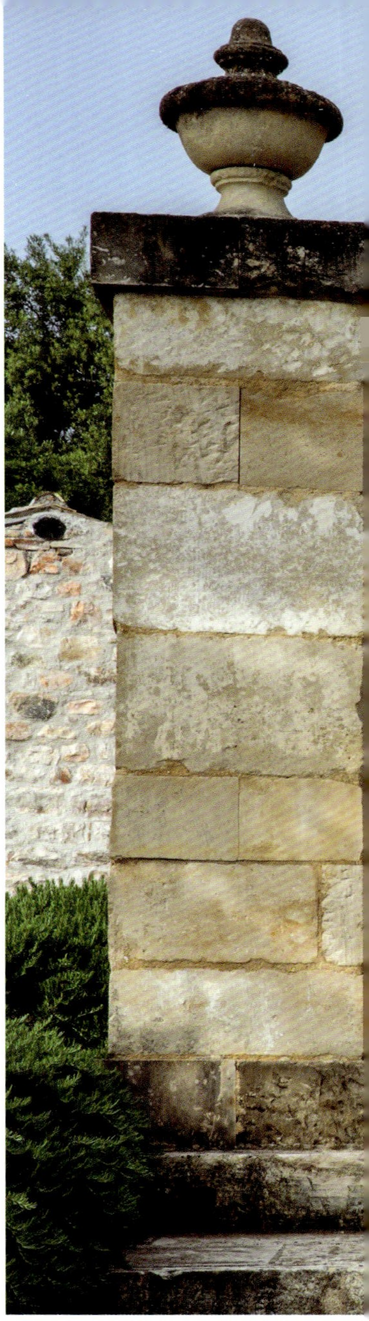

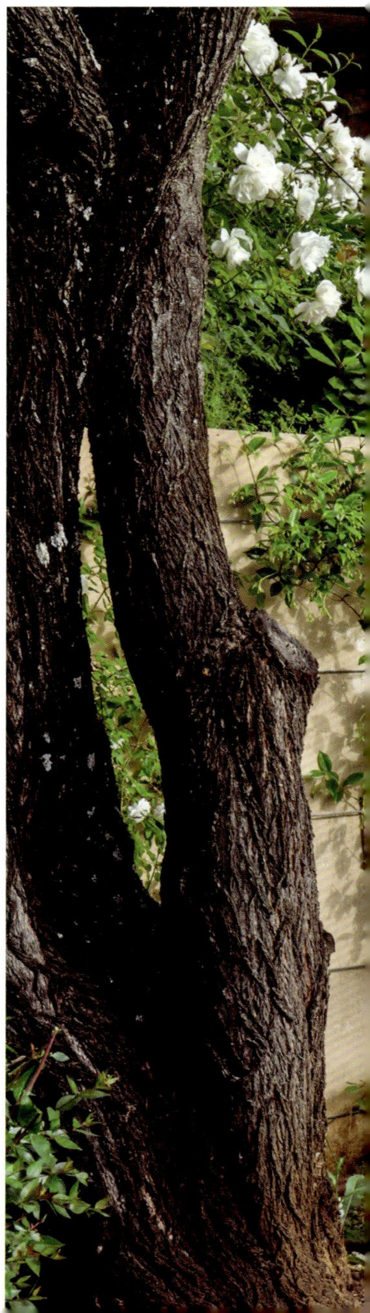

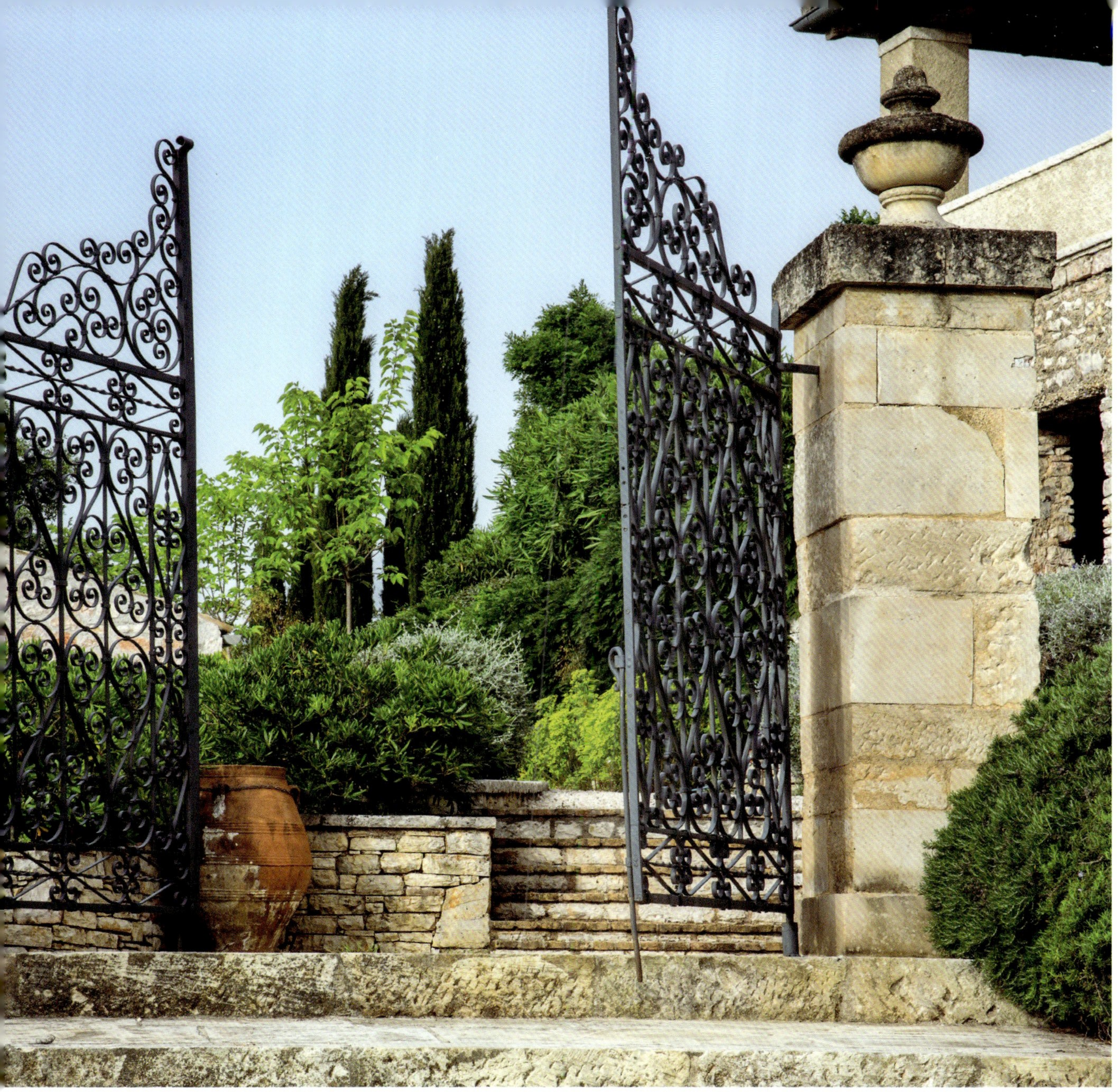

The path to the house leads through this elaborate wrought-iron gate.

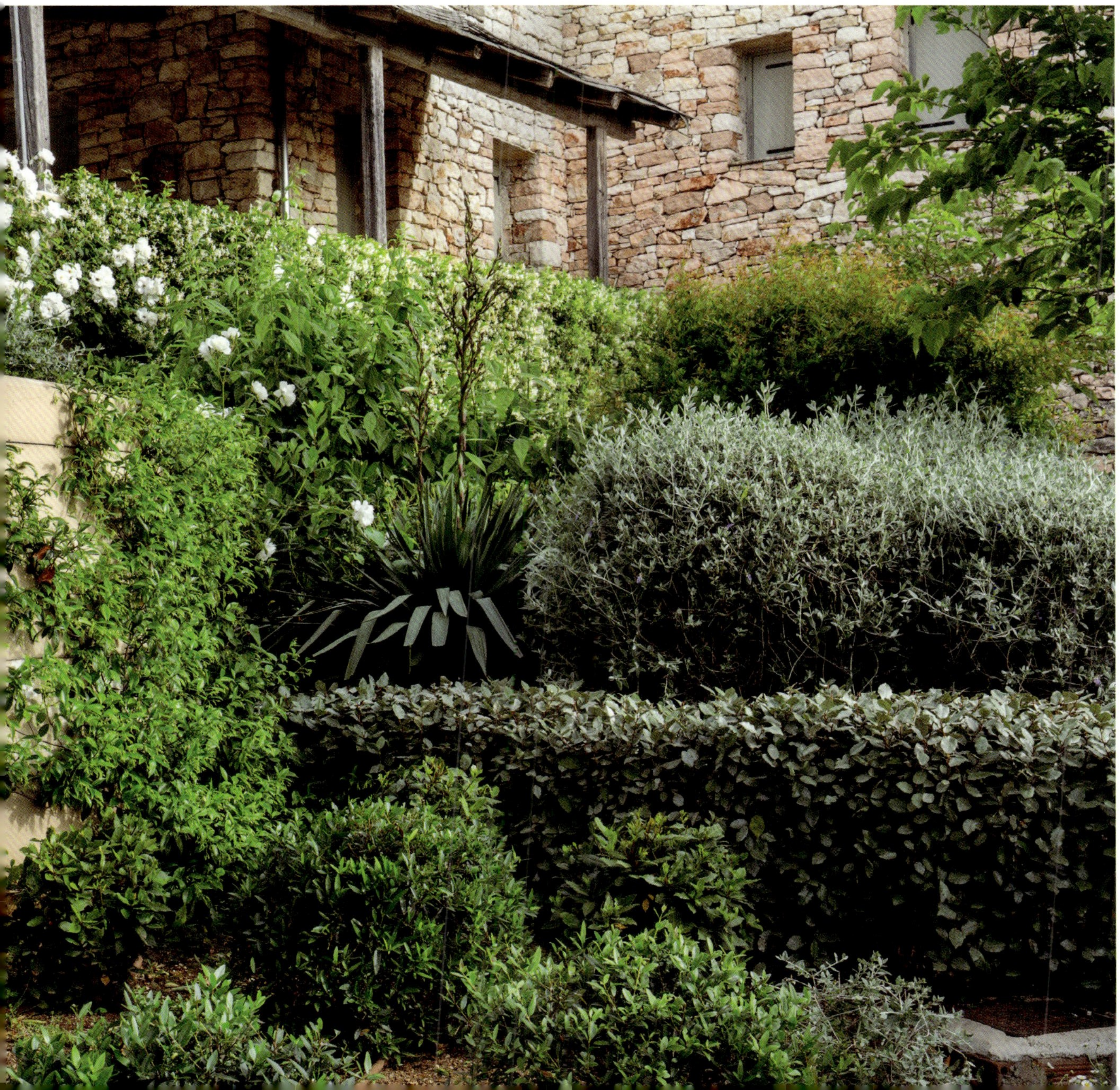

Not far inside the gate is this refreshing space combining white, silver, and green. White roses are combined with star jasmine, myrtle, *Teucrium fruticans*, silvery bronze *Elaeagnus* x *ebbingei*, and blue Spanish dagger yucca.

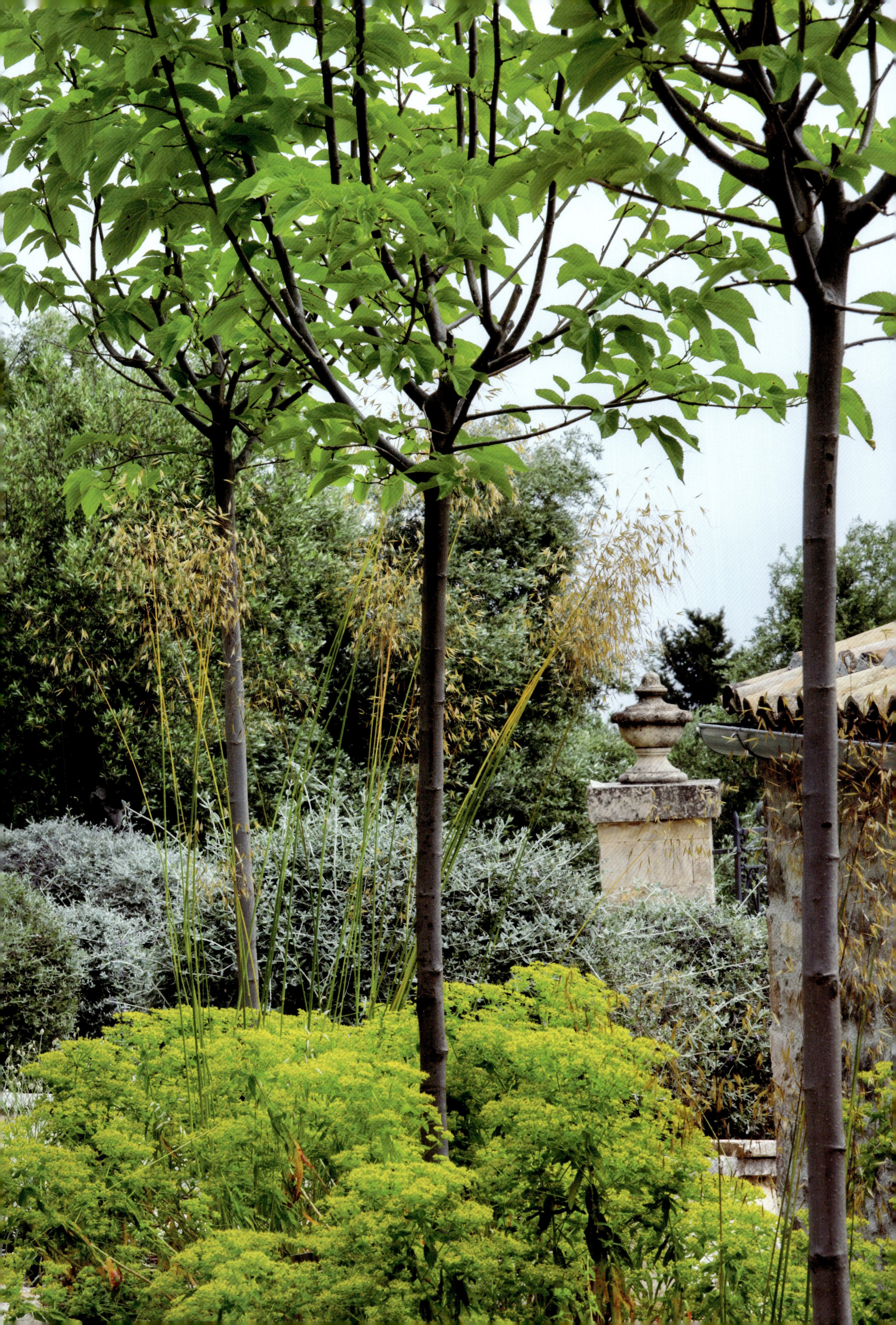

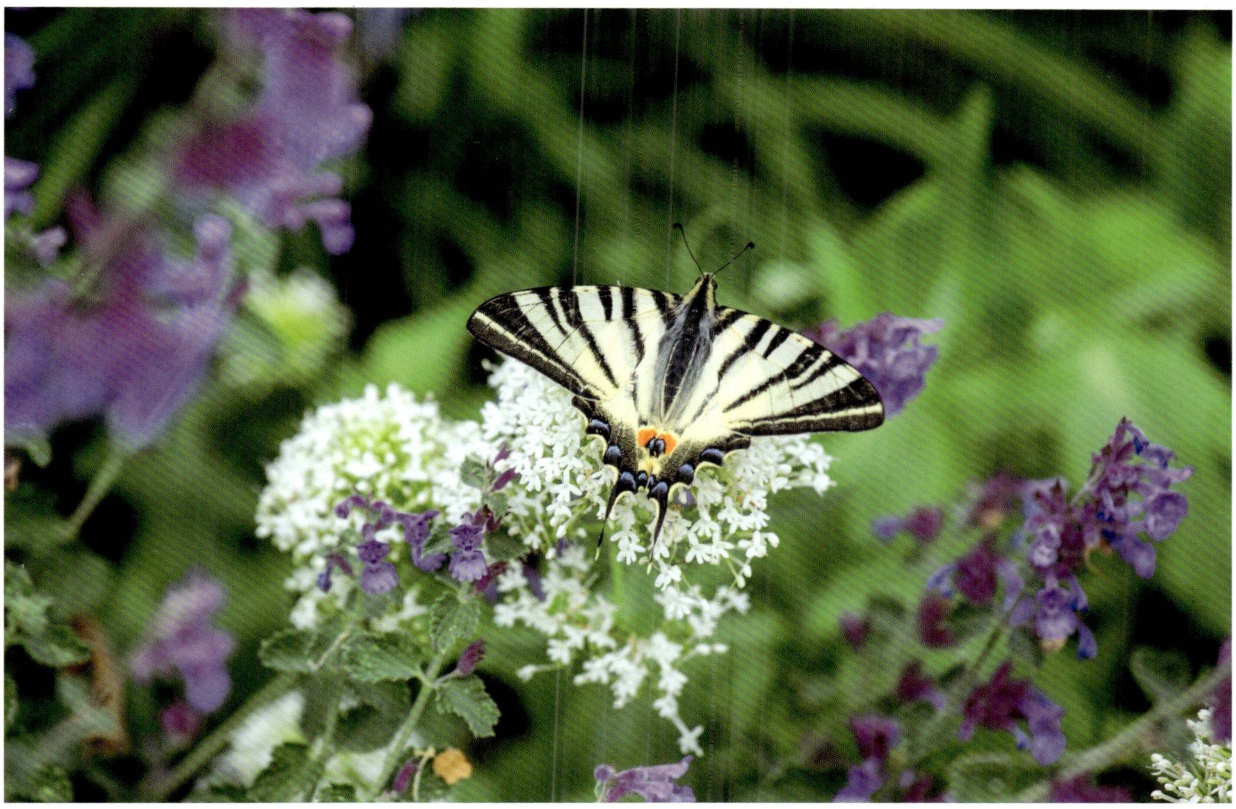

A swallowtail butterfly (*Iphiclides podalirius*) alights on *Centranthus ruber* 'Alba'.

OPPOSITE
Along a walkway lined with fruitless mulberry trees, tall golden oat grass (*Stipa gigantea*) grows with yellow-green *Euphorbia ceratocarpa*; the bright blue flowers of Cupid's dart (*Catananche caerulea*) bloom here in May.

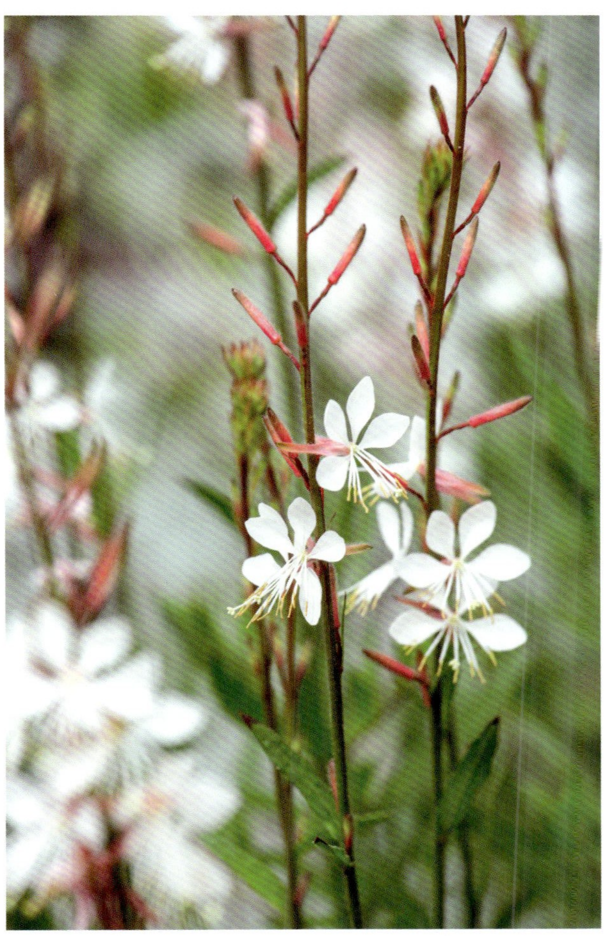

Gaura lindheimeri 'Whirling butterflies'.

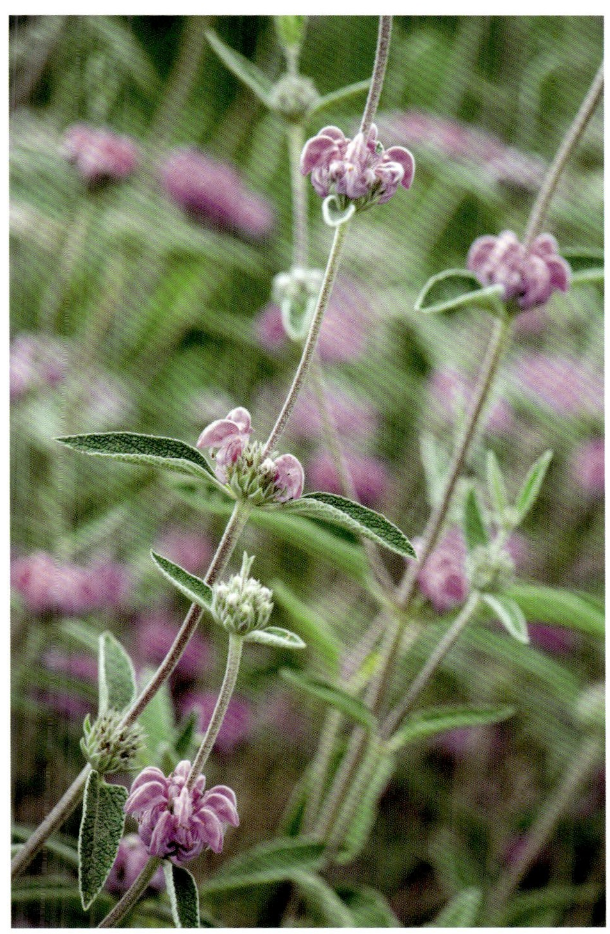

Phlomis purpurea, native to Portugal and Spain, is a close relative of Corfiot native Jerusalem sage (*Phlomis fruticosa*).

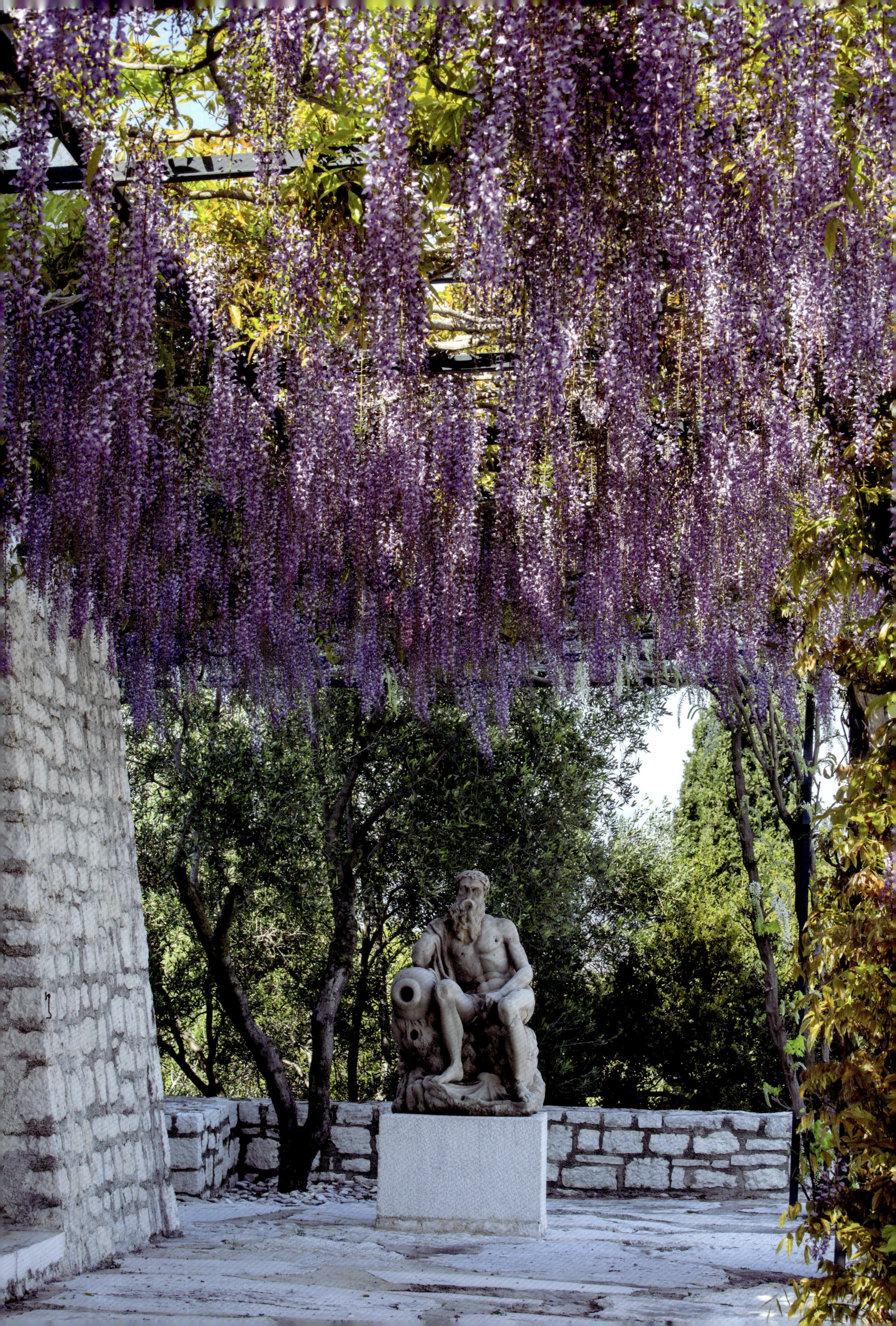

Kanónas and Strongílo

Lord Jacob Rothschild's Corfu estate occupies two peninsulas looking across the Corfu Straits towards the Bay of Butrint. The estate is remarkable for its natural beauty, its subtle enhancements of the wild landscape, and its contrasts between wild and cultivated and between grandeur and intimacy. Mary Keen, who has for many years advised the Rothschild family on landscape design and planting choices, has written that, here '… the point of the "garden" is the place. The light that beguiled so many painters, the glimpses of sea through olives and cypresses, the ancient boles of trees among rocks, the wildflowers in spring and autumn all proclaim this secret paradise beyond the skill of any gardener.'[48]

OPPOSITE
A statue of Neptune on the terrace at Strongílo. The wisteria pergola runs the entire width of the Tower, softening the military style of the architecture.

The estate reflects the love and creativity of three generations of the Rothschild family, all of whom have respected the 'spirit of place' and the power of the natural landscape to speak for itself. Lord Rothschild bought the house at Kanónas for his mother and stepfather, the celebrated Greek artist Níkos Ghíka, in the 1970s. They extended it with the two wings and the courtyards seen today, and within the inner courtyard they planted the plane trees (*Platanus orientalis*) so evocative of shaded village squares in mainland Greece. Lord Rothschild added the immense castle-like Tower at Strongílo, designed by Timothy Hatton Associates with inspiration from the fortresses in Corfu Town. He also commissioned the famous swimming pool, designed by Javier Barba and quarried out of the rock below the Tower. And, in keeping with the intent to let nature speak for itself, he guided the work to expose the stark rock platforms beside the house at Kanónas and to highlight a stalactite grotto on the hillside below the Tower. His daughter Beth, working jointly with Keen, designed the planting below the Tower and around the pool, and his daughter Emmy designed the stone portal near the pool.

OVERLEAF
A dawn view over the pool and across the Corfu Straits. The affinity of the pruned shrubs with the shapes of the hills across the Straits and along the Corfiot coast helps to root the landscape design into its site.

Kanónas is reached on paths through woodland, between box hedges shaded by olive trees, and through an elaborate portico. Inside, in both the outer and the inner courtyards, with their elaborate mosaic paving and arresting display of Classical and later art, the planting is kept very simple. Myrtle and *Westringia fruticosa* are trained as low clipped hedges, *Plumbago auriculata* covers a wall, and lemon

48. Mary Keen, *The Landscape at Kanónas and Strongílo* (Letterpress of Cirencester, 2007).

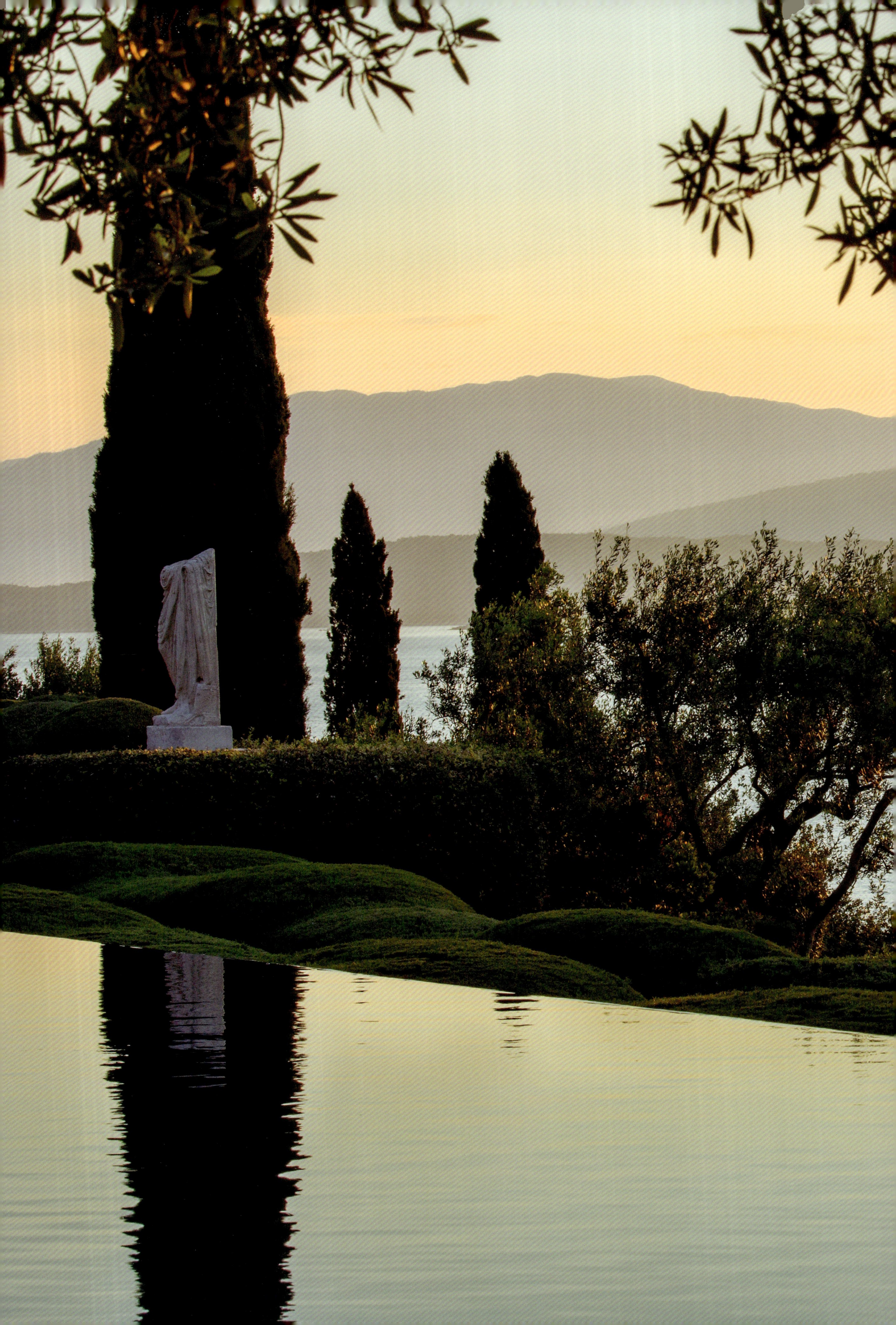

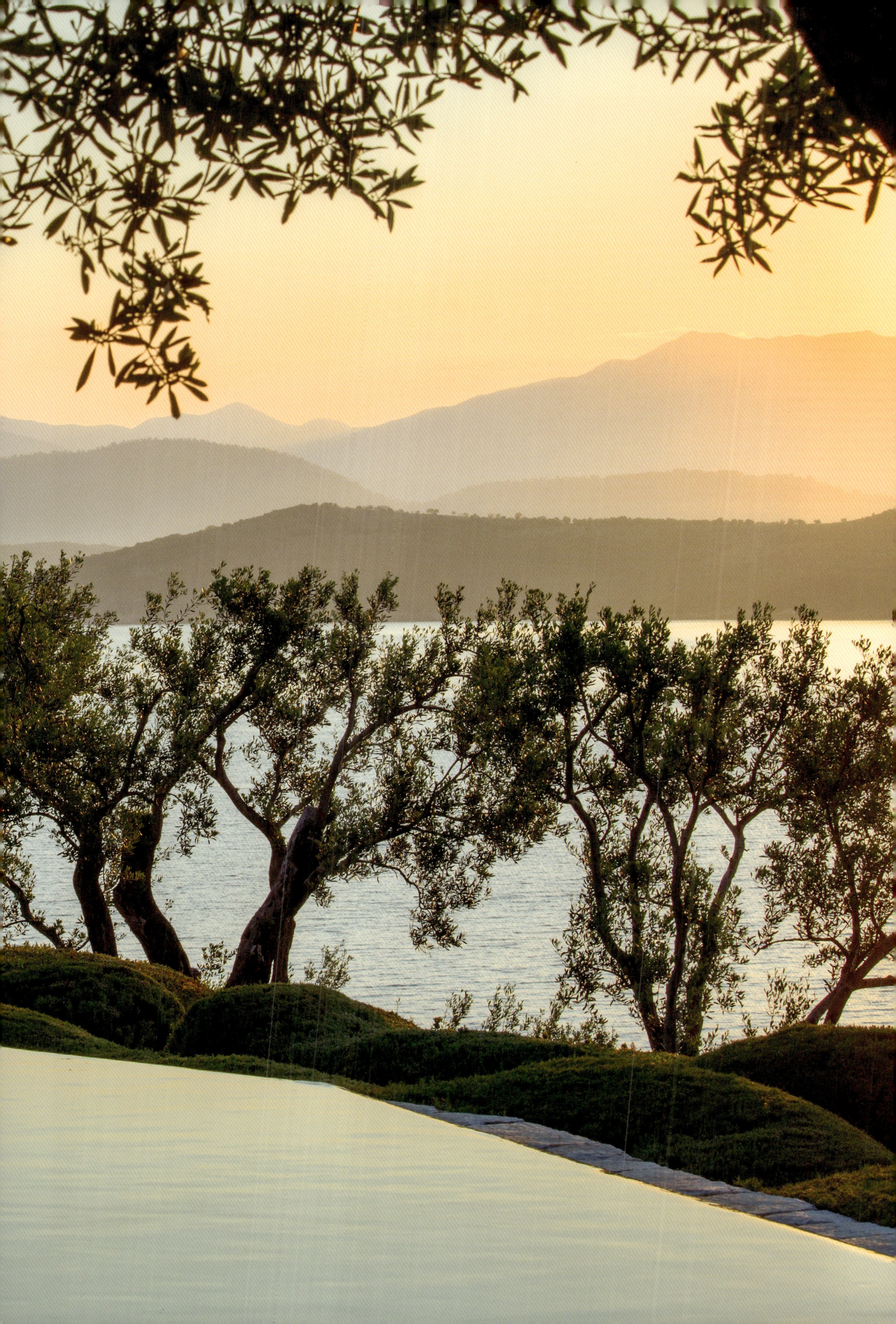

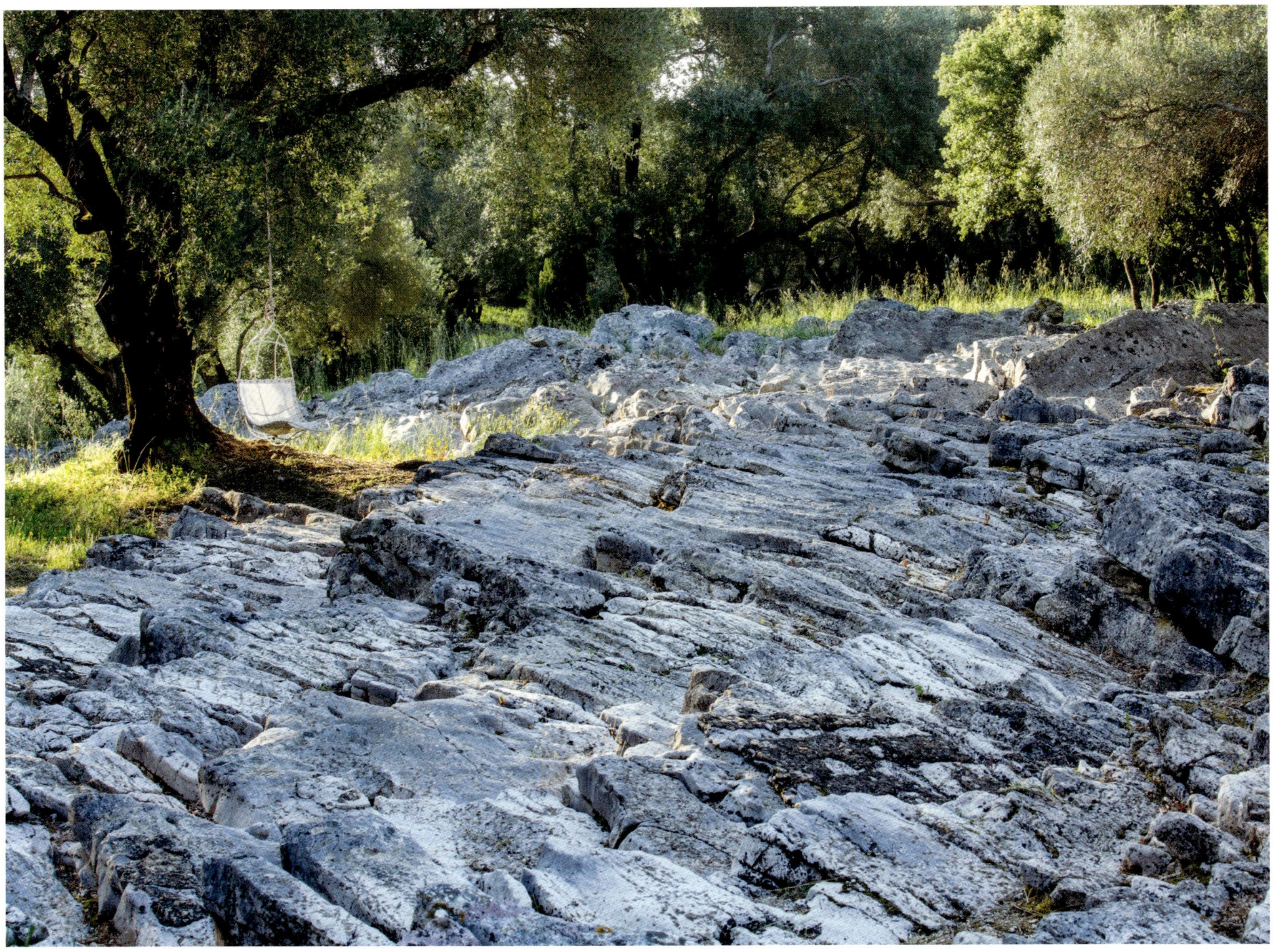

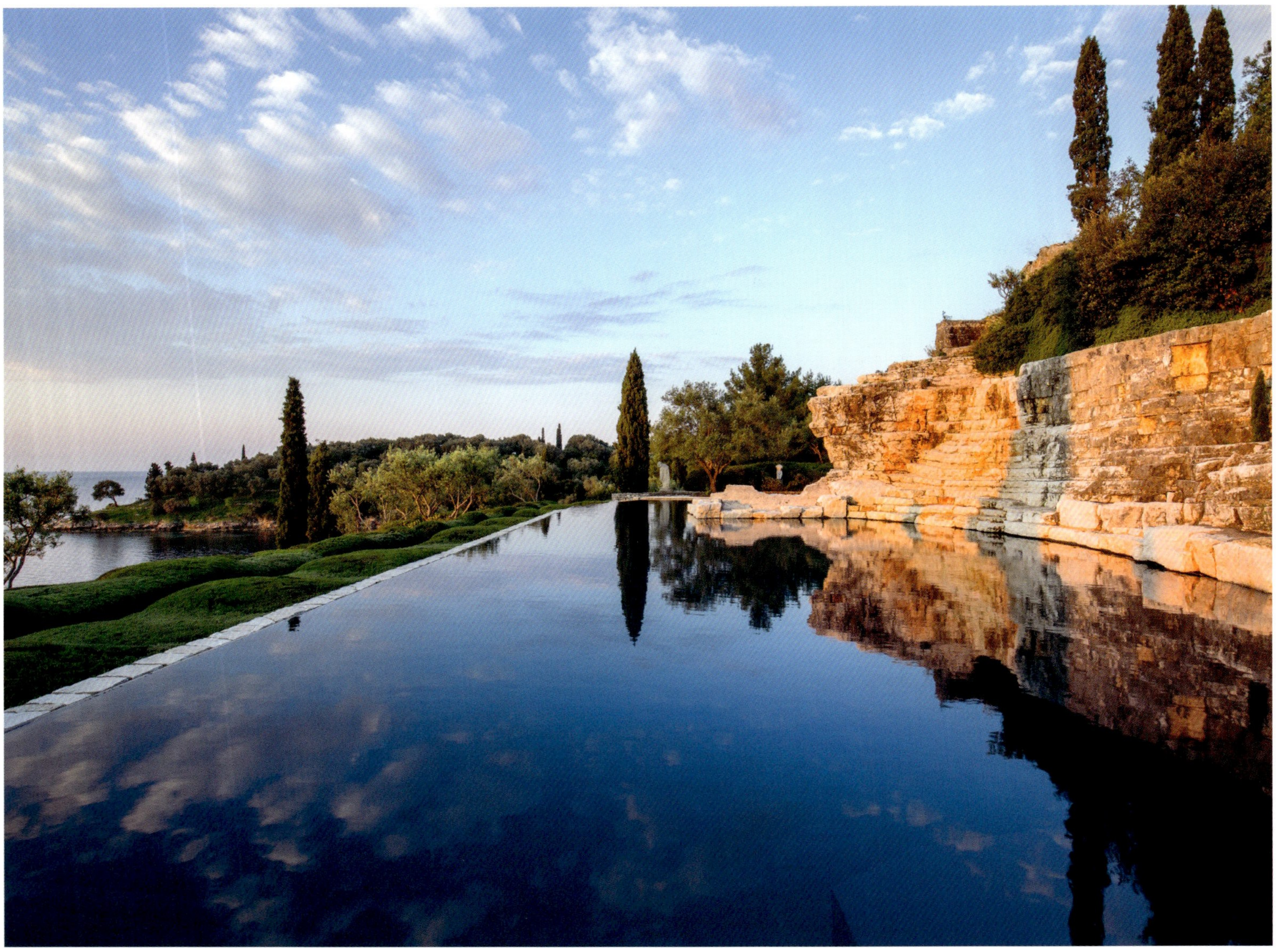

OPPOSITE TOP
In a typical Corfiot combination of raw rock with domestic spaces, this rock platform abuts the house at Kanónas and its wisteria pergola, elegant mosaic paving, and Classical statuary. The rock was exposed at Lord Rothschild's direction.

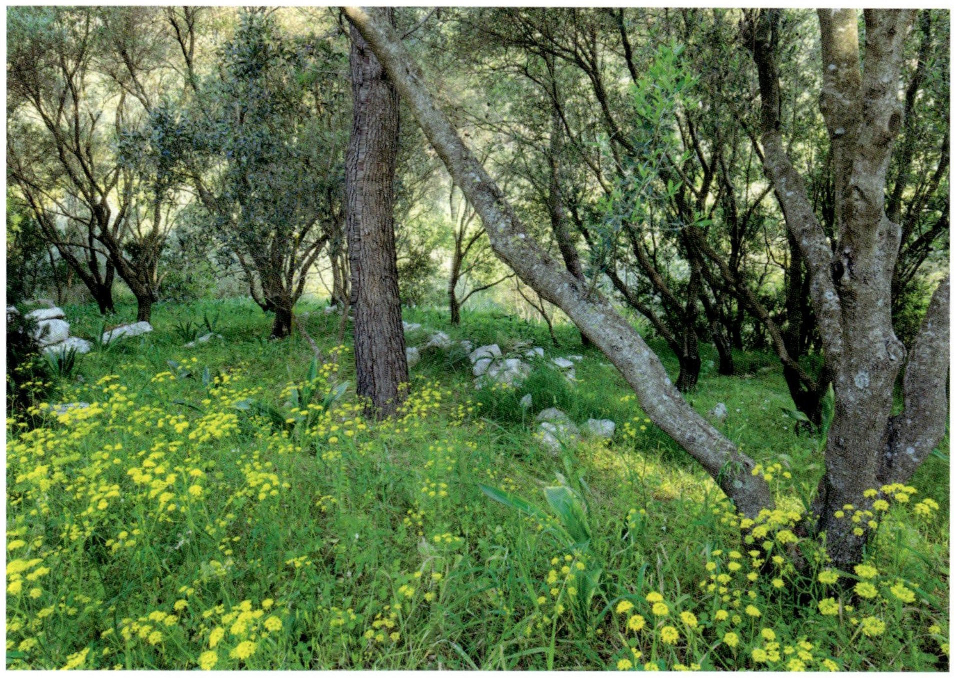

The Rothschild estate is a local leader in the responsible management of olive groves and conservation of the wild landscape. Wild golden-flowering *Malabaila aurea* carpets this olive grove sloping down to the sea.

OPPOSITE BOTTOM
The famous pool at Strongílo, designed by Javier Barba.

trees and agaves are arranged symmetrically in pots. South of the house, a brooding statue of Neptune is dramatised by a dark backdrop of pencil cypresses and a low box hedge. The formal dark green planting here quickly gives way to a more open-textured hedge of grey *Westringia fruticosa* as one turns the corner and the rocky nature of the underlying land increasingly reveals itself.

Miles of paths connect the different parts of the estate. High on the peninsula in front of the Tower at Strongílo, the mood is set by the military architectural style and the exposure of the land to the winds. The paved open forecourt calls to mind a military muster station—or perhaps a parade ground—for several hundred troops. Decorated with cannons and cannonballs, it has commanding views over the sea and up the Butrint Valley opposite. Yet it has been somewhat softened by a gardener's hand: a long pergola is covered with fragrant wisteria, and a large collection of cactus on a table is backed by a whimsical cactus sculpture. Below the forecourt have been planted evergreen and ever-grey native shrubs, along with large grey-blue agaves. From here, a footpath leads down through open woodland, created by artful naturalistic plantings of native kermes oak, holm oak, and bay, towards the swimming pool.

The pool area is approached down an enclosed flight of stone steps and through an exquisite courtyard in Roman style. On a hot summer day one is drawn to linger here, enjoying its cool, damp twilight after the dry heat on the open hillside. Water from a wall fountain splashes into a marble basin. Symmetrically arrayed on the mosaic

OVERLEAF
Miles of paths encourage exploration on foot.

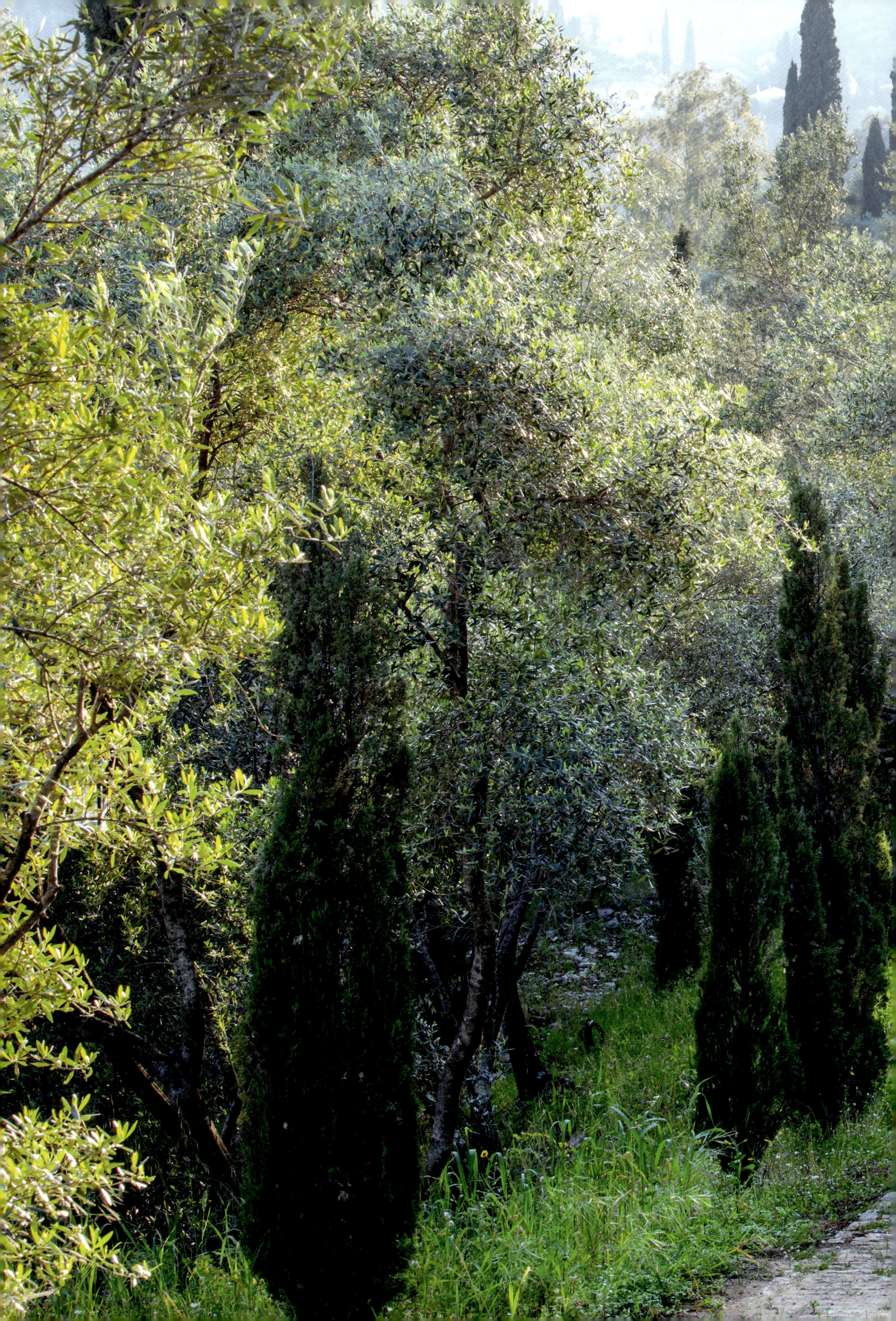

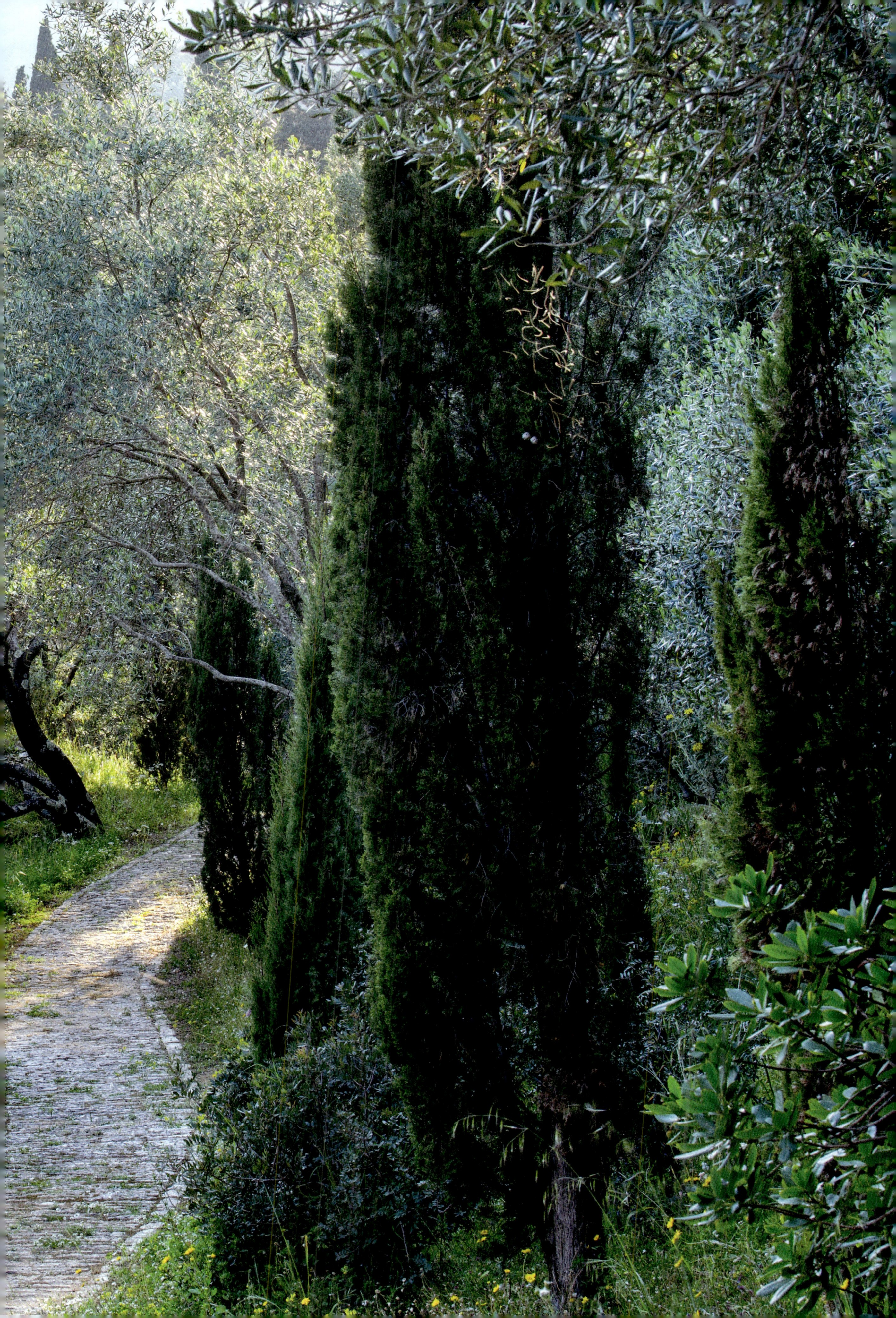

A view from the vegetable garden to the Pink Tower. Original oaks and Judas trees form an integral part of the design.

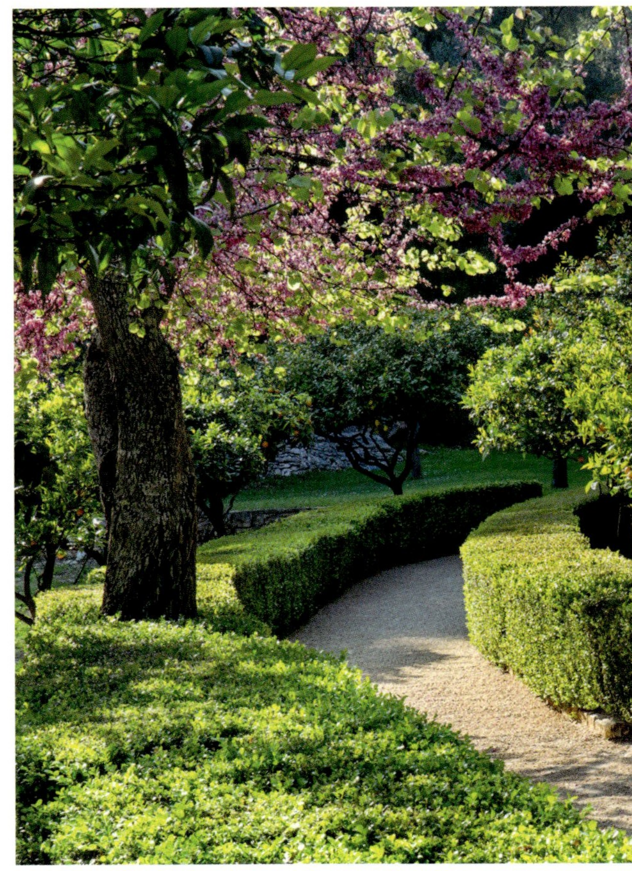

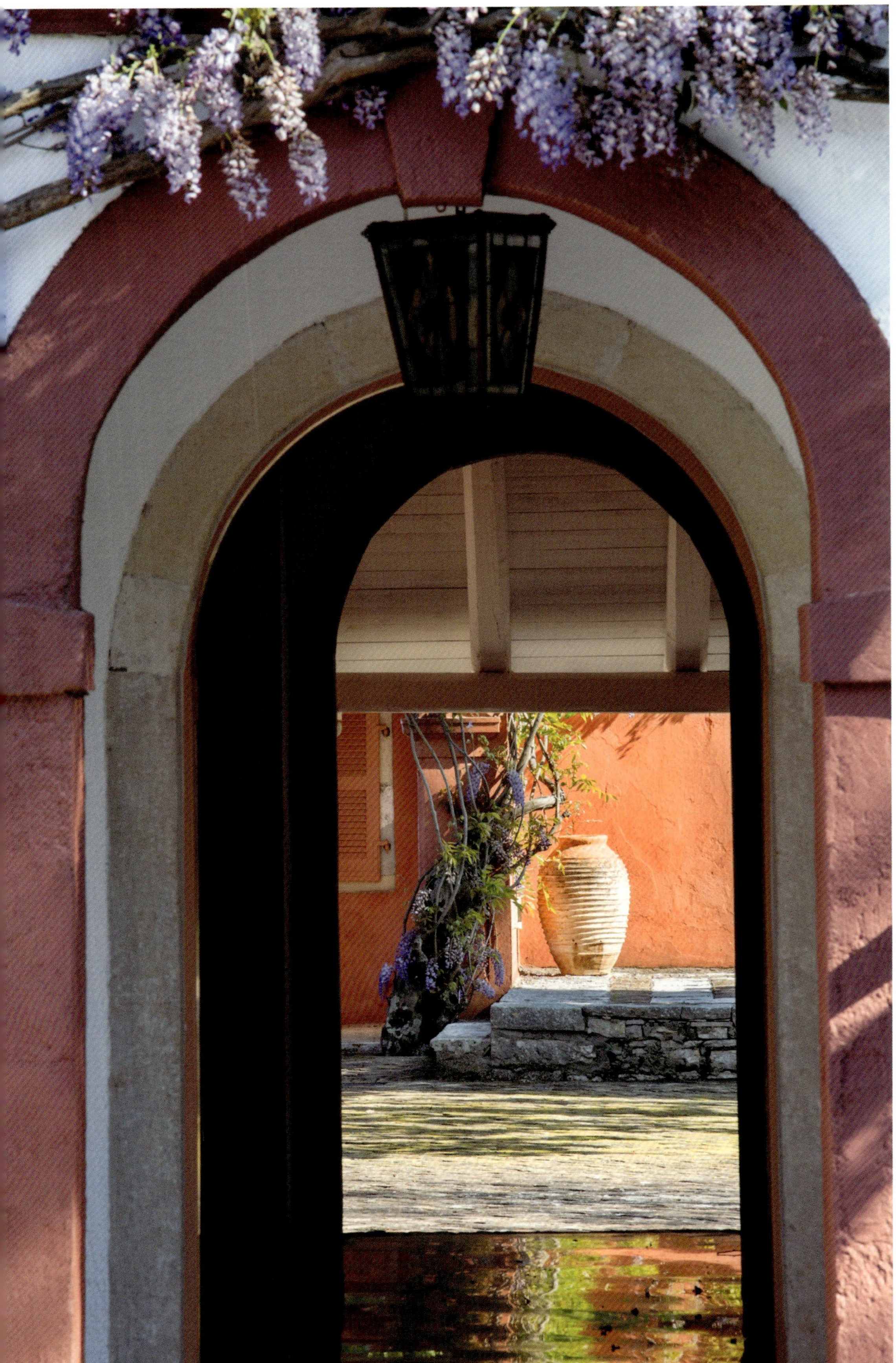

At Kanónas, a view through the loggia to the second courtyard.

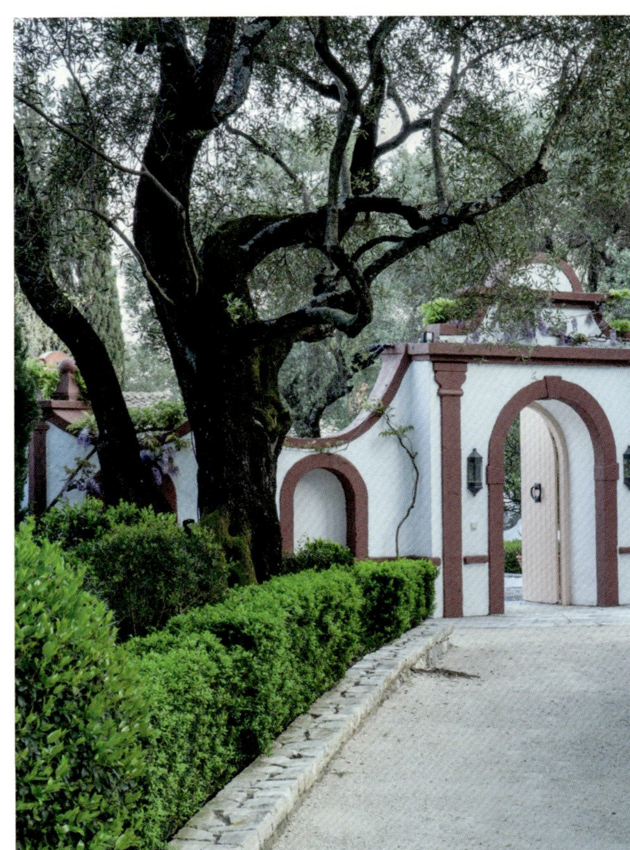

The entrance gate at Kanónas is painted in a reverse-colour version of traditional Corfiot style.

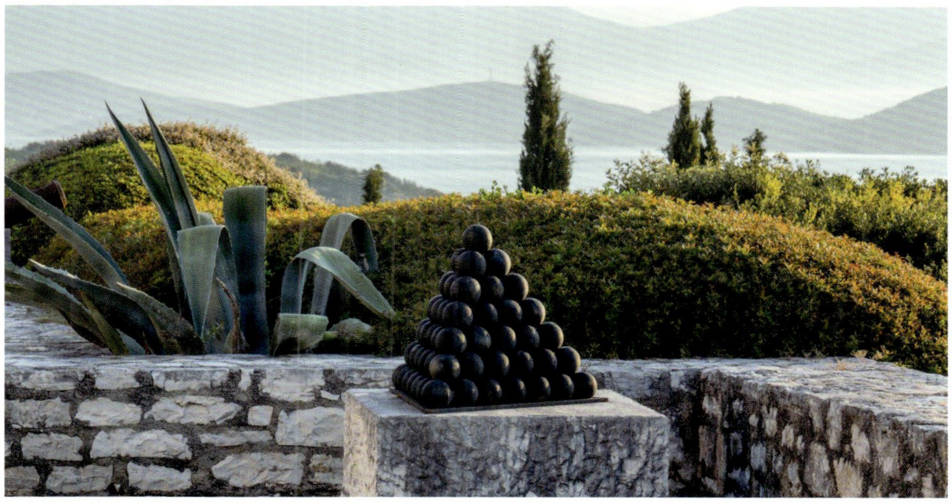

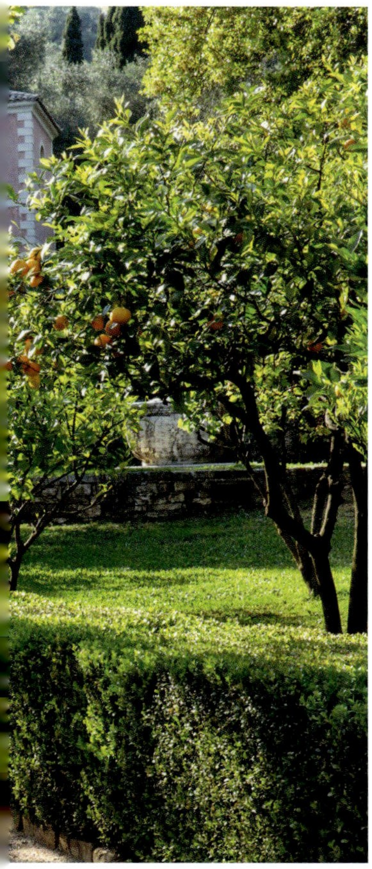

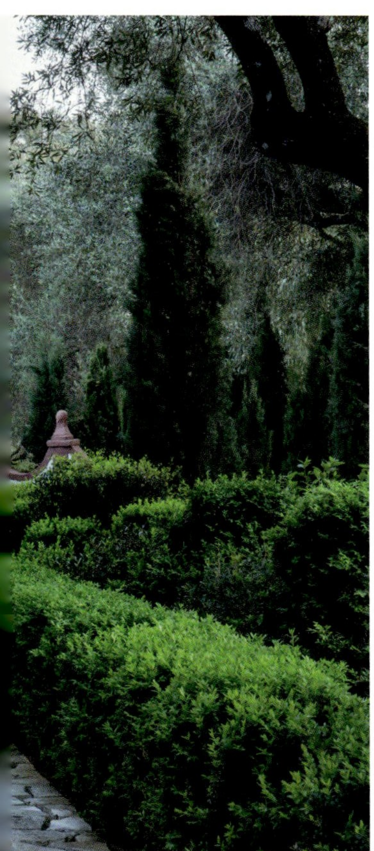

Cannonballs on the wall at Strongílo. Agaves and clipped native shrubs evoking the shapes of the distant mountains have been planted on the hillside below.

pavement are four lemon trees in pots. From here, the way leads into the summer pavilion at the edge of the pool terrace.

Nothing quite prepares one for the first view of the pool: an enormous expanse of dark water contained within untamed rock. Barba has emphasised that, 'Being an admirer of nature it does not feel right to try to compete with it. That is why my designs try to bond with the surroundings instead of standing out.'[49] With its surface sometimes troubled by wind, sometimes perfectly mirroring the crags above it and the cypress and olive trees planted nearby, it is nonetheless always the same colour as the sea spread out not far below. On the crags, curtains of rosemary hang down and pencil cypresses spring from narrow ledges. Enfolding the pool at its far end, and bordering its seaward side, are svelte shapes of cloud-pruned native shrubs and rosemary.

Between the two peninsulas is a flat-bottomed valley containing a luxuriant kitchen garden. After the grandeur and majesty of the Strongílo landscape, it would be hard to imagine a greater contrast than the domestic, almost magical, lushness of this garden. Corfu is a rocky land, but in the miniature Eden here the vegetable beds have only tiny stones. Immaculate bright green rows of lettuces have been carefully mulched with manure; beds lying fallow have been carefully covered with seaweed. In the adjoining orchard, quince, pomegranate, orange, and lemon trees are set in green lawns divided by manicured box hedges.

The estate's gardens are beautifully maintained under the direction of manager Andy Belton.

49. As quoted in Amanda Storey, 'The Barba Legacy', *Dolce Magazine*, 15 September, 2016. See also Nicholas Shrady, 'Greek Drama: Lord Jacob Rothschild's Pavilion on Corfu', *Architectural Digest*, October 1995.

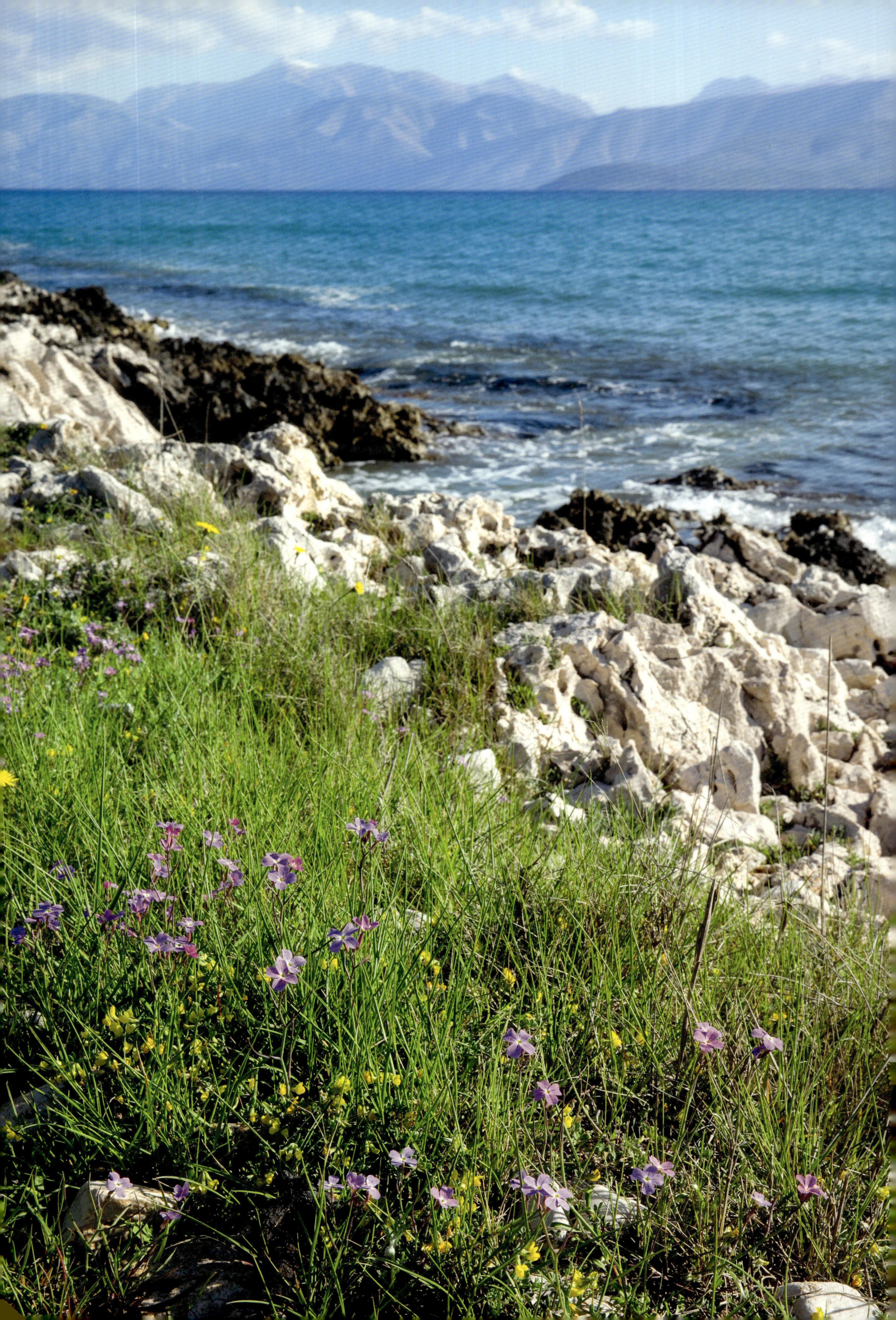

CHAPTER FIVE

The Wild Garden

Because so many of Corfu's contemporary gardens draw inspiration from the wild landscape of this 'garden island', this chapter explores the roots of that inspiration. Corfu's unusually rich range of wild plants (some fourteen hundred species)[50] stems from the island's geographical position at a crossroads: many of these plants have close counterparts in Northern Europe or North Africa, while others are typical of mainland Greece and Italy. It is also a product of Corfu's relatively mild and damp climate, which encourages vigorous plant growth, and the wide range of soils and microclimates, which provide a wide diversity of natural habitats. The chapter surveys the varied natural landscape across the island, with its long history of dialogue between man and the land; follows the procession of wildflowers through the year; and illustrates some local culinary and medicinal uses of wild plants.

OPPOSITE
Multi-coloured Virginia stocks (*Malcolmia maritima*) bloom among the rocks at Aghios Spiridón.

THE CORFIOT LANDSCAPE

Corfu's plant habitats vary dramatically. The windswept summit of the island's highest point, Mount Pantocrátor, feels much higher than its 906 metres because it is so close to the sea—views of which abound in all directions—and because the surrounding limestone karst is so barren. But less than an hour's drive from this somewhat lunar landscape are hillsides densely forested with oak and chestnut, fertile plains along the north coast, broad sandy beaches backed by rolling dunes, flat coastal meadows filled with flowers in spring, wetlands surrounding the Antiniótissa Lagoon, and the soaring mudstone cliffs of Cape Drástis. In the centre of the island, the fertile Rópa Valley grows lush and green, with water flowing through thickly reeded channels even in the height of summer, while on the west coast at Palaiokastrítsa the land falls dramatically hundreds of feet to the sea, and in the southern salt pans at Lefkímmi, flamingos congregate.

People have been shaping Corfu's landscape for thousands of years, by felling and burning the original forest trees and pasturing animals—changing whole ecosystems in the process—but also by

50. O. Borkowski, *Übersicht der Flora von Korfu* (Braunschweig, Germany: Braunschweiger Geobotanische Arbeiten I, Braunschweiger, 1994). See also the Flora Ionica project website at https://floraionica.univie.ac.at/index.php?site=1

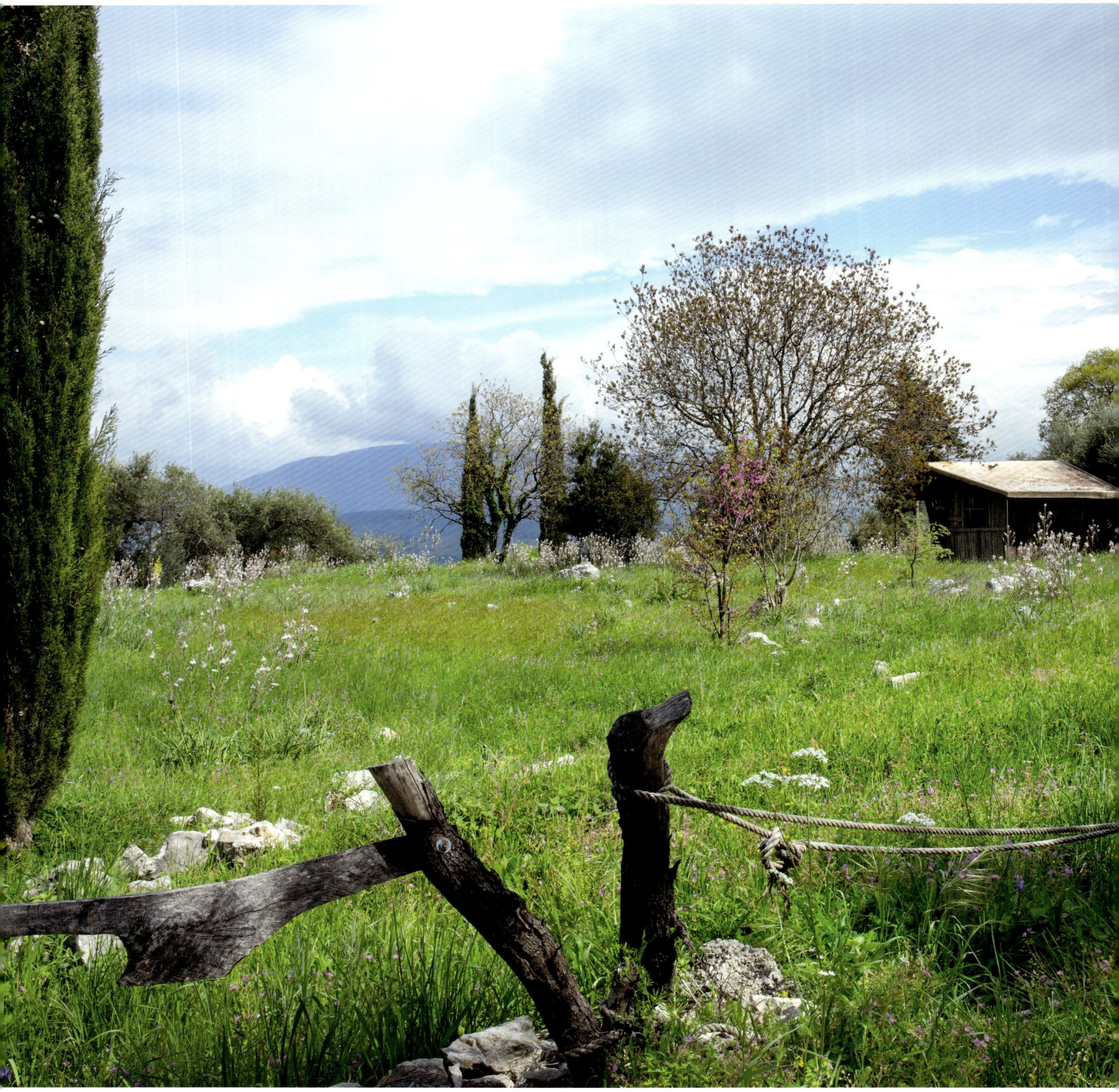

A mountain meadow
above Pórta.

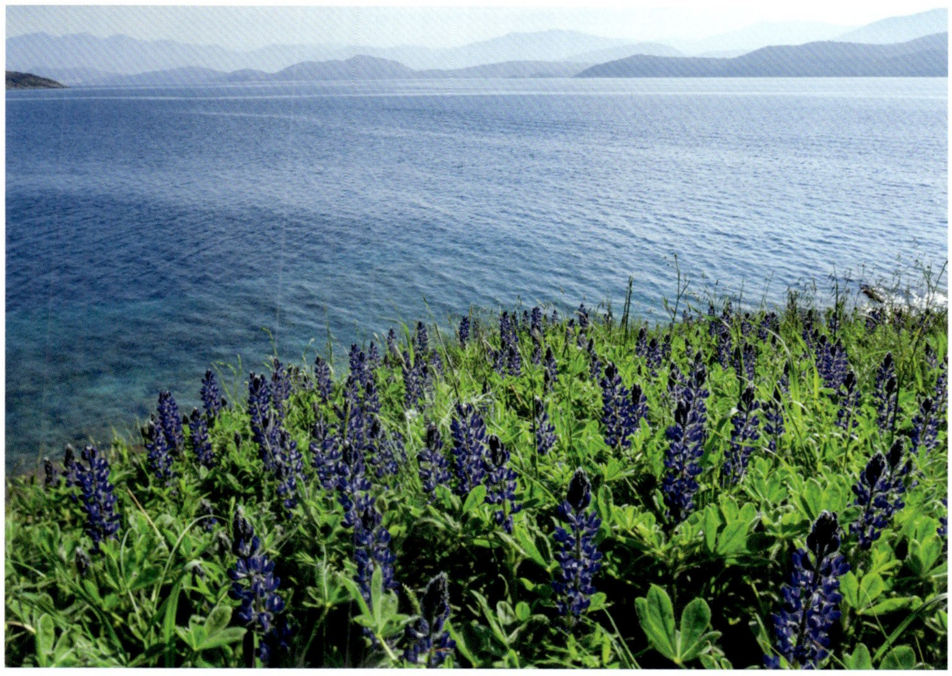

Blue *Lupinus varius* grows thickly on a headland in eastern Corfu.

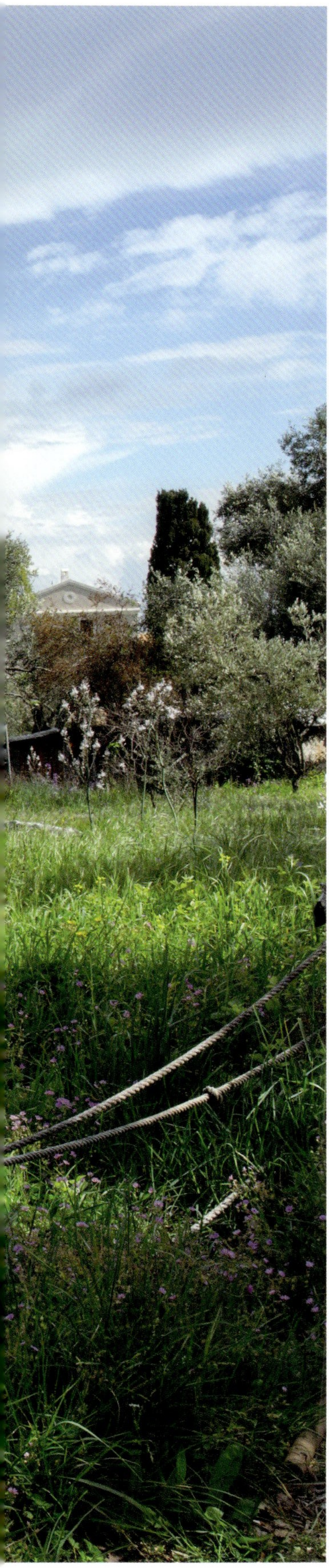

OVERLEAF Woodland borders a farm on Mount Pantocrátor. Along with cypresses and Judas trees are turpentine trees (*Pistacia terebinthus*), wild pears (*Pyrus amygdaliformis*), and oaks—mainly *Quercus pubescens* and *Q. aegilops*.

terracing hillsides to protect them from erosion and by introducing new species for cultivation. Manmade aspects like olive groves and ancient stone terraces and walls now merge with the natural landscape as if they had always been there.

In the earliest recorded times, Corfu was famous for its oaks, which were thought to be sacred to Zeus, and both Homer and Classical poets refer to the island's rich woodland. But in Roman times and again under Venice and during the Napoleonic Wars, Corfu's forests were raided for shipbuilding. Except on slopes in central Corfu, little of them remains. Trees were also cleared for fuel, and to make space for grazing sheep and goats, and—starting in the fourteenth century—growing olives. Original ecosystems were further weakened by repeated fires, both natural and human-induced.

Nowadays, deep woodlands of oak and chestnut, interspersed with cypresses, persist mainly on hillsides too high for olive cultivation. And in upland ravines, thickets remain of holm oak and sweet bay, wild pear and hawthorn (*Crataegus laciniata*). Together they suggest what the ancient vegetation might have been like.

Corfu's more common types of natural landscape are shrubland and scrub. Shrubland, or *maquis*, in some places is the local climax vegetation in its own right, but more often it marks the first stage in the degradation of woodland. It consists of densely growing evergreens, such as kermes oak (*Quercus coccifera*), tree heather (*Erica arborea*), strawberry tree (*Arbutus unedo*), Mediterranean buckthorn (*Rhamnus alaternus*), bay (*Laurus nobilis*), lentisc (*Pistacia lentiscus*), mock

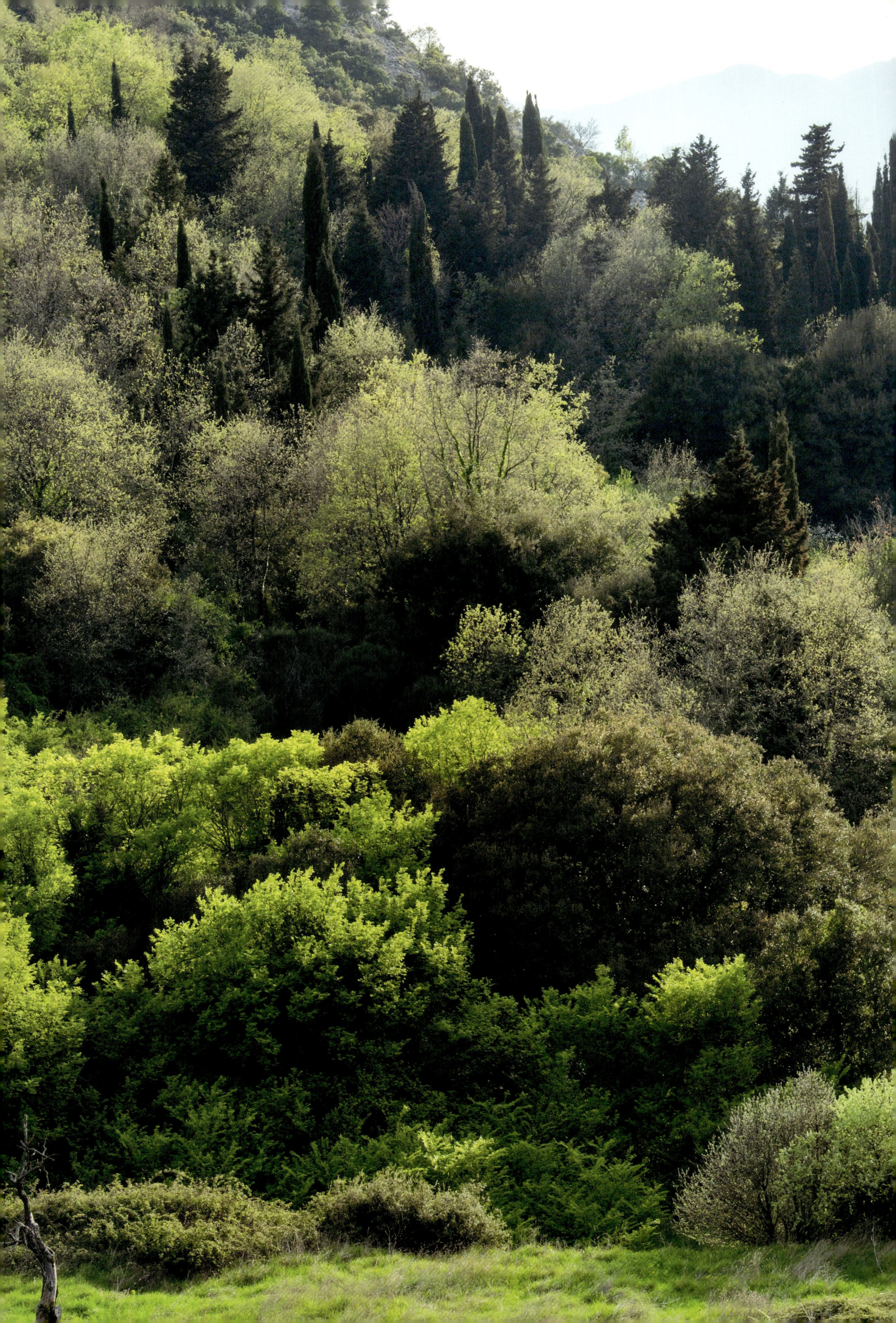

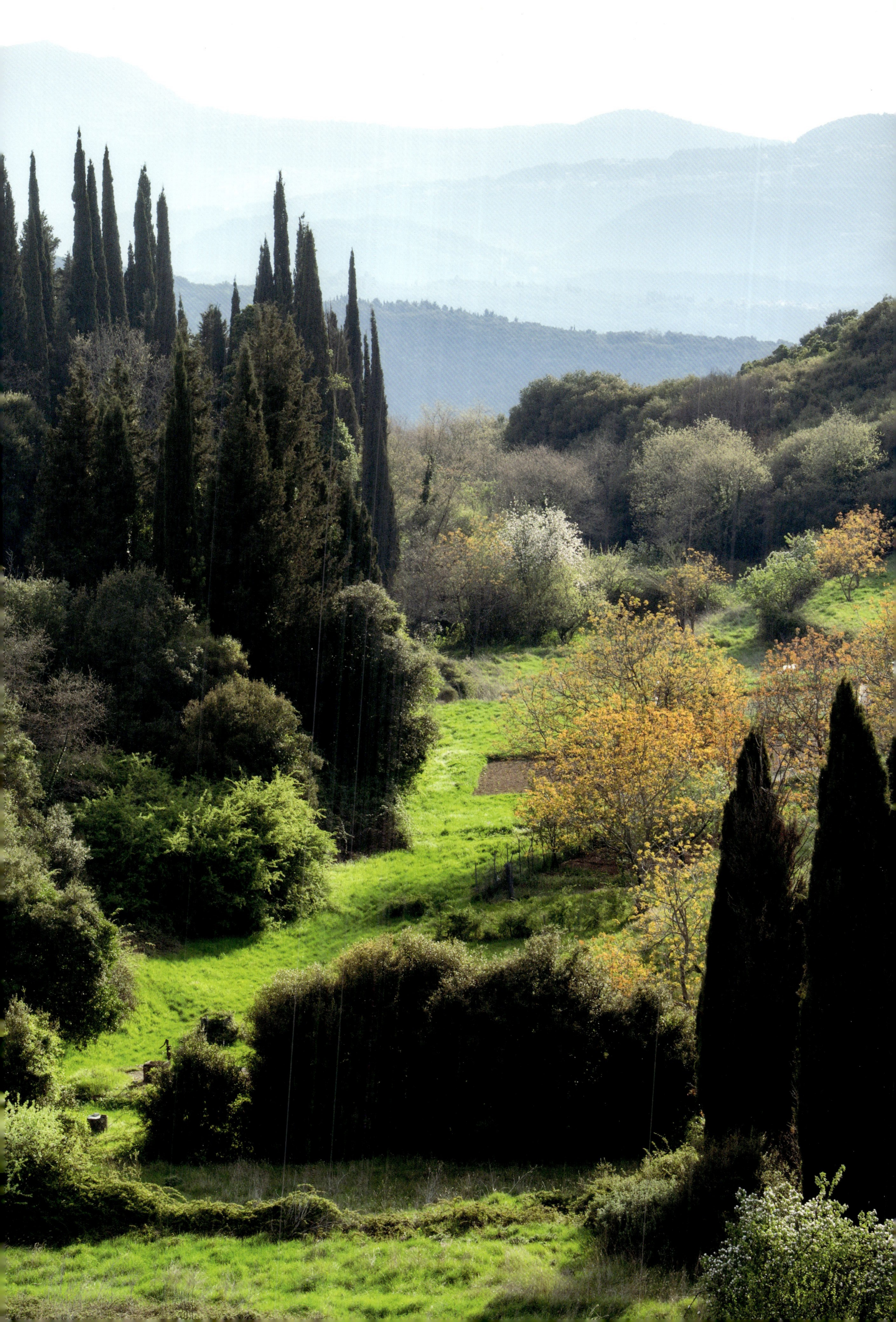

Dense oak woodlands, like these near Aghi Déka and Varypatádes, persist on hillsides too steep for cultivation.

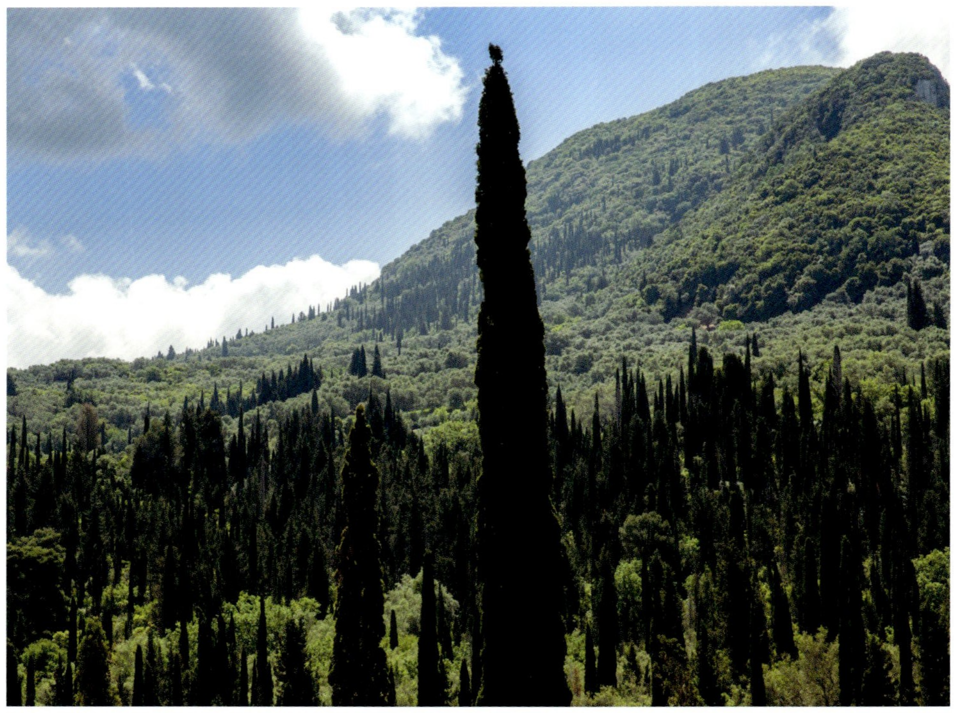

OPPOSITE TOP
Goats and sheep, roving through olive groves and across wilder hillsides, play an important role in maintaining the natural vegetation, as they have for centuries, nibbling just enough to make the plants robust and allowing them to perpetuate themselves.

privet (*Phillyrea angustifolia*), wild olive (*Olea silvestris*), and myrtle, as well as the deciduous turpentine tree. Some of Corfu's areas of *maquis* are at sea level, as in Eremítis in the northeast, while others extend up to about six hundred metres.

When the *maquis* itself degenerates, the result is *phrygána*, or scrub—the degraded drought-proof vegetation found on thin, stony, limestone soils. Areas of scrub exist at coast level, for example in the windswept area west of Aghios Spiridón on the north coast, but they are much more common on uplands. Typical scrubland plants include Jerusalem sage (*Phlomis fruticosa*), Mediterranean sage (*Salvia fruticosa*), spiny broom (*Calicotome villosa*), tree medick (*Medicago arborea*), thorny burnet (*Sarcopterium spinosum*), cistus, thyme, and savory. Being notably less dense than *maquis*, the *phrygána* is much richer in flowering plants, including orchids and bulbs. In autumn, winter, and spring it is alive with flowers.

The island earned its living from farming until forty years ago, and much of the land is still printed with old cultivation patterns. Olives have been grown in Corfu since mythical times,[51] but under the Venetians they provided the backbone of the colonial economy.[52]

OPPOSITE BOTTOM
Unlike the young, immaculately tended olive groves of Greece's Kalamáta region, Corfu's groves appear more like forests, with huge trees several hundred years old and each with a unique character. The Corfiot olive, *Olea europaea* var. "craneomorpha", or beautiful crown, grows naturally to fifteen to twenty metres. Its local name, *Lianólia*, refers to the thin shape of its fruit.

51. Homer says that when shipwrecked Odysseus landed at Phaeacia, 'he crept beneath two shoots of olive that grew from a single stock—the one an ungrafted sucker, while the other had been grafted'. Homer, *The Odyssey*, Book V, translated by Samuel Butler. 52. In the fourteenth century, to speed the adoption of the crop they had introduced, 'the Venetians gave ten gold pieces for every grove of a hundred olive trees planted'. Lawrence Durrell, 'Corfu', in *The Greek Islands* (London and Boston: Faber, 1978). See also Augustus Sordinas, 'Olive Presses', in Frank Giles, ed., *Corfu: The Garden Isle*, p. 265.

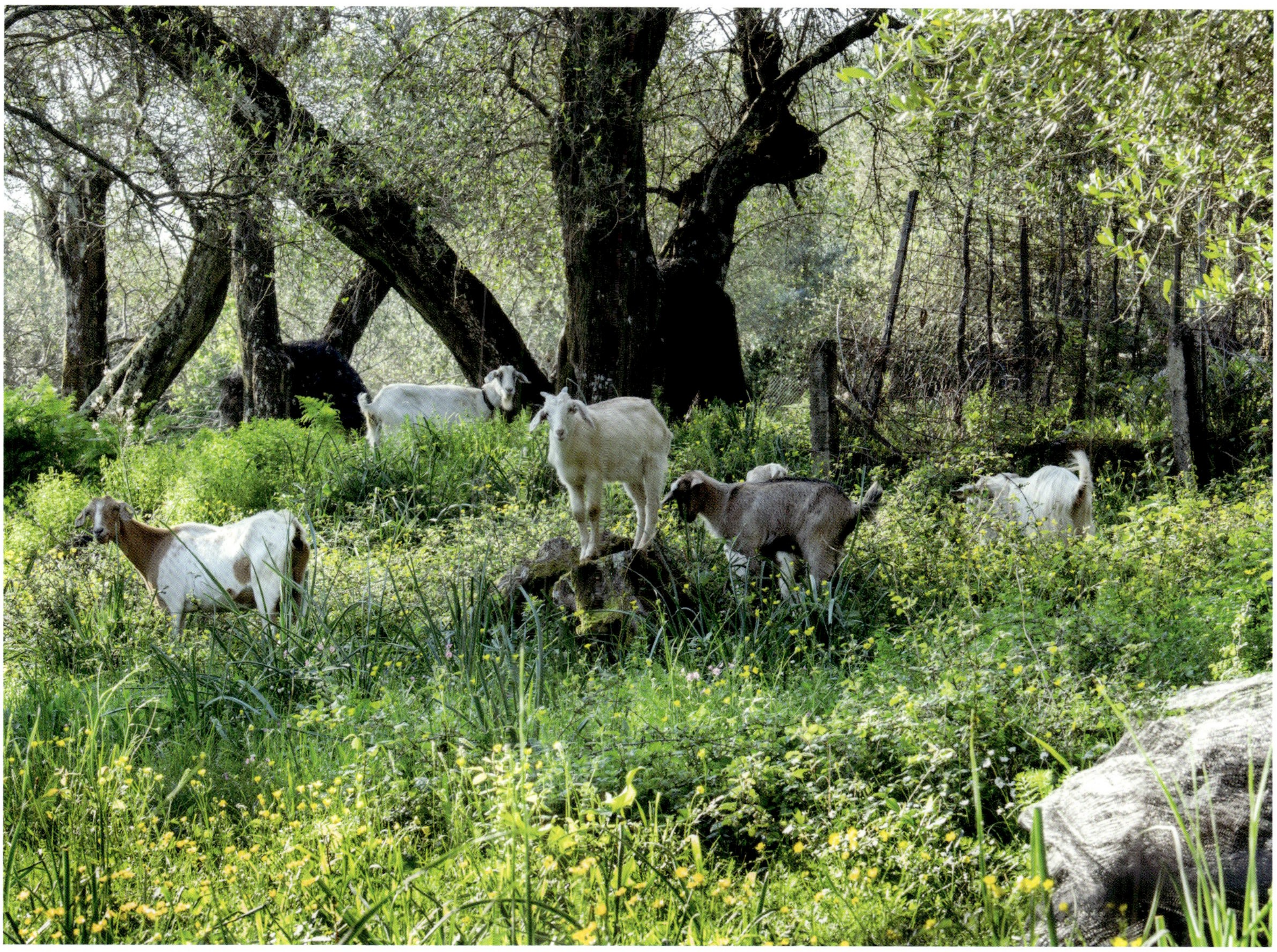

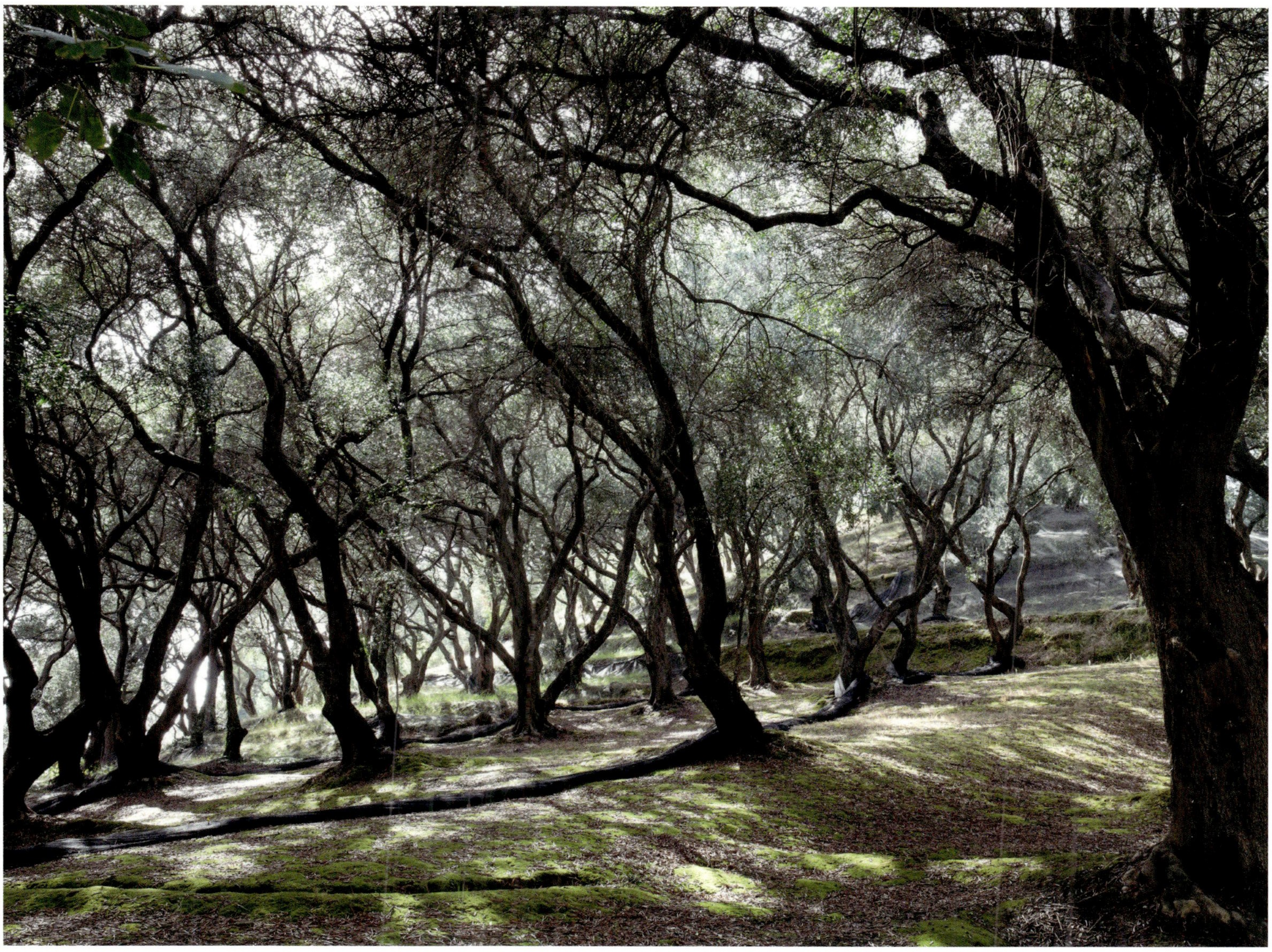

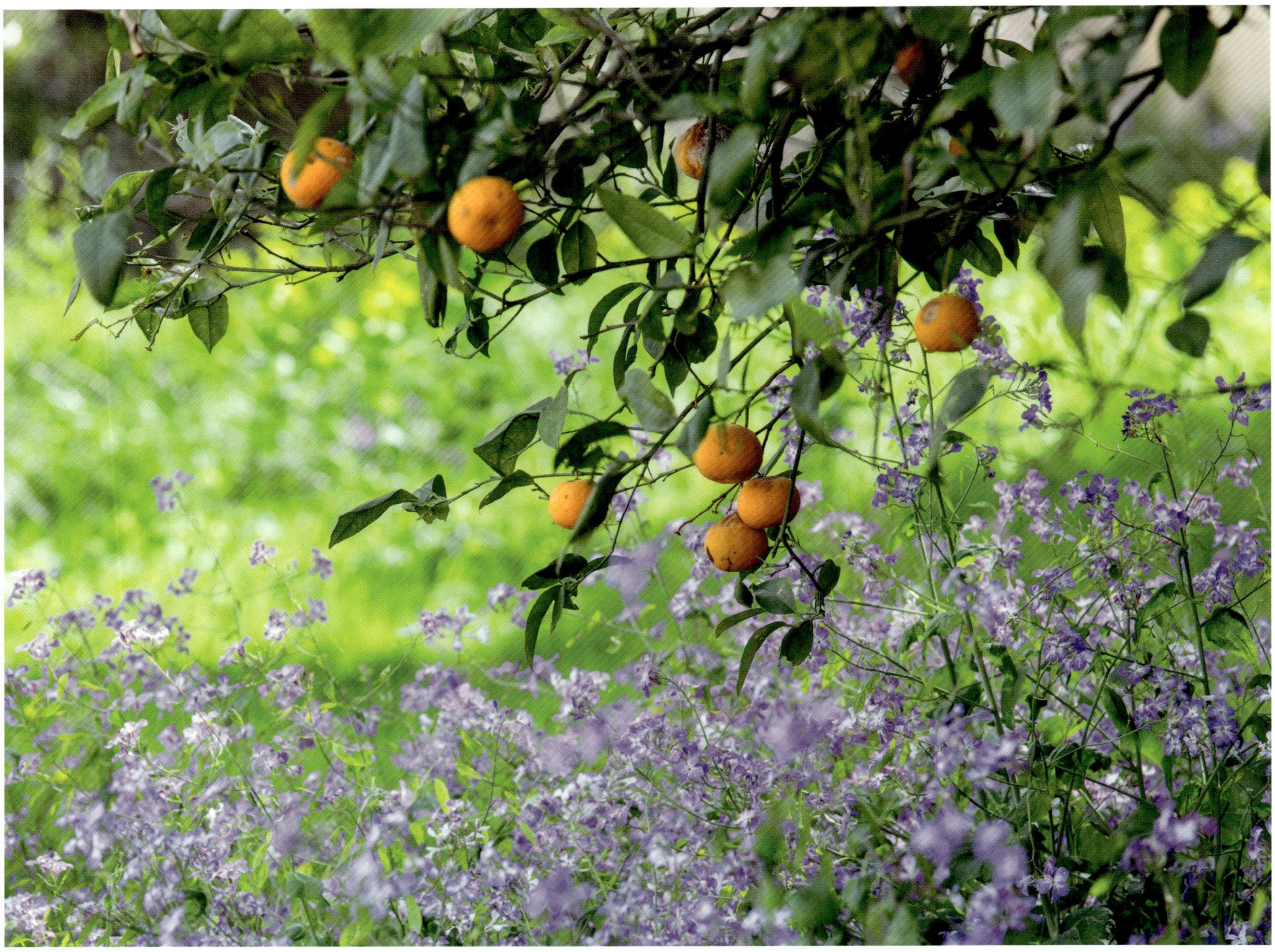

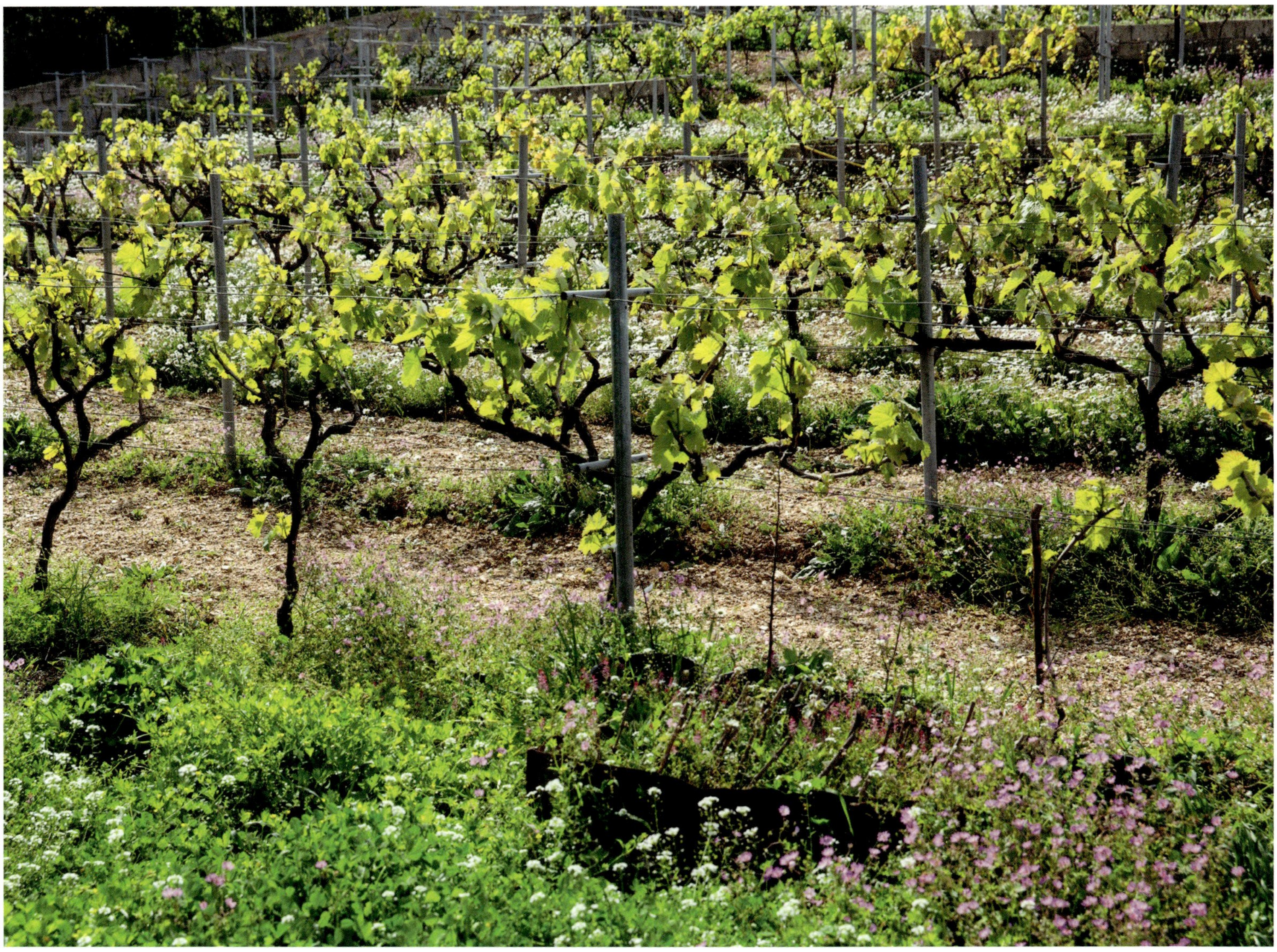

Planted in regular grids and still numbering more than three million, the olives cover more than half the landscape; they speak of centuries of human dialogue with a rough land. Sadly, Greece's economic difficulties mean that many of the ancient trees are now being felled for household fuel and to be shipped off for use in Italy's pizza ovens.

Rows of vines—an economic crop here since pre-Roman times—stretch out across the wide Rópa Valley and crowd on to small handmade terraces on the northern slopes of Mount Pantocrátor. Vegetable plots and enclosed fields and orchards provide geometric patterns in the northern and southern plains. And, in the folds of the high country, the fan-shaped patterns of ancient crop terraces can still be seen, some now thickly overgrown with bracken.

Old texts give us insights into how the agricultural landscape has evolved. British traveller Fynes Moryson, who visited in 1596, reported that 'The island Corfu inhabited by Greeks is very fertile, yielding plenty of fruits, corn, wine, currants'.[53] Visiting a little later, George Sandys found 'the whole adorned with groves of oranges, lemons, pomegranates, fig trees, olives, and the like, enriched with vines and abundance of honey'.[54] A traveller in 1845, walking up from Ipsos to the summit of Mount Pantocrátor, depicted 'a steep ascent through olive woods, and over a barren rocky country, where the industry of the natives was very apparent, for every spot of level ground, however small, was cultivated'.[55] He also noted that 'Grain for about four months' consumption is also raised, the rest is procured from the Black Sea' and that 'The suburbs [of Corfu Town] were formerly richly planted with olive and mulberry trees but they were cut down by the French in order to clear a space before the fortification'.[56]

Today, plants no longer cultivated persist in the wild landscape. Oats, seeding themselves along the margins of olive groves and roads, probably were introduced from the Near East in the Bronze Age. They stir the childhood memories of Corfu's elderly, from hard times when people saved the seeds from year to year to grow the grain as a winter crop on tiny terraces under individual olive trees.[57] Wild parsnip, native to Eurasia and cultivated by the Romans, grows profusely around ancient settlements, and the dye plant woad flowers in spring along the Roman road below Trimódi.

OPPOSITE TOP
In northern Corfu, mauve-flowering honesty (*Lunaria annua* subsp. *pachyrhiza*) is common in orchards and along roadsides.

OPPOSITE BOTTOM
A family vineyard in Kokkokílas.

53. Fynes Moryson, *An Itinerary Concerning His Travel to the Twelve Dominions* (Glasgow: James MacLehose and Sons, 1617), Vol. II., p. 110. 54. George Sandys, *Sandys Travels: A Relation of a Journey begun in An. Dom. 1610* (London, 1621), p. 3. 55. John Murray (publisher), *A Handbook for Travellers in the Ionian Islands, Greece, Turkey, Asia Minor, and Constantinople* (London: John Murray, 1845), p. 9. 56. Ibid., p. 3. 57. Sophocles Sarakinós, in conversation.

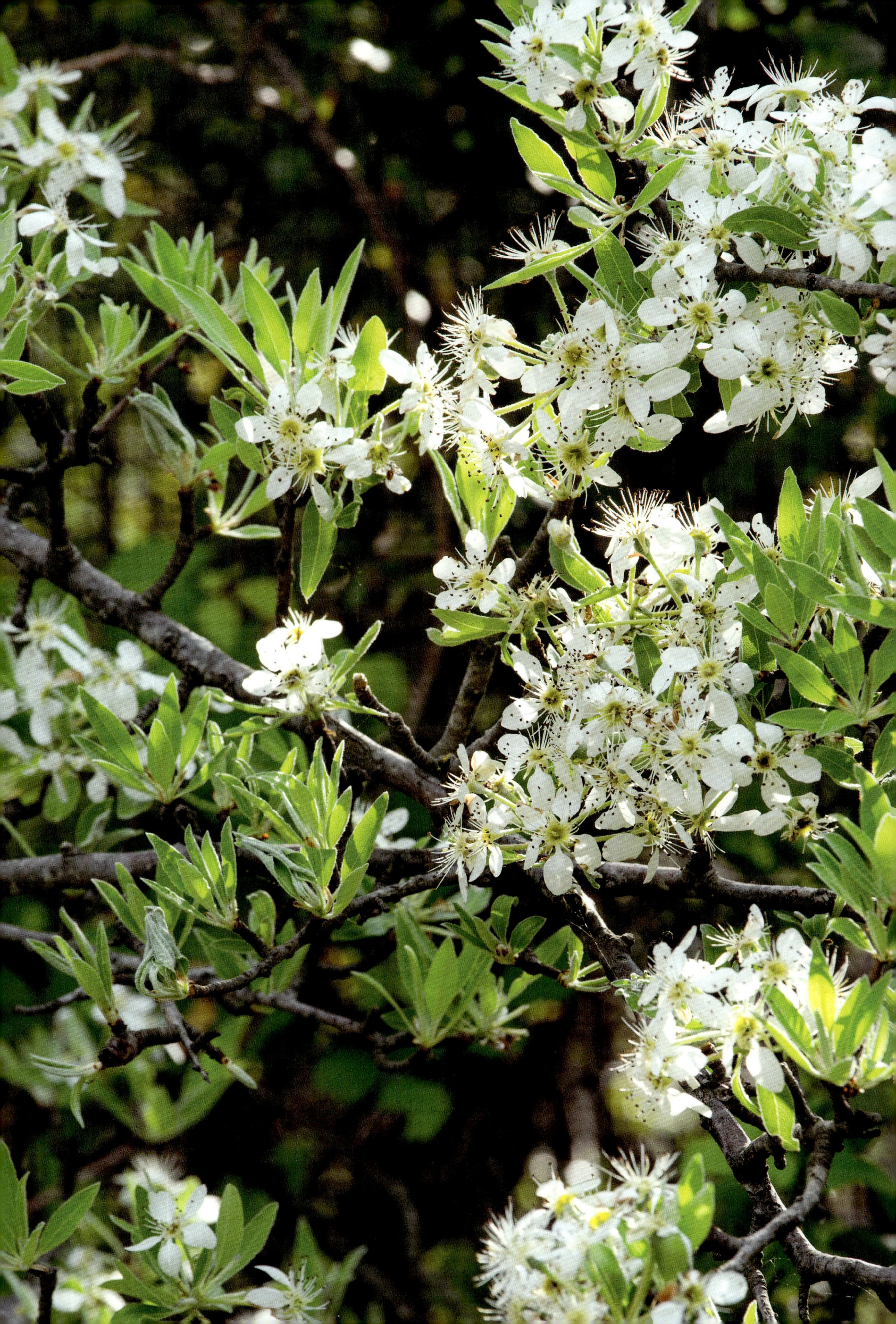

WILDFLOWERS THROUGH THE YEAR

Some would say that spring in Corfu begins with the almond blossom. Naturalised for centuries, almond trees, with their profusion of white flowers, are a familiar January sight in northern Corfu amid the brilliant green of pastureland, or against dark hillsides forested with oaks still shivering in their withered last-year's leaves.

OPPOSITE
Wild pear blossom (*Pyrus amygdaliformis*).

From January on, the island's procession of flowers unfurls and swells, beginning discreetly at low altitudes and then spreading into the high hills, rushing onwards to a climax by mid-April, then shrinking away at the onset of summer drought.

Close to the coast, the evergreens of the *maquis* have been growing actively all winter. The early spring sees frothy white tree heather and the blooms of laurustinus (*Viburnum tinus*), like little clumps of snow, along with sharply defined sprays of blackthorn blossom (*Prunus spinosa)*, against the deep green of myrtle, strawberry trees, and the bright shoots of newly sprouting buckthorn. New bracken fronds poking through bramble thickets bring to mind landscapes much further north. Sweet violets (*Viola odorata*) nestle in the lush greenery along the roadsides, interspersed with large-flowered southern daisies (*Bellis sylvestris*), magenta *Anemone pavonina*, and the first pink dove's-foot cranesbills (*Geranium molle*). In open areas on the north coast, and in the central Rópa Valley, meadows of wild *Narcissus tazetta* bloom under a turbulent February sky, the bulbs surprisingly resilient to the boggy conditions in winter. And in some coastal areas, the big lime-green mop-heads of Mediterranean spurge (*Euphorbia characias*) are in full flower. The species name of this spurge comes from the Greek for rock, *harakás,* denoting the plant's preferred habitat.

Soon the olive groves across the island are alive with crimson anemones and the mysterious green and black snake's-head iris (*Hermodactylus tuberosus*), along with several varieties of arum, including the pretty friar's cowl (*Arisarum vulgare*)—green with maroon stripes on the cowl and purple spots on its stem—and the stranger-looking *Biarum tenuifolium*, whose long brown-purple tongues emerge leafless and questioningly from the soil. More open grassy areas and woodland margins are dotted with Greek star of Bethlehem (*Ornithogalum atticum*), blue grape hyacinths and, occasionally, the rarer crocus-leaved romulea *(R. bulbocodium*)—white with a yellow eye, looking like a mix between a crocus and a tulip. In sheltered mountain hollows, the fragile stems of Algerian iris (*I. unguicularis*) push their way out from carpets of moss and grass, their exquisite flowers looking much too delicate to withstand the ferocious rain and hail of the season. Lower down, the

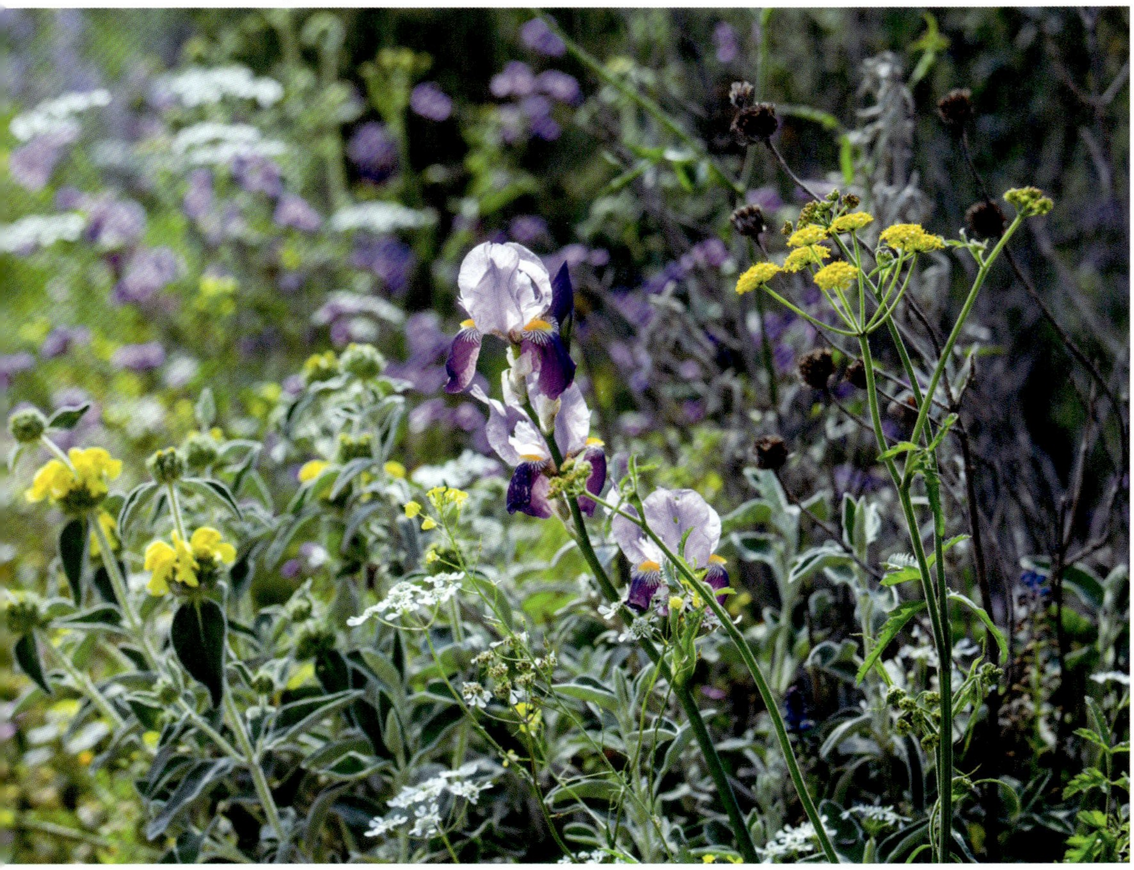

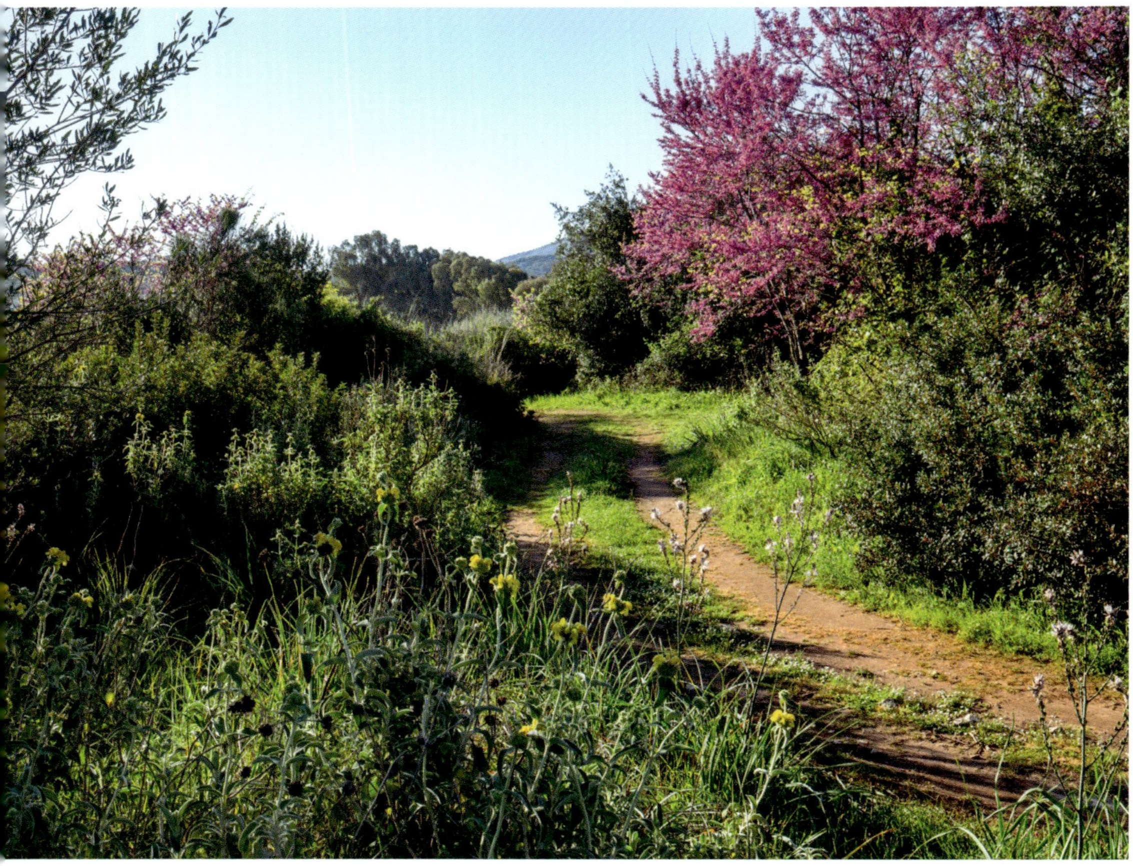

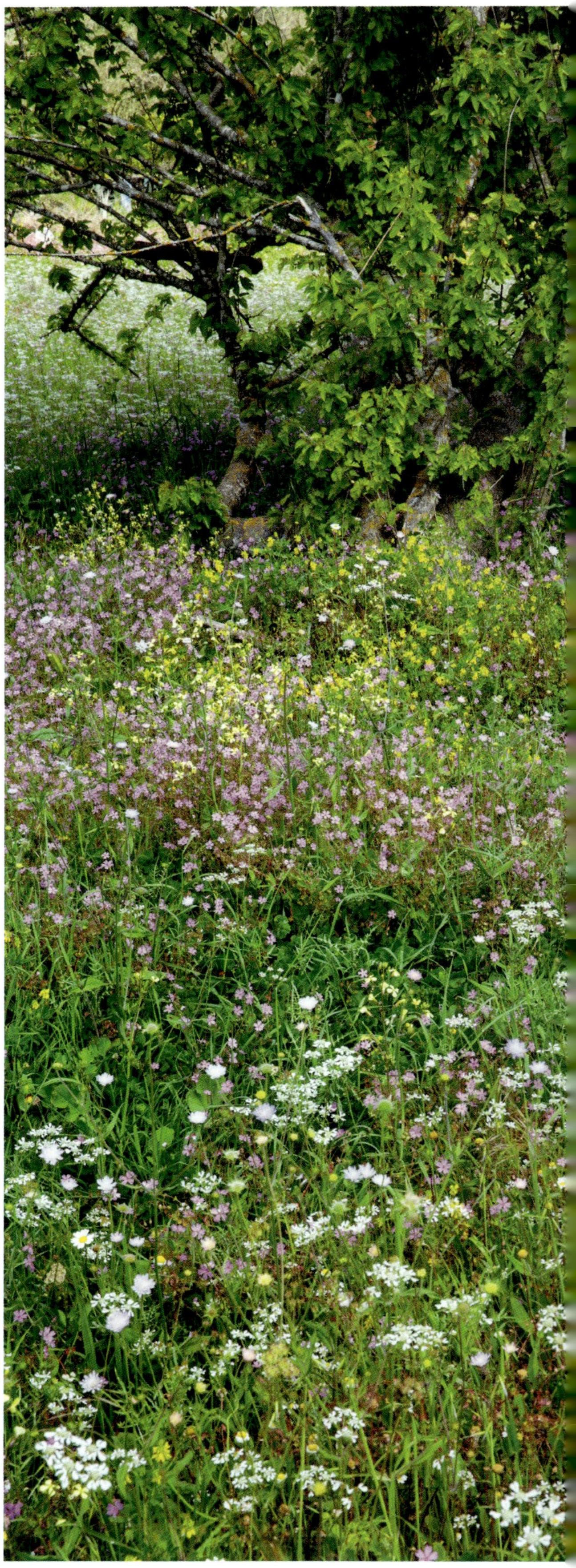

Scrubland at the coast near Aghios Spiridon, with Judas trees, lentisc, yellow-flowering Jerusalem sage, and hollow-stemmed asphodel.

In a mulberry orchard in south Corfu, the carpet includes the white umbels of *Tordylium apulum*, chamomile (*Matricaria chamomilla*), pink dove's-foot cranesbill (*Geranium molle*), and yellow bird's-foot trefoil (*Lotus corniculatus*).

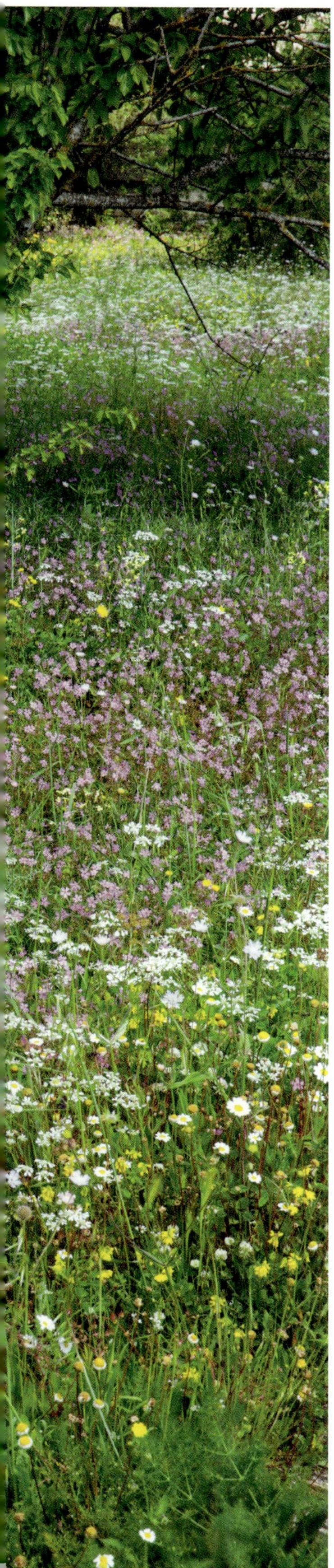

biggest of Corfu's orchids, robust but fragrant giant orchid (*Barlia robertiana*), is beginning to flower, as are the first white bearded irises.

By March, spring is in full swing. Roadsides are lined with the brilliant mauve of honesty and, above, the magenta flowers of Judas trees and the white of wild pears. On hillsides and along coastal footpaths, spiny broom adds bursts of brilliant yellow to the mix. In meadows and olive groves, mauve iris-like Barbary nut (*Gynandriris sisyrinchium*) appears through the rapidly lengthening grass. White-blossoming quince and purple bearded iris flower in the overgrown gardens of abandoned farmhouses. Orchards are carpeted with Queen Anne's lace (*Tordylium apulum*), along with blue-flowering borage, which smells of cucumber when crushed; bugle (*Ajuga reptans*); the ubiquitous crimson dove's-foot cranesbill; and the highly invasive Bermuda buttercup (*Oxalis pes-caprae*). Acid yellow, this last came originally from South Africa and is said to have been introduced to Malta as an ornamental plant in the early nineteenth century; quite likely it came to Corfu accidentally with the Maltese stone that the island's British rulers imported for their monumental buildings.

Almost everywhere in open places, including vineyards and old farm terraces, March sees drifts of white daisy-flowered Greek chamomile (*Anthemis chia*), with faces upturned to the sun. In the mountains, bright patches of yellow-flowering Jerusalem sage echo the colour of the yellow asphodels (*Asphodeline lutea*), with their spikes of six-pointed star-shaped flowers. Less decorative are the hollow-stemmed asphodels (*Asphodeline fistulosus*); ragged plants with greyish-green leaves and greyish-white flowers, they quickly colonise overgrazed pastureland. Sheep and goats avoid them because of the needle-like crystals the leaves contain. It is this plant that grew in the Elysian Fields of antiquity, where the god of the underworld sheltered the powerless souls of the dead.

April is an exciting month for orchid lovers. Inhospitable-looking places like the grass verges at the airport outside Corfu Town, or the edges of a football field in northern Corfu, are host to deep-purple loose-flowered orchids (*Orchis laxiflora*). Coarse gravel at the edges of mountain roads is a habitat of choice for early spider orchids (*Ophrys sphegodes*), with their green or purplish sepals and petals and brown pouch-shaped lip. Woodland margins are good places for man orchid (*Acera anthropophorum*) and the pretty white or deep purple Provence orchid (*Orchis provincialis*). Coastal paths in eastern Corfu display pyramidal orchid (*Anacamptis pyramidalis*), four-spotted orchid (*O. quadripunctata*) with its crimson stems, and wavy-leaved monkey orchid

OPPOSITE TOP
Both purple and white irises (*I. germanica* and *I. florentina*) are naturalised in Corfu.

Smyrnium rotundifolium enlivens woodland margins and shaded roadsides with its acid-green colour and distinctive whorled stems.

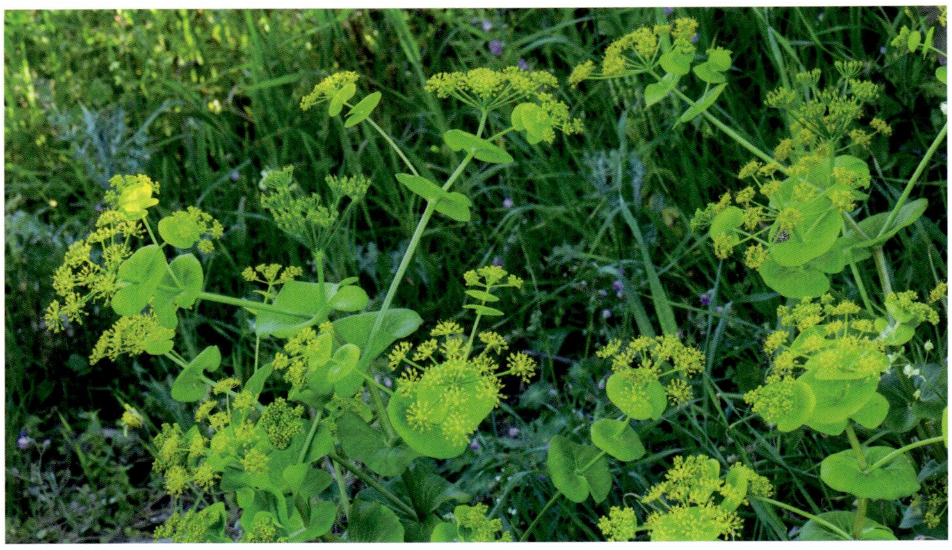

Bearded iris and *Smyrnium rotundifolium* bloom together in April.

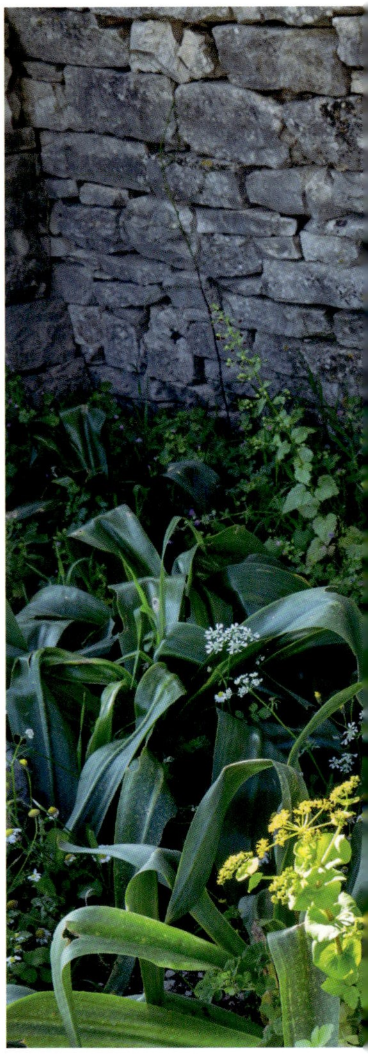

(*Ophrys italica*), the shape of whose pink flower resembles a monkey with a phallus. According to Baumann, this orchid 'can be taken as the symbol of the god of fertility Priapos, protector of gardens and vineyards'.[58] Scrubland and pine woods in southern Corfu provide good habitats for violet limodore (*Limodorum arborvitum*), along with horseshoe orchid (*Ophrys ferrum-equinum*) and Provence orchid. Mountain grasslands now see bee orchids (*Ophrys bombyliflora*) and the first flowers of several types of tongue orchid (*Serapias*), with their strange cowl-like sepals, and the elegant two-toned butterfly orchid (*Orchis papilionacea*).

By mid-April the island is carpeted almost everywhere with flowers. Along sunny roadsides, the deep blue of *Anchusa cretica* mingles with white chamomile and crimson cranesbill. Big drifts of pink and yellow flowers in orchards and olive groves have a surreal quality, as if someone from Disneyland had painted them. Along the shoreline, thousands of Virginia stocks bloom in varied shades of pink and purple. Hillsides and cliffs explode in yellow from Spanish broom and flares of copper from the new leaves of turpentine trees. Mountainsides turn carmine under a covering of tiny-flowered Calabrian soapwort. Damp lowland meadows are lush with honeywort (*Cerinthe retorta*) and yellow flag iris (*Iris pseudacorus*).

May is spring's last month of luxuriant growth. While the early-spring bloomers begin to die back, the plants that start flowering now are more heat tolerant. Cistus and wild roses give a glorious show in white and shades of pink in open grassland and the edges of the *phrygána*. Drifts of crimson field gladiolus are a spectacular sight in

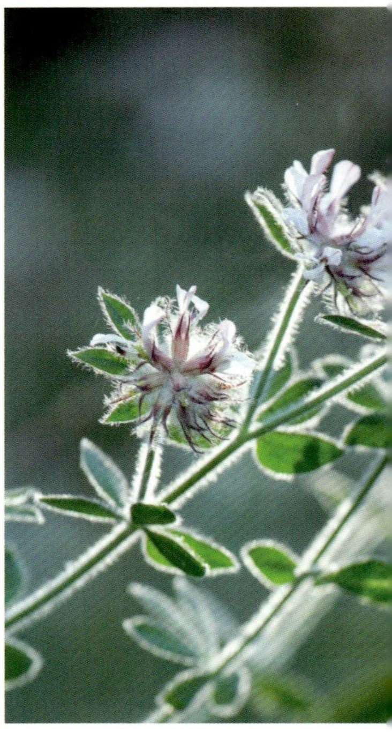

Dorycnium graecum, a member of the clover family, grows in *maquis* and woodland.

58. Hellmut Baumann, *Greek Wild Flowers and Plant Lore in Ancient Greece* (London: The Herbert Press, 1986), p. 210.

Common spring flowers of olive groves, the iris-like Barbary nut (*Gynandriris sisyrinchium*) with dove's-foot cranesbill (*Geranium molle*).

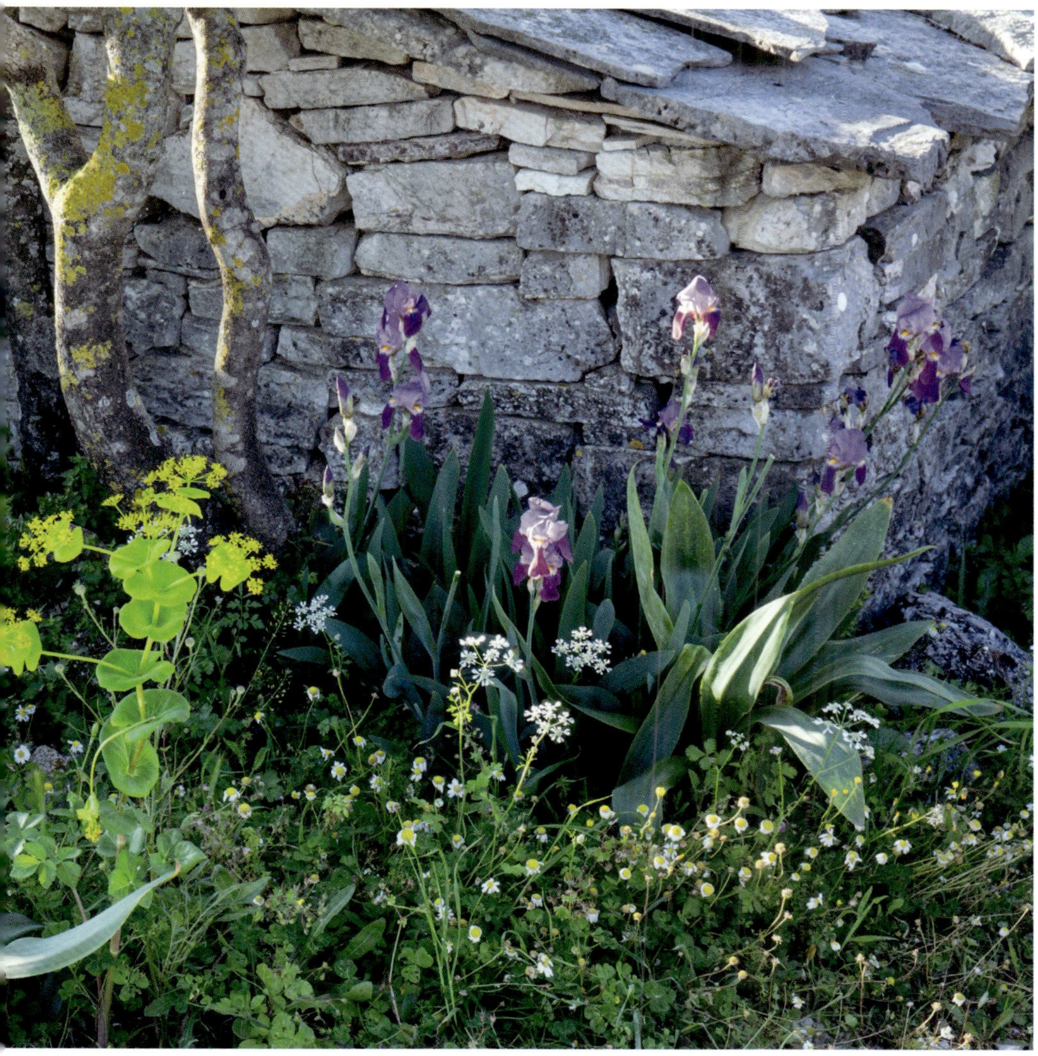

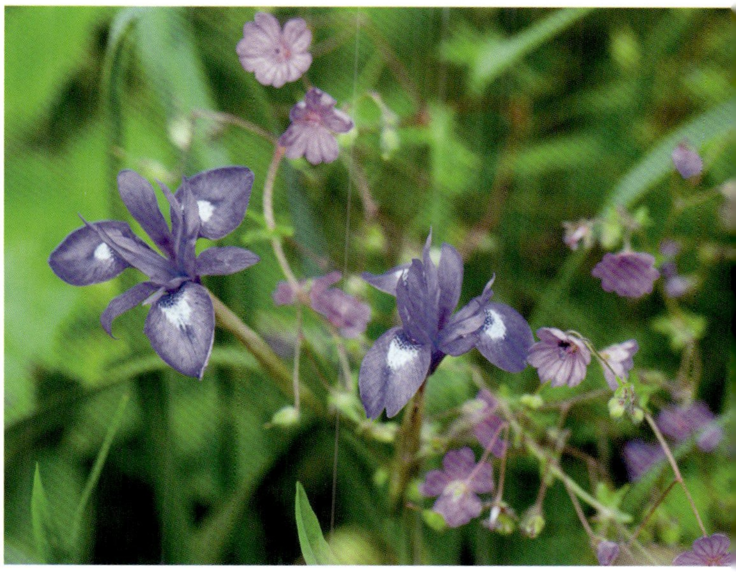

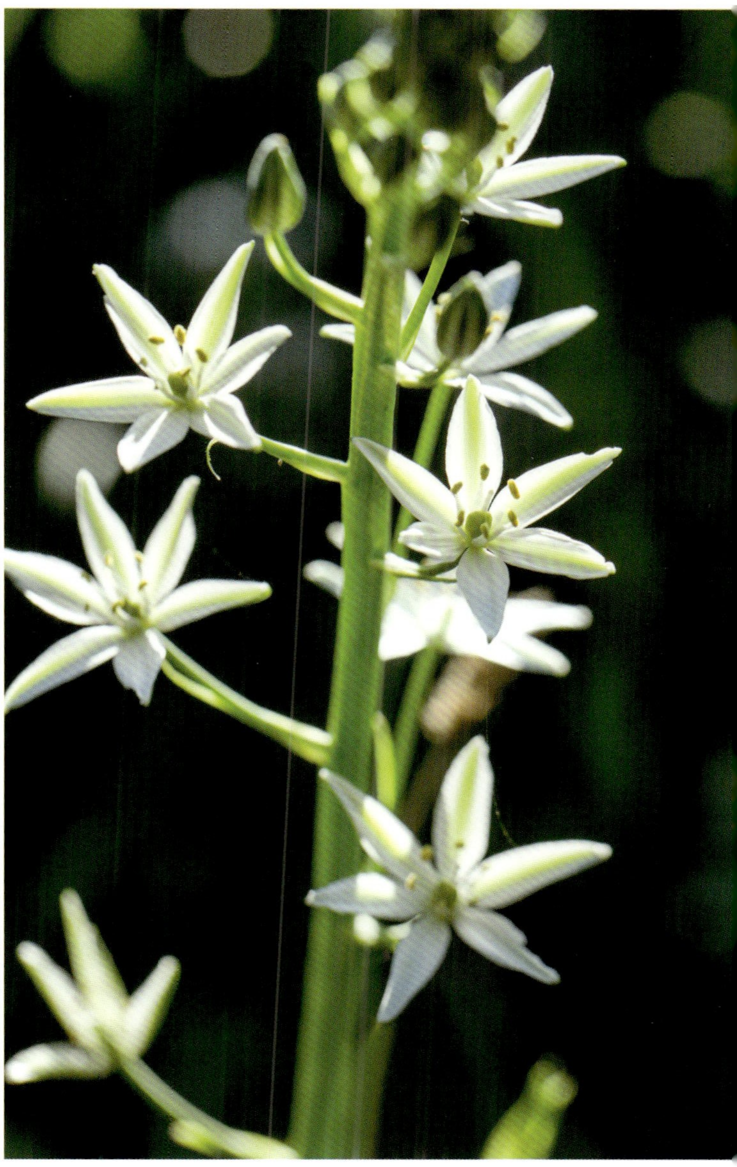

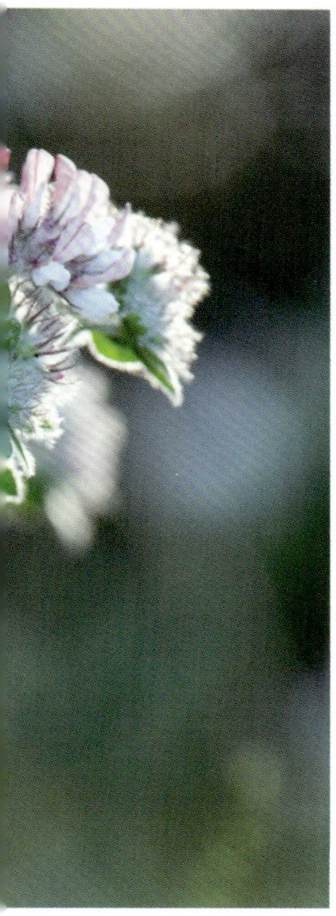

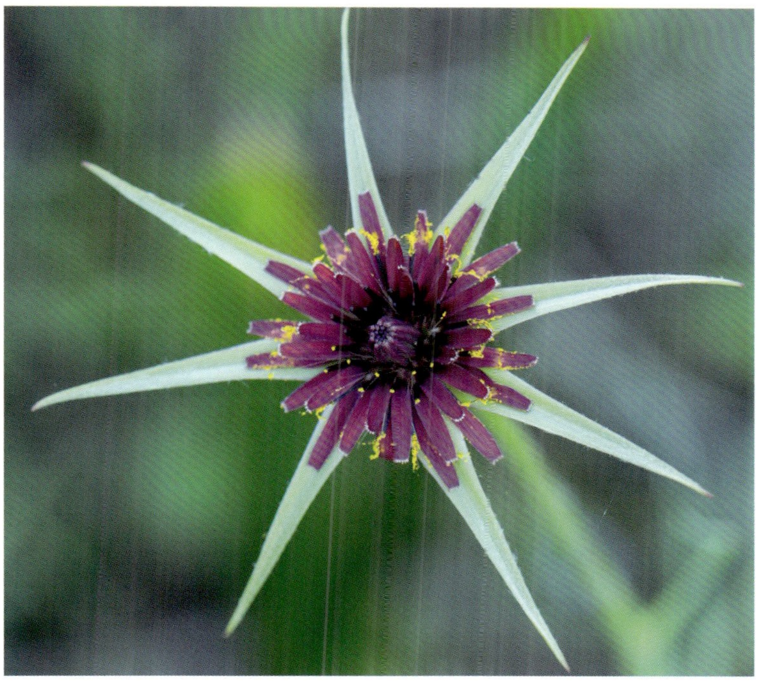

Salsify (*Trachopogon porrifolius*), a plant of the *maquis* and open places, whose roots are regarded as a choice vegetable.

Star of Bethlehem (*Ornithogalum narbonense*), a common spring flower in shady places.

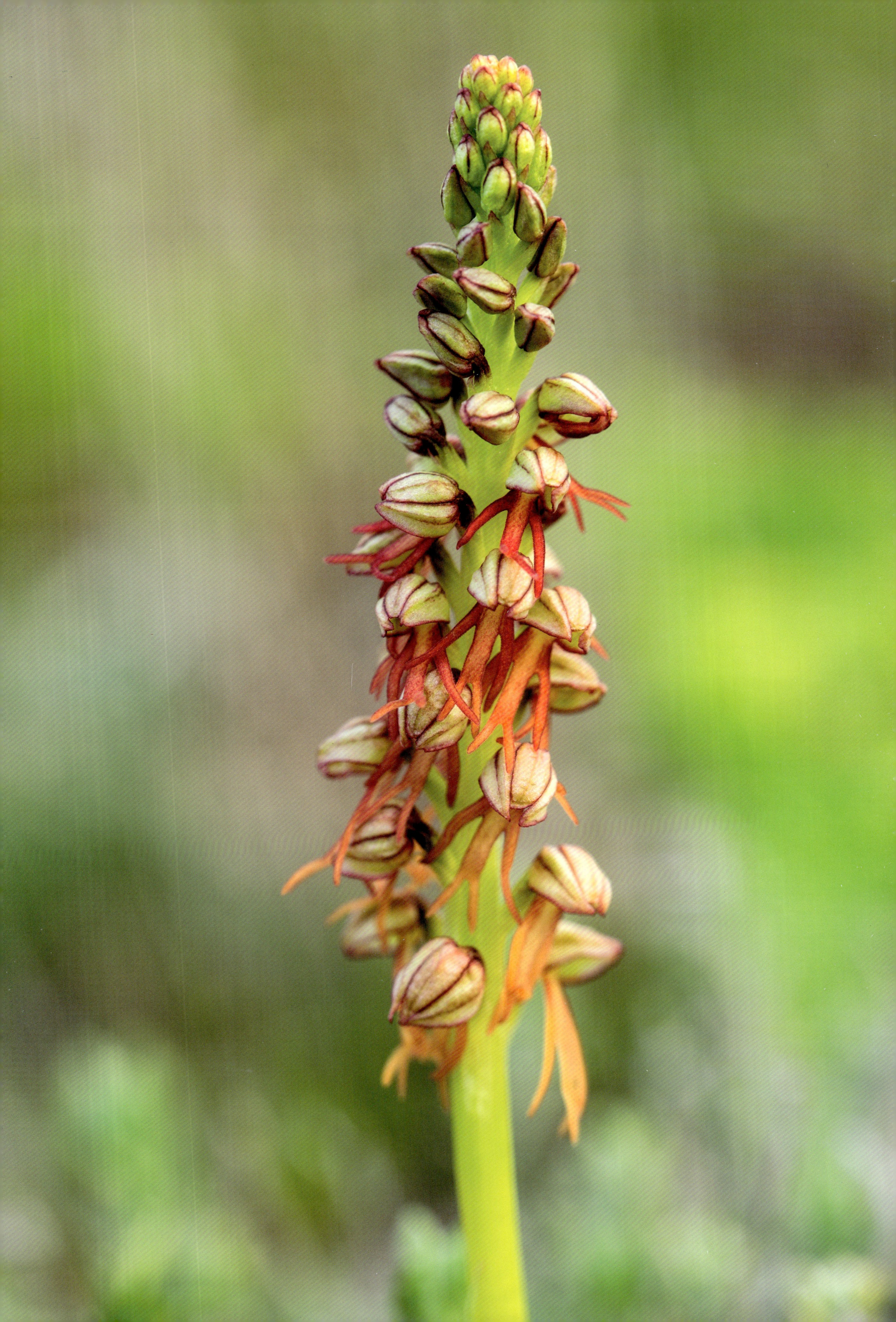

Pyramidal orchid
(*Anacamptis pyramidalis*).

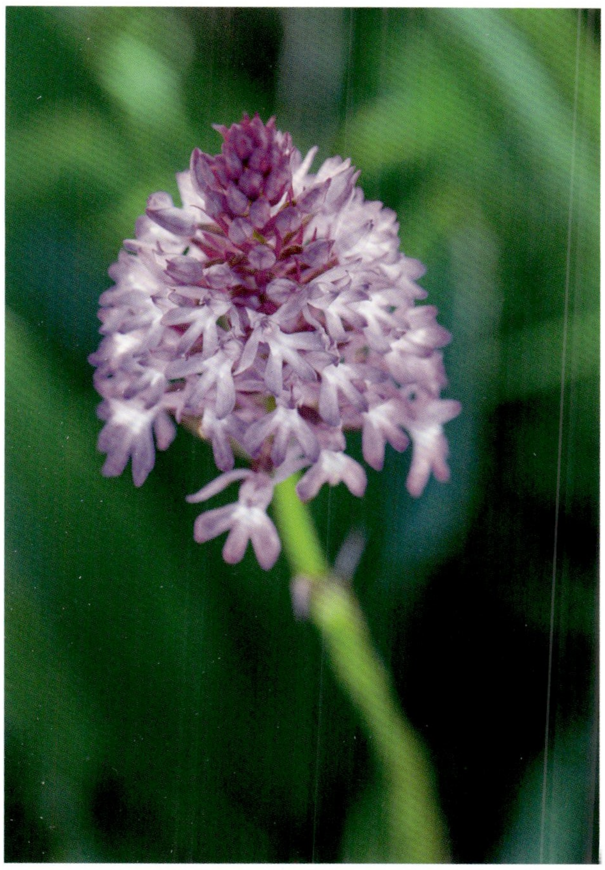

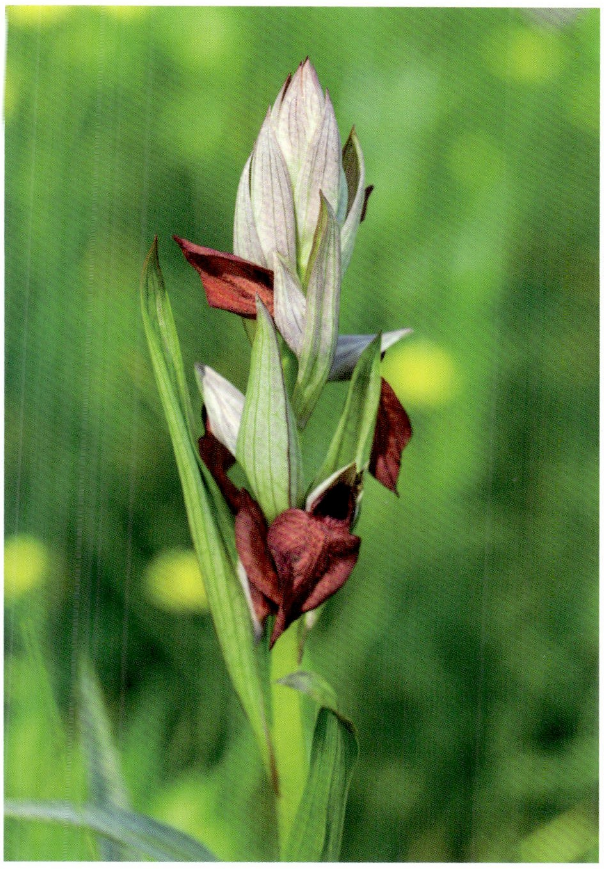

Heart-flowered orchid
(*Serapias cordigera*).

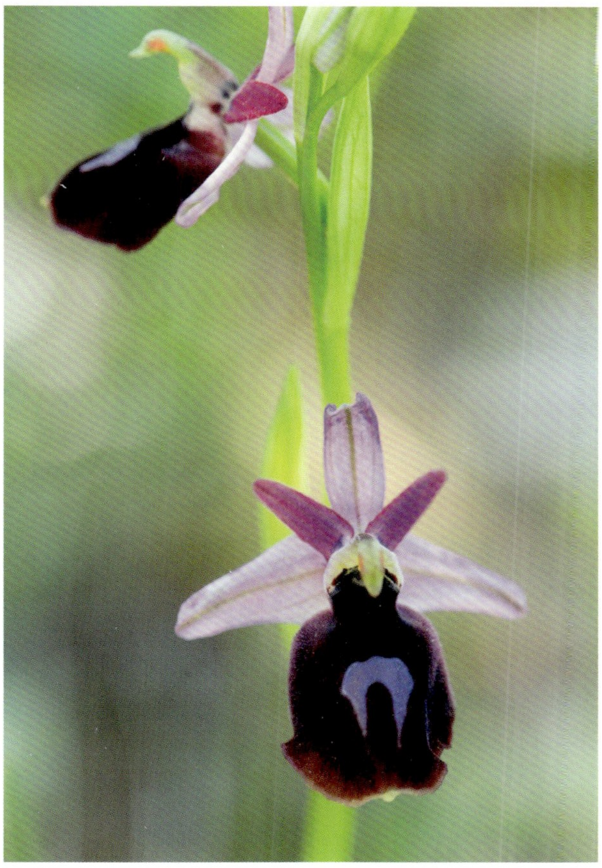

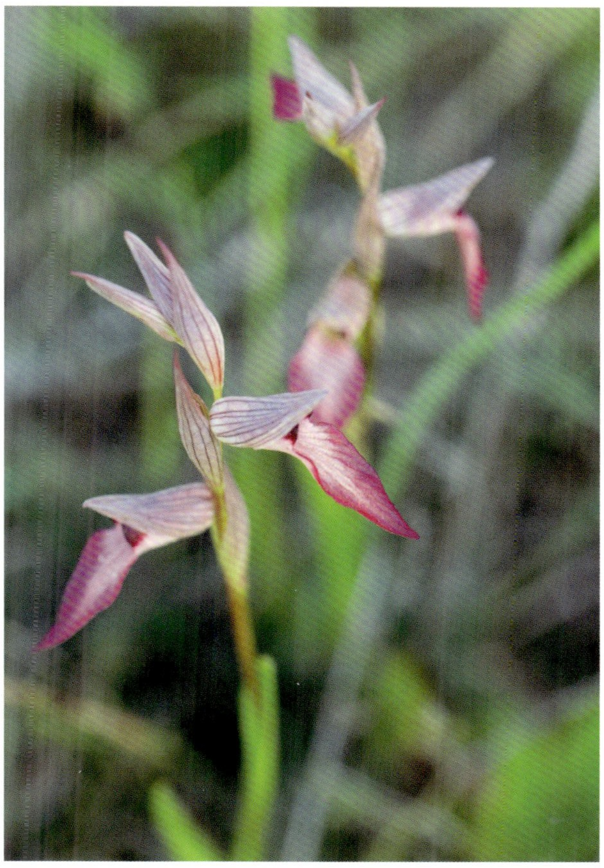

Tongue orchid
(*Serapias lingua*).

Horseshoe orchid
(*Ophrys ferrum-equinum*).

OPPOSITE
Man orchid
(*Aceras anthropophorum*).

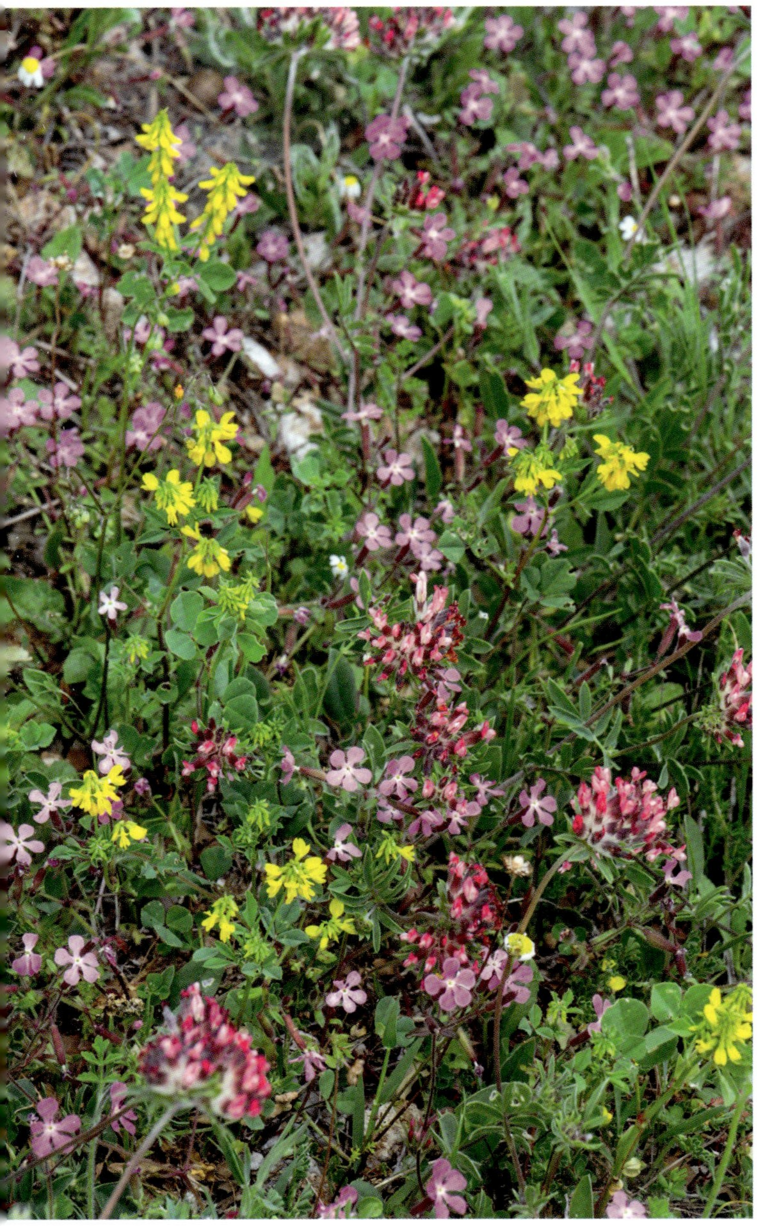

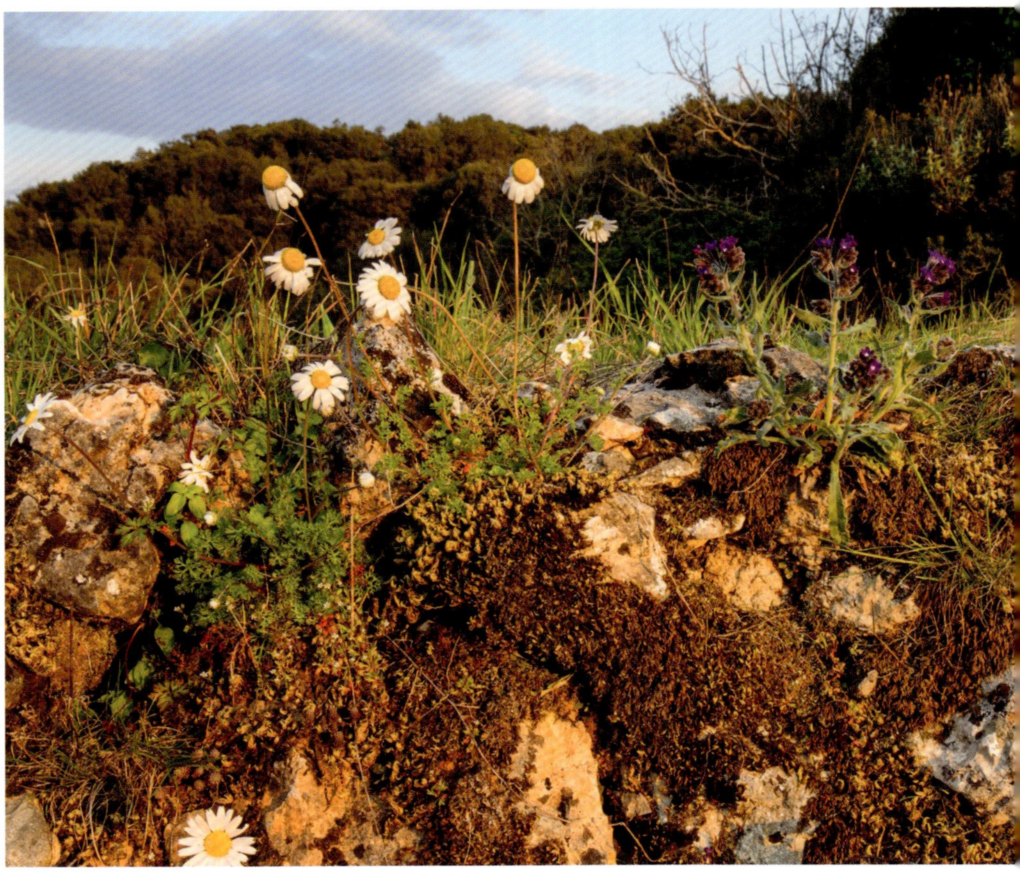

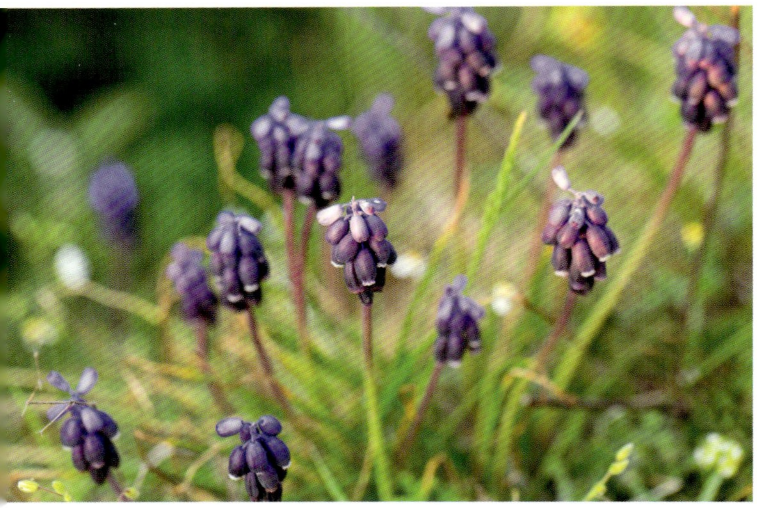

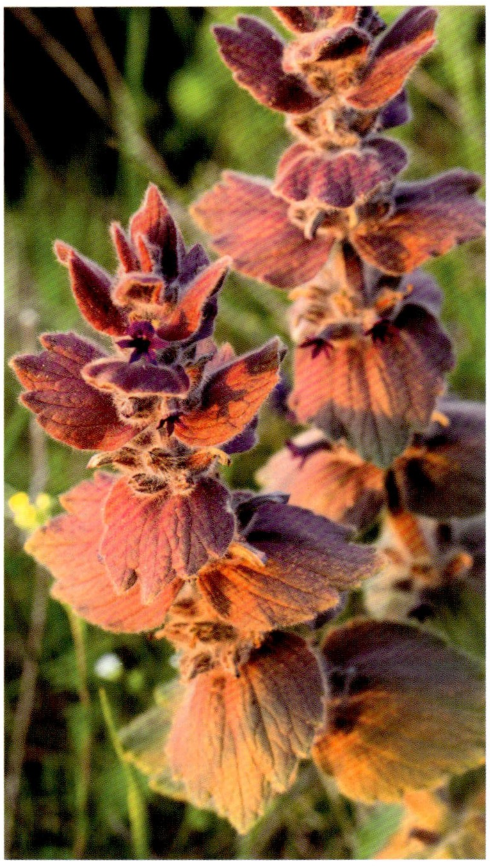

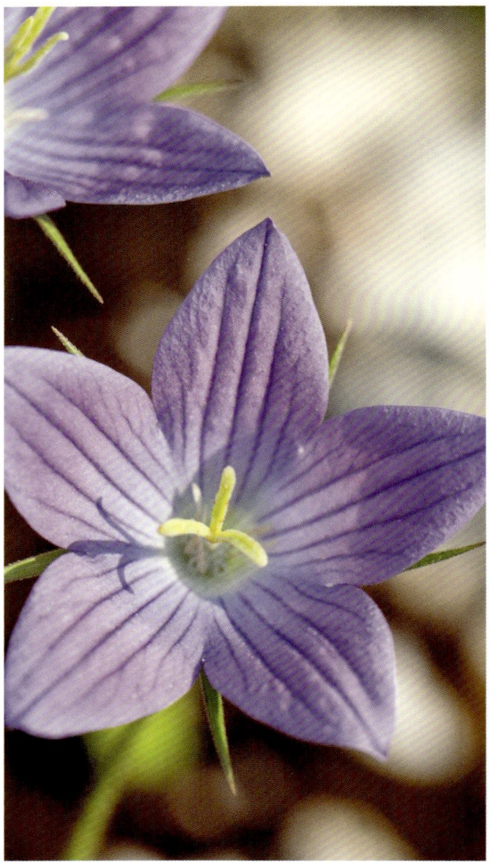

Several types of grape hyacinth are native to Corfu. *Muscari neglectum*, seen here, blooms near Petália in April.

Eastern bugle (*Ajuga orientalis*) in evening light.

Spreading bellflower (*Campanula patula*) blooms in open places and is a not-unwelcome garden weed.

Houndstongue (*Cynoglossum hungaricum*), with intense purple flowers, shares a wall with scented mayweed (*Matricaria chamomilla*).

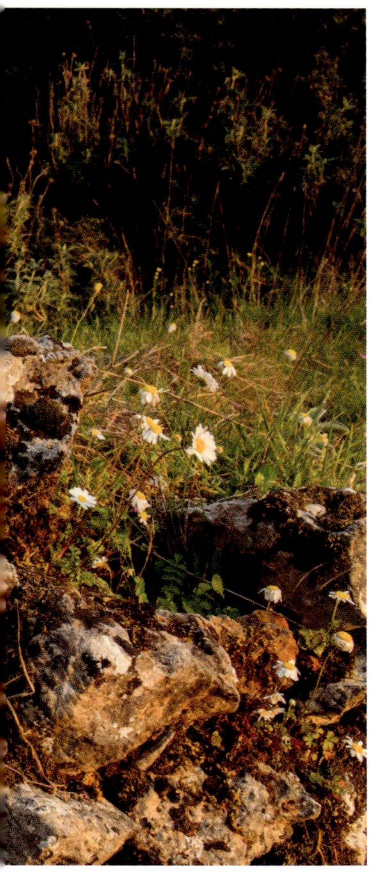

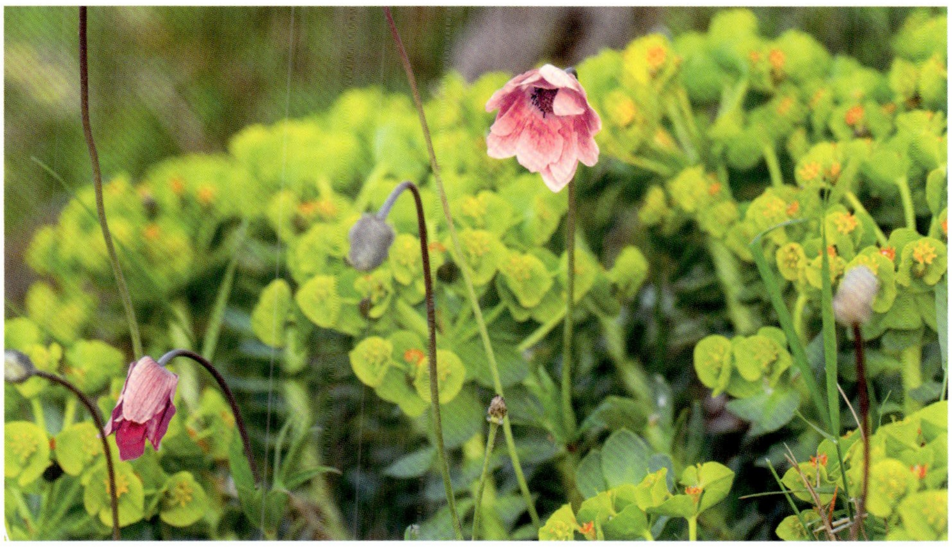

Two plants familiar in cultivation, crimson *Anemone pavonina* and *Euphorbia myrsinites*, grow wild on Mount Pantocrátor.

damp meadows. Capers display their big pink flowers, bursting forth from the old walls of the forts in Corfu Town or from rock platforms sprayed by the sea. Prickly pear (*Opuntia ficus-indica*) puts out yellow cup-shaped flowers, their buds looking like so many fat toes on a foot. Mountain walks yield wonderful combinations of colours and forms: yellow-green *Smyrnium rotundifolium*, with its strange, seemingly sculpted, collars and stiff umbels of flowers, grows among young green bracken leaves, scarlet poppies (*Papaver rhoeas*), white Queen Anne's lace, and deep purple fodder vetch (*Vicia villosa*); new shoots of fuzzy grey Jerusalem sage push their way between the flowers of pink kidney vetch (*Anthyllis vulneraria*) and yellow tuberous hawkbit (*Leontodon tuberosus*). In waste ground, spectacular thistles including purple *Galactites tomentosa* are establishing their dominance for the summer, along with prickly teasels (*Dipsacus fullonum*), whose generic name comes from the Greek *dipsa* (thirst)—perhaps because the plant was traditionally used to treat diabetes, whose symptom is thirst.

June sees more spiny, spiky plants flowering: globe thistle (*Echinops spinosissimus*), with amethyst flowers set among silver leaves; *Eryngium creticum*, with metallic blue leaves and flowers; yellow-flowered Spanish oyster plant (*Scolymus hispanicus*); and *Acanthus spinosus*—its deep green, silver-patterned leaves impervious to grazing animals and lethal to hikers. Tall pink hollyhocks (*Althaea rosea*) flower in open ground and in the margins of olive groves, along with blue scabious (*Scabiosa atropurpurea*). Various mulleins are flowering now too—notably the very tall *Verbascum macrurum* whose characteristic spires punctuate the mountain landscape. By late June, most of the island's grass has dried to a brittle golden beige. Aromatic mountain plants hold their own as temperatures rise; those in flower include summer

OPPOSITE TOP Mediterranean kidney vetch (*Anthyllis vulneraria*), Calabrian soapwort (*Saponaria calabrica*), and bird's-foot trefoil (*Lotus corniculatus*) form colonies in open rocky places. Calabrian soapwort is quick to recover after a wildfire, carpeting blackened hillsides with tiny crimson flowers.

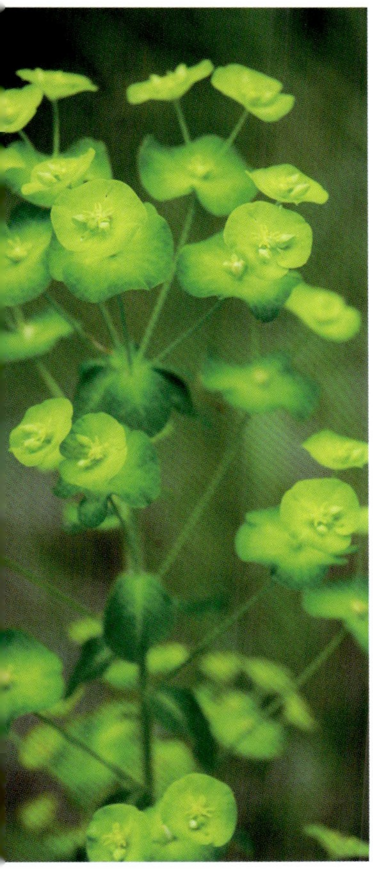

Euphorbia amygdaloides, familiar as a garden plant, makes large colonies in open woodland and on shaded slopes.

savory, thyme, marjoram, calamint (*Calamintha nepeta*), and oregano. On rock walls and on mountain roadsides, *Campanula versicolor* produces tall spikes of mauve bellflowers. Chaste tree (*Vitus agnus castus*) comes into flower at coast level, growing in open streambeds and sometimes in pebbles just above the tideline. *Agnos* (Greek) and *castos* (Latin) both mean chaste; the plant was traditionally considered an anaphrodisiac and sedative, though nowadays it is seen as a useful amphoteric—bringing balance to the body's hormonal and reproductive system.[59] Giant fennel (*Ferula communis*), its feathery leaves familiar along roadsides, may have made two metres of growth since the early spring. Its stem is full of inflammable pith that smoulders very slowly without burning the outside of the stalk; Prometheus reputedly used these stems to bring fire to the human race,[60] and it may have provided the original Olympic torch.

OPPOSITE
Households use aromatic Mediterranean sage (*Salvia fruticosa*) to cure a broad range of ills.

In high summer inland, most plant growth stops. By now the land is parched, and the crickets deafening. But along the island's shoreline new flowers are emerging. Coastal marshes and muddy salt flats are hazed over with sea lavender (*Limonium graecum* with pink flowers and *L. vulgare* with lavender-blue ones). At Almirós on the north coast, spectacular fringed trumpets of sea daffodil (*Pancratium maritimum*) emerge white and leafless from the sand just above the tideline. On the dunes around the Korissión and Antiniótissa Lagoons are blue-grey sea holly (*Eryngium maritimum*) and horned poppy (*Glaucium flavum*) with its big bright yellow flowers.

September sees the first harbinger of 'the little spring' that follows the start of the autumn rains: dry olive groves and grasslands are suddenly pierced by the tall leafless flower spikes of sea squill (*Urginea maritima*). This plant's Greek name, *skýlokremida*, or dog onion, refers to the massive brown bulb, nearly the size of a football, which can be seen protruding from the ground. Sea squill was used locally as a rat poison; it contains cardiac glycoside, which is used in the treatment of bronchitis and asthma and to make the blood-thinner warfarin.

In early October, as the ground dampens, carpets of golden *Sternbergia sicula* emerge from the underbrush on sunny banks and rocky places. Though easily mistaken for a crocus, this is actually a member of the daffodil family, as can be seen from the papery bract below the petals. In more secluded places, carpets of pink ivy-leaved cyclamen emerge from the newly sprouting grass and moss. Crocuses are plentiful: white *Crocus boryi* is common along coastal and mountain

59. Eléni Christoforátou, in conversation with the author. 60. Vangelis Papiomitoglu, *Wild Flowers of Greece* (Athens: Mediterraneo Editions, 2006).

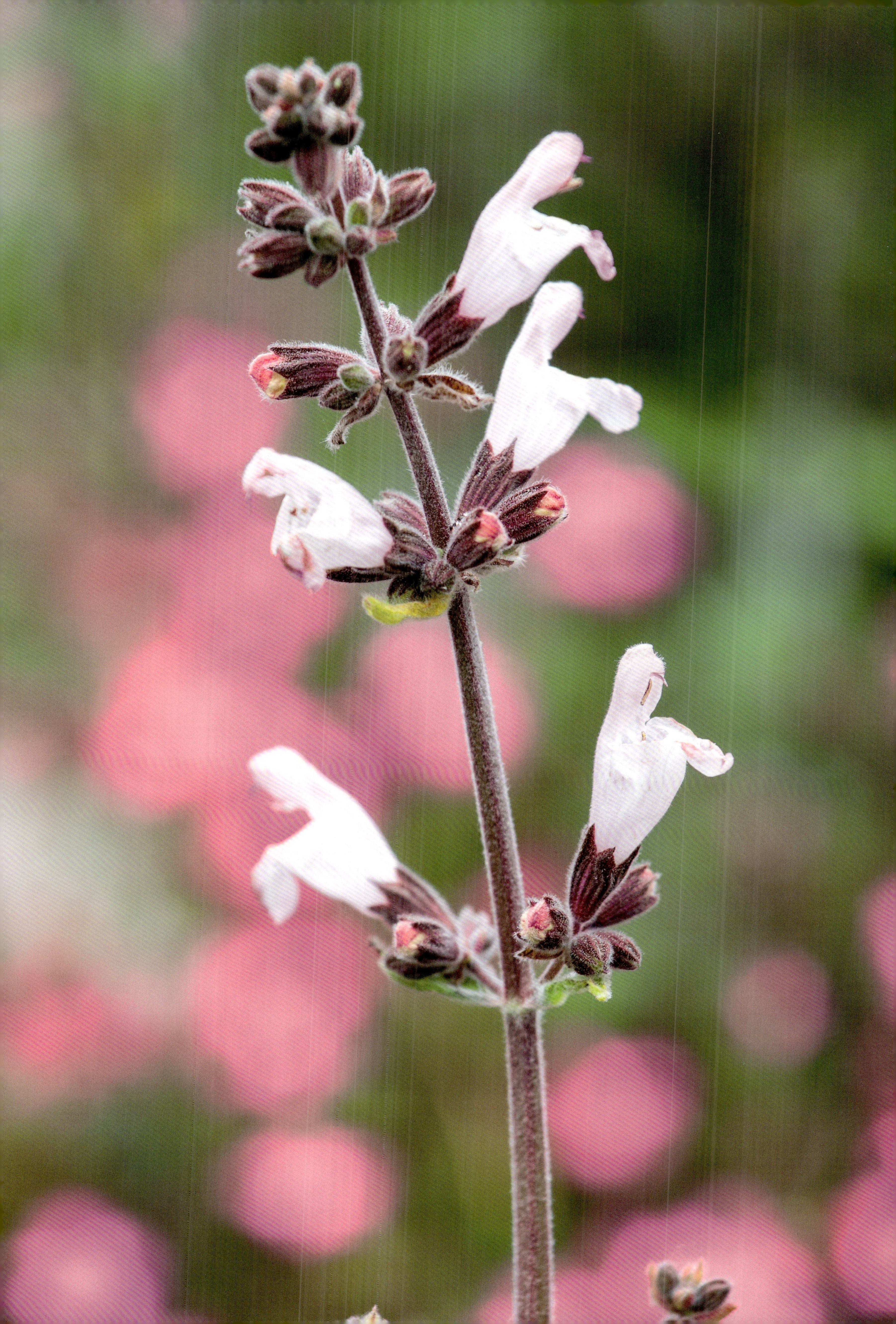

Giant reed (*Arundo donax*) on the beach at Arillas. Known locally as *kalamáki* or little bamboo, its canes are widely used for shading pergolas.

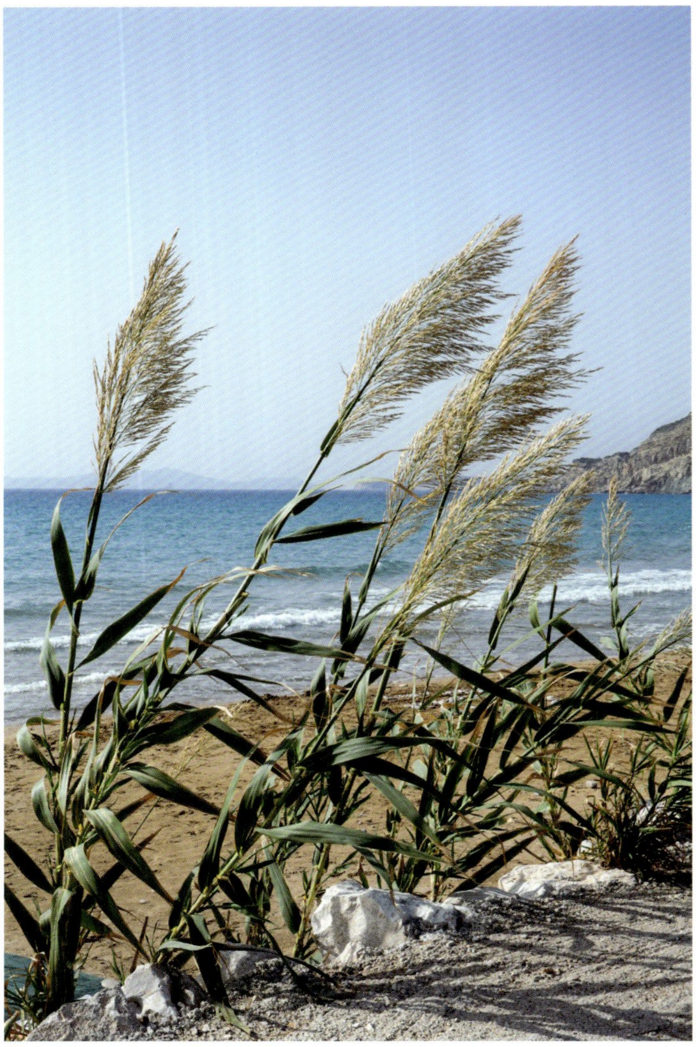

Crocus boryi, one of the first crocuses to flower in autumn.

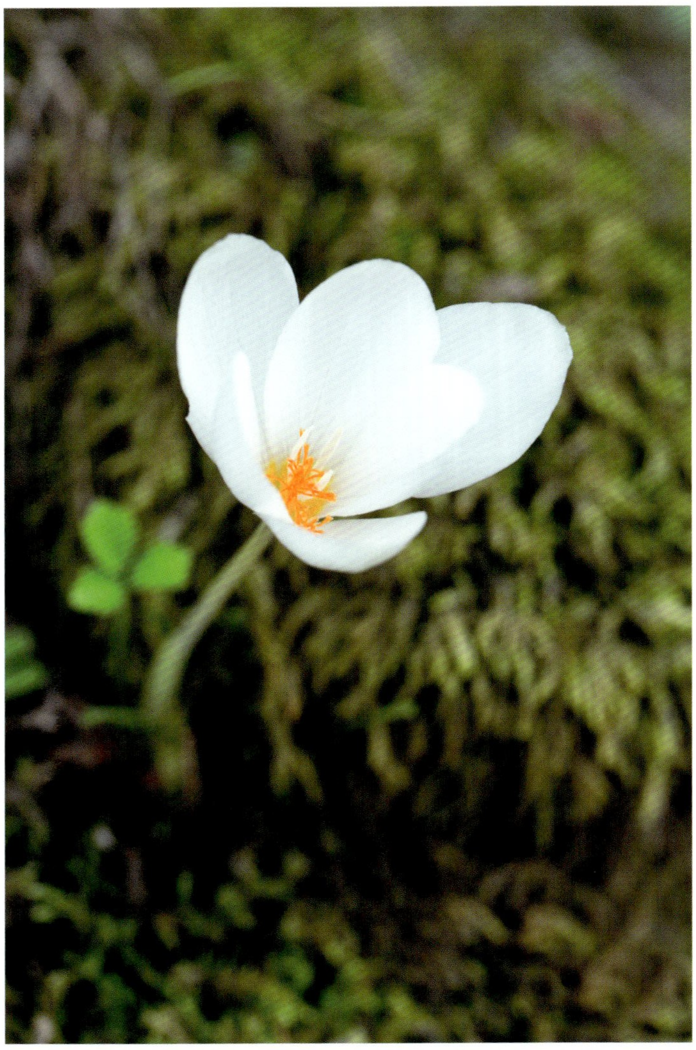

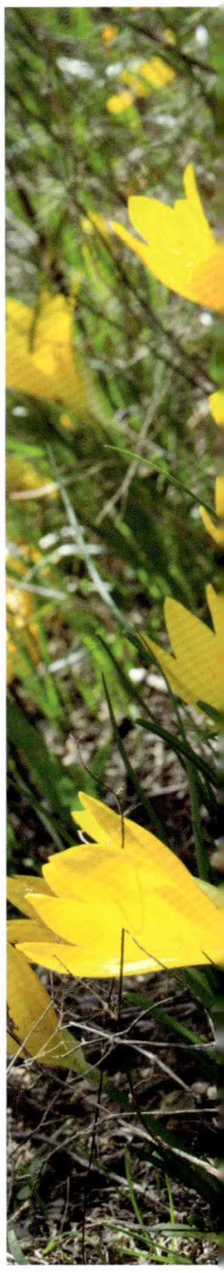

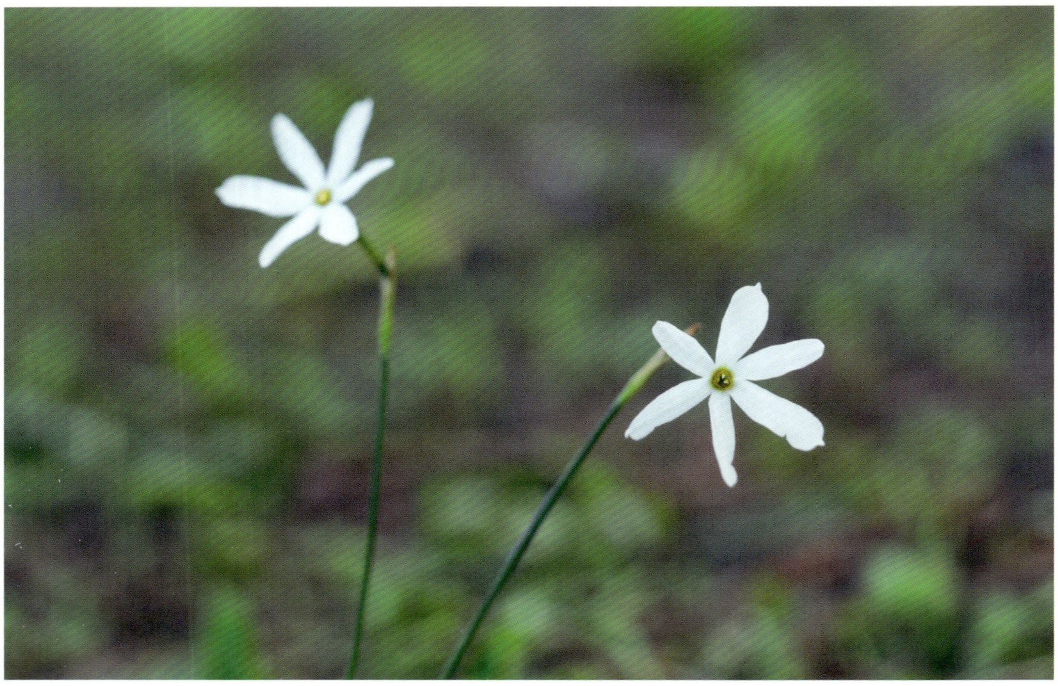

Diminutive, sweetly scented *Narcissus serotinus* emerge in olive groves after the first autumn rains.

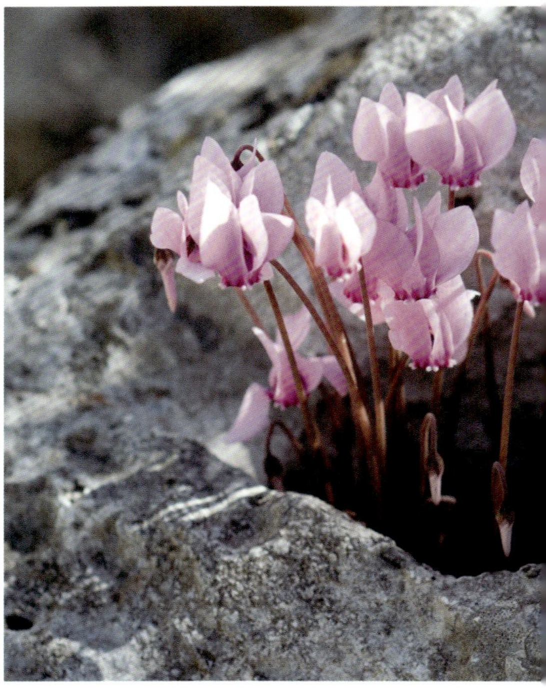

Ivy-leaved cyclamen (*Cyclamen hederifolium*) flower in early autumn in olive groves and open woodlands and along roadsides. This one has seeded itself in a rock cranny.

Carpets of *Sternbergia sicula*, a member of the daffodil family, appear in September and October.

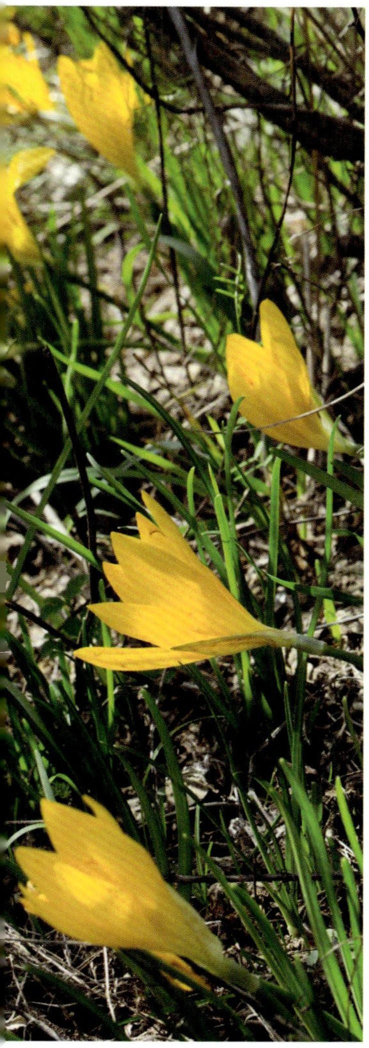

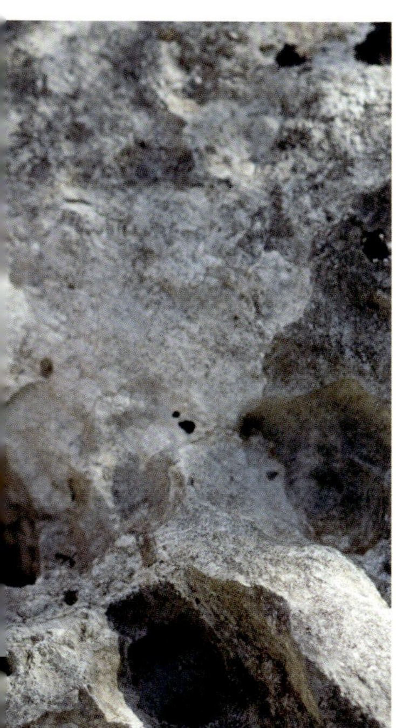

Yellow horned poppies (*Glaucum flavum*) on the beach at Avláki.

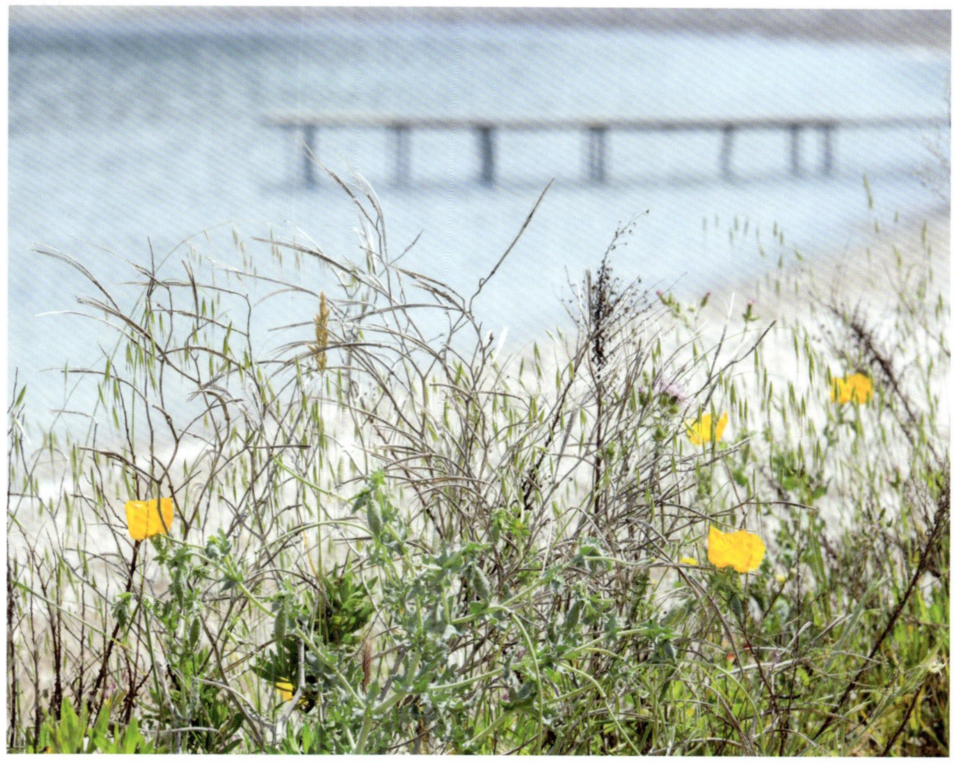

paths, and in well-drained grassy areas the exquisite *C. biflorus* subsp. *melantherus*, with starry mauve flowers and unusual black stamens, sometimes keeps company with lady's tresses orchid (*Spiranthes spiralis*). Under olive trees and in thickets—in a good year—one may find the ground starred with tiny *Narcissus serotinus* nodding on slender stems. Open roadsides and the seashore blaze with yellow fleabane (*Dittrichia viscosa*), a medicinal plant that is a characteristic feature of the landscape in autumn.

As the year progresses through November into December—months with high proportions of rainy days and dwindling hours of daylight—fewer and fewer plants are flowering, though many are growing actively in response to the abundant moisture. Judas trees and carobs drop their leaves, exposing bundles of dark brown pods wrapped around their trunks and branches. In deep hollows in oak and chestnut woodland, where the ground has stayed damp all summer, snowdrops (*Galanthus reginae-olgae*) begin to bloom in early November; their long-stemmed flowers mostly appear before the leaves. Oak leaves begin to yellow and fade. Chestnuts fall to the ground, to be eaten by martens and mice or harvested by people with tough fingers or thick gloves. Olives ripen and are raked from the trees, or allowed to fall into nets spread on the ground. The bright flowers of common daisy and field marigold (*Calendula arvensis*), starting to appear before Christmas, are harbingers of the coming spring.

Field gladiolus (*Gladiolus italicus*), one of the island's most beautiful wildflowers, blooms in olive groves and meadows in May.

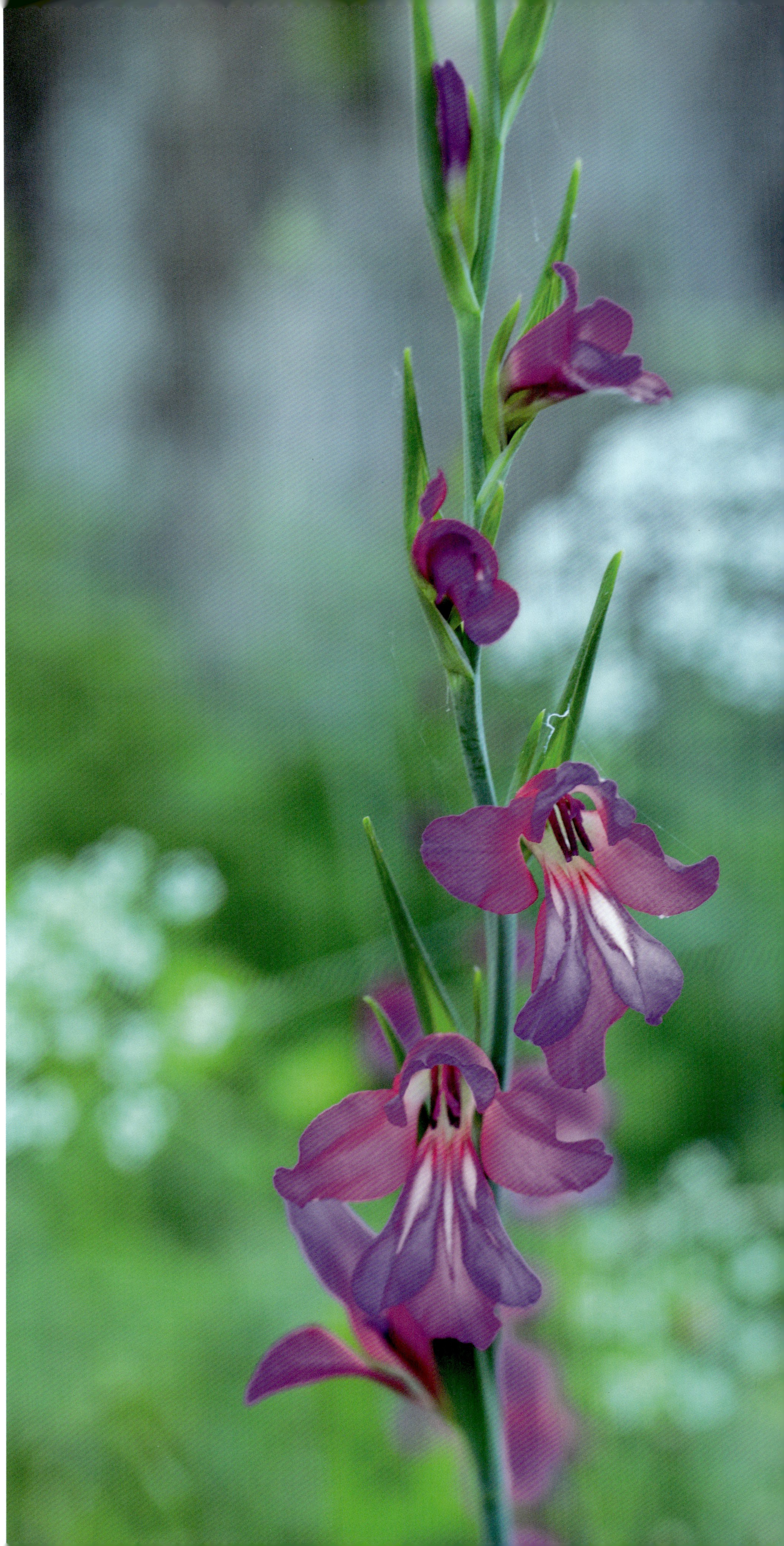

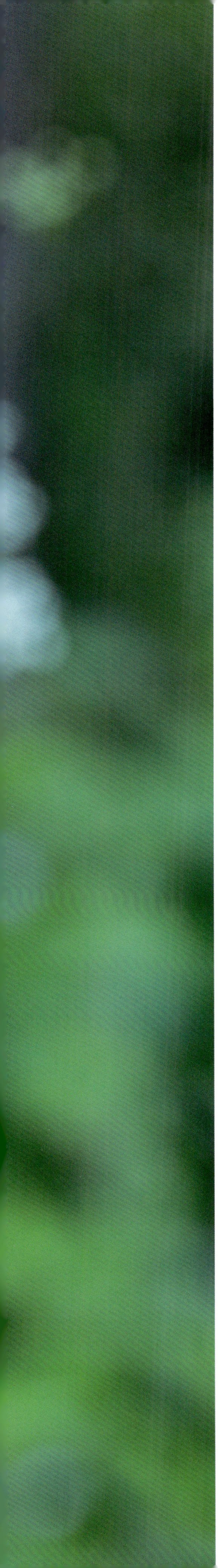

USEFUL PLANTS

Wild greens. Gathering wild plants—*hórta*—for food is a big tradition in Corfu, as it is in much of mainland Greece.[61] Elderly couples carrying bags and kitchen knives venture along country lanes, and sometimes a whole family on a Sunday outing will leap out of a car to clip shoots of wild asparagus, chicory, or dandelion. *Hórta* may simply be boiled or made into pies or recipes such as *Tzigaréli*, with leeks and hot spices. The greens favoured include dandelion; wild mustard (*Sinapis alba; tsinápi* in Greek); wild spinach; Neapolitan garlic (*Allium neapolitanum; skórdo*); borage (*Borago officinalis; fournáki*); wild asparagus (*Asparagus acutifolius*; *sparángia*); new shoots of butcher's broom and black bryony (*Tamus communis; ovriá*); chicory; common mallow (*Malva sylvestris*); and the new leaves of wild parsnip (*Pastinaca sativa*), *Malabaila aurea*, and white-flowered Queen Anne's lace (*Tordylium apulum; moscholáchano*). Culinary fennel (*Foeniculum vulgare; málatho*) is another essential element of *hórta*. Its young stems and leaves are cooked with fish or with broad beans and artichokes, and in some parts of the island are a key ingredient of Easter-time *mayeirítsa* soup.

Other edible plants of Corfu include several coastal ones. Glasswort (*Salicornia europaea; almirícha*) is an unremarkable-looking plant of salt marshes like those at Lefkímmi, and is sometimes also seen above the shoreline on pebbly beaches. Its young jointed stems taste rather like asparagus, and its high content of mineral salts makes it very nutritious. Rock samphire (*Crithmum maritimum*), with thick fleshy leaves and umbels of yellow flowers, grows on cliffs and in crevices of sea walls. In spring, before the leaves become tough, they can be steamed for salad or pickled like gherkins. Fishermen used to take rock samphire on long voyages as protection against scurvy; it contains aromatic oils, mineral salts, iodine, and vitamin C. Capers have been a valuable food since ancient times. The flower buds are collected before they open, in May to July, and the fleshy fruits after August. Pickled in brine with vinegar, both are locally popular as an accompaniment to fish and in salads. Common purslane (*Portulaca oleracea; glystrídha*) is a welcome roadside weed that also appears in summer vegetable beds and pots of ornamental flowers, growing very fast from seed. Its fat juicy leaves provide a good salad when more fragile greens have shrivelled away from drought. Locally it is considered good for both the digestion and the heart.

61. Tragically, though, there seems to be a notable increase in the use of glyphosate herbicide in olive groves, killing the wild vegetation and reducing the diversity of species, and risking leaching into the water supply and poisoning the olives.

Starting in ancient Egypt, woad (*Isatis tinctoria*) was for centuries the staple source of the blue dye indigo.

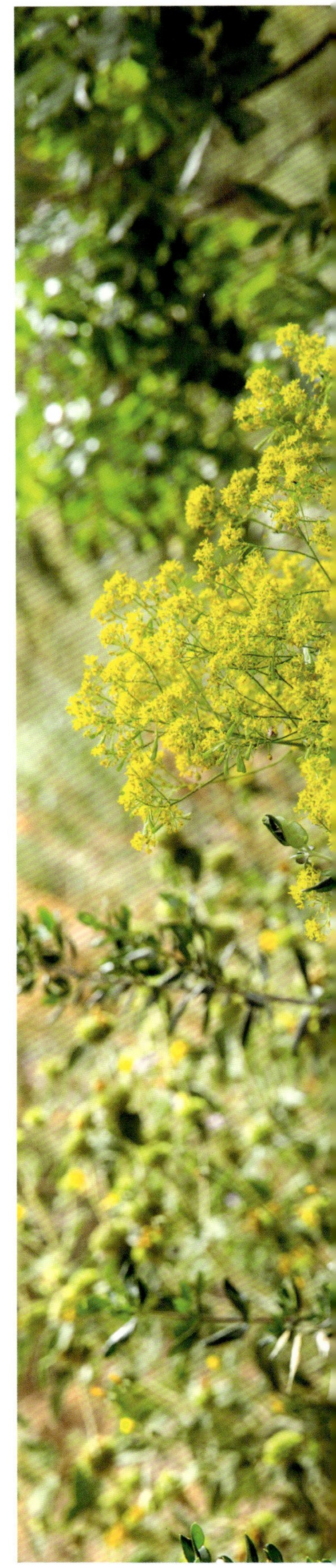

Plants for flavours and cures. Many of Corfu's wild aromatic herbs are used in cooking and in traditional medicine.[62] Oregano (*Origanum heracleoticum*) is at the heart of much local cooking. Its generic name derives from the ancient Greek *óros* and *gános*: mountain splendour. Sprigs are collected in full flower at the height of summer and then hung up in a cool dark place to dry. In August, the shepherds' pick-up trucks that lumber up the mountain roads with water for sheep and goats return piled high with bunches of so-called *rígani* for sale or use at home. Marjoram (*Origanum majorana*), with its somewhat milder flavour, flowers May to July and is also widely used.

Native thymes include common thyme (*Thymus vulgaris*), flowering April to July, and the woodier highly decorative *Thymus capitatus*, flowering April to September. Summer savory (*Satureja thymbra*), a low woody plant that flowers March to June, is often confused with thyme; much-branched and grey with hairs, it has distinct whorls of pink flowers, rather than thyme-like rounded or oblong flower heads. Savory is used in cooking but also to treat diarrhoea, mouth ulcers, and intestinal parasites.

In the north of the island, shrubby Mediterranean sage (*Salvia fruticosa*) makes large colonies on open hillsides and cliffs and at the edges of the *maquis*. It is harvested for drying in April to June, when growth is at its peak. Sage has a long history as a therapeutic plant. Its Latin name, *Salvia*, comes from salvare, meaning to save, and nowadays sage infusions are recommended locally for relieving colds and flu, sore throat, and tonsillitis; sage oil is used to treat mouth ulcers. Felty germander (*Teucrium polium*) is a tough, low-growing aromatic plant of dry rocky places, with leaves covered by protective grey fuzz; it is toxic but, taken wisely as an infusion, is considered good for the digestion; its Greek name, *panayóhorto* (holy herb), evokes its beneficent properties.

Aromatic bay (*Laurus nobilis; dáfni* in Greek) grows in thickets at the margins of woodlands and in mountain ravines, flowering February to April, and is much favoured in local cooking. Oil of bay is used to soothe strains and bruises, and as a hair conditioner.

The most common plant used locally for first aid for wounds is yellow fleabane (*Dittrichia viscosa*). Known as *krouziá*, it still has a place in some family medicine cabinets for its microbial properties and ability to stop bleeding. The felty leaves of this sticky, highly aromatic plant can be rubbed on skin or clothes to protect against insects. Spread

62. For much of the information on local traditional medicine in this section I am indebted to conversations with herbalist Eléni Christoforátou.

Poultices of pitch trefoil (*Psoralea bituminosa*), with its characteristic smell of tar, once featured as a remedy for snake bite.

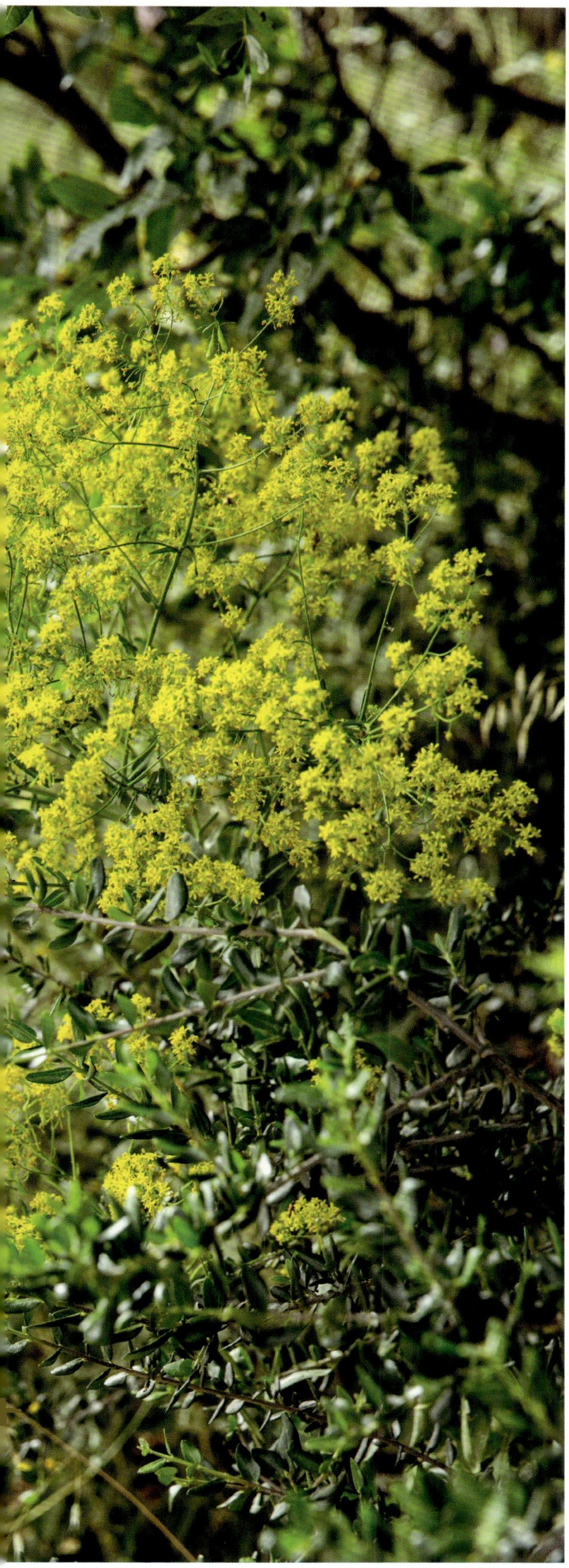

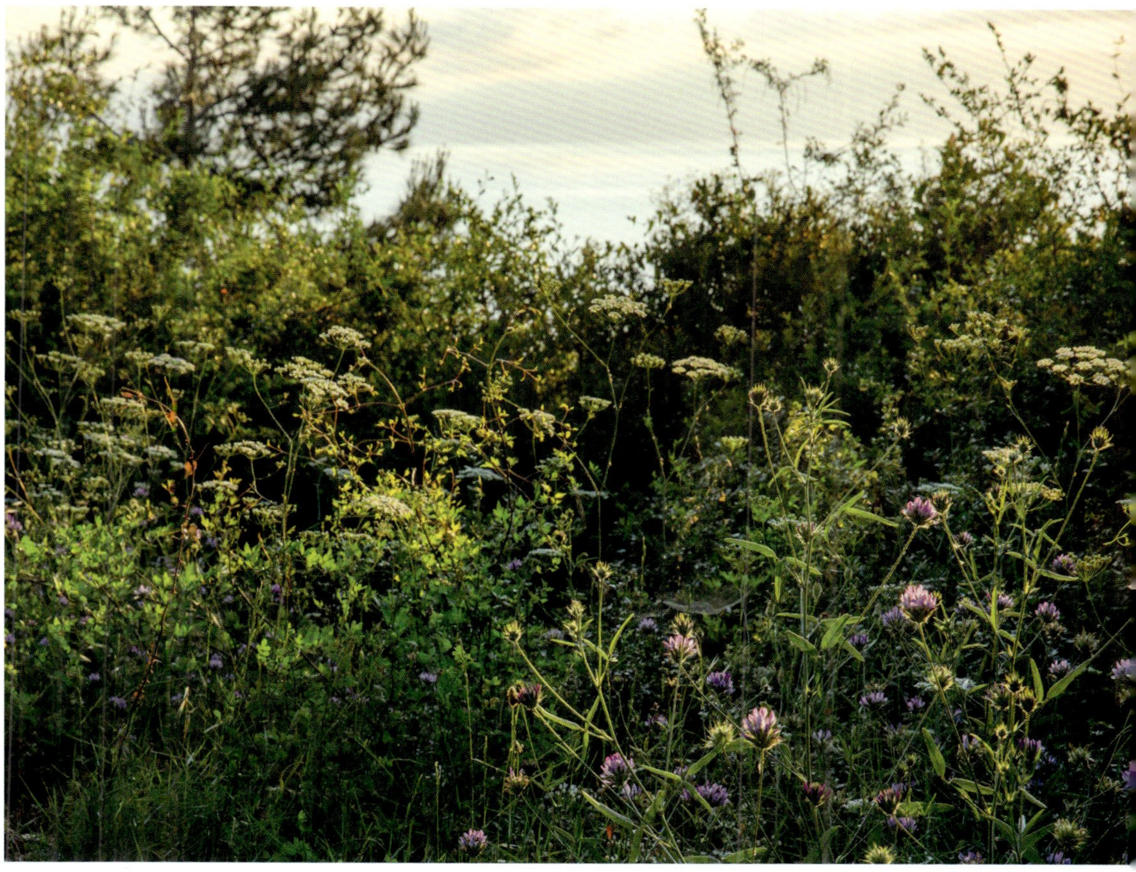

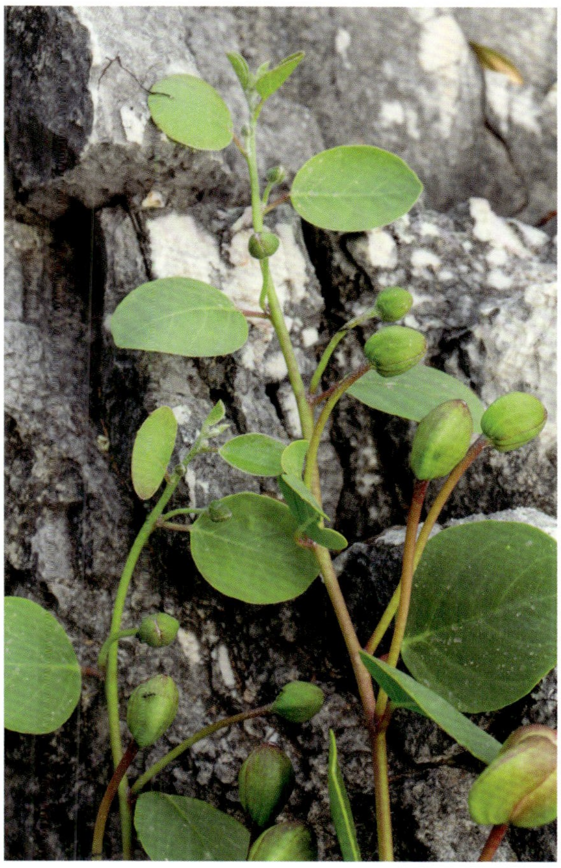

Capers (*Capparis spinosa*), whose pickled buds are a popular condiment, are common on rocks and stone walls in coastal areas of Corfu.

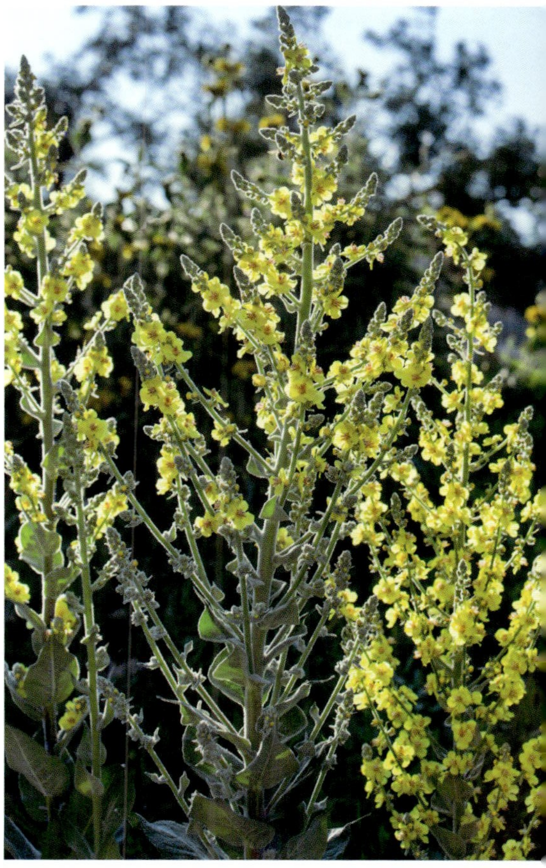

Dried leaves of *Verbascum graecum* had several traditional uses. They could be spread over drying figs to prevent them from rotting, and could be twisted for use as lamp wicks.

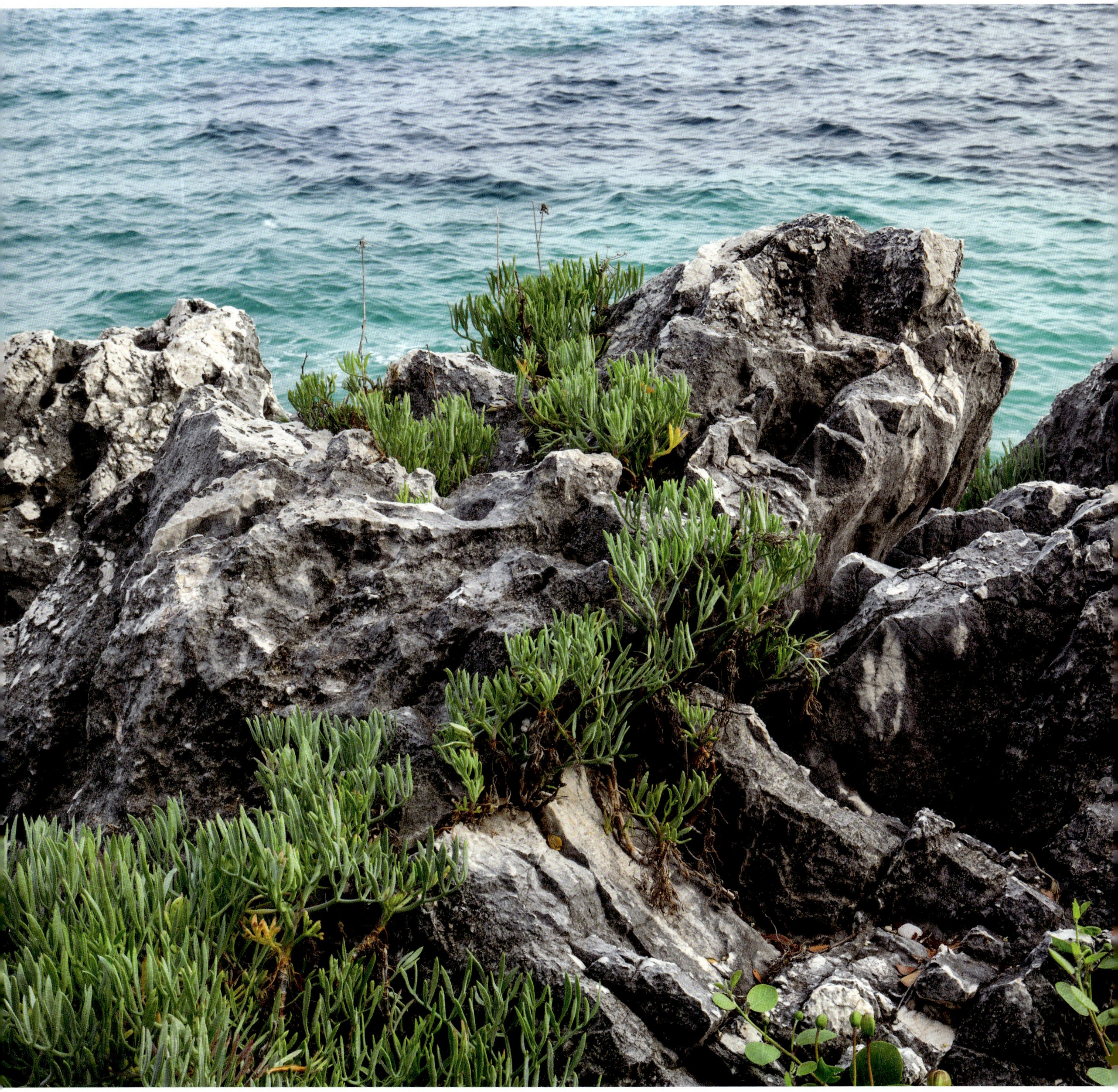

Rock samphire (*Crithmum maritimum*), a seaside plant valued for its high vitamin C content.

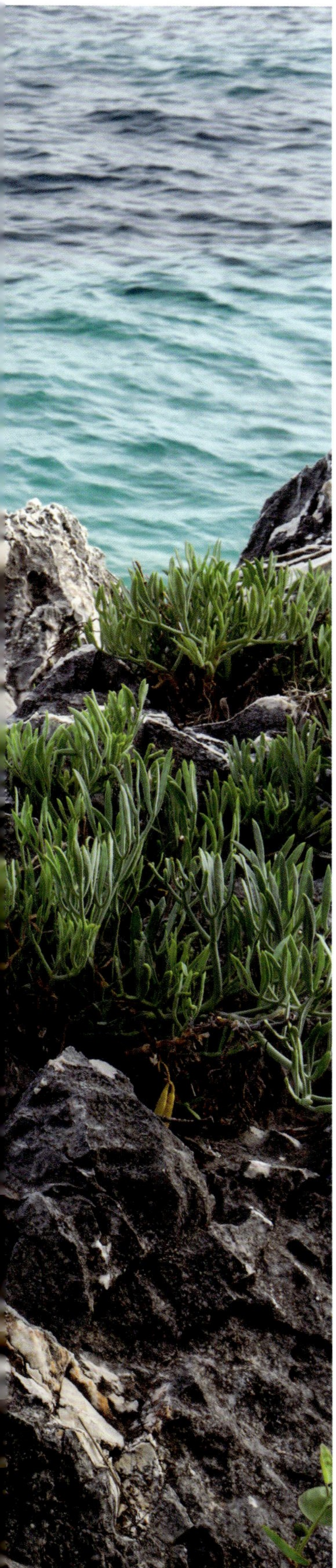

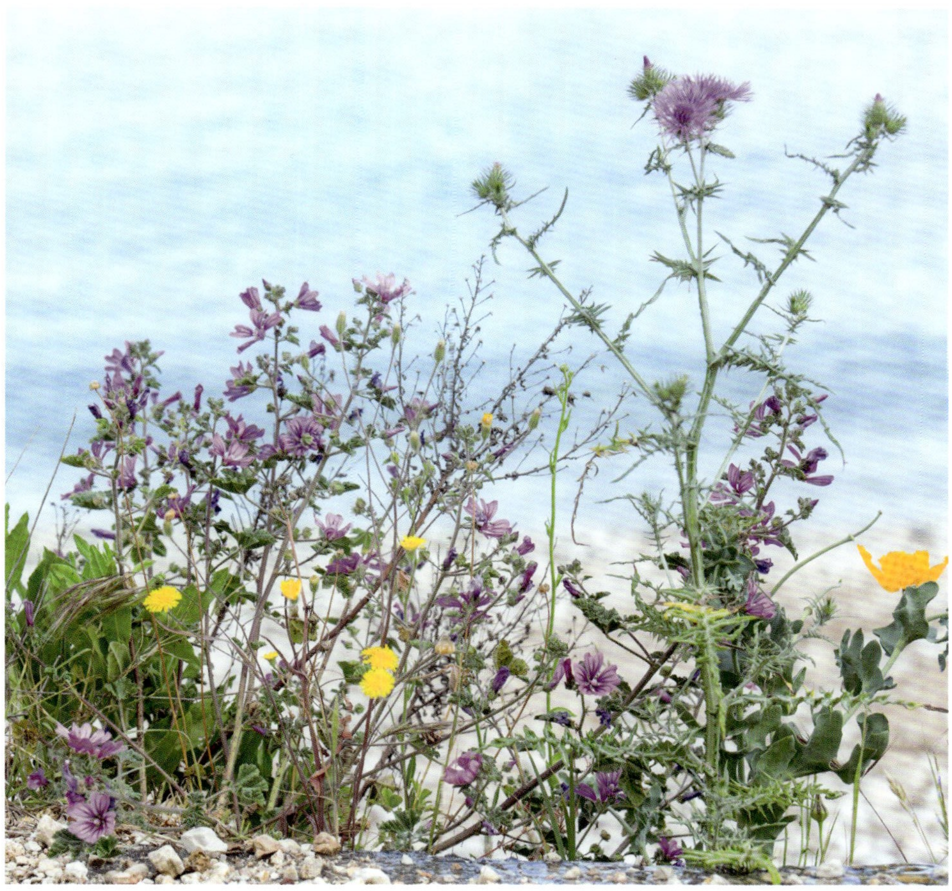

Common mallow (*Malva sylvestris*), whose spring leaves and stems are a popular ingredient of *hórta*, grows on roadsides and in open ground.

over stored potatoes, the dried leaves help to repel mice and insects.

Most Corfiots know and still use pretty pink European centaury (*Centaurium erythraea*), locally called *pharmakoúli* or 'little medicine', as a household remedy. This very bitter plant is an effective substitute for quinine to bring down a fever. It was much used to treat malaria, which remained quite common in rural Corfu until the mid-twentieth century. Compresses are dipped in a pot with vinegar diluted in water and applied to the forehead and wrists.

Several plants in the chamomile group grow in Corfu. *Anthemis chia* (*Margaríta* in Greek) is the common large-flowered white daisy with feathery foliage found throughout the island in spring. Better for drying and tea making is the smaller-flowered scented mayweed (*Matricaria chamomilla*); its distinguishing feature is that its white rays turn downwards soon after the flowers open. Both these plants grow in cultivated fallow and waste ground, olive groves, vineyards, and roadsides, sometimes occurring in large drifts. Infusions of dried chamomile are used locally to treat colds, constipation, skin disorders, and hangovers. Chamomile tea relaxes and can help induce sleep. Medical research has shown that chamomile heals wounds and burns, acting as an anti-inflammatory.

OVERLEAF
Common poppy (*Papaver rhoeas*) at the edge of Avláki beach.

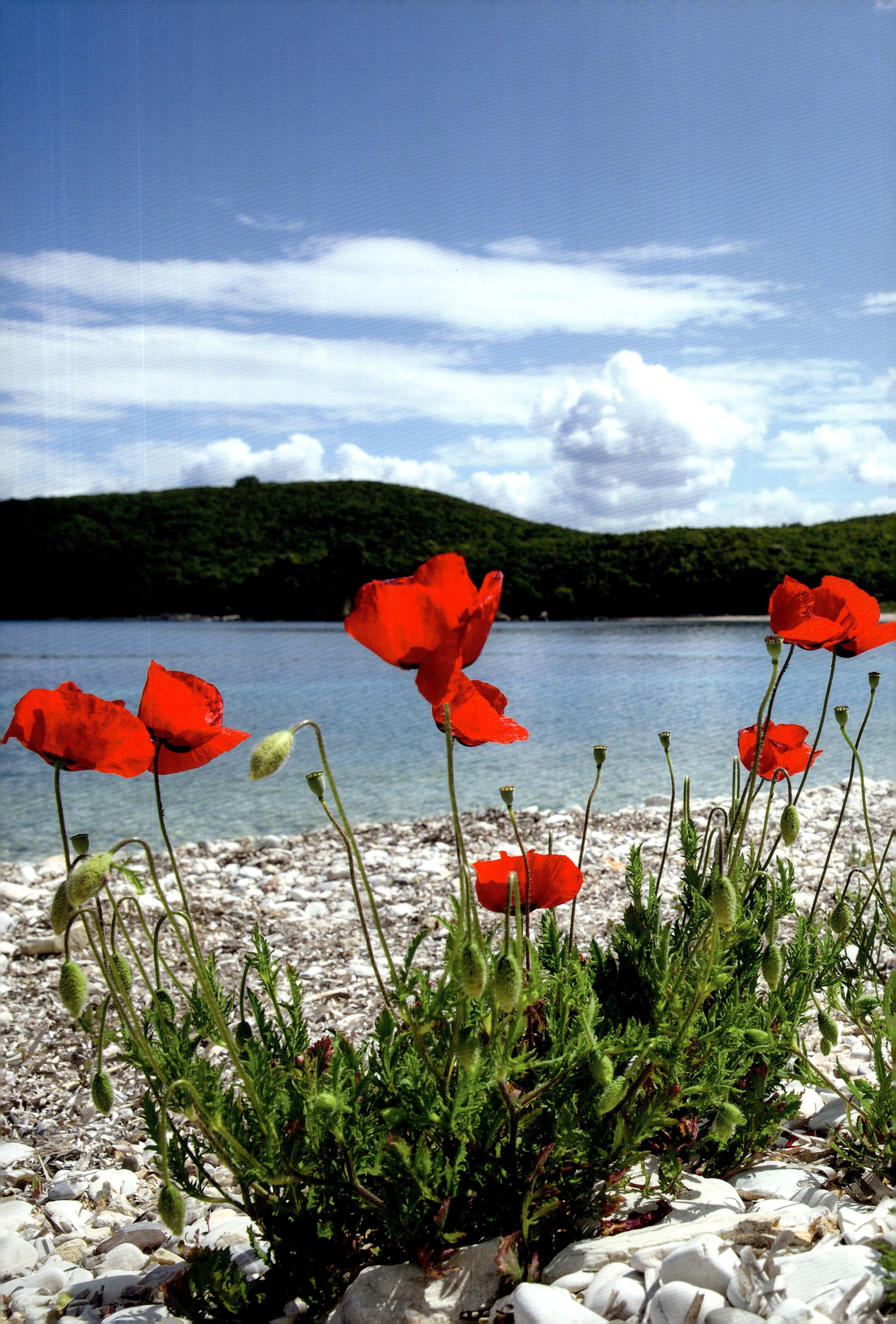

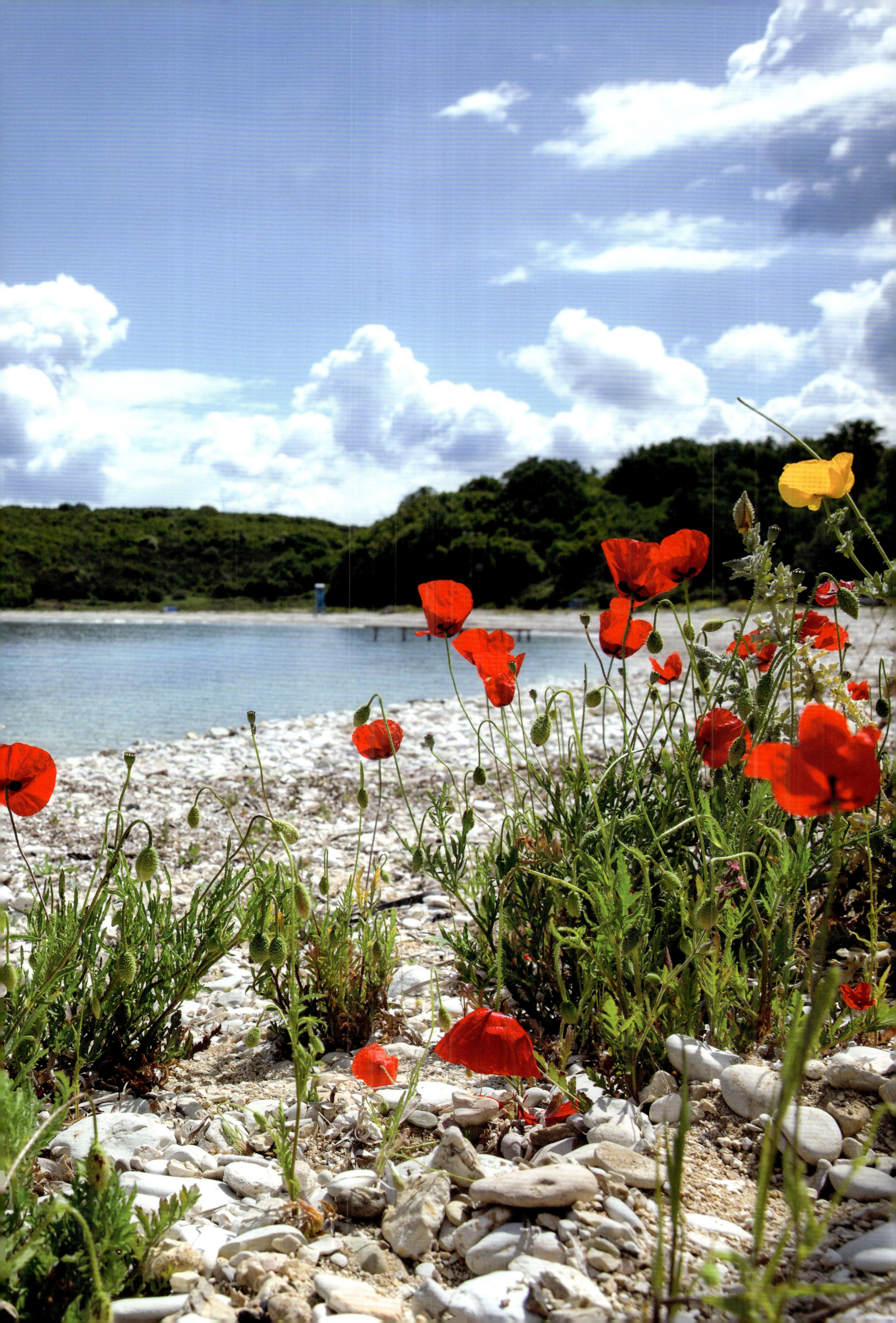

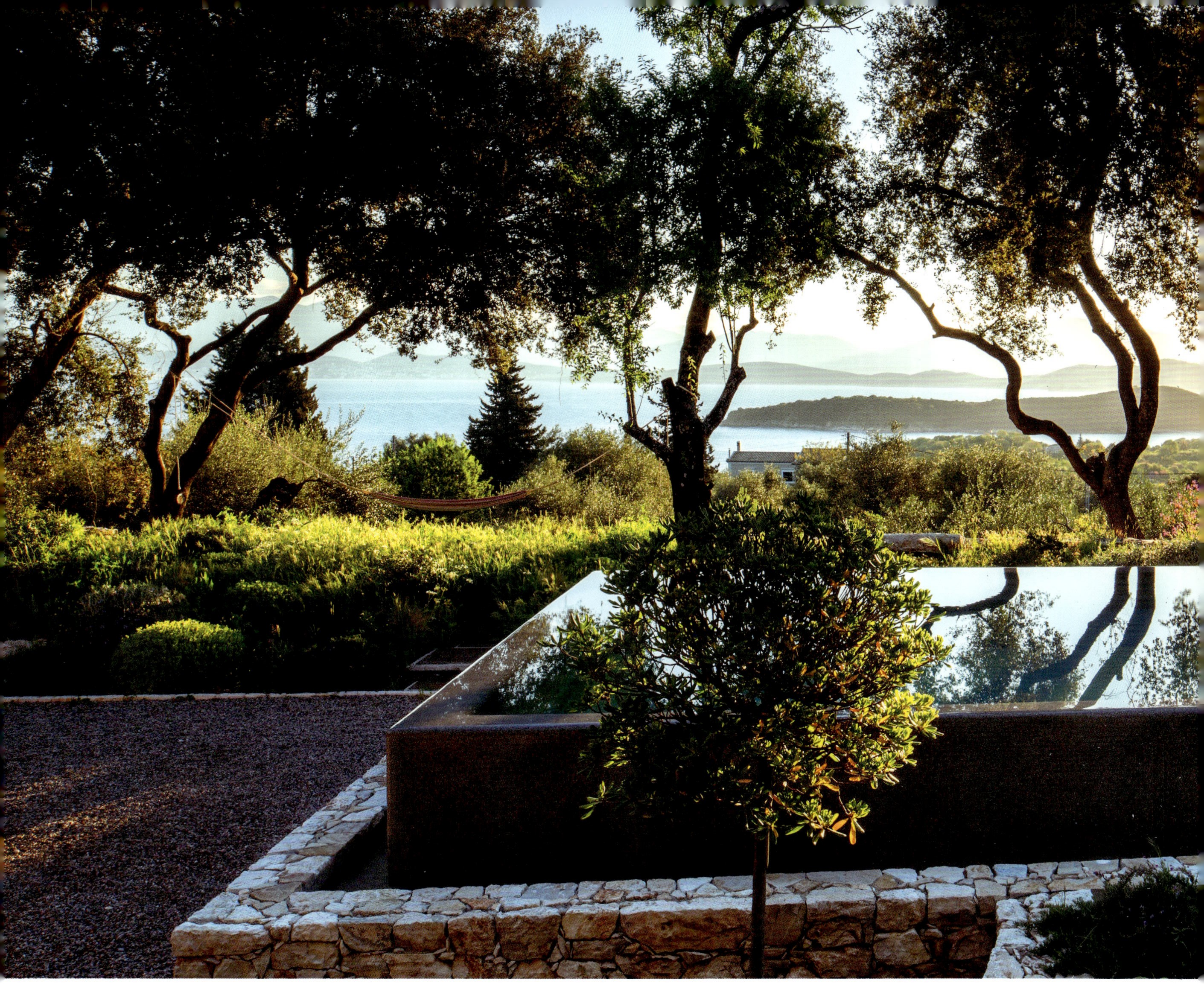

WORKS CITED

ATKINSON, S. 1911. *An Artist in Corfu*. London: Herbert and Daniel; Boston: Dana Estes.

BAUMANN, H. 1986. *Greek Wild Flowers and Plant Lore in Ancient Greece*. London: The Herbert Press.

BLAMEY, M., and GREY-WILSON, C. 1988, second edition 2008. *Wild Flowers of the Mediterranean*. London: A. and C. Black.

BORKOWSKI, O. 1994. *Übersicht der Flora von Korfu*. Braunschweig University, Germany: Braunschweiger Geobotanische Arbeiten I. Braunschweiger.

BRUCE, J., 2017. 'High and dry: landscape architect Thomas Doxiádis on how Greece's commercialism and climate drove him to re-establish native species', *Financial Times*, 5 November.

CHATTO, B. 1978. *The Dry Garden*. London: Orion Press.

DOWE, J., L. 2010. *Australian Palms: Biogeography, Ecology, and Systematics*. Collingwood, Australia: CSIRO.

DURRELL, G. 1978. *Corfu: Garden of the Gods*. London: Harper Collins.

DURRELL, L., 1945 and second edition 2000. *Prospero's Cell*. London: Faber.

———, 1978. 'Corfu', in *The Greek Islands*. London and Boston: Faber.

FILIPPI, O. 2008. *The Dry Gardening Handbook: Plants and Practices for a Changing Climate*. London: Thames and Hudson.

———, 2016. *Planting Design for Dry Gardens*. Filbert Press. Filbertpress.com

GAY, J. 2016. 'Island Life', *Garden Design*, January.

GILDEMEISTER, H. 1995. *Mediterranean Gardening: A Waterwise Approach*. Gruibingen: Moll. Reissued 2003, Berkeley and Los Angeles: University of California Press.

———, 2004. *Gardening the Mediterranean Way*. New York: Harry N. Abrams.

GILES, F., ed., 1994. *Corfu: The Garden Isle*. UK: John Murray; USA: Abbeville Press.

GROVES, R. H., and DI CASTRI, F. eds., 1991. *Biogeography of Mediterranean Invasions*. Cambridge, UK: Cambridge University Press.

HOMER, *The Odyssey*. Translated by Samuel Butler.

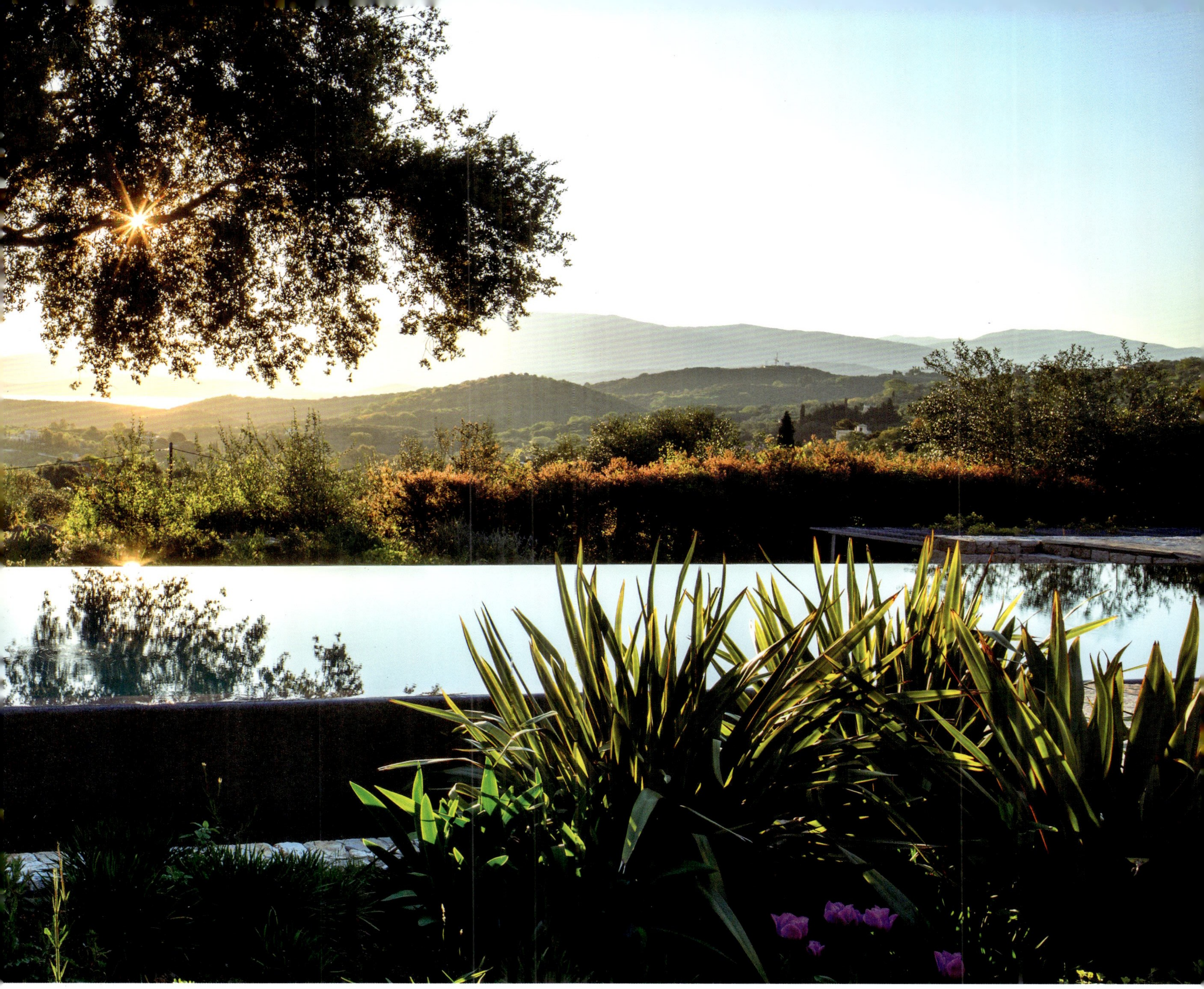

JONES, L. 2000. *The French Country Garden*. London: Thames and Hudson.

———, 2011. *Nicole de Vésian Gardens: Modern Design in Provence*. Paris: Actes Sud.

———, 2012. *Mediterranean Landscape Design—Vernacular Contemporary*. London: Thames and Hudson.

KARAMOUTSOS, K. D., 2010. *Archontikés Agrikíes Kerkyraïkés* (Manor Houses of Corfu—in Greek) in six volumes. Athens: Ekdóseis Papazísi.

KEEN, M. 2007. *The Landscape at Kanónas and Strongílo*. Cirencester, UK: Letterpress of Cirencester.

KHANSARI, M., REZA MOGHTADER, M., and YAVARI, M. 1998. *The Persian Garden: Echoes of Paradise*. Washington, DC: Mage Publishers.

LLOYD, C. 1970. *The Well-Tempered Garden*. London: Harper Collins.

MORYSON, F. 1617. *An Itinerary Concerning His Travel to the Twelve Dominions*, Vol. II. Glasgow, UK: James MacLehose and Sons.

MURRAY, J. 1845. *A Handbook for Travellers in the Ionian Islands, Greece, Turkey, Asia Minor, and Constantinople*. London: John Murray.

PAISIDOU-LAZARIDOU, D. 1997. *Noble Houses of Corfu*. Thessaloniki: Altintzis.

PAPIOMITOGLU, V. 2006. *Wild Flowers of Greece*. Athens: Mediterraneo Editions.

SANDYS, G. 1621. *Sandys Travels: A Relation of a Journey begun in An. Dom. 1610*. London.

SHRADY, N. 1995. 'Greek Drama: Lord Jacob Rothschild's Pavilion on Corfu', *Architectural Digest*, October.

SHERRARD, E. ed., 1988. *Edward Lear: the Corfu Years—A Chronicle Presented through his Letters and Journals*. Evia, Greece: Denise Harvey.

SILVA-PANDO, F. J., and PINO-PEREZ, R. 2016. 'Introduction of Eucalyptus into Europe', *Journal of Australian Forestry* 79 (4).

SOURTZINOS, G., n.d. *Corfu: A Journey through the Ages*. Third Edition. Corfu, Greece: Historical Folklore Society of Corfu.

STOREY, A. 2016. 'The Barba Legacy', *Dolce Magazine*, 15 September.

XENOPHON, *A History of My Times*. London: 1966 Penguin Classics edition.

Note: Plants are listed by their English names, with Latin equivalents in parentheses. Italic page numbers indicate photographs.

Note: Italic page numbers indicate photographs. Plants and their Latin names are detailed in the Index of Plant Names.

ACKNOWLEDGEMENTS

Many people gave generous help in the making of this book. In particular, my deep gratitude goes to the owners of the gardens featured, to Mary Keen for writing the Preface, Christopher Grey Wilson for his expert review of Chapter 5, María Nikoloúzou and Eléni Christoforátou for sharing their knowledge of the Corfiot flora and curative uses of local plants, and Dária Koskorou and Eléni Sarakinós for insights on Corfu's history. I thank Calí Doxiádis for her confidence in this project and for her astute observations on garden design trends as well as on the evolution of the Corfiot landscape. I thank Eos Boúas, Jehanne Legrand Theódotou, and Patricia Manessi for valuable suggestions, introductions, and unforgettable shared explorations; Anastasía Kostándi of Vístonas and Elvíra Myrilla of Lefkímmi for advice on vegetable- and fruit-growing in their areas and on local culinary uses of wild plants; and the designers of some of the gardens featured, for explaining their inspirations and approaches. Several of these individuals gave incisive comments on an earlier draft, teaching me much in the process, but remaining errors and infelicities are my own. I thank Lisa Birman for her excellent editing and Professor Phil Cleaver, graphic designer extraordinaire, for the design of the book. Working with my co-author Marianne Majerus was a privilege, and I am grateful not only for her beautiful photographs but also for her dedication, professionalism, and the fun we had working together. Last, I thank my husband Adil Kanaan and my family and close friends for their creative ideas, practical support, and unflagging encouragement.

I deeply appreciate the financial support of Tanqia International (http://elwan.com/infrastructure-company/tanqia-siyana/), arranged by its CEO Ibrahim Elwan to help cover the printing costs of the volume.

Rachel Weaving
Washington DC, January 2018

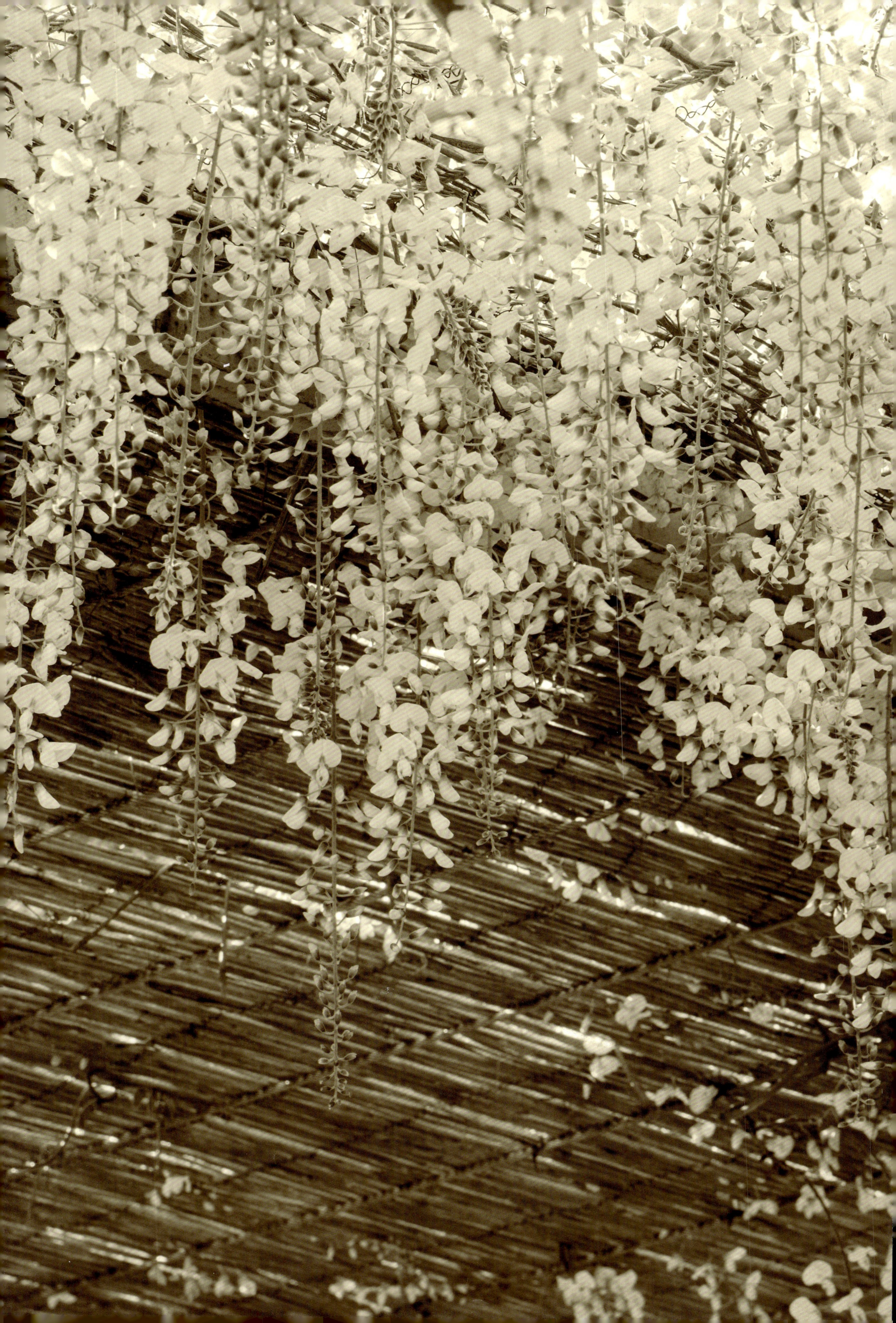